INTRODUCTION TO
RISK MANAGEMENT AND INSURANCE

The Prentice Hall Series in Finance

Adelman/Marks
Entrepreneurial Finance

Andersen
Global Derivatives: A Strategic Risk Management Perspective

Bekaert/Hodrick
International Financial Management

Berk/DeMarzo
Corporate Finance*

Berk/DeMarzo
Corporate Finance: The Core*

Berk/DeMarzo/Harford
Fundamentals of Corporate Finance*

Boakes
Reading and Understanding the Financial Times

Brooks
Financial Management: Core Concepts*

Copeland/Weston/Shastri
Financial Theory and Corporate Policy

Dorfman/Cather
Introduction to Risk Management and Insurance

Eiteman/Stonehill/Moffett
Multinational Business Finance

Fabozzi
Bond Markets: Analysis and Strategies

Fabozzi/Modigliani
Capital Markets: Institutions and Instruments

Fabozzi/Modigliani/Jones/Ferri
Foundations of Financial Markets and Institutions

Finkler
Financial Management for Public, Health, and Not-for-Profit Organizations

Frasca
Personal Finance

Gitman/Joehnk/Smart
Fundamentals of Investing*

Gitman/Zutter
Principles of Managerial Finance*

Gitman/Zutter
Principles of Managerial Finance—Brief Edition*

Goldsmith
Consumer Economics: Issues and Behaviors

Haugen
The Inefficient Stock Market: What Pays Off and Why

Haugen
The New Finance: Overreaction, Complexity, and Uniqueness

Holden
Excel Modeling in Corporate Finance

Holden
Excel Modeling in Investments

Hughes/MacDonald
International Banking: Text and Cases

Hull
Fundamentals of Futures and Options Markets

Hull
Options, Futures, and Other Derivatives

Hull
Risk Management and Financial Institutions

Keown
Personal Finance: Turning Money into Wealth*

Keown/Martin/Petty
Foundations of Finance: The Logic and Practice of Financial Management*

Kim/Nofsinger
Corporate Governance

Madura
Personal Finance*

Marthinsen
Risk Takers: Uses and Abuses of Financial Derivatives

McDonald
Derivatives Markets

McDonald
Fundamentals of Derivatives Markets

Mishkin/Eakins
Financial Markets and Institutions

Moffett/Stonehill/Eiteman
Fundamentals of Multinational Finance

Nofsinger
Psychology of Investing

Ormiston/Fraser
Understanding Financial Statements

Pennacchi
Theory of Asset Pricing

Rejda
Principles of Risk Management and Insurance

Seiler
Performing Financial Studies: A Methodological Cookbook

Shapiro
Capital Budgeting and Investment Analysis

Sharpe/Alexander/Bailey
Investments

Solnik/McLeavey
Global Investments

Stretcher/Michael
Cases in Financial Management

Titman/Keown/Martin
Financial Management: Principles and Applications*

Titman/Martin
Valuation: The Art and Science of Corporate Investment Decisions

Van Horne
Financial Management and Policy

Van Horne/Wachowicz
Fundamentals of Financial Management

Weston/Mitchel/Mulherin
Takeovers, Restructuring, and Corporate Governance

INTRODUCTION TO RISK MANAGEMENT AND INSURANCE

Tenth Edition

MARK S. DORFMAN
(1945–2006)
University of North Carolina at Charlotte

DAVID A. CATHER
Penn State University

PEARSON

Boston   Columbus   Indianapolis   New York   San Francisco   Upper Saddle River
Amsterdam   Cape Town   Dubai   London   Madrid   Milan   Munich   Paris   Montreal   Toronto
Delhi   Mexico City   Sao Paulo   Sydney   Hong Kong   Seoul   Singapore   Taipei   Tokyo

Editor in Chief: Donna Battista
Editorial Project Manager: Jill Kolongowski
Editorial Assistant: Elissa Senra-Sargent
Director of Marketing: Maggie Moylan
Marketing Manager: Jami Minard
Senior Managing Editor: Nancy H. Fenton
Senior Production Project Manager: Kathryn Dinovo
Senior Manufacturing Buyer: Carol Melville
Cover Designer: Jonathan Boylan

Manager, Rights and Permissions: Michael Joyce
Permissions Specialist, Project Manager: Jill C. Dougan
Cover Image: © Caitlin Mirra/Shutterstock
Media Project Manager: Lisa Rinaldi
Full-Service Project Management: MPS Limited
Printer/Binder: Edwards Brothers Malloy
Cover Printer: Lehigh-Phoenix Color/Hagerstown
Text Font: Times Ten LT Std

This product includes copyrighted material of Insurance Services Office, Inc., with its permission. This product includes information which is proprietary to Insurance Services Office, Inc. ISO does not guarantee the accuracy or timeliness of the ISO information provided. ISO shall not be liable for any loss or damage of any kind and howsoever caused resulting from your use of the ISO information.

Credits and acknowledgments borrowed from other sources and reproduced, with permission, in this textbook appear on the appropriate page within text.

Microsoft and/or its respective suppliers make no representations about the suitability of the information contained in the documents and related graphics published as part of the services for any purpose. All such documents and related graphics are provided "as is" without warranty of any kind. Microsoft and/or its respective suppliers hereby disclaim all warranties and conditions with regard to this information, including all warranties and conditions of merchantability, whether express, implied or statutory, fitness for a particular purpose, title and non-infringement. In no event shall Microsoft and/or its respective suppliers be liable for any special, indirect or consequential damages or any damages whatsoever resulting from loss of use, data or profits, whether in an action of contract, negligence or other tortious action, arising out of or in connection with the use or performance of information available from the services.

The documents and related graphics contained herein could include technical inaccuracies or typographical errors. Changes are periodically added to the information herein. Microsoft and/or its respective suppliers may make improvements and/or changes in the product(s) and/or the program(s) described herein at any time. Partial screen shots may be viewed in full within the software version specified.

Microsoft® and Windows® are registered trademarks of the Microsoft Corporation in the U.S.A. and other countries. This book is not sponsored or endorsed by or affiliated with the Microsoft Corporation.

Many of the designations by manufacturers and sellers to distinguish their products are claimed as trademarks. Where those designations appear in this book, and the publisher was aware of a trademark claim, the designations have been printed in initial caps or all caps.

Cataloging-in-Publication Data is on file at the Library of Congress.

10 9 8 7 6 5 4 3

ISBN 10:   0-13-139412-6
ISBN 13: 978-0-13-139412-4

To Jen, Jon, Will, and my parents, Skip and Dean

Brief Contents

Contents

Preface

Over thirty years and nine editions, Mark Dorfman's *Introduction to Risk Management and Insurance* has provided thousands of students a comprehensive, well-written introduction to the risk and insurance discipline. The tenth edition of this text builds upon Mark's fine work by keeping pace with the increased importance of risk management and insurance in business and society. Every chapter in the tenth edition has been updated to reflect recent changes in industry practice, product innovation, and regulation. In particular, the tenth edition refocuses its attention on corporate risk management, reflecting its growing importance in today's economy.

NEW CHAPTERS IN THE TENTH EDITION

Risk management has recently received increased attention in corporate boardrooms across the world. Some of the increased attention resulted from recent large losses (such as the September 11, 2001 terror attacks and the "Great Recession" of 2008), increased regulation (such as the Sarbanes-Oxley Act of 2002), and calls for more extensive disclosure of a firm's risk management practices by influential parties like the New York Stock Exchange and Standard and Poor's. Many business schools presciently anticipated the heightened importance of risk management, creating risk management and insurance departments decades ago. While this book has included chapters on risk management since its first edition, this tenth edition has been reorganized to first describe the broad scope of the risk management discipline, followed by an examination of the role of private insurance, social insurance, and employee benefits within a risk management context.

Risk management means different things to different people. The description of risk management used in the tenth edition of this book remains consistent with its earlier editions, as it is a process that has been used successfully by corporate risk managers for many years. This traditional process is also consistent with descriptions of the enterprise risk management process that have been proposed more recently by the **Casualty Actuarial Society**, the **Risk and Insurance Management Society**, and the **Committee of Sponsoring Organizations of the Treadway Commission**.

The book starts with a new five-chapter section on the risk management process, with each chapter focused on a key step in the risk management process.

- Chapter 1 introduces **insurance**, the **risk management process**, and the concept of **Enterprise Risk Management (ERM)**. It defines key terms used throughout the book and identifies factors that have increased society's need for protection from risk.

- Chapter 2 discusses the **identification of loss exposures**, a key first step in the risk management process. The chapter describes the variety of **property, liability** and **personnel** risks (such as **workers compensation** and **employee benefits** programs) found in most firms. It also introduces the broad array of **financial, operational**, and **strategic** risks addressed in many ERM programs.

- Chapter 3 discusses **risk assessment**, the next step in the risk management process. Using simple examples and no confusing symbols or equations, the chapter explains how to calculate key **risk measures** (e.g., variance, standard deviation), and shows how insurers and self-insurers reduce risk and more accurately forecast losses through **risk pooling**. It also differentiates between **loss frequency and severity**, showing how each affects a firm's average loss.
- Chapter 4 describes the **risk handling techniques** available to address **pure risks**, including **loss control** (e.g., avoidance, prevention, and reduction), **risk transfer** (e.g., insurance, contractual transfer, and limited liability), and **loss financing** (e.g., insurance, self-insurance, and retention). It also examines the selection of risk handling techniques based on frequency, severity, and firm size.
- Chapter 5 describes the **risk handling techniques** available to address **speculative risks**, with discussion focused on **diversification** and **hedging** techniques. It introduces the concepts of covariance and correlation, and shows how ERM applies **portfolio theory** to aggregate and diversify the risks within a firm.

ORGANIZATION OF THE TENTH EDITION

The tenth edition is organized into six sections. The material covered in the ninth edition has been extensively updated and rewritten, and can generally be found in sections two through six, as described below. Also noted below are significant changes and new material added since the ninth edition.

- Chapters 1–5 examine the **risk management process**, as described above. It examines the traditional model of risk management used by corporate risk managers for decades, as well as more recent interpretations used in ERM.
- Chapters 6–10 describe **insurance as a risk handling technique**. This section maintains the unique balance of theory and practice found in the earlier editions of this book. New material added to this section since the ninth edition includes updated material on insurer profitability, the shifts in market share in the insurance industry resulting from demutualization, and a discussion on the competitive structure of the insurance industry.
- Chapters 11–13 focus on **personal insurance protection for property-liability loss exposures**. New to this edition is a discussion of the latest versions of the Insurance Services Office (ISO) Personal Auto Policy and the ISO Homeowners 3 Special Insurance Policy, both found as appendices in the book.
- Chapters 14–19 discuss **personal life-health insurance and employee benefits**. This section begins with an introduction to personal financial planning, followed by discussions on life insurance, annuities, health insurance, and employee benefits. The tenth edition contains a completely updated discussion on health insurance. New material added to this section includes a discussion on adverse selection in the individual health insurance markets, a revamped discussion of long term care insurance, the Patient Protection and Affordable Care Act, and a description of high-deductible healthcare plans and health savings accounts.
- Chapters 20–21 examine several types of **social insurance** available in the United States, including Social Security, unemployment insurance, and workers compensation programs. An updated description of the benefits currently available from these programs is provided.

- Chapters 22–23 focus on **commercial property-liability insurance**. This section includes updated discussions of workers compensation, property insurance, and liability insurance. New to this edition is a description of the latest version of the Insurance Services Office (ISO) Commercial General Liability policy, which is also provided as an appendix to this book.

CHANGES FROM THE NINTH EDITION

Readers familiar with the ninth edition of this book will find that this material has been extensively updated and significantly reorganized in the tenth edition. To simplify the transition between editions, the following table shows where the material from the ninth edition can be found in the tenth edition.

Chapter number in the ninth edition	Chapter number in the tenth edition
Ch. 1 Fundamentals and Terminology	Ch. 6 Fundamentals of Insurance Ch. 3 Risk Assessment and Pooling
Ch. 2 Defining the Insurable Event	Ch. 7 Insurable Perils and Insuring Organizations
Ch. 3 Risk Management	Ch. 1 Introduction to Enterprise Risk Management and Insurance; Ch. 2 Risk Identification Ch. 4 Risk-Handling Techniques: Loss Control, Risk Transfer, and Loss Financing Ch. 5 Risk-Handling Techniques: Diversification and Hedging
Ch. 4 Insurance Companies	Ch. 7 Insurable Perils and Insuring Organizations
Ch. 5 Insurance Occupations	Ch. 8 Insurance Functions
Ch. 6 The Insurance Market: The Economic Problem	Ch. 9 Insurance Markets: Economics and Issues
Ch. 7 Insurance Regulation	Ch. 10 Insurance Regulation
Ch. 8 Insurance Contracts	Ch. 11 Insurance Contracts
Ch. 9 Basic Property and Liability Contracts	Ch. 11 Insurance Contracts
Ch. 10 Homeowners Insurance (HO)	Ch. 13 Homeowners Insurance (HO)
Ch. 11 The Personal Auto Policy	Ch. 12 The Personal Auto Policy
Ch. 12 Professional Financial Planning	Ch. 14 Professional Financial Planning
Ch. 13 Life Insurance Policies	Ch 15 Life Insurance Policies
Ch. 14 Standard Life Insurance Contract Provisions and Options	Ch. 16 Standard Life Insurance Contract Provisions and Options
Ch. 15 Annuities	Ch. 17 Annuities
Ch. 16 Medical Expense and Disability Income Insurance	Ch. 18 Health Insurance and Disability Income

(Continued)

(*Continued*)

Chapter number in the ninth edition	Chapter number in the tenth edition
Ch. 17 Advanced Topics in Risk Management	Ch. 5 Risk-Handling Techniques: Diversification and Hedging Ch. 11 Insurance Contracts
Ch. 18 Commercial Property Insurance	Ch. 22 Commercial Property Insurance
Ch. 19 Commercial Liability Insurance	Ch. 23 Commercial Liability Insurance
Ch. 20 Bonding, Crime Insurance, and Reinsurance	Ch. 8 Insurance Functions Ch. 22 Commercial Property Insurance
Ch. 21 Employee Benefits	Ch. 19 Employee Benefits
Ch. 22 Social Security	Ch. 20 Social Security
Ch. 23 Unemployment and Workers' Compensation Insurance	Ch. 21 Unemployment and Workers' Compensation Insurance

BOOK OBJECTIVES AND INTENDED AUDIENCE

The goals of this tenth edition are twofold. The first is to increase the readers' understanding of the role of risk management and insurance in dealing with events that can adversely affect people, families, firms, and other organizations. In turn, it is hoped that this better understanding will stimulate critical thinking and sound reasoning as society chooses the public policy options that best address these issues into the future.

In keeping with previous editions of this text, this book was written as an introductory undergraduate text on insurance and risk management. No prerequisite course work is expected of the reader. The sequence of chapters is designed for instructors who cover course material in both insurance and risk management. However, the organization of the chapters in the book is flexible, and instructors who prefer to focus solely on insurance can skip over chapters 2 through 5 without a loss of continuity.

IMPORTANT FEATURES OF THIS BOOK

Teaching risk management and insurance can be challenging, as the course material is very diverse, spanning the fields of economics, statistics, finance, business law, and business ethics. This book consistently uses several pedagogical tools to help the reader better understand this diverse discipline. Every chapter begins with a list of *learning objectives* that provides the reader an overview of the topics discussed in the chapter. *Key terms* are printed in bold to alert the reader to important concepts and definitions. *Insight boxes* are included in the chapters to provide interesting examples and applications of concepts discussed in the chapters. *Tables and figures* are strategically placed throughout the book to illustrate in greater detail the concepts discussed in the chapters. Each chapter concludes with a *summary* to reinforce the ideas discussed earlier in the text. Students can answer the *review questions* and *objective questions* found at the end of each chapter to hone their understanding of key concepts discussed earlier in the chapter. Answers to the objective questions for students to check their work can be found as an appendix. *Discussion questions* are also provided at the end of each chapter to facilitate open-ended discussion of broader issues. *Selected references* are cited at the end of each chapter for readers who want to read more about the material discussed in the chapter.

ADDITIONAL INSTRUCTOR RESOURCES AND SUPPLEMENTS

In addition to features within this book, a variety of resources are available for instructors using this book. Instructors can download these resources for free at the Instructor's Resource Center, at www.pearsonhighered.com/dorfman. Professors must register on the Web site to access the book's resources.

Richard Corbett of Florida State University (emeritus) revised the Instructor's Manual for the tenth edition. Each chapter of the Instructor's Manual includes the following six sections: (1) Suggested Classroom Time, (2) Chapter Overview, (3) Lecture Outline, (4) Answers to Review Questions, (5) Answers to End-of-Chapter Objective Questions, and (6) Ideas for Instructors and Teaching Methods.

Revised by Tom G. Geurts at George Mason University, a PowerPoint presentation is also available for download from the Instructor's Resource Center.

Also revised by Professor Geurts, a test bank is available for instructors. The test bank includes true/false, multiple choice, and essay questions. The test bank can be downloaded as Microsoft Word files or as files for the TestGen program, an easy-to-use testing software that allows instructors to view, edit, and add questions. WebCT and Blackboard conversions are also available.

ACKNOWLEDGEMENTS

It is an honor to join Mark Dorfman as the new co-author of the tenth edition of this book. Mark was a great educator, both as an instructor in the classroom and more universally as the author of an excellent textbook. Few authors have the talent and the commitment to publish a textbook for thirty years, and I look forward to continuing Mark's good work.

As Mark notes in the Acknowledgements to the ninth edition, many distinguished classroom instructors and successful business practitioners have made valuable contributions to this book over the years, including the following:

Khurshid Ahmad	Robert Nagy
Eugene Anderson	James R. Newell
Robert Atchley	Max Oelschlaeger
Kenneth Black, Jr.	Daniel J. Pliszka
Mark Cross	Jochen Russ
Karl C. Ennsfellner	Barry Schweig
John Fitzgerald	A. Frank Thompson
Elizabeth Grace	Steven Tippins
Robert P. Hartwig	Peter Townley
Cheri Hawkins	Peter Walters
George L. Head	William Warfel
Barbara Blundi Manaka	Steven Weisbart
David Marlett	Brenda Wells
Robert J. Myers	Eric Wiening

In addition, I join with Mark in acknowledging two other people who have made vital contributions to this book over its first thirty years. Saul Adelman, Mark's colleague at Miami University of Ohio, has worked on the Instructor's Manual for the text in the past and made countless suggestions for improvements of the manuscripts.

Mark's wife, Marcia Dorfman, provided her consistent support, valuable proofreading skills, and talents as a professional librarian throughout the first nine editions.

I would also like to thank a number of people for their contributions to this tenth edition. Barbara Manaka (Temple University), Elizabeth Grace (San Jose State University), and Eric Wiening (Olivet College) reviewed early drafts of the first several chapters of this book, providing helpful guidance for the direction for the text. Lars Powell (University of Arkansas – Little Rock) reviewed the entire book, providing invaluable comments and suggestions for improvements to the text. Richard Corbett (Florida State University) wrote the instructor's manual for the tenth edition of the book.

The editorial and production staff at Pearson has provided exceptional support and guidance. Special thanks are due to Donna Battista, editor in chief at Pearson, for her support of this project. The production team of Kathryn Dinovo, Lynn Lustberg, and Jill Kolongowski were professional, prompt, and patient – a textbook writer's dream team.

Finally, I wish to thank my family – my wife, Jen, and my sons, Jon and Will – for their constant support, incredible patience, and never-ending good cheer during this entire project.

Dave Cather

About the Authors

MARK S. DORFMAN (1945–2006)
University of North Carolina at Charlotte

Mark Dorfman taught introductory risk management and insurance classes for more than 35 years at the following universities: University of Illinois, Miami University (Ohio), the University of Arkansas at Little Rock, the University of North Carolina at Charlotte, the Wirtschaftsuniversität Wien (The Business and Economics University of Vienna, Austria), the University of Ulm, Germany, and Audencia University in Nantes, France. Even after 35 years, he still enjoyed teaching; sharing ideas with students was one of his life's great joys. He believed teaching risk management and insurance to students was very important. He always kept students in mind when writing this book and wanted them to find the writing style "user-friendly."

Mark was born in Chicago and attended Chicago public schools. His undergraduate degree is from Northwestern University. The University of Illinois awarded his Master of Science and Doctor of Philosophy degrees. Mark held high offices, served on boards of directors of several academic and nonacademic institutions, and wrote extensively in the major risk management and insurance academic journals.

DAVID A. CATHER
Penn State University

Dave Cather received his PhD in Risk Management and Insurance from the University of Georgia. He is clinical associate professor of Risk Management at Penn State University. Prior to joining the faculty at Penn State, he was a faculty member at the Wharton School of the University of Pennsylvania from 1987 to 2003, and he continues his affiliation at that school as a part-time lecturer. He was also a member of the faculty of Temple University and Bowling Green State University, his undergraduate alma mater. He has won multiple teaching awards over his career, including the 2008 Les Strickler Innovation in Instruction Award presented by the American Risk and Insurance Association. His research has been published in a variety of journals, including the *Journal of Risk and Insurance*, *Risk Management and Insurance Review*, the *Journal of Banking and Finance*, *CPCU Journal,* and *Best's Review*. Before starting his academic career, he worked in the property-liability insurance industry as a licensed independent agent.

1

Introduction to Enterprise Risk Management and Insurance

After studying this chapter, you should be able to

- Explain why interest in risk management is growing among corporations
- Describe the different classifications of risk in the risk and insurance industry
- Explain how risk aversion affects risk-taking behavior
- Describe the ways that firms and individuals protect themselves from risk
- Describe the risk management process
- Describe the scope of corporate enterprise risk management activities

In "The Decade in Management Ideas," their 2010 review of management over the prior ten years, the editors of the *Harvard Business Review* identified *Enterprise Risk Management (ERM)* as one of the "most influential management ideas of the millennium (so far)." While they jokingly acknowledged that their assessment is a bit premature because the millennium is only a few years old, they correctly observed that risk management has risen dramatically in importance since 2000. The term *ERM* has become synonymous with the business world's increased awareness of risk and the need to manage it effectively.

The origins of ERM can be traced to well before 2000. **Corporate risk management**, the process of protecting the earnings power and the assets of a firm from the financial losses resulting from negative events like property damage or lawsuits, is a precursor to ERM that became popular after World War II.[1] Traditionally, corporate risk managers have protected their firms from these losses using techniques such as risk financing, which includes insurance and noninsurance techniques; loss control, and risk transfer.

Recently, however, firms have broadened their view of risk, realizing that risk managers are not the only people responsible for dealing with risk within corporations. Auditors and accountants are responsible for ensuring that financial statements accurately reflect the financial status of the firm and are not plagued by errors or fraud. A firm's financial officers work to reduce the firm's vulnerability to price changes in a variety of markets, such as interest rates, currencies, and commodities. Operational

---

[1] See Chapter 2 in Williams et al. (1997) for a detailed description of the evolution of the risk management discipline.

managers guard against events that disrupt the normal operations of the firm, and strategic planning officers position the firm to best compete against its rivals. Firms are increasingly recognizing that it is not best for any of these functions to operate in disconnected "silos" that are isolated from each other and beneath the radar of the corporate board. **Enterprise risk management (ERM)** is thus a process that examines all these risks *collectively* and elevates the analyses to the highest level in the corporation: the corporate boardroom.

WHY INTEREST IN RISK MANAGEMENT IS GROWING

Why are firms and individuals increasingly concerned about risk? Each of the following factors has heightened public concern about risk management.

Catastrophic Loss Events

Since 2000, the United States has suffered two of the deadliest disasters in its history—the September 11, 2001 terror attacks and the landfall of Hurricane Katrina in August 2005, resulting in the deaths of 2,973 and 1,836 people, respectively. Excluding wars, the United States had not experienced a tragedy of such deadly proportions since the early 1900s. Both events prompted widespread debate by citizens and public officials on how to best protect the country from similar events in the future.

Concern about catastrophes is not solely a U.S. phenomenon, however. Catastrophic events of even greater magnitude have occurred recently across the world. The 2004 tsunami along the coastline of the Indian Ocean killed a quarter million people. Since 2000, catastrophic earthquakes have struck Japan, Haiti, Pakistan, and China, killing hundreds of thousands more. Terrorism is a global concern as well, with recent attacks across Europe, Japan, India, and much of the rest of the world.

Corporate Financial Failures

The past several years have been plagued by inept corporate risk management resulting in massive financial losses, not only for poorly managed corporations but also for a much wider group of individuals beyond them. In the early 2000s, the U.S. economy endured a wave of corporate scandals, as bankrupt firms such as Enron were found to have grossly overstated their earnings and provided incorrect financial data to the investment community. A few years later, the U.S. banking system collapsed due to overinvestment in real estate and real estate derivatives. The failure of the banking system triggered "The Great Recession," as the United States fell into its steepest recession since the Great Depression of the 1930s. From 2007 to 2009, U.S. stock markets declined in value by over 50 percent, and financial markets in many other international financial markets suffered losses of similar magnitude.

The political fallout that erupted in the wake of these financial collapses prompted a call for improved risk management and stronger financial monitoring of corporations. Angry about the corporate corruption of the late 1990s, the U.S. Congress in 2002 passed the Sarbanes-Oxley Act, a law that brought sweeping changes to corporate governance and financial accounting standards. Two years later, the accounting profession also proposed a model for ERM that elevated the responsibility for risk management to the level of the corporate board of directors.

INSIGHT BOX 1-1

Enron and Arthur Andersen: How Corporate Fraud Increased Interest in Risk Management

If you are studying enterprise risk management for the first time, you might be wondering why the accounting profession is such a strong proponent of the ERM movement. To answer this question, we need look no further than when the Enron Corporation declared bankruptcy in 2001, with dramatic repercussions on Arthur Andersen, the public accounting firm that conducted the audit of Enron's financial statements.

To most U.S. investors, Enron will be forever linked to the notion of corporate fraud. Formed in 1985, Enron was an energy company headquartered in Texas that enjoyed phenomenal financial success during the 1990s. Enron's reported revenues grew from $9.2 billion in 1995 to $100.8 billion in 2000, a period that coincided with the deregulation of several energy markets. In the wake of Enron's bankruptcy in 2001, evidence emerged to suggest that the firm's rapid growth was fueled not by its ability to capitalize on deregulation but instead by questionable accounting practices. For example, Enron recognized as income the discounted cash flow from highly questionable long-term contracts, a practice that greatly inflated its revenue flows. The firm also minimized its reported liabilities by moving its debt off its balance sheet and into special-purpose entities that it did not own (such as limited partnerships) but financially secured with Enron assets.

In response to its bankruptcy, financially devastated investors, who had unknowingly based their investment decisions on Enron's fraudulent financial statements, sued the firm in hopes of recovering their losses. By the time the lawsuits were filed, however, there was little of value left in Enron. Unable to collect from Enron, plaintiffs brought suits against Arthur Anderson for failing to report Enron's dire financial condition accurately in its audit of the firm. The mounting lawsuits filed against Arthur Andersen as a result of the Enron case and several other corporate fraud cases proved more than the firm could withstand, and it dissolved in 2002.

Because Arthur Anderson was one of "big five" public U.S. accounting firms at the time of Enron's collapse, its demise was a body blow to the accounting profession. Public accounting firms walk an uneasy tightrope. While they are paid by the companies that they audit, the information that they provide in their reports benefits a larger audience: namely, the entire investing and credit community. Their work becomes especially difficult when they must report negative financial information about a client, because such information often triggers lawsuits against the client by disgruntled investors. If the client is financially impaired and the audit firm is found not to have satisfied the duty of care that it owes to investors and lenders, it may be sued as well.

By improving upon the methods that firms use to manage their risk, as well as the ways they monitor and report such risks, the accounting profession can protect itself better from adverse litigation. Perhaps more important, improving risk management practices and reporting reduces the chance that firms will suffer financial losses, not to mention providing better information to the investment and lending community.

Source: P. M. Healy and K. G. Palepu, "The Fall of Enron", Journal of Economic Perspectives, Vol. 17, no. 2, Spring 2003 pp. 3–26 and R. Ball, "Market and Political/Regulatory Perspectives on Recent Accounting Scandals," Journal of Accounting Research, Vol. 47, No. 2, pp. 277–323.

Shrinking Employee Benefits

Most U.S. workers rely heavily upon the employee benefits and wages provided by their employers; these wages and benefits protect workers from a variety of personal loss exposures. During the 2008 economic recession, the U.S. unemployment rate increased to over 10 percent as firms went out of business or laid off workers in response to declining revenues. In an effort to cut expenses, many employers also scaled back valuable employee benefits like health insurance and pension plans. Without employee benefits, workers felt increasingly at risk of being unable to afford to retire or pay for the growing cost of medical care.

These losses were the focus of considerable media coverage, but they overshadowed some of the less dramatic exposures to loss that people bear in the ordinary course of their lives. Losses from auto accidents, deaths, and lawsuits typically affect a small number of people and thus receive less public attention than more catastrophic events. Nonetheless, these individual losses are just as financially devastating to the victims.

Large-scale natural disasters, investment losses, and relatively minor traffic accidents are quite diverse but share a common characteristic: they can all cause us financial harm and interrupt our ability to carry out the tasks of daily life. This book examines how firms and individuals can better protect themselves from these and other types of risks through the use of insurance and risk management.

METHODS OF CLASSIFYING RISK

The term *risk* refers to the variation in possible outcomes that can result from an uncertain event based on chance. Risk has several definitions and uses across different academic disciplines. Even among professionals in the insurance and risk management industry, the ambiguous nature of risk has made it difficult to develop a single definition of the term. Instead, we will define several characteristics of risk that are widely used to classify risk in the insurance and risk management community.

Pure Risk vs. Speculative Risk

Exposures to risk that can cause financial loss for firms and individuals can be classified as either pure or speculative risks. **Pure risks** are loss exposures that can result in two possible financial outcomes: The person or firm exposed to the risk suffers a financial loss, or the financial position will remain unchanged. Pure risks offer no opportunity for financial gain. Most of the catastrophic events we discussed earlier—terrorism, flood, or earthquakes—are examples of pure risks. Many of the events that can result in damage to property are also pure risks, such as fires or windstorms. Employee benefits programs also protect workers from pure risks, such as unexpected medical expenses, unemployment, and disability.

Unlike pure risks, **speculative risks** are loss exposures that can result in three financial outcomes: A person exposed to the risk will suffer a financial loss, receive a financial gain, or find his or her financial status unchanged. The decision to invest your money in the stock market is an example of a speculative risk because your wealth will increase, decrease, or remain constant as a result of the investment. Speculative risks also include the risk borne by entrepreneurs who start their own businesses or a firm that decides to introduce a new product line. Other speculative risks result from the potential gains or losses associated with price movements of foreign currencies, interest rate changes, or commodities such as grains, precious metals, or oil.

Large corporations are routinely exposed to a wide variety of both speculative and pure risks.[2] Risk managers often find it helpful to differentiate their loss exposures into these two risk categories because they will use different methods to handle each of them.

Diversifiable Risk vs. Non-diversifiable Risk

It is also helpful to classify loss exposures based on whether the risk can be reduced through diversification. A number of risk-bearing financial institutions, such as insurance companies and investment funds, help their clients by providing them a way to diversify their risks with those of a large number of other clients. In its simplest form,

---

[2] Some people working in the risk and insurance industry use the term *risk* to mean the person or item exposed to loss. So you may hear an insurance agent say, "We'll insure that risk for $1,000." Another common practice is to use the term *risk* as a synonym for the cause of the loss exposure. Thus, an agent may offer to sell you insurance from the *risk* of fire. While these references initially seem to add to the ambiguity associated with the word *risk*, their meaning becomes evident within the context of the sentence in which they are used.

risk diversification is a process in which the financial losses of a few members in a group are spread across a much larger number of people in the group who have not suffered a loss. Thus, while the owner of a small home would be devastated financially if her $100,000 house was completely destroyed by a fire, if that homeowner were one of the 20,000 customers protected by a fire insurance company, each customer's share of that loss would equal the affordable sum of $5.

Crucial to the success of such risk-bearing arrangements is making sure that there are a large number of clients to share the risk, and that the risk is not likely to cause a large number of group members to suffer a loss at the same time and thus financially overwhelm the group. In this regard, we will find it helpful to classify risks based on whether they satisfy these diversification characteristics.

In insurance, diversification is achieved through the use of **risk pooling**, also known as the use of the **law of large numbers**. Most common types of insurance, such as auto and life insurance, offer protection from risks well suited to diversification via risk pooling because the loss usually affects only one person, not a large number of clients in the same risk pool. On the other hand, several of the catastrophic risks described at the beginning of this chapter—floods, wars, and unemployment—tend to be **non-diversifiable** risks for insurers because they often result in financial losses for a large number of people in the risk pool at the same time. Private insurers rarely offer insurance for non-diversifiable risk, recognizing that their financial strength could be harmed if such a catastrophic loss occurred.

Risk diversification is also used in the field of finance. For example, an investor who invests all his cash in the stock of a single company will suffer a huge loss if that firm's stock price decreases. On the other hand, that same investor is exposed to far less risk if he purchases stock from a larger number of companies because it is much less likely that all the companies will decline in value simultaneously. For this reason, financial advisors urge investors to hold a **well-diversified portfolio** of investments because many of the speculative risks that can cause financial harm to a single firm (such as the failed launch of a new product or a loss of market share to a competitor) are **diversifiable** if the remaining investments in the portfolio are unaffected.[3]

Unfortunately, the impact of some types of investment risks, such as inflation or recession, is not limited to a single firm but instead adversely affects a large number of firms in an investment portfolio or even an entire market. These risks exhibit the characteristics of non-diversifiable risk in an investment portfolio.[4]

Table 1-1 provides some examples of diversifiable and non-diversifiable risks within the pure and speculative risk categories, focusing on the loss exposures that we've described so far in this chapter. Notice the differentiating characteristic of diversifiable risks is that they are generally firm-specific; that is, they affect only one or a small number of group members while the remaining firms in the group remain unaffected. Thus, our ability to reduce the adverse effects of non-diversifiable risks is limited because these risks affect such a large number of firms within the diversification risk pool.

---

[3] In addition to these speculative risks, many of the pure risks that affect only a single firm (such as a lawsuit or plant fire) can also be diversified in investment portfolios. Based on this fact, some skeptics question whether well-diversified stockholders really value risk management efforts because these investors may be able to eliminate such risks more efficiently through portfolio diversification, as discussed in Chapter 5.

[4] Readers who have taken a class in finance may be familiar with the concepts of non-diversifiable and diversifiable risks but know them by other names. Some texts refer to diversifiable and non-diversifiable risk as *non-systematic* and *systematic* risk, or *firm-specific* and *market* risk.

TABLE 1-1 Some Diversifiable and Non-Diversifiable Risks

	Diversifiable Risk	*Non-Diversifiable Risk*
Pure risk (insurer risk pool)	• Building fire • Auto accident	• Unemployment • Flood
Speculative risk (investment portfolio)	• (Failed) launch of new product • Changes in input prices (corn, gas)	• Economic recession • Global inflation

RISK AVERSION

Many people feel uncomfortable when faced with a decision that involves risk because it represents a situation in which they might suffer a financial loss. As a result, they shy away from choices that expose them to risk when they have the chance to do so. **Risk aversion** refers to the behavioral tendency, when facing a choice between risky alternatives, to prefer to take less risk rather than more.

Risk aversion generally is considered an appropriate strategy for dealing with pure risks because there is no financial reward for bearing them. Risk aversion is also one of the primary reasons that individuals and some firms purchase insurance and otherwise engage in risk management activities. The objective of today's risk managers is not to eliminate *all* sources of pure risk that might endanger their firms, however. That is simply impossible, and no firm or organization can operate today without bearing at least some exposure to risk.

A policy of risk aversion may not be the best way to deal with speculative risk, however, because such a strategy often reduces a person's ability to earn increased financial gains. For example, many investments exhibit a **risk-return trade-off**, by which an investor can expect to receive increased financial returns for bearing higher levels of risk. The long-run returns to investors from riskier investments like common stock are thus higher than the returns from less risky investments like government securities. Corporations similarly engage in speculative risks like developing new products or entering new markets in the hopes of increasing the returns for the owners of the firm. As these examples suggest, firms and individuals that exercise good judgment in choosing speculative risks can profit from such activities.

PROTECTION FROM RISK: INSURANCE, EMPLOYEE BENEFITS, AND RISK MANAGEMENT

How can individuals and firms protect themselves from the financial harm caused by these types of loss exposure? The available means vary considerably across the globe, depending upon each country's level of economic development and financial prosperity.

NO PROTECTION

People living in industrialized countries often fail to appreciate the importance of risk protection in their daily lives, but in fact products like insurance are crucial in stabilizing an economy. Many less-developed economies offer few ways for individuals and firms to protect themselves from loss exposures because they have poorly developed risk and insurance infrastructures. Individuals living in these countries have little choice but to rely upon their families, churches, tribes, or villages for assistance. In times of catastrophic loss, impoverished countries often rely upon humanitarian aid from other nations to help pay for the costs of emergency medical care and related expenses.

The United Nations Conference on Trade and Development has recognized the development of an insurance industry as a vital component in the economic development of emerging countries. Unfortunately, insurance is not widely available in all countries, as emerging economies account for only 11 percent of the world's insurance market, with industrialized countries accounting for the remaining 89 percent.[5]

PERSONAL INSURANCE PROTECTION

In countries with well-developed financial services industries, insurance products usually provide financial protection for some, but not all, types of financial risk exposure. Indeed, in many parts of the world, individuals have been able to buy insurance products to protect themselves from loss for several centuries.

Insurance is a financial agreement in which an individual pays a fee (known as a *premium*) to transfer the financial consequences of his insured losses to a risk pool administered by an insurer. There are two major sources of insurance protection. **Social insurance** is protection available to consumers through programs administered and funded by governmental bodies. For example, Social Security is the largest federal social insurance program available to U.S. citizens. On the other hand, **private insurance** is sold to consumers through a variety of independently owned and operated insuring organizations, such as stock insurers and mutual insurers.

Private insurance cannot protect consumers from all risks. For example, losses from wars, unemployment, and other catastrophic events are so potentially large that private insurers cannot offer protection without risking their own financial ruin. In other cases, imperfections in insurance markets cause the supply of insurance to fall short of the demand, thus forcing consumers to find other means of protection. Paradoxically, many individuals and firms with urgent needs for insurance protection often are unable to buy it because their high likelihood of suffering insured losses forces private insurers to increase their premiums to unaffordable levels. To address these problem areas, governmental bodies often create social insurance programs to help fill the need for essential insurance products that are unavailable in the private insurance sector.

EMPLOYEE BENEFIT PLANS

U.S. workers also rely upon **employee benefit plans**, nonwage compensation provided by their employers, as a source of protection from a number of personal pure risks. Several different types of personal insurance protection typically are provided, including health insurance, life insurance, disability insurance, and a number of different types of retirement programs [defined benefit plans and 401(k) plans]. Employee benefits account for approximately 30 percent of the total compensation paid by employers in the United States, and they are many employees' sole source of protection against these types of personal risks. [Bureau of Labor Statistics, 2010]

Employers offer these benefits for a variety of reasons. Many companies offer these insurance arrangements as a means to attract and retain talented workers, a practice that dates to the mid-1900s. At that time, labor unions were strong advocates for expanding employee benefit compensation, in part because the insurance protection provided to workers in the form of employee benefits received favorable tax treatment, a practice that largely holds true today. Group insurance plans commonly are included in employee benefit programs because these arrangements often have lower administrative expenses than insurance sold to individual workers, making it more cost-effective for an employee to be covered through group insurance than through an individual policy.

---

[5] Please see United Nations Conference on Trade and Development (2007), p. 13.

Despite these advantages, employers have gradually scaled back the insurance coverage that they provide through employee benefits, citing high costs as the reason. Many now question whether employers will be able to continue their current practice of providing insurance protection through employee benefit plans.

CORPORATE RISK MANAGEMENT

Due in part to the limitations of insurance markets, many firms have become less reliant upon insurance as a primary means of protecting themselves from loss exposures, and some have actively sought out noninsurance alternatives that can protect their organizations from financial harm. In recognition of the variety of techniques—both insurance and noninsurance—that firms can use to protect themselves from loss, these efforts are known by the broader term *risk management*. Firms began embracing risk management at an increasing rate during the last half of the twentieth century. Today, nearly every major firm across the globe has a corporate risk management department, as do a large and growing number of smaller firms and organizations.

THE RISK MANAGEMENT PROCESS

The **risk management process** is a systematic approach by which an organization can identify and manage its exposures to risk in ways that best fit its strategic goals. The process has proven to be quite versatile. Corporate and non-corporate entities (such as state and local governments and nonprofit organizations) have designed their risk management programs around the process, and it has recently been adapted for use in the enterprise risk management initiatives of many firms, as we discuss later in this chapter. An outline of the risk management process is shown in Figure 1-1.

While no two risk management departments operate in exactly the same way, most can follow the same general process, described in the five steps listed here.

ESTABLISH THE GOALS OF RISK MANAGEMENT

The first step in the process is to set the objectives of the risk management function so they are consistent with the strategic goals of the organization. Strategic goals can vary greatly across firms and non-corporate organizations. The objectives of a multinational corporation are often different from goals of a nonprofit charity, and

FIGURE 1-1 Steps in the Risk Management Process

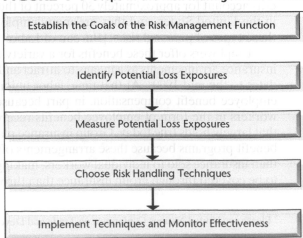

Establish the Goals of the Risk Management Function

Identify Potential Loss Exposures

Measure Potential Loss Exposures

Choose Risk Handling Techniques

Implement Techniques and Monitor Effectiveness

management's willingness to incur losses is lower for nuclear power plant operators than for firms in less-hazardous industries.

Despite their differences, however, risk managers across all disciplines generally share a common goal: to ensure that the organization will survive if it suffers a significant financial loss. Most risk managers also strive to minimize the chance that an unexpected event will disrupt the normal operation of their organizations or impede its growth. Once these basic objectives have been satisfied, however, many organizations tailor their risk management goals to fit their unique characteristics and capabilities.

IDENTIFY POTENTIAL LOSS EXPOSURES

After setting its objectives, the risk management department must next identify all possible exposures to loss. This step requires that the risk manager be intimately familiar with all aspects of the firm. If the manager overlooks a loss exposure and that exposure results in a financial loss, the firm will usually bear the cost of that loss.

It is difficult to summarize the wide variety of loss exposures encountered by risk managers because risk exposures vary dramatically across firms and industries. Nonetheless, a common approach to pure risk identification identifies four distinct types of risk:

- **Property risks** are losses to a firm that result from the destruction of or damage to property, including both **tangible property**—physical assets like buildings, vehicles, and inventory—and **intangible property**—intellectual property like copyrights, patents, and research and development.
- **Liability risks** are loss exposures in the form of monetary judgments owed to plaintiffs who were harmed financially by the negligent acts of the organization.
- **Human resource risks** are losses incurred by the firm as a result of the death, injury, or discontinuation of employment of key employees. These risks may also result from legal obligations that the organization owes to its employees, such as workers' compensation, as well as from the cost of employee benefit plans.
- Finally, **indirect losses** are financial losses that often result from any of these circumstances, such as a reduction in revenues incurred when the firm's business is interrupted due to a property or liability loss.

MEASURE POTENTIAL LOSS EXPOSURES

After identifying the loss exposures of the organization, the risk manager must next take steps to quantify the financial impact of each. This step is difficult in that the risk manager must forecast the future: She does not know whether the loss will occur, nor does she know the size of the loss if it should occur. Two quantitative measures of the loss exposure are especially useful: the frequency of the loss exposure and the severity of the loss. The **frequency** of the loss exposure measures the number of losses that might occur over a given period of time. The **severity** of the loss is a measure of the size of the loss if the loss is assumed to occur. The risk manager often will rely on the firm's prior loss experience to estimate future loss frequency and severity.

CHOOSE THE MOST EFFICIENT METHODS TO HANDLE THE LOSS EXPOSURES

The methods that organizations can choose to deal with their loss exposures are referred to collectively as **risk handling techniques**. A variety of risk handling techniques are available, and risk managers often use more than one to address a specific loss exposure. These techniques often are categorized into three broad categories: loss control, loss transfer, and loss financing.

- **Loss control** activities are designed to limit financial loss by reducing the frequency of loss, its severity, or both. Risk managers rely heavily on loss control so long as its benefits exceed the costs. Also known as *risk control,* loss control activities include risk avoidance, loss prevention, and loss reduction. When a firm practices **risk avoidance**, it simply does not engage in the activity that can result in financial loss. For example, a firm may choose to cancel the introduction of a new product line or end the production of an existing one because it could cause harm to its customers. **Loss prevention** activities help lower the frequency of losses, such as training workers to perform certain work-related activities like driving or lifting heavy objects in a safe manner, using security guards in banks, or printing warning labels on drugs or chemicals. **Loss reduction** activities mitigate the severity of losses, such as installing sprinkler systems in buildings to control fire losses or physically separating two key manufacturing facilities so they cannot be harmed by the same loss event. Recognizing that loss prevention efforts are not 100 percent effective, loss reduction activities aim to minimize the impact of losses if they should occur.

- **Loss transfer** activities include techniques that shift the financial consequences of a loss onto a third party and away from the organization that suffers the loss. Many common contracts include elements of loss transfer. Thus, a tenant often will assume some responsibility for the liability risk of its rented building through a property lease, or a manufacturer may transfer to its customers or its trucking firm the risk that goods will suffer damage during shipment. A number of loss-financing contracts, including insurance and hedging, also use loss transfer, as we discuss in Chapter 4 Methods of Handling Risk.

- **Loss financing** techniques are arrangements that an organization can use to pay for the cost of uncertain loss events that may occur sometime in the future. Simply put, if an organization cannot transfer the financial consequences of a loss exposure to a third party or use loss control to reduce the risk to an acceptable level, it must arrange a way to pay for the losses if they occur. Some risk financing activities can be carried out *internally* by a firm's risk management department, such as paying losses from internal cash flows through a **risk retention** program, or arranging more formalized financing through a **self-insurance** program. Others involve paying a fee to an *external* third-party risk-bearing institution to assume financial responsibility for some portion of the firm's losses, such as buying insurance from a commercial insurer.

Note that the use of third-party risk-bearing institutions incorporates risk transfer as well as risk financing because these institutions assume financial responsibility for the losses transferred to them by the risk manager. Third parties often rely on some form of risk diversification to absorb risk, and they frequently are an attractive alternative because they are more cost-efficient than their customers in bearing risk.

IMPLEMENT THE CHOSEN RISK-HANDLING TECHNIQUE AND MONITOR ITS EFFECTIVENESS

Much of the daily work in a risk management department involves implementing and then managing the risk-handling methods selected by the firm. The risk management environment changes rapidly. Large corporations constantly introduce new products or services, acquire or sell operations, and adjust their capital costs. Markets for insurance and noninsurance techniques also are subject to significant fluctuations in prices and supply. Changes in insurance and risk management regulation also can require quick adjustments in risk management strategy. For all these reasons, risk managers must continually monitor and occasionally adjust their firms' methods of handling risk.

ENTERPRISE RISK MANAGEMENT

In the wake of the corporate scandals of the early 2000s, several influential voices in the global business community called for improvements in the ways that firms manage and report on their risks. One of the most ambitious proposals was a report published in 2004 by the Committee of Sponsoring Organizations (COSO) of the Treadway Commission, entitled "Enterprise Risk Management—Integrated Framework." This report, sponsored and written by several accounting professional groups, reflected a growing concern in the financial and accounting communities that firms needed to upgrade the methods that they use to monitor, manage, and protect themselves from risk, as well as the way they report their risk management efforts to the public. The COSO report has been well received in the business community, especially among organizations that are responsible for providing corporate financial information to investors, such as stock exchanges and rating agencies.

In spite of growing support, however, the business community has not coalesced around a single, universally accepted definition of enterprise risk management.[6] Proponents instead generally describe ERM as having the following characteristics:

- **A top-down corporate focus.** ERM calls for elevating the oversight of corporate risk management to the highest level of the firm: the corporate boardroom.
- **A broad scope of loss exposures.** ERM examines a wide variety of risk within the firm, encompassing traditional pure (or hazard) risk, financial risk, operational risk, and strategic risk.
- **A portfolio perspective.** ERM evaluates risk using a portfolio approach, examining correlations among risks and capitalizing on cases in which different risks move in opposite directions to cancel each other out.
- **A systematic process of risk identification, assessment, and treatment.** Proponents of ERM, including the authors of the COSO report, advocate that organizations adopt a systematic process modeled after the risk management process described earlier in this chapter.

A common feature across most ERM programs is that their scope extends beyond pure risk management, also known as hazard risk management in the ERM literature, to encompass such areas as financial risks, operational risks, and strategic risk,[7] which are described in greater detail here. Insight Box 1-2 also provides some highly publicized examples of recent corporate loss events in each of the areas of risk.

- **Hazard risks** are the adverse financial losses associated with pure risks. As we discussed in the previous section of this chapter, these risks often are related to property losses, liability losses, human resource losses, and the indirect or consequential losses that can result from any of these types of loss exposures.

---

[6] One possible reason for this lack of uniformity is that ERM is difficult to define in a concise way. For example, COSO offers a commonly cited (but hardly concise) definition of ERM: "A process effected by an entity's board of directors, management, and other personnel, applied in a strategic setting across the enterprise, designed to identify potential events that may affect the entity and manage risk within its risk appetite to provide reasonable assurance regarding the achievement of entity objectives."

[7] The COSO report was drafted by several professional groups from the accounting industry, and focuses heavily on accounting issues related to risk management (e.g., reliability of financial reporting, compliance with laws and regulations). Other key stakeholders with interest in enterprise risk management (e.g., the Casualty Actuarial Society, the Institute of Internal Auditors Research Foundation, the Risk and Insurance Management Society) have offered ERM models that include failures of accounting and internal control systems and regulatory noncompliance as risk areas within the financial or operational risk categories, the approach followed in this book.

INSIGHT BOX 1-2

Examples of Recent Loss Events in Each ERM Risk Category

Hazard Risks

- *Property damage:* destruction of the World Trade Center Towers in the November 11, 2001 terrorist attacks
- *Human resource and indirect losses:* lost concert ticket revenue incurred by concert promoter AEG Live due to the unexpected death of Michael Jackson
- *Liability losses:* lawsuits filed by Toyota owners alleging damages from auto accidents caused by accelerator problems

Operational Risks

- *Product quality issues:* Dell's recall of laptop computers due to defective batteries
- *Supply chain disruption:* Reduced production for global automakers resulting from a 2011 earthquake in Japan that damaged the factories of their parts suppliers
- *Financial system failures:* Enron's fraudulent accounting practices

Financial Risks

- *Price risk:* Fluctuations in jet fuel prices that inspired Southwest Airlines to launch a jet fuel hedging program
- *Uncompetitive cost structures:* U.S. automakers' employee benefit costs
- *Credit crisis:* The U.S. banking industry's failure to recognize the 2007 real estate crisis

Strategic Risks

- *New technology:* The growing market share that Apple has earned at the expense of traditional computer manufacturers
- *Emerging consumer trends:* The bankruptcy of several retailers (Circuit City, Eddie Bauer, Linens 'N Things) in 2008–9 due to a steep decline in consumer spending
- *Reputation risk:* Mattel's efforts to maintain consumer confidence after recalling toys painted with lead paint

---

- **Operational risks** are risks related to the success or failure of an organization's systems or processes, technology, or people. Examples include the malfunction of essential processes like accounting systems, whether from intentional fraud (such as at Enron) or from poorly trained personnel. Operational risk also includes factors that reduce product quality and customer satisfaction, such as supply chain failures, faulty product design, and inadequate customer service. In most organizations, the management of operational risk is the responsibility of the chief operating officer (COO).
- **Financial risks** like currency fluctuations, changes in commodity prices, and changes in interest rates often arise in the course of the organization's efforts to secure capital and minimize the cost of its operations. Other examples include credit risk (the risk that entities owing money to the organization might fail to pay) and asset risk (the risk that assets held by the firm might decrease in value). In most firms, the chief financial officer (CFO) is responsible for financial risk management activities.
- **Strategic risks** are contingencies that affect the organization's ability to achieve its goals or mission statement. For corporations, these include risks associated with a firm's ability to compete with its rivals, maintain brand value, and protect its reputation. Because these risks ultimately can dictate the success or failure of a firm, the chief executive officer (CEO) typically assumes responsibility for strategic risk in most corporations.

ERM and the Chief Risk Officer The growing interest in ERM has increased recognition of risk managers and elevated their positions on their firms' organizational charts. It has also prompted many corporate boards of directors to acknowledge the new breadth and complexity of today's corporate risk environment and the risk manager's role in dealing with operational, financial, and strategic risks.

A growing number of firms have thus created a new title for the person responsible for this function, the **chief risk officer (CRO)**. Consistent with the recommendation of the COSO report, the CRO is a senior C-level position comparable to the CFO or the COO, who reports to the CEO. The CRO also works closely with those members of the board of directors who are responsible for the oversight of corporate risk management activities. The skills required of the CRO are considerable and can include prior experience in such diverse disciplines as engineering, accounting, manufacturing, financial modeling, strategic planning, law, information technology, insurance, or risk mitigation.

Summary

In this chapter, we have examined the factors leading to the growing interest in corporate enterprise risk management. Enterprise risk management applies the traditional risk management process across four areas of risk: hazard risk, financial risk, operational risk, and strategic risk. ERM efforts encompass both pure and hazard risk, as well as diversifiable and non-diversifiable risk. The ERM concept recognizes that traditional behavioral tendencies toward risk aversion may be appropriate when dealing with pure risk, but they may not be appropriate across the wider spectrum of risks included within the ERM framework. With only minimal adjustments, however, the traditional risk management process has been adapted to fit the broad range of risk encompassed within the enterprise risk management framework.

Review

1. Describe how the scope of risks encompassed in enterprise risk management differs from those of traditional corporate risk management.
2. Explain why interest in risk management has increased dramatically in the United States in recent years.
3. How did the corporate scandal at Enron prompt the accounting profession to take a leading role in the call for improvements in corporate risk management?
4. Describe the difference between pure and speculative risks. Provide an example of each.
5. Describe the process of risk diversification, noting the two conditions that must exist for diversification to be effective.
6. Explain why auto and life insurance are two types of risk that are well suited to diversification by insurers through the use of risk pooling.
7. Explain why damage from floods and wars are two types of risk that are not well suited to diversification by insurers through the use of risk pooling.
8. Financial advisors encourage investors to hold a well-diversified portfolio of investments. Explain whether this level of diversification can protect an investor if
   a. one of her stock holdings is a firm with an unsuccessful new product launch, or
   b. the global economy falls into a recession.
9. Describe the concept of risk aversion. Is it an equally appropriate strategy for dealing with pure and speculative risks?
10. Describe the alternatives available to people and firms across the globe to protect themselves from adverse loss exposures.
11. How does social insurance differ from private insurance? In your answer, explain why some loss exposures are insured better through social insurance than through private insurance.
12. Explain why it may be advantageous for people to get insurance protection from employee benefit plans instead of buying individual insurance policies.

13. List and briefly describe the five steps in the risk management process.
14. Describe four different types of risk that need to be addressed by the risk manager in a typical corporation. Discuss whether each of these four types of risk are equally important across different industries.
15. Describe the difference between loss frequency and loss severity.
16. Describe the three broad categories of risk-handling techniques used by risk managers. In your answer, provide at least two specific examples of each technique.
17. Explain why it is necessary to monitor the effectiveness of the chosen risk-handling techniques of the risk management process on a continuous basis.
18. While no single, universally accepted definition of ERM exists, describe four characteristics that commonly are attributed to a well-designed ERM program.
19. List and describe the four areas of risk encompassed in an enterprise risk management program. For each risk area, provide an example of a recent risk event that has been described in the popular business media.

Objective Questions

1. Which of the following have led to a growing interest in risk management?
   a. The terrorist attacks of September 11, 2001
   b. Corporations that filed fraudulent financial statements that overstated earnings
   c. Shrinking wages and employee benefit plans during the 2008 recession
   d. All of the above
2. Auto collision claims are an example of which of the following?
   a. Pure risks that can be diversified across a large group of drivers
   b. Speculative risks than can be diversified across a large group of drivers
   c. Pure risks that cannot be diversified across a large group of drivers
   d. Speculative risks that cannot be diversified across a large group of drivers
3. Which of the following is not a speculative risk?
   a. An investor who invests in common stock
   b. An entrepreneur who starts a new company
   c. A business that develops a new product line
   d. A lawsuit filed against a firm by a client who slips on the firm's icy steps
4. Risk aversion . . .
   I. is the tendency of a person to prefer less risk instead of more risk when faced with risky decisions.
   II. is a more appropriate strategy for pure risks than for speculative risks.
   a. I only
   b. II only
   c. both I and II
   d. neither I nor II
5. Which of the following statements about insurance is correct?
   a. Insurance is available in all countries across the world.
   b. Insurance is a common technique used by individuals to protect against risk.
   c. Private insurance is available for non-diversifiable risks like unemployment.
   d. a and b are correct
   e. b and c are correct
6. Which of the following statements about employee benefits are correct?
   I. Workers are granted favorable tax treatment on the employee benefits that they receive from their employers.
   II. Employee benefits account for over half of the compensation paid by employers in the United States.
   a. I only
   b. II only
   c. both I and II
   d. neither I nor II
7. Which of the following is a step in the risk management process?
   a. Identifying all possible sources of financial loss
   b. Setting the goals of the risk management program
   c. Choosing the most efficient ways to handle the firm's loss exposures
   d. Measuring the frequency and severity of all loss exposures
   e. All of the above
8. The owner of a building inserts a provision in its lease that makes its tenant legally responsible for clearing snow and ice from the building's sidewalks. This provision is an example of which of the following?
   a. Loss prevention
   b. Loss reduction
   c. Loss transfer
   d. Self-insurance
9. ACA is a leading global automaker. ACA has to stop production of a popular vehicle when a labor strike

shuts down the factories of BBB Company, the sole supplier of auto transmissions to ACA. The lost production resulting from this supply chain disruption is an example of a(n) _____ that is borne by ACA.

a. hazard risk
b. financial risk
c. operational risk
d. strategic risk

10. Which of the following is not a characteristic of an ERM program?

a. The decisions of the ERM department are monitored by the firm's board of directors.

b. The ERM program focuses only on pure risk.
c. The ERM department evaluates the loss exposures of the firm as a portfolio of risk.
d. The ERM department typically uses a systematic process modeled after the risk management process to identify, assess, and treat the firm's risks.

Discussion Questions

1. Discuss the events that led to the development of the concept of enterprise risk management. Was the growth of ERM prompted primarily by an expansion of risk management activities within corporations, or was it forced upon firms by external events?

2. Describe the differences between the scope of traditional corporate risk management activities and the range of activities encompassed in enterprise risk management.

Selected References

Bureau of Labor Statistics, "Employer Costs for Employee Compensation—June 2010."

The Committee of Sponsoring Organizations (COSO) of the Treadway Commission: "Enterprise Risk Management—Integrated Framework Executive Summary," September 2004, retrieved March 27, 2001 at http://www.coso.org/

Kirby, Julia. "The Decade of Management Ideas", *Harvard Business Review*, January 1, 2010, retrieved July 7, 2011 from http://blogs.hbr.org/

United Nations Conference on Trade and Development. *Trade and Development Aspects of Insurance Services and Regulatory Frameworks,* 2007, page 13.

Williams, C. Arthur Jr., Michael L. Smith, and Peter C. Young. *Risk Management and Insurance*, 7th ed. (New York: McGraw-Hill Inc. 1995), Chapter 2.

2

Risk Identification

After studying this chapter, you should be able to

- Explain why risk identification is a vital step in the risk management process

- Identify some common characteristics used to classify risk

- Explain the difference between direct and indirect losses

- Describe the wide variety of property risk exposures borne by firms

- Describe the legal system used in the United States to resolve liability issues

- Describe the negligence standard used in tort liability claims

- Describe three types of human resource risks

- Define and provide examples of hazard, operational, financial, and strategic risks, as they are commonly used in enterprise risk management (ERM).

The ultimate objective of the ERM function in most large firms is to handle risks in ways that are harmonious with the strategic plan of the organization. This objective can be achieved on several levels. At a minimum, the risk manager should take steps to assure the survival of the firm and to minimize the interruption to the firm's normal operations that may be caused by a financial loss. At its best, however, an organization with a well-functioning ERM program attempts to understand how the risks that cause financial losses are interconnected to each other, recognizing that large organizations face many risks.[1] In this sense, setting the ERM goals of the organization, the first step in the risk management process, relies heavily on a comprehensive identification of all the risks of the firm, the second step of that process.

This chapter focuses on the identification of loss exposures that might arise from the risks borne by the firm. Because the process of identifying loss exposures is synonymous with identifying the risks that cause such losses, the terms *loss identification* and *risk identification* often are used interchangeably in the risk and insurance industry. Risk identification has changed significantly in recent years as risk managers have

---

[1] An important concept in ERM is the idea that a firm should view all its risks collectively to capitalize on risks that offset each other at little or no cost to the firm. Additional discussion on this portfolio approach is presented in Chapter 5.

taken responsibility for a wider variety of risk categories and ERM programs have grown more popular.

Risk identification is arguably the most critical step in the risk management process because firms that fail to identify key risk exposures often have to pay for their oversights if the overlooked risk results in a financial loss. Even the best managed firms can occasionally overlook a key loss exposure—for instance, few U.S. firms had plans in place to address losses from terrorist attacks prior to September 11, 2001—but thorough monitoring of a firm's risk environment will help to assure that such oversights occur infrequently.

Risk managers often use a variety of techniques to complete the ambitious task of identifying their firm's vulnerability. Internal information from analysis of financial statements, communication with managers, surveys administered within the organization, and onsite inspection can provide a useful assessment. Risk managers also can obtain external information from risk consultants, agents and brokers, and risk management trade associations such as the Risk and Insurance Management Society. The best means of staying on top of the risks in the firm is to be involved intimately in all aspects of the organization and maintain frequent communication with its key managers.

USEFUL METHODS OF RISK CLASSIFICATION

As a risk management department develops a list of its firm's loss exposures, it notes several aspects of the risks that cause those losses because these characteristics will influence the strategies used by risk managers to treat such risks.

External vs. Internal Risks

It is helpful to know whether a loss exposure is caused by a risk that is located within or outside the firm. Risk managers often are better able to deal with internal risks, such as fires or injuries to workers, because these risks are more likely to be under the manager's control. By contrast, external risks can be troublesome because they are largely beyond the control of the risk manager. For example, due to the random and often catastrophic nature of natural disasters, earthquakes and floods pose a great challenge to risk managers.

An especially daunting challenge is dealing with external losses that are not random, but consciously planned by parties outside the firm. For example, losses from terrorism and Internet sabotage are very difficult to deal with because terrorists and hackers can study a firm and attack it at a point where its defenses are most vulnerable. Conscious acts are not always criminal in nature, of course. Thus, many firms suffer significant losses at the hands of competing firms in their industries that intentionally exploit the weaknesses of their rivals to increase their own market share and profitability.

Pure and Speculative Risks

ERM traces its roots to efforts to protect firms from harm arising from pure risks, but in recent years it has expanded its scope to speculative risks as well. Clearly, both categories of risk can cause great financial harm. A risk manager must recognize whether its firm's losses are caused by pure or speculative contingencies, however, because the incentives for firms to engage in activities that expose them to the two types of risk are quite different. In particular, risk managers must be more tolerant of the negative outcomes from speculative risk because all firms are exposed to downside risks in their efforts to earn the returns generated by speculative business ventures. This risk/return tradeoff is irrelevant to pure risks, however, because a firm cannot profit from its exposure to pure risk.

DIRECT AND INDIRECT LOSSES

Another key consideration in risk identification is recognizing the full financial scope of the loss exposures of the firm. Many financial losses have two components: direct loss and indirect loss. In the case of property loss exposures, **direct loss** is the financial loss that immediately results from the damage or theft of such property. Thus, the direct loss incurred by a firm as a result of a fire to one of its buildings includes the portion of the building damaged in the fire, as well as smoke damage to the remaining portion of the structure and water damage resulting from the use of fire hoses in fighting the blaze.

Indirect loss is the financial loss that often results as a consequence of the direct loss. Many indirect losses start immediately upon the occurrence of a serious loss event—the time at which the firm suspends its normal operations—and continue over time until the firm is able to resume its business as usual. The size of the indirect loss typically is measured by the reduction in revenues and the increased expenses incurred as a result of the direct loss. For example, a small retailer may suffer a significant reduction in sales if one of its four stores were to close for a month for repairs after a fire. Similarly, the owner of an apartment complex could suffer a significant loss of rental income due to a fire in one of its buildings. Because the size of the indirect loss often is directly related to the period of time that a business has been interrupted, these losses frequently are called **business interruption** losses.

Indirect losses do not result solely from damage to property. For example, a drug manufacturer that must recall a popular drug because the product has a harmful side effect often will be the target of lawsuits (the direct loss), but it also may suffer a sizable loss of revenues (the indirect loss) because it is no longer able to sell the drug or because consumers become wary of buying any of the firm's products. Similar indirect losses occur in other industries as well, as is shown in Insight Box 2-1.

INSIGHT BOX 2-1

Mattel Toy Recall

In the summer of 2007, Mattel Corporation, the world's leading toy company, discovered that some of its popular products had been finished with lead-based paint. The most notable of these was a toy car modeled after Sarge, a character from the movie *Cars*, for which Mattel had obtained licensing rights from Pixar. An investigation of the incident revealed that the manufacturer, based in China, had hired a subcontractor to paint its assembled toys, but the subcontractor had neglected to use the non-lead-based paint specifically designed by Mattel for the toy.

Recognizing the potential harm that could arise from this problem, Mattel quickly announced a recall of the improperly painted toys, which it expanded after testing revealed that many more toys were affected than originally thought. The total cost of the toy recalls at the end of 2007 equaled $110 million.[2] While the recalls prompted a wave of panic among parents, Mattel's quick action to discuss the matter publicly and conduct the recalls minimized the damage to the reputation of the firm.[3]

Ironically, even though Mattel agreed in a class-action settlement to provide ongoing medical monitoring of those children exposed to the lead paint, few children were publicly acknowledged to have suffered harm.[4] In this instance, the indirect loss arising from a supply chain issue became a much larger issue than the direct loss from liability.

---

[2] Matthew Garrahan, "Mattel Looking for a Brighter Future After Weathering Storm," *Financial Times,* February 6, 2008, p. 27.

[3] Chrystia Freeland, "View from the Top: Mattel's Bob Eckert," Published February 15, 2008 on FT.com (http://www.ft.com/).

[4] Patti Waldmeir, "Too Much Safety in America's Playrooms: [USA 1ST EDITION]," *Financial Times* November 28, 2007.

Experienced risk managers recognize that a significant loss can result in both direct and indirect losses and that an indirect loss can be larger than the direct loss that caused it. A risk management plan must identify both types of losses and consider ways of dealing with both types of financial losses as well.

IDENTIFICATION OF PURE RISKS

We begin by focusing on pure risks, also known as *hazard risks*. These risks have been the traditional focus of risk managers, and we can classify them broadly into three categories: property risks, liability risks, and human resource risks.

Property Risks

Risk managers focus considerable attention on identifying loss exposures that can cause financial harm to the property of their firms. **Tangible property** refers to physical assets of value to the firm. Within this category, buildings, plants, stores, and related structures often are classified as real estate or **real property**. **Business property** includes such items as building contents, inventory, equipment, supplies, furniture, computers, and communications equipment. Vehicles, planes, and other transportation equipment are also important categories of property.

Intangible property refers to assets that are not physical in nature, but whose value to the firm is associated with such essential needs as the legal rights to intellectual property (copyrights or patents), capabilities and skill sets (research and development or human capital), and measures of competitive economic value (reputation or brand awareness). Although it is challenging to measure its value sometimes, intangible property has grown in importance in many industries, and protecting it or intangible property from harm has become an area of considerable risk management attention.

For example, as shown in Insight Box 2-2, a recent survey of risk managers identified protecting the reputation of their firm as their most difficult risk management challenge. If its reputation is damaged, a firm can suffer declining earnings, smaller market share, lower credit ratings, and an inability to attract and retain talented employees.

Firms also are susceptible to severe losses that result from damage to the property *of others* because the complexity and interconnectedness of today's business environment makes risk identification increasingly difficult. For example, many firms rely heavily upon *supply chains*, complex production systems consisting of multiple assemblers, part suppliers, and transportation firms, to manufacture their products. Manufacturers can gain a number of benefits from including multiple parties in a supply chain, such as reduced production costs or higher-quality components. Supply chains can complicate the ERM process, however, because risk managers must not only protect their own organizations from harm but also take steps to avoid supply chain disruptions that may occur if one of the supply chain members suffers a loss due to ineffective risk management. A variety of firms have suffered sizable financial losses recently from supply chain disruptions, ranging from auto assembly plants shut down by a shortage of auto parts to product recalls necessitated by safety concerns related to toys painted with lead paint or containing other dangerous components. Risk managers thus have identified supply chain risks as another challenging risk management dilemma (see Insight Box 2-2).

To demonstrate further the complexity of risk management in today's business world, consider the number of parties who can suffer financially from the loss of a single building. For example, a fire loss in a large department store in a shopping mall

---

INSIGHT BOX 2-2

A Survey of Risk Managers' Most Challenging Risks

A recent international risk management survey of 320 organizations across 29 countries suggests that firms are focusing greater attention on increasingly complex and dynamic risks. Described below are the four risks that were identified most frequently as a concern by the respondents. Also provided is the percentage of the firms that reported that they were not appropriately prepared to deal with the risk.

Reputation risk was the most frequently identified concern among the surveyed organizations. More than half the surveyed firms (52 percent) indicated that they were not "risk ready" to deal with an event that could harm the reputation of their firm. As was noted in the report, it can take years for an organization to build a favorable reputation, but it can be destroyed overnight.

Business interruption was the second most frequently identified concern among the respondents. This finding suggests that firms are concerned that an adverse event could affect their firms' earnings and disrupt their normal operations significantly, resulting in a large indirect loss for the firm. Of the respondents, 30 percent reported that their firms were inadequately prepared to handle a business interruption episode.

Third-party liability was the third most frequently reported concern. Litigation is becoming a global concern as countries around the world are experiencing increased costs in satisfying their legal duties to others. One-quarter of the responding organizations indicated that they were not ready to address such litigation.

Disruptions or supply chain failures were also a major concern for the surveyed organizations. Over a third of the respondents (37 percent) indicated that their organizations were not prepared to deal with a supply chain failure, reflecting the complexity of protecting a firm from adverse outcomes that frequently arise away from the site of the risk managers' organization.

Based on *Aon, Global Risk Management Study 2007: Extract of Key Findings*, April 24, 2007. (Retrieved on May 19, 2011 from www.aon.com).

---

can result in a financial loss to the owner of the store and the tenant who rents the store from the owner, especially if the tenant receives economic benefits, like low rent or great location, that are not available elsewhere. The lender who lent money to the storeowner to buy the building also may suffer financially, recognizing that the damaged storeowner is more likely to default on the loan. In addition, neighboring stores that rely on the large store to attract customers to the shopping mall might suffer financial loss. Clearly the interconnected nature of business networks can complicate the risk management process.

Liability Risks

Another major area of concern for risk managers is corporate **liability risk**, or the risk that a firm may be legally responsible for the harm that it caused to another person. If a firm's actions harm another person, the injured party can sue the negligent party for the damages suffered as result of those actions. Liability risks sometimes are overlooked because you cannot see a lawsuit in the same way that you see a burned home or a damaged car. Yet a $100 million lawsuit can be far more costly than a direct property loss.

TORT LIABILITY IN THE UNITED STATES

The U.S. legal liability system is patterned after the legal system used in England. The concept of legal liability arises from the general rule of English common law that people are responsible for any loss or injury that they cause another to suffer. The law creates three categories of situations in which one person injures another.

First, **breach of contract** is a failure, without a legal excuse, to perform contractual duties. Second, local, state, and federal laws define **criminal acts**, which are wrongs against society that are punishable by fines or imprisonment. Finally, **torts**, or civil wrongs, are unreasonable conduct toward another person. The same action, such as reckless driving, may be both a criminal and a civil wrong. Although punishment for a criminal wrong may include making restitution to the injured party, it often does not. Therefore, the victim must file a successful tort action in an appropriate civil court to collect payment for injury.

In tort cases, two parties are involved in civil litigation, or what is more commonly known as a *lawsuit*. The **plaintiff** is the party claiming injury, and the **defendant** is the party from whom the plaintiff seeks a financial award. People, businesses, government units, and other organizations all can be plaintiffs or defendants in a lawsuit.[5] A lawsuit begins in a *civil trial court*. The designation of civil trial courts varies across states and may be known as a *court of common appeals*, *superior court*, *district court*, or *circuit court*. Appellate courts may be asked to review the decisions of trial courts if the losing parties believe trial procedures were unfair or that the law was applied improperly in their case. Appellate court rulings can be appealed to state (or sometimes federal) supreme courts on the same basis.

Whether a defendant has acted negligently is usually a *question of fact*. It is the role of the jury in a lawsuit to ascertain the facts after its review of the evidence presented in the case. In turn, based upon those facts, a judge applies the appropriate legal remedy. The courts are not always consistent. Two juries may view the same evidence but reach different conclusions about the facts. Conduct by a defendant may be viewed as reasonable in New York City but unreasonable in rural states. The point, however, is that no one can determine the outcome of a lawsuit until a jury has settled the questions of fact.

NEGLIGENCE

While the courts apply a variety of tort rules across different legal situations, one of the most common rules used in lawsuits against individuals and firms is negligence. A standard of negligence is applied in a variety of situations, including auto liability, medical malpractice, or the duty that a building owner owes to a guest. **A negligent act** is something that a reasonable person would not do, or the omission of something a reasonable person would do, that results directly in some injury to another person.[6] To establish a case of negligence, the law requires the plaintiff to prove the following four points:

1. *Legal duty:* The defendant owed a legal duty to the plaintiff. Thus, in an auto accident situation, the defendant has a legal duty to drive within the speed limit.

2. *Breach of legal duty:* It must be shown that the defendant failed to satisfy the legal duty. Thus, if the defendant is speeding twenty miles per hour above the speed limit, the court will likely find that he or she has breached the legal duty.

---

[5] Courts also can impose liability for the negligent acts of other parties. *Vicarious liability* means that a person is liable because of another person's acts. For example, assume that Jack B. Nimble lends his car to Johnnie B. Good, and Johnnie then causes an accident with Jack's car. Jack might be held liable if it can be shown he was negligent in lending his car to someone he knew or should have known was a poor driver. (Johnnie also would be liable in this example.) More commonly, vicarious liability arises for businesses when parties hired as contractors injure others.

[6] A review of many court cases in which the concept of the reasonable person has been applied leads to the definition of a **reasonable person** as one who has normal possession of all faculties and senses, who is honest and moderate in all activities, and who thinks, speaks, and acts based on reason. Violating the reasonable person standard can result in a court imposing legal liability for a person's direct acts or omissions of actions.

3. *Injury or damage:* The plaintiff must show that he or she suffered property damage or bodily injuries, such as a cut, broken bone, physical pain, or similar physical impairment of a bodily function. In the case of our auto accident, the medical expense and pain and suffering incurred by the defendant are examples of injuries.

4. *Proximate cause:* The plaintiff must show that his or her injuries would not have occurred but for the defendant's failure to satisfy his or her legal duty. Thus, the plaintiff would need to demonstrate that he or she would not have suffered such medical expenses unless he or she had been involved in the accident.

Based on the facts presented in support of these four requirements, the court will make a **judgment**, the official decision of the court as to the rights of the parties to a lawsuit. If the plaintiff fails to establish any one of the elements of negligence, or if the defendant establishes a successful defense, the court will not award the plaintiff a favorable judgment. Conversely, if the plaintiff establishes each of the four elements of a negligent act to the satisfaction of the judge and jury, the plaintiff is entitled to a favorable judgment, usually a specific sum of money. The judgment is enforceable by officers of the court. Thus, if the court finds that the defendant must pay the plaintiff $100,000, the plaintiff can expect the court to enforce this decision.

Consider the following negligence claims:

- A customer contracts salmonella food poisoning after dining at a restaurant and sues the owner of the restaurant for medical expenses related to the resulting illness.
- A hotel guest is injured because a lightbulb in a hallway is burned out, causing the guest to trip over a chair. The injured guest's suit claims that the hotel operator was negligent for not replacing the bulb and for leaving a chair in the hallway.
- A driver injured in an auto accident sues the manufacturer of the vehicle, claiming that a design flaw increased the chance that the car would catch fire if struck in the rear by another vehicle.

TYPES OF DAMAGES

A court can award two types of damages: compensatory and punitive. **Compensatory damages** are payments set by the court to restore the victim to the same financial condition after an injury that he or she was in before the injury. There are two types of compensatory damages. **Special damages** are *economic* damages incurred by the plaintiff, including such items as medical expenses, the past and estimated future wages lost by the plaintiff due to injury, and the cost to repair property damage. **General damages**, sometimes called *noneconomic* damages, are awards made to the plaintiff for hard-to-measure items like pain and suffering or the emotional distress resulting from the death or injury of a loved one. Both types of compensatory damages are difficult to calculate, but because of their noneconomic nature, general damages for such losses as pain and suffering or emotional distress are especially hard to value. Despite this complication, general damages can be sizable because they often are calculated as some multiple of the special damages, such as two times the award for special damages.

Punitive damages are awards made to plaintiffs not as compensation for injuries suffered, but as a means of punishing defendants for outrageously offensive acts. Punitive damages usually imply **gross negligence**, cases in which the defendant willfully disregarded the potential harm inflicted upon the defendant by his or her actions.

While punitive damages are awarded in a relatively small percentage of all lawsuits, they have posed a significant risk to many firms historically due to their severity. For example, a California court awarded six plaintiffs injured in an auto accident $4.9 billion in punitive damages to punish the car manufacturer for its gross negligence in failing to take action to correct a defect in the design of the car.[7]

DEFENSES IN A NEGLIGENCE SUIT

A defendant has two main lines of defense against a charge of negligence: contributory negligence and assumption of the risk. The jury also will rule in favor of the defendant if the plaintiff fails to prove any of the four elements of a negligent act.

Contributory Negligence Defendants traditionally have been able to counter a negligence lawsuit with the defense of **contributory negligence** if they can show that the plaintiff's own negligence contributed to or led to the injury sustained. If the plaintiff has been negligent, however, that does not relieve defendants of their duties; rather, it means that because both parties are at fault, neither will be allowed recovery from the other. For example, assume that the plaintiff fails to signal a turn while driving and his car is hit in the rear by an oncoming car that was speeding. If the defendant, the driver of the speeding car, establishes that the plaintiff contributed to the loss by failing to signal, she may be able to protect herself from judgment. In this circumstance, neither plaintiff nor defendant could recover from each other under the contributory negligence rule.

The contributory negligence rule is harsh; even slight negligence on a plaintiff's part can relieve a grossly negligent defendant of responsibility for an accident. As a result, most states have applied a modification of the rule called **comparative negligence**, which allows plaintiffs some degree of recovery even if they contributed to their own injuries. Some states allow the plaintiff to recover damages proportionate to the defendant's negligence. Other states allow the plaintiff to recover only when he or she is responsible for 49 percent or less of the damage. In all cases, the comparative negligence rule allows the plaintiff a better chance for recovery than the contributory negligence rule and thus greatly increases the number of judgments awarded by the courts.[8]

As an example of recovery under the comparative negligence rule, assume that the plaintiff, Moe D'Laun, a landscape architect, sustains $100,000 damage in an automobile accident, and a court decides that Moe was 30 percent responsible for the accident. Under the comparative negligence rule, Moe would recover $70,000. Under the contributory negligence rule, he would recover nothing.

---

[7] See "GM Attempts to Get $4.9 Billion Judgment in Suit Thrown Out," *Wall Street Journal*, July 30, 1999, Eastern edition: p. 1. While critics have called for the U.S. Supreme Court to provide guidance to the lower courts in setting more reasonable awards, the Court has chosen instead to identify awards that it deems inappropriate and return those cases to the lower courts for review. For example, see *State Farm Mutual Automobile Ins. Co. v. Campbell*, WL 1791206 U.S. (2003).

[8] The doctrine of last clear chance is another modification of the contributory negligence rule. In general, when a plaintiff's negligence contributes to the loss, nothing may be collected if the court applies the contributory negligence rule. The last clear chance doctrine is an exception to the contributory negligence rule. This doctrine states that if the defendant had a clear chance to avoid injuring the plaintiff, then the plaintiff can collect despite having made a contribution to the loss. For example, assume that the plaintiff, Denton Fender, was waiting to make a left turn but failed to use his turn signal. Assume that the defendant, Manuel Transmission, had a clear chance to avoid the accident but hit Denton anyway. In this case, the sequence of events in court would likely be that (1) the plaintiff, Denton, establishes negligence; (2) the defendant, Manuel, establishes contributory negligence on Denton's part; and (3) the plaintiff then establishes that the defendant had a clear chance to avoid the accident despite the plaintiff's negligence. Assuming no further legal steps by the defendant, the plaintiff would receive full recovery.

Assumption of the Risk Another common-law defense available to the defendant in a lawsuit is establishing that the plaintiff knowingly assumed the risk of injury. For example, most fans at a professional baseball game know that they face a risk of being injured by a ball that is hit into the crowd by a baseball player. Thus, the owner of a baseball stadium could defend itself from a lawsuit filed by an injured fan by calling upon the **assumption of the risk** doctrine.

Human Resource Risks

Risk managers also focus considerable attention on minimizing their firms' exposure to **human resource risks**, financial losses arising from the loss or injury to employees and key people associated with the firm. Three aspects of human resource risks merit particular attention: protecting the firm from the loss of unique talent that is difficult to replace, workers' compensation exposures, and employee benefit exposures.

Loss of a Key Person/Employee Who is Difficult to Replace Firms often incur sizable financial losses when a key person is unable to complete his or her job because of death, sickness, or other factors that result in the discontinuation of employment. Perhaps the most common exposure that firms face in this risk area is the loss of a top executive such as the chief executive officer (CEO) or chief financial officer (CFO) because it is often very difficult and expensive for firms to find replacements for senior-level talent. Larger corporations often are less vulnerable to this risk than small corporations because they can make plans to replace the missing executive by promoting an internal subordinate, a process known as **succession planning**. Smaller firms have fewer internal candidates from which to pick, but this fact makes planning all the more vital for these firms.

Certain industries also are more vulnerable because they rely on irreplaceable talent. The loss of an important sports star or entertainer can affect the financial success of his or her employer dramatically, with significant indirect losses in the form of delayed or cancelled performances, lost ticket revenues, or decreased sales receipts. A recent example occurred after the sudden death in 2009 of entertainer Michael Jackson, as described in Insight Box 2-3.

Workers' Compensation A top priority in nearly all risk management programs is protecting employees from harm, a concern based on financial and legal considerations. Firms are required by law to provide workers' compensation benefits to their employees and to satisfy the statutory requirements of workplace safety regulations like the Occupational Safety and Health Act (OSHA). Workers' compensation protection includes payments to injured workers for medical expenses and lost wages they incur as a result of a work-related injury, as well as death benefits to the dependents of a worker who dies as a result of injuries suffered on the job.

Employee Benefit Programs The human resource risk concerns of corporate risk managers often extend beyond protecting workers from harm on the job and include the design and management of corporate employee benefit programs. Most risk managers are very familiar with how insurance companies operate and thus are helpful in designing employee benefit programs that rely heavily on group insurance arrangements. In addition, the coverage available from workers' compensation benefits and the benefits from health insurance are very similar. In firms that employ a large number of employees, the methods used to finance workers' compensation coverage is similar to those used to finance employee benefits, and risk managers often are uniquely qualified to manage such financing programs.

INSIGHT BOX 2-3

Human Resource Risk and Indirect Loss: The Death of Michael Jackson

On June 25, 2009, singer Michael Jackson died in the midst of rehearsals for his comeback event, fifty sold-out concerts at London's O2 Arena that were scheduled to start that July 13. In the week following his death, which prompted a worldwide outpouring of grief for the "King of Pop," concert promoter AEG Live was reported to face a loss of as much as $494 million as a result of the cancellation of the concerts. AEG Live's parent company, AEG, owns the O2 Arena.

A report indicated that Jackson's death might trigger the biggest event-cancellation claim in insurance history.[9] According to the report, AEG Live had not been successful in securing insurance for all fifty concerts and instead was able to insure only the first twenty-two, for $214 million. Insurers were said to have been reluctant to cover the later concert dates, concerned about whether Jackson was healthy enough to complete all fifty performances. Randy Phillips, the company's CEO, was quoted in the London press as saying that his firm would self-insure the rest of the concerts.

AEG Live offered a full refund to fans holding tickets to the concerts, which had generated $85 million in sales revenue. Music executives suggested that as many as half the tickets might never need to be refunded because fans would prefer to keep them as souvenirs, as had occurred for concerts that were cancelled due to the deaths of Elvis Presley in 1977 and Kurt Cobain in 1994.[10] Ticket refunds accounted for only a portion of the loss incurred on the event, however, because AEG Live had purchased insurance for other vendors who had contracts in place in support of the concerts.

AEG Live held $17.5 million in life insurance coverage on Jackson through Lloyds of London, which was designed to cover accidental death, including drug overdose but not including death by natural causes.[11] In an exclusive interview with Billboard.biz, Randy Phillips indicated that the company had incurred $23–$25 million in production costs. Industry sources indicated that AEG Live also had paid Jackson $10–$20 million in advance.[12] Phillips worked hard to find replacement acts to play in the O2 Arena in July and August, Europe's slowest concert months. In financial terms, the loss of revenue from the cancelation of the late summer shows was the hardest to mitigate, as O2 Arena vacancies later in 2009 and in 2010 could be filled by other acts more easily.

But the lost revenues "probably [are] miniscule in comparison to the value of the intellectual property we own," Phillips said.[13] AEG Live holds more than 100 hours of audio and video footage of Jackson's rehearsals, enough material to make two live albums (Jackson never released a live recording), two 3-D "mini-movies" about "Thriller" and "Earth Song," and a pay-per-view event. "We own the intellectual property," Phillips told Billboard.biz. "It is our responsibility and fiduciary duty to the [Jackson] estate to monetize as much of these assets as we can . . . because the majority of the profit would go to the estate."

In August 2009, AEG Live entered into an agreement with Columbia Pictures, in which Columbia purchased the video footage of Jackson's rehearsals from AEG Live.[14] The deal enabled AEG Live to recoup its losses from the cancellation of the concerts. In October 2009, Columbia later released *Michael Jackson's This Is It*, a documentary based on the footage. The film became the highest-grossing concert film in history, bringing in over $260 million at box offices worldwide.

---

[9] See P. Gusman, "Will Insurers Pay for Jackson's Concerts?" *National Underwriter P&C*, July 6–July 13, 2009, p. 7.

[10] See L. Pleven and E. Smith, "U.S. News: Jackson Promoter Plans Massive Refund," *Wall Street Journal* (Eastern edition), June 29, 2009, p. A4.

[11] See "AEG Live Releases Michael Jackson Rehearsal Footage," Associated Press, July 3, 2009, retrieved from cnbc.com on March 9, 2010 (see *http://www.cnbc.com/*).

[12] See R. Waddell, "Exclusive: AEG Live CEO Addresses Michael Jackson Fallout," Billboard.biz, retrieved on March 9, 2010, from *http://www.billboard.biz*.

[13] Ibid.

[14] Christman, E., Donahue, A., Mitchell, G., Peoples, G., & Waddell, R. (2010). Profit, and loss. *Billboard, 122*(25), 19–19.

ENTERPRISE RISK MANAGEMENT RISKS

The scope of most ERM programs extends well beyond traditional pure risk management to encompass such areas as financial risks, operational risks, and strategic risk.[15] With the exception of hazard risks, the remaining risk categories encompass a wide variety of speculative risks. Let's look at each of these risk categories using a real-life example of ERM in practice.

Figure 2-1 depicts a sample of the wide variety of ERM risks at General Motors, a large U.S. automaker. Examples of the common types of risks appear in the four risk categories, demonstrating how ERM focuses on identifying the full portfolio of risks that affect the firm, as well as the interrelationships among them. This figure also shows why ERM is especially challenging to coordinate and implement: The employees responsible for managing these risks are spread across a variety of corporate activities, including finance, accounting, treasury, operations, information technology, strategic planning, regulatory compliance, and traditional risk management.

The figure is arranged from top to bottom to indicate whether risks are internally generated or arise from external sources like weather or industry competitors. As we've seen, ERM departments typically are able to control the financial causes of internal risks better than external risks.

Hazard Risks Hazard risks include the direct losses arising from property, liability, and human resource risks, as well as the indirect losses associated with these events. Because losses from hazard risks serve only to decrease the value of the firm

FIGURE 2-1   General Motors ERM Risk Vulnerability Map (Internal to External Risks Ranked from Top to Bottom)

Hazard Risks	*Financial Risks*	*Operational Risks*	*Strategic Risks*
Product liability	Inadequate financial control	Accounting system failure	Ethics violations
Workers' compensation	Debt, credit rating	HR risk: key skill shortage	Inadequate management oversight
Loss of key facility	Health care, pension costs	IT system failures	Loss of intellectual property
General liability	Credit risk or default	Product recall issue	Poor technology decisions
Tornado, wind damage	Adverse change in regulation	Logistics provider failures	Attack on brand loyalty
Terrorism, sabotage	Currency fluctuations	Supplier failure to deliver	New or foreign competitors
Heavy rain, thunderstorm	Economic recession	Utilities failure: power, water	Negative media coverage

Based on Debra Elkins, "Managing Manufacturing and Supply Chain Risks in Global Automotive Operations," presented on March 18, 2005, at the North Carolina State University Enterprise Risk Management Roundtable.

---

[15] For example, see Slywotzky, Adrian J., and John Drzik. 2005. "Countering the Biggest Risk of All," *Harvard Business Review* 83, no. 4: 78–88; Walker, Paul L., Shenkir, William G., and Barton, Thomas L. 2002. "Enterprise Risk Management: Putting It All Together," Institute of Internal Auditors Research Foundation, Altamonte Springs, FL; Shenkir, William G., and Paul L. Walker, "Enterprise Risk Management and the Strategy-Risk-Focused Organization," *Cost Management* 1 May 2006: 32–38; and Colquitt, L. Lee, Robert E. Hoyt, and Ryan B. Lee, 1999."Integrated Risk Management and the Role of the Risk Manager," *Risk Management and Insurance Review* 2: 43–61.

and destroy its assets, it is easy for employees to agree that it is sound business practice to mitigate these risks.

External forces like adverse weather and other acts of nature cause many of the hazard risks identified by the automaker in Figure 2-1. These risks are random events that are largely beyond the control of the firm. Other risks, like injuries to workers or lawsuits, result from forces more easily controlled by parties within the firm.

Financial Risks Risks included in the financial risk category of Figure 2-1 are largely managed by the accounting, treasury, and financial divisions of the firm. In many firms, the senior executive with ultimate responsibility for financial risks is the CFO. Unlike hazard risks, many financial risks are speculative risks in which changes in a financial market could work for or against the firm.

Many risks in this category are attributable to fluctuations in value, as determined by financial markets. For example, many firms are vulnerable to **price risks** in the form of adverse changes in interest rates, foreign currency exchange rates, or commodity prices, such as the price for petroleum products, grains, ores, or electricity. Price risks can affect key **input costs**, the price a firm pays to buy raw materials used in production or operations, or **output costs**, the prices at which the firm can sell its goods or services.

Firms that extend credit to customers or other parties are also exposed to **credit risk**, the risk that the borrower will not satisfy its financial obligations. While most firms have some exposure to credit risk through their accounts receivables or the extension of trade credit, financial firms like banks are especially vulnerable. While price risk is largely outside the control of the firm, credit risk is driven more internally by the firm's decisions to extend credit. Similarly, a number of the financial risks are variables within the control of the firm, such as the automaker's cost structure and the factors influencing its debt and credit ratings.

Note that General Motors identifies the costs of its health care and pension plans, two important components of its employee benefit program, as key financial risks, reflecting a growing corporate concern about how to finance such programs over the long run.

Operational Risks Operational risks arise from events that prevent a firm from conducting its normal scope of operations. While loss exposures in this risk category vary widely across firms, they are usually attributable to inadequate internal processes and controls, internal system failures, and human or management error. In many firms, the chief operating officer (COO) is ultimately responsible for losses caused by operational risks.

A notable exposure in this risk category is monitoring for accounting fraud and the related problem of a failure in the firm's accounting system. After numerous corporate accounting scandals during the early 2000s, Congress passed the Sarbanes-Oxley Act in 2002, bringing sweeping changes to the accounting profession. The act included a requirement that firms must describe in their financial statements the systems that they have in place to identify risks that could cause financial harm, providing a regulatory mandate for improved corporate risk management. General Motors includes accounting fraud as an operational risk because it is attributable to a failure in an internal accounting system.[16]

---

[16] By contrast, many firms include fraud and accounting system failure in other risk categories. For example, some recognize it as a financial risk because these concerns are clearly relevant to the financial and accounting activities of the firm. Other firms have added a fifth risk category to Figure 2-1, often called *compliance risk,* to include a firm's obligation to comply with regulatory requirements like Sarbanes-Oxley, as well as other types of regulated activities.

Another major area of concern for the automaker is the interruption of its business due to supply chain disruptions like damage to the production facilities of a key supplier (a parts manufacturer suffers a fire loss and cannot ship its parts to an assembly plant), an operational shutdown of a common carrier (a labor strike by the union representing workers in the transportation or shipping industries), or adverse events that disrupt the routine operation of the firm (a crippling snowstorm or massive power failure). Supply chain disruptions can prove to be particularly difficult to handle if they occur off the premises of the risk manager.

Strategic Risks In highly competitive industries, firms often focus considerable attention on monitoring their rivals in an effort to identify and exploit their weaknesses. Thus, strategic risks often are the result of conscious, premeditated plans by competitors to increase market share by taking advantage of the vulnerability of a rival, rather than random events such as natural disasters or catastrophic weather.

The strategic risks shown in Figure 2-1 reinforce the need to address these competitive risks as well as other events that can harm the firm's ability to compete, such as souring relations with suppliers or customers or the creation of powerful new rivals through mergers and industry consolidation. Many strategic risk concerns relate to factors that can decrease a firm's brand value, such as problems related to product quality, changing customer demands, or negative media coverage. While most of these factors are traced to events occurring outside the firm, internal factors such as budget overruns, poor technology decisions, and lax management oversight also affect the ability of the firm to compete successfully against its rivals.

Many strategic risks are related to preserving the value of the intangible property within the firm. Concerns about protecting brand value, media image, customer relations, and reputation are major concerns not just for automakers, but for nearly all firms today.

Summary

The identification of loss exposures is perhaps the most critical activity carried out by a risk management department because it is necessary to identify the complete spectrum of loss exposures facing an organization before developing a comprehensive strategy to handle such risks. This chapter has described many of the more common risks encountered by organizations today, including such pure risks as property, liability, and human resource risks, as well as the indirect losses that each of these risks can cause. More recently, the growing popularity of ERM programs has expanded the scope of today's risk management departments to encompass operational, financial, and strategic risks as well.

After an organization has identified its risks, it must next examine each loss exposure in greater detail to ascertain the statistical characteristics of their losses. This process is called *risk assessment*. Chapter 3, "Risk Assessment and Pooling," will describe how an organization can calculate several statistical measures for the types of loss exposures described in this chapter, thus proceeding through the third step in the risk management process.

Review

1. Explain how risk identification has changed in recent years, as well as the reasons for the change.
2. Provide an example of an internal and external risk for a large automaker.
3. Consider the losses resulting from a large fire loss to a commercial building. Provide two examples of direct losses commonly associated with a fire, as well as two examples of indirect losses.

4. List and briefly describe the three broad categories of hazard risks.
5. Define and provide two examples of tangible and intangible property.
6. Provide two examples of situations in which risk managers are concerned about damage to the property of others.
7. What differentiates torts from liability for criminal acts and breach of contracts?
8. List and briefly describe the four requirements that a plaintiff must prove when suing a defendant in a negligence case.
9. Describe the difference between compensatory and punitive damages.
10. Describe two common-law defenses that are available to a defendant in a negligence lawsuit.
11. Describe the difference between contributory and comparative negligence.
12. List and briefly describe the three broad categories of human resource risk found in most firms.
13. Define and briefly describe the differences between the four categories of risk found in an ERM program.
14. What is price risk? In your answer, describe the difference between input costs and output costs.
15. Explain why failures of accounting systems can be considered a financial risk or an operational risk in two different organizations.

Objective Questions

1. An earthquake is an example of
   a. an internal pure risk
   b. an internal speculative risk
   c. an external pure risk
   d. an external speculative risk

2. Which of the following is not an example of a direct loss resulting from a fire at Bubba's Bar-BQ, a Southern-style restaurant?
   a. $6,000 of smoke damage to the furniture and furnishings in the restaurant.
   b. $18,000 in fire damage to the kitchen of the restaurant.
   c. $30,000 in lost revenues resulting from a 45-day closure of the restaurant.
   d. $3,000 in damaged electrical wiring caused by water used to fight the fire.
   e. All of the above are direct losses from the fire.

3. Which of the following statements about intangible property is correct?
   I. Examples of intangible property include a firm's brand value and its reputation.
   II. Because it pertains to the ability of the firm to compete against its rivals, the duty to protect intangible property belongs to the corporate CEO, not the risk manager.
   a. I only   b. II only   c. both I and II
   d. neither I nor II

4. Bobby slips on an icy sidewalk when entering Skip's sporting goods store. Bobby requires $12,000 of medical treatment for the head injury that he suffered in the fall. Bobby goes to court to attempt to collect the medical costs from Skip. This legal action is an example of which of the following?
   a. A criminal act
   b. A breach of contract
   c. A tort
   d. None of the above

5. Which of the following is not a requirement that the plaintiff must prove to the courts in a negligence case against a defendant?
   a. The defendant owed the plaintiff a legal duty.
   b. The plaintiff suffered some sort of property damage or bodily injury.
   c. The defendant failed to satisfy a legal duty that he owed to the plaintiff.
   d. The defendant committed a crime in the way that he interacted with the plaintiff.

6. Amy wins a lawsuit from Tess for injuries suffered in an auto accident. Included in the judgment is $40,000 in compensation for pain and suffering. Pain and suffering is which of the following?
   a. An example of special damages
   b. An example of general damages
   c. An example of punitive damages
   d. An example of property damages

7. Which of the following is not an example of a corporation's human resource risk?
   a. A large company's concerns about finding a person to replace its sick CEO
   b. The cost of providing workers' compensation benefits to an employer's work force
   c. Paying for the medical costs of customers injured by the corporation's products
   d. The cost of providing employee benefits to workers of a corporation

8. Scary Airlines, a large commercial airline, suffers a huge loss of profitability due to a 30 percent increase in the cost of jet fuel. The risk that caused this loss is an example of which of the following?
   a. A hazard risk
   b. A financial risk
   c. A strategic risk
   d. An operational risk

9. Gamer Industries suffers a 22 percent decline in quarterly revenues after a longshoreman's strike prevents the firm from shipping its new video game product to its international markets. The risk that caused this loss is an example of which of the following?
   a. A hazard risk
   b. A financial risk
   c. A strategic risk
   d. An operational risk

10. Sleeper Film Company estimates that it loses about 2 percent of its annual sales revenues as a result of counterfeiters selling bootleg copies of the movies that it produces. The risk that caused this loss is an example of which of the following?
    a. A hazard risk
    b. A financial risk
    c. A strategic risk
    d. An operational risk

Discussion Questions

1. Refer to Insight Box 1-1 in Chapter 1 (on p. 3), describing the risk management problems associated with Enron's fraudulent financial accounting. If Enron's risk manager organized its ERM program into hazard, operational, financial, and strategic risks, as described in Figure 2-1, into which risk area does fraudulent accounting best fit?

2. Legal scholars often suggest that a prime goal of the tort liability system is to deter firms from engaging in risky behavior that could cause harm to others. Explain how such a goal can lead to more effective ERM and how the U.S. tort liability system encourages firms to achieve this goal.

Selected References

Casualty Actuarial Society, Enterprise Risk Management Committee, "Overview of Enterprise Risk Management," May 2003.

Colquitt, L. Lee, Robert E. Hoyt, and Ryan B. Lee, 1999, "Integrated Risk Management and the Role of the Risk Manager," *Risk Management and Insurance Review* 2: 43–61.

The Committee of Sponsoring Organizations (COSO) of the Treadway Commission: "Enterprise Risk Management—Integrated Framework Executive Summary," September 2004, retrieved March 27, 2010 at http://www.coso.org/

Economist Intelligence Unit, "Best Practice in Risk Management: A Function Comes of Age," 2007, retrieved April 28, 2011, at http://graphics.eiu.com/

Elkins, Debra, "Managing Manufacturing and Supply Chain Risks in Global Automotive Operations" presented on March 18, 2005, at the North Carolina State University Enterprise Risk Management Roundtable.

Shenkir, William G., and Paul L. Walker, "Enterprise Risk Management and the Strategy-Risk-Focused Organization," *Cost Management* 1 May/June 2006: 32–38.

Slywotzky, Adrian J., and John Drzik, 2005, "Countering the Biggest Risk of All," *Harvard Business Review* 83, no. 4: 78–88.

3

Risk Assessment and Pooling

After studying this chapter, you should be able to

■ Explain how probability distributions can be used to calculate the expected value, variance, and standard deviation of a loss exposure.

■ Explain how risk managers and insurers can use prior loss data to estimate probability distributions for the frequency and severity of losses.

■ Calculate the average loss, given probability distributions for the frequency of losses and the severity of losses.

■ Use the process of convolution to calculate the average loss.

■ Demonstrate how the process of risk pooling can be used to reduce risk.

■ Describe the characteristics of the normal distribution that are useful in risk pooling.

■ Use confidence intervals to demonstrate how insurers and risk managers can use risk pooling to decrease their cost of risk management.

In this chapter, we discuss the third step in the risk management process, the assessment of risk. After a risk management department has identified the broad range of risk exposures that can affect the financial status of its organization, it must focus next on estimating the financial impact of each risk. It can be challenging to predict the expected financial outcome of each future risk exposure; but having an accurate forecast of future losses better ensures that the firm can budget appropriately for such financial considerations and select the optimal risk-handling techniques. It also enables the risk manager to better monitor the current year's loss experience against prior years' losses to detect changes or trends in risk exposures before they result in increased financial harm.

After a brief review of some basic statistical concepts, we will demonstrate how firms can calculate two key statistical measures used to evaluate loss exposures: the frequency with which losses occur and their severity. We will see that risk managers often look at data on past losses to estimate their underlying loss probability distributions and to forecast such losses in the future. We'll discover how these loss distributions in turn can help quantify risk objectively, using measures like the variance and standard deviation of a firm's loss distribution. Finally, we examine risk pooling, the process that insurance companies and many self-insured corporations rely on to reduce risk.

BASIC STATISTICAL CONCEPTS

Risk assessment relies heavily on concepts developed in the field of statistics. Thus, we will find it helpful to review briefly some basic statistical terminology.

Random Variable

Risk managers are responsible for forecasting the outcomes associated with their company's exposure to risk. That can mean predicting such unknown values as the number of auto accidents caused by company drivers, the amount of money owed to injured workers as a result of workers' compensation obligations, or the average loss in revenue associated with an unexpected closure of one of the firm's retail outlets due to a fire. Random factors like highway driving conditions, the severity of worker injuries, and the effectiveness of a store's fire sprinklers can affect these measures. Thus, each is a **random variable**, or a variable whose future value is not known with certainty.

Probability Distributions

A **probability distribution** is a table or graph that shows all possible outcomes for a random variable, as well as their respective probabilities of occurring. We know in advance the probability distributions for some random variables, such as the number that will result from a given roll of a die:

Value on die	1	2	3	4	5	6
Probability	1/6	1/6	1/6	1/6	1/6	1/6

When we don't know the probability distribution of a random variable in advance, we must estimate it, often from prior experience or industry data. For example, consider Rick, the owner of Rick's Restaurant, a fine restaurant doing business in a large city on the East Coast. Based on conversations with attorneys, risk consultants, and other restaurant owners, Rick estimates that he has a 10 percent chance of losing a $100,000 lawsuit in the next year, compared to a 90 percent chance that he will not be sued.[1] Thus, Rick's loss distribution is shown below:

Loss outcome	$0	$100,000
Probability of loss outcome	0.9	0.1

All probability distributions share some important characteristics, and these traits are reflected in both of the above distributions. For example, the maximum probability for any one outcome of a random variable will always be less than 1.0, and the minimum probability for any one outcome is always greater than zero. The probability distribution also must include all possible values of the random variable with probabilities

---

[1] Please note that while the risk of being sued is uncomfortably high in some areas of the country, it is unlikely that most small firms have such a high chance of getting sued. We only use the 10 percent figure to keep the math simple in this example. This example also ignores the legal costs incurred in defending the claim in court, which can add up to a considerable additional expense.

greater than zero, regardless of how small their chance of occurrence may be. We can be sure that we have accounted for all values of such random variables if the sum of their probabilities equals 1.0. Finally, we can use the information provided in a probability distribution to calculate several important measures in risk management, including the expected value, the variance, and standard deviation.

Expected Value

One of the more important goals of risk assessment is to calculate the expected financial outcome associated with each of a firm's exposures to risk. Thus, when assessing the financial impact of a firm's pure risks, a risk manager is interested in calculating a measure of the long-run average loss that he or she should expect in the future. We calculate this measure of the **expected value** of a loss exposure with the information provided in a probability distribution.

We can find the expected value of the random variable by multiplying each possible outcome of the variable shown in a probability distribution by its corresponding probability of occurring, and then summing these products across all outcomes in the distribution. For example, based on his loss distribution, Rick can calculate his **expected loss**, the expected value of the loss distribution, by multiplying both possible loss outcomes by their corresponding probability of occurrence and summing the product across all loss outcomes:

$$\text{Expected loss} = \$100,000 \times 0.1 + \$0 \times 0.9 = \$10,000 \qquad \text{(Eq. 3-1)}$$

An insurer would use the $10,000 expected loss as a starting point in calculating the premium that it needs to charge Rick to insure his liability risk. Alternatively, if Rick were trying to save money toward the payment of such liability losses, setting aside $10,000 per year would cover the loss over a long-term time frame.[2]

Variance and Standard Deviation

We also can use the data shown in a probability distribution to calculate two measures of risk: variance and standard deviation. The **variance** measures how the outcomes of a random variable vary around the expected value of that variable. Here are step-by-step instructions, with the results shown in Table 3-1.

1. Subtract the expected value of the random variable ($10,000, from Eq. 3-1) from each possible outcome of that variable (as shown in Column 3).
2. Square the differences found in Step 1 (as shown in Column 4).

TABLE 3-1 Calculating the Variance Using Data from a Probability Distribution

Column 1	*Column 2*	*Column 3*	*Column 4*	*Column 5*
Loss Outcomes	*Probabilities*	*Loss Outcome − Expected Loss (Col. 1 − $10000)*	*Squared Differences (Col. 3 × Col. 3)*	*Squared Difference × Prob. (Col 2 × Col 4)*
$0	0.90	−$10,000	100,000,000	90,000,000
$100,000	0.10	$90,000	8,100,000,000	810,000,000
	1.00			900,000,000

---

[2] Of course, this plan is a bit risky, as Rick would need to save for ten years without suffering a loss before he had accumulated enough money to pay for the loss if it occurs. The inability to accumulate enough money in a short period of time to pay for large self-funded loss savings plans helps to explain why insurance is often a popular loss financing technique.

3. Multiply each of the squared values in Step 2 by their probability of occurring (as shown in Column 5).

4. Sum up all the products found in Step 3 (as shown at the bottom of Column 5).

The variance is 900,000,000, the sum of the values shown in Column 5.

A limitation of using the variance to measure risk is that it is not measured in the original unit of currency that we used to measure the loss. For example, due to the squaring of differences shown in Column 4 of the table, the variance appears in "squared dollars" rather than in dollars. To correct for this limitation, we use a second measure of risk that is closely related to the variance, the standard deviation. The **standard deviation** is the square root of the variance and thus is measured in dollars. Thus, we find that Rick's risk, as measured by the standard deviation, equals $30,000, or the square root of the variance, 900,000,000.

The variance and standard deviation measure the degree to which the actual losses from a loss distribution deviate from the expected loss. Both measures are thus valuable to insurers and risk managers because they can be used to calculate a margin for error around estimates of expected losses. We use both measures later in this chapter to show how insurers and risk managers can reduce risk through risk pooling.[3]

RISK ASSESSMENT: ESTIMATING LOSS FREQUENCY AND LOSS SEVERITY

Risk managers routinely make decisions about how to handle risk based on their assessment of its statistical properties. In this section, we demonstrate how risk managers can calculate two aspects of financial risk, loss frequency and loss severity, and use these measures to assess the risk exposures of their firms. We will focus on pure risk exposures because these are often the type that can interrupt a firm's normal course of operations and cause financial harm. We'll also demonstrate how risk managers can estimate useful measures of risk from in-house loss data.

Suppose that Rebecca, the risk manager for a large car rental firm, wants to estimate the per-car average cost to repair damage from collisions and other related causes of loss in her vehicle fleet for the coming year. If she has kept accurate information about the amounts of damage incurred in the past year, she can calculate the average loss as:

$$\text{Average loss} = \frac{\text{total dollar amount of losses}}{\text{total number of cars}} \qquad \text{(Eq. 3-2)}$$

While this equation is a useful starting point, we can make a minor algebraic change to obtain even better information about this loss exposure:

$$\text{Average loss} = \left(\frac{\text{total amount of losses}}{\text{total number of accidents}}\right) \times \left(\frac{\text{total number of accidents}}{\text{total number of cars}}\right) \text{(Eq. 3-3)}$$

$$= \text{Average loss severity} \times \text{Average loss frequency} \qquad \text{(Eq. 3-4)}$$

---

[3] Readers who need to brush up on the calculation of the expected value and risk measures discussed in this section often find it helpful to work with a familiar probability distribution, such as the dice example presented earlier. In support of this effort, note that the expected value on a dice roll equals 3.5 and the variance and standard deviation measures equal 2.92 and 1.71, respectively.

TABLE 3-2 Loss Frequency Data and Estimated Probability Distribution

Column 1	Column 2	Column 3	Column 4
No. of Losses per Car	*Number of Cars*	*Total Number of Losses*	*Estimated Probability*
0	910	0	0.91
1	80	80	0.08
2	10	20	0.01
	1000	100	1.00

This expanded equation of the average loss illustrates two key components of loss.[4] The first term on the right of the equal sign measures loss severity, and the second term measures loss frequency. The **severity** of the loss represents the average size of the loss, measured across the portion of the firm's vehicle fleet that suffered an accident in the past year. A variety of factors can affect the expected value of the severity of the loss, such as the original value of the car (damaging an expensive car costs more than damaging an inexpensive car) or the design (some cars are designed to withstand impact better than others).

The second component of total losses is the **frequency** with which losses occur, here the average number of losses per car in a year. Factors that influence loss frequency include traffic density and highway conditions.

To demonstrate the relationship between frequency and severity, suppose that our risk manager Rebecca has gathered the information shown in Columns 1 through 3 of Table 3-2 about the number of losses incurred by her fleet of 1,000 cars in the past year. She can use this data to find the frequency of losses two ways. First, she can simply estimate the average loss frequency per car by dividing the total number of losses, the sum of Column 3, by the total number of cars, the sum of Column 2. She finds that the estimated mean number of losses suffered per car is 100 losses divided by 1,000 cars, or 0.1 accidents per car. (Note that 10 unlucky cars in the fleet were involved in two accidents during the year, accounting for 20 percent of the 100 losses.)

The data in the table also provides Rebecca a way to estimate the probability distribution of the frequency of losses. For example, based on the data shown in the second column, 910 of the 1,000 cars had no accidents last year, suggesting that there is an estimated 91 percent chance that any given car in the fleet will suffer no loss in the coming year. We can estimate the probability that a car will have one or two losses in the coming year using the same process. Recognizing that a fleet of 1,000 cars represents a large sample of cars, Rebecca can thus feel confident that her estimated frequency distribution, as shown in Columns 1 and 4, is a close approximation to the unknown distribution of the number of accidents per car, also known as the **loss frequency distribution**. Based on this distribution, we can find the expected value of the loss frequency per car by multiplying each value in Column 1 by its respective probability, as shown in Column 4:

Average frequency $= 0 \times 0.91 + 1 \times 0.08 + 2 \times 0.01 = 0.10$ accidents per car

Thus, the average frequency that we find using the probability distribution is the same as the average frequency using the raw data, as described above.

---

[4] See Denenberg, H.; R. Eilers, J. Melone, and R. Zelten, *Risk and Insurance,* 2d ed., (Englewood Cliffs, NJ: Prentice-Hall, 1974)

TABLE 3-3 Loss Severity Data and Estimated Probability Distribution

Column 1	Column 2	Column 3	Column 4	Column 5
Range of Loss Amount	Midpoint Dollar Amount of Loss	Number of Losses	Total $ Amt. of Losses	Estimated Probability
$1–4,000	$2,000	75	$150,000	0.75
$4,001–8,000	$6,000	20	$120,000	0.20
$8,001–12,000	$10,000	5	$50,000	0.05
TOTAL		100	$320,000	1.00

Rebecca can also use data she gathered on the 100 cars involved in accidents last year, as shown in Columns 1 through 4, to estimate the severity per car. While data on loss frequency is discrete (it has integer values of 2 losses, 1 loss, or 0 losses), data on loss severity is continuous because loss values can take a wide variety of dollar amounts ranging from $1 up to the full value of the vehicle. To simplify the severity data, Rebecca can sort the loss data into ranges and estimate the average loss based on the midpoints of the ranges, as shown in Column 2 of Table 3-3.

We estimate the average severity per accident by simply dividing the total amount of losses, the sum of Column 4, by the total number of losses, the sum of Column 3. Thus, the estimated severity, or loss amount per accident, is the $320,000 of total losses divided by 100 losses, or $3,200 per accident. Rebecca also can use the data shown in Columns 1–4 to estimate the **loss severity distribution**. Thus, for example, she estimates that if a car is in an accident, there is a 75 percent chance of suffering $2,000 in damages because the data in Column 2 indicates that 75 of the 100 cars in an accident incurred $2,000 in damages last year. Estimating the rest of the severity probability distribution using this approach, we find that 20 percent of the cars suffered damage in the $6,000 range and 5 percent of the losses fell in the $10,000 range. In turn, we can find the average loss severity by multiplying each loss amount value shown in Column 2 by its respective probability, as shown in Column 5:

$$\text{Average severity} = \$2,000 \times 0.75 + \$6,000 \times 0.20 + \$10,000 \times 0.05$$
$$= \$3,200 \text{ per accident}$$

Based on the above figures, our risk manager can now find the average loss per car using two separate methods. She can simply divide the total number of cars (1,000) into the total dollar losses incurred by the fleet, $320,000, yielding an estimated $320 loss per car. Alternatively, she can estimate the average loss per car by multiplying the average severity per accident by the average loss frequency per car:

$$\text{Average loss/car} = \text{average severity} \times \text{average frequency}$$
$$= \$3,200/\text{accident} \times 0.10 \text{ accidents/car} = \$320/\text{car}$$

Obtaining information about the frequency and severity of losses is very important in risk management; we need both factors to select the risk-handling technique that is best suited to a particular loss exposure. Risk managers also can use certain techniques to alter probability distributions applicable to the frequency or severity of losses. For example, by installing a fire sprinkler system in a building, a risk manager can decrease the maximum severity of a fire loss.

CONVOLUTION

Another way to show how the firm's losses are related to loss frequency and severity is to construct the loss distribution through the process of convolution. **Convolution** calculates all possible combinations of losses indicated by the frequency and severity loss distributions, as well as their corresponding probabilities of occurring.

Let's look at the car rental example again. Based on the frequency distribution shown in Table 3-2 and the severity distribution shown in Table 3-3, we show all possible combinations of losses, as well as their respective probabilities, in Table 3-4. Thus, as you can see in Row A, we know that the probability of no loss occurring equals 0.91, as indicated by the frequency distribution shown in Table 3-2. We find the probability of all other losses by multiplying the probability corresponding to the frequency of the loss by the probability corresponding to the severity. Thus, Rows B, C, and D show the three possible loss outcomes that can arise if only one loss occurs, as we see in the severity distribution in Table 3-3. In each case, we calculate their probabilities by multiplying the probability of each severity value, as shown in the fifth column of Table 3-3, by 0.08, the probability that the loss frequency equals 1.

Showing the possible ways that two losses can occur takes a bit more calculation. There are nine possible combinations (Rows E through M) that two losses can occur, reflecting the fact that there are three possible loss amounts for the first loss and for the second loss. We can thus find the probability for each combination of losses by multiplying three separate values: the probability for the severity of the first loss, the probability for the severity of the second loss, and 0.01, the probability from the frequency distribution associated with two losses occurring. These joint probability calculations are shown for each possible loss value in the far-right column of Table 3-4.

Because the sum of all probabilities shown in the fifth column of Table 3-4 equal 1.0, we know that all possible combinations of two, one, and no losses are considered in the probability distribution. Also note that expected value for probability distribution shown in Table 3-4 (the sum of the entries in column 6) is $320, the same value that

TABLE 3-4 All Possible Loss Combinations Calculated Using Convolution

Row	Loss 1	Loss 2	Total Loss	Probability	Total Loss × Probability	Joint Probabilities
A	–	–	0	0.910000	0.0	
B	2,000	–	2,000	0.060000	120.0	.08 × .75
C	6,000	–	6,000	0.016000	96.0	.08 × .20
D	10,000	–	10,000	0.004000	40.0	.08 × .05
E	2,000	2,000	4,000	0.005625	22.5	.01 × .75 × .75
F	2,000	6,000	8,000	0.001500	12.0	.01 × .75 × .20
G	2,000	10,000	12,000	0.000375	4.5	.01 × .75 × .05
H	6,000	2,000	8,000	0.001500	12.0	.01 × .20 × .75
I	6,000	6,000	12,000	0.000400	4.8	.01 × .20 × .20
J	6,000	10,000	16,000	0.000100	1.6	.01 × .20 × .05
K	10,000	2,000	12,000	0.000375	4.5	.01 × .05 × .75
L	10,000	6,000	16,000	0.000100	1.6	.01 × .05 × .20
M	10,000	10,000	20,000	0.000025	0.5	.01 × .05 × .05
TOTAL				1.000000	320.0	

we found when we multiplied the average frequency by the average severity. Thus, the probability distribution that results from the convolution process reinforces the fact that a firm's losses reflect the combined effects of frequency and severity.

Although the convolution process is quite easy to carry out for the simple severity and frequency distributions shown above, calculating all possible combinations of losses and their respective probabilities by hand becomes tedious for more complicated severity and frequency distributions. As a result, risk managers often rely on computer simulation techniques to complete the convolution process for complex loss distributions.

DIVERSIFICATION OF RISK USING RISK POOLING

Now that we've examined the measurement of risk using the variance and standard deviation, we look at how risk can be diversified away through the technique of risk pooling. **Exposure units** are the persons or objects (such as buildings, autos, and firms) exposed to risk. The more exposure units in a pool, the more accurately the insurer can predict any individual unit's risk of loss. **Risk pooling**, then, is the ability to reduce each exposure unit's risk by making more accurate predictions about a large pool of units.

Change in Risk Through Pooling

To demonstrate the pooling concept, we return to our discussion of Rick, the owner of Rick's Restaurant. Recall that Rick estimates that he has a 10 percent chance of losing a $100,000 lawsuit in the next year, compared to a 90 percent chance that he is not sued, resulting in the following loss distribution:

Loss outcome	$0	$100,000
Probability of loss outcome	0.9	0.1

Based on this loss distribution, the expected value of Rick's liability risk equals $10,000 with a standard deviation equal to $30,000, as we showed in Table 3-1.

Now consider what happens to Rick's risk if he agrees to pool his risk with Vic, a second restaurant owner. Assume that both parties have *homogeneous* risk characteristics; that is, they exhibit the same level of risk, represented by Rick's liability loss distribution. Also assume that each pool member's loss experience is statistically *independent* of the other member's.[5] Finally, each person entering the pool agrees to pay the **mean loss of the pool**, calculated by adding all losses incurred by pool members and dividing by the number of people in the pool.

By joining the pool, Rick is faced with a new loss distribution because he is now responsible for paying the mean loss measured across all pool members. Because there are only two people in the risk pool, we can list easily all possible combinations of losses between Rick and Vic (Table 3-5).

TABLE 3-5 Calculation of All Possible Loss Combinations (Pool Size of 2)

Rick's Loss	*Vic's Loss*	*Total Loss*	*Mean Loss*	*Probability*
0	0	0	0	.9 × .9 = .81
100,000	0	100,000	50,000	.1 × .9 = .09
0	100,000	100,000	50,000	.9 × .1 = .09
100,000	100,000	200,000	100,000	.1 × .1 = .01

---

[5] For a more detailed discussion of statistical independence and correlation, see Chapter 5.

Based on the data shown in the fourth and fifth columns of Table 3-5, we can create a new **mean loss distribution** for the pool.[6]

Mean loss outcome	$0	$50,000	$100,000
Probability of mean loss outcome	0.81	0.18	0.01

Note that the expected value of the mean loss distribution equals $10,000, calculated as:

Expected value of mean loss $= 0 \times 0.81 + 50,000 \times 0.18 + 100,000 \times 0.01 = \$10,000$

We show the mean loss distribution in the first two columns of Table 3-6 and use this data to calculate the variance of the mean loss distribution, shown as the sum of the entries in Column 5.

Based on the figures shown in Table 3-6, we find that the standard deviation of the mean loss distribution equals $21,213.20, calculated as the square root of the variance of 450,000,000 as shown at the bottom of Column 5.

By comparing Rick's expected loss and risk in the pool versus not in the pool, we can see the benefits of pooling:

- The expected value of Rick's unpooled loss distribution is $10,000 and the standard deviation of his unpooled loss distribution is $30,000.
- The expected value of Rick's pooled mean loss distribution is $10,000 and the standard deviation of his pooled mean loss distribution is $21,213.

So long as all pool members have homogeneous risk characteristics, each has the same expected loss that he or she would have individually. Thus, pooling offers no opportunity for an individual to reduce his or her future expected loss payout. Rick's *mean loss remains the same*; it is $10,000 whether he is in or out of the pool.

On the other hand, pooling will result in a *reduction of risk*. We routinely measure risk in insurance and risk management using the standard deviation of the loss distribution. Note that the standard deviation of Rick's unpooled loss distribution was $30,000, but his measure of risk decreased to $21,213.20 when he entered the pool. In other words, Rick incurs less risk by joining the risk pool because the standard deviation of the mean loss distribution is smaller than standard deviation of the unpooled loss distribution. Perhaps most importantly, the probability of the largest loss amount,

TABLE 3-6 Calculation of Variance of Mean Loss Distribution (Pool Size of Two)

Column 1	*Column 2*	*Column 3*	*Column 4*	*Column 5*
Mean Loss Outcomes	*Probabilities*	*Loss Outcome − Expected Loss (Col. 1 − $10,000)*	*Squared Differences (Col. 3 × Col. 3)*	*Squared Differences × Prob. (Col 2 × Col 4)*
$0	0.81	−$10,000	100,000,000	81,000,000
$50,000	0.18	$40,000	1,600,000,000	288,000,000
$100,000	0.01	$90,000	8,100,000,000	81,000,000
	1.00			450,000,000

[6] Note from the data shown in Table 3-6 that the probability that a $50,000 mean loss occurs equals 0.18, the sum of the two 0.09 probabilities associated with the two loss combinations that result in a total loss equal to $100,000. These data, when combined with the 0.81 chance of no loss and the 0.01 chance of a $100,000 mean loss, yields the three possible outcomes in the mean loss distribution. For more discussion on this intuitive approach to explaining risk pooling, see Harrington and Niehaus (2004).

TABLE 3-7 Risk Reduction Through Pooling as the Size of the Pool Increases

Pool Size	Mean	Standard Deviation	Normal Distribution
1	$10,000	$30,000	No
2	$10,000	$30,000/2^{0.5} = $21,213$	No
4	$10,000	$30,000/4^{0.5} = $15,000$	No
36	$10,000	$30,000/36^{0.5} = $5,000$	Yes
100	$10,000	$30,000/100^{0.5} = $3,000$	Yes
900	$10,000	$30,000/900^{0.5} = $1,000$	Yes

$100,000, has decreased dramatically, from 10 percent to 1 percent because it is extremely unlikely that Rick and Vic will both lose a lawsuit in the same year.

A further reduction in risk will result from increasing the size of the pool. Table 3-7 shows how the standard deviation decreases with an increased number of pool members. As shown in Column 3, we can define the relationship between risk, as measured by the standard deviation of the mean loss distribution, and pool size, as shown in Column 1, with a simple formula: *the risk faced by any one object in a pool will equal its unpooled standard deviation divided by the square root of the number of pool members.* For example, pooling four exposure units reduces risk by one-half, and a pool size of 100 results in a standard deviation of $3,000, one-tenth of the unpooled standard deviation before joining a pool. In this manner, Rick can reduce the risk associated with being sued by joining a pool with other restaurant owners facing similar risk.[7]

Rick also can use pooling to decrease his cost of bearing risk, as shown below.

Normal Distribution

As shown in the rightmost column of Table 3-7, when the number of objects in a risk pool is fairly large, say over thirty, we can assume that the mean loss for that risk pool is normally distributed. Normally distributed random variables exhibit several unique statistical characteristics that are useful in risk pooling. First, if we plot the values of the mean loss (in dollars) on the x-axis and probability corresponding to the loss amounts on the y-axis, the resulting graph, commonly called the **normal curve**, will be shaped like a bell, as shown in Figure 3-1. The center of the normal curve will correspond to the mean, or expected value, of the mean loss, with probabilities for all other values of the expected value distributed symmetrically around the center, but decreasing in probability as we move farther away from the expected loss.[8]

Second, a statistical relationship exists between the standard deviation and the area under the normal curve:

- The range of values found by adding and subtracting one standard deviation to the mean of the random variable accounts for 68.26 percent of the area under the curve.

---

[7] Again, note that two assumptions must be met for this formula to hold true. First, all objects in the pool must exhibit **homogeneous** risk characteristics. Second, the losses of all pool members must be **independent** of each other. If the losses of the pool participants are correlated, this formula does not hold and the risk faced by the participants will be higher.

[8] For an intuitive interpretation for why the curve is bell-shaped, suppose that an insurer calculated the mean liability loss for a sample of 100 restaurants from Rick's risk pool, and then repeated this sampling process over and over again. The most common value for the mean across all the samples will be $10,000, the expected value of the loss distribution. Means that are slightly different from $10,000 will occur slightly less frequently, and so on.

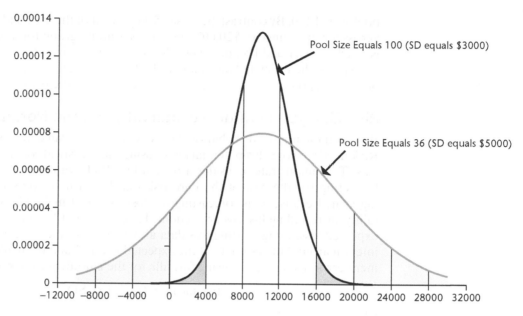

FIGURE 3-1 Normal Curves of the Mean Loss Distribution Based on Pool Sizes of 36 and 100 Exposure Units (SD denotes standard deviation)

- The range of values found by adding and subtracting two standard deviations to the mean of the random variable accounts for 95.44 percent of the area under the curve.
- The range of values found by adding and subtracting three standard deviations to the mean of the random variable accounts for 99.74 percent of the area under the curve.

We can demonstrate the statistical relationship between the standard deviation and the expected loss graphically, focusing on the fact that 95.44 percent of the area under the normal curve must fall within a range of two standard deviations above and below the mean value. For simplicity, we assume that an insurer estimates the mean loss and standard deviation of Rick's risk pool using prior loss statistics, and their estimates are consistent with the data shown in Table 3-7.[9] Based on these data, the mean loss distribution for a pool of 36 restaurants is compared to the mean loss distribution for a pool of 100 restaurants in Figure 3-1. Note that both risk pools are normally distributed and centered around $10,000, the expected loss. For the mean loss distribution based on a pool size of 36, the unshaded area two standard deviations above and below the expected loss ($10,000 ± 2 × $5,000) ranges from $0 to $20,000, based on a standard deviation equal to $5,000. On the other hand, because the standard deviation for a pool size of 100 is $3,000, not $5,000, the unshaded area two standard deviations above and below the expected loss ($10,000 ± 2 × $3,000) is much smaller, ranging from $4,000 to $16,000. To ensure that 95.44 percent of the area under the curve fits within this narrower range, the shape of the normal distribution for the larger pool size is taller and thinner. Thus, there is a much higher probability that the insurer's estimated mean loss will fall very close to the actual expected loss of $10,000 for the normal curve associated with a

---

[9] In practice, insurance risk pools typically are much larger; we assume small pool sizes to simplify the calculations. With such small pool sizes, it is also unrealistic to assume that an insurer could estimate the expected loss and standard deviation of its risk pools without some measurement error.

pool size of 100. By contrast, because 95.44 percent of the area under the curve is spread across a wider range of $20,000, the corresponding graph for a pool of 36 restaurants is much shorter and broader. Thus, for smaller pool sizes, there is an increased probability that the estimated mean loss will fall some distance away from the expected loss of $10,000, potentially resulting in a miscalculation of the premium for the pool.

Risk Charges, Confidence Intervals, and the Normal Distribution

Based on the normal distribution discussed above, we can determine how much money Rick needs to cover his potential losses using the statistical concept of confidence intervals. To demonstrate, consider a person like Rick who is faced with the prospect of budgeting for the cost of the pure risk that his firm is exposed to during the coming year. Because he is forecasting the loss, he must make allowances for the uncertainty surrounding his loss projections. He can do that by (1) estimating the mean, or expected loss, using existing loss data about the risk, and (2) calculating a confidence interval around the estimate of the expected loss to build in an allowance for measurement error, using the following formula for the **confidence interval**:

$$\text{Est. mean} \pm (k) \times \text{Est. SD} \qquad \text{(Eq. 3-5)}$$

where

- *Est. mean* is the estimate of the mean loss, which typically is calculated using loss data from previous years;
- *Est. SD* is the estimated standard deviation, calculated using loss data from previous years; and
- k is a specified number of standard deviations that is added and subtracted to the estimated mean loss to reflect the uncertainty resulting from forecasting losses.

For example, we know from our earlier discussion that if losses are normally distributed, 95.44 percent of the area under the normal curve will fall within two standard deviations of the expected loss. By equating the area under the normal curve to the probability that the estimated mean loss falls within that area, we know that setting k equal to 2.0—that is, adding and subtracting two standard deviations to the estimated mean loss—will provide us a confidence interval that includes the true mean loss 95.44 percent of the time.[10] Calculated in this manner, the product of k multiplied by the standard deviation is often called the **risk charge**, and it represents a margin for error that is added and subtracted to the estimate of the mean loss to allow for the measurement error arising from estimating an unknown variable.

We can use confidence intervals to determine the amount of money that Rick needs to hold in reserve to meet his obligation to the risk pool. There is randomness in estimating a loss that may occur in the future because the loss can be bigger or smaller than the estimated mean value. Our principal concern, however, is making sure that we have enough funds to pay for the loss if it turns out to be bigger than its expected value. In this regard, we typically focus on the upper tail of the confidence interval (that is, the sum of the estimated mean loss plus the risk charge) to make sure that we have enough funds if the loss turns out to be larger than the expected loss amount.

---

[10] While statistical standards vary across industries, it is common to set confidence intervals at a level of confidence at or near 95 percent. In this regard, the 95.44 percent level of confidence associated with a k value of 2.0 is widely used. Another common standard is to set k equal to 1.96, thus resulting in a confidence level that is exactly equal to 95 percent. We can increase our level of confidence by expanding the range of our confidence interval. Thus, referring back to our discussion of the statistical characteristics of normal distributions, by setting k equal to 3.0, we increase our confidence level to 99.74 percent because we are much more confident that our estimated mean loss will fall within this very wide range.

Keeping in mind that the standard deviation of the mean loss distribution decreases as pool size increases, we calculate 95.44 percent confidence intervals for different sized pools:

- With 36 objects in the pool, the confidence interval is $10,000 ± (2.00) × ($5,000) or a range of values from $0 to $20,000

- With 100 objects in the pool, the confidence interval is $10,000 ± (2.00) × ($3,000) or a range of values from $4,000 to $16,000.

- With 900 objects in the pool, the confidence interval is $10,000 ± (2.00) × ($1,000) or a range of values from $8000 to $12,000.

Thus, if Rick's business is one of 900 restaurants included in a risk pool, he can be 95.44 percent certain that a cash reserve of $12,000 will be sufficient to cover his obligation to the risk pool. Note that this $12,000 is only $2,000 above the expected loss. It is also far less than $20,000, the amount Rick would need to set aside in his budget if he participated in a smaller risk pool of 36 restaurants. This $8,000 difference thus represents the benefits arising from participating in a larger risk pool, corresponding to the dramatic reduction in the standard deviation of the mean loss distribution associated with increased pool sizes.[11]

Practical Considerations in Using Risk Pooling

When consumers purchase such insurance products as life and auto insurance, insurers generally use risk pooling to minimize both the risk and the premiums they charge. These products satisfy the assumptions underlying our discussion of risk pooling. Insurers can sort consumers into homogeneous risk categories, often based on simple risk-classification variables like age or gender. Likewise, the independence assumption is generally satisfied because consumers of these products are not usually plagued by widespread catastrophic losses in which one event can result in a loss that affects a large number of policyholders in a pool.

On the other hand, insurance is often not available for risks that violate the assumptions underlying risk pooling. For example, insurers cannot use pooling to reduce risk when the number of the exposure units is small, in part because they have insufficient data with which to forecast losses. Likewise, some types of risks are difficult to insure because the losses are not independently distributed and can financially ruin an insurer.[12] Insurers thus do not typically offer protection for risks like floods, war, or unemployment, which are subject to catastrophic episodes in which large numbers of policyholders are affected adversely at the same time.

Finally, insurance companies do not have exclusive rights to risk pooling. Risk managers have increased their use of this technique dramatically as an alternative to buying insurance. For example, large employers with thousands of employees often use pooling to self-insure some of their areas of risk, especially workers' compensation and employer-sponsored health insurance.

---

[11] A common question that arises when discussing pooling is whether an individual can calculate a confidence interval for his or her loss exposure in the same manner as described in this section. For example, if Rick calculated his personal risk charge by multiplying 2.00 times $30,000 (the value of his unpooled standard deviation), would he be 95.44 percent certain that his loss in the coming year will fall within the resulting confidence interval ($10,000 ± [2.00] × [$30,000] or $10,000 ± $60,000)? One can argue against this approach for two reasons. First, note that the upper tail of the resulting confidence interval is $70,000, a large (and perhaps unaffordable) sum to hold in reserve in a checking account. Second, as suggested from the rightmost column in Table 3-7, we cannot assume that the assumption of normality holds true for pool sizes less than thirty. In this regard, the level of confidence corresponding to this confidence interval is much less than 95.44 percent because we cannot assume that the loss is normally distributed.

[12] The issues associated with a lack of independence and positively correlated losses are discussed in greater detail in Chapter 5.

Summary

This chapter has discussed risk assessment, or the statistical methods that risk managers use to measure risk objectively. In the first portion of the chapter, we demonstrated how to calculate two common risk measures, the variance or standard deviation, and discussed how each calculation can be used to assess the degree to which the different values of a random variable vary around the expected value of that variable. We next demonstrated how to use calculations of loss frequency and loss severity to forecast the expected value of the loss. Finally, we discussed how organizations can use risk pooling to reduce the risks of their exposure units, and how insurers and risk managers can take advantage of pooling to decrease their costs of bearing risk.

Risk assessment plays a key role in risk management because individuals and organizations often use measures like the frequency and severity of losses to determine the best way to handle risk. In Chapter 4, "Risk-Handling Techniques," we will describe the different ways to handle pure risk, and discuss how organizations can use measures of the frequency and severity of losses to select the best technique to handle their loss exposures.

Review

1. Explain why flipping a coin is a random variable, and show the probability distribution of outcomes that can result from a single flip of a coin.

Use the following information to answer Questions 2 and 3.

Scary Airline predicts that the annual probability of one of its jets being destroyed in a crash is 1 in 10 million. If destroyed, the value of the property damage to the plane equals $50 million. Assume that there are no partial losses; the plane is either destroyed in a crash or suffers no loss.

2. Show the physical damage loss distribution for Scary Airline's planes.
3. Calculate the expected value of the physical damage loss.
4. Show the calculations for the variance and the standard deviation, as described in footnote 3.
5. Describe the difference between loss severity and loss frequency. In your answer, give an example of a loss control technique (as described in Chapter 2, "Risk Identification") that can be used by the owner of an apartment complex to reduce the severity and the frequency of fire losses.

Use the following information to answer Questions 6 and 7.

Sue is analyzing the workers' compensation (WC) losses of the employees in her firm that occurred over a one-year period, based on the following data.

Number of WC Claims Filed/Worker	Number of Workers	Total Number of Claims
0	850	0
1	100	100
2	50	100

6. Use the information in the table to find the average frequency of losses per worker.
7. Use the information in the table to estimate a probability distribution for the frequency distribution of losses per worker in a year.

Use the following information to answer Questions 8 and 9 below, which pertain to Questions 6 and 7.

Range of Loss Amount	Midpoint Dollar Amount of Loss	Number of Losses	Total $ Amt. of Losses
$1–2000	$1,000	180	$180,000
$2001–10,000	$6,000	20	$120,000
Greater than $12,000	NA	0	0

8. Use the information in the table to find the average severity per claim.
9. Use the information in the table to estimate a probability distribution for the loss severity per claim.
10. Using your answers from Question 7 and Question 9, use convolution to find the average loss.
11. Al's Toy Store faces the following probability distribution of fire losses in its store over the next year:

Probability	.85	.10	.05
Loss	$0	$20,000	$40,000

Calculate the expected value and standard deviation of Al's losses for the year.

12. Refer to Question 11. Assume that Al pools his losses with Ed's store, which has an identical loss distribution. Ed's losses are independent of Al's. Al and Ed agree to split the total losses in the pool equally. Show the revised probability distribution for the mean loss from the pool.
13. Refer to Questions 11 and 12. Calculate the expected value and standard deviation of the pooled mean losses.
14. Insurers combine a large number of exposure units in the process of risk pooling. Describe the effect of increasing the size of the risk pool on the mean loss of the pool and on the standard deviation of the mean loss in the pool. In your answer, assume that the losses of all the exposure units in the pool are independent and homogeneous.
15. Describe the shape of the normal distribution, indicating the statistical relationship between its mean and its standard deviation.
16. Describe the concept of a risk charge as the term is used in the calculation of insurance premiums. Is the risk charge affected by an increase in the number of exposure units in a risk pool?
17. List and briefly describe two examples of loss exposures that are not well suited to risk pooling, and explain the reasons why risk pooling is not effective for these loss exposures.

Objective Questions

1. A(n) _____ is a table or graph that shows all possible outcomes for a random variable, as well as their respective probabilities of occurring.
   a. variance
   b. expected value
   c. standard deviation
   d. probability distribution
2. Which of the following statements about probability distributions is not correct?
   a. The maximum probability of any one outcome must be less than 1.
   b. The minimum probability of any one outcome must be greater than zero.
   c. The sum of the probabilities across all outcomes must equal 1.
   d. All the above statements are correct.
3. Joe faces a 25 percent chance of a $1 million loss and a 75 percent chance of no loss. Joe's expected loss equals:
   a. $0
   b. $25
   c. $250,000
   d. $1 million
4. All of the following are statistical calculations used to measure risk EXCEPT:
   a. variance
   b. standard deviation
   c. expected value
   d. All the above are measures of risk.
5. The process of convolution
   I. uses the probability distribution for loss frequency in the process of forecasting the average loss
   II. uses the probability distribution for loss severity in the process of forecasting the average loss
   a. I only b. II only c. both I and II
   d. neither I nor II

6. Which of the following statements best describes the calculation of a confidence interval (CI) for the estimate of the value of the mean loss?
   a. The CI is found by adding and subtracting a risk charge to the forecasted value of the mean loss.
   b. The CI is found by taking the square root of the variance of the loss.
   c. The CI is found by multiplying the value of each possible outcome of a probability distribution by its probability of occurring, and summing all the resulting products.
   d. None of the above provides a good description of the process of calculating a CI.
7. Which of the following statements about risk pooling is correct?
   I. By joining an insurance risk pool, the insured becomes financially responsible for the mean loss of the pool instead of his or her own personal risk exposure.
   II. By joining an insurance risk pool, the insured can decrease the expected loss that he or she must pay to finance her exposure to loss.
   a. I only b. II only c. both I and II
   d. neither I nor II
8. Assume that Fred faces a potential liability exposure. The standard deviation of the probability distribution for the loss equals $12,000. Assume that Fred joins a risk pool with 899 other people with the same loss distribution whose losses are independent of each other. As one of 900 pool members, Fred's risk equals which of the following?
   a. $0
   b. $400
   c. $900
   d. $1200
   e. None of the above

9. Which of the following statements regarding the use of risk pooling is correct?
   I. Insurers can use risk pooling to diversify risk in products like auto or life insurance.
   II. Risk managers cannot use risk pooling to reduce risk because they do not have sufficient number of homogeneous and independent exposure units.
   a. I only   b. II only   c. both I and II
   d. neither I nor II

10. Which of the following statements about the normal curve is correct?
    a. The mean of the normal curve is located at the center of the curve.
    b. The shape of the normal curve is symmetric around the mean.
    c. The normal curve is shaped like a bell.
    d. All the above are correct.

Discussion Questions

1. Discuss two methods that can be used by risk managers to forecast the average loss associated with a particular loss exposure, assuming that the firm has a large data base of prior losses.
2. Describe two types of pure risk for which the technique of risk pooling can be used to reduce risk effectively, as well as two types of pure risk in which the technique cannot be used effectively. In your answer, briefly describe the characteristics of the pure risks that make them well (or poorly) suited for risk reduction through pooling.

Selected References

Denenberg, H., R. Eilers, J. Melone, and R. Zelten, 1974, *Risk and Insurance*, 2d ed. (Englewood Cliffs, NJ: Prentice-Hall).

Doherty, N., 1985, *Corporate Risk Management: A Financial Exposition* (New York: McGraw-Hill).

Harrington, S. E., and G. R. Niehaus, 2004, *Risk Management and Insurance*, 2d ed. (New York: McGraw-Hill).

4

Risk-Handling Techniques: Loss Control, Risk Transfer, and Loss Financing

After studying this chapter, you should be able to

- Describe the three broad categories of risk-handling techniques: loss control, risk transfer, and loss financing.

- Differentiate between loss prevention and loss reduction, two broad types of loss control.

- Describe methods that can be used to transfer risk away from the firm, including insurance, contractual transfer, and the use of limited liability ownership forms.

- Differentiate between external and internal loss-financing techniques.

- Describe the advantages and disadvantages of insurance as a risk-handling technique.

- Describe the alternatives available to firms that want to finance losses internally.

- Describe how loss frequency and severity affect a firm's choice of risk-handling techniques.

The preceding two chapters discussed two key steps in the risk management process: the identification of risks that can harm an organization financially, and the methods that risk managers use to measure and assess those risks. In this chapter, we move to the next step in the risk management process, examining the different ways available to handle the pure risks of the firm.[1] More specifically, we discuss three methods for handling risk: loss or risk control, risk transfer, and loss financing (see Figure 4-1). We also describe different risk management conditions under which each of these risk-handling techniques is well suited.

Risk managers consider several factors when choosing how best to handle the risks facing their organizations. The first of these are the frequency and severity of the losses caused by the risk, as risk managers generally will use the risk assessment measures discussed in Chapter 3, "Risk Assessment and Pooling," to choose how best to handle the

---

[1] We examine different methods of handling speculative risks in Chapter 5.

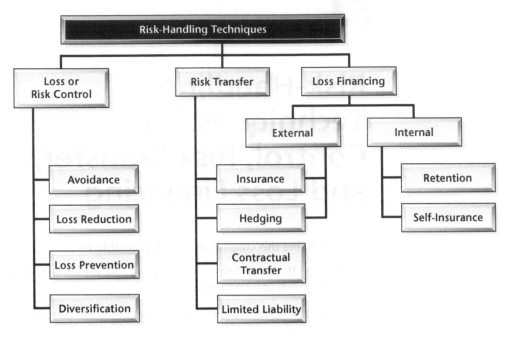

FIGURE 4-1 Methods of Handling Risk

risk in question. A second consideration affecting a firm's selection of its risk-handling techniques is its size. Small firms and individual consumers usually rely upon insurance as their primary means of financing their loss exposures, while larger national and multinational corporations are less dependent on insurance and often have a wider variety of non-insurance risk-handling alternatives available to them. Finally, the supply of insurance has great influence on a firm's choice of risk-handling techniques, as firms rely more heavily on non-insurance techniques when the supply of insurance is inadequate.[2]

LOSS OR RISK CONTROL

All organizations incur costs because they are exposed to risks that can result in unexpected losses. These costs include insurance premiums, uninsured losses, business interruption, and other indirect losses, as well as the costs incurred by the organization to control each of these expenses. The risk manager often has some ability to control the severity and frequency of these costs through the use of loss control. Also known as **risk control, loss control** refers to risk-management activities that help reduce the expected losses incurred by an organization.

We can classify loss-control efforts into two categories: loss prevention and loss reduction. **Loss prevention** reduces the frequency with which losses occur. **Loss reduction** decreases the severity of the loss if it does occur. In practice, many common

---

[2] Several sectors of the United States economy have endured insurance shortages since 2000, including a shortage of terrorism insurance after the September 11 attacks, a medical malpractice liability insurance crisis, and a shortage of homeowners insurance in hurricane-prone states. Some risks are not readily insurable, as we discuss in Chapter 7.

loss-control activities, such as worker training seminars, the hiring of security staff, and preventive maintenance of machinery and vehicles, do not fit neatly into just one category because they simultaneously reduce both loss frequency and severity.

Loss Prevention

Familiar examples of loss-prevention activities include the use of tamper-resistant packaging, safety education programs, and warnings printed on drugs or dangerous chemicals. As a rule, when the frequency of loss is high, risk managers should consider loss-prevention activities; however, these measures are cost-effective only if their cost is lower than the benefits realized from fewer loss occurrences.

Large firms often hire loss-control engineers to identify sources of loss or injury and to prescribe corrective action. Some losses can be traced to workplace hazards such as poor layout of work areas, inadequate lighting or ventilation, poor maintenance, or insufficient computer security. Other losses are related more directly to human errors, such as bad judgment, inadequate training or supervision, or lack of attention to safety requirements. Firms can develop and implement loss-control programs to deal with all these problems, but it takes a strong commitment by management and constant attention by the risk manager to reach the desired goals.

A risk manager's first goal in a loss-prevention program is to reduce or eliminate the chance of death or injury to people. Making decisions pertaining to the value of human lives can be complicated, however. Establishing engineering solutions or using cost-benefit analysis raises the ethical problem of measuring the benefits of saving human lives. It's also tough to evaluate the effectiveness of many loss-prevention activities, like immunizations and anti-pollution reforms, because the economic benefits may not be realized for many years, and even then they may be quite difficult to measure.

Sometimes the best method of dealing with an exposure to loss is the strategy of **avoidance**: simply not engaging in the risky activity. In practice, avoidance may mean not introducing a new product, ending the production of an existing risky product, discontinuing some operations, or choosing not to do business in locations where a given peril is present. Many U.S. firms avoid investing in foreign countries with high political risk. They prefer to forgo profits instead of bearing the risk that their property may be confiscated or their employees harmed.

Some risks are unavoidable. Neither firms nor individuals can avoid the risk of bankruptcy, a liability suit, or death. Avoidance is also not feasible if the risk in question generates most of or all the revenue for the individual or organization exposed to loss (unless the organization has decided to cease operations). In other cases, avoidance is not necessary; most exposures to loss can be reduced. Beyond these exceptions, however, avoidance is often the best, and sometimes the only, practical alternative for handling a risk, especially when both the frequency and severity of loss is high.

Loss Reduction

Despite the best loss-prevention efforts, some losses typically will occur. Effective loss-reduction activities aim to minimize their impact. Loss-reduction activities are most appropriate when the severity of loss is high. Like loss prevention, however, loss reduction is justified only when the savings exceeds the cost. An excellent example of a loss-reduction device is an automatic fire sprinkler system, which prevents the spread of fires by showering newly started fires with water, thus reducing their severity. Sprinklers often pay for themselves in a short time through reduced fire insurance premiums. Other loss-reduction devices include firewalls and fire doors, airbags in vehicles, and salvage operations.

A simple way to reduce losses is through **duplication**, or redundancy, a process in which an individual or firm reduces its exposure to risk by holding multiple copies of a key resource or asset. Duplication is especially effective when the cost is low, such as when a student saves multiple copies of her master's thesis on her laptop, her universal serial bus (USB) flash drive, and in her e-mail as an attachment. Duplication is also a cost-effective way to avoid situations in which a firm's normal operations are highly dependent on a single asset or vendor, especially when a loss to that asset or vendor could significantly hurt the company financially. For example, firms with extensive supply chains often maintain multiple vendors whenever possible, thus minimizing their exposure to supply-chain interruptions that could result when an exclusive vendor suffers a loss that restricts its ability to supply the firm. For more discussion of the role of duplication in preventing supply chain interruptions, see Insight Box 4-1.

Duplication is closely related to **physical separation**, a loss-reduction practice in which a firm designs its operations around multiple locations that are physically far from each other, thus reducing the chance that a single adverse event like a fire or storm could disrupt all operations. From a production-engineering standpoint, it may be more cost-efficient to build a 100,000-gallon-a-day ice cream plant rather than two 50,000-gallon-a-day plants. However, if the ice cream maker built two distant plants, a loss to one would not jeopardize the functioning of the other. The same reasoning holds for warehouses and even trucks. As these examples suggest, when planning the size of an operating unit, it is helpful to include discussions about the risk of loss along with the more typical production and engineering considerations.

Firms can also limit the severity and variability of their losses through **diversification**. For example, larger corporations often sell a variety of products and services

---

INSIGHT BOX 4-1

The Value of Redundancy: How a Strike by Chinese Workers Led to a Supply-Chain Interruption for Honda

During May 2010, Chinese workers in a large auto parts plant that produced transmissions for Honda vehicles went on strike, asking for a 50 percent increase in wages. The strike received international media attention and was covered by China's state-owned media, which had never before broadcast reports of labor unrest in the country. Unauthorized labor organization is illegal in China, and observers wondered whether the Chinese government had permitted media coverage of the strike to show that Chinese workers were growing dissatisfied with their role as a source of low-cost labor for global manufacturers.

Many manufacturers maintain multiple vendors of key components in their supply chains or make other arrangements to ensure an adequate supply of parts, such as holding a buffer stock of parts. Unlike most manufacturers with complex production supply chains, however, Honda had relied solely on the striking plant for transmissions and had not arranged to have a second

Chinese supplier of auto transmissions for its assembly plants in the country. One report noted that Honda had not expected strikes in China because unauthorized labor organization was illegal in the country.

The work stoppage and resulting shortage of transmissions forced the closure of four other Honda auto assembly plants in China for more than a week, halting normal production of approximately 3,000 cars per day. A Honda representative indicated that the firm was prepared to ship transmissions to China from its Japanese plants if the strike continued, but the firm was able to arrange a labor agreement with the striking workers by agreeing to increase their wages by 24 percent (from around $220 per month to $280 per month, which is more than double the minimum wage in that part of China).

Based on "Chinese Workers Demand Higher Pay," Louisa Lim, interviewed by Renee Montagne for National Public Radio on June 1, 2010. Transcript downloaded from www.npr.org on June 2, 2010.

to diversify their sources of revenue. They can offset a decline in the revenue of one product line with increased sales from another product, making overall revenue flow more stable over time. Diversification thus helps reduce risk and, if properly executed, reduces severity by reducing the chance that all sources of revenue simultaneously decrease. The strategy of diversification is also used heavily in investments, as we discuss in Chapter 5, "Risk-Handling Techniques Using Diversification and Hedging."

Loss Control and Federal Regulatory Agencies

A variety of federal regulators mandate that firms in the United States meet minimum safety standards. Loss-control engineering increased in importance with the passage of the Occupational Safety and Health Act (OSHA). This federal law promotes a safe working environment for employees by creating two duties for employers. One is to remove all recognized hazards from the work environment, and the second is to comply with the standards for a safe working environment as published in bulletins from the Department of Labor. Because OSHA levies heavy fines for noncompliance with these standards, including imprisonment in certain cases of employee fatalities, loss-prevention activities have taken on added importance.

The program provides for on-site reviews by OSHA inspectors. It also requires extensive recordkeeping by employers to detail occupational injuries that result in death or injury or require significant medical treatment. The law also requires that employers enforce safety regulations rather than merely posting signs or providing safety equipment.

The *Consumer Product Safety Commission (CPSC)* is a federal agency responsible for regulating the safety of products sold to consumers. The Consumer Products Safety Act requires manufacturers and retailers to notify the CPSC of any product hazard of which they become aware. The commission has an electronic network for sharing information about dangerous products. In addition, it sets safety standards for some products such as lawnmowers. Once the CPSC has developed the standards, makers of these products must certify that their output complies. Noncompliance can result in fines, penalties, and even imprisonment.

The U.S. *Environmental Protection Agency (EPA)* regulates firms whose activities may damage the environment. Various federal environmental protection acts impose loss-prevention duties on businesses, especially companies using toxic chemicals.[3] The amended Clean Air Act, for example, requires organizations emitting air pollutants to get a permit from the EPA. If the organization does not and subsequently pollutes the air, the EPA can shut down the establishment. If a firm gets the required permit but violates the provisions of the Clean Air Act, the EPA can impose fines for each day a violation occurs.

RISK TRANSFER

Risk transfer refers to a variety of widely applied techniques that a risk manager can use to shift the financial responsibility for losses away from his or her organization and onto a third party. We can classify transfer techniques into three broad categories:

---

[3] These acts include the Comprehensive Environmental Response Compensation Liability Act (also known as *Superfund*), the Superfund Amendments and Reauthorization Act, the Clean Air Act, and the Water Pollution Control Act. A description of these acts can be found at http://www.epa.gov/lawsregs/laws/.

risk transfers to risk-bearing financial institutions, contractual transfers, and transfers involving limited liability.

A **risk-bearing financial institution** provides value to its customers by allowing them to transfer their financial risks to the institution in exchange for a fee. Examples include insurance companies and markets for risk-hedging contracts, like the Chicago Board of Trade, New York Mercantile Exchange, or Eurex. Capitalizing on their size and unique capabilities to reduce risk, these institutions generally can bear risk more cost effectively than their customers. These risk transactions span two broad categories of risk-handling techniques: risk transfer and loss financing. Thus, customers not only transfer their risks to the institution but also finance the cost of the loss through these transactions. Because of their loss-financing characteristics, we discuss these loss-transfer techniques in greater detail in the next section.

Unlike insurance and hedging, non-institutional **contractual transfer agreements** typically do not reduce the underlying risk but simply transfer the consequences of risk to another party. For example, many sales agreements include clauses that transfer ownership of the goods from the manufacturer to the buyer as soon as the goods are moved off the manufacturer's premises. These clauses enable the manufacturer to transfer the risk that the goods are damaged during shipping to the buyer or the common carrier transporting the goods, such as a trucking company or ocean cargo shipping firm. Similarly, **exculpatory clauses** are clauses in business contracts that transfer risk between contracting parties. For example, contracts for security systems and fire alarm services often include exculpatory clauses in which the customer gives up the right to sue the service provider for damages sustained because of an alleged defect in the product or service, under the expectation that the customer will buy insurance protection for such damages.

Hold-harmless agreements are contracts entered into prior to a loss, in which one party agrees to assume a second party's financial responsibility should a loss occur. For example, a railroad may require a manufacturer to assume financial responsibility for accidents before building a spur line on the manufacturer's property. In other cases, vendors request hold-harmless agreements before selling a manufacturer's goods. Likewise, contractors may require subcontractors to provide the contractor with liability protection in the event that they are sued because of the subcontractor's activities.

Businesses also can transfer risk by taking advantage of the limited liability protection provided to the owners of certain types of business organizational forms. Under the doctrine of **limited liability**, business claimants, such as creditors or the plaintiffs in a lawsuit, cannot attach to the personal assets of the owner of that business because by law their claims are limited to the assets of the firm. Traditionally, business owners could obtain limited liability protection only by incorporating their business, and business claimants could attach to an owner's personal assets (assuming the assets of the firm were insufficient to satisfy such claims) if his or her firm was a sole proprietorship or partnership. More recently, however, most states have modified their laws to provide limited liability protection to a broader variety of organizational forms of business, including limited liability partnerships (LLPs) and limited liability companies (LLCs). As we discuss in Insight Box 4-2, the owners of many partnerships and small businesses have recently organized their firms to take advantage of limited liability protection, thus shielding their personal assets from lawsuits.

INSIGHT BOX 4-2

Changing Partners(hips): The Growth of Limited Liability

For many newly hired graduates in the professional services, from accounting to law, a traditional career goal is to become a partner in the firm, a promotion that recognizes professional achievement and earns high compensation. In recent years, however, the title of partner has come with some additional risk, including the risk of losing one's personal assets through an adverse legal judgment against the partnership.

Two or more people who want to form a business together traditionally have had two options for organizing their firm: a partnership and a corporation. Of the two, corporations typically require more administrative effort to start, but they provide an advantage that partnerships do not: limited liability protection. As this chapter explains, the doctrine of limited liability means that business claimants, such as creditors of the firm or plaintiffs suing the firm, generally do not have a legal right to attach to the personal assets of the owners of the firm. Although the owners of small corporations face adverse tax rules compared to partnerships (critics note that the owners of small corporations are "double taxed," because corporate income is taxed at the corporate tax rate and then the owners pay an additional personal tax on the dividends that they receive as compensation), limited liability is an especially attractive feature of the corporate business form.

Many professional service firms, including law firms, accounting firms, medical practices, architectural firms, and engineering firms, traditionally have been formed as partnerships. Unlike the owners of corporations, partners are unable to protect their personal assets from business claimants. Instead, if the assets of the partnership are insufficient to meet its claimants' needs, a claimant can attach to the personal assets of the partner. Moreover, if a claimant is filing a sizable lawsuit, a partner's responsibility for damages extends to the claims against his or her fellow partners. Thus, if the courts find that a surgeon was negligent in causing severe harm to a patient during a surgical procedure, the injured patient can attach to not only the assets

of the doctor who performed the surgery, but also the other physicians in the practice.

In the face of increasing litigation risk in the United States in the 1980s, the owners of many partnerships called for reform. As a result, two new organizational forms were created: the limited liability partnership (LLP) and, more recently, the limited liability company (LLC). These hybrid organizations shield the owner's assets from claimants *and* avoid the adverse income tax rules applicable to corporations.

Many existing partnerships switched to the limited-liability hybrids to capitalize on their ability to better protect partners from lawsuits. For example, prior to 1992, professional accounting standards generally required public accounting firms to operate as a partnership. These standards were relaxed in 1992, and within two years, all the leading U.S. audit firms had switched to a limited-liability hybrid. A senior executive of Ernst and Young explained the reason his Big Four accounting firm became an LLP: "Organizing as a limited-liability partnership would put us on a level playing field with corporate America. . . . We can't attract people [to work for the firm if they are] worried about losing their homes in the case of a disaster. . . . The accounting profession is getting murdered by the litigation that has overtaken us in the last few years."

During the 2000s, the popularity of the LLC organizational form grew rapidly. Practitioners report that LLCs have become the organizational form of choice for most new business startups. Early research supports these reports, indicating that 58 percent of the new businesses created nationally from 2004 to 2007 were LLCs, compared to 39 percent for corporations, the next most popular organizational form.

Based on "Partnership Shift Seen for Big Accounting Firms." THE NEW YORK TIMES, July 28, 1994; and R. Chrisman, "LLC's Are the New King of the Hill: An Empirical Study of the Number of New LLCs, Corporations, and LPs Formed Between 2004–2007 and How LLCs Were Taxed for Tax Years 2002–2006." FORDHAM JOURNAL OF CORPORATE & FINANCE LAW, 15.2 (2010): 459–89.

LOSS FINANCING

When organizations are unable to transfer risk to third parties or to control their exposure to loss, they must find a way to pay for their losses. **Loss financing**, a third broad class of risk-handling techniques, includes a variety of strategies. Traditionally, insurance and hedging have been two of the most common methods to finance loss costs externally. Organizations can also adopt a variety of internal self-financing options, including risk retention, self-insurance, and captive insurance.

Insurance

For centuries, consumers have relied upon insurance to pay for unexpected losses. We've seen why insurers often hold a comparative advantage over their smaller customers in bearing such losses: because they can use risk pooling to better predict the mean losses across all pool members and thus charge lower premiums (as discussed in Chapter 3). As a result, it is often less expensive for many consumers to transfer their risks to an insurer for a premium than to bear the risks themselves. Insurance is, therefore, the foundation of the risk management programs of most individual consumers, as well as most small and medium-sized businesses and non-business organizations.

The value of insurance as a loss-financing mechanism is especially apparent in light of the uncertain timing of large losses. Consider a highly profitable small business that faces a 1 percent chance each year of suffering a $500,000 fire loss. While in theory the firm could plan to save $100,000 per year over five years to build a fund to pay for the loss (ignoring interest), it would not have enough cash, in spite of its high profitability, if the 100-to-1 fire event occurred in year two of the savings campaign. Such financing considerations are even more important to less-profitable organizations that are unable to save large sums of money for such losses.

Insurance is an especially appropriate risk-management tool for a firm when its loss frequency is low and the severity of a potential loss is high. When the frequency of losses within a firm is low, its risk manager generally has insufficient data with which to forecast losses, making risk reduction through pooling infeasible. High severity means that firms are also less likely to have enough funds available internally to bear the risk of suffering a large loss. Many situations facing both smaller firms and individuals meet these two criteria of low frequency and high severity, and thus insurance is widely purchased. Even large firms will face certain risks that can be characterized by low-frequency, high-severity loss exposures and thus require insurance.

Firms and individuals also buy insurance for reasons that are unrelated to risk pooling. In some cases, the law may require them to. For example, employers are required to provide workers' compensation benefits to employees, and drivers must purchase auto liability insurance. Lending institutions often require consumers to buy insurance on autos or real estate as a condition of borrowing money to purchase such items; in these cases, the insurance protects the lender's collateral interest in the items should they be damaged or destroyed. A large firm may need certain services that the insurer offers, such as loss-control inspections or loss-settlement expertise. Finally, exposure to any extremely large potential losses generally requires insurance protection. The combined effect of these forces creates a fairly consistent level of demand for insurance products.

Unfortunately, the supply of insurance is sometimes insufficient to meet the demand. Some types of risks—such as earthquakes, war, or unemployment—are not commercially insurable because the maximum losses associated with these risks are too big for even the largest insurers to bear without causing them financial distress. If insurers have insufficient pricing information available for a particular loss exposure, they typically will be unwilling to sell insurance protection from that risk. Insurance shortages also can result from ineffective insurance regulation, such as efforts to hold premiums below the price levels necessary to cover an insurer's costs.

From an accounting point of view, the purchase of insurance offers several financial advantages. Businesses can write off the cost of insurance premiums as a tax-deductible expense at the time they pay the premium. Most small to medium-sized businesses buy guaranteed cost insurance, which means that the price of insurance is fixed for the duration of the policy, thus leading to a more-stable risk-management budget. On the other hand, insurance can be costly. The *loading charge*, a fee to cover the administrative expenses incurred by the insurer, can account for more than a third of the premium charged for many types of insurance. And for consumers with poor previous loss experience, the cost of insurance can be very high, reflecting their high probability of suffering losses in the future.

After deciding to insure a particular loss exposure, the risk manager still faces many decisions, including choosing an insurance agent or broker, choosing an insurance company, and choosing an insurance policy. A risk manager who decides to use the services of an insurance broker often will work with the broker to develop specifications for the insurance program. After buying an insurance policy, the risk manager's work is still incomplete; he or she must make sure that the company does not violate any terms of the insurance agreement. For example, if the contract is conditioned on the company's employing a security guard or maintaining a fire sprinkler system, the risk manager must be sure these conditions are met. If a loss occurs, the risk manager must report the loss to the insurer promptly and comply with all the post-loss contractual requirements. If the claims payment offered by an insurer is inadequate, the risk manager, acting with the company's legal staff, must negotiate an acceptable payment with the insurance company. As these examples suggest, the use of insurance as a risk-management tool includes much more than purchasing an insurance policy.

Insurance with Deductibles

The purchase of insurance can greatly affect a consumer's behavior regarding risk because insurance policyholders often have less incentive to prevent losses if they know that their insurers will be paying for them. *Moral hazard* refers to this tendency of policyholders to engage in behavior that increases the expected loss payouts of an insurer. Insurers are very mindful of the costs related to moral hazard and often include clauses in insurance policies to control such behavior. A common example is a contractual provision stating that the policyholder must deduct a specific dollar amount, called the **deductible**, from any insurance claim that he or she is requesting the insurer to pay. In this way, the insurer attempts to control moral hazard by making the consumer financially responsible for at least a portion of his or her insured loss.

Individuals and small businesses with limited budgets often buy insurance with relatively small deductible amounts, such as $1,000 or less; however, larger firms can afford to pay bigger deductible amounts. As a result, they often can negotiate a lower premium from an insurer in exchange for assuming responsibility for a larger deductible on their policies. Insurers are willing to reduce the price for insurance with bigger deductible amounts for several reasons. First, larger deductibles lower the insurer's costs because it does not have to pay for small losses that fall below the deductible amount, nor does it incur administrative expenses for handling such small claims. The insurer also pays a smaller amount on each loss because the policyholder is responsible for a higher deductible amount. Because of these pricing factors, larger firms and organizations can use their willingness to bear higher deductibles as a means to negotiate a decreased price for insurance.

For large businesses with sufficient financial resources to absorb very high amounts of losses, a useful risk-handling technique is **high-deductible insurance protection**, insurance coverage designed with a very large deductible, such as $100,000 to $500,000 per loss. Under this plan, the insurer pays all losses incurred by the policyholder up to the coverage limit of the policy but then bills the policyholder for either the deductible or the sum of all the paid losses, whichever is less.[4] The insured receives a significant premium discount in exchange for assuming the high deductible. Properly designed, this arrangement enables the insured firm to decrease its premiums while maintaining insurance protection for unexpectedly large loss events. High deductibles are popular with larger firms that are required by law to satisfy compulsory insurance requirements, such as workers' compensation, but want to minimize their costs while doing so.

Hedging

Like the purchase of insurance, **hedging** is a risk-handling technique that combines the financing of risk with the transfer of risk. Risk managers of financial institutions, such as banks and mutual funds, and of firms dealing in commodities, such as grain companies, petroleum refiners, and soft drink bottlers, include hedging as an important risk-management tool. Unlike insurance, however, hedging strategies deal with speculative risk, which offers the opportunity not only for financial loss but also for financial gain. We therefore defer our discussion of hedging to Chapter 5, when we examine the ways that firms handle speculative risk exposures.

Risk Assumption or Retention

In **risk assumption**, the party exposed to the risk of loss bears the consequences of that loss. Also known as *risk retention*, risk assumption is often a deliberate decision that firms make with a full understanding of the consequences of a potential loss, knowing that they will bear these consequences. It is a typical strategy when loss costs are relatively small and can be financed comfortably from current cash flow. For example, firms often assume the risk of losing items of relatively small value, such as hand tools or plates used by a restaurant.

While most organizations can bear the cost of broken plates and hand tools easily, some firms assume losses of significantly greater size. The ability to assume risks that can result in larger losses largely depends upon a firm's financial capacity and its appetite for risk. A small family business thus may find it difficult to absorb the cost of a vehicle destroyed in an accident, but a national package delivery firm may retain such losses on a routine basis. Similarly, a large international oil company might assume the loss of a $250-million oil tanker if its quarterly profits average $8 billion.

Sometimes organizations have little choice but to assume certain financial risks. We've seen above that the deductible provisions in many insurance policies require the insured to assume some financial responsibility for a predefined portion of a loss, and firms often must assume financial responsibility for damage caused by earthquakes or floods because property insurance policies typically exclude these causes of loss from coverage.

In contrast, firms sometimes assume risk out of ignorance, such as by failing to identify a potential loss exposure before loss occurred or because they failed to carry out the risk-management process effectively. Other firms find that they have assumed risks because of gaps in their insurance program because they underestimated the severity of a loss or because no one conducted a thorough evaluation of the risk-management activities of a newly acquired firm. None of these errors exemplify sound risk-management practice.

Some firms may give accounting recognition to the expenses of assuming risk by maintaining an unfunded loss reserve account. These bookkeeping entries provide no cash in the event of loss, nor are any tax deductions available until a loss is paid. The purpose of this approach is to recognize the cost of assumed risks in the firm's accounting

---

[4] This arrangement differs from a **self-insured retention** program, in which the insured firm pays for all losses up to a certain dollar threshold, after which the insurer takes over loss payment.

system and thus provide a more realistic view of the firm's financial position. Other firms may finance their losses through the use of **funded risk assumption**, setting aside a cash, or near-cash, investment fund to use when losses occur, or arranging contingent lending agreements with a bank. This funding may supplement a plan to finance small losses from current cash flow. It provides an extra margin of safety if several assumed losses occur in a short period of time or during a period of reduced cash flow.

The accounting treatment of losses assumed by a firm is quite different from the treatment of insured loss costs. Assumed losses are a tax-deductible expense, but they can be deducted only at the time the loss is paid, even if the firm has prudently arranged financing before the losses occur. Because loss events occur randomly, the cash flows resulting from a risk assumption program typically exhibit more variability than the smooth amortization of insurance premiums. Unlike insurance, risk assumption also requires more attention and time from the risk-management department, which must investigate losses, arrange payment, and carry out many of the support services otherwise provided by insurers.

Self-insurance

Under certain conditions, medium-sized to large organizations can self-insure their financial loss exposures. **Self-insurance** is a risk-handling technique in which a firm retains and finances its losses internally based on forecasts generated from the pooling of losses within the organization. It requires a business to combine a sufficient number of its own similar exposures to predict the losses accurately. The firm also must make adequate financial arrangements in advance to provide funds to pay for losses when they occur.[5]

Due to its considerable statistical and financing requirements, self-insurance is typically a viable risk-handling technique for only a narrow range of loss exposures that exhibit high frequency but low to moderate severity. For example, two types of risk that are often self-insured by many large-sized organizations are workers' compensation and employer-sponsored health insurance. Large firms can self-insure all or some of their health insurance or workers' compensation costs because they can pool the loss experience of many employees, improving their ability to forecast losses accurately.[6] Because workers' compensation is mandated by law, regulators have established detailed requirements for firms that want to self-insure to better assure that these benefits are financed adequately.

Captive Insurers

One way to finance the losses in a self-insurance program is to create a **captive insurance company**, or captive, an insurance subsidiary formed as a separate company to write the insurance for its parent firm. The captive's parent may be one company, several companies, or an entire industry. Captives often are formed in locations like Bermuda or the Cayman Islands, where insurance regulation is less restrictive and less costly than in the United States. Several states, such as Vermont and Colorado, also have become popular places to form captives, often by modifying their insurance regulations to increase their attractiveness for this purpose.

---

[5] Risk assumption, deliberate or unplanned, should not be confused with self-insurance. Unless a firm forecasts and makes adequate financing arrangements for its self-insurance fund, a true self-insurance system does not exist.

[6] Workers' compensation loss exposures are an especially attractive candidate for self-insurance because these losses are often paid over a period of several years. Thus, a self-insured firm can earn investment income on the assets held in support of the loss reserves of the firm during this time.

One motive in forming a captive is to enable the parent to retain for investment the premiums that it otherwise would pay to a commercial insurer. A second is to save the overhead and profits that otherwise would be earned by commercial insurers. A third, and controversial, motive is to take advantage of differences in the tax rules applicable to parents and insurers.

Under federal income tax guidelines, a parent company cannot deduct self-insurance funding until losses are paid, while it can deduct commercial insurance premiums when they are paid. Therefore, parents have argued in court that payments to their captives are not self-insurance arrangements but instead premiums paid to a third-party insurer. If that were the case, parents could recognize insurance premium payments to captives as a current business expense while the captive insurer reported them as insurance income. The Internal Revenue Service (IRS) disagreed with this reasoning for many years with its "economic family doctrine," arguing that payments to a parent's captive should not be deductible for the parent because such payments involve no transfer of risk outside the economic family of the parent firm. During the early 1990s, however, the courts moderated the strict position of the IRS, allowing premiums paid to an affiliated captive to be deductible when the captive provided substantial insurance coverage to other outside parties unaffiliated with the parent. In the late 1990s, the courts further moderated these rules to allow the deduction of premiums paid by a corporate affiliate of a parent firm into a captive that insured other affiliates owned by the same parent. Ultimately, the IRS abandoned the economic family doctrine in 2001[7] and currently evaluates premium deductibility on a case-by-case basis. A key factor determining whether premiums paid to a captive are deductible is whether the captive also insured enough risk from nonaffiliated third parties to permit risk reduction across all the members of the pool, considerations that are consistent with the discussion of risk pooling found in Chapter 3.

Beyond these motivating factors, many organizations find that using captives provides benefits that are not available from commercial insurance, such as more cost-effective loss-control or claims-settlement services. Some parent companies suggest that captives offer cash flow advantages, such as the avoidance of premium taxes, and the ability to consolidate subsidiaries' insurance needs under one insurance program. Thus, in areas such as automobile liability exposure, maintaining a self-insurance facility might be considerably less expensive than having each subsidiary company purchase its own coverage.

Of course, there are other cost factors to consider when deciding whether to use a capture insurer. First, commercial insurance companies often provide their customers with valuable services in both loss-prevention engineering and claims settlement. These services must be purchased or provided internally if a captive is used. Second, a business must hire competent management to administer the captive insurer, and experienced talent is not widely available. Third, the creation of a captive can require a significant amount of startup capital that the parent must pay.

CHOOSING AN APPROPRIATE RISK-HANDLING TECHNIQUE

So far in this chapter, we have examined the variety of ways that organizations can handle their exposures to pure risk. We next discuss how they can select the best techniques to fit a given type of loss exposure, integrating our discussion of risk assessment in Chapter 3 with what we have just learned. Generally, identifying the best

---

[7] Revenue Ruling 2001-31, 2001-1 CB 1348.

TABLE 4-1 The Selection of Risk-handling Techniques, Based on Frequency and Severity

	Low Severity	*High Severity*
High Frequency	Self-insurance (for larger firms) and loss control	Avoidance (if possible) and loss control
Low Frequency	Risk assumption and loss control	Insurance and loss control

risk-handling technique is a matter of determining how frequently losses occur and how big they are when a loss occurs.

Shown in Table 4-1 is a generalized approach for selecting the optimal risk-handling technique based on the frequency and severity of loss exposure. To simplify, we classify loss exposures in a 2-by-2 matrix, with high and low frequency on the vertical axis and high and low severity on the horizontal axis. Keeping in mind that it is unrealistic to assume that all individuals and organizations will handle their different risks in identical ways, we can use this table as a useful summary of some common risk-handling tendencies.

Low-frequency, low-severity losses are commonly assumed or retained by many organizations because their cost generally can be paid from cash accounts without causing financial issues. If the organization is concerned that larger than expected losses may occur, it can choose to arrange for supplemental internal loss funding to provide an additional means of financing. Because the organization is bearing the cost of retained losses internally, it also will use loss control whenever the cost is lower than resulting reduction in loss costs.

Low-frequency, higher severity losses are insured by many organizations. Insurers generally can use risk pooling to reduce risk by combining a large number of exposure units. Loss-control efforts, especially loss-reduction techniques, are also useful, and insurers often reward a reduction in losses with a reduction in premiums.

High-frequency, low-severity losses are often self-insured by large organizations that possess enough exposure units to reduce risk effectively through pooling. Self-insurance also requires that the organization prearrange financing to cover the cost of expected self-insured losses. Because the firm is paying for losses internally, it also will use loss control to reduce losses when its cost is offset by the reduction in losses. Loss prevention is especially advisable to reduce the frequency of losses. Unlike large organizations, however, smaller firms may choose to insure high-frequency, low-severity losses because they do not have enough exposure units to reduce risk effectively through pooling, or they lack the financial resources to self-fund these losses.

High-frequency, high-severity losses are potentially catastrophic. As a result, most organizations attempt to avoid such risks if they can anticipate them with sufficient lead time. Loss-reduction and loss-prevention activities are also advised. Corporations dealing with high-frequency, high-severity losses face direct and indirect costs that can force them to restructure their operations dramatically in an effort to generate enough cash to pay for their mounting losses. In the worst-case scenario, the troubled firm may be forced into bankruptcy, where it attempts to reorganize and pay for its loss obligations without defaulting on its existing financial obligations to employees, bondholders, and other corporate stakeholders.

Summary

This chapter has examined the variety of alternatives available to individuals and organizations when considering how to handle pure risks. Organizations use loss-control techniques to decrease their exposure to financial loss in two ways: by reducing the frequency at which losses occur and by reducing the severity of losses if they should occur. Risk-transfer techniques shift the financial responsibility for losses away from the organization and onto another party, such as an insurer or some other third party via contractual arrangements. Loss-financing techniques are arrangements that can be used to pay for losses, including external sources of financing like insurance, and internal arrangements such as risk retention or self-insurance programs. As shown in Table 4-1, no single method can solely be used to handle all risks. Instead, risk-handling needs vary depending on firm size and on the frequency and severity characteristics of the loss exposure.

Once the risk management department has selected the best technique with which to handle its loss exposure, it must take the steps to implement that technique. For example, if a large firm decides to self-insure a loss exposure, it must hire actuarial consultants to forecast losses, arrange financing to pay for expected losses, and assemble a staff or hire third parties to manage the self-insurance program. If a firm plans to purchase insurance protection from a loss, it must determine the amount of insurance to buy, consider whether it will hire a broker to assist in soliciting bids from insurers, and develop a process to determine which insurer best fits the firm's needs. In this regard, proper execution of a well-developed risk management plan will enable the firm to reduce its susceptibility to financial losses arising from pure risk.

Review

1. How is loss prevention different from loss reduction? Give some examples of each.
2. Describe the conditions in which avoidance is an appropriate risk-handling technique.
3. What is OSHA, and how does it relate to a firm's risk-management program?
4. Describe how firms use contractual transfer methods to handle risk. Provide two examples.
5. Describe how firms can use limited liability as a means to protect themselves from risk.
6. Describe the advantages and disadvantages of using insurance as a loss-financing technique.
7. Describe the role of deductibles in insurance contracts.
8. How does self-insurance differ from risk assumption as an internal loss-financing technique?
9. What are the potential advantages (and disadvantages) of a self-insurance program?
10. Describe the benefits associated with using captive insurers as a loss-financing technique.
11. Describe how loss frequency and loss severity affect a firm's choice of risk-handling techniques.

Objective Questions

1. A pharmaceutical firm recalls a popular drug after a study reveals that it causes deadly side effects, and later announces that it will no longer sell the drug. This decision is an example of which of the following?
   a. avoidance
   b. self-insurance
   c. loss prevention
   d. contractual transfer
2. Installing airbags in automobiles is an example of which of the following?
   a. avoidance
   b. loss reduction
   c. loss prevention
   d. limited liability
3. ABC Mills agrees to assume the financial responsibility for losses caused by a local railroad as part of an agreement to build a railroad sidetrack next to ABC's silos. This exemplifies which of the following?
   a. limited liability
   b. an exculpatory clause
   c. hold harmless agreement
   d. avoidance

4. Insurance is frequently used as a risk-handling technique for _____ losses.
   a. high frequency, high severity
   b. high frequency, low severity
   c. low frequency, high severity
   d. low frequency, low severity

5. Which of the following statements regarding deductibles in insurance policies is correct?
   I. Deductibles decrease moral hazard behavior by policyholders.
   II. Increasing the deductible in an insurance policy can help decrease the policy premium.
   a. I only   b. II only   c. both I and II
   d. neither I nor II

6. An insurance policy with a deductible is an example of which of the following?
   a. risk transfer
   b. risk assumption
   c. both a and b
   d. neither a nor b

7. Self-insurance is frequently used as a risk-handling technique for _____ losses.
   a. high-frequency, high-severity
   b. high-frequency, low-severity
   c. low-frequency, high-severity
   d. low-frequency, low-severity

8. Cellar-Dwellers, Inc. is a construction firm that specializes in building residential basements. The firm estimates that thieves steal 1,000 cement blocks from the firm's work sites each year, which it pays for out of its current cash accounts. This financing arrangement exemplifies which of the following?
   a. loss reduction
   b. loss prevention
   c. risk retention
   d. self-insurance

9. Captive insurers . . .
   I. often are used to finance the self-insured losses of a large corporation
   II. often are located in locations like Bermuda or the Cayman Islands
   a. I only   b. II only   c. both I and II
   d. neither I nor II

10. The federal law that promotes a safe working environment for workers is:
   a. Superfund
   b. Equal Opportunity Act
   c. OSHA
   d. CERCLA

Discussion Questions

1. Explain why insurance is more commonly used as a risk-handling technique by smaller firms than by bigger corporations.

2. Refer to Table 4-1 on page 59. Unlike the other two categories of risk-handling techniques, loss control is used across all four quadrants of the table. Explain why loss control is appropriate across such a wide spectrum of losses.

Selected References

Head, G. L. (ed.), 1995, *Essentials of Risk Control*, 3d ed., vol. 1 (Malvern, PA: Insurance Institute of America).

Trieschmann, J. S., R. E. Hoyt, and D.W. Sommer, 2005, *Risk Management and Insurance*, 12th ed. (Mason, OH: Thomson-Southwestern).

Williams, C., M. L. Smith, and P. C. Young, 1995, *Risk Management and Insurance*, 7th ed. (New York: McGraw-Hill Inc.).

5

Risk-Handling Techniques: Diversification and Hedging

After studying this chapter, you should be able to

- Describe and identify several risk-bearing financial institutions.

- Calculate the covariance and correlation between two exposure units.

- Calculate the expected value, variance, and standard deviation for a portfolio consisting of a group of exposure units.

- Describe the risk management services provided by risk-bearing financial institutions to their customers.

- Describe how firms can use hedging to handle several types of speculative risk.

- Describe how viewing risk in a portfolio context can result in improved risk management decisions.

The growth of enterprise risk management (ERM) has vastly expanded the responsibilities of today's corporate risk managers. While corporate risk management traditionally has focused on pure risks, risk managers are increasingly dealing with an ever-expanding array of loss exposures, including a growing variety of speculative risks. For the corporate risk management function to continue evolving, risk managers need a firm understanding of the techniques available for handling such new loss exposures.

This chapter examines two common approaches to handling speculative risk: risk diversification and hedging. Risk diversification applies risk-reduction concepts from portfolio theory to the wider range of exposures borne by corporate risk managers. Through the judicious use of hedging, firms also can reduce their vulnerability to a variety of financial risk exposures.

RISK-BEARING FINANCIAL INSTITUTIONS

Bearing risk collectively, as a member of a group, is an essential risk-handling technique that offers several advantages to organizations exposed to financial losses. Risks that could result in the financial ruin of a single person or firm typically are less financially devastating for a large group, especially when all group members do not experience the same negative consequences simultaneously. Large groups often can bear risk in a more cost-efficient manner than individuals; they can afford to hire advisors with risk-bearing expertise or obtain data to become better informed about the risk. Perhaps the most important advantage, however, is that the technique results in **risk diversification**, a process in which risk can often be reduced by combining individual exposure units into a group and sharing the average loss experience for the group across all group members.

Often large financial institutions organize and manage the infrastructure necessary to diversify the risk of their group members. Examples include:

- Pension plans: employer-sponsored plans designed to accumulate and invest money saved for a group of employees over their working lives, which in turn is used to pay the cost of retirement benefits to each retiree until his or her death.
- Mutual funds: an investment arrangement in which clients reduce their investment risk by joining other investors to buy a well-diversified portfolio of investments, typically managed by professional investment managers.
- Insurance companies: firms that reduce their policyholders' exposure to pure risk through the use of risk pooling (see Chapter 3, "Risk Assessment and Pooling").

Collectively, these organizations can be described as **risk-bearing financial institutions**, or financial organizations that assume the risks of large groups of customers, using risk diversification to reduce the risk within these groups. Customers benefit because these large organizations typically can absorb risks more effectively than the customers could on their own.

COVARIANCE AND CORRELATION

To see how institutions can reduce risk through diversification, we need to understand how the risk exposure of one group member is related to the risks of all other members in the group. To do this, we'll use some ideas familiar from Chapter 3—expected value, variance, and standard deviation of random variables. We'll also introduce two other definitions—the covariance and correlation coefficient.

Consider one of the most common examples of risk diversification: risk reduction in an investment portfolio.[1] A common practice in investing is to purchase stocks on the basis on their forecasted return in the future, as estimated by stock market analysts. For example, shown in the first four columns of Table 5-1 are the forecasted annual returns[2] for a pair of stocks under two economic scenarios: The economy enjoys high growth, or it falls into a recession. For simplicity, we assume each of these two "states of the economy" has a 50 percent chance of occurring.

---

[1] Much of the research conducted on risk diversification was focused originally on investment risk. This work is particularly applicable to several aspects of corporate risk management. As was noted in Chapter 1, most employers provide pensions or 401(k) plans to their workers as an employee benefit, and the cost of these plans is financed in part by the investment income earned on pension assets. Employees also apply these same diversification lessons in their personal investment activity. In addition, the theoretical underpinnings of investment portfolios can be applied to risk pooling, as is shown later in this chapter. Thus, insurers diversify risk across their groups of customers, and large firms diversify risk in self-insured risk pools.

[2] Consistent with financial literature, Return = annual change in market value/market value at the beginning of the year. Thus, assuming no dividend, if the value of a stock was expected to increase from $10 at the beginning of the year to $12 at the end of the year, the expected return would be estimated as 20 percent, or (12–10)/10. For stocks paying a dividend, we modify this formula to reflect the additional return from the dividend payment. Thus, Return = (annual change in market value + dividends)/market value at the beginning of the year.

TABLE 5-1 Calculating the Covariance Using Data from a Probability Distribution

State of Economy	*Column 2* *Probability*	*Column 3* *Stock A Returns* R_A	*Column 4* *Stock B Returns* R_B	*Column 5* $R_A - E(R_A)$	*Column 6* $R_B - E(R_B)$	*Column 7* *Col. 2 × Col. 5 × Col. 6*
Growth	0.5	22	14	6	6	18.00
Recession	0.5	10	2	−6	−6	18.00
TOTALS	1.0					36.00 = Cov$_{AB}$

The expected value and the standard deviation for the two stocks are shown below, where we've calculated each measure using the formulas described in Chapter 3:

- Expected return for Stock A: $.5 \times 22 + .5 \times 10 = 16$ percent
- Standard deviation of returns for Stock A: $[.5 \times (22 - 16)^2 + .5 \times (10 - 16)^2]^{0.5} = 6.0$ percent
- Expected return for Stock B: $.5 \times 14 + .5 \times 2 = 8$ percent
- Standard deviation of returns for Stock B: $[.5 \times (14 - 8)^2 + .5 \times (2 - 8)^2]^{0.5} = 6.0$ percent

Investors naturally are interested in the expected value of the returns of the stocks, as shown above. But an equally important consideration is how the returns of Stock A, denoted R_A, are interrelated to the returns of Stock B, denoted R_B. Do the returns of the two stocks move up and down together, or do they move in different directions? This interrelationship is measured by the **covariance** of returns for Stock A and Stock B, as shown in Table 5-1.

We calculate the covariance between the returns of the two stocks using a three-step process:

1. For both stocks, calculate the expected value of the returns, as shown in the preceding paragraph.
2. Subtract the expected value of the return for Stock A, denoted $E(R_A)$, from the returns for that stock in each state of the economy, as shown in Column 5. Make the same calculations for Stock B, as shown in Column 6.
3. For each state of the economy, multiply the difference in returns for Stock A (Column 5) by the difference in returns for Stock B (Column 6) by the probability of occurrence (Column 2), as shown in Column 7. The sum of the products shown in Column 7 is the covariance.

As shown in Table 5-1, the covariance for the returns of Stock A and Stock B, denoted Cov$_{AB}$, equals 36.00, the sum of the values shown in Column 7.

As its name suggests, the covariance measures how two random variables, like the returns yielded on two stocks or the insured losses for two stores in a retail chain, co-vary, or move relative to each other. The covariance calculated in Table 5-1 has a positive sign because the returns for Stock A move in tandem with Stock B. Thus, both stocks are expected to perform their best in a growing economy, and both are expected to yield their lowest return during a recession. If the returns of the two stocks move in opposite directions, the covariance is negative.

While the information conveyed by the covariance is helpful, its practical use is largely limited to telling us whether the relationship between the stocks is positive versus negative).[3] To address this shortcoming, we use a slightly modified version of the measure, called the **correlation coefficient**, denoted Corr_{AB}:

$$\text{Corr}_{AB} = \frac{\text{Covariance}_{AB}}{\text{Standard deviation}_A \times \text{Standard deviation}_B} \qquad \text{(Eq. 5-1)}$$

Returning to our example, the correlation coefficient between the returns of Stock A and the returns of Stock B equals 36/36.00 or 1.0, where the denominator is the product of the standard deviation of the returns of Stock A (6.0 percent) and the standard deviation of the returns for Stock B (6.0 percent).

Because it measures the covariance of the returns relative to the product of the standard deviations of those returns, the correlation is simply a numeric ratio that can be no lower than –1.0 and no higher than 1.0. If two random variables have a correlation equal to 1.0, as they are in Table 5-1, we say they are exhibiting *perfect* positive correlation. Conversely, if the correlation between two random variables equals –1.0, the variables are perfectly negatively correlated. Values of the correlation near 1.0 (–1.0) are exhibiting strong positive (negative) correlation, and values equal to 0 are uncorrelated.

The ability to reduce risk through diversification depends heavily on the degree of correlation found across all members in the risk group. As a result, we next examine three different types of correlation: positive correlation, zero correlation, and negative correlation.

Positive Correlation

Values for correlations that are greater than zero reflect positively correlated items. Positively correlated random variables tend to move in the same direction. The highest possible value for a correlation is 1.0, a value that reflects perfect positive correlation. As was shown in Table 5-1, the returns of Stocks A and B were perfectly positively correlated.

Negative Correlation

An example of negative correlation between the returns of two stocks is shown in Table 5-2. Notice how the returns move in opposite directions.

TABLE 5-2 Negatively Correlated Stock Returns for Stocks C and D

State of Economy	Column 2 Probability	Column 3 Stock C Returns (R_C)	Column 4 Stock D Returns (R_D)
Growth	0.5	10	40
Recession	0.5	30	0
TOTAL	1.0		

---

[3] As a measure of the interrelationship between two random variables, the covariance is somewhat limited. It tells us only the direction of the interrelationship between the two stocks based on whether its value is positive or negative. In addition, the value of the covariance is not calculated in the original units of measurement, but it is in fact the product of Column 5 and Column 6 in Table 5-1, or a squared value of the random variable. Clearly a discussion of the "squared returns" of Stock A and Stock B is not very intuitive. Finally, because the size of the covariance is unbounded, it is difficult to determine whether its value is large or small without gathering additional information about its mean, variance, etc.

- Expected return for Stock C: $.5 \times 10 + .5 \times 30 = 20$ percent
- Standard deviation of returns for Stock C: $[.5 \times (10 - 20)^2 + .5 \times (30 - 20)^2]^{0.5} = 10.0$ percent
- Expected return for Stock D: $.5 \times 0 + .5 \times 40 = 20$ percent
- Standard deviation of returns for Stock D: $[.5 \times (40 - 20)^2 + .5 \times (0 - 20)^2]^{0.5} = 20.0$ percent
- $\text{Covariance}_{CD} = 0.5 \times (10 - 20) \times (40 - 20) + 0.5 \times (30 - 20) \times (0 - 20) = -200$

- $\text{Correlation}_{CD} = \dfrac{\text{Covariance}_{CD}}{\text{Std. deviation}_C \times \text{Std. deviation}_D} = \dfrac{-200}{10 \times 20} = -1.0$

The economic conditions in which Stock C is expected to yield its highest return coincides with Stock D's worst returns, and Stock D is expected to perform best when Stock C's returns are lowest. Negatively correlated random variables offer a great opportunity for risk reduction through diversification, as we'll see in the next section.

Zero Correlation

Two random variables may also be uncorrelated, as shown by the returns of Stocks E and F in Table 5-3. By definition, if two random variables are statistically independent of each other, their correlation equals zero, a condition we often find among many types of insurable risks, such as the risk of fire and of traffic accidents.

- Expected return for Stock E: $.33 \times 15 + .33 \times 11 + .33 \times 10 = 12$ percent
- Standard deviation of returns for Stock E: $.33 \times (15 - 12)^2 + .33 \times (11 - 12)^2 + .33 \times (10 - 12)^2]^{0.5} = 2.16$ percent
- Expected return for Stock F: $.33 \times 9 + .33 \times 3 + .33 \times 12 = 8$ percent
- Standard deviation of returns for Stock F: $[.33 \times (9 - 8)^2 + .33 \times (3 - 8)^2 + .33 \times (12 - 8)^2]^{0.5} = 3.74$ percent
- $\text{Covariance}_{EF} = .33 \times (15 - 12) \times (9 - 8) + .33 \times (11 - 12) \times (3 - 8) + .33 \times (10 - 12) \times (12 - 8) = 0$
- $\text{Correlation}_{EF} = \dfrac{\text{Covariance}_{EF}}{\text{Std. deviation}_E \times \text{Std. deviation}_F} = \dfrac{0}{2.16 \times 3.74} = 0$

TABLE 5-3 Uncorrelated Stock Returns for Stocks E and F

State of Economy	Probability	Stock E Returns (R_E)	Stock F Returns (R_F)
Growth	0.33	15	9
Status quo	0.33	11	3
Recession	0.33	10	12
TOTAL	1.00		

RISK DIVERSIFICATION

To explain risk diversification, let us look at the definitions of the expected value and the variance of the risk-bearing group.[4] The expected value of the group is simply a weighted average of the expected values of each group member. Thus, for a group consisting of two members, EV_G, the expected value for the group equals

$$EV_G = W_1 \times EV_1 + W_2 \times EV_2 \qquad \text{(Eq. 5-2)}$$

where W_1 and W_2 represent the weight or proportion of the group that consists of the first and second group members, and EV_1 and EV_2 is the expected value for the first and second members. For example, referring back to Table 5-1, the expected value of the return on a stock portfolio consisting of equal amounts of Stock A and Stock B equals 12 percent, calculated as the 0.5 weighting times the 16 percent return on Stock A, plus a 0.5 weighting times the 8 percent return on Stock D. Similarly, based on the figures in Table 5-2, the expected value of a portfolio consisting of equal weightings of Stock C and Stock D equals 20 percent ($0.5 \times 20 + 0.5 \times 20$).

While the calculation of the expected value of the group is very intuitive, the definition for the variance of the group is less straightforward. The variance for a risk group denoted Var_G and consisting of two random variables is a weighted sum of the variances of the random variables *plus* a weighted value for the correlation between them:

$$Var_G = W_1^2 \times SD_1^2 + W_2^2 \times SD_2^2 + 2 \times W_1 \times W_2 \times SD_1 \times SD_2 \times Corr_{12} \quad \text{(Eq. 5-3)}$$

where W_1 and W_2 denote weighting variables that reflect the proportion of the portfolio that consists of random variables 1 and 2, respectively; SD_1 and SD_2 denote the standard deviation for random variables 1 and 2, respectively; and $Corr_{12}$ denotes the correlation between random variable 1 and random variable 2. Despite its length, the extra complication involved in calculating Equation 5-3 is worth the additional effort because the variance of the risk group is often less than a weighted average of the variances of its components. We can trace the reason for the reduction in risk to the term on the far-right side of Equation 5-3. Simply put, if the value of the correlation is less than 1.0, the inclusion of the correlation term in Equation 5-3 offers an opportunity to reduce risk via diversification in the risk group.

Equipped with formulas to calculate the expected value and the variance of risk-bearing groups, we can examine how risk diversification is affected by correlation.

Case 1: Risk Diversification in Negatively Correlated Groups

The optimal conditions for reducing risk through diversification occur when the random variables combined in the risk group are negatively correlated. For example, refer to Table 5-2, which shows the returns for two stocks exhibiting perfect negative correlation. The expected return for a portfolio consisting of equal weights of Stock C and Stock D equals 20 percent, as we noted above. Using Equation 5-3, we find that the variance for a portfolio consisting of equal amounts of Stock C and Stock D equals

$$Var_{CD} - .5^2 \times 10^2 + .5^2 \times 20^2 + 2 \times .5 \times .5 \times 10 \times 20 \times -1.0 - 25$$

---

[4] The term *risk-bearing group* refers in general to the group that is formed as part of the risk diversification process. Risk-bearing groups also are referred to in more specific terms depending on the risk being diversified; e.g., insurance policy owners are grouped into *risk pools*, stocks are grouped into *investment portfolios*, etc.

An investor thus can reduce her risk considerably by holding a portfolio of negatively correlated investments. More specifically, by holding equal amounts of Stock C and Stock D, she sets the variance of her portfolio at 25, resulting in a standard deviation for the portfolio of 5 percent, much smaller than the standard deviation of either Stock C or Stock D alone (10 percent and 20 percent, respectively).

In fact, because Stock C and Stock D are perfectly negatively correlated, an investor can eliminate the risk in her portfolio completely by holding an optimal amount of each. To demonstrate, first note that when our investor holds equal amounts of both stocks in her portfolio, the standard deviation of the portfolio equals 5 percent, and the expected return for the portfolio equals

$$EV_{CD} = W_C \times EV_C + W_D \times EV_D = .5 \times 30 + .5 \times 0 = 15 \text{ percent during a recession, and}$$

$$EV_{CD} = W_C \times EV_C + W_D \times EV_D = .5 \times 10 + .5 \times 40 = 30 \text{ percent during economic growth}$$

Now let's assume that the investor tinkers with the weighting of the two stocks in the portfolio a bit. Note that by holding two-thirds of the portfolio in Stock C and one-third in Stock D, she can eliminate the risk in her portfolio completely:

$$EV_{CD} = W_C \times EV_C + W_D \times EV_D = .667 \times 30 + .333 \times 0 = 20 \text{ percent during a recession}$$

$$EV_{CD} = W_C \times EV_C + W_D \times EV_D = .667 \times 10 + .333 \times 40 = 20 \text{ percent during a}$$
$$\text{growing economy}$$

By adjusting the stock weightings, the investor has locked in a 20 percent return regardless of the uncertainties of the economy. Portfolio risk is eliminated because the expected return is the same regardless of whether the economy grows or falls into a recession. To confirm, note that when we recalculate the variance of the portfolio to reflect the revised weightings, risk is eliminated and the variance equals zero:

$$Var_{CD} = W_C^2 \times SD_C^2 + W_D^2 \times SD_D^2 + 2 \times W_C \times W_D \times SD_C \times SD_D \times Corr_{CD}$$
$$= .667^2 \times 10^2 + .333^2 \times 20^2 + 2 \times .667 \times .333 \times 10 \times 20 \times -1.0 = 0$$

Thus, we find that combining random variables that are negatively correlated offers great opportunities for risk reduction through diversification. Moreover, *under conditions of perfect negative correlation, risk can be eliminated completely.*

Case 2: Risk Diversification in Positively Correlated Groups

While combining negatively correlated random variables dramatically reduces risk, combining random variables that are perfectly positively correlated does *not*. For example, consider the returns for Stock A and Stock B discussed earlier. The correlation between them equals 1.0, as shown in Table 5-1. Holding an equal weighting of both stocks will result in an expected return equal to 12 percent ($.5 \times 16 + .5 \times 8$), as defined in Equation 5-2. We can calculate the variance of the returns for such a portfolio using Equation 5-3 as follows:

$$Var_{AB} = W_A^2 \times SD_A^2 + W_B^2 \times SD_B^2 + 2 \times W_A \times W_B \times SD_A \times SD_B \times Corr_{AB}$$
$$= .5^2 \times 6^2 + .5^2 \times 6^2 + 2 \times .5 \times .5 \times 6 \times 6 \times 1.0 = 36$$

and the standard deviation of the returns for the portfolio thus equals 6, the square root of the variance. Thus, *creating a risk group consisting of random variables that are perfectly positively correlated offers no reduction in risk* because the standard deviation of the portfolio is equal to the standard deviation of the returns for each stock.

Note that many random variables are positively correlated (and hence greater than zero), but the value of their correlation is less than 1.0. For these random variables, risk reduction through diversification is possible, but it will be far smaller than the reductions possible when diversifying a group of negatively correlated random variables. For example, many mutual funds diversify investment risk across a portfolio of positively correlated stocks.[5] We also examine the limits to risk reduction in groups of positively correlated random variables in the next section.

Case 3: Risk Diversification in Uncorrelated Groups: Insurance Risk

While we've focused on investments in discussing diversification so far, the expected value and variance formulas apply equally well to other risk groups. For example, consider our discussion of insurance risk pooling in Chapter 3. An underlying assumption was that the potential losses of all the exposure units in the pool were independently distributed. This means the correlation among them equals zero. Setting the correlation equal to zero in equation 5-3 results in a simple equation for Var_P, the variance of the insurance pool:[6]

$$Var_P = W_1^2 \times SD_1^2 + W_2^2 \times SD_2^2 \qquad \text{(Eq. 5-4)}$$

where W_1 and W_2 represents the weight or proportion of the pool that consists of the first and second group members, and SD_1 and SD_2 are the standard deviations of losses for the first member and the second member. Given Equation 5-4, we can show how the pooling method used in insurance enables insurers to diversify risk.

RISK POOL WITH TWO EXPOSURE UNITS

Recall from Chapter 3 our example of Rick and Vic, the two restaurant owners who agreed to share their exposure to liability risk jointly in a two-person risk pool. Each restaurant owner faced a mean loss equal to $10,000 with a standard deviation of $30,000. Because each owner's mean loss is simply the expected value associated with the liability risk, we can use Equation 5-2 to calculate EV_P, the expected value resulting from this risk pool:

$$EV_P = W_1 \times EV_1 + W_2 \times EV_2 = .5 \times -\$10,000 + .5 \times -\$10,000 = -\$10,000$$

where the 0.5 weightings reflect the fact that each restaurant owner shares the losses in the risk group equally and –$10,000 equals the expected loss amount for each owner. In turn, we can use Equation 5-4 to calculate Var_P, the variance of the risk pooling arrangement when all the losses of all pool members are independent of each other:

$$Var_P = W_1^2 \times SD_1^2 + W_2^2 \times SD_2^2 = .5^2 \times \$30,000^2 + .5^2 \times \$30,000^2 = 450,000,000$$

---

[5] See Insight Box 5-1 for more details on mutual funds and (non) systematic risk (and how they pass some risk to investors).

[6] For an early discussion on how portfolio theory can be applied to the insurance mechanism, see Sharpe (1981). More extensive discussion on the topic is also found in Doherty (2000).

INSIGHT BOX 5-1

Mutual Funds and the Diversification of Investment Risk

A compelling example of the U.S. consumer's desire for risk diversification is the explosive growth in mutual funds. A *mutual fund* is an investment fund that collects investment capital from a large group of investors and invests it in a well-diversified pool of investments. Mutual funds invest in a wide range of assets, including equity funds, which invest in common and preferred stocks; bond funds, which invest in bonds issued by corporations and governmental institutions; and hybrid or blended funds, which invest in both stocks and bonds.

Financial Assets of Leading Financial Institutions, 1990–2010 (in trillions)

Year	Commercial Banks	Mutual Funds	Private Pensions	Life Insurers	Government Pension Funds	Property-Liability Insurers
2010	$14.4	$10.2	$5.7	$4.9	$2.8	$1.4
2005	$9.8	$8.0	$5.4	$4.4	$2.7	$1.2
2000	$6.7	$6.2	$4.5	$3.1	$2.3	$0.8
1995	$4.5	$2.7	$2.9	$2.1	$1.3	$0.7
1990	$3.3	$1.1	$1.6	$1.4	$0.7	$0.5

Based on Federal Reserve Board, Statistical Releases, "Flow of Funds Accounts," various years.

As this table shows, the assets held by mutual funds grew quickly from 1990 to 2010, surpassing those held by private pensions and life insurers over that time. Among financial institutions, only commercial banks held more assets than the mutual fund industry in 2010. Much of the growth in mutual funds came from individual investors, who invested large sums during the bull stock market of the 1990s. Another source was retirement contributions that employers made to employee benefit programs, many of which were invested in mutual funds.

By gathering huge amounts of investment capital from millions of investors, most mutual funds can purchase widely diversified investment portfolios. When an investor contributes money to a mutual fund, she or he purchases only a small fraction of the value of the fund, but the fraction is very well diversified. Thus, a small investment of $100 in an equity mutual fund is spread across hundreds of stocks, resulting in the purchase of a fraction of a share of each security. By contrast, that same $100 investment is not large enough to buy even a single share of some of the highest-priced stocks in the market, thus offering far less opportunity for risk diversification.

The commissions per share that investors must pay to buy small amounts of stock are much higher than the costs that mutual funds incur when buying large blocks of stock. Mutual funds thus can take advantage of the lower transaction costs of their "large block" trading to offer small investors a more cost-effective method of investing. Finally, investors also benefit from participating in mutual funds because they are managed by experienced, well-trained investment professionals.

Most stock price changes are positively correlated over time, moving in tandem in response to market-wide factors like changes in interest rates and the growth rate of the economy. These price-change risks are non-diversifiable because they are common across a large percentage of the securities in the markets. Mutual fund managers understand that they cannot eliminate such risk, and thus they do not guarantee investors a return. But they *can* diversify away the negative consequences of firm-specific risks like poor strategic decisions, unsuccessful product launches, and lawsuits,[7] and such diversification is highly valuable to small investors.

---

[7] Because many sources of firm-specific risk also are addressed by corporate risk managers, well-diversified stockholders are doubly protected from such loss exposures. Some skeptics suggest that investors should view the risk-management activities of the firm as an unnecessary expense because such activities are redundant with the cost-efficient risk diversification available through a well-diversified investment portfolio. Such arguments ignore the fact that risk-management activities are valued by other parties who are less able to diversify away risk, such as employees of the firm or customers who depend on the firm for a continuous supply of goods or services.

Thus, the standard deviation of the risk pool equals $21,213.20, the square root of 450,000,000. In short, Equations 5-2 and 5-4 yield results that are identical to the risk-pooling example in Chapter 3: The two-firm pool consisting of Vic and Rick has an expected value of –$10,000 (where the negative sign reflects the expected loss for each party) and a standard deviation equal to $21,213.

RISK POOL WITH MORE THAN TWO EXPOSURE UNITS

While the example of Vic and Rick shows the usefulness of modeling risk pools as portfolios, insurers do not limit the size of their risk pools to only two members in real life. Fortunately, Equations 5-2 and 5-4 are easily modified to accommodate a larger risk pool consisting of n independent exposure units:

$$EV_P = W_1 \times EV_1 + W_2 \times EV_2 + \cdots + W_n \times EV_n \text{ for all } n \text{ exposure units} \quad \text{(Eq. 5-5)}$$

$$Var_P = W_1^2 \times SD_1^2 + W_2^2 \times SD_2^2 + \cdots W_n^2 \times SD_n^2 \text{ for all } n \text{ exposure units} \quad \text{(Eq. 5-6)}$$

For instance, if Vic and Rick were able to attract into their pool two additional restaurant owners with homogeneous liability exposures independent of their own, the expected value of the losses in the four-firm risk pool would equal

$$EV_P = .25 \times -\$10,000 + .25 \times -\$10,000 + .25 \times -\$10,000 + .25 \times -\$10,000$$
$$= -\$10,000$$

and the variance of the risk pool would equal

$$Var_P = .25^2 \times 30,000^2 + .25^2 \times 30,000^2 + .25^2 \times 30,000^2 + .25^2 \times 30,000^2$$
$$= 225,000,000$$

The standard deviation of the four-firm pool is thus equal to $15,000 (or the square root of 225,000,000), half the standard deviation of the loss faced by any single member. As this example shows, combining independent, and hence uncorrelated, exposure units in a risk pool results in a significant reduction in risk with relatively modest pool sizes because *the standard deviation of the risk pool varies inversely with the square root of the number of independent exposure units in the pool.*

The standard deviations associated with bigger risk pools are shown horizontally across the top row of Table 5-4. Note that with large pool sizes, they decrease to levels approaching zero. Thus, for a risk pool of 10,000 exposure units, the standard deviation is only 300, which is 1 percent of the risk borne by any single member of the pool. With an infinitely large pool, the measure of risk equals zero, demonstrating that insurers can eliminate risk completely through the diversification of independent pool members.

Correlated Loss Exposures and Insurance Complications

Keep in mind that we can use Equation 5-4 to calculate the variance of the risk pool only if insured losses are distributed independently, so that correlation equals zero. If the losses from an insurance risk pool are positively or negatively correlated, we must include these values in the calculation of the variance of the pool, as we showed in

TABLE 5-4 The Standard Deviation in Risk Pools with Independent and Positively Correlated Losses (in dollars)

Size of Pool	1	2	4	100	10,000	Infinite
Independent	30,000	21,213.20	15,000	3,000	300	0
Correlation = 0.1	30,000	22,248.59	17,102.63	9,904.54	9,491.10	9,486.83

Equation 5-3. In particular, positively correlated exposure units pose a difficult challenge for insurers because they limit the ability to decrease risk through diversification.

The figures shown in Table 5-4 demonstrate how the existence of positive correlation among exposure units can hamper risk diversification. In the bottom row (Correlation = 0.1) of the table, we calculate the standard deviations for risk pools of increasingly larger sizes, where each pool member is assumed to be homogeneous with Rick but whose losses are positively correlated at a 0.1 level.[8] Comparing these measures of risk to the top row, the measures of risk associated with uncorrelated loss exposures, reveals a "good news–bad news" scenario. The good news is that insurers can reduce the risk of losses in positively correlated risk pools by increasing the number of exposure units in the pools. Thus, as measured from left to right in the bottom row, the standard deviation decreases from more than $22,000 with a pool of two, to $9,491.10 for a pool size equal to 10,000.

The bad news is that the standard deviations for the correlated risk pool across all pool sizes will always be greater than that for the pool of independent exposure units. Perhaps more importantly, the standard deviation of the correlated risk pool will never fall below $9,486, the value in the bottom row corresponding to an infinitely large pool. In short, the risk for positively correlated risk groups decreases as pool size increases, but it cannot be diversified away as effectively as in pools of independent loss exposures.

Why would losses be positively correlated in a risk pool? Simply stated, positive correlation arises when a common factor or condition causes a large number of pool members to have a loss. For example, in Rick and Vic's risk pool above, positive correlation could result if the court system made a legal ruling that applies across many business owners. Many potentially catastrophic natural disasters, such as floods and earthquakes, are positively correlated because they affect scores of people and firms simultaneously. Not surprisingly, these loss exposures are often excluded from coverage in many insurance contracts because insurers are not willing to expose themselves to a financially catastrophic loss event.

ADDITIONAL BENEFITS FROM RISK-BEARING FINANCIAL INSTITUTIONS

Thanks to diversification, insurers can charge their customers lower premiums and investment groups can spread their portfolios across a wide variety of investment holdings. Looking beyond diversification, risk-bearing financial institutions provide other benefits to their members as well:

- **Professional management:** Financial institutions hire professional managers and advisers with expertise and training in managing financial risk.
- **Administrative services:** Financial institutions often can provide the essential administrative services needed to carry out the risk-bearing activity (such as

---

[8] To calculate the standard deviation values shown in the bottom row of Table 5-4 without assuming independence, we must adapt Equation 5-3, the variance for a pool of two correlated exposure units, to accommodate a larger number of pool members. Note that Equation 5-3 is simply a sum of the two weighted variance terms for each of the two members in the pool plus the weighted covariance of the two group members (where the covariance equals the correlation between the two pool members multiplied by their respective standard deviations). For larger risk groups, we similarly sum up all the variances of each pool member plus all the covariance terms from all possible pairs of members in the pool. To simplify matters in a manner that is consistent with the way insurers bear risk, assume that each member of the pool is equally weighted and that each member's standard deviation is equal, in keeping with the assumption of homogeneity discussed in Chapter 3. Under these assumptions, the formula for the variance of a risk pool consisting of n homogeneous exposure units equals $sd^2/n + [(n-1)/n] \times corr \times sd^2$, where n denotes the number of pool members, sd is the standard deviation for each pool member, and $corr$ is the correlation of losses. For additional discussion, see Doherty (2000).

claims handling services by insurers or buying and selling securities in investment funds) more cost-effectively than the individual members of risk groups can.

- **Investment in information:** Financial institutions obtain the data necessary to make well-informed risk-bearing decisions.
- **Investment in infrastructure:** Financial institutions obtain essential resources, like reinsurance or trading floors, that are useful in bearing risk.

For the many individuals and business owners who do not have the expertise or resources to dedicate to these types of risk-bearing activities, a risk-bearing group is therefore more cost-effective.

HEDGING OF SPECULATIVE FINANCIAL RISK

In addition to diversification, a second technique that often is used to handle speculative risk is hedging. **Hedging** is taking two financial positions simultaneously whose gains and losses will offset each other for the purpose of limiting risk. It encompasses many types of transactions. For example, we can view the purchase of insurance as the hedging of risk. When an insured firm has a loss, it gains the right to collect insurance proceeds. The firm has hedged its loss exposure because the event that causes the damage (loss) causes an offsetting gain (the claim against the insurer).

Recent innovations in financial products enable today's risk managers to construct a wide variety of hedging arrangements. In this section, we describe how firms can use hedging to limit their exposure to several types of financial risk. We start with a basic introduction to some of the financial risks that are commonly hedged, followed by several examples that illustrate how hedging can address a variety of financial risk management problems.

Commonly Hedged Financial Risks

Large corporations routinely hedge a variety of speculative risks that can result in significant financial losses.

Currency risk is the loss potential caused by unfavorable fluctuations in the value of domestic currency relative to foreign currencies. Here is a simple example (we look at a more extended example below). Assume that in January, $1 purchases 3 euros (€; the currency used by most countries in the European Union), and in October, $1 purchases only 2€. During this period, the dollar has lost one-third of its value against the euro. If a U.S. importer needed to deliver 6€ million to obtain some inventory from a European exporter, it would pay $2 million in January (6€ million/3) but $3 million in October (6€ million/2). The currency fluctuation has required a $1 million additional payment for the importer, or, expressed differently, a $1 million loss.

Interest rate risk is the loss potential caused when changes in interest rates reduce the market value of fixed-income securities, such as bonds. Generally speaking, when interest rates rise, the value of fixed-income securities falls. When interest rates fall, fixed-income securities gain value. The longer their time to maturity, the more volatile is the market price for fixed income securities.

Commodity price risk refers to fluctuations in the prices for a wide variety of commodity products, including petroleum, metals, and agricultural products like grains and livestock. Firms that sell commodities face **output price risk** because changes in market prices affect the price at which they can sell their products. By contrast, firms that use commodities in the manufacturing of the products they sell face **input price risk** because changes in commodity prices can increase or decrease their manufacturing costs.

Derivative Securities and Other Financial Transactions

Frequently, hedging relies on derivative securities. A **derivative security** is a financial instrument whose value is based on (derived from) the value of an underlying financial asset or commodity. For example, a **futures contract** is an order placed by a trader in advance to buy or sell a commodity or financial asset later at a specified price. Futures contracts, which are a type of derivative security, are themselves traded in organized commodities and securities markets as contractual agreements between traders and speculators. Risk managers use futures contracts to provide a hedge when an increase or decrease in a commodity's price can reduce profits.

Consider an airline that must buy jet fuel in large amounts each month, as well as the oil refiner that will sell the fuel. Assume that it is March and oil sells for $50 a barrel. Both the airline and the refiner are profitable at this price. If the price rises to $60 a barrel, the refiner's profits increase while the airline's profits decrease. An opposite result occurs if the price of oil drops below $50 a barrel: The airline's profits increase while the refiner's profits decrease. Assume that the risk managers of both companies want to hedge their positions. The airline can buy a futures contract that gives it the right to purchase oil at $50 a barrel in November. To buy the contract, the airline must pay $1 for each of the 10,000 barrels that it plans to purchase in November. To hedge its position, the refiner can sell a contract that would have forced it to sell a barrel of oil at $50 a barrel in November. Assume that by selling this contract, the refiner earns $2 a barrel for each barrel that it commits to sell.

If the price of oil rises to $60 a barrel in November, the right to purchase oil through a futures contract at $50 a barrel is worth $10 a barrel. Relative to its position in March, the airline loses money when it buys 10,000 gallons of fuel at $60 a barrel, but its loss is reduced by the increase in value of its futures contract.[9] Thus, the risk manager has hedged the potential loss resulting from the adverse price change of oil. By contrast, at $60 a barrel, the refiner will be forced to honor its commitment to sell oil at $50 a barrel, but its loss is reduced by the $2-a-barrel price that it received from selling the contract in March.

If the price of oil falls to $40 a barrel in November, the airline profits from the lower price of oil, but it loses the money that it paid to guarantee the purchase of oil at $50 a barrel. The refiner loses profits if it sells oil at $40 a barrel, but it gains when the option that it sold for $2 a barrel expires.

In this way, the risk managers of a firm dealing in commodities use futures contracts to hedge the firm's exposures to losses caused by adverse commodity price fluctuations. Hedging is not limited solely to the use of futures contracts; several other types of derivatives are also available.

Forward contracts are similar to futures contracts, but they are not traded on organized exchanges. **Currency swaps** occur when two companies lend each other currencies. When the two swapped currencies are at different interest rates—one a fixed rate and the other a variable, or floating, rate—this is an **interest rate swap**.

Traded options create a legal right to buy or sell a commodity or a financial asset at an agreed-upon price for a specific period. The **option holder**, also known as the party with the *long position*, has the right to buy or sell under the agreed terms. The **option writer**, also known as the party with the *short position*, is obligated to buy or sell based on the choice of the option holder. A **call option** is an option to buy an underlying asset. A **put option** is an option to sell an underlying asset. A call option has value if the holder can buy the asset (say, 100 shares of stock) for less than the prevailing market price. A put option has value if the holder can sell the stock above the prevailing

---

[9] The airline's $10-a-barrel gain on the futures contract is reduced by the $1 a barrel that it paid for the contract in March.

market price. For the holder of the long position, puts acquire value when the price of the underlying asset falls. Thus, buying a put is a hedge against falling asset prices.

Two Examples of Financial Risk Management

Let us look at two examples of how firms can use options and other derivative securities to hedge financial risks.

AN INTEREST RATE RISK EXAMPLE

Six months ago, Acme Bank aggressively sought and attracted new deposits by offering one-year certificate of deposit (CD) rates that were slightly higher than the competition's. Acme invested the deposits in fixed-rate loans with an average maturity of five years. The CDs, on the other hand, will mature in six months. Acme is concerned that interest rates will rise, forcing it to pay higher rates to retain the deposits. Because the five-year loans have a fixed interest rate, raising the rate that it must pay on the CDs will reduce the bank's profitability. Management decides to hedge against the risk of rising interest rates by selling U.S. Treasury futures contracts. If interest rates rise, the value of the futures contracts will fall, enabling the bank to repurchase the contracts below the selling price. The profit on the futures transaction will help to offset the higher interest rates that will have to be paid to depositors. If interest rates fall, the benefit of paying lower interest rates to depositors will be reduced by a loss on the futures transaction.

A CURRENCY RISK EXAMPLE

Global, Inc. is a large manufacturer of computerized industrial equipment. A total of 40 percent of its sales are to European steel mills. Ordinarily, the steel mills place advance orders with Global via contracts that specify the types and dimensions of the equipment to be produced. The contracts also require the price to be paid in euros and stipulate that the mills place a 10 percent deposit with each order. Production time usually varies between four and nine months. Global's corporate treasurer is concerned that the euro might depreciate against the dollar before delivery is made. In other words, when the equipment is delivered and payment is received in euros, those euros may convert to fewer dollars than expected when the contract was signed. Because Global pays its production costs in dollars, the foreign exchange loss would result in lower profits. Management decides to hedge the risk by selling a forward contract in euros for roughly the amount of euros that it has contracted to receive. The forward contract effectively fixes the dollar value of the euro, and hence of the equipment contract. Although Global would not benefit if the euro appreciated against the dollar, neither does it lose if the euro depreciates against the dollar because the risk manager has taken a position in financial markets that is the opposite of Global's manufacturing contract. If the manufacturing position loses, the financial position gains, and vice versa.

Hedging and Correlation

In the case of both Acme Bank and Global, Inc., risk managers can effectively hedge their financial risk to speculators in the financial markets, offsetting the adverse financial consequences of their unhedged risk. In other words, the derivatives are effective because they are *negatively correlated* with the firm's underlying risk.

Like mutual funds and insurers, hedging speculators charge a fee for their services and may assume great risks from their hedging activities. The cost of derivatives will vary across time and market forces. Speculators are not alchemists; they cannot offer derivatives that set prices for currencies or commodities independent of the underlying market price for those goods. Instead, they must cultivate an understanding of the factors that affect the supply and demand of their derivative products and their underlying securities.

ENTERPRISE RISK MANAGEMENT AND RISK PORTFOLIOS

The models described in this chapter have clear implications for advocates of ERM. When ERM is carried out at the level of the corporate boardroom, the board is better able to monitor and manage the risks of the entire firm in a portfolio setting. As we have shown in this chapter, bundling risks into portfolios offers numerous advantages.

Perfect Positive Correlation Among Risk Exposures Is Unlikely

As we noted in Table 5-1, bundling risks into groups will not be advantageous if all the risk exposures exhibit perfect positive correlation. Fortunately, the random nature of business activity within a firm leads to less than perfect positive correlation. Business cycles do not occur in lockstep fashion across the globe or within certain markets, and firms always face different demand patterns, regional factors, and seasonal influences. So long as the correlation among risks is less than perfectly positive, there is opportunity for risk reduction.

Natural Diversification Occurs Across Uncorrelated Risks

Allowing each business unit of a firm to manage its risk in an isolated "silo" unco-ordinated with the other units of the firm often can lead to suboptimal results. In some cases, risks may naturally offset each other across the varied activities of a large firm, and firms therefore should replace their silo approach with a coordinated ERM program. When risks naturally cancel each other out to some degree, risk-handling techniques like insurance or hedging are less necessary, thus offering opportunities to reduce the cost of corporate risk management.

A prime example of such natural risk diversification is the relationship between hazard risk and other risks that are correlated to financial markets. For instance, firms often find that some of their financial risks are highly correlated with movements in the economy. A rapidly growing economy thus may result in higher interest rates and higher input prices for commodities like oil due to increased demand. Hazard risks are unlikely to follow suit, however, because most are uncorrelated with the financial markets. Thus, pure risk events like hurricanes, earthquakes, and other natural losses tend not to follow the movements of other economically sensitive markets. This makes combining hazard risk with other financial risks analogous to pooling uncorrelated exposure units.

Bundling Negatively Correlated Risk Exposures Dramatically Reduce Risk

The reduction in portfolio risk that results from the hedging of negatively corre-lated financial risk exposures explains the wide use of derivatives by corporations. However, corporate hedging activities rely heavily on contracts with independent third parties outside the control of the firm, and the supply and the price of hedging instruments can vary widely over time. As a result, the management of corporate hedging activities frequently requires a great deal of time and money.

Can firms count on internal negative correlations across their other risk exposures as a means to reduce their aggregated risk? Management must invest the necessary time and energy to evaluate its risks collectively to avoid overlooking natural hedg-ing relationships. Perhaps more importantly, firms that adopt an ERM framework are better able to identify and nurture strategic opportunities that reduce risk across all their operations.

Risk Management at the Boardroom Level Increases Consistency and Negotiating Power

Managing risk on a corporate boardroom level also can decrease the probability of adverse surprises because it is easier to maintain consistency across all business units instead of allowing subsidiaries to set their own risk standards. In addition, by aggregating and coordinating risk management activity on a corporate boardroom level, a firm is better able than its smaller business units to negotiate more favorable terms with certain risk-bearing institutions.

Summary

Diversification and hedging techniques are uniquely useful risk-handling techniques within an ERM program. Risk diversification reduces risk by combining a large number of random variables in a risk group whose members are not perfectly positively correlated. Diversification is even more effective when the group includes random variables that are negatively correlated. Hedging strategies reduce exposure to loss through the purchase of contracts yielding payoffs that are negatively correlated to the firm's underlying risk. By viewing all the firm's risk from the corporate boardroom as a portfolio, a chief risk officer (CRO) can take advantage of natural hedging opportunities where risks from different areas of the firm cancel each other out.

Review

1. Risk-bearing financial institutions diversify risk by combining a large number of exposure units in a risk group. Describe the types of exposure units found in the risk groups of an insurer, a mutual fund, and a pension.

2. Describe the difference between the covariance and the correlation.
   For the next six questions, use the following table, which shows the expected returns from six different stocks in three different states of the economy.

State of Economy	Probability	Return for Stock A	Return for Stock B	Return for Stock C	Return for Stock D	Return for Stock E	Return for Stock F
Growth	1/3	30	3	15	24	0	18
Status Quo	1/3	22	1	3	6	3	3
Recession	1/3	20	4	−3	−6	6	−3

3. Calculate the covariance and correlation for the returns for Stock A and Stock B.
4. Based on Equation 5-3, describe the impact of including Stock A and Stock B in a stock portfolio on the portfolio's risk.
5. Calculate the covariance and correlation for the returns for Stock C and Stock D.
6. Based on Equation 5-3, describe the impact of including Stock C and Stock D in a stock portfolio on the portfolio's risk.
7. Calculate the covariance and correlation for the returns for Stock E and Stock F.
8. Based on Equation 5-3, describe the impact of including Stock E and Stock F in a portfolio on the portfolio's risk.
9. Explain why insurance risk pooling is most efficient when the losses from the policyholders in the risk pool are distributed independently.
10. Discuss why perils like earthquake damage or unemployment are not insured easily by private insurers.

11. Looking beyond risk diversification, discuss some of the additional benefits that risk-bearing financial institutions offer their customers.
12. What is the difference between output price risk and input price risk?
13. What are the types of loss that are dealt with through the use of hedging in financial risk management? Describe the tools that are available to managers dealing with financial risks.
14. From the viewpoint of the option holder, what is the difference between a call option and a put option?
15. Based on Equation 5-3, explain why hedging is a useful risk-handling technique.
16. Under what conditions will the bundling of risk exposures yield no reduction of risk?

Objective Questions

1. Currency risk is defined as which of the following?
   a. the loss of value when a domestic currency can buy less in terms of a foreign currency
   b. the loss in value of a currency due to changes in domestic interest rates
   c. the loss in value of a currency due to random changes in gross domestic product (GDP)
   d. the loss of currency caused by theft
2. A contract to buy or sell a commodity that is traded on securities markets in advance is called which of the following?
   a. an option
   b. a forward contract
   c. a futures contract
   d. a swap
3. Which of the following statements about ERM is correct?
   I. ERM encompasses the management of hazard risk and financial risk.
   II. ERM does not encompass the management of financial losses from derivatives.
      a. I only   b. II only   c. both I and II
      d. neither I nor II
4. If you hold a call option,
   a. you have the right to sell something at a specified price in the future.
   b. you have the right to buy something at a specified price in the future.
   c. you have a legal duty to sell something at a specified price in the future.
   d. you have a legal duty to buy something at a specified price in the future.
5. A(n) ____ is not a risk-bearing financial institution.
   a. insurance company
   b. mutual fund
   c. pension
   d. limited liability partnership (LLP)

6. Opportunities for risk reduction are greatest when the correlations among exposure units in a portfolio are which of the following?
   a. 1.0   b. –1.0   c. 0
   d. slightly less than zero
7. Which of the following does not affect the risk in a portfolio consisting of two stocks?
   a. The weighting, or percentage of the portfolio, for each stock.
   b. The standard deviation of the returns earned on the two stocks.
   c. The correlation of the returns of the two stocks.
   d. All of the above affect the risk in the portfolio.
8. For insurance risk pools in which exposure units exhibit a 0.1 correlation, which of the following is true?
   I. As the size of the risk pool increases, the standard deviation of the mean loss decreases.
   II. As the size of the risk pool becomes extremely large, the standard deviation of the mean loss equals zero.
      a. I only   b. II only   c. both I and II
      d. neither I nor II
9. In 2010, which of the following was the largest risk-bearing financial institution (based on assets)?
   a. mutual funds
   b. life insurers
   c. private pensions
   d. property-liability insurers
10. Which of the following statements regarding correlated risks is correct?
   I. Stock prices tend to be positively correlated to marketwide economic events.
   II. Natural disasters like hurricanes are positively correlated to prices in the stock markets.
      a. I only   b. II only   c. both I and II
      d. neither I nor II

Discussion Questions

1. Discuss the validity of the following statement: Diversification is a useful technique for handling speculative risk, but it cannot be used to handle pure risk effectively.

2. From the viewpoint of a proponent of ERM, explain why the traditional "silo" approach to corporate risk management is flawed.

Selected References

Doherty, Neil, *Integrated Risk Management: Techniques and Strategies for Reducing Risk* (New York: McGraw-Hill, 2000).

Sharpe, William, *Investments*, 2nd ed. (Englewood Cliffs, NJ: Prentice-Hall, 1981).

6

Fundamentals of Insurance

After studying this chapter, you should be able to

- Define insurance from a financial and legal perspective.

- Explain how an insurance system operates.

- Distinguish among a loss, a hazard, and a peril.

- Differentiate between social insurance and private insurance.

- Describe the leading types of insurance in the property-liability and life-health industries.

- List the components of an insurance premium.

- Discuss the costs and benefits of the insurance system from society's standpoint.

Purchasing insurance is one of the most critical transactions individuals and businesses make to protect themselves from financial harm. In the 1943 *South-Eastern Underwriters Association* decision by the U.S. Supreme Court, Justice Hugo Black wrote, "Perhaps no modern commercial enterprise directly affects so many persons in all walks of life as does the insurance business. Insurance touches the home, the family, and the occupation or business of almost every person in the United States." Clearly, many aspects of the insurance transaction merit study and thought.

In this chapter, we introduce and define insurance. We describe how the insurance mechanism redistributes the cost of insured losses across all members of an insurance risk pool and how social insurance programs differ from private insurance programs. The chief component parts of insurance premiums are also described, followed by a discussion of the costs and benefits of insurance to society.

INSURANCE DEFINED

Experts do not always agree on the definitions of risk management and insurance terms. In fact, many court cases have attempted to define these terms over the years, with millions of dollars hanging in the balance. If a transaction is labeled as insurance, it is subject to regulations, accounting rules, and tax laws. Sometimes it qualifies for favorable tax treatment, such as making the premium a tax-deductible expense. The scope of insurance is not obvious; some examples of contracts that can fall within or outside the definition of insurance include warranties, service contracts, and the portions of rental car agreements that discuss vehicle damage. Despite these complications, the definitions we offer below are generally accepted and lay the foundation for material covered throughout the text.[1]

Financial Definition

The first definition of insurance is a financial one. Recall from Chapter 1 that *insurance* is a financial agreement that transfers the risk of insured losses to a risk pool administered by an insurer. The insurer redistributes the cost of such losses across all pool members. The pool thus combines all the potential losses from the customers of an insurer and then transfers the cost of the predicted losses back to those exposed. Certainty of financial payment from a pool with adequate resources and accurate ability to predict losses are the hallmarks of the insurance transaction.

Unexpected economic losses have always occurred, and they would occur even if the insurance transaction never had been developed. Through the operation of an insurance system, however, we can predict combined losses. Because insurance allows a group's (but not an individual's) losses to be predicted with reasonable accuracy, it also allows the cost of losses to be financed and redistributed in advance.

In a typical insurance agreement, the insurer assesses its customer a **premium** charge, the price of insurance that is based on the expected cost of insured losses. An insurance system redistributes the cost of losses by collecting a premium payment from every participant (insured person or organization) in the system. In exchange for the premium, the insurer promises to pay the insured's claims in the event of a covered loss. Generally, only a small percentage of the insured group suffers losses. Thus, an insurance system redistributes the costs of losses from the unfortunate few members experiencing them to all the members of the insurance system who pay premiums, as shown in Insight Box 6-1.

An insurance system can operate because most people find the risk of suffering a large loss unpleasant to consider. Because they are *risk-averse*, they are willing to pay a relatively small but certain premium to avoid having to pay a relatively large uncertain loss. For example, if Horace Mann does not purchase insurance, he may be uncertain about whether he will have to pay for fire losses to his home. He is uncertain because he does not know in advance whether his house will burn or, if a fire occurred, how severe the damage would be. Once he has purchased fire insurance, however, it becomes certain that Horace will *not* have to pay for any fire losses to his home because the insurance company will pay for such losses. In this case, the homeowner has transferred his uncertainty to the insurance company.

Legal Definition

In legal terms, insurance is a contract in which one party agrees to compensate another party for losses covered by the contract. We call the party agreeing to pay for the losses the *insurer* or *insurance company*. The party whose loss causes the insurer to make a claim payment is the **insured, policyholder**, or **policy owner**. The insurance contract is called a **policy**, and the insured's possibility of loss is that party's **exposure to loss**. Using these legal terms, we say that the insured transfers the exposure to loss to the insurer by purchasing an insurance policy.

---

[1] For an extended discussion of the definition of insurance and its regulatory implications, see Government Accountability Office, "Definitions of Insurance and Related Information" (GAO-06-424R; February 2006).

INSIGHT BOX 6-1

A Simple Mathematical Example of an Insurance System

Assume that 1,000 Midwestern farmers want to join together to form an insurance risk pool to protect themselves against the loss of their barns by fire. None of the farmers knows whether he or she will suffer a fire in the coming year, but each knows that such a loss could result in the failure of their family business. They learn that in the past, fire losses caused damage each year equal to 1 percent of the value of such barns. Based on this fact, the fraction *Dollars of fire damage divided by the dollar value of exposed property* equals 1 percent.

If each farmer has a barn worth $80,000, then 1,000 such barns have a value of $80 million (1,000 × $80,000). Based on the damage prediction of 1 percent, the expected losses for the farmers' insurance pool will thus equal $800,000 (0.01 × $80,000,000). Focusing solely on the cost of insured losses (for now, we assume that the pool has no operating expenses, that the actual losses equal the expected losses, and that no investment income is earned on premiums paid in advance), then the cost of membership in the pool is $800 per farmer. We calculate this premium by dividing the $800,000 in losses by the 1,000 insured farmers in the insurance pool, as summarized below:

- Number of barns insured = 1,000
- Value of each barn = $80,000
- Number of barns expected to burn this year = 1 percent of 1000 = 10

- Total value of property in insurance pool = $80,000,000
- Predicted losses at the rate of 1 percent of total value = $800,000
- Predicted loss allocated per farmer = $800,000/ 1,000 = $800

To illustrate how a fire insurance pool redistributes the costs of losses, consider Farmer Jon, who paid the $800 premium along with the other 999 farmers. If Jon is one of the ten unfortunate farmers who suffer a fire in the coming year, he faces the prospect of losing $80,000 and possibly his family's livelihood. Instead, as a member of the insurance pool, he will receive $80,000 to pay for the replacement of his barn. As you can now see, each insured paid a small part of the $80,000 loss experienced by one member. In one sense, the insurance company operates like a big checkbook. The insured members make the deposits (premiums), and the insurer writes the checks to the (hopefully) small number of members suffering losses.

Because it is unlikely that each farmer's barn will be worth exactly $80,000, we can compute the cost of insurance based on each $100 of value. Each $100 of insurance will cost the insured $1 ($800,000/800,000, or dollar value of losses per hundreds of dollars of exposures). Thus, a farmer with a $45,000 barn would pay $450 for a one-year membership in the pool (450 × $1, or hundreds of dollars of value times premium cost per $100). A farmer with a $65,000 barn would pay $650.

Based on the financial and legal considerations described above, insurance can be defined as follows:

> An insurance contract is a contractual relationship in which one party, the insurer, is paid a premium by the other party, the insured or policy owner, in exchange for the insurer's promise to compensate the insured in the event the latter suffers a financial loss described under the contract, more commonly known as an insurance policy.

Insurance is a branch of contract law. The insurance policy, like all contracts, creates rights and related duties for those who are parties to it. For instance, it gives the insured the right to collect payment from the insurer if a covered loss occurs. The insurer has a duty to pay for such losses. The insurer also has the right to collect premiums, and those wanting their coverage to continue have the duty to pay them. The insurer has the right to specify the rules and conditions for participating in the insurance pool, and the insured has the matching duty to obey them if he or she expects to collect for losses. In analyzing an insurance contract, remember that a right created for one party represents a duty for the other party. Generally, however, an insurer legally cannot force an insured to pay premiums or meet other conditions set forth in the contract, but it may cancel the insurance or deny claims if the conditions are unmet or premiums are unpaid.

LOSS, PERIL, AND HAZARD

In everyday conversation, we often refer to terms such as *loss*, *peril*, and *hazard* interchangeably, but these words take on a particular meaning when used to describe insurance.

Loss

Insurance policies are written carefully to specify the situations in which insurers will or will not pay the claims requested by their policyholders. An insured *loss* can be described as an undesired, unplanned reduction of economic value. By contrast, the word *expense* refers to planned losses, such as the burning of fuel or wear and tear on machinery.

The **chance of loss** is the *probability* of suffering a loss, expressed as a fraction. The numerator is either the actual or the expected number of losses; the denominator is the number of units exposed to loss. If we expect 3 of 1,000 houses to be destroyed by fire, the expected chance of loss is 3/1,000, or 0.003. We may or may not accurately know the chance of loss in a given case before a loss occurs. If we are referring to the predicted chance of loss, we divide the expected number of losses by the number of exposure units. This fraction is called the *a priori* chance of loss. If we are looking backward over time, we can divide the actual number of losses by the total number of exposures. This fraction is called the actual, or *ex post*, chance of loss.

It is the possibility or the chance of loss that creates the need for insurance. If there were no possibility of loss, or if losses were certain to occur, insurance would not exist. In the first instance, there would be no need for it. In the second, there would be no element of uncertainty about losses, and the result would be expenses rather than losses. Expenses should be handled by methods other than insurance.

Peril

A **peril** is defined as the cause of the loss. Examples of perils include fires, tornadoes, heart attacks, and criminal acts. Insurance policies provide financial protection against losses caused by insured perils. However, many causes of loss are not insurable, and insurance contracts focus much attention on specifying which perils are and are not insured. Insurers call policies that specifically identify a list of covered perils **specified-perils** or **named-perils** contracts. An alternative is the **open-perils** contract, in which the insurer agrees to cover all causes of loss except those that are specifically *excluded* in the policy.

Defining the full scope of damage covered as part of the insured peril can be complicated. In insurance, the **proximate cause** of a loss is the first peril in a chain of events that results in a loss. The loss would not have occurred without this step. Generally, if the proximate cause of the loss is an insured peril, the insurer will pay the claim and the related damages associated with the unbroken chain of events (for example, smoke or water damage resulting from an insured fire loss) started by the occurrence of the peril. However, if the proximate cause of the loss is an excluded peril, the insurer will not pay the claim. Because it raises questions of fact, the proximate cause of a loss sometimes must be determined by a court.[2]

---

[2] After Hurricane Katrina, for example, determining whether the cause of destruction was wind (a covered peril) or flood (an excluded peril) was an important issue for many homeowners living in beachfront properties along the Gulf of Mexico that were destroyed by the 2005 storm.

Hazards

Hazards are conditions that increase the frequency or the severity of losses. **Physical hazards** are conditions related to the physical environment in which a loss event may occur, while **moral hazards** are behavioral activities that increase the frequency or severity of losses. Storing gasoline in a garage is an example of a physical hazard. The storage of the gasoline usually will not cause a loss. The gasoline, however, will make fire losses that do occur more severe. Poor lighting in a crime-prone area is also a physical hazard in that theft losses may be more frequent than would be the case if better lighting were available. The poor lighting by itself would not cause the loss, but to the extent that it makes theft more frequent, it is a hazard. Sometimes hazards increase both the frequency and severity of losses, as would be the case if an automobile is driven too fast for existing conditions.

If an individual engages in behavior that increases the losses that insurers must pay, the loss results from **moral hazard**. In economics, the tendency of policyholders to engage in riskier behavior (such as drivers who have insurance choosing to drive fast because they know that insurance will pay if such behavior results in a loss) is viewed as a form of moral hazard. Another example is **insurance fraud**, a situation in which a person causes or exaggerates a loss to collect insurance proceeds. If somebody burns down a building to collect insurance, the fire causes the damage, but moral hazard is responsible for the increased frequency of loss. If a thief steals $5,000 but the insured storeowner reports a $20,000 loss to the insurance company, the $15,000 fraud committed by the insured results from the moral hazard.[3]

Insurers try to minimize moral hazard by selecting their insureds carefully and by including contractual provisions in insurance policies that decrease an insured's incentives to cause or exaggerate a loss. For example, many contracts require insureds to pay the first specified number of dollars of a loss or a percentage of each loss to decrease the insured's tendencies toward moral hazard. Also, insurance contracts do not cover losses that can be proved were caused by an insured's fraud.

INSURANCE AND RISK REDUCTION

Insurance plays a critical role in the management of risk for all types of organizations, ranging from large multinational corporations to smaller families and individuals. Based on the definitions of risk described in Chapter 1, insurance traditionally has been used to address the risk of suffering a financial loss from a pure, diversifiable loss exposure. For example, many of the loss exposures that are routinely insured, including fire, life, and liability, result from pure risk. In each case, the policyholder is confronted with two scenarios: suffering a financial loss or maintaining his or her existing financial status without a loss. There is no opportunity to profit from the loss. Each of these perils can be described as a loss that is easily diversifiable across a pool of insureds because the occurrence of a financial loss by one claimant is independent of the others in the risk pool.

An insurance system can operate successfully—and reduce risk—only when it can predict losses accurately. Insurance pools reduce risk by applying a mathematical principle called the **law of large numbers**. Simply put, the law states that the greater the number of observations of an event based on chance, the more likely the

---

[3] The insurance literature sometimes differentiates between morale and moral hazard, where *morale hazard* is defined as unconscious, unintentional behavior that increases the size of the insured loss, while *moral hazard* is conscious, intentional (and often illegal) behavior increasing the loss amount.

actual result will approximate the expected result. For example, suppose that the managers of an insurance risk pool expect 1 percent of its members to experience a loss, based on historical records of losses. Assuming that the prior losses are a good representation of the loss they are estimating, the law of large numbers states that the greater the number of exposures in the pool, the more likely the 1 percent loss figure will be realized. By applying the law of large numbers, the insurance company can predict accurately the dollar amount of losses per pool member that it will experience in a given period. The relative accuracy of the company's predictions increases as the number of exposures in the insurance pool increases. We can state this same idea with more mathematical rigor by noting that when the exposures in the insurance pool are independent and have the same loss potential (i.e., they are homogeneous), the riskiness of the pool tends toward zero as the number of exposures tends toward infinity. (We provided an intuitive numerical example of risk pooling in Chapter 3.)

If insurers can predict losses accurately, they can forecast their costs and allocate them across all pool members in advance, charging an appropriate premium. Note that the law of large numbers allows accurate predictions only of broad groupwide results. It does not allow us to predict accurately what will happen to a particular exposure in the group (Luis's house or Sue's life).

PRIVATE AND SOCIAL INSURANCE PROGRAMS

U.S. consumers obtain insurance protection from two primary sources: social insurance programs and private insurance programs. **Social insurance** programs are insurance plans sponsored by a government body and described by statute. Federal or state laws typically require certain defined populations to participate in a social insurance program. While these programs are financed in part by premiums or taxes assessed on the participants, they often are supplemented by subsidies provided by the governmental sponsor.[4] The following programs are among the better-known federal insurance activities:

- The U.S. Social Security Administration (SSA) administers the trust funds paying retirement, disability, and survivor benefits (*www.ssa.gov/*).
- The Federal Deposit Insurance Corporation (FDIC) insures bank deposits up to $250,000 (*http://www.fdic.gov/*).
- The Department of Labor administers unemployment benefits through the Unemployment Trust Fund (*www.dol.gov/dol/topic/unemployment-insurance/index.htm/*).
- The Department of Labor insures corporate pensions through the Pension Benefit Guarantee Corporation (PBGC; *www.pbgc.gov*).

Private insurance consists of insurance plans that are offered by nongovernmental insurance organizations, defined by insurance contracts (rather than by statute), and financed by their insureds. Without the subsidization of a governmental body, private insurers rely on the premiums that they assess upon the plan participants, as well as the interest that they earn by investing these premiums, to cover the claims that they pay. While several different types of insurance organizations compete in the insurance marketplace, stock and mutual insurers account for most of the insurance sold in the

---

[4] See Actuarial Standards Board, "Actuarial Standard of Practice #32: Social Insurance," January 1998, retrieved on July 6, 2011, from *www.actuarialstandardsboard.org*.

United States. (We will provide a more detailed description of the different types of insurers and their operational objectives in Chapter 7.)

The discussion of insurance in this book will generally focus on the private insurance industry. Private insurers offer many different types of insurance products, as discussed below.

TYPES OF INSURANCE

The U.S. private insurance industry is very large, generating more than $1 trillion in premium revenue in 2008.[5] The private insurance market consists of the life and health insurance industry and the property and liability insurance industry.

Life and Health Insurance

Life and health insurers sell products that protect insureds from a variety of perils that can affect a person's life adversely. Because each of these perils can cause great financial harm to an individual person, they often are called **personal risk** exposures. For example, **life insurance** provides protection from the peril of death, paying a sum of money upon the death of the insured to a beneficiary named in the policy (for example, the insured's spouse or another family member). Conversely, for insurance consumers concerned about outliving their life savings, the peril in question is old age or living too long, which can be insured by an insurance contract called an **annuity**. When properly designed, an annuity can guarantee that the insured will continue to receive a predefined amount of money until his or her death, no matter how long the insured survives.

Health insurance provides protection from the additional medical expenses incurred by a policy owner as a result of the perils of sickness or accident. **Disability income insurance** provides protection from the peril of disability, or the lost wages that result from the inability to work due to illness or injury.

Consumers can purchase individual insurance policies to protect themselves from each of the abovementioned perils. It is also common for many consumers to receive protection from these perils from group insurance contracts. **Group insurance plans** are designed to protect multiple people as members of a designated group (for example, employees working for a common employer or the members of an auto club) under a single insurance contract. Employers often provide group insurance coverage to their employees in employee benefit programs.

Property and Liability Insurance

The property and liability insurance industry encompasses a number of categories of insurance. For example, there are many different types of **property insurance policies**, each of which is designed to protect policyholders from damage to different types of property, including commercial buildings, personal property, commercial equipment, houses, and their contents. **Liability insurance** protects insured parties by paying for the legal judgments that they may owe to claimants, as well as the cost to defend the insured from such litigation. Legal judgments may result from situations in which the insured caused bodily injury to the claimant or damaged the claimant's property.

---

[5] Insurance Information Institute, *The Insurance Fact Book*: 2010, p. 14.

Marine insurance protects property in transit from damage. **Ocean marine insurance** covers property transported by ship, and **inland marine insurance** covers property transported by planes, trains, or trucks. The property and liability insurance industry also includes **auto insurance**, as well as **workers' compensation**, which pays lost wages and medical expenses to employees injured on the job. Another type of coverage associated with property insurance is **business interruption coverage**, which provides payment for indirect losses associated with property damage caused by fires and other covered perils.

The property and liability insurance industry is also known as the *property-casualty insurance industry*. **Casualty insurance** encompasses a wide range of insurance protection, including protection against auto, health, workers' compensation, and liability risks.[6]

A common practice in property and liability insurance is to classify the industry based on the type of consumer buying the insurance product. **Personal lines insurance** is insurance designed to serve the personal risk needs of individuals and families. The two largest property-liability insurance products in the United States, based on premium volume, are personal auto insurance and homeowners insurance, both personal lines products.

Commercial lines insurance is insurance tailored to fit the needs of commercial organizations. Commercial liability insurance and workers' compensation are the two biggest commercial insurance products in the United States, ranking third and fourth in overall insurance. Other important types of commercial lines insurance are commercial property policies and commercial auto insurance.

In addition to these standard categories of coverage, insurers sell other interesting types of insurance. The following list conveys only the scope of available insurance possibilities:

- *Weather-related insurance.* Payments can be made for crop-hail damage, rained-out concerts, or too much or too little snow.
- *Change-of-law insurance.* Payments are made if new regulations increase construction costs after contracts are signed.
- *Motion picture completion bonds.* Insureds receive payment if the film is not completed on time. The death of a star or other unforeseen events could cause the insurer to pay.
- *Boiler and machinery insurance.* Many property insurance contracts specifically exclude damage caused by exploding steam boilers. Some insurance companies sell this type of coverage, but in practice what insureds pay for, in addition to the indemnity agreement, is regular inspections of their boilers.
- *Wedding insurance.* The average cost of a wedding in the United States is approximately $20,000.[7] Wedding insurance covers losses arising from cancellation or postponement because of illness of the bride or groom, loss of wedding gifts, or failure of vendors to perform. The insurance provides reimbursement for nonrecoverable expenses, payment of extra expenses, or payment for lost or damaged wedding rings, gifts, or wedding clothes.

---

[6] In actuarial science, professional actuaries can specialize in the casualty insurance industries by passing a series of actuarial exams administered by the Casualty Actuarial Society.

[7] Zhang, J. "Your Money Matters (A Special Report)—I Do ... for Less: As the Economy Shrinks, So Do Wedding Budgets," *Wall Street Journal* (New York), June 8, 2009.

BUILDING BLOCKS OF AN INSURANCE PREMIUM

The calculation of the premiums charged by insurance companies to their policyholders is not a simple process. Unlike companies in many other industries, insurance companies do not know before setting their prices the total costs they will incur to produce their products. Instead, they must forecast their policyholders' losses, or **insured loss claims**, as the starting point for calculating their premiums. Insurers then adjust these calculations to incorporate several other pricing factors, including their estimated administrative costs and potential investment income.

Figure 6-1 provides a summary of the building blocks of insurance premiums, including the following components:

- The estimated cost of insured loss claims
- The estimated cost to pay for the administrative expenses of the insurer, also known as the insurer's *loading expense*
- The estimated investment income earned by the insurer on the premiums received from policyholders
- A fair rate of return for the owners of the insurer

Insured losses are the largest expense category built into the premium calculations of most insurance companies. Loss adjustment expenses, or the costs that insurers incur in settling loss claims, are also included as insured losses. Within the property and liability insurance industry, insurers measure the portion of an insurer's premium that pays for insured claims with the **loss ratio**, calculated as the total amount of insured losses paid by an insurer in a given product line divided by the premiums earned by the insurer in that line.

Loading expenses include a variety of overhead costs that insurers incur in administering the insurance mechanism. Examples are employee compensation, investments in technology, commissions paid to insurance marketing representatives, and insurer premium taxes. Insurers measure their loading expenses with the **expense ratio**, calculated as the sum of an insurer's administrative expenses in a product line divided by premiums written in that line.

FIGURE 6-1 Illustrating the Building Blocks of Insurance Premiums Using Data (in $ Millions) from the 2008 Auto Insurance Market

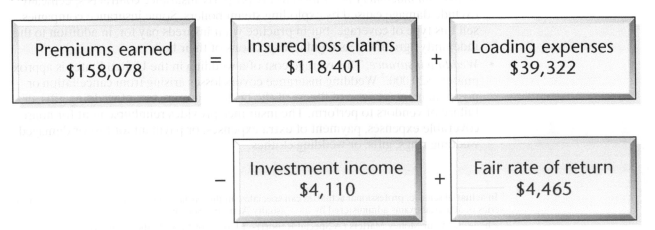

Best's Aggregates and Averages Insurance Information Institute and author calculations.

In addition to premiums received from policyholders, an important source of revenue for insurance companies is **investment income**, income earned by insurers from investments in securities. Because insurers receive the premium payments from their policyholders months or years in advance of paying insured claims, they can earn additional revenue by investing those premiums. Recognizing investment income in premium calculations serves to *reduce* the price of insurance because insurers can use investment income to pay for a portion of their loss claims and loading expenses. Most premiums are invested in low-risk investments such as corporate bonds, bonds issued by state and federal governments, common and preferred stock, and short-term investments.

States that regulate the pricing of insurance generally recognize the need for insurers to earn a **fair rate of return** for bearing the risk of their policyholders. The long-run financial strength of insurers will be compromised if insurers cannot set premiums at a level that allows them to pay their claims and loading expenses. Further, while the randomness of insurance claims can raise or lower returns in any given year, in a competitive financial marketplace, stockholders and other investors will not invest in insurers that fail to provide them a fair rate of return over the long run.

The Building Blocks of Auto Insurance Premiums

We can better appreciate the comparative size of each of the abovementioned building blocks by examining premium and expense data from actual insurance markets. For example, the dollar amounts shown in Figure 6-1 shows premiums and expenses for the U.S. private passenger auto insurance industry for 2008. Note that this industry generated $158 billion in premium revenue that year, 59 percent of this revenue coming from the sale of private passenger auto liability insurance, protection that pays for the damage that an insured driver is responsible for as a result of causing bodily injury or property damage to other parties. The remaining 41 percent was spent on physical damage insurance, such as collision coverage.

In 2008, U.S. auto insurers paid 74.9 percent of their premium income as insured loss claims. This expense includes payments for property damage claims (such as payments to other drivers for damage to their vehicles caused by the insured or damage to the insured's own vehicle), as well as bodily injury damages incurred by people harmed in insured accidents (such as the insured or other people harmed by the insured). In contrast, loading expenses accounted for 24.9 percent of private passenger auto premiums. Approximately one-third of these loading expenses were payments made to insurance marketing intermediaries, such as commissions paid to agents or brokers. State premium taxes, taxes assessed as a percentage of the premium revenues (not the income) of the auto insurer, account for approximately 10 percent of loading expenses. The remaining loading expenses paid for the usual costs of operating a business, such as compensation to employees, office expenses, and the related cost of equipment and information technology.

The auto insurance industry is very competitive, with nearly 900 insurers selling private passenger auto insurance in the United States in 2008. As a result, the profit margins for most auto insurers are very thin. A common measure of insurer underwriting profitability is the **combined ratio**, the sum of an insurer's loss ratio and expense ratio in a given product line, where values less than 100 percent reflect profitable insurance operations. The combined ratio for U.S. private passenger auto insurers in 2008 was 99.8 percent. Thus, the premiums charged in the private passenger auto insurance industry were marginally higher than insured losses and loading expenses in 2008, generating an underwriting income of $355 million on premium volume equal to $158 billion.

Measured as a percentage of earned premiums, insurer investment income generated a 2.6 percent return to private passenger auto insurers in 2008.[8] Combining insurer investment returns with insurer underwriting income yields a pretax income for the industry equal to $4.47 billion, or a rate of return equal to 2.8 percent of insurer premium revenues.

THE BENEFITS AND COSTS TO SOCIETY OF INSURANCE SYSTEMS

While insurance provides many benefits to society, the costs of administering the insurance mechanism are not trivial. We next discuss the costs and benefits of insurance.

Costs

What is the cost to society of operating an insurance system? Would it be represented by the $158 billion of premiums in our prior example? No, because three-quarters of those premiums represent the cost of losses. Assuming that these losses would occur even if no insurance system existed, the cost to society of operating an insurance system includes the cost of the resources that the system uses—the labor, the land, and the capital—but not the cost of the losses. Based on this reasoning, the cost borne by society from insurance is the portion of the insurance premium that pays for administering the insurance mechanism, which we can approximate using the loading expenses of insurers.

A second cost to society from the insurance mechanism is intentional losses such as arson or similar fraudulent attempts to collect insurance proceeds. These costs are attributed properly to an insurance system because the motivation to commit such actions would not exist if insurance companies were not available to pay fraudulent claims. Some losses, however, are less frequent or less severe because the possibility of lower insurance premiums encourages loss-prevention or loss-reduction activities. For example, because insurers provide discounts to policy owners for employing security guards and installing fire sprinklers and smoke detectors, society loses fewer of its resources to fire and theft.

Benefits

What advantages does society gain from an insurance system's operation? How do they compare with the resources used? One of the greatest benefits with which an insurance system rewards society is stability in families. Insurance prevents a family from experiencing the great hardships caused by unexpected losses of property or the premature death of the main income provider. It allows a family to continue its activities in a much more normal fashion after a loss than would be the case if no insurance existed.

Insurance is also very useful to businesses. Insurance aids the planning process because the planner knows that a property loss will not mean financial ruin and that the future of a business cannot be destroyed by a fire, a lawsuit, or the death of a key person.

Insurance aids credit transactions as well because creditors are more willing to lend money if the debtor's death does not make collection of the loan difficult or impossible. Likewise, lenders are more willing to make property or real estate loans if they know that a disaster cannot destroy the financial security behind their loan.

---

[8] Pulled down by the 2008 recession, this return was lower than normal for the industry. Over the ten-year period from 1999 to 2008, private passenger auto insurers earned higher investment earnings, averaging around 4.0 percent.

An economist would give an insurance system high marks because it functions as an antimonopoly device. That is, if no insurance system were available, only the largest businesses could sustain losses and remain in operation. For example, one of the nation's largest chains of grocery stores probably could lose one of its stores in a fire and remain in business, whereas smaller store chains could not sustain uninsured losses as well, and a mom-and-pop grocery probably would have to close permanently if an uninsured fire destroyed its only store. Insurance allows smaller operators in an industry to pool their exposure to loss and thus remain competitive.

Financiers recognize that insurance availability tends to lower a firm's cost of capital because both creditors and investors would charge much more for the use of their money if that money were subjected to the risks associated with natural disasters in addition to normal business risks. In addition, without insurance, firms would have to hold more money in relatively nonproductive near-cash reserves to protect themselves against a rainy day.

Insurance companies, and the organizations that they support, contribute directly to society's welfare in many ways relating to loss prevention and medical research. Among the better-known company-sponsored loss prevention organizations are the Underwriters' Laboratories, Inc. (*www.ul.com/*), National Safety Council (*www.nsc. org/*), and the Insurance Institute for Highway Safety (*www.hwysafety.org/*). Many medical schools and other medical research facilities receive direct support for their work from life insurance companies.

Insurance companies are very important financial intermediaries. Annually, life insurance companies collect billions of dollars in people's savings and reinvest these amounts in the economy. Property insurers also maintain billions of dollars that are invested in our private-enterprise economy. Insurers provide a useful service to savers by evaluating and selecting sound investments, and they provide a service to businesses and governmental units at the local, state, and federal levels. In general, business and government borrowers do not find it practical to use the small savings streams of individuals, but they can use effectively the river of funds made available by insurance companies. In one recent year, insurance companies held an estimated $6 trillion in assets. Financial assets held by insurers include bonds (and other credit market securities), equity securities, cash, policyholder loans (held by life insurance companies), and mortgages.

In conclusion, although it costs society some of its scarce resources to operate an insurance system, and although people cause some losses in an attempt to collect insurance, the benefits society receives from insurance operations far outweigh the costs.

Summary

Insurance is a financial arrangement for redistributing the costs of unexpected losses through a legal contract in which an insurer agrees to compensate an insured for losses. A loss is an undesired, unplanned reduction of economic value. Insurance is not necessary unless a potential policyholder faces a chance of loss, as measured by a fraction whose numerator represents the number of losses and whose denominator represents the number of exposures to loss.

A peril is the cause of a loss. Physical hazards are physical conditions that serve to increase the frequency or severity of perils, and moral hazards are the result of engaging in activities that increase the insured losses paid by insurers.

The law of large numbers allows insurers to predict losses accurately. This mathematical rule states that the greater the number of observations of an event based on chance, the more likely the actual result will approximate the expected result.

The components of an insurance premium are the cost of losses, the expenses of operating the insurance company, the investment earnings available when premiums are paid in advance and a fair rate of return. Insurance provides many benefits to society: stability in families and businesses, easier completion of lending arrangements, improved ability of smaller businesses to survive large losses and compete with larger businesses, provision of capital to businesses and individuals, and active support of loss prevention research. In exchange for these insurance benefits, society bears the cost of operating the insurance mechanism and the cost of intentional and exaggerated claims.

Review

1. The term *insurance* can be defined in both financial and legal terms. How do these definitions differ?
2. How does insurance redistribute the costs of losses?
3. What is the difference between insurable losses and depreciation expenses?
4. Describe the difference between a named-perils policy and an open-perils policy.
5. What is the difference between a hazard and a peril? Give examples of each.
6. Why is it the chance of loss, and not the loss itself, that creates the need for insurance?
7. How does a moral hazard differ from a physical hazard? Give examples of each.
8. Define the law of large numbers. What are its implications for an insurance system?
9. Explain the differences between social insurance and private insurance programs.
10. Describe four types of life and health insurance. In your answer, describe the personal risk that is insured by each type of insurance.
11. In the property and liability insurance industry, describe the difference between personal lines insurance and commercial lines insurance. Give two examples of each.
12. List the four building blocks of an insurance premium. Why are investment earnings included in the calculations?
13. What are the definitions for the loss ratio and the expense ratio? Describe what each ratio measures.
14. In what ways do insurance systems benefit society?
15. What are the major costs of insurance systems?

Objective Questions

1. An insurable loss is:
   a. An event that has not been predicted
   b. An exposure that cannot be measured easily before the event has occurred
   c. An unexpected reduction of economic value
   d. Being without something that one has previously possessed
2. The definition of *peril* is:
   a. An event or condition that increases the chance of loss
   b. The uncertainty concerning loss
   c. A measure of the accuracy with which a loss can be predicted
   d. The actual cause of the loss
3. A moral hazard is:
   a. A loss of faith in the insurance company because it has denied claims
   b. Illustrated by the loss of a wallet to a thief
   c. An act by an insured that increases the losses paid by his insurer
   d. The potential for the insurance company to increase premiums after a loss
4. "A financial arrangement that redistributes the costs of unexpected losses" is the definition of
   a. a derivative security
   b. a mutual fund
   c. insurance
   d. moral hazard
5. A person storing 100 pounds of gunpowder in the basement so that he can load his own shotgun shells is an example of:
   a. a physical hazard
   b. a peril
   c. a moral hazard
   d. an indirect loss
6. The expense ratio is defined as:
   a. Insured expenses divided by insured losses

b. Total expenses divided by written premiums
c. Insured expenses and losses divided by net income
d. Net income divided by total expenses

7. Which of the following is *not* an example of a social insurance program?
   a. Federal Deposit Insurance Corporation
   b. Pension Benefit Guaranty Corporation
   c. Unemployment Trust Fund
   d. Personal Annuity Insurance

8. In property-liability insurance, which of these is *not* considered personal lines insurance?
   a. workers' compensation
   b. homeowners insurance
   c. auto insurance
   d. all are personal lines

9. Which of the following is *not* a component in the calculation of insurance premiums?
   a. estimated loss claims
   b. investment income
   c. loading expense
   d. in fact, all are considered

10. Which of the following is a cost incurred by society through the operation of the insurance mechanism?
    a. insured loss costs
    b. loading expenses
    c. fraudulent loss claims
    d. all the above
    e. b and c

Discussion Questions

1. Provide some important examples of how a privately operated insurance system contributes to a market-based economy.
2. Why are the costs of insured losses not included among society's costs for operating an insurance system?
3. Describe how the premiums charged by insurers are affected by the returns available to the holders of different types of investments.

Selected References

Actuarial Standards Board, American Academy of Actuaries, *Social Insurance*, Actuarial Standard of Practice, Number 32, January 1998.

Government Accountability Office, "Definitions of Insurance and Related Information," Presentation for Committee on Financial Services, U.S. House of Representatives (GAO06-424R), February 2006.

The I. I. I. Insurance Factbook (New York: Insurance Information Instititute), published annually.

7

Insurable Perils and Insuring Organizations

After studying this chapter, you should be able to

■ Describe the characteristics of an ideally insurable loss exposure

■ Explain why a broad group of insureds is needed to assure affordable insurance

■ Describe how risk classification systems operate and how can they result in subsidization in insurance markets

■ Describe the causes of adverse selection in insurance markets

■ Describe the characteristics of a well-designed insurance risk classification system

■ Describe the different types of private insurance companies in the United States

Insurance provides firms and individuals a unique and essential service, the ability to reduce their risk by redistributing the financial consequences of losses across a wide pool of policyholders. This chapter describes the conditions in which the insurance mechanism operates effectively, as well as the circumstances in which risk pooling is not practical or feasible. We also examine the different types of insuring organizations that compete in the insurance marketplace.

The limits of the insurance mechanism are especially relevant for organizations in today's risk management environment. For some perils, such as floods or earthquakes, there is very little insurance available from private insurers to protect victims from significant financial loss. On the other hand, in markets like health insurance, private insurance is available, but many employers and individuals cannot afford it, prompting critics to call for health care reform. As suggested by the public policy debate surrounding these issues, it is necessary to understand fully the circumstances in which the insurance mechanism can and cannot effectively bear risk.

IDEALLY INSURABLE LOSS EXPOSURES

We begin by asking, "From the perspective of a private insurer, what are the characteristics of an insurable peril?" While the answer depends upon the loss exposure in question, the following characteristics are common attributes of insurable perils:

1. A large group of similar items are exposed to the same peril(s)
2. Accidental losses beyond the insured's control[1]
3. Definite losses capable of causing economic hardship
4. Extremely low probability of a catastrophic loss to the insurance pool[2]

These criteria represent the ideal, although in practice, insurance companies provide coverage under less-than-ideal conditions. However, private insurance ventures that depart too far from the ideal are likely to fail or to require financial subsidization from governmental entities. In this section, we look at each criterion of insurability.

A Large Group of Similar Items Exposed to the Same Peril(s)

An insurance company needs to insure a sizable number of policyholders to obtain predictive accuracy, which is the statistical benefit of risk pooling. A common goal among insurers is to accurately predict both the mean frequency and the mean severity of losses. Although the definition of "a large group" depends on several factors, small insurers often can gain predictive accuracy with fairly modest pool sizes measured in the thousands, as was shown in Chapter 3.

The items in an insurance pool need to be similar so that the insurer can calculate a fair premium. For example, brick homes usually will suffer less wind damage than mobile homes. It would be unfair to combine them in the same insurance pool and charge each insured the same premium rate because the owners of brick homes would pay too high a premium, and the owners of mobile homes too low. For the same reason, all members of the insurance pool should face approximately the same level of exposure to loss. Thus, charging all insureds the same rate for coverage from windstorm would be unfair if some buildings were located in a hurricane area and others were not. As we will discuss later, firms typically cannot charge unfair premiums in a competitive insurance market without losing their low-risk insureds.

Accidental Losses Beyond the Insured's Control

Insurers typically cannot insure perils that are under the insured's control without increasing premiums significantly. If policyholders could intentionally cause losses and then collect for the resulting damages, there would obviously be far more claims, and the premiums needed to fund them would be more than honest people would pay. In practice, insurance fraud is against public policy and also is excluded by the wording of insurance contracts. Thus, an insurance company will not pay for an insured's intentionally caused losses such as arson or theft, if discovered.

---

[1] From the insured's standpoint, losses must be accidental. For example, if an insured deliberately took two different types of medicine that were incompatible with each other, the unintended fatal results would be accidental from the insured's standpoint. The term *accident* is difficult to define precisely, but unintended results are implied.

[2] Insurance consumers also require an economically feasible premium, one that a sufficient number of average insureds can afford. An affordable premium allows the law of large numbers to operate. If premiums are high because the insurer cannot predict the risk or an insufficient number of policyholders participate in the risk pool, only those most exposed to loss will purchase coverage. We discuss this problem later in this chapter.

Non-fraudulent losses arising from an insured's negligence, such as when his bad driving causes an accident, *are* insurable. In this case, the insured did not intend to cause the accident, even though he may have driven in a negligent manner. The differentiation between accidental losses and intentional acts is sometimes subtle. For example, insurers consider suicide an intentional and thus uninsured loss if it occurs within a year or two of the purchase of a life insurance policy because it is assumed that suicidal tendencies existed in the insured at the time of purchase. If suicide occurs after the first year or two, however, the loss is considered accidental and presumed to be the result of mental illness that manifests itself after the time of purchase.

Health and disability insurers often take steps to control their policyholders' actions when they can result in increased loss claims, especially those attributed to malingering, or extending the insured period during which losses are paid, after an illness or accident. Many health and disability policies require the insured to pay for a portion of the covered expenses, specifically to reduce the motivation to remain hospitalized unnecessarily. Likewise, policies replacing income while an insured is disabled replace only a percentage of the lost income, such as 66 percent, to provide an incentive to return to work. When losses produce no regret for the policyowner, the number of insured claims often will increase.

Nonaccidental or expected reductions of economic value, such as wear and tear, are not insurable events. It would be difficult for insurers to insure such losses without increasing premiums to unaffordable levels.

Definite Losses Capable of Causing Economic Hardship

Insurable events must be definite and verifiable. Otherwise, insurer and insured would argue frequently about whether a loss has occurred. Thus, an individual can be insured against the loss of a house as the result of a fire, but not as the result of its being haunted. More realistically, health insurers often limit payments for mental illness, in part because of the frequent difficulty of determining the beginning, presence, or absence of the covered condition.

Termite damage usually is not insured by property insurance contracts because determining when the loss occurred and the extent of damage can be difficult. Termite damage, being gradual, also presents a moral hazard because homeowners with an infested residence might knowingly allow the damage to continue in anticipation of a large-scale replacement of an old structure with a new one. Termite exterminators often guarantee their work and agree to pay for subsequent damage if the treatment fails. However, they usually do so only after a thorough inspection and chemical treatment. Moreover, their guarantee is usually contingent on follow-up inspections. The whole transaction is more in the nature of a service contract or a warranty, neither of which is viewed as insurance in most states.

The damage caused by insurable events also must be measurable in economic terms. The loss of a loved pet can cause a family much grief, but we cannot measure such discomfort economically. Thus, insurers exclude the loss of pets in homeowner's insurance contracts. In contrast, the loss of racehorses or valuable breeding livestock represents an insurable exposure because the damage can be measured economically. In fact, insurance companies write a significant amount of livestock insurance in the United States.

Insurance operates most successfully when the potential damage caused by a peril is severe enough to cause economic hardship to the policyholder. Insuring inexpensive items, especially if losses are frequent, would result in premium charges equal to or greater than the potential damage, which makes such insurance unattractive. As a rule, insurance should be purchased only when losses are large and uncertain. This rule is known as the **large-loss principle**.

Low Probability of Catastrophic Loss

Loss exposures with catastrophic potential are usually not insurable events. We define a **catastrophic loss exposure** as a potential loss that is unpredictable and capable of producing an extraordinarily large amount of damage relative to the assets held in the insurance pool, but the definition of this term is open to interpretation and depends on how "extraordinarily large" is defined.[3] For example, before Hurricane Andrew struck Florida in 1992, many insurance companies felt that damage from one hurricane was not likely to be catastrophic relative to the amount of assets in the insurance pool. Afterwards, many insurers changed their opinion and tried to withdraw this coverage from the market.

Catastrophes occur when a single event, or a related series of events, affect a large number of the exposure units in the insurance pool. That is, catastrophic loss potential exists when insured losses are not independent, or when a loss to one exposure unit implies a loss to many others.

In addition to their potentially devastating financial impact, many catastrophic losses exhibit two other troublesome characteristics. First, many catastrophic losses from natural disasters tend to be focused in specific geographic areas. For example, earthquakes and floods are not problems in many parts of the United States but occur with greater frequency in certain loss-prone areas, such as along fault zones or coastlines. Outside these areas, most people face minimal risk from these events, and therefore they are less willing to pay a premium to protect themselves from such perils. Second, catastrophic losses are difficult to predict accurately. While science is making progress in modeling catastrophic losses, events such as climate change and increased economic development in loss-prone areas are complicating these forecasting efforts.

BROAD EXPOSURE TO LOSS AND INSURER DEATH SPIRALS

Insurance systems operate successfully when a large number of insureds are exposed to loss and the price of insurance is small relative to the potential loss. Because they are risk-averse, most people are willing to pay a relatively small, certain price to avoid a relatively large, uncertain loss. People have a price, however, beyond which they will not pay to transfer a risk.

Following this logic, if earthquake insurance were cheap—for example, $1 for $20,000 of protection—it is likely many people would purchase it. As soon as the price is raised, some people who think an earthquake is an unlikely source of loss for them will drop out of the insurance pool rather than pay. Thus, most non-Californians in the United States probably would not pay more than a nominal sum for earthquake insurance despite the existence of potentially devastating earthquake zones in some areas of the country beyond California (such as the New Madrid fault in Missouri). The first group to drop out of the pool, therefore, will be those exposures most favorably situated relative to the peril. Their exit will force the premium rates upward.

As we described in Insight Box 6-1 in Chapter 6, property insurance companies calculate their rates based on a fraction equal to the estimated dollar value of losses divided by the dollar value of insured property. When the most favorably situated exposures leave the pool, the denominator of the fraction becomes smaller, while the numerator stays mostly unchanged. This effect produces a higher premium. For example, assume that $1 million worth of losses are to be spread over $100 million worth of property value. The cost of such insurance will be $1 for each $100 of property value. If $25 million worth of property leaves the pool and losses remain the same, the $1 million of losses must be spread over $75 million of property, producing a premium of $1.33 for each $100 of property value.

The 33 percent increase in rates caused by the favored group's departure has an identical effect on the next most favored group, and its members will leave the pool

---

[3] The General Accountability Office's definition of the term *catastrophe* is also open-ended: "Term used for statistical recording purposes to refer to a single incident or a series of closely related incidents causing severe insured property losses totaling more than a given amount." See General Accountability Office, "Catastrophe Risk: U.S. and European Approaches to Insure Natural Catastrophe and Terrorism Risks (GAO-05-199, February 2005, p. 69).

because the premium rates now exceed their valuation of the protection. As each of the marginal members of the pool leaves, the premium rates are forced upward, and every time more members leave, yet another group of members sees the insurance protection as a poor value. This process can become a vicious circle of premium increases, commonly called an **insurer death spiral**, that stops when the pool contains an overwhelming number of high-risk members; namely, policyholders who will pay a high price to transfer their risk because they are very susceptible to the peril.

At this point, an insurance system will break down completely because instead of transferring the cost from the few who experience it to a large pool of insureds, it must make the transfer among only those likely to experience loss. When the cost of operating the insurance pool is added to the cost of the losses transferred, the premiums will be too great relative to the potential loss, even for those wanting to remain in the pool. Thus, an insurance system will fail when only those individuals most exposed to loss want insurance protection.

So far, we have described the characteristics of insurable perils in fairly general terms. Insight Box 7-1 provides a more specific discussion of insurable risk, examining whether the property loss caused by tornadoes is an insurable peril.

INSIGHT BOX 7-1

Are Losses from Tornadoes Insurable?

According to the NOAA, a tornado is a violently rotating column of air that extends from a thunderstorm and makes contact with the ground. Severe tornadoes are capable of producing damaging winds in excess of 200 miles per hour. During the spring of 2011, a massive tornado outbreak occurred in the southeastern portion of the United States. The initial insured damage for the 2011 storms was estimated to cost as much as $8 billion, and the storms that spring killed well over 500 people. The deadliest tornado strike on record in the United States occurred in 1925, killing 695 people in Missouri, Illinois, and Indiana.

Despite the severity of these losses, many people are surprised to learn that property damage caused by tornadoes exhibits the characteristics of an insurable peril. Here is why:

- *A large number of similar items—including homes, businesses, and vehicles—are exposed to tornado damage:* Tornadoes have occurred in every state in the United States, so the population exposed to loss is quite large. Tornadoes also occur fairly frequently, enabling insurers to better forecast their frequency and severity.

- *Tornadoes are accidental losses beyond the control of the insured policyholder:* While building and

homeowners can take steps to limit their exposure to tornadoes (using a weather radio during stormy weather or building a tornado safe room in a basement), they cannot control tornadoes.

- *There is definite loss capable of causing economic hardship:* Tornadoes can destroy a building or structure, causing sizable economic harm. While weather researchers often examine wind damage to determine whether it was caused by tornado or straight-line wind, both are covered as wind damage under property insurance policies.

- *The probability of catastrophic loss is low:* While tornadoes clearly can cause great economic harm to a homeowner, the scope of the destruction is generally quite localized, limited to a fairly narrow geographic path. Thus, unlike the more widespread damage caused by floods or wars, losses from tornadoes can be insured.

- *The desire to purchase tornado coverage is not limited to a small segment of consumers who are most likely to suffer a loss:* Because tornadoes occur in every state, all building owners are vulnerable to a tornado loss and thus have a need for insurance.

Based on "Tornadoes," Insurance Information Institute, retrieved February 25, 2001 at www.iii.org; "Severe Weather," National Oceanic and Atmospheric Administration, retrieved May 13, 2011 at http://www.noaawatch.gov/themes/severe.php; "AIR Worldwide Estimates Insured Losses from the Severe Thunderstorm Outbreak of April 22–28 at between USD 3.7 and 5.5 Billion" by Kevin Long, AIR Worldwide, May 9, 2011; "U.S. Spring Storms of 2011," Eqecat retrieved June 2, 2011 at http://www.eqecat.com. Please note that at the time this book was printed, only preliminary reports of the damage caused by the 2011 tornadoes, and the reaction from the insurance industry, were available.

RISK CLASSIFICATION AND INSURABLE EVENTS

A generally accepted principle of insurance is that each insured and each class of insureds should bear its fair share of the insurance pool's losses and expenses for an event to be insurable in the private market. Economists measure this *mathematically fair price* (also known as the *actuarially fair premium*) for insurance using the expected value of an insured's losses, as was described in Chapter 3.[4] Because the mathematically fair price is not known with certainty and must be estimated, insurers have developed **risk classification systems** that are used to sort policyholders into different pricing groups based on their risks of suffering insured losses. Once they have classified policyholders into large, homogeneous groups, insurers can forecast more accurately the expected losses of customers within these risk classes. Without careful risk classification, many events that otherwise would be insurable would become uninsurable, as described below.

Subsidization

In theory, each insured's mathematically fair share of losses is based on the expected loss for the insured person's risk class. **Subsidization** occurs if each insured does not pay the mathematically fair price for insurance. If the insured is paying more than the mathematically fair price, the insured provides the subsidy. If the insured is paying less than the mathematically fair price, the insured receives a subsidy.

When *significant* subsidization occurs, the results can be so unfair that low-risk insureds have an incentive to either switch insurers or forgo the insurance. For example, assume that the annual fair mathematical cost for $1,000 of life insurance for a 20-year-old man is $1.79, and that the cost for similar protection for a 40-year-old man is $3.53. (Rates for men and women are different.) Assume that both men were joined by thousands of others of the same ages in one insurance pool, and every man in the pool was charged an average rate of $2.66 [($1.79 + $3.53)/2]. The 20-year-olds would be paying $0.87 too much and the 40-year-olds would be paying $0.87 too little. Now $0.87 might not seem too great a sum, but it is about 50 percent of the original price.

When the 20-year-olds realize that they are subsidizing the 40-year-olds, they will seek and join another insurance pool designed specifically for 20-year-old men and charging a rate appropriate for them. When the 20-year-olds leave the original pool, the rate for the 40-year-olds must rise closer to their fair level of $3.53. Significant subsidization cannot exist for long in a competitive market because some insurers will offer lower rates to people paying too much for coverage.

In practice, charging all policyholders the same rate, reflecting average experience, results in good policyholders subsidizing bad ones. A competitive marketplace tends to control such cross-subsidies, however, as rival insurers attempt to gain market share by identifying low-risk policyholders who are paying too much for insurance and offering these insureds discounts that reflect their lower expected losses. Thus, competition results in safe driver discounts for good drivers and lower life or health insurance rates for nonsmokers. As these examples suggest, competition reduces subsidization in the insurance market.

The operation of this process has a limit. As insurers increasingly differentiate between risk classes, the number of people assigned to each class becomes smaller and smaller until, at some point, the law of large numbers cannot operate satisfactorily. If it

---

[4] We focus only on the expected loss to keep the discussion simple. As was noted in Chapter 6, premium calculations include several other factors in addition to the expected loss.

were so narrowly defined, the insurance pool would become too small to allow sufficient predictive accuracy; therefore, some subsidization does occur in all insurance pools. For example, even if it could be shown that a driver with six accidents is a more favored exposure than one with seven accidents, it is unlikely that competitive forces would produce an insurer specializing in providing insurance for people with exactly six accidents. Thus, drivers with six accidents are charged the same rate as those with seven, and subsidization occurs. Competition thus serves to reduce or minimize subsidization, not to eliminate it. In practice, insurers try to achieve a balance between the small groups required for fairness and the large numbers of exposures needed for predictive accuracy.

Adverse Selection

The use of risk classification requires that insurers have access to accurate information about the risk characteristics of their customers. Insurers are unable to use risk classification effectively under conditions of *asymmetric information*, or situations in which one party in an insurance transaction has more relevant information than another. When policyholders have better information than an insurer about their risk levels, they can take advantage of it through a process called **adverse selection**, or **anti-selection**. For example, adverse selection occurs when a person with deteriorating health tries to buy health insurance at low prices without telling the insurer of their medical problems, or when someone tries to purchase fire insurance immediately after a disgruntled neighbor threatens his property. Adverse selection raises serious ethical and moral questions, but it is an ever-present fact in the insurance market.

If insurers made no attempt to put applicants for insurance in different risk classes, a predictable result would occur. Applicants for insurance with a greater-than-average chance of loss would certainly apply for insurance at a rate that did not fairly reflect the insurer's exposure to loss. If these above-average-risk applicants succeed in purchasing insurance at average rates by concealing their high-risk characteristics, the insurer will suffer financial losses from adverse selection. This does not mean that above-average-risk applicants cannot buy insurance. Insurers often accept exposures with a greater-than-average chance of loss, but they are careful to charge those applicants above-average premiums commensurate with their higher chance of loss. Insurers thus select insureds very carefully, charging each a rate based on its own expected loss.

PRINCIPLES OF RISK CLASSIFICATION

Insurers use risk classification to minimize subsidization and adverse selection. The guiding principle applied when establishing risk classes has been that each insured should bear the mathematical fair share of the pool's losses and expenses, but this rule can produce controversial results. In fact, some measures that discriminate fairly in the mathematical sense produce results that most of society would consider offensive. Race is such a variable. Even though insurers have used race in the past to predict mortality, many people would object strongly to using it to set insurance rates today.

How can we determine if a variable is appropriate for use in risk classification? We can evaluate rate classification factors on the following four points: separation and homogeneity of the classes, reliability, incentive value, and social acceptability.

Separation and Class Homogeneity

If the insurer has constructed its risk classes carefully, *separation* among the classes will result; that is, each class will have a significantly different expected loss. Moreover, each member within a given class will have approximately the same chance of loss, providing for *class homogeneity*. This rule prevents combining males aged 20 and 40 in the same life insurance pool and causes a mathematically fair insurance exchange.

Reliability

To ensure *reliability,* information about a risk classification variable should be easily obtainable and not subject to manipulation by the insured. Thus, classifying drivers based on age and gender meet this standard, but asking an applicant how many miles he drives each year or whether he uses drugs or alcohol would not work as well because the insured can provide false information. If working with less-than-ideal risk classification criteria, insurers often seek independent verification of information provided by applicants.

Incentive Value

If insurers construct their risk classes carefully, insureds can be rewarded for maintaining clean driving records, applying successful loss-prevention measures, or otherwise achieving below average loss potential. The reward, or *incentive,* is better insurance rates.

Social Acceptability

The *social acceptability* criterion indicates that the use of risk classification variables that violate social norms regarding discrimination is inappropriate, especially when they are beyond the control of the insured. In practice, it is a very challenging criterion to work with. First, who is to decide what is socially acceptable—the courts? Congress? Insurance regulators? Further, social acceptability can be at odds with the other risk classification criteria we've discussed. What do we do when the desirability of mathematically fairness conflicts with a socially desired outcome?

Two examples of risk classification variables that are no longer used by insurers are race and gender. Insurers voluntarily eliminated race as an underwriting criterion because of the unacceptable social implications of this practice. Several years later, the courts addressed gender in two landmark pension cases, the *Manhart* case and the *Norris* case. The result was to equalize pension payments to similarly situated men and women and disregard differences in life expectancies. These rules apply only to pension plans, not to individual life insurance and annuities, where gender-distinct mortality tables are still used.[5]

An ongoing controversy focuses on genetic testing of insurance applicants. **Genetic testing**, the use of technology to examine an individual's genes, has the possibility of identifying people with a high susceptibility to certain diseases. Whether insurers should be allowed to charge a 25-year-old man a higher-than-average premium because genetic testing suggests a greater-than-average chance of death from a disease at age 45 remains a question of social policy. As such testing becomes increasingly accurate (as it has in recent years), society will have to weigh a fair insurance premium in the balance with social acceptability. On the one hand, many people

---

[5] *City of Los Angeles, Department of Water and Power* v. *Marie Manhart*, U.S. Supreme Court, 1978 (434 U.S. 815). *Arizona Governing Committee for Tax Deferred Annuity and Deferred Compensation Plans, etc., et al. Petitioners Nathalie Norris, etc.*, U.S. Supreme Court, 1982 (No. 82-52).

have a genetic predisposition to one or another potential illness, and society may find excluding them or discouraging them from purchasing insurance too high a price to pay for more accurate underwriting. On the other hand, insurers are concerned that people with knowledge of their genetic predisposition to disease may engage in adverse selection.

Using a person's credit history to underwrite insurance, or **credit scoring**, is another area of controversy. Evidence suggests that people with a bad credit history also produce more losses for homeowners or automobile insurance and therefore should pay higher insurance premiums. However, critics argue that using credit scores tends to raise insurance costs for low-income and minority people more than for other groups, prompting a call to ban the use of credit scores in insurance pricing. Although subsequent research (e.g., FTC 2007) was generally unable to substantiate these criticisms, a few states now restrict the use of such scores.

The considerations described above have great bearing on insurability and the pricing of insurance. An equally important factor in making affordable insurance available to the public is the existence of a healthy and responsive insurance industry. A variety of insurers do business in the United States, as described below.

TYPES OF INSURANCE COMPANIES

Several types of insurers provide insurance to policyholders in the United States. While a clear majority of policyholders buy insurance from either stock insurance companies or mutual insurance companies, other types of insurers include Lloyd's of London and reciprocal exchanges. One feature that differentiates these types of providers from one another is their ownership structure, which influences several aspects of insurer operations, including the objectives of the insurer, who receives the profits and suffers the losses from insurance operations, and how the insurer is managed.

Stock Insurance Companies

A **stock insurance company** is similar to most other large corporations in that stockholder-owners provide the capital to establish and operate the corporation through the purchase of stock issued by the insurer. The shares of most publicly owned stock insurers are traded on the New York Stock Exchange (NYSE) or on the NASDAQ stock exchange. As the owners of the stock insurer, stockholders are entitled to the profits of the firm, but only after all other parties who have contractual relations with the firm (for example, policyholders, employees, taxing authorities) have been satisfied. On the other hand, if the insurer suffers significant losses, a stockholder's loss is limited to the amount invested in the stock of the troubled insurer. Stockholders also may sell their shares (their ownership interest) in the company if they choose to do so. By exercising their right to vote, they elect the directors of the firm, who in turn hire the management of the insurer.

Mutual Insurance Companies

Mutual insurance companies are nonprofit corporations whose owners are the policyholders insured by the corporation.[6] These policyholders have rights similar to those of owners of for-profit corporations. For example, they can vote to elect the directors

---

[6] The Web site of the National Association of Mutual Insurance Companies (NAMIC), a trade association of mutual property insurance companies, is (*http://www.namic.org/*). This site contains information about recent insurance legislation and other areas of interest to mutual insurance companies and their insureds.

of the corporation, who then appoint the management of the firm. Policyholders also can vote on important business matters, such as making changes in the corporation's bylaws or other key strategic decisions.

One significant difference between stock and mutual insurance companies is that it is possible to own an interest in a stock company and not purchase insurance from it, or to be insured by the stock insurer and not have an ownership interest in it. Neither of these positions is possible in a mutual insurer, in which the policyholder is both customer and owner.

A second difference is that mutual insurers have less access to sources of financial capital than stock insurers. Stock insurers can raise capital to finance their operations through the sale of stock, while mutual insurers cannot. Mutual insurers are thus more reliant than stock insurers upon retained earnings generated from profitable insurance operations as a source of capital.

While mutual insurance companies legally are nonprofit corporations, this does not mean they are run inefficiently. Quite the contrary—many operate as efficiently as any for-profit company. Like all other companies, mutual insurers vary considerably in performance.

Based on the manner in which they set premiums, mutual insurers can be classified as either advance premium or assessment mutual insurers. In an **advance premium mutual**, policyholders pay their premiums when their insurance begins and become eligible for a dividend when the insurance period ends. Mutual insurance companies pay dividends only when they experience fewer losses or lower expenses than predicted or have greater investment earnings than projected. If their policyholders incur unexpectedly large amounts of insured losses or the value of the insurer's investments falls dramatically, the insured-owner's dividends will decrease. In this sense, when individuals or businesses purchase insurance from a mutual insurance company, they become owners and share in the financial outcome of ownership, whether favorable or unfavorable. However, advance premium mutual insurance companies cannot require their policyholders to cover unmet claims.

For most mutual life insurance companies, favorable operating results are the norm, fortunately. As a rule, a built-in dividend arises because the annual premium is higher than needed to pay all expected losses and expenses. When, as anticipated, fewer losses occur than were predicted, the policyholder receives a dividend. Unlike dividends from profit-making corporations, this dividend does not represent new income to the policyholder; rather, it represents the return of part of the premium. In this sense, the initial premium from a mutual company has a safety factor that can be returned to the policyholder if nothing unexpected occurs during the year. The Internal Revenue Service (IRS) calls the dividends paid by mutual insurance companies a return of premium, and they are not subject to federal income tax.

Assessment mutuals provide primarily fire and windstorm insurance for farmers and small towns. As a result, they account for a much smaller amount of premium volume than advance premium mutuals. Under the assessment system, insured members may or may not pay a premium when the insurance period begins, but they become liable to pay their fair share of the insurance company's losses and expenses when the period ends. An insured's liability in an assessment mutual may or may not be limited, and potential purchasers should determine their maximum liability before purchasing insurance.

Demutualization occurs when a mutual insurer changes its legal form to a stock company. While demutualization activity has occurred sporadically in the United States for decades, one of the prime reasons for making this switch in recent years was the passage of the Gramm-Leach-Bliley Act of 1999 (GLB), which allowed commercial banks and investment banks to compete in insurance markets. Facing increased competition after the Act was passed, a number of mutual insurers converted to a stock insurer ownership structure, in part because stock insurers have more flexible capital structures than mutual insurers. While a stock company can raise capital by selling common or preferred stock, a mutual company cannot. Lack of flexibility in raising funds can prove to be a problem if a mutual company needs large amounts of funds to arrange mergers or acquisitions or to offset bad investment results. As a result, many of the largest mutual life insurance companies demutualized around the time that GLB was passed.

Other Types of Insurers

LLOYD'S OF LONDON

Lloyd's of London is not an insurance company; it is a large insurance marketplace. Historically, it has been one of the world's most important markets for insurance and today, it is a leading supplier of marine insurance, aviation insurance, and reinsurance. Started in 1688 in a coffeehouse operated by Edward Lloyd, Lloyd's of London is a meetingplace where sellers of insurance, called *syndicates*, deal with customers hoping to buy insurance. Each syndicate is operated by a syndicate manager, who represents a collection of Lloyd's members.

Until the early 1990s, membership in the Lloyd's society was limited exclusively to wealthy individuals who were referred to as *names*. The names participated in Lloyd's with unlimited liability, meaning that they were personally responsible for the claims that they insured. After suffering severe losses during the late 1980s and early 1990s, the syndicates modified the requirements for membership so that today, both individuals and corporations can be members of Lloyd's, and both have only limited liability for the obligations to their policyholders.

Each syndicate is a separate legal entity that accepts loss exposures for its own account. The General Insurance Standards Council of Lloyd's provides internal government for the syndicates, but each is relatively free to accept, reject, and price its own exposures. Lloyd's provides internal control through an annual audit of each member. All premiums initially are placed in a premium trust fund, from which claims and expenses are paid. After three years, the syndicate members receive their profits from the fund or are forced to meet assessments if resources are inadequate.

Lloyd's of London is perhaps best known to the public as a source for unique and specialized insurance products, as detailed in Insight Box 7-2.

THE RECIPROCAL EXCHANGE

One definition of the word *reciprocal* is "mutual." In a **reciprocal exchange**, each insured insures every other insured and in turn is insured by every other member of the exchange. A reciprocal exchange, thus, is like a mutual insurance company because the policyholders insure each other on a nonprofit basis. The difference is that a reciprocal exchange is unincorporated.

An **attorney-in-fact** manages a reciprocal exchange. This person is responsible to the policyholders for providing all the administrative services needed to operate the organization. While a reciprocal exchange is a nonprofit organization, the manager is paid for providing the services. Thus, he or she has an incentive to see the operations of the exchange grow and prosper. In practice, because reciprocals insurers tend to sell only one or a few types of insurance products, they do not provide a large proportion of the total insurance written in the United States.

INSIGHT BOX 7-2

Lloyd's of London: Insurer of the Stars

In contrast to its conservative British roots, Lloyd's of London has a colorful history of insuring many unique types of loss exposures. In particular, entertainers and athletes have purchased insurance through Lloyd's of London for a variety of risks. Here is a sampling:

- Troy Polamalu, the all-pro football player for the Pittsburgh Steelers, insured his hair for $1 million in 2010.

- Supermodel Heidi Klum insured her legs for $2 million while serving as a spokeswoman for the shaving products division of Braun, the German electronics company.

- Irish folk dancer Michael Flatley insured his legs for $39 million.

- Singer and musician Bruce Springsteen bought $6 million of coverage on his voice.

- Soccer star David Beckham insured his legs for $195 million in 2006.

Celebrity insurance is not purchased solely for publicity. "We are providing business interruption insurance for service industries," said Jonathan Thomas, active underwriter for Syndicate 1607 with Creechurch International Underwriters. Celebrity insurance takes one of two forms. "Genuine protection policies generally protect against lost money in the event a celebrity becomes disabled, thus forcing a show or event to be shut down or delayed." The second coverage "includes a modest true risk transfer, [but its] main purpose is public relations." The second type may also "include some disfigurement coverages."

Based on Maria Sciullo, "Eat Your Heart Out, Samson: Troy's Hair Worth $1 Million," *Pittsburgh Post Gazette*, September 1, 2010; Lori Chordas, "Body Guards," *Best Review*, March 2005, pp. 88–89; and "The Ultimate Risky Business: How Lloyd's of London Insures Its Own Future," *Knowledge at Wharton*, November 24, 2009, retrieved May 10, 2011 at http://knowledge.wharton.upenn.edu.

FRATERNAL INSURERS

Fraternal beneficiary societies, which are nonprofit groups organized around a common bond (such as religions or community service) to aid and benefit their members, provide their members with life and health insurance protection. Because of their service to their members and their community, these societies often are exempt from federal income taxes. Fraternal insurer make up a small proportion of the total life insurance owned by the U.S. public, accounting for around 1 percent of the direct premiums written in the life-health insurance industry.

SAVINGS BANK LIFE INSURANCE

Through most of the 1900s, federal banking laws prohibited banks from competing in other financial service industries, such as the insurance industry. For many years, however, state-chartered savings banks have been permitted to sell savings bank life insurance (SBLI) in a handful of East Coast states. Especially popular in Massachusetts and surrounding states, SBLI is noteworthy in that it was one of the first types of life insurance to be sold successfully by a noninsurance entity.

MARKET SHARE TRENDS ACROSS TYPES OF INSURERS

The differences in ownership structure among different types of insurers help to explain how the markets for many insurance products have developed historically. Many policyholder-owned insurers like mutual insurers and reciprocals were born when key groups of customers—such as farmers, military personnel, and factories that invested heavily in loss control—created their own insurance companies because they felt their low levels of risk deserved less costly premiums. Thus, many policyholder-owned insurers were formed not as investment opportunities for their customers, but instead as an arrangement to assure that their policyholders could buy essential insurance products at reasonable prices.

Most policyholder-owned insurers operating in the United States today were formed decades or even centuries ago, when large portions of the country's insurance industry were in their infancy. Since that time, the insurance industry has grown into a mature and competitive industry that is better able to satisfy its consumers' insurance needs. Financial markets also have grown during that time, making it easier to form new insurers and enabling existing insurers to better access additional capital as needed. As a result of these two factors, stock insurers have become the predominant type of private insurance organization in the United States today.

The data shown in Figure 7-1 and Figure 7-2 reflect the premium revenue received by different types of insurers in the U.S. life-health and property-liability insurance industries in 1998, a year before the passage of GLB, and 2008. Stock and mutual insurers are clearly the leading types of insurers over that time. In the property-liability insurance industry, stock insurers, mutual insurers, and reciprocal exchanges have maintained fairly consistent market shares from 1998 to 2008. During that same time period, however, the market share of stock insurers has increased dramatically in the life-health insurance industry, as many of the largest mutual insurers demutualized in the early 2000s. Thus, the portion of the market insured by stock insurers increased from 65 percent in 1998 to 84 percent in 2008 because numerous large mutual insurers converted to stock insurers over that time.

Much of this chapter has focused on the characteristics of insurable risks and the operation of the insurance risk pools, but it has not addressed the activities required to carry out these operations. In the next chapter, we describe the variety of insurance functions necessary to administer the insurance mechanism.

FIGURE 7-1 Net Premiums Written (in $ Billions) by Type of Life-Health (L-H) Insurer

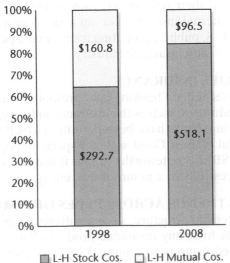

FIGURE 7-2 Net Premiums Written (in $ Billions) by Type of Property-Liability (P-L) Insurer

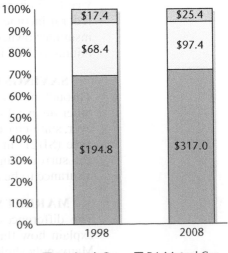

Based on Premium data obtained from Best's Aggregates and Averages, Property-Liability Editions, 1999 and 2009 and Best's Aggregates and Averages, Life-Health Editions, 1999 and 2009.

Summary

An insurance system works best when the following four criteria are met: (1) A large number of similar items in the insurance pool are exposed to the same peril; (2) the losses insured against are accidental; (3) the losses are definite once they occur and of sufficient severity to cause economic hardship; and (4) a low potential for catastrophic losses exists, especially ones likely to occur in a limited geographic area.

Exposures to catastrophic losses in a limited geographic area cannot be insured privately because when only those parties most exposed to loss want coverage, the insurance system breaks down. The premium becomes unacceptably high, and the large numbers needed for predictability are not present. High premiums also can result when applicants have better information about the risk levels than their insurers because they may be able to engage in adverse selection to buy insurance at prices below those commensurate with their risk levels.

Subsidization in an insurance pool results when the better risks pay more than their fair share to compensate for losses while the poorer risks pay too little. Competition among insurers helps to minimize subsidization as rival insurers offer lower prices to policyholders who are paying too much for insurance.

Legally, an insurance organization may take several different forms. It may incorporate as a stock or a mutual insurance company, or it may be unincorporated as a reciprocal exchange. The insureds may be the owners, as they are in the mutual insurance company. The owners need not buy insurance from the company they own, as is the case in a stock insurance company. Regardless of the form of legal organization, the function of any insurance system is to redistribute the costs of the losses from the few insureds that experience them to all who are exposed to them.

Review

1. Which of the following exposures to loss would be a likely basis for an insurance system? Explain why the exposures would or would not qualify as a basis for insurance.
   a. The potential loss of domestic pets
   b. The potential loss of farm animals
   c. The potential loss of a person's memory
   d. The theft of a college student's textbooks
   e. The loss of a valuable stamp collection
   f. The possible rainout of a baseball game
2. What is the definition of a catastrophic loss?
3. Why are certain crime losses, such as the theft of furs and jewelry, a more difficult exposure to insure than fire loss? (Refer to ideal insurance transactions.)
4. What difficulties would be present in combining a group of men and women of the same age in the same life insurance pool?
5. What would happen to an insurance system in which the insureds were indifferent to the occurrence of losses?
6. Why are floods and earthquakes difficult to insure in a privately operated insurance system?
7. What is adverse selection? How do insurers try to prevent adverse selection?
8. Explain the statement that adverse selection causes subsidization.
9. Explain the four major principles of risk classification.
10. What is meant by incentive value in a risk classification scheme?
11. Why is it difficult for insurers to satisfy the social acceptability of risk classification criteria?
12. Explain why the legal organization of an insurance system is important to the consumer.
13. Describe the differences between stock insurers, mutual insurers, and reciprocal exchanges.
14. Why are the dividends on mutual insurance company policies not subject to the federal income tax, while dividends paid by stock insurers to their owners are subject to the tax?
15. How does an advance premium mutual insurer differ from an assessment mutual?

Objective Questions

1. The criteria for ideally insurable losses include all the following except:
   a. definite losses
   b. accidental losses
   c. a small carefully defined group of exposures
   d. low probability of catastrophic loss

2. One reason that floods have not been insured in the United States is:
   a. The damage is easily retained by most building owners, so they do not buy insurance.
   b. The federal government wants to discourage people from living in flood plains and thus has invalidated all flood insurance coverage.
   c. Private insurers cannot attract a broad risk group because people living in areas not prone to flooding are unlikely to want to buy protection.
   d. Insurance companies do not know how to define the peril of flood.

3. According to _____, insurance should be bought only when losses are significant and uncertain:
   a. the central limit theorem
   b. the rule of adverse selection
   c. the law of large numbers
   d. the large-loss principle

4. Which of the following perils is not privately insurable because of its catastrophic loss potential?
   a. termite damage
   b. theft
   c. arson
   d. nuclear contamination

5. Insurers cannot use credit scores as a risk classification variable in several U.S. states because their use does not satisfy which of the requirements of risk classification variables?
   a. separation and homogeneity
   b. reliability
   c. incentive value
   d. social acceptability

6. If only those most exposed to loss try to buy insurance, the insurance pool will fail because:
   a. Insurance agents will not sell the coverage.
   b. The coverage will be too cheap for insurance companies to make money.

   c. The premiums are likely to be more than most people could afford—perhaps even greater than the cost of the losses.
   d. The potential for fraudulent losses will undermine the insurance underwriting.

7. Incentive value in a risk classification scheme means:
   a. Insureds have a financial incentive to prevent losses.
   b. Insurers have a financial incentive to find a better class of insureds.
   c. Agents have an incentive to sell more insurance.
   d. Insureds have an incentive to purchase the cheapest insurance.

8. Stock insurance companies have all the following characteristics except:
   a. ownership by people who are not necessarily insureds of the company
   b. management elected by owners
   c. all profits and losses from insurance operations passed on to the insureds
   d. being incorporated

9. The largest and most frequently found form of mutual company is the _____ mutual:
   a. assessment
   b. reciprocal
   c. perpetual
   d. advance premium

10. Lloyd's of London is a very important source of what type of insurance coverage?
    a. fire
    b. marine
    c. life
    d. war

11. The reciprocal exchange is managed by a(n):
    a. attorney-in-fact
    b. broker
    c. syndicate manager
    d. director of insurance

Discussion Questions

1. List some examples of exceptions that you have heard of or read about to the guidelines set forth for ideal insurance exposures. Do these exceptions have any features in common?

2. Explain why the answer to the question "What is an insurable event?" may change over time.

3. If you were to begin a bicycle insurance company to insure all the bikes in the United States, what form of organization would you choose? Explain your answer.

Selected References

Actuarial Standard Board, Actuarial Standard of Practice Number 12, "Risk Classification (for All Practice Areas)," December 2005, Doc. Number 101.

Best's Aggregates and Averages, Life-Health Edition, 1999 and 2009 (Oldwick, NJ: A. M. Best Company).

Best's Aggregates and Averages, Property-Liability Edition, 1999 and 2009 (Oldwick, NJ: A. M. Best Company).

Federal Trade Commission. "Credit-Based Insurance Scores: Impacts on Consumers of Automobile Insurance," July 2007.

General Accountability Office, "Catastrophe Risk: U.S. and European Approaches to Insure Natural Catastrophe and Terrorism Risks (GAO-05-199, February 2005).

The I. I. I. Insurance Factbook, 2011 (New York: Insurance Information Institute).

Myhr, A. E., and J. J. Markham, 2004, *Insurance Operations, Regulation, and Statutory Accounting*, 2nd ed. (Malvern, PA: American Institute for Property Casualty Underwriters/Insurance Institute of America).

8

Insurance Functions

After studying this chapter, you should be able to

- Describe the differences between insurance agents and brokers

- Describe how direct marketing and e-commerce has affected traditional insurance marketing

- Identify a loss adjuster's responsibilities

- Explain the insurance underwriter's functions

- Describe the activities carried out by insurance actuaries

- Describe the role of traditional business functions like finance and accounting in insurance

- Describe the reinsurance function and explain why insurers use reinsurance

In the preceding chapter, we described several types of insurers, all of which need the services of many different professionals. In this chapter, we examine the internal functions of insurance companies and what they contribute to the overall operations of the insurance company.

Many of the functions described in this chapter are also potential career opportunities. Insurers and reinsurers routinely are hiring for entry-level positions in actuarial science, underwriting, marketing, information technology, and claims administration. The insurance industry employs well over 2 million workers in the United States.

INSURANCE AGENTS AND BROKERS

Insurers have traditionally relied upon a marketing system that uses salespeople to contact consumers, and most consumers buy insurance using an insurance agent or broker. These marketing intermediaries perform an essential service to their customers, providing advice and expertise about the fields of insurance and financial services. This section describes the differences between agents and brokers, as well as their legal role as intermediaries in insurance transactions.

Agency Law

A deeper understanding of the occupation of insurance agent begins with an understanding of agency law.[1] An **agent** is a person authorized to act for another person. The agent may create, perform, or terminate a contract for another person. The person on whose behalf the agent acts is the **principal**. By law, the agent's acts become the acts of the principal. Any person who legally can enter a contract can appoint an agent. By law, an insurance company, like other companies, is considered a person. Generally, the insurance company is the principal employing or contracting with the insurance agent.

The law defines several duties that agents owe their principals. Among these are the duty of loyalty (agents must not further their own interest at their principal's expense), the duty of care (that is, the duty not to be negligent), and the duty to obey instructions. If the agent has an interest in matters that are adverse to the principal's interest, the agent must inform the principal. An agent cannot serve two principals having adverse interests unless both principals consent. The agent has the duty to inform the principal of all relevant information and to keep a proper account of all money or other assets. The agent has a duty of reasonable care, meaning the agent should not attempt to do business he or she cannot perform properly. The principal has the duty of paying for the agent's services and honoring all other agreed-on commitments to the agent.

An **agency contract** between the insurance agent and the insurance company establishes the rights and duties of each party. Through the agency contract or agreement, agents receive **actual authority** from their principals. The written appointment of an agent is an example of **express authority**, which in this case provides details of the agent's duties and responsibilities. **Incidental authority** to do things normally required to accomplish the specified acts accompanies express authority. That is, the express authority identifies specific acts that an agent may do; incidental authority covers all the details necessary to accomplish the agent's work, which are too numerous to itemize in an agency contract.

Some insurance agents have only the authority to solicit business for their principal, the insurance company. Others can bind their principal to insurance contracts. **Binding authority** refers to the ability of an agent to create a valid and binding insurance contract on behalf of his or her insurer. With this power, agents can start insurance contracts locally before submitting them for home-office approval. Insurance companies call agents whose authority is limited to the solicitation of business *special* or *soliciting agents*. Agents with the authority to bind their principals to contracts are called *general agents*. This term is especially common in property insurance, where agents with binding authority are the norm.

So long as the agent acts within the scope of the express authority, the principal is bound by the agent's actions. If agents go beyond the scope of their authority, substantial legal issues may arise. To protect themselves from the legal judgments related to these issues, insurance agents need to purchase errors and omissions liability insurance. This coverage, sometimes called *professional liability insurance*, provides payment if a third party is injured by the insurance agent's mistakes. Not only does this insurance pay legal judgments against negligent insurance agents, but the insurer also provides funds for the agent's legal defense, even if the lawsuit is groundless.

---

[1] See Douglas R. Richmond, "Insurance Agent and Broker Liability," *Tort Trial and Insurance Practice Law Journal* (Fall 2004, pp. 1–58) for a comprehensive discussion of many of the issues summarized in this section.

Insurance Brokers

An insurance **broker** is a legal representative of the insurance consumer with the limited authority to find an insurance company willing to accept an applicant's application for insurance. The insurance applicant hires the broker and is the principal, while the broker acts legally as an agent for the applicant. The insurance broker's function is similar to that of the real estate broker who is hired to find a buyer for a client's house. That is, the broker helps to bring two parties together to complete a transaction. Many brokers are also licensed as insurance agents.

Insurance brokers are used most commonly in commercial insurance. Businesses often have unique property or liability exposures or require insurance contracts written to their specifications. A broker can help write the specifications for the insurance or even assemble the insurance program and then find an insurer willing to provide the coverage. Businesses also employ brokers when designing their employee benefit plans, such as their group life and health insurance.

Most individual needs for insurance can be met with standard coverage and do not require a broker's service. However, people with poor driving records, substandard health, or other high-risk characteristics may need a broker to find an insurer willing to accept the exposure. Because brokers shop for insurance on a daily basis, they have information about pricing and coverage availability that is unknown to businesses and individuals who shop for insurance only annually.

The broker earns a commission, a percentage of the premium the insurer charges the principal (the insured). This compensation practice can result in a conflict of interest for the broker; the broker receives a bigger commission from a larger premium, but the broker's client incurs higher costs. To avoid such conflicts of interest, fee-based compensation for brokers has grown more common in recent years. Many brokers also offer a variety of other services on a flat-fee basis, including expertise in loss control and the management of self-insurance programs.[2]

Licensing Requirements

All states have laws requiring people who sell insurance to have a license to engage in this activity. By requiring a license, the state can help protect the public from uneducated, incompetent, and unscrupulous people. Licensed agents typically are required to be at least eighteen years old, to have no felony convictions, and to pass an examination demonstrating knowledge of the industry. Generally, states require people to participate in classroom instruction before taking the required insurance examination. Many states require agents to participate in continuing education classes to maintain their licenses after passing the licensing exams.

In addition to the state insurance license, life insurance agents selling variable annuities or variable life insurance — products that have significant investment characteristics — must qualify for a federal security dealer's license. To get a security dealer's license,

---

[2] In the fall of 2004, New York State attorney-general Eliot Spitzer made some serious accusations of fraud and conflict of interest against some of the largest insurance brokers in the United States. The brokers were accused of bid rigging and of collecting substantial "contingent commissions." The bid-rigging charges arose from the practice of submitting fraudulent or "artificial" high bids that made the bid of the insurance company that the broker selected and recommended appear to be the best choice. The contingent commissions issue arose from the volume of business that the broker directed to particular insurers, thus violating their duty to their principal of not self-dealing at the buyer's expense. Volume-based commissions are found in other industries, but the size of these commissions and the fact that they were not transparent to the insurance applicants provided the basis of the legal complaint. Following the investigation and legal charges, many large insurance brokers announced that they would no longer accept contingent commissions. Several of the brokers also paid large fines to settle the legal complaints.

life insurance agents must pass one or more examinations administered by the National Association of Security Dealers (NASD). The large amount of knowledge and training needed to become eligible for both licenses better assures that sales personnel are qualified to advise clients properly.

Property and Liability Insurance Agents and Brokers

Because several important differences distinguish the duties of a life insurance agent from those of a property and liability insurance agent, we describe them separately.

Property and liability insurers traditionally have used two main marketing channels: the independent agency system and the direct writing system. **Direct writer** insurers use agents who represent only one insurer and thus are often called *exclusive agents* or *captive agents*.[3] These agents receive most if not all of their compensation in the form of commissions, calculated as a percentage of the premium charged for an insurance policy.

Independent agents are independent contractors who represent multiple different insurers. Thus, they may place a client's homeowners insurance with one company and auto insurance with another. Unlike the agents working for a direct writer, independent agents own the legal right to renew their clients' insurance business, a valuable intangible asset known as the *renewal* or *expiration rights*. If an independent agent's relationship with a particular insurer is severed, the agent retains the right to renew the affected business with a different insurer in his or her agency, thus maintaining his list of customers. This ownership right in the business affects the way that agents are compensated. Independent agents earn the same percentage commission on both the initial premium payment and subsequent renewal payments, while direct writer agents typically earn higher commissions on the initial premium payment than on renewal payments.

Life Insurance Agents and Brokers

AGENTS

The marketing of life insurance has been an area of continuous change for the past several decades. From before World War II through the 1970s, it was common for life insurance agents to make sales visits to clients' homes to arrange relatively large amounts of individual life insurance coverage. Today, this type of service is increasingly rare, especially for low- and lower-middle-income people. Now, many individuals who previously identified themselves as life insurance agents call themselves "professional financial planners." These financial planners believe that the new identification better reflects the fact that they can offer a wider range of services than a traditional life insurance agent.

The function of the life insurance agent most familiar to the public is to motivate people to apply for coverage. Although the property-liability agent can, and often does, have the legal authority to bind a principal to an insurance contract, the life insurance agent never has this authority. Why not? The insurer can cancel most property insurance contracts so long as it provides the policyholder with sufficient advance notice, but life insurance contracts cannot be canceled except for nonpayment of premiums. To minimize the chance that its agent may fraudulently or mistakenly create an erroneous policy that cannot be corrected, the power to bind the life insurance company remains with the home office.

---

[3] Experts make a technical distinction between exclusive agents and direct writing agents. *Exclusive agents* are not employees of the insurer; rather, they are independent contractors who agree to place all their business with one insurer. Direct writing agents are employees of one insurer.

BROKERS

The brokerage function operates in life insurance much as it does in property insurance. Like property brokers, life brokers evaluate the market for their clients and may deal with many different insurers. They may place their clients' life, disability, and annuity insurance business with three separate insurers.

Even traditional agents sometimes may act as a broker, for instance to find an insurer willing to accept the exposure for a client with impaired health or a hazardous job. If an applicant is turned down by the home office, then the soliciting agent may act as a broker for a client in poor health and try to find an alternate company willing to provide coverage.

An Insurance Agent's Duties

Many people assume that the sole duty of an insurance agent is to sell insurance. In fact, the role requires much more. A good insurance agent must be able to inform clients, motivate them to take a specified course of action, provide service before and after losses, and exercise judgment in selecting clients for the insurance company.

Providing consumers with service and information is at the heart of the agent's job. Explaining the features of the coverage provided in the insurance contract, which can be complex and difficult to understand, is one of the agent's most important functions. A good agent also must provide information about related areas. For instance, the life insurance agent must know about and be able to explain certain aspects of the federal income tax and the unified transfer (gift and estate) tax laws. He or she also must be familiar with Social Security and other government benefits. The property insurance agent must be intimately familiar with losses that are and are not covered under insurance policies. He or she also must be familiar with certain aspects of real estate law and very familiar with property values. Again, providing consumers with factual information that they can understand is an important job function.

Motivating consumers is often more of a challenge for the life insurance agent than the property insurance agent. Most U.S. consumers have little choice about buying automobile insurance because it is required by law. Mortgage providers similarly require their mortgage holders to buy homeowners insurance as a condition for lending. On the other hand, many consumers are less aware of the need for adequate life insurance, and the purchase is not usually required by law or by lenders. Thus, the agent must demonstrate to prospective consumers the financial loss that a family would suffer in case of premature death and motivate them to protect their families.

Insurance agents must use judgment in submitting applications to their companies. Insurers call this process *field underwriting*. The agent must be familiar with a company's requirements for acceptable applications. If substandard risks (for example, people who are obese or drivers with three recent accidents) are unacceptable to the insurer, the agent must not submit such applications. Nor should the agent submit applications after detecting the presence of moral hazard.

The insurance agent should give clients continuous service. Before losses have occurred, the property agent must provide information to clients and see that their coverage is complete and accurately reflects the value of the covered property or potential liability. After a loss, a client's needs are usually greater, and the agent again must provide information and counsel. Births, changes in financial markets, new debts, divorce, the accumulation of a sizable estate, changes in Social Security laws, and many other factors change customers' needs for life insurance. The life insurance agent should provide clients with a regular review of their insurance needs and compare it to the amount of insurance they own.

Aside from this rather long list of duties, there is something an agent must *not* do: practice law. To prevent unqualified people from advising the public, states have made it a crime for any person other than a licensed attorney to give legal advice. This crime is called the *unauthorized practice of law*. Life insurance agents must be familiar with this rule, especially if they sell insurance for estate planning purposes. It would thus be permissible for an agent to explain to a client the benefits of having a valid will or the tax benefits to be gained from using a life insurance trust. But it would be a crime for the agent to draft either the will or the trust for the client, or to offer legal advice on the effect of recent court rulings on a client's existing documents.

Insurance Direct Marketing

In some lines of insurance, the traditional insurance marketing model is losing market share to direct marketing efforts. **Direct marketing** includes mail and telephone solicitations, solicitations aimed at affinity groups (such as all the employees of a company, or university alumni groups), or Internet solicitations. For example, in automobile insurance, it is estimated that direct marketing accounted for about 30 percent of the policies sold. Term life insurance, a type of life insurance that provides short-term protection for a limited period of time (for example, five or ten years) also has been sold successfully using direct marketing techniques.

The term **e-commerce** describes the use of the Internet to automate insurance and other transactions. From an insurer's viewpoint, e-commerce allows cost-cutting efficiencies and direct contact with customers. From a consumer's viewpoint, it allows transactions to occur at a time and place of her choosing. Moreover, if providers pass savings along to consumers, e-commerce results in lower insurance costs. Because personal automobile insurance and term life insurance are frequently purchased and relatively simple, they have been the two most popular insurance products sold on the Internet. The Internet also lends itself to comparing prices, with price-conscious consumers of auto and term life insurance proving to not be especially brand-loyal.[4]

LOSS ADJUSTERS

After a loss, the insured must notify the insurance company. This notice represents a claim for payment. Before settling the claim, the insurer will conduct a claims investigation. Insurers call the person conducting the investigation a **loss adjuster**, a claims adjuster, or a claims auditor. Loss adjusting is most important in property insurance, where many losses are partial and where the extent of property damage is not always clear. Loss adjusting generally is not a problem in life insurance because insurers make no payment for partial losses and pay the full amount due after receiving proper notification of the insured's death. Life insurance companies do conduct investigations in cases involving death claims that arise shortly after policies are purchased. Life insurers also use loss adjusters to investigate some claims for accidental death benefits, disability income benefits, and health insurance benefits. Nevertheless, we devote this section of the chapter to property and liability claims adjusting.

The property adjuster investigates reported losses, determines whether the insurer is liable to pay the claim, or recommends that the insurer deny the claim if the facts suggest this is appropriate. Much of the loss adjuster's work is done outside the office, usually at the scene of the reported damage. In some cases, the adjuster needs only the fire marshal's report or the reports of police officials to complete an investigation. If the loss represents a substantial amount of money, the loss adjuster will form a personal opinion of the facts.

---

[4] A study investigated the quality of life insurance advice given on the Internet; the results were questionable. See Mark S. Dorfman and Saul W. Adelman, "An Analysis of the Quality of Internet Life Insurance Advice," *Risk Management and Insurance Review*, Vol. 5, No. 2 (Fall 2002).

One of the first questions the adjuster examines when a claim is filed is whether the insurance company is responsible for paying for the loss. In some cases, the claimant reports the loss to the wrong company or reports property as destroyed that is different from the property covered in the insurance policy. Occasionally, insureds make claims after policies expire or after the time for premium payment has elapsed. Adjusters also will reject claims when losses are caused by perils, such as floods, that are specifically excluded from coverage in the insured's policy. In some cases, the adjuster may determine that fraud by the insured is involved in the loss, in which case the insurance company never pays for the damage.

Once satisfied that the insurer should pay for the loss, the adjuster must determine the dollar amount of the damage. Often adjuster and insured can agree on the amount of the claim, but sometimes the insured thinks the amount of loss is greater than the adjuster finds reasonable. The adjuster, who evaluates claims daily, is typically more familiar with the value of property and does not have the insured's personal attachment to the destroyed property. Thus, a basis for an honest difference of opinion exists. If the insured and adjuster cannot agree on the amount of the claim, appraisal or arbitration provisions in property insurance policies provide for resolving disputes without court litigation. Insurers settle most valid claims without arbitration or suit, however, because most insurers expect their loss adjusters to settle claims fairly with no unnecessary reduction in payments for legitimate losses.

Because it would be impractical to keep an adjuster near the scene of every possible automobile accident or to send adjusters all over the country to investigate claims, insurance companies often use loss adjusters who are not their own employees. Instead, they hire the services of an **independent adjuster** or an independent **adjustment bureau**. When an Indiana insurance company must pay a claim for an accident in South Carolina, it hires an adjuster near the accident to complete the investigation.

Independent adjusters are agents of insurers. A **public adjuster** is an agent of the insured. Although most insureds do not feel the need to hire an adjuster, in cases of complicated losses, either commercial or personal, insureds may feel that a fairer settlement will be forthcoming if an adjuster is representing their interests. Public adjusters are often found in larger cities.

In some instances, particularly losses involving liability claims, insurers initially may not be sure if the insured's claim is covered. For example, the insured's policy may exclude losses arising from an insured's intentional acts that injure others. However, it may take a court trial to determine if a particular act was in fact intentional. In such complicated situations, insurers may assume the liability unconditionally, may deny the claim outright, or may pursue the claim but reserve the right to deny coverage at a later point when adequate information becomes available to make a correct decision. If an insurer decides to take the third route, it must give the insured adequate notice of the insurer's **reservation of rights** and carefully meet other legal formalities.

Letters informing the insured that the insurer is reserving certain rights are not denials of coverage. They represent notice from the insurer to the insured that the insurer is not certain that coverage exists, but that the insurer plans to proceed with the loss adjustment, and perhaps the legal defense, as if the coverage existed. The insurer also is putting the insured on notice that certain events may occur in the future that may cause the insurer to reevaluate its position.[5]

---

[5] Without notice that the insurer is reserving its rights, courts well might find that an insurer acted in bad faith if it began paying the cost of a legal defense but later ended those payments or even sought to recoup the expenses that it already paid. It also might be considered bad faith if the insurer did not inform the insured that, despite paying for a legal defense, it reserved the right not to satisfy a settlement or legal judgment. In many states, if a court finds that an insurer handled a claim in bad faith, it can increase the damage award assessed against the insurer.

UNDERWRITERS

One of the most challenging tasks in an insurance company is underwriting new business. An **underwriter** reviews applications for insurance and then either accepts them at an appropriate rate or rejects them. This person makes a decision based on criteria set by the insurer's management (such as no drivers insured with three previous accidents or no fire insurance offered to restaurants), and on his or her own personal experience and judgment. The underwriter must be a skillful judge of people. If an applicant has a history of behaving in ways that increase moral hazard, the underwriter probably will decline the insurance, no matter how sound the property or how healthy the person.

The goal of underwriting is to produce a pool of insureds, by categories, whose actual loss experience will closely approximate the expected loss experience of a given hypothetical pool of insureds. For example, assume that an underwriter is told that a pool of exposures with specified characteristics (say brick buildings located no more than five miles from a fire station) will produce a loss rate of 1 percent of the value of the insured property. The underwriter's objective should be to place in this pool only exposures whose characteristics match the specifications. If the underwriter does the job well, the loss ratio of the insureds accepted will approximate closely the expected 1 percent figure. Of course, in any given year, deviation from the expected loss ratio is likely. In the long run, however, if the underwriter performs well, the expected and actual results should be close. Putting applicants for insurance in the classification or pool that reflects the mathematically fair costs of their losses most closely is the essence of good underwriting.

The underwriter must be alert to the possibility of adverse selection (the tendency for individuals who are more likely to suffer a loss to try to buy their insurance at average rates that do not truly reflect the above-average cost of their exposure). Adverse selection is especially a concern to underwriters when applicants can conceal information about their increased probability of suffering a loss (such as withholding information about prior losses or engaging in hazardous activities) from the insurer. If undetected by the underwriter, these asymmetric information situations can result in reduced underwriting profitability. Recognizing that the possibility of adverse selection is always present, the underwriter must screen all applications for insurance carefully.

Contrary to some opinions, the underwriter is not supposed to reject so much business that the insurer experiences no losses. If the underwriter rejects all but the exceptionally safe exposures, much desirable business has been turned away. Insurance companies expect losses, and it is just as much an underwriting error to reject profitable business as it is to accept loss-prone business. Instead, the function of the underwriter is to accept applicants so that the losses paid by the insurance company closely match the losses that the company expected to pay. High-risk applicants are not necessarily uninsurable, but when insurers accept such applicants, they must charge a premium that reflects the insured's increased costs. To charge standard rates would mean asking the standard risks to subsidize the substandard risks, a practice that can result in the insurance company's collapse (as discussed in Chapter 7).

The underwriter's performance is judged primarily on the quality rather than the quantity of successful applications produced, whereas the agent is compensated based on quantity of production. Conflict between the two parties is more apparent than real, however. If the agent knows that a company will not accept a certain class of business, he or she should not submit such applications. Likewise, if the agent is aware of moral hazard, he or she should never submit that business. Ultimately, the agent knows that if he or she consistently submits applications that result in an above-average number of claims, the company will end the agency relationship.

Property Insurance Underwriting

Selecting insureds properly and charging them a fair price is the chief goal of underwriting. In underwriting and rating property for fire insurance, for example, the underwriter considers such factors as the type of construction (for example, brick or wood), the occupancy or use of the building (commercial or residential), the exposure to fires that may originate from surrounding properties, the fire protection provided by the community in which the property is located, and any safety features incorporated in the property, such as fire sprinklers or alarms.

A driver's age, the use to which a vehicle will be put, the driver's accident and moving violation record, and the driver's gender have all been used to determine the premium for an applicant when underwriting auto insurance. The application supplied by the potential insured provides a starting point for gathering underwriting information. Public records of traffic violations are also available. These data are verified by insurance employees and supplemented with third-party data from such sources as credit-rating agencies or data clearinghouses.

Life Insurance Underwriting

The primary factors determining an insured's life insurance premium are his or her age, gender, and health. To account for the first two factors, life insurers have developed *mortality tables*, statistical tables tabulated from large samples of previously insured policyholders, that can be used to forecast an insurance applicant's life expectancy given his or her age and gender. Based on the law of large numbers, a life insurance underwriter can assume that if a sufficiently large number of applicants in a given age and gender category are combined, the insurance pool will experience a death rate consistent with the figures shown in its mortality tables. Insurers usually use medical examiners to determine an applicant's health. The life insurance underwriter will also be interested in the insured's occupation, hobbies, total amount of life insurance owned, general financial condition, and any indications of a moral hazard. Like the property insurance underwriter, the life insurance underwriter must be alert to the possibility of adverse selection.

The **Medical Information Bureau,** or **MIB** (http://www.mib.com/), was formed in 1902 by physicians who were medical directors of several life insurance companies. The MIB provides a central location for storing information about life, health, and disability insurance applicants. The data is primarily medical, such as blood pressure and other test results, but it also includes data on bad driving records and dangerous hobbies. The information is in coded form, and the MIB protects its confidentiality. All member companies submit reports on their applications to the MIB, and all are able to request MIB reports to assist in the underwriting process. Consumers must authorize the MIB review in writing during the application process. They also have a right to request a review of their MIB file and make corrections if needed.

ACTUARIES

Actuaries are skilled professionals who apply their extensive training in mathematics and statistics to solving insurance problems. The insurance industry relies on actuaries to forecast the claim costs for different lines of insurance; and in turn, insurers use these forecasts when calculating the premiums for prospective customers when they apply for insurance. Actuaries make projections of the future based on historical results, probabilistic models, and their own judgment.

Insurers rely on actuaries to compile loss statistics, to develop insurance rates, to calculate dividends, and to evaluate the financial strength of the insurance company.

Actuaries develop rates by reviewing past statistics and projecting future results. The price of an insurance policy is set before the loss costs are known; it is the challenge of actuarial science to predict these costs.

Part of the challenge of the actuary's job is developing rates that are fair to all insureds. Brick houses are less prone to fire losses than wooden houses, so the two are charged different rates. Women aged twenty-one have lower mortality than do women aged sixty-five, so they pay different life insurance rates. As the actuary tries to draw finer and finer distinctions (for example, between drivers with three accidents versus four accidents, or between persons twenty-five pounds overweight and persons thirty-five pounds overweight), the challenge becomes greater. Remember that the law of large numbers relies on the numbers in question being sufficiently large. Thus, the actuary's task is to develop distinctions treating all members of the insurance pool fairly by ensuring that they are similar, while at the same time keeping the pool big enough to preserve the predictability of large numbers.

In addition to developing rates, insurance companies need actuaries to calculate and analyze operating results or profits, calculate dividends, and develop scientific loss reserves. All of these calculations require estimates of unknown factors.

Professional actuarial societies recognize the achievements of experienced actuaries who demonstrate their expertise in the discipline by passing a rigorous series of examinations. The Fellow of the Society of Actuaries (FSA) designation is earned by those working in the life–health insurance area (http://www.soa.org/). Actuaries working in the non–life insurance area pass the examinations leading to the Fellow of the Casualty Actuary Society (FCAS) designation (http://www.casact.org/). The exams are challenging; it can take an actuary several years to become a fellow. Many companies reward their actuaries for completion of these exams with promotions and extra compensation.[6]

OTHER OCCUPATIONS

So far, we have defined several functions that are unique to the insurance industries. Insurance also requires the skills of more traditional areas of business, but professionals in these disciplines must adapt their skills to fit the unique features of the insurance industry.

Attorneys represent the insurance company's interest in lawsuits against insureds, against other insurers, and against other parties claiming that the insurer's actions injured them or their interests. Attorneys assist in developing the wording of insurance policies and deal with regulatory bodies, explaining the company's viewpoint and arguing the company's position at regulatory hearings. Life insurers rely on a legal staff to assist agents in underwriting advanced cases involving estate planning and employee benefits and to advise on other company activities. No insurance company could operate without an attorney's services.

Financial managers carry out critical functions for insurers. For example, they prepare budgets and coordinate the company's cash inflows and outflows. Financial managers are also responsible for the investment of company funds, which can run into billions of dollars. Because of their very large cash flows, insurers require a staff of well-trained financial analysts to assist in making financial management decisions.

---

[6] There are ample employment opportunities for actuaries. Not only do insurance companies need actuaries, but so do regulating agencies and consulting companies working in the area of pension plans and other employee benefits. Readers interested in learning more about becoming an actuary should visit the following Web site: (http://www.beanactuary.org/).

The unique nature of the insurance industry requires *accounting* processes that are different from those in many other industries. Most of an insurer's liabilities consist of **loss reserves**, estimates of the claims owed to policyholders, and insurance accounting practices have been adapted to address the uncertainty associated with reserving. Insurance contracts, especially life insurance contracts, can have very long durations, and expensing the usual and substantial initial costs of selling the insurance over the life of the contract can complicate income recognition. The unique features of the insurance industry have thus necessitated the development of unique accounting rules known as Statutory Accounting Principles (SAP), which differ from the Generally Accepted Accounting Principles (GAAP) rules used in other industries.

Insurance company operations can encompass a diverse range of other activities as well. Property insurers need architects and engineers to evaluate the potential for loss in various factories, apartment buildings, and shopping malls. Life insurers need physicians to assist in evaluating applicants for insurance. Most insurers need people skilled in information systems to handle the large amounts of data generated by an insurance company's operations. Insurance companies also need administrative assistants, clerks, marketing personnel, and many other skilled people to carry on their operations.

REINSURANCE[7]

Reinsurance is a transaction in which one insurance company obtains insurance from another to protect itself against losses sustained under policies that it has issued. Both life and nonlife insurance companies engage in reinsurance transactions. The company that sells the insurance to the policyholder is called the **primary insurer** or **ceding company**. The company from which the primary insurer obtains reinsurance is the **reinsurer**. The reinsurer agrees to indemnify the primary insurer as specified in the reinsurance contract.

For example, assume that the Nevada Mutual Property Insurance Company sells a $225 million property insurance policy to Miseryloves Company and reinsures a part of this coverage with the Colorado Reinsurance Company. Nevada Mutual is the primary insurer (and also the ceding company), and Colorado Reinsurance is the reinsurer. If an insured loss occurs at Miseryloves Company, it reports the claim to the Nevada Company. The Nevada Company pays the claim and, assuming that the claim is sufficiently large, it in turn seeks payment from its reinsurer, Colorado Reinsurance. Figure 8-1 illustrates this relationship.

We call the two basic arrangements between primary companies and reinsurers *facultative* or *treaty* reinsurance. A **facultative reinsurance** arrangement occurs when a primary insurer makes a separate agreement each time that it needs reinsurance by entering the reinsurance market and negotiating the terms of the coverage and the premium that it will pay.

A **treaty reinsurance** arrangement, also called **automatic reinsurance**, sets up a standing relationship between a primary insurer and a reinsurer in which a portfolio of the primary insurer's exposures is covered by reinsurance, without specific arrangements for any particular exposure. The treaty between the parties is subject to (non) renewal, but while it is in force, the primary insurer is committed to cede, and the reinsurer is committed to accept, all the business covered by the treaty. Treaty reinsurance accounts for a majority of the risk that is reinsured globally.

---

[7] Information about reinsurance can be obtained at the Reinsurance Association of America Web site: (http://reinsurance.org/).

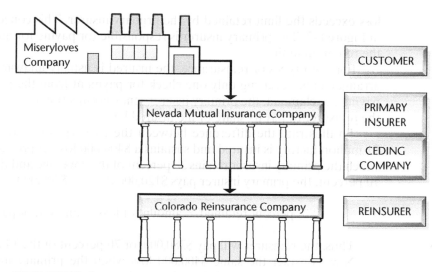

FIGURE 8-1 Reinsurance Arrangement

Reinsurance Coverages

Reinsurance coverages have some elaborate and strange-sounding names, such as *pro rata quota share treaty reinsurance* or *excess-of-loss per risk reinsurance*. Reduced to simple and understandable dimensions, however, there are two types of reinsurance arrangements: (1) proportional coverages, known as *pro rata reinsurance*; and (2) excess-of-loss coverage.

Pro rata reinsurance means that the primary insurer and the reinsurer proportionally divide the losses, premiums, and expenses. For example, the primary insurer may retain 40 percent of the coverage and cede the remaining 60 percent. Income and expenses are then pro-rated; that is, shared in the same proportions. This concept is illustrated in Figure 8-2.

In contrast to pro rata reinsurance, in which the reinsurer shares part of every loss, **excess-of-loss reinsurance** coverage commits the reinsurer to pay only when the

FIGURE 8-2 Reinsurance Coverages

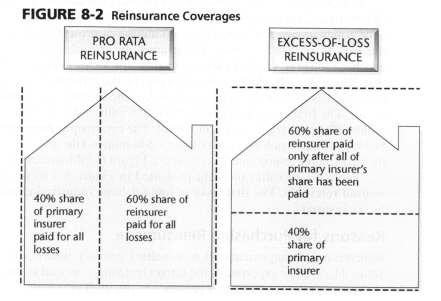

loss exceeds the limit retained by the primary insurer. This concept also is illustrated in Figure 8-2. The primary insurer is responsible for paying for all losses falling below the retention limit.

For both types of reinsurance, the insured is usually unaware of any reinsurance arrangements, receiving only one check for payment from the primary insurer. After paying the claimant, the primary insurer sends notification to the reinsurer, requesting the reinsurer to pay its share of the insured loss.

To illustrate the difference between the two types of coverage, assume that a $1 million factory is insured and sustains a $400,000 loss. If pro rata coverage exists in which the primary insurer retains 30 percent of the coverage and the reinsurer provides 70 percent, the primary insurer pays $120,000 (0.30 × $400,000 = $120,000, or

$$\text{percent retained} \times \text{amount of loss} = \text{amount of payment}$$

Thus, the reinsurer will pay $280,000, or 70 percent of the $400,000 loss.

Now consider the same $400,000 loss when the primary insurer has purchased excess-of-loss coverage, and the reinsurer has agreed to pay for all losses in excess of $300,000. (The loss retained by the primary company may be expressed either as a dollar amount or as a percentage of the exposure.) The primary insurer will pay $300,000, its retention limit. The reinsurer will pay $100,000 ($400,000 − $300,000, the excess of the loss beyond the amount retained by the primary insurer).

Both pro rata and excess-of-loss coverage can be arranged on a facultative or a treaty basis. Thus, we might describe a *pro rata facultative reinsurance arrangement* or a *pro rata treaty reinsurance arrangement*.

One type of excess-of-loss reinsurance arrangement deserves special attention. **Catastrophe reinsurance** is distinguished by very high retention limits for the primary carrier before the catastrophe reinsurer becomes liable. Catastrophe reinsurance also has very high upper limits on the reinsurance policy, with increments of coverage often expressed in the millions of dollars. For example, a policy might provide $10 million of coverage after a $5 million loss has been incurred and paid by the primary insurer or the insured. Part of the primary insurer's retention with respect to the catastrophe reinsurance frequently may be reinsured, creating layers of coverage.

For example, assume that a primary insurer provides $40 million of the $100 million of coverage required by an oil refinery, and buys a $100 million catastrophe reinsurance policy to cover the remaining $60 million of protection. The refinery self-insures the first $5 million of losses. The primary insurer also purchases reinsurance from another reinsurer, the first excess reinsurer, for losses in excess of $15 million and less than $40 million. If a $100 million loss occurs, the primary insurer will pay $10 million, calculated as the first $15 million of loss less the $5 million self-insured by the refinery owner. The first excess reinsurer will pay $25 million: $40 million (its upper limit) – $15 million (the primary insurer's retention). The catastrophe reinsurer pays the remaining $60 million: $100 million (size of loss) − $40 million (the amount of coverage provided by the primary insurer and its reinsurer). Figure 8-3 illustrates this result.

Table 8-1 modifies the data presented in Figure 8-3 to show the refinery's self-insured retention. The first layer of loss for large industrial exposures is often borne by the insured.

Reasons for Purchasing Reinsurance

Reinsurance arrangements allow (smaller) primary insurers to use the marketing, actuarial, or other expertise of the (larger) reinsurer, as well as the financial strength of the reinsurer, to enhance their presence in the market.

FIGURE 8-3 Layers of Insurance and Reinsurance Coverage

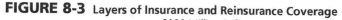
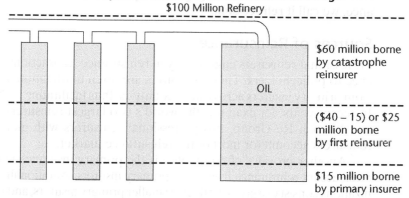

$100 Million Refinery

$60 million borne by catastrophe reinsurer

($40 – 15) or $25 million borne by first reinsurer

$15 million borne by primary insurer

TABLE 8-1 Layers of Coverage for $100 Million Refinery (Amounts in $ Millions)

Catastrophe (top) layer	60, excess of 40
First excess layer	25, excess of 15
Primary coverage	10, excess of 5
Self-insured retention	5, per occurrence

Reinsurance also enables the primary insurer to keep its exposures similar in size. After the primary insurer sets an internal retention limit, it retains all exposures up to that limit, reinsuring the amounts that exceed it. For example, a life insurer may retain a maximum of $100,000 of insurance on any one life. If it were to sell a policy in an amount greater than $100,000, it would reinsure the difference. Keeping its exposures similar in size means that no single loss can upset the insurer's loss predictions. Imagine what would happen to an insurer with 999 lives insured for $100,000 and the 1,000th life insured for $10 million. If the 1,000th life were the one lost, the insurer's predictions for loss payments would be inaccurate. In more formal terms, the variation in loss potential is greatly increased if greatly disproportional coverage is written on just a few lives. Thus, reinsurance allows for stability in operating results.

Another reason to reinsure is to reduce the size of potential loss, and therefore the size of the loss and unearned premium reserves the primary insurer needs to maintain. Limiting reserves is an important consideration for a small but growing insurer. Thus, reinsurance facilitates growth.

In property insurance, reinsurers pool risks across countries and even continents, thus facilitating geographic diversification of risk. If primary insurers in the United States were unable to spread their losses abroad, many domestic insurance companies might not be able to remain solvent if a catastrophic occurrence struck the United States.

Reinsurance also allows a primary insurer with limited surplus to accept larger exposures than it otherwise could. The ability to accept a wider range of exposures is a valuable service that a company can offer its insureds, and one that allows its agents to compete for more business. In this sense, reinsurance improves relationships between a company and its agents.

Reinsurance benefits consumers because the financial strength of the reinsurer bolsters the primary insurer. It also allows the primary insurer to predict operating results more accurately and manage growth more efficiently. The reinsurer in turn can profit from the insurance transaction without necessarily marketing a product to the public. Because reinsurance has proven to be such a workable idea, it is not surprising that reinsurers themselves engage in the practice. When a reinsurer purchases reinsurance, we call it **retrocession**.

Sources of Reinsurance

Professional reinsurers engage only in reinsurance transactions; they do not sell insurance to policyholders. These reinsurers are often multinational firms that assume risk from primary insurers across many countries, thus facilitating global risk diversification. In recent years, for example, the world's two largest reinsurers were Swiss Re Group and Munich Re Group, two professional reinsurers with global scope. Professional reinsurers account for most of the reinsurance market.

Another provider of reinsurance is the primary insurance market. Primary insurers often accept reinsurance from other primary insurers. Additionally, many insurance organizations consist of a group or fleet of smaller primary insurers, and reinsurance agreements between affiliated primary insurers in a fleet are common. A third source of reinsurance is self-insurance subsidiaries of noninsurance companies. In addition to providing insurance for the parent company, these companies also provide reinsurance facilities to other Finally, the Lloyd's of London is a fourth source of reinsurance coverage.

Summary

Insurance agents and brokers bring buyers and sellers of insurance together. The agent represents the insurance company. The broker represents the purchaser of insurance. Agency law governs the relations between agents and insurance companies, as well as brokers and consumers.

In property insurance, the two basic types of agent are those who are employees of direct writers and those who work as independent agents representing several different insurance companies. The life insurance agent most familiar to the public is known as the *special* or *soliciting agent*. The agent's assignment is to secure applications for insurance. Life insurance agents do not have the power to bind their company.

The duties of an insurance agent are much broader than merely selling insurance. A good agent provides clients with information and service both before and after a loss. The agent exercises judgment about which applications for insurance to submit to the insurer. The occupation of insurance agent has provided thousands of men and women with rewarding careers.

The loss adjuster's work begins once a claim for payment reaches the insurer. The adjuster must investigate the claim, report the findings to the insurer, and negotiate a fair settlement if the claim is approved. Many adjusters work for independent adjustment bureaus rather than directly for insurance companies.

Underwriters must select and rate applications for insurance. They must be constantly alert to the possibility of people who are more likely than average to experience a loss applying for insurance at standard rates. The results of such adverse selection are losses greater than the insurance company anticipated when rates were formulated. The result of good underwriting is to have the insurer's actual experience closely match the expected experience, not to keep the insurer from paying any claims at all.

The actuary is the insurance company's mathematician and statistician. Actuaries develop the pricing methods used in the various kinds of insurance that the company offers. The actuary's skills are needed to calculate the company's profits and the dividends that it pays. No insurance company could operate without the services of an actuary. Many other talents are needed to make an insurance company run. Attorneys, financiers, accountants, marketing personnel, and many other skilled professionals are required to allow the insurance operation to perform its crucial tasks.

Most insurance companies purchase reinsurance to limit their exposure to catastrophic loss and to stabilize their financial performance. Most of the risk ceded by primary insurers to reinsurers is reinsured through treaty reinsurance arrangements. Facultative reinsurance is used to reinsure more individualized exposures on a case-by-case basis. Reinsurers diversify risk on an international scale, assuming risk from primary insurers across the globe.

Review

1. What duties do principals owe their agents? What duties do agents owe their principals?
2. Explain the basis for conflict between the insurance agent and the home-office underwriter. In practice, why are such conflicts often not a problem?
3. Describe the differences between an insurance agent and an insurance broker. Are these differences important to the insurance consumer?
4. Why do life insurance agents and property insurance agents have different grants of authority?
5. Describe the differences between an independent agent and a direct writer.
6. Evaluate the success of direct marketing and e-commerce in insurance marketing.
7. What purpose does a "reservation of rights" letter serve?
8. Should a good job of loss adjusting always involve the claims adjuster negotiating the lowest possible dollar amount of claims settlement?
9. What incentive does the insurer have to settle claims fairly?
10. Why do insurance companies hire independent loss adjustment bureaus?
11. Why must the underwriter be concerned about adverse selection?
12. Describe the functions carried out by actuaries in most insurance companies.
13. What are the reasons that reinsurance is so widely purchased by insurers?
14. What is the difference between a facultative and a treaty reinsurance arrangement?
15. What does "25, excess of 15" mean in a reinsurance arrangement?
16. What type of exposures would encourage a life insurance company to purchase catastrophe reinsurance?

Objective Questions

1. The definition of agent is a person:
   a. Working for another person
   b. Authorized to act for another person
   c. Signing a contract for another person
   d. Substituted for a person's rights and duties
2. A broker is:
   a. The agent of the insured
   b. The agent of the insurance company
   c. Neither the agent of the insurance company nor the insured, but his or her own agent
   d. Never used in life insurance
3. Independent loss adjusters:
   a. Are technically agents of the insurance company whose loss they are adjusting
   b. Are technically agents of the insured
   c. Are neither agents of the company nor of the insured, but independent of both
   d. Are independent of the company, but only until the claim is settled
4. A fire insurance underwriter considers all of the following in setting prices EXCEPT:
   a. the materials used to build the structure
   b. the activities undertaken by the person or business using the building
   c. the quality of the fire protection services provided by the local government
   d. in fact, all of the above are considered
5. The responsibilities of the _____ function include calculating the value of insurer reserves and examining trends in insured loss data to forecast future premiums.
   a. underwriting
   b. actuarial
   c. marketing
   d. loss adjusting
6. Pro rata reinsurance occurs:
   a. If the reinsurance is automatic
   b. If the reinsurance must be negotiated each time it is purchased
   c. If the reinsurer pays only for losses in excess of the stated amount
   d. If the reinsurer and primary insurer share losses on a proportional basis
7. _____ is a transaction engaged in by two insurers who agree to share premiums and losses.
   a. Suretyship
   b. Reinsurance
   c. Bonding
   d. Primary insurance
8. Treaty reinsurance means:
   a. The primary insurer must cede business and the reinsurer must accept business during the period covered by the treaty.
   b. Each case of reinsurance requires separate negotiations.

c. The primary insurer and the reinsurer must sign the International Reinsurance treaty.

d. All losses must be settled by the terms of the U.S. pro rata treaty.

9. Assume an excess-of-loss reinsurance arrangement with the primary insurer retaining the first $10 million of loss, and the reinsurer providing $50 million of coverage. Assume that a $50 million covered loss occurs. Based on this data, which of the following statements is true?

a. The primary insurer and reinsurer each pays $25 million for the loss.

b. The primary insurer pays $40 million; the reinsurer pays $10 million.

c. The primary insurer pays $10 million; the reinsurer pays $40 million.

d. The primary insurer and reinsurer each pay $50 million, and the insured collects $100,000.

10. The insurance company purchasing insurance from the reinsurer is called:

a. The first insurer

b. The selling insurance company

c. The retrocessionaire

d. The ceding insurance company

Discussion Questions

1. What do you think would be the most difficult aspects of the job of a(n): life insurance agent, property-liability insurance agent, loss adjuster, actuary, and property insurance underwriter?

2. Explain why an insurer's obligation to pay may be an issue before the loss is adjusted, and why this leads to the insurer having to reserve its rights before the adjustment proceeds.

3. If you were a large business owning $10 million worth of property, would you want your primary insurer to buy reinsurance? If so, would you prefer to deal with a small primary insurer who reinsured your risk, or a large primary insurer who did not purchase reinsurance?

Selected References

The I. I. I. Insurance Factbook, 2011 (New York: Insurance Information Institute).

Myhr, Ann E., and James J. Markham, *Insurance Operations, Regulation, and Statutory Accounting*, 2nd ed., 2004 (Malvern, Pa.: American Institute for Chartered Property Casualty Underwriters).

9

Insurance Markets: Economics and Issues

After studying this chapter, you should be able to

- Describe the forces of supply and demand that affect the price of insurance

- Discuss whether insurance markets exhibit the characteristics of a competitive market

- Describe the methods used to assure that high-risk insurance applicants can obtain insurance

- Discuss the factors that limit a consumer's understanding of insurance

- Describe the decisions that consumers must make in the purchase of insurance

- Describe how the courts, the law, and the insurance commissioner provide consumer protection in the insurance market

This chapter examines the economic forces affecting insurance markets, providing a framework to better understand some common problems affecting insurance supply and demand. A **market** is a place where buyers and sellers transact business. While most markets involve only buyers and sellers, insurance markets often include a third party: insurance regulators. The sellers of insurance products are insurance companies and, more specifically, their agents and marketing representatives. Buyers of insurance include businesses and individuals, as nearly every adult American purchases one or more types of insurance. Insurance **regulators** include governmental officials who influence insurance transactions through our legislative, executive, and court systems.

Regulation affects insurance markets in different ways. For example, regulation affects insurers by setting the financial and legal requirements of new insurers, by monitoring the financial strength of insurers, and by setting in place the laws and standards that define appropriate competitive behavior in doing business with consumers. Regulation affects consumers, too. For example, legislation that mandates the purchase of insurance, often called **compulsory insurance laws**, requires drivers to buy auto liability insurance or employers to provide workers' compensation benefits to their employees. Regulators understand that if consumers are required to buy insurance, it may be necessary to take steps to better assure that such protection is readily *available* and that its price is *affordable*. In addition, regulation often is focused on protecting segments of the insurance-buying public, especially if those consumers are poorly informed about how to buy insurance wisely or if they are unable to make sound buying decisions because they lack vital information about the product.

To understand the insurance market and some of its problems better, we turn to the fundamental topic of the law of supply and demand. We will limit our discussion of the topic in this chapter to matters related to common imperfections in insurance markets.

SUPPLY AND DEMAND

Economic theory suggests that the most efficient distribution of society's scarce resources would occur if prices were set in a perfectly competitive market. In this context, *efficient* means that nobody's welfare could increase without decreasing the welfare of somebody else. In this perfectly competitive world, one equilibrium price prevails which satisfies both producers and consumers and maximizes welfare. This point is shown as price P1 and quantity Q1 in Figure 9-1. In the diagram, the demand curve slopes backward, indicating that consumers purchase less insurance as the price rises. Less insurance may be the result of lower quantity purchased, higher deductibles, or coverage of more limited perils. The supply curve (a short-run curve in this case) slopes forward, showing that insurers will provide more insurance as prices rise. If any other price except the equilibrium price, P1, were tried tentatively by producers or consumers, dynamic forces would set in, readjusting the price up or down to P1. A freely competitive market, for insurance or other goods, serves as a screening device. People who are most willing and able to pay get what is sold; and firms providing insurance at the least cost supply it.

If the market price were changed from that freely determined by the forces of supply and demand, the economic model predicts that lower total welfare would result. For example, if a monopoly existed or monopoly results were achieved by collusion among suppliers, the price would rise and the quantity demanded would decrease. This relationship is shown as price P2 and quantity Q2 in Figure 9-1. If transactions were made at price P2, consumers would be hurt in two ways. First, some consumers would purchase the good but they would have to pay the higher price. Paying a higher price reduces consumers' welfare. Second, some consumers who would have purchased the good at the freely set price will not make the purchase at the higher price. Because they could not purchase the good at the lower price, the forgone consumption reduces their welfare.

FIGURE 9-1 The Law of Supply and Demand

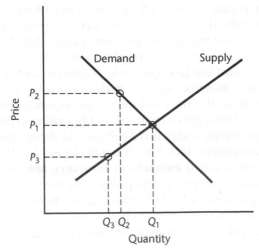

Alternatively, let's assume that the prevailing market price was lowered artificially from the freely determined price, perhaps by regulation. Then, just as in the preceding case, total welfare would be lowered. This point is shown in Figure 9-1 as price P3 and quantity Q3. Here, demand would increase but supply, especially in the long run, would decrease because firms will not supply as much of the good at the lower price. To make the argument clearer, assume that regulation lowered the price below the producers' costs. In the long run, producers would be bankrupt if they sold the product at that price. Even if prices were lowered from the free market price by a small amount, the sellers would attempt to cut back on services or other costs or move to more lucrative areas to maintain profits.

CONDITIONS FOR COMPETITIVE INSURANCE MARKETS

Many markets are not perfectly competitive, so they do not behave as described above. The conditions for a perfectly competitive market include the following characteristics. Provided with each condition is a brief discussion of its pertinence to the insurance industry.

A Large Number of Buyers and Sellers, Such That No Single Buyer or Seller Can Influence Price

This condition is satisfied in most insurance markets. Millions of firms and individuals buy insurance in the United States. There are also a large number of sellers. In 2009, 2737 property-liability (PL) insurers and 1106 life-health (LH) insurers operated in the United States. The four largest PL and LH insurers in 2009 held a combined market share of 27.4 percent and 35.2 percent, respectively, values that are comparable to those found in many other competitive industries.[1]

Freedom of Entry Into and Exit Out of the Market

In a competitive market, there are no barriers impeding new rivals from entering the marketplace to compete with existing competitors. This condition largely holds true for insurance markets. Existing insurers do not hold constrictive rights to their clients, nor are they so large that they are overwhelmingly more efficient than new rivals. While some regulatory requirements (such as holding minimum amounts of initial capital or meeting certain licensing standards) could possibly limit entry, new insurers have satisfied these standards in the past. On the other hand, while regulators have on occasion restricted an insurance company's ability to exit from a market to better ensure that its customers can find another insurer, such actions typically are temporary and generally uncommon.

Sellers Offer Identical and Perfectly Substitutable Products

In perfectly competitive markets, sellers are unable to differentiate their products from other rivals, and thus they cannot command higher prices for their unique goods and services. When evaluating insurance against this standard, some inconsistencies become evident. While many consumers may view insurance as a homogeneous commodity

---

[1] See *2011 Insurance Fact Book,* Insurance Information Institute, p. 24. Please note that the percentage of the market controlled by the four largest insurers often increases when the market is measured on a state basis instead of on a national basis. For additional discussion on measuring an industry's competitive structure with four-firm concentration ratios and other measures, see Chapter 6 of Viscusi, Harrington, and Evans (2005).

good, insurers focus considerable attention on differentiating their products from their competitors. Areas of differentiation include financial strength (as reflected in favorable financial ratings from rating agencies), well-trained agents and service personnel, or the tailoring of insurance protection to fit the unique needs of their customers.

Well-Informed Buyers and Sellers

Information problems sometimes limit competition in insurance markets. Insurance prices are not readily available to consumers, in part because the price depends on the personal risk characteristics of the insurance applicant. Moreover, because insurance pricing requires insurers to forecast the expected cost of losses, they frequently miscalculate their "cost of goods sold." Other pricing problems can be traced to asymmetric information, a condition in which insurers and policyholders do not possess equal information. Thus, moral hazard can result if insureds effectively conceal their intent to engage in behavior that increases the loss costs of their insurers. Adverse selection can result if risky applicants conceal their high-risk characteristics from insurers when applying for insurance (for more on this topic, see Chapter 7).

On balance, while some insurance markets are not textbook examples of competitive markets, most generally exhibit the characteristics of a competitive marketplace. Competition serves consumers well because it provides insurers incentives to keep premiums low and to develop insurance products continually that better satisfy the needs of their policyholders. Recognizing that competition is in the best interests of most insurance policyholders, insurance regulation capitalizes on this industry structure, taking steps to maintain competition among insurers.

ISSUES IN INSURANCE MARKETS: AVAILABILITY AND AFFORDABILITY

Although they generally rely on competition among insurers to maintain an adequate supply of insurance at affordable prices, regulators have been forced to intervene into the free market process periodically. A common trouble spot for insurance regulators is assuring that a sufficient supply of affordable insurance is available for high-risk insurance applicants. For example, the personal auto insurance market for high-risk drivers has been a problem for decades, and some inner-city markets have been unable to maintain an adequate supply of affordable property insurance since the mid-1960s.

High-risk insurance applicants often cannot afford to pay a premium that is sufficient to cover the high cost of the losses in their risk pools. In an effort to provide high-risk insurance consumers affordable insurance premiums, regulators occasionally have limited the premiums that insurers can charge for such customers. Not unexpectedly, the effects of such price regulation resulted in insurers offering a reduced supply of insurance for high-risk applicants, much as insurers will reduce the supply of insurance to Q3 in Figure 9-1 if prices are set at P3. Recognizing the limited effectiveness of such caps on premiums, many states have developed alternative approaches for dealing with the insurance availability issue, as discussed below.

Automobile Insurance

Drivers causing repeated accidents or those convicted of serious driving offenses at first will find their insurance premiums increasing at renewal. If their driving problems continue, they usually find it difficult to buy insurance in the *voluntary* market. That is, without government intervention, many private insurers will not offer insurance voluntarily to these high-risk drivers. The government chooses to intervene in the market because a lack of insurance will not keep the uninsured drivers off the road. Instead, many of these people will drive without insurance and injure more people, with the innocent victims unable to recover compensation for their injuries.

Currently, state governments typically require each insurer voluntarily selling auto insurance to the public to also accept a proportionate number of applications from the unwanted drivers. Therefore, if an insurer voluntarily writes 3 percent of the state's automobile insurance, it also will have to accept 3 percent of the bad drivers in that state. It can charge these drivers a higher rate for coverage, but even the higher rate may not cover the anticipated costs of providing the insurance. The state rules that force insurance companies to insure some percentage of bad drivers are known as **automobile insurance plans** or **assigned risk plans**. Another approach to providing insurance to these drivers is **joint underwriting associations (JUAs)**. In states where JUAs operate, the insurers agree to share the profits or losses of a pool of insurers providing insurance to this group. In all these cases, insurers—who presumably pass some of their costs forward—charge the involuntary market losses to the voluntary market.

Readers may wonder why insurers do not charge the appropriately high premium in the voluntary market. One explanation is that if they did so, many high-risk drivers would not or could not afford to buy insurance. Because many of these drivers will continue to drive without insurance, the cost of the accidents caused by these uninsured drivers likely would be borne by their victims. Thus, the state-mandated subsidy keeps the insurance for high-risk drivers more affordable.

Fair Access to Insurance Requirements (FAIR) Plans

Fair Access to Insurance Requirements (FAIR) plans are designed to deal with the problem of unavailability of property insurance in inner-city areas. FAIR plans have operated since 1968 and now are found in most states, the District of Columbia, and Puerto Rico.[2] There is some variation in rules and coverages offered among the states in the provisions of their respective FAIR plans, but the following characteristics generally apply. FAIR plans guarantee property owners an inspection of their property if they request it. If the property is insurable, an appropriate rate is charged. If the property is uninsurable, the owner must be given written notice of any improvements or loss-prevention measures required to make the property insurable. Once the property is insured, the property owner must maintain it in insurable condition to keep the insurance in force. Nevertheless, owners cannot be discriminated against individually because of factors over which they have no control, such as general neighborhood deterioration.

FAIR plans have been controversial since their beginning, and the success or failure of FAIR plans is hard to measure. Underwriting losses (claims for payments that exceed premiums earned) have occurred in most states in most years with these plans. Critics suggest that these underwriting losses have been passed forward to other property owners, causing them to subsidize inner-city property owners. On the other hand, FAIR plans have increased the welfare of many property owners in hard-to-insure areas who would not otherwise have insurance protection. As suggested by these two divergent viewpoints, the outcome of the debate depends on whether the yardstick is financial or social. The availability of property insurance at affordable rates is important to every property owner, and FAIR plans have helped many people purchase affordable insurance. The social question involves who is to bear the costs for this affordable coverage and how the costs are to be transferred.

---

[2] Insure.com (http://info.insure.com) provides a link that lists all FAIR plans currently operating and provides contact information for each of these plans.

Special Liability Insurance

Several lines of liability insurance have been either unavailable or unaffordable in recent years for certain groups. Included in the list of insurance applicants that have had problems buying insurance are the following:

- Directors and officers of corporations (who have been sued in cases of mergers, failed mergers, disappointing earnings, "cooked books," and bankruptcies)
- Health care providers, especially physicians and hospitals (whose errors and omissions can result in large damage awards)
- Firms that may be financially responsible for polluting the environment (such as those engaged in drilling for oil or gas).

Insurers in these cases behaved as if one or more of the criteria for the ideally insurable exposure were missing. As we described them in Chapter 7, these criteria include broad risk pools, economically feasible premiums, and no catastrophic loss potential.

CONSUMERS AND INSURANCE INFORMATION

Research suggests that one missing ingredient in the insurance market may be a well-informed consumer. Why isn't the insurance consumer well informed? Perhaps it is not clear to consumers that the rewards of making informed decisions are worth the cost of getting the needed information. In addition, consumers may view the cost of getting information about insurance to be unnecessarily high. The cost of obtaining information involves time, effort, and sometimes money—usually in that order. The Internet has lowered some of the cost barriers to obtaining insurance information, but it has not solved the information dilemma.

The cost of getting the necessary information to make effective purchase decisions may be examined in terms of the problems encountered in obtaining this knowledge. Perhaps the main problem in making an informed decision is the insurance contract itself. The typical insurance contract is a complex legal document that is difficult for most consumers to understand. Few people have enough legal knowledge to comprehend the meaning of the wording in a property insurance contract, and a life insurance contract can be even more difficult to grasp. Besides the legal knowledge needed to understand a contract, knowledge of finance is needed to evaluate the cost of a life insurance policy. The industry excuses the legal complexity of insurance contracts as being necessary to reduce misunderstanding or litigation. Nonetheless, in recent years the industry has made significant efforts to write personal insurance policies in simpler language.

It is a generally accepted tenet of industrial organization theory that the more informed the consumer is, the more likely the producer is to add to the consumer's information. Conversely, the more uninformed the consumer appears, the more likely the producer is to withhold information. That is, the well-informed consumer usually is provided facts during a sales presentation, while the uninformed consumer often gets just razzle-dazzle—or even worse.

Informed consumers are more likely to receive not only better marketing information, but also genuine product improvements. Why should a producer spend time and money improving a product when the customer cannot tell the difference between the improved and unimproved version? From this perspective, the responsibility for problems existing in markets in which the consumer remains uninformed lies with both the producer and the consumer. If producers viewed consumers as being well informed, the nature and content of their marketing efforts probably would become more informative. Product innovation would be truly that, not just new coverings on old products. Thus, the price of remaining uninformed includes not only wasted premium dollars, but also little incentive to improve the insurance product.

THE CONSUMER'S CHOICES: COMPANY, AGENT (OR BROKER), POLICY, AMOUNT, AND PRICE

An economist analyzing the consumer's problem in the insurance market would conclude that this purchase is difficult to make knowledgeably. The informed consumer must make five separate choices: company, agent (or broker), policy, amount, and price. We will discuss each of these choices now. One reason that this material is presented so extensively is to demonstrate how difficult it is to be an informed insurance purchaser. In addition, it provides some insight into why many people buy insurance without adequate information or sufficient shopping. Finally, it may help readers to become better-informed insurance consumers.

Selecting an Insurance Company

Consumers should consider two criteria when choosing an insurance company: its financial strength and its ability and willingness to provide service before and after a loss.

An insurance policy is a promise. Like all promises, it is worth no more than the word and the financial strength of the person or company making it. Therefore, the first priority in choosing an insurance company is to find a financially strong company. Consumers can get a professional opinion of the financial strength of most insurance companies from the ratings provided by financial ratings firms. Firms that provide ratings of insurance companies include A. M. Best Company (http://www.ambest.com/), Standard & Poors (http://www.standardandpoors.com), Moody's Investor's Services (http://www.moodys.com/), and Weiss Research (http://www.weissratings.com/). Insurance companies with high ratings have historically had a much stronger history of paying the insurance claims of their policyholders than insurers with low ratings. However, the following points list some critics' concerns about relying too heavily on an insurer's financial rating when making a purchase decision:

- The ratings firms often do not agree among themselves on a specific insurance company's merits.[3]
- All ratings firms can make and have made mistakes.
- One letter grade cannot sum up an insurance company's operations accurately.
- Companies with high ratings can sell policies that are not the most efficient choices.
- Ratings are estimates; they are no guarantee of the future.

Other sources of information about specific insurance companies include insurance agents, state insurance regulators, and satisfied or dissatisfied customers. All these sources may be subject to biases, however. Agents may have a monetary interest in recommending a company. Dissatisfied customers may be victims of their own misunderstanding. Moreover, stories about a few unhappy customers are more likely to receive public attention than the successful handling of thousands of claims in which

[3] Steven W. Pottier and David W. Sommer, "Property-Liability Insurer Financial Strength Ratings: Differences across Rating Agencies," *Journal of Risk and Insurance* (December 1999; Vol. 66, No. 4), pp. 621–42.

customers were satisfied by their insurer's efforts. State insurance regulators may be forced to limit their comments because of the sensitive and potentially influential nature of their statements.

Once a financially sound company is identified, the consumer should determine the insurer's reputation for fairness and promptness in settling claims and its reputation for providing service. An agent's motivation to provide good service comes from the company. If the company stresses good service, the agent is more likely to provide it than if the company appears indifferent.

Selecting an Insurance Agent

A good insurance agent has considerable knowledge of the protection being offered and also understands related areas of personal finance. A good agent is a person of integrity who puts a client's interest before his or her own. Good agents communicate clearly, so the insured understands the needs that the insurance fulfills and the rights and duties that the contract creates.

Evidence of an agent's knowledge is found in the ability to answer questions clearly. If the agent cannot answer a question immediately, he or she knows where to get the answer. Some agents have earned professional designations, which involves studying for and passing a series of examinations that test an agent's expertise on in-depth insurance topics. Traditional professional designations include the **Chartered Life Underwriter (CLU)** and **Chartered Property Casualty Underwriter (CPCU)**. Life insurance agents who have expanded their practice into professional financial planning also can earn the **Certified Financial Planner (CFP)** designation.[4]

It is difficult for a consumer to form an opinion about an agent's trustworthiness. A useful Internet resource is the Web sites of the state insurance departments, which list the names of agents who have been disciplined or have had their license revoked for unethical or illegal behavior.[5]

We have noted previously that more and more consumers purchase insurance products through a direct marketing channel such as the Internet rather than use a local insurance agent. However, just as in any purchase, the insurance buyer using the Internet should take steps to ensure that the seller is reputable and meets all the criteria—especially that of financial strength—for selling a high-quality product.

Selecting an Insurance Policy

To choose a good insurance policy, the consumer must understand his or her need for insurance. Only then can it be determined whether a particular policy meets this need. By definition, a good insurance policy is one that meets the consumer's needs without providing more insurance than is required. In choosing a good property and liability insurance policy, the consumer's selections are standardized. Standard policies are well suited to fit the needs of most consumers, and insureds with unique insurance needs, such as money-making hobbies or unusual property (such as expensive artwork, extensive gun or coin collections, or a large greenhouse), can amend the standard policy to tailor the coverage to their needs.

Choosing a good life insurance policy is more difficult than choosing a good insurance policy in other areas because life insurance policies are not standardized. Some policies combine savings with protection; some policies offer purely protection. Often

---

[4] The respective Web sites for the organizations sponsoring these designations are as follows: CFP (http://www.cfp.net/become/), CLU (http://www.theamericancollege.edu), and CPCU (http://www.cpcusociety.org/).

[5] A link to all state insurance departments can be found at http://www.naic.org/.

a company's policies are combined with a variety of clauses and endorsements, many of which are described in Chapter 15. Due to the complexity of life insurance coverage, applicants are advised to become familiar with the different types of policies and forms because an informed consumer knows the correct questions to ask and can understand the answers.

Selecting the Proper Amount of Insurance

Choosing the proper amount of insurance, like choosing the proper policy, begins with knowledge of the consumer's individual need for insurance. The need for insurance is related to the severity and the frequency of a potential loss. In property insurance, the need for protection usually is based on either the acquisition cost or the replacement value of a physical asset. This need can be calculated. In cases of business income insurance or liability claims, estimates of potential losses are needed. It has been suggested that people tend to buy too much insurance for low-severity, high-frequency losses but tend to purchase inadequate coverage for high-severity, low-frequency exposures. An example of such a mistake would be to buy a service contract on a new car extending the warranty several years while simultaneously driving with the minimum amount of liability coverage. The most that one could lose in terms of a car repair bill is far less than the most that one could lose in a liability suit.

In choosing the proper amount of life or disability insurance, the starting point is the consumer's financial goals. How much money would this person need to solve financial problems if death or disability were to occur immediately? The second step involves determining the amount of available assets to meet these needs. Available assets include existing life insurance policies, individual savings, Social Security benefits, and group life insurance provided by employers. If a gap exists between financial needs and available assets, this gap is the appropriate amount of life insurance to purchase. For the purposes of this chapter, it suffices to note that making an informed purchase of the proper amount of life insurance often is a complicated procedure.[6] Despite the difficulty in choosing the proper amount of insurance, some commonsense rules apply:

- First, insure those exposures to loss that are most likely to cause the greatest amount of damage.
- Never expose more to loss than you can afford to lose.
- Never risk a great loss (a high percentage of your assets) in exchange for a small gain (saving the insurance premium).

Paying the Right Price

Useful hints for consumers will help them to pay the right price, but few absolute rules exist. The right price is the one that provides the consumer with the greatest amount of insurance after considering the other four criteria just described. That is, the right price for insurance is not necessarily the lowest price. The lowest price may come from a company whose financial strength is questionable. It may come from a company that too frequently resists or denies its insureds' legitimate claims. It may come from an insurer whose agents are not trained adequately or from a company whose policies offer coverage that is less valuable than that offered by other companies. For these and other reasons, the consumer first should consider all the other criteria mentioned and then search for the right price.

---

[6] Chapter 14, "Professional Financial Planning," describes the "needs-based purchase" of life insurance in detail.

One rule in finding the right price is to engage in comparison shopping. Considerable price variation exists for comparable insurance policies offered by similar insurers. The need for shopping is present in both life and property insurance.

Conclusion

Being an informed insurance consumer is not easy. However, shopping for insurance on the Internet has become a productive source of information on price and other aspects of insurance in recent years. Several Web sites have side-by-side comparisons of many insurance companies and the insurance premiums that they charge. Initial research suggests that price shopping on the Internet is proving to be an effective way to lower a consumer's insurance costs. However, as we have just suggested, the insurance with the lowest cost may not be the best "bargain."

It is worthwhile for the consumer to make informed purchase decisions. If you consider the imperfections in the insurance market caused by uninformed consumers, or if you consider that many Americans spend more than $1,000 each on homeowners insurance, automobile insurance, and life insurance every year, you can understand that being an informed consumer does not cost—it pays. Moreover, the dividends earned by the informed consumer continue for years.

CONSUMER PROTECTION: THE ROLE OF THE COURTS, THE LAW, AND INSURANCE COMMISSIONERS

Insurance regulation can come from one of three sources: the courts, state insurance law (and, to limited extent, federal law), and state insurance commissioners. Transactions in the insurance market cannot be understood without appreciating the role of regulation. This chapter provides an overview of regulation that is just sufficient to see the interface between regulation, buyers, and sellers. We present more specific details of insurance regulation, its history, and current policy in Chapter 10, "Insurance Regulation."

The Courts

If an insured believes that he or she has not received what the insurance contract promised, he or she has the opportunity to bring a case to court. If the court is convinced that the insured has not been dealt with fairly, it can force the insurance company to correct the situation. The usual reason for litigation is the insurer's denial of the insured's claim for payment. That is, after a claim is denied, the insured sues the insurer for breach of contract.

An insurer may deny claims for many reasons. The insured may have attempted to defraud the insurer, or the loss may have been caused by an excluded peril in the policy. The contract may not be in force because the insured did not pay premiums, or the coverage may have been suspended because an insured violated a contract condition. Most of these grounds for claims denial raise questions of fact. Were the premiums paid promptly? When was the notice of cancellation mailed? What, in fact, was the proximate peril causing the loss? A jury in court often must resolve questions such as these. It is the function of the court to protect the legitimate rights of both insured and insurer. On the one hand, if an insurer were to pay claims that should be denied, it would hurt the interest of all members of the insurance pool by increasing costs. On the other hand, the denial of valid claims is intolerable, and courts can prevent such an injustice. Thus, the role of the court is to protect the legitimate rights of both parties to an insurance contract.

The doctrine of **stare decisis** gives court decisions in a particular case added weight if the decision is considered to set a precedent. The literal translation of the term *stare decisis* is "to stand by decisions." In practice, the doctrine means current court decisions will be consistent with previous decisions involving the same, or essentially similar, facts. For example, if a state court sets a precedent deciding that the term *animal* includes birds and fish, that precedent will be followed in that state the next time the issue arises in litigation. If a court in another state (jurisdiction) decides that a contract meaning to exclude bird damage must specify birds and animals separately, that decision will be precedent-setting in that state. *Stare decisis* adds certainty to the outcome of litigation and may in fact reduce litigation if people have a better understanding of how the courts would view their position in a legal dispute. It also greatly enhances the role and power of the court in the area of consumer protection.

The Law

The insurance laws (codes) of the various states provide consumers with essential protection. They establish rules of conduct, requiring some behaviors and forbidding others. For instance, Article 24 of New York State's revised insurance code is titled "Unfair Methods of Competition and Unfair and Deceptive Acts and Practices." One part of this article states, "No person shall engage in this state in any trade practice which is defined . . . to be an unfair or deceptive act or practice." The article goes on to define several prohibited unfair or deceptive acts or practices. The list includes (1) issuing or circulating false literature, (2) making false statements or rumors about insurance institutions, and (3) making incomplete comparisons between insurance contracts.

New York's Article 24 is an example of a law that prohibits direct abuse of consumers. In some broad sense, all insurance law is designed to protect the consumer's interest. Rules and regulations governing company solvency, licensing of agents, approval of policy forms, licensing of insurance companies and rate regulation all promote and protect consumer rights. The law, however, is fairly rigid. It can deal only with issues in general. It can mark out boundaries between acceptable and unacceptable behavior. For dealing with particular problems on a daily basis, however, a more flexible institution is needed. The state insurance commissioner is this flexible institution. The combination of state insurance law and the actions of the state's insurance commissioner provide a state with insurance regulation.

The Insurance Commissioner

Every state has an insurance commissioner, an administrator in charge of insurance regulation. This person's responsibilities include interpreting and enforcing the state's insurance code. In most states, the governor appoints an insurance commissioner; in a few states, the commissioner is elected. Commissioners typically are granted broad powers to regulate the business of insurance in their states. These powers reflect the commissioners' specialized expertise in insurance matters, as most legislators and judges are less familiar with the insurance industry.

Two important differences exist between the role of the courts and the role of the insurance commissioner. First, unlike courts, the commissioner can initiate action even before a complaint is brought by an insured. Second, a court will decide if the Very Mean Insurance Company has been unfair in denying the claim of John Consumer. If the insurance commissioner becomes convinced that the Very Mean Insurance Company is denying many insureds' claims unfairly, however, the commissioner has the duty to correct this situation or withdraw this company's license to conduct business. The courts protect individual consumers from injustice, while the commissioner protects *all* the state's insureds from injustice.

Summary

This chapter has examined how consumers, insurers, and regulators interact in insurance markets. Insurance markets generally exhibit the characteristics of competitive markets, and insurance regulation relies heavily upon the natural forces of supply and demand that are found in a competitive market to serve insurance consumers in the United States effectively. Occasionally, insurance markets fall out of equilibrium, signaling a situation in which regulatory intervention is needed.

Historically, availability and affordability problems have occurred when providing insurance to poor drivers, inner-city property owners, and individuals and businesses needing some specific types of liability insurance. In the first two areas, which have been longstanding problems, measures have been enacted to create an involuntary market. In these cases, insurers voluntarily writing the good risks have been forced to accept some percentage of the less-desirable exposures. In automobile insurance, such plans are called *automobile insurance plans* or *assigned risk plans;* in property insurance, these plans are called *FAIR plans*.

The insurance consumer often is not well informed when making this purchase. Acquiring the needed information takes time and effort. The costs of making uninformed purchases include wasting money on the wrong policy, buying from the wrong company, and paying the wrong price. An uninformed consumer causes other market imperfections as well. The industry has no incentive to improve products or even to provide educational information to uninformed consumers. Thus, the consumer must accept some responsibility for the insurance industry's performance. To make an informed choice, the consumer must choose all the following: a good insurance company, a good agent or broker, a good insurance policy, the right amount of protection, and the right price.

The courts, the law, and the insurance commissioner protect the insurance consumer. The courts protect insureds or insurers from particular injustices. The law determines the boundary between acceptable and unacceptable behavior. The insurance commissioner interprets and enforces the law for the benefit of all consumers.

Appendix: The Insurance Underwriting Cycle

Underwriting cycles are pricing cycles that commonly occur in many insurance markets. Underwriting cycles are characterized by prolonged periods of time in which insurers compete by reducing their prices, followed by sudden and often dramatic increases in premiums across the industry. Historically, the events that have triggered the end of the intense price-cutting phase of an underwriting cycle often have been unexpected catastrophic losses, such as the September 11, 2001 terror attacks. Such events often prompt insurers to increase premiums by expanding their pricing models to include cost factors (such as the increased risk of more terrorist attacks) that were not included in their prior premium calculations.

This appendix describes underwriting cycles and their financial impact on insurance markets. Before we can show how underwriting cycles affect insurance industry operating results, however, we must first define some useful measures of property insurance financial performance.

Written premiums are the total premiums collected by an insurer during a specific period such as a year. **Earned premiums** are the percentage of an advance premium payment that belongs to the insurance company. The insurer may not earn some of the written premiums until many months after it receives the premium payment. For example, if an insured pays a year's insurance premium on January 1, by March 1 the insurer has earned only two months' worth of premiums. The difference between the written and earned premiums equals the **unearned premiums**. The premiums for March through December would be unearned in our example.

The **loss ratio** is the incurred losses (those losses reported to the insurer and adjustment expenses on these losses) divided by earned premiums. Simply put, the loss ratio is the percentage of the earned premium paid for losses and loss adjustment expenses, and it is often used to measure an insurer's underwriting profitability. The **expense ratio** is the total expenses (except loss adjustment expenses) divided by written premiums. This measure of an insurer's loading expenses often is used to measure an insurer's administrative cost efficiency. The **combined ratio** is the sum of the loss and expense ratios. It summarizes, in one number, the underwriting experience of the company or the industry.[7] If the ratio is below 100, the company's underwriting experience was profitable. If the ratio is more than 100, then the insurance underwriting was unprofitable.

The data in Table 9-1 presents the pattern of cash flow of the U.S. property insurance industry and the underwriting cycle from 1997 to 2007. Despite a combined ratio exceeding 100 percent for seven of the years shown, the property insurance industry's after-tax net income was positive (that is, the industry earned a profit) each year except 2001. The profit came about because investment earnings exceeded underwriting losses. If companies expect their investment performance to be strong enough to overcome underwriting losses, they sometimes quote lower prices for insurance and use "liberal" underwriting; industry commentators call this a **soft market**.

Sometimes an unprofitable underwriting year coincides with an unprofitable investment year, as happened in 2001. The terrorist attacks on September 11, 2001, caused the most insured damage in history, and those losses also had a negative impact on an already weak investment market. When bad investment returns combine with unprofitable underwriting, capital usually leaves the insurance industry, leading to a **hard market**. In a hard insurance market, insurance companies raise their prices and are more "conservative" in their underwriting. Conservative underwriting means insurers are very careful and often do not offer coverage to the most risky exposures. For their lower-risk exposures, insurers may offer less coverage for a given premium or require a higher premium for continuing the same levels of coverage.

Readers can see the pattern of the **underwriting cycle** of the property insurance industry illustrated in the data in Table 9-1 by tracking the combined ratio shown at the bottom of the table. The underwriting cycle involves a soft market leading to reduced

industry profitability, which in turn leads to a hard market and increased profitability. The increased profitability means more capital is available in the industry and competition becomes more intense, which in turn leads back to a soft market and the cycle repeats itself. As shown in Table 9-1, price competition led to increasingly lower profits from 1997 to 2001, as the combined ratio increased each year over that time span. The September 11, 2001 attacks reversed this price trend, as the combined ratio for the industry steadily improved from 2002 to 2006.

As suggested above, an insurer's financial performance during an underwriting cycle often is affected by anticipated investment income. In practice, the anticipation of investment earnings leads some companies intentionally to price their insurance below the level of expected losses because anticipated investment income is expected to be large enough to make up for the premium shortfall. Other insurers expect to make a profit on both their insurance and investment functions, but even these insurers allow expected investment income to modify their insurance rates.

Cash flow underwriting describes the practice of trying to attract new business by pricing insurance "at a loss." The theory underlying cash flow underwriting is that investment income can more than offset underwriting losses. Thus, it may be possible for an insurance pool to pay more than $1 in claims for every $1 that it collects in premiums and still be profitable, so long as investment earnings more than offset the excess cost of paying claims. Although relatively high investment returns allow success with this strategy in some years, intense competition and lower available investment returns can cause insurers to experience net losses in other years.

The figures in Table 9-1 demonstrate how anticipated investment income affects underwriting performance. An insurer's taxable income recognizes two sources of investment income. *Net investment income* is a measure of the income received by insurers from their investment holdings, consisting primarily of interest payments from bonds and dividends from stock holdings. *Realized capitals gains (losses)* measure the returns earned by insurers on the sale of their investments. Thus, the sum of an insurer's net investment income and its realized capital gains and losses reflects the combined impact of investment income on insurer profitability. Note that insurers' combined ratios were well above 100 percent during the late 1990s and early 2000s, as

---

[7] Readers interested in the topic of evaluating insurance company operating results are directed to this article: "Measuring Underwriting Profitability of the Non-Life Insurance Industry," published by the Swiss Re as Sigma No. 3/2006, at their Web site (http://www.swissre.com/).

TABLE 9-1   Financial Results for the U.S. Property-Liability Insurance Industry ($ Billions)

	1997	1998	1999	2000	2001	2002	2003	2004	2005	2006	2007
Written Premium	276.6	281.6	287.0	299.7	323.5	369.7	404.4	423.3	425.9	443.8	444.3
Earned Premium	271.5	277.7	282.9	294.0	311.5	348.5	386.3	412.6	418	435.8	442.8
Losses Incurred[a]	163.8	175.3	184.5	201.0	234.5	238.8	238.7	246.4	256.6	231.3	245.9
Loss Adjustment Expense	34.0	36.5	37.7	37.8	40.9	44.8	50.0	53.2	55.1	52.5	52.5
Other Underwriting Expense	74.9	77.9	80.8	82.6	86.2	93.8	100.7	106.4	109.7	117.3	120.4
Policyholder Dividends	4.7	4.7	3.3	3.9	2.4	1.9	1.9	1.6	1.9	3.4	2.5
Underwriting Gain (Loss)	(5.8)	(16.8)	(23.4)	(31.2)	(52.6)	(30.8)	(4.9)	5.0	(5.3)	31.4	21
Investment Income	41.5	39.9	38.6	40.7	37.7	37.2	38.6	39.6	49.8	52.4	55.2
Operating Income (Loss)	35.5	23.4	13.9	9.9	(13.8)	5.6	33.8	44.1	45.5	85	75.2
Realized Capital Gains	10.8	18.0	13.7	16.2	6.6	(1.2)	6.6	9.3	11.9	3.5	8.8
Federal Income Tax	9.5	10.6	5.4	5.5	(0.2)	1.3	10.3	14.7	10.7	22.4	19.8
Net Income After Tax	36.8	30.8	22.2	20.5	(6.9)	3.0	30.0	38.7	46.7	66.2	64.3
Loss Ratio[b] (as %)	72.8	76.3	78.5	81.2	88.4	81.4	74.7	72.6	74.6	65.1	67.4
Expense Ratio (as %)	27.1	27.7	28.1	27.6	26.7	25.4	24.9	25.1	25.8	26.4	27.1
Combined Ratio (as %)	101.6	105.6	107.9	110.1	115.9	106.7	99.6	97.7	100.3	91.6	94.5

[a]Incurred losses include sums already paid and estimates of amounts to be paid.
[b]The loss ratio includes adjustment expenses.
Based on Insurance Services Office, Best's Review, Best's Aggregates and Average; Insurance Information Institute, Business Insurance; and author's calculations. Net Income Figures may not balance due to rounding or omission of miscellaneous items.

insurer investments were yielding sufficient income to make up for underwriting losses. By contrast, as interest rates decreased in the mid-2000s, insurance underwriting standards became much more conservative as insurers charged more for insurance protection. In fact, the insurance industry's underwriting results were generally profitable from 2004 through 2007 for the first time in several decades.

Review

1. Most markets consist of buyers and sellers. The chapter suggests that the insurance market has three participants. Who is the third participant, and what is its role in the market?
2. What are the requirements for a perfectly competitive market? What is one of the main benefits of perfect competition?
3. Describe an aspect of insurance that is not consistent with the characteristics of competitive markets.
4. If insurers colluded and raised the price of insurance, what would you predict would be the effect on the quantity of insurance sold? Explain your answer.
5. If the government made insurers lower the price of insurance 25 percent, what would you predict would be the effect on the quantity of insurance sold? Explain your answer.

6. What is a FAIR plan? How does it work?
7. Explain the purpose of assigned risk plans and JUAs in automobile insurance.
8. Describe the problems caused by uninformed consumers in the insurance market.
9. How does the role of the courts differ from the role of the insurance commissioner in protecting the consumer?
10. Describe the important factors to consider when choosing an insurance company.
11. Why is the lowest-priced insurance protection not necessarily the best one to buy?
12. What information do financial ratings firms provide? What are some potential problems with their ratings?
13. Explain three commonsense rules for choosing the proper amount of insurance.

Objective Questions

1. All the following criteria are specified in the model for perfect competition except:
   a. Government regulation
   b. Numerous independent sellers
   c. Numerous well-informed buyers
   d. Freedom of entry and exit
2. To make automobile insurance available to high-risk drivers, various states have used each of the following approaches except:
   a. JUAs
   b. Federal mandatory plans
   c. Assigned risk plans
   d. Auto insurance plans
3. The most important choice that a consumer must make when purchasing insurance is:
   a. The lowest price
   b. The most coverage available
   c. Coverage from a company of unquestioned solvency
   d. Coverage from a company with the widest array of policy alternatives
4. *Stare decisis* means:
   a. All things considered.
   b. Stand by things that are decided.
   c. Innocent parties prevail.
   d. It is impolite to stare.

5. All the following parties are participants in the insurance market except:
   a. Insurance buyers
   b. Insurance companies
   c. Government regulators
   d. The Federal Reserve
6. Insurance consumers can get information about the financial strength of insurance companies from:
   a. The Federal Reserve
   b. Financial ratings firms
   c. Credit information bureaus
   d. Public policy organizations (PPOs)
7. Which of the following designations cannot be earned by insurance agents?
   a. HMO
   b. CLU
   c. CPCU
   d. CFP
8. In most states, the insurance commissioner is:
   a. Elected
   b. Impeached
   c. Appointed by the governor
   d. Appointed by the president

Discussion Questions

1. Why is the role of regulation in the insurance market so extensive?
2. Do you think FAIR plans or automobile insurance plans represent legitimate government intervention in the insurance market? Explain your position.
3. Do you think consumers should assume much of the responsibility for promoting their own welfare in the insurance market, or do you think the government should do more?

Selected References

The I. I. I. Insurance Factbook, 2011 (New York: Insurance Information Institute), published annually.

Viscusi, W. Kip, Joseph E. Harrington, and John M. Vernon, 2005, *Economics of Regulation and Antitrust*, 4th ed. (Cambridge: MIT Press).

10

Insurance Regulation

After studying this chapter, you should be able to

- Describe the administrative process used to regulate insurance

- Explain the reasons that the insurance industry is regulated

- Identify the important landmarks in the history of insurance regulation

- Describe the regulatory activities of state insurance departments, including solvency regulation, rate regulation, investment regulation, and regulation of agents and insurance officers

This chapter continues the discussion at the end of the previous chapter, in which we covered the role the government plays in protecting the insurance consumer. The government supervises the insurance industry to protect consumers and to address imperfections in the insurance markets. Depending on your perspective, insurance *regulation* (or insurance *supervision*, as it is known in Europe) may be viewed either as a form of governmental consumer protection or as government interference with transactions between insurance buyers and sellers. Today, some people favor more governmental regulation of insurance, and others favor less.

In its simplest form, regulation can be viewed as the rules by which the game is played. The rules for a game, such as football, result in two things that on the surface appear contradictory but in reality are not—a loss of freedom and the creation of freedom. For example, in football, a rule against illegal blocking means that a player loses the freedom to block another whose back is turned. But it also means all players have gained some freedom from being hit while their backs are turned. If the rule is broken, as is often the case, the offending team incurs a penalty. Insurance regulations operate in a similar way, by restricting some freedoms to create others. The freedom to market any insurance policy, for example, is restricted. Policy forms must be approved before they are sold to the public. At the same time, this restriction creates a freedom for the consumer—to remain unhindered by undesirable policy forms when making a purchase decision.

THE ADMINISTRATION OF STATE INSURANCE REGULATION

Insurance regulation in the United States involves all three branches of government. The legislative branch is responsible for writing and revising laws pertaining to the insurance industry. The governing federal insurance law is the **McCarran-Ferguson Act**. In a most unusual outcome for a federal law, the McCarran-Ferguson Act turns the regulation of the insurance industry over to the states. (We present the history and reasons for the McCarran-Ferguson Act later in this chapter.) As a result, each of the fifty states has its own insurance code, as do Washington, D.C., Puerto Rico, American Samoa, Guam, and the U.S. Virgin Islands.

A second important party in insurance regulation is the judicial branch, which includes a variety of courts, such as state and federal, original jurisdiction, and appellate courts. Courts interpret and apply regulation to the different parties involved in insurance transactions, which includes insurance companies, policy owners, and insurance regulators. By interpreting the law, a court validates regulation and applies it to the unique circumstances of each trial that it hears. Courts, however, never initiate regulation. They react only when matters are brought to their attention.

While the legislative and judicial branches are critical components in insurance regulation, most of the daily administration of insurance regulatory matters is carried out through the executive branch of the government by state insurance regulators. In most states, these regulators are insurance commissioners, but they are called superintendents of insurance or directors of insurance in other states. The insurance commissioner conducts the day-to-day administration of a state's insurance laws by applying them to specific cases.

State Insurance Regulation

At present, each state has its own insurance laws and its own administrator responsible for regulating the insurance market within the boundaries of the respective laws. One result of regulation by the various states and U.S. territories is that companies operating on a national basis must comply with more than fifty potentially different sets of rules and regulations. Even when regulations are similar, insurers with national operations must get more than fifty different approvals for rates and policy forms.

Within this framework of insurance regulation by the states, the extraterritorial rule of New York State stands out. In 1939, New York made the **Appleton rule** part of its insurance code. Put simply, the rule states that insurance companies doing any business in New York State must be in substantial compliance with all of New York's rules in whatever state they do business, not just in New York. Because most of the largest life and non–life insurers conduct business in New York, the New York insurance code has an impact well beyond the state borders: Consumers who are not New York residents get the benefit of New York legislation if they deal with an insurer that does business in New York.

The National Association of Insurance Commissioners (NAIC)

The National Association of Insurance Commissioners (NAIC) is a private, nonprofit association of state insurance commissioners created to enhance uniformity in insurance regulation. The organization meets formally three times a year to consider matters of common concern. Between scheduled meetings, its subcommittees consider special problems. A key function of the NAIC is to develop model bills for the various states to introduce in their own legislatures. Because many states often adopt such model legislation, this function increases the uniformity of insurance codes across the states.

We now have developed the basis for a more-thorough definition of **insurance regulation**: the rules of the insurance market, as established by law, administered by public officials, and interpreted by the courts, all for the purpose of promoting and protecting the public interest.

THE REASONS FOR INSURANCE REGULATION

The insurance transaction between consumer and insurer is made in a comprehensively regulated market. Insurers generally are not free to write any contract they choose, are not free to charge any price they choose, and, for some types of personal insurance, must accept insureds that they did not freely choose.

The insurance industry is regulated extensively for several reasons. The financial strength of insurers is regulated because of the potentially severe financial impact that insurer insolvency can have on customers. Regulation also addresses the unequal knowledge and bargaining power of the buyer and seller, as well as the forecasting uncertainties related to insurance pricing. Some level of regulation promotes certain social goals. Each of these reasons is discussed below.

Insurer Insolvency

Insurance is a contingent promise to be delivered in the future, a promise worth no more than the company standing behind it. Promoting insurer solvency is, therefore, the most important goal of insurance regulation. **Solvency**—the insurer's ability to pay all its legal obligations—makes the result of the insurance transaction certain and predictable. Maintaining insurer solvency can be difficult if many policyholders suffer insured losses simultaneously, such as when a hurricane or other large loss event occurs. Consumers generally cannot evaluate or monitor insurance company solvency because insurance accounting and actuarial procedures are too technical and complicated. Therefore, the government monitors insurer solvency on the public's behalf.

A second reason for promoting solvency is the potentially catastrophic costs that can result from an insurer's insolvency. These costs include houses destroyed with no funds to rebuild, liability suits with only personal assets available to satisfy judgments, and widows left with dependent children and unfulfilled financial plans. The scope and severity of such problems explain why an insurer's solvency is of utmost concern to the public, and hence to regulators.

A third explanation for solvency regulation is that life insurance companies (and, to a much smaller extent, property insurance companies) are responsible for sizable amounts of consumer savings. Legally, the relationship between insurer and insured is comparable to that of debtor and creditor, but it also bears a close resemblance to the fiduciary arrangement between a bank and its depositor. Fiduciaries are held to strict requirements for their actions because they require public confidence. Because insurers' operations parallel those of fiduciaries, the insurer's solvency is a subject for public regulation.

Reduce Unequal Distribution of Knowledge and Bargaining Power

An insurer has enormous advantages in technical expertise compared to the typical consumer. For example, most insureds do not understand the insurance policy as well as the employees of the insurer that sold it. Because many insureds feel unequal to the insurer when loss adjustment disputes arise, one purpose of insurance regulation is to compensate for this imbalance.

The model for what economists call perfect competition assumes both well-informed buyers and well-informed sellers. As the market moves away from this ideal, competition deteriorates and problems arise, such as different prices for identical goods or higher prices for inferior goods. While both situations occur today in the insurance market despite regulation, many people fear that the problem would occur more frequently if there were no regulation.

The imbalance in knowledge between insurer and insured arises in part because most insurance contracts are long and contain words that are meaningful to lawyers but often not to the public. Regulation prevents dishonest insurers from taking advantage of the consumer's relatively uninformed position by imposing unfair contracts.

Another reason for the knowledge imbalance is the fact that insurance is an intangible good. This makes it difficult for a consumer to evaluate the product's performance until it may be too late to argue about it. For example, if a consumer purchases an inferior coffeemaker, he or she usually discovers the problem shortly afterward, allowing the consumer to return the appliance to the place of purchase for repair or replacement. On the other hand, the insured usually does not find out an insurance policy is problematic until he or she has made a claim for payment—a particularly inopportune time to learn that the policy is inferior. Thus, regulators must help.

Uncertainties of Insurance Pricing

Although the ideal of perfect competition is rarely realized, we often achieve a satisfactory level, or workable competition, in our economy. Competition, however, does not necessarily work to the consumer's advantage in the insurance market. Part of the problem is that insurers must set prices before costs are fully known. Although it is not unusual to lack complete cost details in many other industries, the collection of insurance cost data can take an especially long time because the life insurer or liability insurer might have to wait for decades before their costs are fully known. Because few consumers have the time or expertise to evaluate these costs, regulators instead judge the fairness and adequacy of an insurance company's rates.

Because free price competition cannot be relied on to promote consumers' welfare in the insurance market, solvency regulation substitutes for uncontrolled competition. The issue confronting regulators is how much pricing freedom to allow the industry. There are two main forms of insurance rate regulation: **prior approval rating**, which requires insurers to get approval from the regulator before using a rate, and **competitive rating**, also known as **file and use rating**, which allows an insurer to use whatever rate it chooses after filing the rate and the supporting statistics with the regulator. Competitive rating, the more-popular scheme in the United States, allows the regulator to reject any rates in use without delaying the insurers use of such rates. If the regulator rejects the rates, the insurer must stop using those rates. This approach allows more freedom for insurers to compete on prices but allows the regulator to retain some control. The current directives controlling insurer pricing in the European Union also follow the competitive rating model.

Promote Social Goals

Some insurance regulation is designed to promote social objectives, such as making insurance more widely available (affordable) or ending objectionable discrimination. For example, some people believe that the public should have the right to purchase insurance at affordable rates. This belief has led many states to pass laws forcing insurers to accept riskier applicants or reduce rates below levels that they would have chosen otherwise.

Insurers' blanket rejection of certain exposures, such as inner-city property or drivers with bad driving records, means some people find private insurance unavailable or unaffordable. Presumably, the social goal of making insurance widely available takes precedence over other goals, such as freedom of the insurer to contract with whom it prefers, although it may conflict with the goal of insurer solvency if an insurer is forced to accept too many poor risks at inadequate rates. Likewise, if regulation forces insurers to overlook valid underwriting criteria to make society more equitable, the subsidization that results may conflict with the goal of offering mathematical fairness to all insureds.

THE HISTORY OF INSURANCE REGULATION

When Congress passed a law in 1945 giving the states the power to regulate the insurance market, insurance became an exception to the rule that the federal government regulates industries whose business involves interstate commerce. We next look at the history of insurance regulation to better understand why insurance is regulated by the states.

Paul v. *Virginia* (1869)

Before 1850, Americans did not purchase insurance as frequently as today, and the insurance market was not regulated extensively. The states issued charters for incorporation, and the federal government provided some regulation through postal laws. In *Paul* v. *Virginia* (1869), the Supreme Court heard a case that questioned whether insurance is a transaction in interstate commerce. If so, the Constitution of the United States gave the federal government the power to regulate it. If not, the states would provide the regulation.

In this case, Mr. Paul, an agent of a New York insurer, was convicted of violating a Virginia law prohibiting solicitation of business without a state-issued license. Paul argued that he did not need a license from Virginia because his activities involved interstate commerce. The state, which stood to lose substantial tax revenue on insurance transactions, opposed this argument. It maintained that Paul was a citizen of the state, conducting business in the state, and therefore was subject to state regulation. The Supreme Court agreed with the state's interpretation. Thus, for about the next seventy-five years, the insurance transaction was *not* considered interstate commerce. It was a transaction to be regulated and taxed by the various states.

The Armstrong Investigation (1905) and the Merritt Investigation (1910)

How effective was the regulation provided by the states? From the record, it appears that the states were probably better at taxation than they were at regulation. For example, in 1905, New York State made an extensive investigation, known as the **Armstrong Investigation**, into the life insurance industry. The revelations were scandalous. The investigation revealed abuses such as unethical business acquisition methods, unjustifiable home-office expenses, and unethical political influence. Five years later, New York investigated its fire insurers in the **Merritt Committee Investigation**. The results again revealed many unethical and undesirable occurrences.

These investigations resulted in a new insurance code for New York State. The quality of the regulation by the states was not uniform, however. Some were more effective than others were, and for the next fifty years, few states were as active in insurance regulation as New York.

South-Eastern Underwriters Association (1944)

A **rating bureau** is an organization that collects insurance loss data and provides loss forecasting services to its member insurers.[1] In the mid-1940s, the South-Eastern Underwriters Association (SEUA), a rating bureau that consisted of many insurance companies doing business in the southeastern United States, had a near-monopoly on the property insurance business in those states. To promote and extend its power, the association engaged in boycotts, rate-making conspiracies, tie-in contracts, and other abuses outlawed by federal antitrust legislation. Unfortunately for the consumer, federal antitrust statutes apparently did not apply to these offenses because of the *Paul v. Virginia* decision. In the 1944 **South-Eastern Underwriters Association** case[2], however, the Supreme Court reversed *Paul v. Virginia*, concluding in a 4-to-3 decision that insurance was indeed interstate commerce and that federal antitrust laws applied to insurance company operations.

The SEUA decision did not upset the regulatory picture for long. First, there was no existing federal insurance code, so the SEUA decision left the industry virtually unregulated. Second, both industry and state regulators expressed strong opposition to federal regulation. As a result, Congress passed the **McCarran-Ferguson Act** in 1945.

The McCarran Ferguson Act (1945)

The McCarran Ferguson Act (1945) expressed the intent of Congress to allow the states to continue to regulate and tax the business of insurance by exempting from federal oversight activities that (1) constitute the "business of insurance," (2) are regulated by state law, and (3) do not constitute an agreement or act "to boycott, coerce, or intimidate." Sections of the law declare, however, that if state law does not provide consumers with the type of protection found in the federal antitrust laws and the Federal Trade Commission Act, then federal laws will be applied.

Since its passage, the McCarran Ferguson Act has been the focus of several court decisions. Among the most important cases are those defining the "business of insurance." For example, the collection and sharing of loss data from multiple property insurers, a primary function of insurance rating bureaus, is the business of insurance and thus exempt from federal antitrust laws.[3]

Another Supreme Court case involving the "business of insurance" question occurred in the late 1950s. In the Variable Annuity Life Insurance Co. of America (VALIC) case (*SEC v. Variable Annuity Life Insurance Co. of America*, 1959), the question arose whether the Securities and Exchange Commission (SEC) had the right and duty to regulate various aspects of a new insurance product, the variable annuity. Until an annuitant receives regular payments from the insurer, the variable annuity is similar to a mutual fund. Under the **Investment Company Act of 1940**, the SEC was given responsibility for

---

[1] Rating bureaus sometimes are also called *insurance advisory organizations.*

[2] *United States v. South-Eastern Underwriters Ass'n*, 322 U.S. 533 (1944).

[3] See L. Powell, "The Assault on the McCarran-Ferguson Act and the Politics of Insurance in the Post-Katrina Era," *Journal of Insurance Regulation,* Vol. 26, Issue 3, Spring 2008, pp. 3-21. Since rating bureaus develop advisory rates for use by its members or provide raw data to its members, this practice clearly involves collusion leading up to setting a price and thus would be illegal under federal antitrust law. However, if federal regulations, including the antitrust laws, were imposed, it would have the effect of causing every company to duplicate the costly rate-making and data collection efforts of the others. Federal regulation also would give large companies, with their larger databases, a competitive advantage over smaller companies. Thus, federal regulation, without an antitrust exemption, potentially could rearrange the competitive structure of the industry. As the matter now stands, the largest property insurance rating bureau, the Insurance Services Office, supplies its members and regulatory agencies with loss data but not actual rates. Each company is free to use this loss data combined with its own expense structure to develop its rates.

regulating mutual funds. Thus, the SEC thought it had responsibility for regulating the variable annuity. The insurance companies selling variable annuities felt that they were exempt from SEC regulation under the provisions of the McCarran Act.

In a 5-to-4 decision, the Supreme Court supported the SEC's position that it should regulate variable annuity sales. The majority ruled that during the accumulation period, the variable annuity was not an insurance transaction to any significant extent. The real meaning of the decision was that if insurers engage in transactions that are not "the business of insurance," they lose the McCarran Act exemption from federal regulations.

Gramm-Leach-Bliley Act (1999)

The Gramm-Leach-Bliley Act (GLB) allows financial service holding companies to include a combination of banks, insurance companies, and security dealers. The intent of GLB was to repeal regulation from the 1930s that prohibited commercial banks, investment banks, and insurers from competing in each other's industries. Regulation of each component part of such a holding company follows its historic practice. Thus, the Federal Reserve and the Treasury Department continue to supervise banks, the SEC continues to supervise security dealers, and state insurance commissioners continue to supervise insurance companies.

In congressional debates prior to the passage of GLB, it was suggested that allowing holding companies to compete across all three portions of the financial services market would result in larger firms with broader product lines, and thus opportunities for consumer cost savings from *economies of scale* and *economies of scope*. **Economies of scale** imply lower costs per unit produced as firms become larger. **Economies of scope** imply that it is more efficient for one firm to offer several different types of financial transactions than for separate firms to offer only one type of financial service each. For example, economies of scale could arise if a large firm bought more cost-efficient technology or spread its marketing costs over a larger number of units sold. Economies of scope arise if one visit could result in a mortgage loan, homeowners insurance, and perhaps insurance on the homeowner's life. If nothing else, it may be more convenient for consumers to fill out one form to complete these transactions than to complete three forms from three different financial service providers. So far, it has been difficult to assess whether the goals of GLB have been achieved because problems related to the 2007 banking crisis have disrupted the normal operations of much of the financial services industries.

REGULATED ACTIVITIES

Insurance regulations apply to a wide variety of insurance activities, as described below. Because more than fifty different sets of rules exist, this description is general. Recall that the main purposes of regulation are to maintain the solvency of the insurer, to equalize the imbalance of knowledge and bargaining power between the insurer and insured, to deal with a unique pricing problem that does not allow for free competition, and to promote specific social goals. In general, these regulatory aims can be placed into two categories: (1) to promote insurer solvency and (2) to maintain order in the insurance market.

Legal Reserves and Surplus

From the instant of its formation and throughout its existence, an insurer must comply with the reserve and surplus requirements of the state in which it is domiciled. As we will see shortly, reserve and surplus accounts serve as a cushion of funds, beyond current operating income, available to meet an insurer's financial obligations. If an insurer fails to maintain a prescribed amount of capital, it is placed under the commissioner's supervision until it can be determined whether continued operation of the insurer best serves the public interest. If an insurer's capital and surplus fall below the minimum standard, it is considered financially **impaired**. If an insurer's liabilities exceed the value of its assets, it is **insolvent**.

An insurer needs **surplus**—an excess of assets over liabilities—as a cushion against bad underwriting results (more losses than predicted) and poor investment results (lower earnings than projected). It is probable that every insurer will experience less-than-desirable underwriting or investment results at some time, and an adequate surplus allows an insurer to ride through such a period without injury to its insureds.

Before an insurer is granted a license to operate in a state, it must establish that it has satisfied the state's minimum capital and surplus requirements. These requirements vary from state to state. The fact that many insurance companies have begun operations in recent decades suggests that these requirements are not significant barriers to entering the industry.

The law also requires an insurer to maintain minimum **reserves** on the liability side of its balance sheet. The insurer must maintain offsetting assets on the other side of the statement. By mandating that insurers hold reserves as liabilities, regulators thus require insurers to maintain a certain minimum amount of assets. To better assure the quality of these assets, insurance laws also require the assets held opposite the liability reserves to be invested in conservative investments. Working together, the reserve and the investment requirements are important tools in promoting insurer solvency.

State regulation requires insurers to categorize their assets as *admitted assets* or *nonadmitted assets*. This accounting procedure is different from Generally Accepted Accounting Principles (GAAP) and represents an attempt to evaluate insurers' assets in the most conservative manner. **Admitted assets** are assets that are readily available to pay claims, such as negotiable securities and real estate holdings. State law allows only admitted assets to offset an insurer's liabilities. **Nonadmitted assets** are not available to meet the company's liability to its insureds because they cannot be converted quickly to cash. Examples include such things as office furniture, supplies, and equipment.

PROPERTY INSURANCE RESERVE ACCOUNTS

Property insurers need an **unearned premium reserve** because insureds pay for their insurance in advance, typically one year at a time. For example, when homeowners pay annual premiums, during the first month the insurer earns one-twelfth of the premium and must show eleven-twelfths of the premium in its reserve account. The unearned fraction represents the eleven months that have not passed and for which the premium was paid. In theory, if all insureds terminate their contracts simultaneously at any point, the amount in the unearned premium reserve would be sufficient to return the unearned premium amounts.

The **loss reserve** is set up to account for unpaid losses. The loss reserve is especially important for insurers writing liability insurance, but it also applies to other lines of insurance. The claims covered by this reserve account may be losses that have been reported, but the claim has not yet been paid or losses not yet reported to the insurer. For both unreported and reported-but-unsettled losses, the insurer makes actuarial estimates of expected loss payments. Actuaries call the estimate of unreported losses the **incurred but not reported (IBNR) reserve**. Unreported losses represent unpaid liabilities. In addition to unreported losses, unpaid claims may be the result of an unsettled lawsuit or a claim on which the insurer and insured cannot agree.

By observing years of data, actuaries can estimate what percentage of the losses from a given year will have been settled and what percentage remain to be settled. For example, perhaps after one year, 80 percent of a given year's automobile physical damage claims have been settled, leaving 20 percent of the claims unsettled and requiring a reserve. After two years, perhaps the percentages will be 90 and 10 percent, respectively. By the third year, all the claims will be settled. In comparison, after one year, perhaps only 60 percent of automobile liability claims are settled, with a reserve needed for the remaining 40 percent. Perhaps after three years, because of litigation or other problems, 20 percent of these claims remain outstanding and still require an estimate of their outcome to be held in a reserve.

In liability insurance, many years may pass between the time an insurer is notified that one of its insureds is being sued and the time the case is closed. In some lines of liability insurance, twenty or more years may elapse between the time that an incident occurs and the time that a lawsuit is brought. Another ten or more years might pass before such a claim results in a payment from the insurer to an injured victim. Because the losses they represent can be unresolved for such long periods and may involve large amounts of money, loss reserves are essential to present fairly the accounting statements of liability insurers.

LIFE INSURERS RESERVE ACCOUNTS

Life insurers maintain a **policy reserve** that represents the difference between the mathematical liability of a future death claim and the value of future premiums that the insured will pay the insurer. The policy reserve is best illustrated by reference to a level-premium whole life policy. With this contract, the insurer is obligated to pay a death claim whenever death occurs, and the insured is scheduled to pay regular level premiums for life. Each year, the present value of the death claim increases as the insured ages and the probability of death increases. At the same time, the present value of future premiums decreases as more of the premiums are collected. As the value of the death benefit increases while the present value of future premiums decreases, the policy reserve must increase to keep the equation in balance. This relationship is illustrated in Figure 10-1. Because the insurer must keep investment assets to offset the policy reserve liability, the insureds have financial protection in the event of the insurer's financial weakness.

While our level-premium whole life example focused on one policy, life insurers do not calculate their policy reserves on an individual policy basis in practice. Instead, they consider blocks of similar policies and calculate the reserve for the whole block of business. Likewise, life insurers must keep policy reserves for all types of policies sold.

Since 1992, the NAIC has required life insurers to keep two different reserve accounts to protect insureds from financial weakness caused by poor investment results. The **asset valuation reserve (AVR)** is supposed to act as a buffer that allows insurers to absorb losses arising from sales of assets for less than their cost (capital losses). These losses arise from what financiers call "business risk." The **interest maintenance reserve (IMR)** is designed to allow insurers to absorb losses caused by changes (increases) in interest rates on government securities.

FIGURE 10-1 Life Insurance Reserves

The AVR requires the insurer to consider the riskiness of its holdings of the following asset categories: corporate and municipal bonds, common and preferred stocks, mortgages, real estate, and joint ventures. This reserve does not apply to cash, U.S. government securities, or policyholder loans. The company, based on maximum guidelines developed by the NAIC, must keep a percentage of each category of assets in the AVR. For example, the maximum guideline for the safest bonds is 1 percent of face value, while the formula for the lowest safety category calls for 20 percent of value. For mortgages, the percentage required in the AVR varies from 3.5 percent to 10.5 percent, depending on the delinquency rate of the mortgage class. In all cases, the amount that an insurer has in its AVR is a function of both the NAIC maximum guidelines and its own investment results.

If an insurer's investment results are poor in a particular year, the AVR will increase, but if previous years' results were good, the balance in the AVR may be sufficient to absorb actual realized losses. In fact, one purpose of the AVR is to act as a buffer, so investment declines in a particular year can be dampened. For example, assume that a company began the year with a $10 million balance in the AVR. During the year, the insurer had $1 million in realized capital losses and another $1 million in unrealized losses. The AVR formula might call for a transfer to the reserve of only $800,000 this year, with the balance of the losses to be amortized in future years. Thus, despite $2 million in losses this year, only $800,000 will be charged to operating results.

The IMR applies only to U.S. government securities and guaranteed securities of agencies backed by the credit of the U.S. government. The IMR accumulates interest-related realized gains and losses and amortizes them into an insurer's income over the remaining life of the investments sold. Like the AVR, the IMR acts as a buffer, dampening the effect of a single year's gains or losses on an insurer's operating income.

Neither investment reserve requirements nor any other type of reserve requirement can provide an absolute guarantee of insurer solvency, as history has shown. Reserve requirements, however, should allow an insurer to be financially rehabilitated with much less injury to its insureds than otherwise would be the case.

Regular Audits and Solvency Testing

Every insurance company is required to file an annual statement with the insurance department in each state in which it transacts business, as well as with the NAIC. The various state insurance departments verify these reports by an audit about once every three years. The audit is conducted by the state insurance department of the state in which the insurer is domiciled, joined by representatives of insurance departments of other states. The NAIC audit procedure divides the country into six zones, with one representative from each zone participating in each audit.

In addition to on-site inspection and audit, the NAIC monitors insurer solvency on an ongoing basis using its Insurance Regulatory Information System (IRIS). IRIS is a computer-based testing system designed to spot solvency problems before they result in losses to insureds. Using IRIS, the NAIC calculates twelve ratios based on data submitted by each insurer to be audited. Companies not submitting to this audit are reported to the licensing states.

The main outcome of IRIS occurs when the computer analysis flags any ratios outside a normal range of expected results. Companies with the highest number of abnormal results receive the highest priority for examination by state examiners. After the first-phase computer analysis of IRIS results, a second-phase analysis of companies with four or more ratios outside the normal range occurs. Logical explanations for abnormal ratios may exist, such as solid but rapid growth, a merger of two companies, or unusual investment results. Alternatively, firms with many abnormal ratios also may be in weak financial condition, but if this is caught promptly, insurance departments may be able to take action protecting policyowners' interests.

Regulators also use other sources of information when evaluating insurers, including SEC filings, financial ratings companies' reports, complaint ratios, news articles, and letters from competitors and agents.

In 1992, after the well-publicized failure of three large life insurance companies and the financial weakening of others, the NAIC developed a new **risk-based capital (RBC)** requirement for life insurance companies. RBC differs from the fixed minimum amount of capital standard in that it takes into account differences in an insurer's underwriting and investment practices in developing a surplus requirement for that specific company. For example, consider two insurers similar in size. One company operates very conservatively, whereas the other operates very aggressively. Prior to the adoption of the RBC requirements, both insurers might have the same minimum capital requirement. Under the RBC rules, the aggressive insurer might have to maintain 150 percent more capital and surplus than the conservative insurer. RBC thus sets an estimated amount of capital based on the aggregated risks of the insurer.

Insurer Insolvencies and Guaranty Funds

All states have solvency laws and guaranty funds to protect insureds from losses caused by insolvent insurers. State regulators are likely to intervene in an insurer's independent operations when the company's surplus accounts reach an unacceptably low level or its conduct appears to be jeopardizing the policyowner's interests. Regulators call the first phase of intervention *conservatorship, rehabilitation*, or *receivership*. In this phase, regulators meet with the executives of the troubled insurer to identify the source of the financial problems and develop corrective actions. For example, regulators may limit the insurer's ability to sell more insurance, find a solvent insurer to assume (a portion of) its business, or liquidate the company.

If the insurer's financial condition has deteriorated past the point of rehabilitation, regulators can declare that the insurer is insolvent, thus initiating the liquidation of the insurer. The insurance insolvency process is quite different from bankruptcy because insolvency provides more protection to the interest of the policyholder. If the assets of the insolvent insurer are insufficient to satisfy the claims of the policyholders, regulators can pay for the shortfall using a **guaranty fund**. Managed on a state-level basis by insurance commissioners, the guaranty fund is created to pay for the cost of unpaid claims of insurance policyholders. Guaranty funds vary across the states, with different limits of benefits available to different classes of injured insureds.[4] The NAIC Guaranty Fund Model Act provides some uniformity among the various state laws.

A state's guaranty fund is not prefunded; the financing instead comes from post-insolvency assessments on all insurers doing business in that state. Thus, there is a transfer of funds from solvent insurers to support the insureds of insolvent insurers. The fairness of such a transfer is subject to criticism because the most likely transfer is from insureds purchasing coverage from insurers charging adequate (higher) premiums to insureds of companies charging inadequate (lower) premiums. Critics note that

---

[4] For example, the policyowner's residency at the time the policy was purchased or the insolvency declared may result in different treatment in different states. Some states treat individual policyowners differently from corporate policyowners, and many states exclude large commercial buyers from protection under the guaranty fund.

insureds who already paid a higher price for their insurance now must pay even more to support insureds who chose to purchase insurance at a lower price.

The financial failure of an insurer often results in insureds giving up some contractual rights, including access to their funds for specified periods of time. In some cases of failed life insurance companies, policyowners received lower investment returns than called for in their contracts.

Rate Regulations

Many people fear that open and unrestrained price competition will not work in the insurance market because prices must be set long before the final costs are known. Thus, rate regulation has been substituted for unrestrained price competition in the insurance market.

Many states' insurance codes specify that insurance rates must not be excessive, inadequate, or unfairly discriminatory. *Not excessive* generally means that rates are affordable and not too high compared to insured claims, while *inadequate* means that the rates are not too low. *Not unfairly discriminatory* means that (dis)similar exposures are charged similar (different) prices and insurers cannot use pricing variables that are deemed discriminatory by the courts, such as race or ethnicity.

Rate regulation, however it is approached in a given state, is at the heart of the effort to promote insurer solvency. It also protects the consumer from the disadvantage of unequal knowledge relative to the insurer, particularly in personal lines insurance. Thus, there generally is less regulation of commercial property insurance and reinsurance rates than in pricing personal insurance.

Investment Activities

Insurance companies are not free to invest funds in all available alternatives. Because inferior investments may jeopardize insurer solvency, states have limited the types of investments that insurers may make. State regulation specifies the classes of acceptable and unacceptable investments and the method used to value assets.

Because life insurance companies hold vast amounts of the public's savings, and because life insurance contracts may extend for decades—neither of which generally occurs in non–life insurance situations—life insurers generally are not allowed to make risky investments. Typical restrictions on life insurers include a limit on the total amount of common stock that a company may own. In New York, for example, the limit is about 10 percent of the insurer's admitted assets. Property insurers are less severely restricted from purchasing common stock and do so to a considerable extent. Life insurers offering newer products based on the performance of a portfolio of equity investments may do so within the framework of special rules for these products.

Policy Form Approval

State regulation requires insurers to get a policy form approved before selling the policy to the public. Many states have regulations that apply to policy forms used to sell life, health, property, and other personal insurance coverages. For example, states require cash-value life insurance policy forms to have certain minimum guarantees, require property insurance forms to contain specified provisions, and require health insurance to provide minimum cancellation rights. Many states require explicit labeling for clauses restricting insurance coverage. The purpose of policy form approval is to keep unfair policy forms out of the market. Policy form approval also prevents insurers from subverting rate regulation by reducing claims payments with restrictive policy wording.

Licensing of Insurance Companies

Each state applies its own regulations before granting people a license to begin operating an insurance company. One of the most important of these specifies a required minimum amount of capital and surplus to form a new insurer. Additional rules often require a minimum number of potential policyholders and qualified members of the board of directors. All states have rules governing who may be an insurance company officer. Regulators refer to the state in which an insurer is legally formed as the **state of domicile**. Similarly, before an insurance company domiciled in one state can transact business in another state, it must secure a license to operate from the state in which it wants to do business.

One of the greatest powers wielded by an insurance commissioner is the right to grant an insurer a license to sell insurance in its state. As defined by insurance laws, **admitted insurance** is insurance obtained from insurers licensed by the state in which the insurance is purchased. Consumers can purchase admitted insurance from domestic or foreign insurers. **Domestic insurance** is provided by a licensed insurer domiciled within the state providing the license. **Foreign insurance** is provided by an insurer licensed by a state other than the one in which the insurance applies (such as an Iowa insurer doing business in Illinois). Through its licensing power, a regulator can better assure that domestic and foreign insurers adhere to its state's insurance laws.

Insurance obtained from insurers who are not licensed in the jurisdiction where the policy is purchased or the exposure is located is called **nonadmitted insurance**. For example, **alien insurance** is insurance purchased in the United States from an unlicensed, non-U.S. insurer. Only when insurance is unavailable domestically (i.e., within the insured's state) may it be placed with a nonadmitted insurer. States control such business by requiring agents or brokers to secure a **surplus-lines** license before placing business with nonadmitted insurers. Surplus-lines agents or brokers generally may not place business with a nonadmitted insurer unless they can establish domestic insurance is unavailable. The rationale for surplus-lines regulation is that the state can exercise no control over nonadmitted insurers but can control the excess and surplus-lines agent or broker.

Some large insurance brokers and their large clients argue that surplus-lines regulations add an unnecessary level of regulation and expense to consumers, and that the only insureds who use the nonadmitted market are large industrial companies that have risk management and legal staffs to protect them from undesirable insurers.

Licensing of Agents, Brokers, and Loss Adjusters

All states require insurance agents and brokers, also collectively known as *producers,* to secure a license before transacting business. One of the mandates of the GLB Act caused the states to standardize their approach to licensing agents so that agents can operate across state lines. Some states also require licenses for loss adjusters. Many states require an applicant for a license to pass an examination that evaluates his or her knowledge of the insurance business. Many states now require agents to earn continuing education credits to maintain their licenses. Rules promoting more knowledgeable agents and brokers benefit consumers but may prove to be a hardship on companies relying on untrained or part-time agents.

State insurance codes establish rules outlining unacceptable conduct by an agent or broker. Misrepresentation, including any incomplete comparisons that cause an insured to exchange one insurance policy for another, a practice called **twisting**, is forbidden.

Anti-rebating laws prevent agents from sharing their commissions with an insured. Critics claim that rather than directly protecting the consumer, anti-rebating laws protect insurance agents from having to share their income with the customer. Those in favor of changing the law argue that change will benefit consumers by lowering prices. Those opposed to the change argue that only consumers who are successful bargainers will benefit, causing others to bear the burden of the higher prices. Those opposed to a change also question whether insurance agents would be able to earn adequate income.

Consumer Complaints

The insurance commissioner's office generally has a staff available to deal with consumer complaints against insurers or agents. Today, many state insurance departments maintain Web sites that allow consumers to check on agents and insurance companies and provide a path for lodging complaints. These sites also may contain other useful consumer information about policy forms and special advice for older consumers.

Many complaints are the result of consumer misunderstanding, and it is the regulator's job to treat both insurer and insured fairly. Typically, the regulator forwards a complaint to the insurer and asks for a response within a limited period of time. If an insurer's response is not satisfactory, the regulator can direct a course of action. The insurer is very likely to comply with the regulator's directive, however, because its license to operate is jeopardized by noncompliance.

Taxation

Taxation is a form of regulation that both the states and the federal government have adopted. It is not without problems, however. Some arise because the industry is composed of for-profit (stock) and nonprofit (mutual) competitors. This situation has led to complex income tax formulas, especially at the federal level. A much simpler tax is the state premium tax, which is typically a flat percentage, such as 2 percent, of the premium a consumer pays. The amount of the tax varies from state to state and is often different among the various lines of insurance within a given state. The premium tax is a tax on a necessity; thus, it is a valuable source of income in most states.

The tax on the insurance transaction was justified originally as a source of revenue to supply the funds that the states needed to provide regulation. Today, though, the states collect much more money in tax revenue than they spend on insurance regulation. The consumer's interest probably would be better served if taxes were lower or the money spent on regulation increased. The consumer, however, does not see the premium tax directly because the insurer builds it into the insurance rates.

Summary

Insurance regulation determines how and by whom insurance transactions may be made. Regulation is established by law, administered by public officials, and interpreted by courts when disputes arise. Insurance is regulated by the states, not the federal government. In most states, the title of the chief insurance regulator is the commissioner of insurance. An organization consisting of all state insurance regulators, the National Association of Insurance Commissioners (NAIC), helps to coordinate regulation across the states.

The purposes of insurance regulation are to promote insurer solvency, balance the inequality of knowledge between the insurance companies and consumers, deal with a unique pricing problem requiring some limits on free and unrestrained competition, and promote certain social goals.

In 1869, the states were given the authority to provide insurance regulation by the *Paul v. Virginia* decision of the Supreme Court. In 1944, the Supreme Court reversed itself in the *South-Eastern Underwriters Association (SEUA)* case, holding that insurance transactions were subject to federal regulation, including the antitrust laws. In 1945, Congress passed the McCarran-Ferguson

Act, which allowed the states to continue to provide insurance regulation, because it found state insurance regulation to be in the public interest. In 1999, Congress passed the Gramm-Leach-Bliley Act, allowing financial services holding companies to compete in insurance, commercial banking, and investment banking while retaining the tradition of state-based insurance regulation.

Although the various states have their own rules, all the states regulate the same activities. Among the areas and activities regulated are the following: legal reserves and surplus requirements, investment decisions, the calculation of insurance rates, policy form approval, taxation, and the licensing of companies, agents, and brokers.

Review

1. What does the term *insurance regulation* mean?
2. Why is the solvency of insurers so important to regulators?
3. What is meant by unequal knowledge and bargaining power? Why do regulators have to protect the purchasers of homeowners insurance more than the purchasers of large commercial insurance policies?
4. How does the pricing of an insurance policy for an insurer differ from a bologna manufacturer's pricing its product? Why does the difference in pricing problems require that insurance pricing be subject to regulation?
5. Why might the lowest-priced insurance policy be undesirable from the consumer's standpoint?
6. Describe the two primary approaches to rate regulation in insurance.
7. What was the outcome of the *Paul v. Virginia* case?
8. What effect did the McCarran-Ferguson Act have on insurance regulation? Why was it passed?
9. What is the role of the NAIC? What are its main functions?
10. How did the Gramm-Leach-Bliley Act (GLB) change the competitive landscape of insurance?
11. What are insurance company reserve requirements? How do they work to protect the consumer?
12. Explain the nature of the risk-based capital ratio.
13. Describe the main methods for regulating the investment activities of insurers.
14. Describe the differences between admitted insurers and nonadmitted insurers.
15. Describe surplus-lines markets and explain their role in serving the needs of insurance consumers.

Objective Questions

1. All of the following are reasons why insurance transactions are so carefully regulated EXCEPT:
   a. Insolvent insurers can create serious social-economic problems.
   b. Insurance buyers and sellers have unequal knowledge.
   c. Insurance prices must be set before costs are known.
   d. Insurance company failures were a significant contributing factor to the Great Depression of the 1930s.
2. The first insurance case dealing with the question of state versus federal insurance regulations to reach the Supreme Court was:
   a. The *South-Eastern Underwriters Association* case
   b. The Gramm-Leach-Bliley Act
   c. *Paul v. Virginia*
   d. *Merritt v. New York*
3. The two main regulatory approaches to supervising insurers' prices are called:
   a. Controlled and uncontrolled competition
   b. Free competition and restrained competition
   c. Prior approval and competitive rating
   d. Level loss and expected loss competition
4. The federal law that allows the combination of banks and insurance companies is:
   a. The Federal Insurance Act of 1984
   b. The Gramm-Leach-Bliley (GLB) Act
   c. The McCarran-Ferguson Act
   d. The Federal Banking-Insurance Act of 1984
5. A _____ is created by insurance regulators to pay for the unpaid claims of the policyholders of an insolvent insurance company.
   a. surplus-lines insurer
   b. guaranty fund
   c. loss reserve
   d. foreign insurer
6. If an insurer's liabilities exceed the value of its assets, it is:
   a. Delisted
   b. Demutualized
   c. Impaired
   d. Insolvent

7. Assets that are readily available to pay claims are called:
   a. Admitted assets
   b. Real assets
   c. Accepted assets
   d. Standard operating assets

8. "Insurance provided by a licensed insurer within the state providing the license" is the definition of:
   a. Foreign insurance
   b. State insurance
   c. Local insurance
   d. Domestic insurance

Discussion Questions

1. What arguments would you make for allowing insurers to set their own rates and be regulated by market or competitive forces? What arguments would you make for continuing regulatory approval of insurance rates?

2. What arrangements do you think would best protect the interests of both insureds and insurers with respect to handling consumers' complaints?

Selected References

The I. I. I. Insurance Factbook, 2011 (New York: Insurance Information Institute), published annually.

Myhr, A. E., and J. J. Markham, 2004, *Insurance Operations, Regulation, and Statutory Accounting*, 2d ed. (Malvern, PA: American Institute for Property Casualty Underwriters/Insurance Institute of America).

11

Insurance Contracts

After studying this chapter, you should be able to

- Identify some basic legal vocabulary used in insurance contracts

- List the four essential elements of a valid contract, as applied to insurance agreements

- Describe several features that distinguish insurance contracts from other contracts

- Explain why insurance policies are standardized contracts

- Describe the basic components used by insurers to construct an insurance policy

All insurance purchases involve contracts. Insurance is a distinct branch of contract law, and a general knowledge of contract law is essential to understanding insurance. The first part of this chapter presents some basic vocabulary and rules of contract law in general. The second part demonstrates how insurance exhibits the four basic parts of a valid contract. Next, we explain the special characteristics distinguishing insurance contracts from other contracts. Figure 11-1 provides an outline of the material described in this chapter.

Insurance companies issue standardized insurance policies that are generally the same across large numbers of customers. The last section of this chapter explains why insurers use standardized insurance policies and describes their component parts.

CONTRACT TERMINOLOGY

A **contract** is a legally binding agreement that creates rights and duties for those who are parties to it. If one party to the contract fails to perform its duties without a legal excuse, attorneys say that the contract is *breached*. If a contract is breached, or if disputes arise between the parties about the interpretation of the contract, the issues may be settled by a court. Courts can enforce their judgments and settle contractual disputes using a variety of remedies. For example, a court can require performance of the original contract by the breaching party, or it can direct that the injured party be compensated for damages caused by the breach.

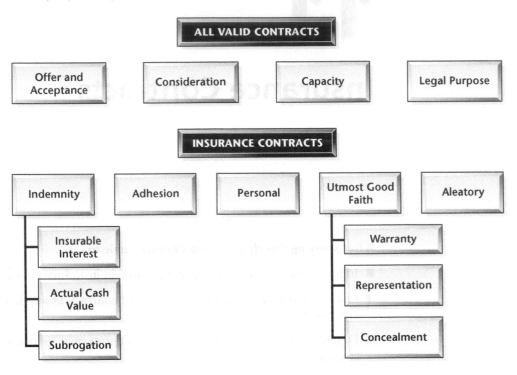

FIGURE 11-1 Distinguishing Characteristics of Insurance Contracts

A **valid contract** is one that a court will enforce. We describe the elements of a valid contract shortly. Two other categories of contracts are voidable and void contracts. A **voidable contract** allows one party the option of breaking the agreement because of a breach by the other party (whether by an act or by an omission of an act). The party with the right to void the contract may choose to have the contract enforced instead. A good example of a voidable contract in insurance is one in which the insured has attempted to defraud the insurer. After the insurer establishes the insured's fraud, the insurer will be released from its contractual obligations. At the insurer's option, the contract can be set aside, or voided.

If, however, an insurer breaches the contract by refusing to pay a valid claim, its insured can go to court to force the insurer to perform. If a court believes an insurer denied the claim in bad faith, it may penalize the insurer for amounts substantially greater than the original amount of damages sustained by the insured.

A **void contract** is one that a court will not enforce because it lacks one or more features of a valid contract. For example, assume that an insurance contract is purchased for an illegal purpose, such as insuring property with the intent of committing the fraud of arson. A court would not enforce such a contract after discovering the illegal purpose. Likewise, if an incompetent person (such as a person declared legally insane) were to enter into an insurance contract, this contract would be considered void from the beginning.

Binder

In property insurance, a temporary contract called a **binder** often is used before the formal insurance policy is issued. The binder must meet all the requirements for a legal contract. It is distinguished by its temporary nature (often 30 days or less). The purpose of the binder is to provide coverage during the time it takes to process an application. A binder may be oral or written. An oral binder, such as one that an agent may give over the telephone, should be followed by a written document, which can be sent via mail, fax, or e-mail in most states, to reduce the likelihood of disputes and to protect the positions of both parties. Normally, written binders will specify the amount of insurance, the period during which the binder is effective, and the parties to the binder.

With respect to oral binders, or contracts, we must define the **parol evidence rule**. This rule provides that after an oral agreement is put in writing, no evidence of additions or conflicts between the oral and written agreements can be introduced in court. That is, the written agreement's terms take precedence over the oral agreement's terms if there is a conflict between the two. For example, if the oral agreement called for $185,000 of insurance and the written agreement provided for $180,000, and assuming that the difference resulted from an ambiguity rather than from a clerical error, the parol evidence rule would support the $180,000 figure.

Conditional Receipt

Binders are not used in life insurance because life insurance agents lack the authority to bind their companies. However, temporary coverage that is contingent on an applicant's ability to present evidence of insurability can be provided by a **conditional receipt**. Life insurance agents give an applicant a conditional receipt when the applicant submits a premium payment with the application. With one common type of conditional receipt, if evidence of insurability exists, coverage begins from the date of the receipt. Evidence of insurability always includes, but is not limited to, good health. Occupation would be another factor. As an example, assume that Francis Drake submits a $400 premium with his application for $180,000 of life insurance. The following day, he takes and passes a medical examination. The next day, he drowns in a fishing accident. Despite the fact that death occurred before the policy was issued, the insurer would make the $180,000 payment because there was a conditional receipt and evidence of insurability.

The main difference between the property insurance binder and the life insurance conditional receipt is the contingent nature of the conditional receipt. The life insurer is not bound to honor claims if the terms of the conditional receipt are not met. The conditional receipt also implies that a premium payment accompanied the application, while property insurers generally do not require an advance premium payment when they issue a binder. In fact, a binder often is required to give the insurer time to calculate the appropriate charge for the insurance.

ELEMENTS OF A VALID CONTRACT

All valid contracts must have the following four elements: offer and acceptance, consideration, capacity, and legal purpose.

Offer and Acceptance

Transactions begin when one person proposes to exchange something of value with another person. The **offer** is the proposal to make such an exchange. If the second person agrees to the exchange, this is **acceptance**. The offer must be reasonably definite and communicated clearly. The acceptance must be unconditional, unequivocal, and communicated clearly.

All parties to a contract must agree to *exactly* the same terms. There must be a meeting of the minds. To create a contract, one party makes an offer to another party to do something or not to do something. The second party may accept or reject this offer or may make a *counteroffer*. When one party makes an offer and the second party accepts it without qualifications, a necessary requirement for a contract is met.

The offer and acceptance may be oral or in writing. The law recognizes both forms of communication. In property insurance, as noted, most states allow oral insurance binders and contracts, but they are usually put in writing as soon as possible to provide protection for both the insured and insurer.

When purchasing insurance, an individual ordinarily completes an application and, in doing so, makes an offer to purchase insurance. If the insurer accepts the offer, it agrees to insure the applicant. Note that insurance agents, though soliciting new business, legally are not offering to sell insurance. Technically, we say that they are inviting the insured to make an offer. If the insurer issues a policy, that indicates acceptance.

Consideration

The value exchanged between the parties to the contract (that is, what each party gives to the other) is the **consideration**. Consideration may take a tangible form such as money, or it may take the form of a promise to do something or not to do it. There must be an exchange of consideration to have a valid contract.

In an insurance contract, the consideration that the insurer gives is a contingent promise to pay the insured. That is, the insurer agrees to make payment only if a covered loss occurs. If such an event does not occur, the insurer need not make payment. In return for the insurer's promise, the insured gives two things—money (premiums) and a promise to follow the provisions and stipulations in the insurance contract.

Most insurance contracts are **unilateral contracts**. That is, only the insurer makes an enforceable promise. The insured does not promise to pay the premiums and cannot be sued for failure to do so. Insureds, however, cannot collect for losses if they do not pay premiums because timely payment of the premium is a condition of the contract. Contracts in which both parties make enforceable promises are called **bilateral contracts**.

Capacity

Not every person has the legal **capacity** to enter into a contract. As a rule, for reasons of social welfare, minors, the insane, and the intoxicated cannot enter into a binding agreement. The purpose of this rule is to keep people from taking advantage of parties who presumably do not have the capacity to understand the agreement that they are making.

State law defines the period of minority as ending at age eighteen. If a thirteen-year-old were to enter into a contract, it would be voidable at the youngster's option. If a minor chose not to void the contract, the youngster could *ratify* or *affirm* it when reaching age eighteen.

Although as a rule minors can disaffirm contracts, they cannot do so when contracting for a necessary good or service. In most instances, courts have held that insurance contracts are not necessities. However, when minors own and operate motor vehicles, own property, or have dependents, the court may consider insurance a necessary purchase that cannot be disaffirmed. Many state laws allow older minors to make binding agreements for insurance.

Insurance companies also must be qualified to enter into contracts. They must have a license to operate in each state where they do business. If an insured suffered financial damages because he or she dealt unknowingly with an unqualified insurer, the insured could look to the court for a remedy. The unauthorized insurer would be subject to fines and penalties.

Legal Purpose

A contract must have a **legal purpose**, a function or intention permitted by law. Contracts having an antisocial purpose are legally unenforceable. No court will aid the parties to such a contract. An insurance policy purchased as a gamble on a famous person's life, or on any life in which the contract owner has no legal interest, is an example of an unenforceable contract. If a person tried to collect proceeds from contracts where an insurable interest was lacking, a court would hold the contract void, as explained later when describing the doctrine of *insurable interest.*

DISTINGUISHING CHARACTERISTICS OF INSURANCE CONTRACTS

All valid contracts must have the four essential features just presented if a court is to enforce their provisions. Insurance contracts are distinctive. They have some unique elements (centering on the contingent promise to pay for covered losses) but share other characteristics (such as subrogation and arbitration conditions) with other business contracts. We now will describe in detail some distinctive characteristics and legal doctrines applying to insurance contracts.

Principle of Indemnity

Insurance contracts provide compensation for an insured's losses. The insured, however, should not profit from an insurance transaction, or else the insurance will provide the policyholder an incentive to cause fraudulent losses or to overstate claims. **Indemnity** means that the insured should be placed in the same financial position after the insured loss as before it. Any departure from this rule should be on the side of undercompensation. Insurers enforce the principle of indemnity through the insurable interest requirement, actual cash value (ACV) settlements, and the operation of subrogation. We will discuss each of these topics separately.

Three Exceptions to the Rule Three exceptions exist to the rule that insurance contracts are contracts of indemnity: life insurance, replacement-cost insurance, and valued insurance.

Life Insurance. Because the economic value of a human life cannot be measured precisely before death, life insurance cannot be a contract of indemnity. A person could not be put in exactly the same financial position occupied before the death of the insured because that position includes unknown future income. Nevertheless, life insurance underwriters are careful not to overinsure by allowing insureds to acquire more life insurance than their financial position justifies. Overinsurance creates an unacceptable moral hazard for life insurers, who do not want their insureds worth more dead than alive. Thus, in practice, life insurance honors the principle of indemnity, but it does not do so legally.

Replacement-Cost Insurance. **Replacement-cost insurance** is written when the insurer promises to pay an amount equal to the full cost of repairing or replacing the property without deduction for depreciation. If an insured loses an old, run-down building and it is replaced by a new building, the insured obviously is better off after the loss. Replacement-cost coverage is a typical feature of homeowners insurance policies and also is found in other property contracts. Because insurance companies are well aware of the potential moral hazard created by writing this coverage, they place conditions and restrictions in replacement-cost contracts to reduce this problem. One typical restriction is a requirement that the insured rebuild, usually at the same location. If no rebuilding is done, the insurer pays the actual cash value of the loss, which can be substantially less than the replacement cost. (We define the term *actual cash value,* or *ACV,* shortly.)

Valued Insurance Policies. A **valued insurance policy** is another exception to the rule of indemnity. Valued policies pay the limit of liability whenever an insured total loss occurs. The value of the insured property is agreed to before the policy is written. If a total loss occurs, it may cause more or less damage than the stated amount. Nevertheless, the stated amount will be paid. Insurers write some ocean and inland marine insurance contracts on a valued basis. The use of valued policies generally is limited to objects for which market value may fluctuate or be difficult to determine accurately after a loss, such as art objects and other collector's items. Underwriters respect the principle of indemnity when writing valued policies and generally require insureds to get appraisals of their property to establish its insurable value.

Insurable Interest

If people could insure property or a life in which they had no financial interest, insurance would become gambling. An insured would be enriched if these losses occurred. Such contracts of insurance were written for a while in England, but the fraud and murder associated with them caused laws to be passed prohibiting the issuance of insurance policies in which the insured lacked interest in the loss. Today's insurance laws hold that no one may collect insurance proceeds without demonstrating a personal loss from the insured event.

Property Insurance In property insurance, one must show a legally recognized form of ownership, such as a title, deed, or another demonstrable financial interest. Insurable financial interests not involving property ownership include bailments, mortgage loans, or other transactions where someone pledges property to secure a loan. In some cases, courts have allowed recovery where the insured had a contract to purchase a structure (or the expectation of inheritance), but the transaction was not complete at the time of an insured loss. This description should make it clear that more than one party may have an insurable interest in the same property. For example, both the owner and the mortgage loan holder may have insurance on the same building.

In property insurance, this interest must be shown to exist when the loss occurs. As noted, a person may purchase insurance on property not yet owned. To collect the insurance proceeds, however, the person must demonstrate a financial loss from the insured event.

For example, assume that Bud and Miller each owns one-half interest in a bar and both are insureds under the same contract. If a loss occurs, each could collect only half the proceeds. Now assume that on October 14, Bud sells his interest to Miller. If a loss occurs on October 15, Bud cannot collect from his insurance policy because at the time of the loss, he had no insurable interest in the property. In other words, he already was entitled to the sale proceeds at the time of the fire. If he were able to receive the insurance proceeds and the sale proceeds, he would be enriched by collecting twice for the same property.

Life Insurance In life insurance, the policyowner must show a recognized interest in having the insured's life continue. This interest must be shown when the policy is purchased. People are presumed to have an unlimited insurable interest in their own lives and may purchase any amount of insurance on their own lives that an insurer will issue. Furthermore, the law presumes that a husband and wife have an unlimited interest in each other's lives. Beyond close family relationships, an insurable interest must be demonstrated; it will not be presumed to exist. Interests that generally can be demonstrated include creditors in the lives of their debtors (but the amount of insurance must bear a reasonable relationship to the debt), business partners in each other's lives, and employers in the lives of their key employees.

Unlike the case of property insurance, the insurable interest must be demonstrated at the time the life insurance is purchased. It need not be shown when the loss occurs. This rule is a choice of the lesser of two evils. On the one hand, divorce removes a spouse's insurable interest. If a policy were to be canceled at this point for lack of insurable interest, the insureds would stand to lose some money. If, for example, the husband were terminally ill, the loss could be substantial. On the other hand, allowing the wife to collect when she no longer has an insurable interest may create a moral hazard. It is somewhat reassuring to know that the law will not allow murderers to benefit from their misdeeds. In the event of a murder, the life insurer, at a court's direction, usually will pay the proceeds to a trust to be distributed to the victim's rightful heirs, excluding the murderer.

In life insurance, another distinction must be made. The owner of the insurance policy, not the beneficiary, must demonstrate the insurable interest. The **owner** of the policy is the party who can enforce the contractual rights, such as naming the beneficiary, assigning the policy, or taking out loans from the insurer. The **beneficiary** is the party who receives the funds at the insured's death. The beneficiary need not have an insurable interest in the insured's life. The owner, however, also may be the beneficiary of the policy.

For example, Father may be the **insured** (the person whose death will cause the policy to mature as a death claim). Mother may be the owner, and Child the beneficiary. In this case, the beneficiary well may have an insurable interest. It is possible, however, to name as the beneficiary of a life insurance policy a charity or the U.S. government, neither of which would be expected to have an insurable interest in the insured's life.

Actual Cash Value

Actual cash value (ACV) generally means replacement cost at the time of loss less depreciation.[1] Equation 11-1 shows this definition mathematically. As noted earlier, the replacement cost of the building is based on the cost to rebuild the structure. It is not based on the price paid to buy the property because prices based on market value also include the value of the land and its location. Location can be an important factor in determining market value, but not replacement cost. For example, it might cost the same amount to build a beautiful home in location A or location B. However, if location B were downwind of a foul-smelling agricultural plant, the home's market value would be less at location B.

$$\text{ACV} = \text{Replacement cost} - \text{Depreciation} \qquad \text{(Eq. 11-1)}$$

Depreciation is expressed as a fraction. The numerator is the number of years the structure was in use. The denominator is an estimate of the structure's useful life. Thus, a building used for 15 years having an expected useful life of 60 years would be one-quarter depreciated (15/60) and three-quarters undepreciated (45/60). This depreciation calculation is not the equivalent of the accounting concept because the accounting

---

[1] Note that if building standards are upgraded between the time that the structure was originally built and the time of the loss, replacement-cost insurance does not cover the extra cost resulting from the higher building standards. Separate insurance must be arranged to cover the increased cost resulting from changes in building codes or ordinances.

concept is based on purchase price, while depreciation for ACV calculations is based on replacement cost and an estimate of the asset's useful life.

Consider a home that has been occupied one-quarter of its useful life. It has a replacement cost of $150,000. (Assume that its historical cost was $100,000, producing an accounting book value of $75,000 on a straight-line basis. The historical cost and accounting book value are irrelevant to the ACV calculation.) Its ACV is $150,000 × 3/4 (the undepreciated amount) = $112,500. As a second example, assume that this building sustains a $50,000 (replacement-cost value) loss. The ACV of this *partial loss* is $50,000 × 3/4 = $37,500.

Sometimes insurers do not use an ACV provision in their policies. In cases where the cost to replace a building is greater than its market value, as is often the case with older buildings, insurers provide coverage based on replacement cost with modern construction techniques. Insurers call this provision **functional replacement**. Thus, functional replacement allows wallboard to be substituted for plaster walls and plastic pipes for copper pipes.

Subrogation

Subrogation is the legal substitution of one person in another's place. Subrogation is supported by the theory that if a person must pay a debt for which another is liable, such payment should give the person who paid a right to collect the debt from the liable party. In insurance, subrogation gives the insurer the right to collect from a third party after paying its insured's claim.

A typical case of subrogation arises in automobile insurance collision claims. Suppose that Lois Steam, the psychologist, is responsible for a collision with Eileen Dover, the architect. Eileen may sue Lois for damages, or she may collect from her own automobile collision insurance. If she chooses to collect from her own insurance, her insurance company will be subrogated to her right to sue Lois. Eileen cannot collect for her loss both from her insurer and from Lois. Thus, subrogation prevents insureds from profiting on their insurance by collecting twice for the same loss.[2] Subrogation also prevents negligent parties from escaping payment for their acts because the injured party has insurance. Insurance policies typically require that the insured cannot take actions that prejudice the insurer's right to subrogation.

Subrogation does not exist in life insurance because life insurance is not a contract of indemnity. Thus, if Karl Marx is killed by his neighbor's negligence, Mrs. Marx may collect whatever damages a court will award for her husband's wrongful death. She also may collect any life insurance proceeds. The life insurer is not subrogated to the liability claim and cannot sue the negligent party.

An insurer has no right to subrogate against its own insured if an insured's negligence results in the insurer paying a claim. First, because insureds have no right to sue themselves, the insurer has no right that could be substituted. Second, the value of the insurance contract would be greatly diminished if an insurer could sue negligent insureds. Such a provision would make most liability insurance valueless. When the insured's negligence causes the destruction of his or her insured property, as is often the case, property insurance also would be useless.

---

[2] If an insurer does receive more compensation than it paid its insured from a subrogation lawsuit, the difference generally belongs to the insured. For example, assume that Eileen collected $4,500 from her insurer because of her collision with Lois. Her insurer reduced the $5,000 damage claim to $4,500 because of a $500 deductible in her collision coverage. The insurer sued for and collected $5,000 from Lois. The insurer then must reimburse Eileen for the $500 deductible. Insurers must compensate their insureds fully for their losses before they can keep any proceeds from subrogation litigation.

Contract of Adhesion

Skilled attorneys working for insurance companies or insurance rating bureaus draft insurance contracts. These attorneys understand the meaning of the words used in insurance contracts and of the drafting and legal history of these contracts. Consumers typically do not have this specialized knowledge. Risk managers of larger organizations and their brokers may have comparable knowledge and information, and in some cases, they may draft their own contracts. However, individuals and small firms cannot bargain with the insurer about the wording of the contract. They may accept the contract unaltered, or they may reject it.

Because such unequal knowledge and bargaining power are perceived to give the insurer a significant advantage over the insured, most states classify insurance contracts as **contracts of adhesion**. Under this legal principle, any language that a court determines is *ambiguous* (open to more than one reasonable interpretation) will be construed against the drafter of the contract.[3] Legal scholars use the Latin phrase, *contra proferentum*, "an ambiguous provision is construed most strongly against the person who selected the language," to describe this outcome. Insight Box 11-1 describes how the courts have applied this concept to cases involving acts of war.

The Personal Feature

Insurance policies are personal contracts, and thus insurance contracts cannot be freely transferred to other parties. When the parties to an insurance contract reach agreement, one of the points they agreed to is to do business with each other. Each has considered the other's character and conduct. For good reasons, neither wants the other party to find a substitute party to the agreement. From the insurer's standpoint, it tries carefully to minimize the moral hazard. Allowing an insured to transfer an insurance policy freely could negate the underwriting efforts. For example, when Mrs. Sand purchased her auto insurance, her insurer considered the fact that she had no previous accidents or speeding tickets. If Mrs. Sand sells her auto to Fred Chopin, she may not transfer her insurance coverage to Fred along with the auto. The insurer wants the right to choose with whom it will do business. Likewise, when Mrs. Sand chose to purchase insurance from the Big Insurance Company, she considered its reputation and its excellent services. She did not choose to deal with the Little Insurance Company, and she may not want her contract transferred to that company.

Assignment The term **assignment** describes the situation in which one party transfers its rights and duties under a contract to another party. In many contractual situations, including insurance, assignment of a contract is allowed. While the assignment of an insurance policy is permitted, insurers reserve the right to refuse a request to assign a policy if it compromises their financial interests. Thus, property insurance policies typically indicate that an assignment is not valid unless the insurer has approved it, as verified by their written consent.

Unlike property insurance policies, life insurance policies can be assigned freely if the insurer is notified properly. A valid assignment of a life insurance policy does not change the life covered by the insurance, but it does change the party who may exercise the benefits of ownership, such as naming a beneficiary.

---

[3] See *Black's Law Dictionary*, 6th ed. (St. Paul, Minn.: West Publishing Company, 1990).

INSIGHT BOX 11-1

What Is a War? How Insurers and the Courts Have Interpreted Ambiguous Wording

The question of whether property damage resulting from warlike acts is covered under property insurance policies offers useful insight on the legal concept of contracts of adhesion. Property insurance policies often exclude damage from war because the potentially catastrophic losses that could result from a major war are uninsurable. Defining the term *war* has proven somewhat difficult, however. For example, in *Holiday Inns Incorporated* v. *Aetna Insurance Company*,[4] the courts addressed whether damage excluded from coverage as an act of war should in fact be paid by the insurer. Aetna issued a policy insuring the Beirut Holiday Inn for:

all risks . . . of direct physical loss or damage . . . except . . . *Loss by war, invasion, act of foreign enemy, hostilities or warlike operations (whether war be declared or not), civil war, mutiny, insurrection, revolution, conspiracy, military or usurped power* [emphasis added].

After the policy was issued, the property was damaged extensively by rockets, grenades, and ensuing fires in heavy fighting between rival ethnic, political, and religious groups. The hotel was closed to guests, and Holiday Inns filed a claim for loss with the insurer. Aetna denied the claim, citing the italicized exclusion. The case then went to court.

The court made the following points. First, under an all-risk policy, the burden is on the insurer to prove that the proximate cause of the loss was excluded. Second, exclusions are given the interpretation most favorable to the insured. Finally, the insurer must demonstrate that the interpretation favoring it is the only reasonable reading of the policy language.

The court defined *war* as "a course of hostility engaged in by entities having at least significant attributes of sovereignty." Because none of the warring factions in Lebanon had sovereignty, the court held that the damage did not arise from war, as strictly defined. After lengthy argument, the court concluded that Aetna had to pay Holiday Inns for the damage.

In the *Holiday Inns* case, the court's reasoning shows the strictness of the application of the doctrine of *contra proferentum* in insurance contracts. It is an excellent demonstration of how costly it can be to use the English language (or any language) imprecisely. Aetna's lawyers were neither unskilled nor unmindful of their objective, yet they still failed to communicate precisely. As shown by this court case, precise use of the English language is a challenging task.

The *Holiday Inns* case was not the final word on the definition of war; the topic has been examined by the courts since that time. For example, the September 11, 2001 attacks on the United States prompted another debate: whether the terror attacks were an act of war and hence excluded from insurance coverage. In the wake of the attacks, the U.S. insurance industry ultimately indicated that it would pay for the $40 billion of losses that resulted, but it would be unable to cover any subsequent terrorist losses because their reinsurers would no longer provide coverage for terrorism. To clarify their limits of coverage, insurers drafted a new policy wording, a so-called terrorism exclusion, and included the exclusion in many of their policies. Many state insurance regulators permitted the exclusion, reasoning that insurers would be unable to bear the cost of future terrorist attacks without reinsurance.[5] Over time, the use of terrorism exclusions decreased after the passage of the Terrorism Risk Insurance Act in 2002, which created a federal reinsurance program to compensate U.S. insurers in the event of subsequent catastrophic terrorism losses.

Utmost Good Faith (Latin: *Uberrimae Fidei*)

Insurance companies rely heavily upon the information provided by insurance applicants to determine their insurability. As a result, the courts hold the person buying insurance to the highest standard of honesty in dealing with the insurer. The penalty

---

[4] *1984 CCH Fire and Casualty Cases*, pp. 430–69.

[5] See C. Oster and M. Schroeder, "Workers Comp Insurance Now Harder to Get," *Wall Street Journal*, January, 9, 2002, p. A3; and "Terrorism: Defining the Threat." Reactions (2007): 1-1. Chapter 8 includes a detailed discussion of reinsurance.

for a lesser level of honesty is the insurer's right to void the contract.[6] This high level of good faith that an insured owes an insurer is reflected in the legal doctrines of warranty, representation, and concealment.

Warranty In insurance terminology, a **warranty** is a statement that something has happened or exists (**affirmative warranty**) or that something will happen (**promissory warranty**). Another distinction sometimes arises between written warranties (known as **expressed warranties**) and commonly understood warranties (known as **implied warranties**).

The traditional doctrine of warranty, which has its origin in ocean marine insurance, is very strict: Any breach of a warranty by an insured allows the insurer to void the contract. For example, a shipowner must warrant that his ship is in seaworthy condition when it leaves the harbor (affirmative warranty), and that it will sail from New York to Amsterdam carrying a cargo of glassware (promissory warranty). If the ship were seriously leaking, if the destination were Japan, or if the cargo were liquor, any one of these deviations would constitute a breach of warranty. Regardless of whether the breach contributed to a loss, the insurer could void the contract under the strict doctrine of warranty.

Because the doctrine of warranty is so strict, it has potential for injuring insureds and working against the ideal to honor reasonable expectations of insureds. Thus, state laws and court decisions have mitigated the harsh effects of this doctrine. Perhaps the simplest method of achieving fairer results is to hold certain policy provisions to be representations rather than warranties, for the rules relating to representation are not so strict.

Representations Before entering an insurance contract, insurers usually ask applicants several questions about the loss exposure. Courts call the applicant's answers, usually found in a formal application for insurance, **representations**. These statements are made to induce the insurer to enter the contract. The general rule with respect to representations is that if the consumer gives false answers and the answers are material to the risk, the insurer can void the contract. The test of **materiality** is a negative answer to the question: Would the insurer have written the same policy at the same price if it had known the truth? For example, when applying for automobile insurance, Denton Fender is asked if he has had any accidents in the past three years or any health problems. He answers "no" to both questions. In fact, he was responsible for two serious traffic accidents and has athlete's foot. The first false response is undoubtedly material; the second is not. If the question is raised in court, all the insurer must do to make its point is to show that it has declined to accept at standard rates any insureds with two previous accidents. If the company consistently charges extra for people with athlete's foot, this representation also would be considered material.

While insurers can void a contract on the basis of misstatements of material facts, it cannot void a policy based on statements of opinion. For example, if a person with undiagnosed cancer states on a health application that he does not have cancer and that person had no reason to believe he had cancer, then a subsequent diagnosis would not be sufficient to void the contract, even though the statement was technically false.

---

[6] Consider the words of one court in describing this doctrine: "It is well established under the doctrine of *uberrimae fidei* that the parties to a marine insurance policy must accord each other the highest degree of good faith. This stringent doctrine requires the assured to disclose to the insurer all known circumstances that materially affect the risk being insured. Since the assured is in the best position to know of any circumstances material to the risk, he must reveal those facts to the underwriter, rather than wait for the underwriter to inquire. . . . The assured's failure to meet this standard entitles the underwriter to void the policy. . . .". See *Knight* v. *United States Fire Ins. Co.*, 804 F. 2d. 9 (2d Cir. 1986).

Concealment **Concealment** is silence when obligated to speak or a failure to disclose material information. Because the insurance contract is one of utmost good faith, the applicant for insurance must reveal all material facts. The best test of the materiality of a concealment is the same as it is for a misrepresentation. Would the insurer write the same contract at the same rate if it knew all the facts? For example, when applying for life insurance, Mary Stuart is asked if she has gone to the doctor in the past three years. She truthfully answers "no." She fails to add that she has had severe chest pains and has collapsed on several occasions but has not sought medical treatment. Under these circumstances, the insurer well may prove a case of concealment and thereby be able to void the insurance policy.

Voiding a contract based on concealment is more difficult for the insurer than voidance for a misrepresentation. In general, the insurer must prove to a jury's satisfaction that the applicant certainly knew he or she was concealing a material fact from the insurer to deceive the insurer. This strict requirement works to the insured's benefit.

In summary, the rules of warranty, representation, and concealment distinguish insurance contracts from other transactions. If an insured deals with an insurer in less than an honorable way, the insured's actions may relieve the insurer of the duty to indemnify the insured if a loss occurs. However, the law and the courts are modifying the strict doctrines and legal technicalities continually so reasonable expectations of reasonable people are honored.

The Entire Contract and Incontestability Clauses

Two important clauses found in life insurance (and sometimes health insurance) policies are related to the question of warranty, representation, and concealment. **Entire contract** statutes require that any statements made by an applicant for life insurance be attached physically to the policy. The policy, with the application attached, constitutes the entire contract between the two parties. One purpose of this provision is to prevent the insured from claiming that the insurance agent or medical examiner recorded information incorrectly. After the contract is signed, the insured is bound by the responses as they are recorded. A second reason for this provision is to prevent insurers from attaching wording to the contract that the insured has not seen, such as the corporate bylaws. This provision is called **incorporation by reference**.

The **incontestable clause** of life insurance policies states that after a given period, usually one or two years, the insurer no longer can contest a policy to void the contract. Thus, if an insured makes a material misrepresentation in applying for life insurance, the insurer must discover the false statement within a limited period of time or else the policy provides coverage anyway. In practice, life insurers review death claims that occur within the contestable period very carefully. If the insurer discovers a material misrepresentation while the policy is contestable, it will void the policy.

The purpose of this clause is to protect the beneficiary from stale claims of fraud. It would be especially difficult for the beneficiary to defend a claim of fraud forty years after the alleged fraud occurred. The defense would be especially difficult when the insured is dead. The incontestable clause is not designed to encourage fraud or cheat life insurance companies; rather, it is an instance of choosing between two undesirable alternatives: allowing collection on an insurance policy even when fraud exists versus depriving some insureds of expected benefits. The law has chosen the first alternative.

The Aleatory Feature

Insurance contracts are **aleatory**; so is gambling. This term means that the parties to the contract know in advance that the dollars they will exchange will be unequal. The insured pays the premium and collects a large sum if a large loss occurs or collects nothing if no loss occurs. The opposite is true for the insurer. In most instances, it collects a premium and pays nothing. In a few cases, it collects a relatively small premium and pays a large amount. The aleatory feature of insurance policies differs from other business contracts, where consideration of equal value is exchanged. We call equal exchange contracts *commutative contracts*.

STANDARDIZATION OF INSURANCE POLICIES

Insurance rating organizations, traditionally known as rating bureaus, prepare standard versions of the most widely used property and liability insurance contracts. Most U.S. insurers use forms prepared by the Insurance Services Office or the American Association of Insurance Services.

Insurance policies are standardized for a variety of reasons. Standardized policies are more economical for the insurer to print and use, which in turn helps reduce insurance rates. It is also more economical to calculate one insurance rate for a standardized policy than many different rates for numerous insurance policies. The meaning of standardized policies is widely known by attorneys, courts, and insurers' employees, and by some consumers, resulting in less insurance litigation. Standardized packaged policies also can reduce adverse selection if insureds buy a preset bundle of coverage rather than just coverage for the exposure most likely to cause a loss. Finally, the standardized policy has the large statistical base needed for rate-making accuracy. That is, because many insurers use the same policy format, their loss and claims expense data can be combined. Combining data would not be logical if each company covered different perils or had different conditions in their individual contracts.

One drawback of standardized policies is the possibility that some needs for insurance may go unmet. Because the standardized policy can be modified by endorsements, the needs of consumers with unusual loss exposures often can be satisfied. By endorsing standardized policies, only the consumers who require the particular coverage are charged for it. If an infrequently needed coverage were included in a standardized policy, all consumers, most of whom would not need the protection, would have to share the cost of coverage.

BASIC PARTS OF AN INSURANCE POLICY

Standard insurance policies are designed to be written using several common parts or contractual components. These components include the declarations page, insuring agreement, deductibles, definitions, exclusions, and endorsements. This section describes each of these parts. Throughout the discussion, we will refer to examples of policy provisions from the Personal Auto Policy (PAP) and the Homeowners (HO) Insurance Policy, two personal insurance policies described in greater detail in Chapters 12 and 13, respectively. Figure 11-2 shows the "building blocks" used to construct an insurance policy, as well as a description of the function of each contractual component.

Declarations

The first element of a property-liability insurance contract usually is the declarations. The **declarations** present the important facts about the coverage provided and personalize the standardized coverage to a particular insured. For example, they specify which house (located at 123 Main Street), which car (VIN 123456789), and which person (John J. Audubon) are covered. The declarations also specify the insurer's limits of

Declarations	Establish "named insured" Provides rating information
Insuring Agreements	Create binding agreement between insurer and insured Subagreements provide specific coverage
Deductibles	Cause insured to bear first dollars of covered losses Control insurance costs and moral hazard
Definitions	Establish meaning of important words found in the policy, thereby reducing room for ambiguity
Exclusions	Limit insurance coverage by specifically identifying perils, people, property, or time period not covered
Conditions	Specify the rights and duties of the insurer and insured under the contract
Endorsements and Riders	Amend contracts to create more coverage

FIGURE 11-2 Building Blocks of Insurance Policy

liability ($350,000 for the house, $1 million for liability), the annual premium, and payments due for shorter (quarterly, semiannual) periods. The declarations are prepared from information that the insured provided in the insurance application.

Insuring Agreement

The **insuring agreement** is the specific language creating the contract. In broad terms, it describes the insurer's and the insured's rights and duties. Often, subagreements are used to identify specific perils covered by the policy or to indicate coverage is provided on an open-perils basis. In the insuring agreement, the insurer states that it provides the insurance described in the policy, and the insured agrees to comply with the conditions of the policy.

Deductibles

Property insurance policies require the insured to pay the first dollars of an insured loss. Insurers call this amount the **deductible**. Several variations of deductible provisions exist.

Policies using a **straight or flat deductible** require the insurer to pay only for the amount of loss in excess of the deductible. For example, if there was a $100,000 loss and a $200 straight deductible, the insured would pay $200 and the insurer would pay the remaining $99,800.

A **percentage deductible** requires the policyowner to pay the first percentage of a loss, for example, 2 percent, with the insurer paying the amount in excess of the deductible. For example, a 2 percent deductible on a $200,000 home destroyed by hurricane wind damage would require the insured to pay $4,000 (.02 × $200,000) and the insurer to pay $196,000 (.98 × $200,000). After Hurricane Andrew in 1992, many insurers in Florida and other states began to use percentage deductibles. Insurance companies can combine the straight and percentage deductibles; for example, they can apply the percentage deductible to hurricane damage but the straight deductible to non-hurricane losses.

Some policies state that the deductible is taken from the loss. Other policies state that the deductible is taken from the claims payment. The difference in wording can produce a different claims payment. For example, an insured may lose $50,000 in property but have only $30,000 in insurance. If a $500 deductible is taken from the loss, the insured files a claim for $49,500 and receives a payment for $30,000, the policy limit. If the $500 reduces the claims payment, the insured receives $29,500.

Deductible provisions serve several purposes. First, they reduce the morale hazard because the insured must pay a small part of every loss. Most insureds presumably do not like to lose the deductible amount, say $500, so they also are not indifferent to insured losses. Second, deductibles eliminate the expenses involved in settling small claims. It is illogical for the insurer to incur $1,000 in expenses to settle a $500 claim. The savings from reduced expenses and payments for small losses are reflected in lower premiums. Therefore, the larger the deductible an insured chooses, the lower the insurance premium. Third, deductibles cause the policyowner to finance some of the loss. In the case of percentage deductibles, for example, the amount of a loss shifted to policyowners can be a significant financial contribution to overall loss costs.

Some insurers encourage insureds to use premium dollars more efficiently by choosing larger deductibles and using the savings to lower premiums or increase policy limits. In personal and commercial insurance purchases, it is wise to consider several combinations of deductible, premium, and policy limit before choosing one.

Definitions

A definition of *war* never appeared in the insurance policy in the *Holiday Inns* v. *Aetna* case discussed in Insight Box 11-1. The court defined the word. Perhaps if the definition had appeared in the policy, the litigation would have been avoided. Insurers often provide **definitions** of words that they consider important or subject to misinterpretation. The definitions may appear as a glossary found at the beginning of the policy or elsewhere in the body of the contract. Common examples include definitions of the parties who are covered under the policy, the types of payments paid by the insurer in the policy, and key terms used throughout the contract.

For example, the PAP includes a definition of the term *occupying*. As a result of the definition, occupying is not defined as simply "being in a car." Instead, the definitions section of the PAP states: "'Occupying' means in, upon, getting in, on, out, or off." The definition thus expands the situations in which insurance protection is provided. Thus, if Mike Angelo, the artist, injures himself when painting the roof of his car, he may be able to claim he was occupying (*upon*) his vehicle. Or, if Shirley U. Jest, the comedian, injures her back while trying to adjust her child's car seat, she may be able to collect for medical expenses resulting from an injury sustained while *in* an auto.

Exclusions

Exclusions identify losses that are not covered. If an insurer denies a claim based on an exclusion and the insured then contests the denial, the insurer has the legal burden of proving that it applied the exclusion correctly. Property insurance exclusions serve several purposes:

- *To eliminate losses arising from catastrophic events.* For example, insurers exclude damage from nuclear radiation or wars.
- *To eliminate losses associated with the moral or morale hazard.* For example, personal insurance policies will not cover losses caused intentionally by the insured.
- *To eliminate coverage not needed by the typical insured.* In these cases, insurers allow an insured who needs special coverage to pay an extra charge to remove the exclusion. For example, the HO policy excludes liability losses arising from business pursuits, but the policy can be endorsed to cover certain business pursuits, such as babysitting, for the occasional policyholder who needs such protection.
- *To eliminate coverage where another policy is specifically designed to provide coverage.* For example, the HO policy excludes coverage from liability claims arising from the ownership, maintenance, or use of most motor vehicles, most watercraft, and aircraft because they are better covered under another policy.
- *To prevent noninsured parties from benefiting from coverage.* For example, the HO policy excludes coverage from benefiting bailees. A **bailment** implies possession of property by a party other than the owner, with the intent of returning the property to the owner. Examples of bailments include property left with dry cleaners or cars dropped off at a repair shop. The party owning the property is the **bailor**. The party in temporary possession of the property is the **bailee**. The intent of this exclusion is to cause the bailee to bear the cost of loss to the goods in its care (for example, the homeowner's fur coat or the driver's repaired auto).
- *To control costs and keep premiums affordable.* This category of exclusions explains why wear-and-tear "losses" are not covered.

Endorsements

Endorsements modify standard insurance contracts. They can add coverage directly or they can add coverage by deleting an exclusion in the standard policy. Sometimes an endorsement can eliminate coverage (for a reduction in premium) or exclude an insured (for example, a teenage driver). Thus, endorsements can be used to tailor the standardized policy to fit the unique coverage needs of the policy owner.

Conditions and General Provisions

The conditions or general provisions section of an insurance policy is included to specify the terms under which insurance coverage is provided by the insurer. In some instances, the conditions create certain obligations upon the policy owner, such as setting the duties that the insured must satisfy to enable the insurer to process claims efficiently, such as promptly notifying the insurer when the loss occurs or cooperating with the insurer by providing information to verify the loss amount. Conditions may also be used to specify detailed information that clarifies the rights of the insurer and the insured in cases such as policy nonrenewal or the calculation methods used to set the value of claims.

Summary

Insurance contracts must meet these four criteria: offer and acceptance, consideration, capacity, and legal purpose. The following characteristics also distinguish insurance contracts from all others: Insurance contracts are contracts of indemnity, contracts of adhesion, personal contracts, contracts of utmost good faith, and aleatory contracts.

An insurance policy describes the legal agreement between insurance company and policyholder. Most policies are standardized contracts that have been extensively examined and interpreted by the courts. The standard parts of an insurance policy include the declarations page, insuring agreement, deductibles, definitions, exclusions, and endorsements.

Review

1. How do binders differ from conditional receipts?
2. What are the important differences between a valid contract, an invalid contract, and a voidable contract?
3. List the four elements of a valid contract. What is the legal result if only three of the four elements are present?
4. Why is legal capacity required to enter into a valid contract?
5. What is indemnity? Identify three ways that the principle of indemnity is enforced in property insurance contracts.
6. Are there any exceptions to the rule that insurance contracts are contracts of indemnity, defined strictly?
7. Describe one difference between life insurance and property insurance in the requirement for insurable interest.
8. Does actual cash value equal fair market value?
9. How does subrogation prevent a person from collecting twice for the same debt or from the same insured injury?
10. Why are the rules on the right to assign a property insurance contract different from the rules on the right to assign a life insurance contract?
11. Why are insurance policies viewed as contracts of adhesion? If an insurer issues a policy that includes ambiguities that an insured challenges in court, how will the courts view the case?
12. What difference does it make to an insured if a false statement made by the insured is considered a warranty or a representation?
13. Explain the advantages of the incontestable clause in life insurance from society's standpoint.
14. What are the advantages of using standardized insurance policies?
15. List and describe the different parts commonly found in an insurance policy.
16. Explain the reasons for including exclusions in an insurance policy.

Objective Questions

1. Choose the one true statement about conditional receipts.
   a. They are used only in property insurance.
   b. They provide permanent coverage when accompanied by the first premium payment.
   c. They are used only in life insurance.
   d. They are used mainly when insuring minors.
2. Each of the following coverages is an exception to the rule of indemnity except:
   a. Actual cash value property insurance
   b. Life insurance
   c. Replacement cost insurance
   d. Valued insurance policies
3. Subrogation in insurance means what?
   a. Losses must be reported in a timely way to the insurance company.
   b. Losses must be considered legally binding.
   c. The insured must pay premiums before losses can be paid.
   d. One party is being substituted for another in terms of legal rights.
4. Because insurance contracts are considered contracts of adhesion, which of the following statements is true?
   a. Ambiguities are construed against the writer of the contract.
   b. Larger losses attach before smaller losses.

   c. The courts will adhere to precedents set in previous cases.

   d. Each party is responsible for providing its own attorney if a breach of contract occurs.

5. What is the impact of the parol evidence rule?
   a. People on parole cannot make valid insurance contracts.
   b. Written evidence takes precedence over oral evidence.
   c. Oral evidence takes precedence over written evidence.
   d. Whichever party speaks first presents the evidence.

6. A temporary property insurance contract is called:
   a. A binder
   b. A parol contract
   c. A rescinded contract
   d. A hypothetical contract

7. What type of insurance policy often is used for artwork and collector's items?
   a. Liability policy
   b. The standard art insurance policy
   c. A valued insurance policy
   d. The commercial marine insurance policy

8. "Replacement cost at the time of loss less depreciation" is the definition of:
   a. The maximum covered loss
   b. Actual cash value
   c. Fair market value
   d. The maximum replacement of loss

9. Insurers use____ to modify a standardized policy to fit an insured's unique coverage needs.
   a. definitions
   b. exclusions
   c. conditions
   d. endorsements

Discussion Questions

1. Discuss the advantages and disadvantages to insurers of the use of standardized policies.

2. Discuss how each of the following upholds or violates the principle of indemnity: subrogation, insurable interest, valued policies, and replacement cost coverage

Selected References

Black, H. C., and J. R. Nolan. 1990 *Black's Law Dictionary* 6th ed. (St. Paul, Minn: West Pub. Co.).

Commerce Clearing House. 1984 *Fire and Casualty Cases* (New York: Commerce Clearing House).

12

The Personal Auto Policy

After studying this chapter, you should be able to

- Explain how the tort liability system applies to automobile accidents

- Describe the key parts of the Personal Auto Policy (PAP)

- Describe the coverage provided under the liability coverage of the PAP

- Describe the coverage provided under the medical payments coverage of the PAP

- Describe the purpose of uninsured motorist insurance coverage

- Distinguish between collision and "loss-other-than-collision" property damage coverage

- Explain how insurers settle losses under the PAP

- Identify the pricing variables used by insurers to determine auto insurance premiums.

This chapter describes the Personal Auto Policy (PAP), a policy form written in simplified English to cover the family automobile.[1] The PAP provides four types of auto insurance protection: Part A—Liability Coverage; Part B—Medical Payments Coverage; Part C—Uninsured Motorist Coverage; and Part D—Coverage for Damage to Your Auto, property damage coverage more commonly known as collision and "loss-other-than-collision" coverage. Nearly all states have compulsory liability insurance laws that require drivers to purchase auto liability insurance, thus making the PAP one of the most widely purchased types of personal insurance coverage. Each type of auto insurance coverage is described in this chapter, followed by a description of the risk classification system used by insurers to set insurance premiums.

---

[1] Most auto insurers issue a PAP form similar to the one developed by the Insurance Services Office (ISO; http://www.iso.com/), the 2005 ISO PAP. The full text is reproduced in Appendix A, and we describe this form in this chapter. I am most grateful to the ISO for its permission to use its copyrighted material in this text.

AUTOMOBILE INSURANCE AND TORT LIABILITY: A REVIEW CASE

To review the tort liability system as it relates to automobile insurance, consider the following case. Assume that Rita Book, a librarian, uses her car to commute to work in the library. As she enters the intersection of Dickens Street and Hugo Way, her car is struck broadside by another car driven by Rex Cars. Rita's car is "totaled" (damage equals $25,000) and, in addition to other injuries, Rita's neck is broken (damage equals $90,000 in medical expenses and $15,000 in lost income). Rex's auto is damaged ($15,000 to the front end), and his skull is cracked. In addition, Rex expects to lose $15,000 of income that he would have earned as a driving instructor.

A driver has a duty of care to act as a reasonable person when operating an automobile. On this basis, Rita (plaintiff) goes to court and sues Rex (defendant) for negligently injuring her. She sues for $230,000 in damages. This amount includes $100,000 for pain and suffering.

In some states, Rex could defend himself in court by trying to establish contributory negligence by Rita. For example, he could try to prove that Rita ran a stop sign before entering the intersection. If such were the case, Rex would have a valid defense and could countersue Rita for the cost of his damages. Or Rex could try to establish that he was trying to escape some great danger to himself and, in the process of the escape, injured Rita. This line of reasoning might provide a valid defense. Rex may also try to establish any other ground to justify his actions or to discredit Rita's actions.

Despite a vigorous defense, assume that a jury finds Rex negligent in the operation of his car. The trial results in a $230,000 judgment in favor of Rita. Because Rex has a PAP, the insurance company will pay for the attorney to defend Rex. The insurer also will pay the judgment on Rex's behalf, up to the policy limits.

Note that as a result of a single auto accident, several different types of damages have occurred. They include physical damage to Rita's car, physical damage to Rex's car, and bodily injury to Rita, resulting in medical expenses, lost wages, and compensation for pain and suffering. The PAP includes coverage for each type of damage. In addition, the PAP is designed to deal with the more complicated issues that can arise in auto accidents. What if Rita was driving a car that she did not own, or if she was on an errand for her employer? What if Rex had no valid insurance, or if he was delivering pizzas on his part-time job?

These questions raise a few of the issues dealt with in the PAP. We will cover many of the answers in this chapter, but our treatment of the PAP is not meant to be exhaustive. Moreover, the answers may change as new policy provisions are introduced and as courts provide new interpretations of policy language. For these reasons, it is important not only to learn the policy language, but also to learn the reasons for the various policy provisions.

PAP DECLARATIONS, INSURING AGREEMENT, AND DEFINITIONS

A specimen copy of the PAP can be found in Appendix A of this book, and readers are encouraged to refer to it as a reference while reading this chapter. The PAP begins with a declarations page, definitions, and insuring agreement, as shown in Figure 12-1. The coverage sections follow, and the policy ends with a section covering the insured's duties after a loss and one containing general policy provisions.

A typical declarations page appears in Figure 12-2. The **declarations** identify numerous pieces of information pertaining to the insurance policy, including the named insured, the vehicles covered, the amount of coverage, the deductibles that apply, the time period over which coverage is provided, and the premium charged for the coverage.

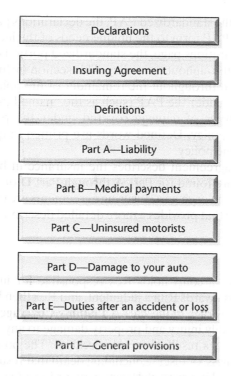

FIGURE 12-1 Personal Automobile Policy Layout

Policyowner: David Cather
22 Main Street
Anytown, USA

Policy Number: ###############
Policy Period: 1/1/2012 to 12/31/2012

Vehicle	Description	Vehicle ID Number
1	2010 Honda Accord	################

Part	Coverage	Coverage Limit	Premium	
A	Liability: Bodily Injury Liability: Bodily Injury Liability: Property Damage	$250,000 each person $500,000 each accident $50,000 each accident		$200
B	Medical Payments	$5,000 each person		$40
C	Uninsured Motorist	$250,000 each person $500,000 each accident		$30
D	Damage to Your Auto 1. Collision loss 2. Loss other than collision	Actual cash value minus 1. $1,000 deductible 2. $500 deductible		$130 $50
	Endorsements to this policy	None		$00
				Total before discount: $450
	Premium discounts: Accident-free			Less discounts: $45
				Total premium: $405

Countersignature Date 1/1/2012 by Ann Agent (authorized representative)

FIGURE 12-2 Sample Declarations Page for a Personal Auto Policy from Pearson Insurance Co.

When attached to the standardized PAP, the declarations page provides the data needed to fit the standard PAP form to the unique needs of the individual policyholder.

After the declarations page, the standardized portion of the PAP begins with definitions that apply throughout the policy. This section includes definitions of important words that are used throughout the remainder of the policy, such as the definition of the parties insured under the PAP (such as the "named insured" and resident "family members"), the types of damage covered under the policy, and covered vehicles insured under the policy. Defined words are printed in quotation marks or boldface print throughout the policy.

The insuring agreement describes the insurance in broad terms. Separate insurance agreements are found for Part A through Part D of the PAP at the beginning of the section describing each part. Insuring agreements are often fairly short, followed by additional wording that provides a more detailed description of the insurance coverage.

PART A—LIABILITY

In our review case, a court holds Rex responsible for injuring Rita to the extent of $230,000. The court awards Rita a judgment, and Rex then looks to his insurer to pay the claim. Rex finds coverage in the Part A **Liability Coverage** of his PAP. Part A provides protection from bodily injury and property damage to any insured person who becomes legally responsible as a result of an auto accident. The policy defines "bodily injury" as "bodily harm, sickness, or disease, including death that results." It also defines "property damage" as "physical injury to, destruction of, or loss of use of tangible property."

The insurer agrees to defend its insured in court, as well as to pay legal judgments on behalf of its insureds, as a part of its auto liability coverage. As a result, the insured does not have to pay for an attorney if sued. Thus, if Rex's defense costs $30,000, the insurer would pay this cost in addition to the $230,000 judgment. In the PAP, the cost to defend an insured does not reduce the money available to pay claims.

The PAP states that the insurer need not provide a defense if litigation arises from an event not covered by the policy. For example, if an injury results while an insured uses a covered auto as a taxi, the insurer is not obligated to pay liability claims or provide a defense because the policy excludes liability coverage for insureds using their autos as public livery vehicles.

Insurers reserve the right to investigate all claims made against insureds and to settle any claims or suits that they deem appropriate. So if the insured clearly was negligent in causing the loss, the insurer can offer the victim a settlement without the insured's consent. The insurer avoids litigation and the defense costs if the victim accepts the settlement. The insurer's duty to defend its insured ends after a claimant has accepted a settlement offer or if an actual payment is made to settle a legal judgment.

Limit of Liability

The declarations page provides a **single limit of liability**, such as $500,000. This amount is the limit for all types of damage that an insured may cause in one occurrence. If judgments exceed this limit, the insured, not the insurer, is responsible for the excess.

The PAP may be written with **split limits** by using an endorsement. When Part A is written with split limits, three separate numbers are indicated in this fashion: ###/###/###. (Insurers typically omit the last three zeros and the dollar signs when referring to the split limits.) The first number is the maximum that the insured will pay for one injured person. The second number is the maximum that the insurer will pay for the injuries sustained by all the people injured in a single accident. The third number is the maximum that the insurer will pay for property damage. For example, consider the split limits of 100/300/50. Under these limits, the insurer pays a maximum of $100,000 to any one injured person and a maximum of $300,000 for any one accident, regardless of the number of injured people. The third number indicates that the insurer will pay up to $50,000 for property damage liability for each accident.[2]

It is very important to have adequate coverage limits. What is an adequate limit? An adequate limit is one large enough to cover any damage you may cause with an auto. If one is responsible for killing a doctor earning $4 million a year, forcing a school bus carrying 30 children off the road (all of whom are injured), or causing a truck loaded with 100 flat-screen televisions to overturn (or even perhaps doing all this damage as a result of a single negligent act), one may be faced with $10 million or more in claims. Because it is rather easy to conceive of situations involving large amounts of damage, experts generally recommend high limits of liability coverage. Moreover, increasing the limit from some minimum specified by the state financial responsibility laws (which can be wholly inadequate) does not increase the insured's overall premium by nearly as much as the percentage increase in coverage. Some commentators believe that the amount of liability insurance people purchase should be a function of the amount of their wealth, meaning that a wealthy person should purchase more liability insurance than a poor person. However, all socially responsible drivers want to compensate their potential victims adequately, and this attitude requires a sufficiently large amount of liability insurance.

Insureds

Under the definition of "insured" listed in the Definitions section of the PAP, the auto policy provides coverage for four categories of insureds that have potential liability arising from the use of an auto. In the first and most commonly used category, the named insured and resident family members are covered for the use of any auto, whether it is owned or borrowed, unless an exclusion applies.

A second category provides coverage to any person using the named insured's covered auto. That is, the car owner's insurance, not the driver's insurance, would pay a claim if the owner let somebody borrow his or her auto. For example, assume that Daniel Boone lets his neighbor, Andy Jackson, borrow his car. As a general rule, coverage on the car involved in the accident is considered **primary coverage**. Insurers providing primary coverage pay first. If Boone's insurance was exhausted by a claim (Jackson was sued for $150,000 and Boone's insurance had a limit of $100,000), then Jackson could turn to his own insurer to pay the remainder of the claim until his own insurance was exhausted. We call Jackson's insurance **excess coverage**. Excess coverage pays after the limits of the primary coverage have been exhausted.

---

[2] In some cases, the single-limit policy will provide more compensation to the insured's injured victims than the split-limits policy. For example, consider a single limit of $500,000 versus split limits of 100/300/50. If the insured's victim, Paul Barer, the mortician, sustained $300,000 in damages, he would receive this amount if the insured had a single-limit policy because it is less than the limit of $500,000. However, he would receive only $100,000 if the insured had 100/300/50 split limits because this contract limits recovery for one individual to $100,000. As a second example, consider the split limits of 250/500/50. Assume that Hannibal Moe, the elephant trainer, causes a collision injuring four people, and they file suit in the following order (the insurer pays claims in the order in which the suits are settled): A's injuries total $400,000, B's equal $100,000, C's amount to $250,000, and D's are $500,000. With split limits, A can collect $250,000, the maximum the insurer will pay for any one person. B will collect $100,000, bringing the total paid by the insurer to $350,000. The remaining $150,000 ($500,000 – $350,000) will go to C. In all, $150,000 of A's claim, $100,000 of C's claim, and D's entire claim will not be satisfied by Hannibal's insurance contract. Not only will Hannibal be liable for the unsatisfied claims of Claimant D, but he also will pay for any additional defense costs because the company's obligation to defend ended after it paid the full limit of liability to Claimant C.

People or organizations other than a driver are often sued due to a driver's negligence. In some of these instances, the PAP will cover the liability of these people or organizations. For example, assume that a fraternity sends one of its brothers, Bozo, to get some liquid refreshments for a party. Assume that Bozo uses his own car to do this. If Bozo causes an automobile accident while returning with the drinks, Bozo's PAP would cover the fraternity's liability. The fraternity's liability arises because Bozo was technically acting as an agent of the fraternity while on this mission. The policy provides coverage to the other parties named in the lawsuit when the insured is driving an owned or a nonowned vehicle.

Exclusions

Part A has several important exclusions relieving the insurer of liability. The PAP divides these exclusions into two sections labeled Part A and Part B.

The exclusions in Part A state that "we do not provide Liability Coverage for any 'insured'":

Exclusion 1: "who intentionally causes bodily injury or property damage." Because intentional injuries are not accidental losses, they are not insurable.

Exclusions 2 and 3: There is no liability coverage for property owned, transported by, rented to, used by, or in the care of a covered person. Two considerations are working here: First, Part A provides liability protection, not property protection, and people logically cannot be liable to themselves. That is, if we cause an auto accident, we cannot turn around and sue ourselves because we destroyed our own property. Second, separate property insurance coverage, such as a homeowners policy, is better suited to provide insurance for the insured's personal property.

For example, assume that Teddy Roosevelt uses his car to deliver his television for repair. While driving to the repair shop, Teddy runs a stop sign and destroys both the television and his car. There is no coverage for the television under the PAP because of these exclusions. Damage to Teddy's automobile, however, is covered by Teddy's PAP under Part D, collision damage. If Teddy had a homeowners insurance policy, presumably he could collect for damage to his personal property, the television (as damage caused by the peril of "vehicles"), for the amount in excess of the deductible.

Exclusion 4: There is generally no coverage if an employee of the insured sustains injury because it is expected that workers' compensation insurance will cover this event.

Exclusion 5: There is no coverage if the auto can be hired by the public to carry persons or property for a fee, but carpooling is permissible.

Exclusions 6 and 7: Excludes coverage for commercial liability exposures involving the automobile and other nonfarming businesses.

Exclusion 8: There is no coverage when a person uses an auto "without a reasonable belief" that he or she is entitled to do so. The issue of what is a "reasonable belief" can be a question of fact to be tried in court.

Exclusion 9: This exclusion eliminates coverage for nuclear-related liability exposures (other than nuclear war), such as possible liability resulting from an accident involving the transport of nuclear material.

Part B of the liability coverage excludes coverage for certain types of vehicles. It states, "We do not provide Liability Coverage for the ownership, maintenance, or use of":

Exclusion 1: Vehicles with less than four wheels (such as motorcycles or mopeds) or vehicles designed for off-road use (such as bulldozers or tractors).

Exclusions 2 and 3: Vehicles, other than those listed on the declarations page as the covered autos, that are owned by the insured or furnished for regular use, such as leased cars, or cars furnished by a business (commonly known as *company cars*). This exclusion causes insureds having vehicles in the excluded categories to declare them and pay a premium if they want insurance on these vehicles.

Exclusion 4: No coverage is available for a vehicle that is "located inside a facility designed for racing." This exclusion removes coverage from insureds engaging in automobile racing. Race car drivers need to purchase separate insurance policies and should not rely on the PAP for coverage of their racing activities.

In summary, the PAP provides the insured with financial protection from lawsuits of people claiming they were injured by an insured. Under the tort liability system, injured parties either must sue the insured or be offered a settlement of the claim before collecting for their injuries. Several exclusions apply to restrict the scope of the liability coverage.

PART B—MEDICAL PAYMENTS

The purpose of the **automobile medical payments** coverage is to pay for relatively small amounts of medical expenses that may be incurred by several types of claimants as a result of a traffic accident. Unlike liability coverage, Part B medical payments are not fault-based; payments are made to eligible claimants without establishing who was legally responsible for causing the accident. The coverage limit for medical payments coverage is usually fairly small; for example, $1,000 to $5,000 of coverage per person. This coverage often eliminates the need of people to sue to recover for their injuries, thus reducing the chance of lawsuits under Part A.

The insuring agreement for Part B provides coverage for reasonable and necessary medical and funeral expenses incurred within three years of an accident that results in bodily injury. Covered persons include the named insured and family members when they are occupying a motor vehicle or are struck by a motor vehicle designed for use on public roads. Passengers in a car listed in the declarations page are also covered. Thus, if Rita Book or her family members are injured when riding in an auto or bus, or as pedestrians, they could look to their insurer for indemnity for medical or funeral expenses up to the policy's limit of liability if the accident resulted from a collision with a vehicle designed for on-the-road use. Alternatively, if Rita is squashed by a bulldozer, plowed under by a farm tractor, or hit by a freight train, there would be no coverage because these vehicles are not designed for use on the road. Injuries sustained while driving or riding a motorcycle are also not covered. Some additional exclusions to the medical payments coverage are also listed, with most exclusions similar to those discussed in Part A, Liability. The "Limit of Liability" section makes it clear that a single limit of liability, stated in the declarations, applies to each insured involved in an accident.

In most states with no-fault auto insurance laws, the named insured, family members, and passengers are provided medical payments coverage through **Personal Injury Protection (PIP)** coverage rather than medical payments coverage. In addition to medical payments, PIP coverage also provides some limited protection for other types of losses. These include loss of income (as a percentage of the injured person's earnings), essential services expenses (such as domestic help or a lawn service to perform services that were carried out by the injured person before the accident), funeral expenses, and survivorship benefits to the dependents of a deceased covered person. More discussion on no-fault auto insurance is provided in the Appendix at the end of this chapter.

PART C—UNINSURED MOTORIST COVERAGE

The purpose of uninsured motorist (UM) insurance is to protect people from financially irresponsible drivers who fail to purchase liability insurance or to have adequate financial resources to compensate people they injure with their automobiles. It is important to recognize that UM coverage is fault-based. Insureds must show they are *legally entitled to recover damages* from a negligent uninsured motorist to receive UM benefits.

Coverage Under the PAP

The insuring agreement for Part C creates a legal right for insureds to collect compensatory damages from their own insurer if the insured is injured by an uninsured motorist, but only for bodily injury. The intention of the insurer not to pay punitive or exemplary damages is stated in the exclusions section of this coverage. The Part C definition of uninsured motorist includes (1) drivers without insurance, (2) drivers with less insurance than the minimum required by state law, (3) hit-and-run drivers, and (4) drivers with coverage provided by insolvent insurers.

In general, suing uninsured motorists, especially hit-and-run drivers, is not a promising source of recovery. Because UM coverage is fault-based, insureds must convince their own insurer that the driver of the uninsured automobile caused the accident. Only when the other driver is negligent is the insured legally entitled to recovery. If the insured cannot establish the uninsured driver's negligence, or if the extent of the damages is subject to dispute, then an awkward situation is created under this coverage. The insured must confront her own insurer to resolve the dispute. In such circumstances, the policy provides for an *arbitration* process to determine if the insured actually is entitled to recover damages, and, if so, in what amount.

The limit of liability for this coverage is found on the policy's declarations page, subject to reduction for any recovery from the negligent driver or from a workers' compensation claim. The exclusions to this coverage are similar to those discussed earlier in this chapter.

The States' Response to Uninsured Motorists

States have generally have approached the problem of accidents caused by financially irresponsible drivers in a variety of ways beyond Part C uninsured motorist protection. All states have **financial responsibility laws**, which require drivers to furnish evidence of financial responsibility to retain their driver's license or their auto registration. Most drivers purchase liability insurance (such as Part A of the PAP), which is acceptable evidence of financial responsibility. Alternative evidence would be a surety bond or a deposit of assets. Drivers must typically establish their financial responsibility after they have been involved in an automobile accident or after they have been arrested for a serious traffic violation.

In addition to financial responsibility laws, most states have passed **compulsory insurance laws**. In these states, drivers must show evidence of purchasing at least the minimum required amount of insurance before the state issues automobile license plates.[3] A few states operate **unsatisfied judgment funds**. These states use revenue collected from license plate sales or from taxes levied on insurers to make payments to injured victims of uninsured motorists.

---

[3] The required minimum limits of insurance coverage vary across the states. In 2011, for example, the minimums ranged from 50/100/25 in Alaska and Maine to 10/20/10 in Florida. For a list of the minimums required across all states, please see http://www.insure.com/ (retrieved July 28, 2011).

Underinsured Motorists

A situation similar to being injured by an uninsured motorist can arise if an underinsured motorist injured the insured. Assume, for example, that Robert F. Lee is injured in an auto accident caused by a driver having the minimum legal amount of insurance, $25,000, and that Robert incurs $600,000 in medical expenses and lost wages. After winning a legal judgment, he collects $25,000 from the negligent driver's insurer. If the negligent driver had no other financial resources, Robert would bear $575,000 of his loss. Now, assume that Robert has $1,000,000 of **underinsured motorists insurance**. In this case, Robert could collect the remaining amount of damages from his own insurer because it defines an *underinsured motor vehicle* as any vehicle that is insured for less than the amount of Robert's Part C, uninsured motorist limits. Underinsured motorist coverage is not part of the basic coverage provided by the PAP and is added to the contract by endorsement for an additional premium.

PART D—DAMAGE TO YOUR AUTO

Part D of the PAP provides coverage for property damage to the policyholder's covered vehicle(s), as listed on the declarations page of the policy. Auto owners often buy Part D coverage, especially for newer vehicles with little depreciation. Drivers who borrow money to pay for their vehicles are also usually required by their lenders to purchase property damage coverage, thus protecting the lender's collateral financial interest if the vehicle suffers physical damage. Once they have paid off their car loans, policyholders often drop the Part D coverages, especially on older autos that are more fully depreciated. Part D does not provide coverage for property damage that the policyholder negligently causes to another driver; such coverage is provided under Part A as property damage liability protection.

Part D offers coverage for "direct and accidental loss" to a covered auto from two different types of physical damage: collision and loss-other-than-collision. **Collision** coverage pays for the damage to a covered vehicle that results from impact with another vehicle or object (such as a guardrail or tree), as well as damage resulting from the upset (such as when the driver loses control and the vehicle goes into the ditch along the highway) of a covered vehicle.

Loss-other-than-collision coverage provides protection from ten specific categories of physical damage: missiles and falling objects; fire; theft or larceny; explosion or earthquake; windstorm; hail, water, or flood; malicious mischief or vandalism; riot or civil commotion; contact with bird or animal; and breakage of glass. Previous versions of the PAP referred to coverage from the loss-other-than-collision perils as *comprehensive* coverage, a term that continues to be used by many professionals working in the insurance industry today.

The coverage for damage to your auto is open-perils coverage. The meaning of the insuring clause is quite clear: If there is a loss and the cause is not excluded, the insurance company pays. A deductible usually applies to the collision coverage and a separate deductible also may apply to the loss-other-than-collision section. Any applicable deductible amounts will appear on the declarations page.

Twelve exclusions apply to this coverage, including damage resulting from wear and tear, war, or radioactive contamination. Many of the other exclusions are familiar to readers by now because they were described earlier in the chapter. Exclusions change over time. For example, an exclusion relating to electronic equipment has changed over time to provide more coverage for innovations such as navigational systems and Internet access systems, as these features have become more common as standard or optional equipment.

Loss Settlement

Insurers adjust losses under Part D on an actual cash value (ACV) basis—that is, replacement cost minus depreciation. In cases where the cost of repair exceeds the market value of the auto, the loss is declared "total," and insurers pay the actual cash value for the vehicle.

The PAP limits the insured's recovery to "the amount necessary to repair or replace the property with other property of like kind and quality." This wording allows insurers to use aftermarket repair parts instead of repair parts made by the car's manufacturer. A common interpretation of this clause suggests that if an aftermarket repair part costs half of an original equipment manufacturer's part, the insured who insists on using original manufacturer parts must bear the additional cost, although case law on this matter varies across the states.[4]

PART E—DUTIES AFTER AN ACCIDENT OR LOSS

Like the conditions of all property and liability insurance contracts, the conditions of the PAP are important, and the insured must comply with them to collect insurance proceeds. The policy states that if the insured fails to comply with the listed duties and the results are prejudicial (harmful) to the insurer, then "[w]e have no duty to provide coverage under this policy."

The policy's language states that in the event of loss, the insured must notify the insurer promptly of how, when, and where the loss occurred. This notice-of-loss requirement allows the company to investigate the loss while the evidence is still fresh. The insured must cooperate with the insurer in settling the loss. That is, the insured must supply evidence, testify at trials or hearings as needed, and help obtain the attendance of witnesses.

The insured must protect the damaged property from further loss. The insurer agrees to pay for reasonable expenses incurred to protect the property. Thus, if an auto went into a ditch, the insurance company generally would pay to have it towed to a garage and stored until it could be repaired. An insured making a claim under Part C, Uninsured Motorist Coverage, for damage attributed to a hit-and-run driver has a duty to notify the police promptly after the incident.

PART F—GENERAL PROVISIONS

Other conditions of the PAP relate to the **territory covered**, which includes Canada, Puerto Rico, and the United States, but not Mexico nor other foreign countries. If a U.S. citizen is temporarily driving in Mexico or other foreign countries, she should buy temporary insurance from an insurer in that country. Assignment of the PAP is invalid without the written consent of the insurer. In addition, the general provisions section also presents the details of each party's termination rights, although state law often affects cancellation of the contract rights of each party.

AUTO INSURANCE PRICING

Personal auto insurers determine the premiums that their policyholders pay using a risk classification system, sorting policyholders into groups of drivers with homogeneous risk characteristics and charging each driver a premium based on the expected

---

[4] An *aftermarket repair part* is a part made by a manufacturer other than the original equipment manufacturer; for example, a hood made by Generic Hoods, Inc., instead of by Ford.

loss of the group. Drivers are sorted on the basis of a variety of pricing variables that measure different aspects of auto insurance costs. While risk classification variables vary among auto insurers, the following rating factors are commonly used by many insurers across the industry.

TERRITORY

Insurance loss costs can vary dramatically across a state, and insurers generally divide a state into different territories to account for these differences. Costs are generally higher for drivers living in major urban areas than for drivers living in suburban areas around major cities. Small towns and rural areas generally enjoy much lower insurance costs. Territory boundaries can differ widely across insurers. As a result, consumers can often uncover lower-priced insurance by comparing premium rates across a large number of auto insurers.

AGE

Auto insurance loss costs vary across drivers in different age categories. Due to their lack of driving experience, youthful drivers generally pay more for auto insurance than older drivers aged thirty to the late fifties, holding other factors constant. Drivers aged sixty and older often pay higher premium rates that are commensurate with their increased average claim costs.

GENDER AND MARITAL STATUS

These two variables are used to increase pricing homogeneity, especially among younger drivers in their teens and twenties. Young male drivers have higher average claim costs than young female drivers, and young drivers who are married have lower average claim costs than drivers who are single. By sorting drivers into subcategories based on gender and marital status, insurers balance the advantages of increased pricing homogeneity against the comparatively smaller disadvantage of working with smaller risk groups.

USE OF AUTO

Auto insurance rating plans typically divide policyholders into categories based on how their vehicles are used, including farm use, business use, vehicles driven to work, and pleasure use (vehicles not used in business or driven to work). Many insurers subdivide the vehicles driven to work category by distance driven; for example, charging workers who live within 10 miles of their workplace less than workers living more than 10 miles from work. Premium charges are directly related to the average mileage for each category. Thus, the amount charged for pleasure use or farm use is less than for the higher-mileage business usage categories.

DRIVING RECORD

Information about prior accidents and traffic violations provides useful data about a driver's future insured loss costs. Thus, risk groups consisting of safe drivers with clean driving records—for example, no accidents or traffic violations over the preceding two to three years—generally have low expected losses. Therefore, these groups are eligible for lower rates than drivers with blemished records. Conversely, risk groups comprised of drivers who are negligent in causing "at-fault" accidents have higher expected losses and pay more for insurance. Many insurers measure this risk with a system that assesses points against a driver's record for every at-fault accident and recent traffic violation, with higher point totals resulting in premium surcharges. For serious traffic offenses, such as drunk driving or vehicular homicide, premium rates can often increase 100 percent or more, and many insurers will cancel the offender's insurance altogether.

INSIGHT BOX 12-1

Consumer Tips for Getting the Most from Your Auto Insurance Dollars

Consumers can take a number of steps to ensure that they are not paying too much for auto insurance:

- **Compare prices across insurers.** The cost of personal auto insurance can vary significantly across different insurance companies. To assure that they are not paying too much for insurance, drivers are recommended to compare the premiums charged by several insurers. (Remember that these prices cannot be shown on a Web site because premiums vary across drivers based on their individual risk characteristics.) Consumers also may find useful information about the insurance prices in their state on their insurance commissioner's Web site, as many commissioners publish an online comparison of the premiums charged by insurers (based on specific types of drivers) licensed in the state.

- **Consider dropping Part D—Physical Damage coverage on older vehicles.** Auto insurers value a vehicle on an ACV basis, where ACV equals the replacement cost minus depreciation. As a result, they will not provide a large loss payout on older cars or cars with high mileage because the depreciation on such vehicles is quite high. Consumers are advised to consider the cost of insuring physical damage coverage on cars with high depreciation. An industry representative notes that one of the most common errors of insurance consumers is mistakenly buying physical damage coverage on a vehicle because they overestimate its ACV.[5] Keep in mind that lenders typically will not permit a car owner to drop physical damage coverage until they have paid off their car loans.

- **Consider increasing physical damage coverage deductibles.** Policyholders buying physical damage coverage should investigate how much money they can save by increasing the size of their deductibles. Premium savings can be sizable, especially for drivers living in geographic areas with high insurance costs.

- **Ask about eligibility for premium discounts.** Insurers offer a growing variety of premium discounts beyond those described earlier in this chapter. For example, many insurers offer loyalty discounts to drivers who have been insured with the insurer for extended periods of time and accident-free discounts to drivers who have not had accidents over several years. A growing number of insurers offer discounts to drivers who have installed certain types of loss control equipment, such as onboard theft monitoring devices. Some insurers offer sizable discounts to low-risk drivers who agree to install global positioning satellite (GPS) devices that enable the insurer to monitor driving activity, such as driving speed, sudden braking, or driving during times of restricted visibility.

- **Adopt low-risk insurance behavior.** While some insurance pricing variables, like gender and age, are largely beyond the control of drivers, others are within their control and offer opportunities for premium savings. Thus, drivers can lower their premiums by reducing the number of miles they drive, moving to an apartment closer to work, cleaning up their driving record, or improving their credit scores.

An important consideration to keep in mind when buying auto insurance is that sometimes the lowest premium is not the best choice. For example, a driver can reduce his premium by buying the minimum coverage permitted in his state, but such actions may be short-sighted if he inflicts catastrophic financial damage to a fellow driver that exceeds his coverage limits, since the negligent driver is responsible for the portion of the damage not covered by insurance. Similarly, drivers should resist buying cheap insurance if the low price is a result of the insurer offering poor claims service. Recognizing that it is difficult for drivers to assess the quality of the service provided by auto insurers, the National Association of Insurance Commissioners (NAIC) offers a Web site (https://eapps.naic.org/cis/) that provides information on the complaints filed against insurers and other relevant operating data.

---

[5] See Spors, K., "Auto Watch: When to Drop Collision, Theft Coverage," *Wall Street Journal*, September 3, 2006, p. A4.

CREDIT-BASED INSURANCE SCORE

These insurance scores are calculated using a scoring formula that uses information found in a driver's credit report. Studies indicate that drivers with favorable insurance scores have been found to incur lower insured loss claims than drivers with unfavorable scores. As a result, drivers with good insurance scores are eligible for lower insurance rates. Supporters of the use of insurance scores explain that these scores are a measure of an intangible but vitally important trait of a driver: financial responsibility. That is, drivers who have excellent credit records because they conduct their financial life responsibly also recognize the value of driving safely and the costs of having accidents. While some critics have argued that the use of insurance scores in setting premiums may be discriminatory toward certain socio-economic groups, most states have approved its use as a pricing variable after extensive statistical analysis.

PREMIUM DISCOUNTS

Auto insurers offer a variety of premium discounts to reward drivers for behavior that reduces insured losses or expenses. For example, a common discount reduces a driver's premiums for having no accidents. Young drivers are eligible for *good student discounts* (responsible students tend to drive responsibly) or for discounts for completing a driver education course. *Multicar discounts* are available on policies insuring more than one vehicle, based on the assumption that each car will have less exposure on the highway than vehicles serving one-car households. Discounts vary widely across insurers. Innovative insurers are continuously watching for ways to discount prices—often linked to the introduction of new risk classification variables that reflect reduced insurer expenses—in the hopes of attracting drivers who are paying too much for insurance because their risk levels are lower than other drivers in their pricing category.

Due to the complexity of insurance pricing, many consumers are unfamiliar with ways that they can make sure they are getting the most out of their insurance premium expenditures. The Web sites of some insurance commissioners' offices in the various states can be very helpful consumer information about auto insurance. Insight Box 12-1 also offers some suggestions.

Summary

Automobile accidents cause billions of dollars in annual damage, including destroyed property, medical and funeral expenses, and lost income. Under the tort liability system, if one person injures another, the injured party (plaintiff) must sue the negligent party (defendant) to collect for the injuries caused by the negligence. Motorists can purchase a package of insurance protection to cover losses related to the ownership and use of an auto. In this chapter, we examined one such policy, the Personal Auto Policy (PAP).

Part A of the PAP provides coverage for an insured who is legally liable for injuring another or another's property. Several important definitions and exclusions—such as intentionally caused injury or business-related claims—apply to this coverage.

Part B of the PAP provides medical expense coverage for the insureds—again subject to limits of liability and relevant exclusions—such as injuries resulting from using vehicles having fewer than four wheels.

Part C protects insureds if uninsured motorists injure them. The various states have passed different types of laws to manage the problem of uninsured motorists, including compulsory liability insurance laws and unsatisfied judgment funds.

Part D provides property protection for the insured's auto. This coverage makes an important distinction between collision and other types of damage.

Parts E and F are general conditions with which insureds must comply to get the benefit of the policy.

Appendix: No-Fault Automobile Insurance

Under the tort liability system, the injured party either must sue the person causing the injury or be offered a settlement of the claim by the defendant's insurer to be compensated for the loss. **No-fault automobile insurance** is an alternative procedure for compensating injured victims of automobile accidents. A central feature of all true no-fault proposals is that people injured in automobile accidents will collect for their injuries from their own insurers. Injuries for which no-fault insurance arrangements provide compensation include lost income, medical expenses, and burial expenses. No compensation is paid for pain and suffering.

Nothing is novel in collecting from one's own insurer. Most insurance is based on the idea that insureds will collect compensation from their own insurer. Thus, if Dangerous Dan McGrew negligently burns down his house, he collects from his own homeowners insurance. If he negligently wraps his car around a tree, he collects from his own automobile insurer. The novel feature of no-fault automobile liability insurance is that McGrew will collect from his own insurer even if Calamity Jane negligently caused his injury. No-fault insurance proposals create the right to collect from one's own insurer. At the same time, these proposals remove the need to sue the negligent party. Thus, pure no-fault insurance would eliminate the need for liability insurance because nobody would have to (or be able to) sue a negligent party to collect for damages.

No-fault insurance does not mean that no one is at fault in causing auto accidents. The name comes from the fact that it is not necessary to prove who is at fault in causing an accident to collect for damages. Under a **pure no-fault** compensation system, all parties involved in an automobile accident receive compensation for their injuries from their own insurer, regardless of who caused the accident. Under the tort liability system, the injured party must sue the negligent party to collect for damages. Such suits to establish the defendant's negligence can be long and complex. No-fault insurance laws are designed to reduce or eliminate negligence lawsuits, facilitate loss payments, and help control the problem of uncompensated victims.

None of the current state no-fault plans is a pure no-fault law; these laws are best described as *modified no-fault laws*. That is, under the current arrangements, after some threshold of damage has been reached, the injured party may revert to the liability system to seek compensation. The threshold may be either a dollar amount such as $2,500 or a **verbal threshold**, such as one eliminating lawsuits unless injury results in death or a serious impairment of bodily function.

To protect residents in a no-fault state from liability suits of nonresidents, the various state laws provide for property damage and bodily injury liability insurance. That is, if a resident of a no-fault state injures an out-of-state resident, the tort liability system provides compensation to the victim. Generally, no-fault insurance is designed to speed the compensation of victims of less-serious traffic accidents by eliminating delays caused by courts and insurance companies in transferring compensation to injured parties.

No-Fault Versus Tort Liability

Both no-fault insurance plans and the tort liability system are designed to compensate the victims of automobile accidents. Under no-fault, injured parties collect from their own insurer for their injuries. Under the tort liability system, the injured party sues the negligent party and collects from the negligent party's insurer. Common criticisms of the tort liability system include:

1. Not enough of the dollars put into the traditional tort liability system are finding their way to automobile accident victims. Fees for a plaintiff's lawyers may run from 25 to 33 percent of the plaintiff's recovery amount. Defendant's attorney's fees, court costs, and insurance company expenses also represent dollars that do not go to victims.
2. Claimants are not always indemnified fairly. Critics of the tort liability system maintain that small claims (sometimes called nuisance claims) often are overcompensated, while large claims are undercompensated.
3. Recovery is often slow. In some states, only about one-half of all claims are settled after two years, and the case backlog is sometimes much longer. Supporters of no-fault insurance claim that this system reduces court congestion and speeds recovery to victims.

4. Proving negligence is often difficult, especially years after an accident occurs. In some cases, the circumstances of the accident are such that negligence cannot be determined easily. (For instance, determining fault in accidents that occur on expressways during rush hour can be challenging.) Over time, witnesses die, move, or their memories fade.

In defense of the tort liability system, supporters use the following arguments:

1. It may encourage good driving because drivers who cause accidents find their insurance premiums increased. In some cases, negligent drivers cause more damage than their insurance will pay for, and they must pay unmet claims from their own assets.

2. Because an adversarial relationship exists between plaintiff and defendant, damages and all other facts have to be proved. Thus, fraud is reduced.

3. In many cases, claims are settled in less than six months, and without litigation. Only a relatively small number of claims actually proceed through the litigation stage.

4. Payments for pain and suffering involve claims for real injuries, and generally they are not compensated by a no-fault system.

5. States that have adopted no-fault auto insurance laws have experienced problems with fraud, overuse of medical services, and increased involvement of attorneys and other professionals.

Review

1. Briefly, how does the tort liability system apply to automobile accidents?
2. Explain the difference between primary and excess coverage in automobile insurance.
3. Several distinct categories of drivers are insured under the terms of the PAP. Identify three categories of drivers covered by the PAP and give examples of each category.
4. Explain whether each of the people described in the following scenario has coverage under Part A of the PAP and say why or why not.

    Bob, the named insured, is an auto mechanic. Bob and his wife, Belle, own and drive a Ford. They have two children, Ben and Bill. Ben, age twenty-six, is in the U.S. Army and comes home to visit about twice a year. Bill is sixteen, lives at home, and has a learner's permit but no permanent driver's license. Ben often rents cars on weekends and drives battle tanks as his military assignments. Bob drives the church van to pick up nondriving members each Sunday. Bob also test-drives vehicles after he has repaired them at his place of employment, Barney's Garage. Bill has been known to lend the family car to his teenage pal, Bubba. Once, Bubba actually lent that car to his girlfriend, Brenda.
5. Does the PAP provide coverage if a named insured drives a nonowned auto? What is the definition of a nonowned auto?
6. What are the four general areas of protection provided by Parts A through D of the PAP?

7. Assume that an insured causes an automobile accident that injures five people and damages one auto. Assume that each of the injured parties successfully sues for $20,000. The damaged auto was worth $10,000. How much would the insurer pay if:
    a. the insured carried 10/20/5 limits?
    b. the insured carried 50/100/5 limits?
    c. the insured carried 100/300/50 limits?
8. Why is damage to an insured's own property excluded under Part A?
9. Identify other major categories of exclusions under Part A.
10. What situations are covered by the medical expense protection part of the PAP? If an insured were struck by a car while walking, would there be coverage under this provision?
11. Why do drivers need uninsured motorists insurance if they have purchased liability and property damage insurance?
12. Explain the difference between an uninsured and an underinsured motorist.
13. What are the insured's major duties after a loss?
14. Do insureds have a right to demand replacement of parts damaged in a collision with parts from the original equipment manufacturer?
15. How does the legal doctrine of subrogation apply under the PAP?

Objective Questions

Assume that Herb Avoir, the vegetarian, owns the PAP discussed in this chapter and reproduced as Appendix B. His policy has the following limits:

A = $100,000
B = $3,000
C = $100,000
D = $250 deductible—collision; $250 deductible—other than collision

Assume that each of the events described in the following situations occurs separately. The actual cash value of Herb's car is $14,500. You are to calculate the amount Herb's insurer will pay.

1. Herb negligently collides with a farm tractor. The tractor is traveling on the highway to get from one farm to another. Herb was at fault. The farmer successfully sues for $80,000 in bodily injury damages and $21,000 in property damage to his tractor. The lawyers charge $10,000 to defend Herb in court.
2. Herb's daughter, Peggy Sue, strikes their home and their second car while learning how to drive. She is sixteen years old and has a learner's permit. Damage to Herb's home is $30,000, and damage to the second car is $15,000. Both vehicles are insured with the same policy.
3. Herb runs a stop sign and collides with a parked car, causing $4,000 of damage to each vehicle.
4. While using his car as a delivery vehicle for a local florist, Herb is struck by an uninsured motorist. He has $15,000 in medical expenses and lost wages. His car is destroyed (replacement value is $16,000).
5. Herb lends his auto to Emmy Lou. Emmy Lou has her own PAP, with coverage identical to Herb's. Emmy Lou runs over and injures a famous baseball player who recently signed a three-year, $27 million contract. Emmy Lou is sued for $32 million. (Answer with respect to Herb's PAP, since both PAPs are the same.)
6. Herb borrows his neighbor's car for a week while the neighbor is on vacation. Unfortunately, Herb did $4,000 damage to the neighbor's car while he was driving it.
7. Herb hits a deer on Door County Highway A. His car is destroyed.

Discussion Questions

1. Describe the different approaches used to address the problem of uninsured motorists.
2. Describe the differences between no-fault and tort liability auto insurance laws.

Selected References

Insurance Services Office, © 2003 Personal Auto Policy, (PP 00 01 01 05)

Shayer, Natalie, 1978, "Driver Classification in Automobile Insurance," in *Automobile Insurance*

Risk Classification: Equity and Accuracy. (Boston: Massachusetts Division of Insurance, Commonwealth of Massachusetts), pp. 1–24.

13

Homeowners Insurance (HO)

After studying this chapter, you should be able to

- Describe the basic coverages provided by the HO insurance forms
- Explain the meanings of words defined in the HO definitions section
- Identify the property perils covered by the HO-3 contract
- Identify the categories of covered persons under the liability section of the HO
- Identify the main property and liability exclusions found in the HO insurance policies
- Describe the effect of underinsurance on HO loss settlements

The decision to buy a home is one of the largest personal investments made by most individuals, and protecting that investment is an important task in personal risk management. As one of the largest product lines in the property-liability insurance industry, homeowners insurance is an important element of economic security to U.S. society. People purchase homeowners insurance (HO) to protect some of their most important assets: their home and its contents, assets they almost certainly cannot afford to lose. Moreover, when people borrow money to purchase their home, lenders require insurance to protect their financial interest in the property. Buying homeowners insurance is thus an essential purchase for most individuals.

This chapter describes homeowners insurance, focusing on the HO-3 homeowners policy, also known as the *special policy*[1]. This policy combines property insurance, comprehensive personal liability insurance, additional living expense coverage,

---

[1] This chapter focuses on a homeowners policy form from the Insurance Services Office (ISO). The ISO HO program consists of six different forms: the Broad form (HO-2), the Special form (HO-3), the Contents Broad form for renters (HO-4), the Comprehensive form (HO-5), the Unit Owners form for condominium owners (HO-6), and the Modified form (HO-8). The ISO forms HO-2, HO-3, HO-5, and HO-8 are used to insure an owner's interest in a home and its contents and provide personal liability coverage. The first two types of HO policies are most widely used, with the scope of the coverage for the HO-3 broader than the coverage of the HO-2. The HO-8 form covers houses having a replacement cost greater than market value, a condition most frequently found in older homes. If these older homes were destroyed, they could be replaced more economically using modern construction techniques (such as using drywall instead of plaster or plastic plumbing instead of copper) without loss in usefulness. HO-8 thus provides for functional replacement rather than replacement with material of "like kind." The authors would like to thank ISO for granting permission to include a copy of the HO-3 policy in Appendix B.

replacement-cost coverage, and medical-expense-coverage-for-others in one convenient, standardized package. A complete copy of the policy is provided in Appendix B. The HO-3 policy is widely used by many insurers. While some larger insurers may use their own proprietary versions of the policy, they are usually quite similar to the HO-3 shown in the appendix.

While the HO-3 is designed for homeowners, other forms are available to protect people who do not own their own homes. For example, the HO-4 form is designed for renters. It does not cover the building in which a renter lives, but it provides coverage for the **personal property** within the building and liability coverage. The HO-6 form covers the property interest, contents, and personal liability of people owning a unit in a condominium or a cooperative building. The HO forms cannot be used to cover mobile homes or house trailers; other, more limited policies are available for this property.

POLICY LAYOUT

Figure 13-1 shows an outline of the HO-3 policy that will be used as sample material throughout this chapter. The HO's front page displays descriptive material that insurers call the *declarations* (Figure 13-2). Based on information provided by the policy-owner, the declarations page shows the name and address of the named insured, the

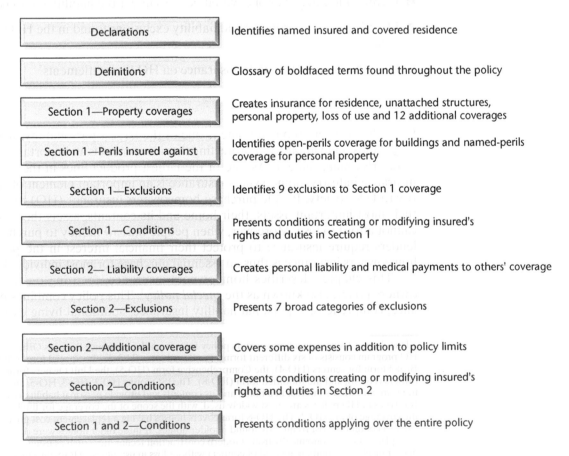

Declarations	Identifies named insured and covered residence
Definitions	Glossary of boldfaced terms found throughout the policy
Section 1—Property coverages	Creates insurance for residence, unattached structures, personal property, loss of use and 12 additional coverages
Section 1—Perils insured against	Identifies open-perils coverage for buildings and named-perils coverage for personal property
Section 1—Exclusions	Identifies 9 exclusions to Section 1 coverage
Section 1—Conditions	Presents conditions creating or modifying insured's rights and duties in Section 1
Section 2— Liability coverages	Creates personal liability and medical payments to others' coverage
Section 2—Exclusions	Presents 7 broad categories of exclusions
Section 2—Additional coverage	Covers some expenses in addition to policy limits
Section 2—Conditions	Presents conditions creating or modifying insured's rights and duties in Section 2
Section 1 and 2—Conditions	Presents conditions applying over the entire policy

FIGURE 13-1 Homeowner's Insurance Policy Layout

Named Insured: David Cather
22 Main Street
Anytown, USA

Policy Number: ###############
Policy Period: 1/1/2012 to 12/31/2012

Mortgagee: ZYX Mortgage Inc., 22 Corporate Way, Anytown, USA

SECTION I (Subject to $1,000 Deductible)

Coverage	Limits of Coverage
Coverage A: Dwelling	$200,000
Coverage B: Other Structures	$20,000
Coverage C: Personal Property	$100,000
Coverage D: Loss of Use	$40,000

SECTION II

Coverage E: Personal Liability (each occurrence)	$300,000
Coverage F: Medical Payments to Others (each person)	$1,000

PREMIUM

Premium before Discounts	$800
Less: Claims-free Discount	−$120
Annual Premium	$680

Countersignature Date: 1/1/2012   by Ann Agent (authorized representative)

FIGURE 13-2 Sample Declarations Page for a Homeowners Policy from Pearson Insurance Co.

time when the policy begins and ends, the maximum limits of the insurance company's liability for the different coverages, the applicable deductible provisions, and other pertinent risk classification information.

The next section of the HO-3 is the *definitions* section, a short glossary that establishes the meaning of several important terms that are used throughout the contract. Most HO policies print the words defined in the definitions section in quotation marks or boldface print.

Two important definitions in the HO-3 are for the named insured and the insured. These definitions determine the parties who are insured under the homeowners policy. The **named insured** is the person whose name is shown as the policy owner in the declarations. The definition of the named insured also includes the spouse of the named insured, so long as the spouse resides in the home. In addition to the named insured, the HO-3 defines an **insured** as any resident relative living in the household. Through this definition, insurance coverage is provided to young children or elderly parents who are living with the named insured. The definition of *insured* generally provides coverage to college students while studying at college away from home. Persons under age 21 in the care of an insured are also covered under the HO-3.

The remainder of the HO-3 policy is divided into two sections, as shown in Table 13-1. Section 1 provides property insurance protection and is divided into four coverages, each with a separate limit of liability. Section 2 provides liability coverage and is divided into two coverages.

TABLE 13-1 Protection Provided by Homeowners Insurance

Type of Coverage	Coverage Limit	Description of Coverage
Section 1, Coverage A: Dwelling	Based on home's replacement cost	Damage to insured's home
Section 1, Coverage B: Other structures	10% of Coverage A limit	Damage to insured's nonattached structures (garage, sheds, etc.)
Section 1, Coverage C: Personal property	50% of Coverage A limit	Damage to contents of home, including coverage on property away from home
Section 1, Coverage D: Loss of use	20% of Coverage A limit	Extra expense of renting quarters after damage from an insured peril prevents the insured from living in the home
Section 2, Coverage E: Personal liability	Minimum of $100,000	Liability for bodily injury to another person, or damage to the person's property
Section 2, Coverage F: Medical payments to others	Minimum of $1000	Medical expenses incurred by others on the insured premises or resulting from actions of the insured away from the premises

SECTION 1—PROPERTY COVERAGES

Section 1 establishes categories of insured property and identifies the losses that are covered and those that are excluded. This section of the policy also identifies several kinds of property subject to maximum limits of recovery.

Coverage A, **dwelling**, covers the insured's home, including structures attached to the dwelling, such as a garage. Coverage A applies to the insured's residence premises shown on the declarations page. A second home or summer cottage, which might be considered a temporary residence, would not be covered if it did not appear in the declarations.

Coverage B applies to **other structures**, such as an unattached garage or shed. It does not cover structures rented or held for rental to any person not a tenant of the dwelling unless used solely as a private garage. Nor does it cover structures used in a business. The insurer's limit of liability for this coverage will not be more than 10 percent of the limit of liability that applies to Coverage A.

Coverage C, **unscheduled personal property**, applies to property usually found in homes, such as furniture, clothes, appliances, and other personal property. Coverage is provided for personal property owned or used by an insured anywhere in the world. The standard limit of liability for this coverage is 50 percent of the limit of liability that applies to Coverage A.

Coverage D, **loss of use**, pays for extra expenses if a covered loss prevents the insured from living in the home. Thus, if a loss covered under Section 1 makes a part of the insured premises where the insured resides not fit to live in, the insurer covers any increase in living expenses necessary to maintain a normal standard of living. The limit of liability for this coverage will not be more than 20 percent of the limit of liability that applies to Coverage A. Some insurers set this limit equal to 30 percent.

For example, assume that Jack and Jane Rabbit lose their house in a fire. They subsequently move to the Hutch Motel while their home is being rebuilt. Their increase in expenses includes the motel bill ($3,500), the increase in their food cost (prefire food cost = $800, postfire restaurant food cost = $2,000, for an increase of $1,200), and miscellaneous increase in expenses = $1,000. Coverage D would pay the total increase in expenses of $5,700 ($3,500 + $1,200 + $1,000).

Discussion

The HO package is **divided coverage**. Each coverage (A through F) is treated separately. Dollars may not be transferred among the various coverages. The maximum amount that the insured could collect is the sum of all the coverages. Thus, if a property loss is total, an insured theoretically could collect the total amount of Section 1, Coverages A through D. If an insured needs additional protection, Coverages B, C, or D can be increased prior to a loss, for an additional premium charge. Coverage cannot be reduced below the specified percentages.

As an example of the coverage percentages, assume that a homeowner, Phil Harmonic, the orchestra director, purchases $100,000 of insurance on his dwelling (Coverage A). Coverage B (other structures) automatically equals $10,000. If Phil had an elaborate unattached enclosed swimming pool worth $25,000 on his property, Coverage B would have to be increased. Coverage C automatically equals $50,000 (50 percent of $100,000). Again, if the homeowner had more than $50,000 in personal property, this coverage would have to be increased. Coverage D automatically equals $20,000 (20 percent of Coverage A), and it also can be increased if needed.

Sometimes the question is raised whether a specific item is real or personal property. If it is real property, it is covered under Coverage A. If it is personal, it is covered under Coverage C. The English common-law rule is that land and anything permanently attached to land is **real property**. Thus, built-in appliances or built-in bookcases are real property.

Special Limits of Liability

The special limits section sets a maximum dollar amount that an insured can recover when a specifically identified property is damaged or stolen. For some property (jewelry, for example), the special limits apply only to loss by the peril of theft; losses from other perils are covered without the special limit applying. With other property (for example, money, bank notes, and coins), any loss is subject to the specified limits. The special limit for each category is the total limit for each loss for all property in that category. Special limits do not increase the Coverage C limits.

Some of the property that is subject to special limits of coverage are provided limited coverage because it is difficult to determine the size of the loss after an insured peril occurs. Thus, the HO-3 provides only $200 on "money, bank notes, bullion, gold other than goldware, silver other than silverware, platinum other than platinumware, coins, medals, scrip, stored value cards, and smart cards." Thus, if Alan claims that his life savings of $2 million, hidden between the mattresses of his bed because he does not have faith in the banking system, was destroyed by fire, the insurer need provide only $200 of payment rather than sift through the ashes of Alan's burned-out bedroom to determine the exact amount of currency lost. "Securities, accounts, deeds, evidences of debt, letters of credit, notes other than bank notes, manuscripts, personal records, passports, tickets, and stamps" are similarly subject to a limit of $1,500. The homeowner can increase these special limits for an additional premium if she has a greater need for coverage.

Other property is subject to special limits of coverage because the property is highly susceptible to loss. For example, theft coverage is limited on several items commonly stolen by thieves. The HO-3 thus provides only $2,500 for stolen firearms and related equipment and $1,500 for stolen jewelry, watches, furs, and precious and semiprecious stones. The policy similarly provides $2,500 for "loss by theft of silverware, silver-plated ware, goldware, gold-plated ware, platinumware, platinum-plated ware, and pewterware." Again, the homeowner can increase these special limits for an additional premium.

The HO-3 offers some limited coverage for items that are better covered under other policies. Electronic apparatus, such as laptop computers and their accessories used primarily for business, are covered for $1,500 while away from the residence premises. Other types of business property are provided $500 coverage while away from the premises and $2,500 coverage on the insured premises. The policy provides $1,500 coverage for watercraft and their related equipment, as well as $1,500 for trailers and semitrailers not used with watercraft. Insureds with property valued far more than these limits are recommended to arrange separate insurance coverage, such as commercial property insurance or watercraft insurance.

Additional Coverage

The additional coverage portion of Section 1 provides protection from several loss exposures that, while not property losses, are nonetheless often suffered by homeowners. For example, in the event of an insured loss, the HO-3 covers the cost to remove the debris from the loss and the expense to protect the property from further damage. Property removed from the residence because it was endangered by an insured peril and subsequently damaged or stolen at the removal site is covered. Fire department service charges also will be reimbursed. All these exposures are covered by insurers to support the efforts of insureds to limit the size of insured losses.

Other additional coverages provide protection from a variety of losses that are commonly incurred by families. Credit card fraud and similar frauds are covered for a limited amount. Coverage is available for damage to trees and shrubs, although losses from ice and wind are not covered. Glass or safety glazing material is covered. Certain loss assessments in cooperative-type buildings are paid up to a $1,000 limit. Coverage of a landlord's furnishings, which is limited to $2,500, is useful for homeowners renting an apartment on the residence premises. Loss due to collapse is covered.[2] Grave markers are covered for damage up to $5,000.

SECTION 1—INSURED PERILS

Property insurance policies specify insured perils using one of two basic formats. A policy using a named-perils approach specifically lists the perils that are covered as insured losses. By contrast, the open-perils approach states that it will cover direct physical loss to covered property unless it results from a list of specific excluded losses. Both formats are used in the HO-3 policy.

Coverages A and B of the HO-3 use an open-perils approach to specify the perils covered by the policy. They state that the policy will cover direct physical loss to covered property unless the damage results from a list of specific excluded losses. Examples of the losses excluded from coverage under the open-perils format includes freezing of a plumbing, heating, air conditioning, or sprinkler system; the pressure, weight, freezing, or thawing of water or ice; theft of materials from a dwelling under

---

[2] Collapse was a named peril in prior versions of the HO insurance program, but it is now included as additional coverage. Collapse is hard to define because it can have many different causes. The HO policy only covers collapsed structures (fallen down as opposed to settling, cracking, etc.) if it can be shown that the cause of the collapse is not excluded from coverage under the policy. Some courts require that a structure actually must fall into rubble before declaring the peril to have occurred. Other courts have declared buildings collapsed that have suffered significant structural weakness but have not actually fallen down. Moreover, some courts have introduced the doctrine of *concurrent causation*. This rule states that the HO policy provides coverage when a loss arises from two separately identifiable perils, one covered (for example, collapse as defined in older homeowners policies) and one excluded (for example, underground water pressure). These concurrent-causation-theory decisions led to deliberate treatment of losses associated with collapse as an additional coverage. To be covered, the collapse must be attributable to the perils covered by the homeowners policy; decay; insect or vermin damage hidden from view; weight of contents, equipment, animals, or people; weight of rain on a roof; or, under certain conditions, defective materials or methods of construction.

TABLE 13-2 Insured Named-Perils Coverage for Personal Property in the HO-3 Policy

Named Perils	
Fire or lightning	Theft
Windstorm or hail	Falling objects
Explosion	Weight of ice, snow, or sleet
Riot or civil commotion	Accidental discharge or overflow of water or steam
Aircraft	Sudden and accidental tearing apart, cracking, burning, or bulging
Vehicles	Freezing
Smoke	Volcanic eruption
Vandalism and malicious mischief	Sudden and accidental damage from artificially generated electrical current

construction; mold, fungus, or wet rot; and a variety of uninsurable perils (e.g., wear and tear, mechanical breakdown, smog, and pollution).

For Coverage C of the HO-3, personal property is covered on a named-peril basis. A list of the sixteen perils insured is shown in Table 13-2. Policy owners are covered for losses to personal property caused by any of these perils. Please note that the description of these sixteen perils in the HO-3 are sometimes quite detailed, reflecting efforts by insurers to limit reimbursement only to those loss situations that satisfy the requirements of insurability.

Consumers often ask why they should buy an HO-3 policy instead of a less-expensive HO-2 policy, which offers named-perils coverage for Coverages A and B. Policies that specify perils using a named-perils format, while less expensive, provide less coverage than those using an open-perils format. This follows from the fact that under an open-perils format, the insurer pays for all losses except for the small number listed as exclusions under the policy. In addition, if legal disputes arise about whether a loss is covered by a policy using the named-perils format, established principles of insurance law put the initial burden of proof on the insured to demonstrate which covered peril caused the loss. Assuming that the insured has met this burden, the insurer then can indicate whether any exclusions apply. With an open-perils contract, however, the initial legal burden shifts to the insurer to prove that an exclusion applies, increasing the odds that a disputed loss will be covered.

SECTION 1—EXCLUSIONS

Section 1 of the HO-3 policy excludes coverage from several perils. These exclusions apply to the open-perils format used to insure dwelling and other structures, as well as the named perils format used to insure personal property. In addition, several types of property are excluded, too. As was noted in Chapter 7, "Insurable Perils and Insuring Organizations," insurance policies contain exclusions for a variety of reasons. We discuss some of these reasons below, providing examples of excluded perils as appropriate.

Exclusions to eliminate losses arising from catastrophic events: Insurers will exclude perils from coverage if such perils could result in catastrophic losses that potentially threaten the survival of the insurer. Thus, perils such as earth movement, water damage from floods, war, and nuclear hazards are excluded from coverage.

Exclusions to eliminate losses associated with moral hazard: Insurance premiums could become unaffordable if insurers did not use exclusions to limit their exposure to moral hazard. Thus, insurers will not cover intentional losses committed by the insured, nor will they pay claims arising from the neglect of the insured to take action to save and preserve property at the time of loss. Similarly, insurers will not cover losses resulting from the failure of the insured to adequately maintain the premises. For this reason, mold is often excluded from homeowners property coverage unless it occurs as a result of an insured peril (such as the accidental discharge of water from a plumbing or heating system).

Exclusions to eliminate coverage not needed by the typical insured: Many of the items described above in the "special limits of coverage" section are limited in coverage because most policy owners do not need extensive protection. By contrast, policy owners with coverage needs in excess of the special limits can pay an additional premium to increase their coverage limits.

Exclusions to eliminate coverage where another policy is specifically designed to provide coverage: The HO-3 excludes coverage for property that is better insured under another insurance policy. Thus, the policy excludes from coverage motor vehicles and equipment, business property, business data stored in computers, and personal property insured elsewhere, such as in a personal property floater.

Exclusions to control costs and keep premiums affordable: For example, the **ordinance-or-law exclusion** eliminates coverage for additional expenses if current zoning laws or building codes prevent rebuilding a structure comparable to the damaged home, thus requiring the homeowner to incur additional cost to bring the home "up to code." For an additional payment, this exclusion can be removed by endorsement. Likewise, insurers will not pay for losses resulting from the failure of power or utility service because it is not an insurer's responsibility to pay claims on behalf of the utility provider.

SECTION 1—CONDITIONS

The relationship between an insurer and its policyholder can be complex, requiring a clear and detailed description of the rights and obligations of both parties. The conditions portion of the HO-3 specifies these details. Some of the most important conditions are described below.

Loss Settlement

The **loss settlement** provision requires careful study because it presents several alternative paths to determine the amount of payment made to the insured in the event of loss. These paths are shown in Figure 13-3, in which the language of the policy with respect to recovery for buildings (Coverage A) and other structures (Coverage B) is illustrated.

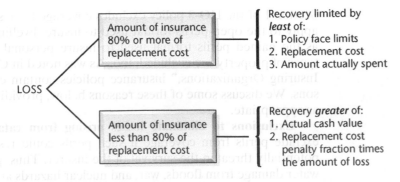

FIGURE 13-3 Loss Settlement under the HO-3 Contract

The loss settlement condition indicates that the insurer's payment for personal property under Coverage C will be based on the lesser of the actual cash value (ACV) of the property or the cost to repair or replace the property. Buildings covered under Coverage A or B are valued on the basis of their replacement cost, without deduction for depreciation. Items such as awnings, household appliances, carpeting, outdoor equipment, structures that are not buildings, and grave markers are valued on an ACV basis as well.

Replacement Cost and Coinsurance

The loss settlement provision of HO-3 contains a penalty provision that applies if the insured has purchased less insurance than 80 percent of replacement cost. The HO penalty provision is similar to the coinsurance provision commonly found in commercial property insurance policies. The purpose of both the **coinsurance clause** and the HO loss settlement clause is to make underinsurance unattractive to the insured. Both clauses provide for the insured to pay a penalty based on the amount of underinsurance, as shown below.

Many property policies contain a clause requiring the insured to purchase a minimum amount of insurance if the insured wants full coverage on all losses. If the insured purchases less than the minimum amount, there will be only partial recovery for losses. In the HO policy, the minimum amount of insurance is stated as a percentage of the replacement cost of the insured property.

To determine whether the insured has met the coinsurance requirement on the dwelling, insurers use the following rules:

- If the amount of insurance purchased, divided by 80 percent of the replacement cost of the home, is equal to or greater than 1, then the insurance company will pay the replacement cost of the loss minus the deductible. The maximum amount paid will be the coverage limit.

- If the amount of insurance purchased, divided by 80 percent of the replacement cost of the home, is less than 1, the larger of the following two is paid (but no more than the policy limit of coverage): (1) The ACV of the loss less the deductible, or (2) the result of

$$\frac{\text{Amount of insurance}}{80\% \times \text{Replacement cost of building}} \times (\text{Replacement cost of loss} - \text{the Deductible})$$

If the first term in the equation is less than 1, the insured will bear a portion of the loss. The insured is said to be a "coinsurer of the loss." If the fraction is equal to or greater than 1, the insurer will pay the full amount of the loss up to the amount of insurance purchased.

To demonstrate the coinsurance clause mathematically, assume that Queen Victoria owns a $1 million castle-like house, and it would take $1 million to replace the house with a comparable one. The market value of the palace may be more or less than the replacement cost depending on many facts, including its location. Assume that her insurance policy has an 80 percent replacement-cost clause, and that Queen Victoria purchases $600,000 of insurance. Ignoring the deductible provision for the sake of simplicity, if there is a $200,000 loss, the insurer will pay:

$$\frac{\$600,000}{80\%(\$1,000,000)} \times \$200,000 = \$150,000$$

Thus, Queen Victoria will pay $50,000 and the insurer will pay $150,000 of the $200,000 loss.

If a total loss occurs, the formula produces the following $750,000 result:

$$\frac{\$600,000}{80\%(\$1,000,000)} \times \$1,000,000 = \$750,000$$

However, Queen Victoria has only $600,000 of insurance, so $600,000 is the maximum amount that she can collect for this loss. In all property insurance policies, the insurance proceeds are restricted to the policy limits.

Reconsider this example, but assume that Queen Victoria purchases $800,000 of insurance. All other facts remain unchanged. In the case of a $200,000 loss, she now collects $200,000 because the fraction $800,000/$800,000 equals 1. In the case of a total loss, she will collect $800,000 because the $800,000 insurance policy is less than the $1 million loss.

Assuming that she was underinsured, and the ACV of Queen Victoria's home produced a larger loss payment than the coinsurance formula, she would receive an ACV settlement. For example, assume that the home was 95 percent undepreciated and that there was a 50 percent coinsurance deficiency. The ACV settlement would be greater than the coinsurance penalty and Queen Victoria is entitled to the greater of the two settlements. Never forget, however, that the policy's limit of liability is the maximum that an insured can recover. Also, the deductible provision applies to all loss settlements, even though that was not illustrated in the foregoing examples.[3]

People often ask why the HO requires coverage equaling only 80 percent of replacement cost rather than 100 percent. One answer involves the effects of inflation on construction costs. If 100 percent coverage were required (and some reporting forms used in commercial insurance do require this amount of coverage) and inflation equaled 1 percent (or any other amount) a month, insureds initially purchasing adequate coverage would face a coinsurance penalty after the first month. After a year, they would face a 12 percent penalty. Thus, to avoid the coinsurance penalty, the HO requires coverage that equals at least 80 percent of replacement cost, but careful insureds will purchase 100 percent coverage with an "inflation guard" endorsement that increases coverage on a regular basis to offset the effects of inflation. Insureds who initially purchase only 80 percent coverage will be penalized after a short period of rapid inflation. As our example pointed out, even without inflation, an insured with only 80 percent coverage will be assuming 20 percent of all total losses.

Mortgage Clause

The HO **mortgage clause** protects creditors making loans secured by the insured property. A mortgage is evidence of a debt. It is the security agreement when a loan is made on real estate. A mortgage gives the lender (mortgagee) a legal interest in the

---

[3] What is the reason for the coinsurance requirement? It exists to keep insurance rates fair. Property insurance rates are expressed as an amount per $100 of value, such as $0.30 per $100. However, in homeowners insurance, small losses (e.g., a windstorm blows shingles off the roof) occur much more frequently than total losses (a tornado destroys the home). Because the probability of a loss to the first $100 of a house's value is greater than the probability of a loss to the last $100 of value, the cost of insurance for these two different $100 segments should be different. In practice, they are not. The rate is $0.30 per $100 for all the $100 segments. The $0.30 per $100 figure is the average cost and results in a fair price only when the insured purchases an amount of insurance equal to the full property value.

If property owners, recognizing that most losses are partial, purchased insurance equal to only 50 percent of the value of the covered property, they may think that they transferred the most significant part of the risk to the insurer. Without the coinsurance penalty, they would have an advantageous deal. If the average rate ($0.30 per $100) was paid, the insured would be paying a rate below the rate mathematically appropriate to the amount of risk transferred. The coinsurance requirement of property insurance policies prevents insureds from taking advantage of the insurer's average rate structure. If someone purchases insurance equal to 50 percent of the value of the property when the insurer requires 80 percent coverage, that insured will receive only partial recovery for a loss.

mortgaged property. If the borrower (mortgagor) defaults on the loan agreement, the mortgagee may foreclose on the mortgage and sell the property to satisfy the debt. Both the mortgagor and mortgagee, therefore, have an insurable interest in the property. Using a mortgage clause, both parties are economically protected under a single policy. The mortgage clause spells out the rights of the mortgagee to receive payment from the insurer if an insured loss occurs, thus eliminating the need for the lender to buy separate coverage on the mortgaged property.[4]

SECTION 2—LIABILITY COVERAGES

Section 2 provides liability protection and is divided into two coverages. Coverage E provides protection from adverse legal judgments that can result when the insured is held responsible for the bodily injury or property damage suffered by a claimant. Coverage F provides for medical payments to those injured by an accident occurring at the insured's premises or resulting from the insured's activities. Both coverages are discussed below.

Coverage E: Personal Liability

In general, Coverage E commits the insurer to pay for successful judgments against its insured resulting from the nonbusiness activities of the named insured and household residents. It agrees to provide the insured with an attorney to defend lawsuits. The insurer retains the right to make a settlement with a claimant if the insurer concludes a settlement is appropriate. Under Coverage F, the insurer agrees to pay for medical expenses to persons other than the insured.

As an example of the protection provided by Coverage E, assume that an insured homeowner named Rimski, while unloading his shotgun, accidentally blows a hole in a car belonging to Korsakov. Whether the accident happens at home or away from the resident premises is not a question because coverage applies anywhere in the world.

Korsakov could sue Rimski to collect for the damage negligently done to his automobile. In this example, where the damage is definitely the responsibility of the insured (Rimski), the insurer usually will try to settle with the injured third party (Korsakov), thereby avoiding litigation. In other cases, in which an insured's responsibility for injuring another is not clearly established, the insurer may choose to defend the insured in court. The decision to try to settle a claim or to defend an insured rests with the insurer in the HO contract.[5]

---

[4] To illustrate the mortgage clause, consider the case of Genghis O. Kahn. Genghis recently purchased a $250,000 house in Ephraim, Wisconsin. He used $50,000 of his own money for a down payment and borrowed $200,000 from the Eighteenth National Bank of Ephraim. To secure the loan, he mortgaged his new home to the bank. If an uninsured loss occurred, Genghis not only would lose his $50,000 down payment, but also he still would owe the bank $200,000. The bank would have some land and a pile of ashes as security for a $200,000 loan. Considering the nomadic ways of Genghis, these ashes would not be great security. To protect the bank's interest, the bank could require Genghis to purchase insurance and add the Eighteenth National Bank as an additional insured. If, however, any action on the part of Genghis (such as an attempt to defraud the insurer) were to result in suspension of the coverage, the bank could lose its insurance protection. As a second alternative, the bank could purchase its own insurance, but it is costly for a lender to insure mortgaged property separately. Rather than rely on either of these options, the standard mortgage clause economically covers the interests of both mortgagor and mortgagee under one policy. As is shown in Figure 13-2, the name of the mortgagee is shown on the declaration page of the homeowners policy.

[5] By contrast, in many professional liability insurance policies such as medical liability insurance, the insured (whose professional reputation may be at issue) can prevent an insurer from trying to settle a claim without litigation.

The insurer's duty to make payment on its insured's behalf is not exactly coincident with its duty to defend its insureds. Payment is required only for covered acts. A legal defense is required even for false, fraudulent, or groundless lawsuits.

Coverage F: Medical Payments to Others

Unlike the liability coverage of the homeowners policy, Coverage F provides medical payments coverage to injured parties without establishing the negligence of the named insured or resident family members. This coverage provides a limited amount of medical payments coverage to a person who is injured while on the insured location with the permission of the insured, or away from the insured location if the loss originated from the insured location (for example, a neighbor harmed when the insured's dead tree falls on the neighbor's home). It also covers medical expenses arising from bodily injury off the insured location resulting from the activities of the insured, an animal owned by the insured, or a residence employee of the insured while employed by the insured.

The coverage pays for reasonable and necessary medical expenses incurred within three years of an accident. The standard amount of protection available from Coverage F is set at $1,000 per person, but an insured can increase the coverage limit by paying an additional premium. By providing immediate reimbursement of medical expenses to injured claimants without determining negligence, this coverage helps to reduce the likelihood that a person injured in an accident will file a lawsuit against the insured.

SECTION 2—EXCLUSIONS

Coverages E and F are open-perils coverages. Due to the differences between property losses and liability claims, however, the liability exclusions for Section 2 are not the same as the property damage exclusions found in Section 1. The liability exclusions are described below, along with a brief explanation why each type of liability risk is not covered.

Exclusions to eliminate coverage when another policy is designed to provide coverage: The insurance industry has developed specialized types of liability insurance policies for different liability loss exposures. For example, separate auto, watercraft, and aircraft liability insurance policies have been designed to cover motor vehicle, watercraft, and aircraft liability, respectively. Because of the specialized nature of liability insurance, Section 2 of the homeowners policy excludes coverage for motor vehicle liability, watercraft liability, aircraft liability, and professional liability (such as medical malpractice liability insurance for a physician or comparable liability protection for architects, attorneys, and other professionals). Damage to property owned or rented to the insured is also excluded because it is better covered by property insurance.

Business liability exposures are not covered under the homeowners policy, as commercial business policies are better suited to cover such exposures. This exclusion does not apply to certain specific cases in which (a portion of) the insured location is rented to others (for example, a homeowner rents his spare bedroom to a graduate student) or to an insured under the age of twenty-one who runs a part-time business with no employees (for example, a teenage child of the insured who does baby-sitting or lawn-mowing in the neighborhood). This business exclusion has been a topic of numerous legal disputes between insurers and their policyholders and some insurers are willing to cover incidental business liability by endorsement. Rather than run the risk of not having protection, insureds engaging in business activities should consider buying an appropriate endorsement for their HO policies to cover these activities or an appropriate business liability policy.

Exclusions to eliminate losses associated with moral hazard: The liability section of the HO-3 excludes from coverage liability resulting from intentional acts, including situations in which an intentional act results in unintended harm to a victim. Similarly, personal liability resulting from the transmission of communicable diseases, sexual molestation, corporal punishment, physical or mental abuse, and the use, sale, manufacture, delivery, or possession of controlled substances is excluded, an exclusion that precludes liability coverage for activities that law-abiding homeowners and their insurers do not want to subsidize.

Exclusions of uninsurable perils: Liability arising from war or nuclear related risks is excluded to eliminate the chance of insuring a potentially catastrophic loss event.

SECTION 2—ADDITIONAL COVERAGES

The additional coverages section of Section 2 pays for expenses in support of the protection offered under Coverages E and F. In the hope of averting a lawsuit, first-aid expenses to others are covered, as are payments of up to $1,000 for damage to the property of others. This section also covers expenses incurred by the insured in the defense of a lawsuit, including interest on judgments and reasonable expenses incurred by the insured, such as lost wages or travel expenses.

SECTION 2—CONDITIONS AND SECTIONS 1 AND 2—CONDITIONS

The end of the HO-3 consists of two portions: conditions that apply to Section 2 of the policy and conditions that apply to the entire policy. The Section 2 conditions focus primarily on those activities that must be carried out by the insured to assist the insurer in defending against a lawsuit, such as promptly notifying the insurer of the suit, forwarding all summons and legal requests to the insurer, and providing evidence to the insurer.

This portion of the policy also discusses the insurer's total liability for an insured occurrence. Liability insurance policies generally provide for the full limit of liability for each occurrence. In addition, there usually is no further premium to be paid. It is important to read all insurance policies carefully, however, to determine how the payment of a claim affects the policy limits for subsequent losses.

The conditions section applicable to the entire policy addresses a number of items discussed in Chapter 11, "Insurance Contracts," including subrogation, assignment (which is invalid unless the insurer has given written consent), concealments, and fraud. Much of this portion of the policy addresses the cancellation and nonrenewal of the policy, although many states have adopted policies on cancellation and nonrenewal that supersede the standardized wording found in the HO-3 policy.

Summary

The HO series provides a combination of property insurance, personal liability insurance, and additional living expense protection. In this chapter, we used the HO-3 to illustrate the principles of insurance policy construction for homeowners. More generally, homeowners insurance policies designed for policyholders who own their own home (the HO-2, HO-3, HO-5, and HO-8) consist of two sections.

Section 1 provides coverage for damaged property. Property covered includes the house and its attached structures (Coverage A), unattached structures like sheds or garages (Coverage B), and the contents of the house (Coverage C). Coverage D in Section 1 covers additional living expenses incurred by the insured when forced out of the home by damage from an insured peril.

Section 2 consists of two coverages. Coverage E provides the insured protection from personal liability, paying for bodily injury to another party or property damage to another person's property. Coverage F pays for medical payments incurred by other parties that arise on the insured's premises or away from the premises as a result of the activities of the insured.

Each coverage part of the homeowners policy consists of an insuring agreement, followed by exclusions and conditions. The exclusions limit coverage to insurable loss events by excluding losses that are better covered under other policies, not needed by the typical insured, catastrophic perils, or too costly to insure affordably. The conditions of the policy explicitly state the rights and obligation of both insurer and insured to ensure that the policy can meet its intended purpose: to provide a package of property, liability, and indirect loss coverages that protects homeowners from a wide variety of personal loss exposures.

Review

1. Describe some individuals who are protected by the HO who are parties to the contract. Distinguish the named insured from other insureds. Describe some covered people who are not parties to the contract.
2. List the four coverages found in Section 1 of the HO. Give an example of a loss covered by each section.
3. List the two coverages found in Section 2 of the HO. Give an example of a loss covered by each section.
4. What is the relationship between the ordinance-or-law exclusion and building codes?
5. Why is the mortgage clause of the HO desirable from a lender's viewpoint?
6. What is the difference between a named-perils policy and an open-perils policy?
7. Referring to the previous question, is one format always preferable over the other?
8. Why do property insurance policies contain exclusions? Illustrate your answer with examples from the HO.
9. Will an exclusion result in partial recovery?
10. Why are limits placed on coin, stamp, and gun collections in the HO? Can this kind of property be insured?

Questions 11–15 are related.

11. Assume that John Marshall owns a $150,000 home, which covers the replacement cost of the structure.

(Ignore the deductible clause and consider just the coinsurance requirement.) If John purchased $120,000 of insurance, how much would he collect for a partial loss of $40,000? For a total loss of $150,000?

12. If John purchased $100,000 of insurance, how much would he collect for a $40,000 loss? How much would he collect for a total loss? (Again, ignore the deductible clause.)

13. Now, assume that John Marshall purchased $50,000 of insurance on his $150,000 home. How much would he collect for a partial loss of $40,000? How much would he collect for a total loss? (Again, ignore the deductible clause.)

14. Now, assume that all the conditions of the loss settlement clause of the HO apply to the case. Assume that John has $100,000 coverage on his $150,000 house, which has been used for only one-eighth of its estimated useful life. How much would John collect for a $40,000 partial loss? How much would be collected for a total loss?

15. Finally, given the same amount of coverage as in the preceding question, if John's home had been used for seven-eighths of its estimated useful life, how much would John collect for a $40,000 partial loss?

16. Under the HO, will a theft loss in April mean less coverage available for a fire in July?

Objective Questions

Assume that Bill Blanton owns the HO-3 policy described in this chapter and reproduced in Appendix A. The limits are as follows:

Type of Coverage	Coverage A	Coverage B	Coverage C	Coverage D	Coverage E	Coverage F
Coverage Limit	$120,000	$12,000	$60,000	$24,000	$100,000	$5,000

A $250 deductible applies to Section 1, Coverages A–D. The replacement cost of Bill's home is $130,000, the contents are valued at $70,000, and the home is 30 percent depreciated. Your assignment is to compute the amount that Bill will collect in each of the following circumstances. (Assume that each event occurs separately.)

1. Bill's house and all its contents are destroyed by a tornado. It takes six months to rebuild the home, and Bill's additional living expenses amount to $12,000.
2. A neighbor's eight-year-old child accidentally releases the brakes on his family's pickup truck, sending it crashing into Bill's home. Damage to the home amounts to $15,000. The truck is destroyed. Its ACV before the loss was $22,000. The child and Bill both suffer a broken arm. Medical expenses amount to $5,000 for each person.
3. Bill's unattached tool shed burns, destroying the shed (damage = $7,000) and the lawn-care equipment inside (damage = $3,000).
4. Bill negligently starts a fire while cooking. His home and all the contents are a total loss. It costs Bill an additional $14,000 to live in a rental home while his house is being rebuilt.
5. While burning leaves, Bill causes his neighbor's house to burn (damage = $70,000).
6. While playing golf, Bill's ball hits another golfer in the head. Bill yelled a warning before the victim, Bob, was hit. Bob claims not to have heard the warning and sues Bill for $60,000 in medical expenses, $6,000 in lost wages (because he couldn't perform his work for three months), and $100,000 for pain and suffering. Assume that Bob wins the case, and it costs an additional $20,000 to provide Bill with a legal defense.
7. While his son is away at college, his stereo is stolen from his dorm room (damage = $1,500).
8. While carrying his television to the basement, Bill drops it. It is a total loss (damage = $850).
9. Bill is a certified public accountant working from his office at home. He is sued for negligence in preparing Al's income tax. The suit is successful, and Al wins a $40,000 judgment.

Selected References

Insurance Services Office, Inc., 2010, *Homeowners 3— Special Form HO 00 03 05 11* (2010).

14

Professional Financial Planning

After studying this chapter, you should be able to

- Describe the five steps of the financial planning process

- Understand the role that life insurance plays in the early adult years of a financial plan

- Understand how to prepare financially for retirement during the middle adult years

- Describe the estate planning process that takes place in the later adult years

- Explain the reasons that businesses buy life insurance products

- Describe some aspects of the taxation of life insurance benefits

For many Americans, planning for the future is a key financial concern. Among the typical questions they face are the following: How much money will my family need in the event of a premature death? How much money do I need to save for retirement? What is the most tax-efficient way to hold these savings? Increasingly, Americans have been turning to financial planning professionals for advice and help to complete their personal financial plans. This chapter centers on a description of the financial planning process and gives special attention to the role insurance products play in the solution to personal financial problems.

The knowledge needed by professional financial planners is very broad and includes an understanding of income taxes, estate taxes, Social Security, investments, annuities, insurance, and employee benefits. While this textbook introduces these subjects, mastering each of them requires a great deal of time and study, and in far greater depth than can be presented in an introductory textbook. In this chapter, we focus primarily on the role of life insurance in personal financial planning. This chapter includes sections on the taxation of life insurance and on the use of life insurance to solve business continuation problems.[1]

---

[1] Professional financial planners must have a far broader understanding of taxes than those issues involving life insurance contracts. However, we present just this area of taxation because of the insurance focus of this introductory textbook. The chapter introduces the complex subject of business life insurance because financial planners often recommend the use of life insurance to preserve the value of business interests. As in the taxation section, the scope of this introductory textbook allows us to present only a summary of this topic.

This chapter divides the financial life cycle into three segments: the early adult years, the middle adult years, and the later adult years. We illustrate the financial planning process by describing the crucial financial problems that planners and their clients must solve during these periods. During the early adult years, the two main objectives of many financial plans are to provide adequate funds for families should wage earners die prematurely and to provide adequate funds for a child's college education. During the middle adult years, people typically direct their financial plans toward saving for retirement. During the later adult years, financial plans must allow for the most efficient transfer of property and wealth from the owner to survivors. Overall, professional financial planning is about problem solving, setting financial goals, and executing strategies to achieve them.

THE PROFESSIONAL FINANCIAL PLANNING PROCESS

Before developing a financial plan, the professional financial planner must establish a relationship with a client. Early in the process, planners should make clear how they charge for their services and make any other disclosures needed to keep the relationship on the highest ethical level. Choosing a financial planner is not easy, but consumers are typically well served by planners with experience and strong educational credentials. Several professional associations offer degrees or certificates recognizing educational achievements of financial planners. Some of the more widely recognized financial planning credentials are the **Chartered Financial Consultant (ChFC)**, **Certified Financial Planner (CFP)**, and the **Personal Financial Specialist (PFS)**.[2]

The financial planning process can be outlined in five steps, as described below.

Step 1: Motivate and Educate Clients

Overcoming the public's tendency to avoid completing a financial plan is a difficult problem. Reasons why people avoid planning include not knowing where to start and not understanding the importance of getting an early start on their financial plans. Therefore, people need education and motivation to overcome inaction and begin to solve their financial problems.

Step 2: Collect Information

People need to collect relevant data and records to complete useful financial plans. Typically, planning begins with a statement of net worth and a cash flow statement or budget. One use of a cash budget is to control spending and increase savings. The cash budget is the heart of the financial plan and can be developed from tax returns and checkbook records. Cash budgets also provide the foundation for estimating future needs.

Planners need to know how property was acquired (for example, by purchase or by gift), when it was acquired, who the legal owners are, and the owner's adjusted cost basis in the property. The **adjusted cost basis**, simply put, is the net cash outflow for purchased property; this figure usually includes the purchase price and any expenses incurred to acquire the property. Determining the cost basis can be complicated, especially for gifted or inherited property.

---

[2] For more details, see *http://www.theamericancollege.edu/financial-planning/chfc-advanced-financial-planning*, *http://www.cfp.net/*, and *http://www.aicpa.org/*, respectively.

Planners also need to know their client's attitude toward accepting financial risk, in part because financial planning requires a trade-off between risk-and-return alternatives. Planners need a careful assessment of the client's attitude toward risk to make recommendations that are well suited to a particular client. High-risk plans for risk-averse people, or low-risk plans for aggressive investors, are not likely to be followed. Unfortunately for planners, people's reaction to risk is difficult to measure, may change over time, and depends on the situation.

Step 3: Develop Goals

With the statement of net worth and cash budget in hand, a family can develop its financial goals. It is important to be thorough, considering all sources of wealth, income, and estimated expenditures. People and families must consider and rank their needs and desires. Most people find their assets and income inadequate to satisfy all their needs and wants. Developing a financial plan forces people to identify the goals they value most and allows them to set a course to achieve their goals. Often financial planners recommend separating goals into short-, intermediate-, and long-term goals. Goal setting allows people to compare actual results with expected results and to keep goals from conflicting with each other. For example, some people might have short-term goals (buying a house, sending children to private schools, taking vacations) that cannot be reached with current income and may jeopardize intermediate goals (such as financing college educations) and long-term goals (saving for retirement). Good communication between planners and clients, and among family members, is needed to set realistic goals.

Many people need to begin a savings plan. People need savings to fund such things as college educations, their retirement, real estate, and the costs of emergencies. A savings plan also implies the presence of an investment strategy for the savings. A common strategy focuses on an **asset allocation plan**. Using an asset allocation plan, a person identifies what percentages of assets will be held in low-risk investments, such as money market funds and certificates of deposit (CDs); and what percentage will be held in higher-risk investments such as mutual funds (which were discussed in Chapter 5). The asset allocation will reflect a person's attitude towards risk, and regular reallocation is required because market fluctuations will shift the actual proportions in an investment portfolio away from the desired target ranges.

Step 4: Implement Plans

Financial planning often results in the need to make changes. In some cases, people need legal documents such as a will. Many people also will need to purchase more life insurance. Data on the average amount of life insurance Americans own reveal many people have relatively low amounts of coverage.[3] The next section of this chapter describes a model for calculating the amount of life insurance needed in a personal financial plan.

Step 5: Review and Update Plans

Plans change. People get raises, have more children, assume responsibility for their parents, get divorced, and inherit wealth. Intelligent planning requires accommodating all such changes into the financial plan, which means regular and frequent plan reviews.

---

[3] Readers can find life insurance data at *http://www.acli.com/*. For an international perspective on the "protection gap," please see "Mortality Protection: The Core of Life," SIGMA No. 4/2004, published by the Swiss Re. The Swiss Re Web site is (*http://www.swissre.com/*).

THE EARLY ADULT YEARS: CALCULATING LIFE INSURANCE NEEDS

There are no set boundaries for the "early adult years." The characteristics of this period include first jobs, first marriages, children, and an accumulation of debt, including mortgage loans on first houses. In cases where families have formed, especially families with young children, life insurance becomes a key ingredient of a sound financial plan. There is no substitute for life insurance. It is a guarantee of future purchasing power if people die prematurely. That is, life insurance allows children to be educated and mortgage loans to be repaid even if a wage earner dies during the early adult years. Many families with children want to provide them with a college education. Financing a college education can be a significant expense for most families, one that they should address in the early adult years. The best financial plan for financing a college education requires both a savings plan and a plan for premature death protection.

The Needs-Based Purchase of Life Insurance

A needs analysis can identify the financial problems caused by a premature death. Many financial planners believe people should purchase life insurance on a needs basis rather than as an attempt to replace lost earnings. A **needs-based purchase** means that people purchase life insurance in an amount equal to the difference between the assets required to complete a financial plan and the assets available to meet the needs.

Life insurance policies with a savings feature that can be used to keep premiums affordable in later years are called **permanent policies**, or **cash value life insurance**. **Term insurance** has no savings element and provides coverage for only a limited number of years. *Permanent needs* for life insurance are not a function of time; these needs exist at all ages. *Temporary need* life insurance comes to a projected end and is designed to meet needs that exist for only a portion of a person's life.

Here is a typical list of needs for postdeath resources. Those needs marked with a (*P*) are permanent needs; those with a (*T*) are temporary needs (though keep in mind that *temporary* does not necessarily mean short-term; some temporary needs may last for years).

- **A burial fund (*P*):** Funeral and final illness expenses may amount to more than $15,000. This need is present at any age, so it is permanent.

- **An education fund (*T*):** At present, four years of undergraduate education may cost from $25,000 to more than $200,000. College costs have risen almost twice as fast as other items in recent years. This need no longer exists after the education is complete, so it is temporary.

- **An income fund (*T*):** In families, the greatest need ordinarily would be for regular income to meet daily expenses during the dependency period. The need is greatest if the wage earner's death leaves a dependent spouse and children. If either the children or the spouse would work after the wage earner's death, the income need is reduced. This need does not exist after children become financially independent or surviving spouses receive retirement income, so this need is temporary.

- **A debt-retirement fund (*T*):** If they are homeowners, most young families have a large mortgage debt. Other large debts arise from unpaid credit card balances and purchases of vehicles on credit. Frequently, people purchase life insurance to repay these debts if the breadwinner dies prematurely. Not all loans and debts are legally payable when a person dies. Many people, however, do not want their survivors to face regular debt installment payments after the family's main source of income disappears. After people repay their debts, this need does not exist, so it is temporary.

FIGURE 14-1   An Equation for the Needs-Based Purchase of Life Insurance

- **An estate preservation fund (P):** The costs of settling an estate (burial costs, court costs, attorney fees, federal transfer taxes, and state death taxes) reduce the funds available for heirs. Life insurance can replace the shrinkage caused by these expenses. For people with large amounts of assets, the goal of estate preservation often creates a need for life insurance because large estates might be subject to the federal unified transfer tax, described in more detail later in this chapter. This need exists throughout life (unless the deceased's estate is very liquid), so it is permanent.

After financial planners calculate the total need for postdeath funds, they calculate the total assets available to meet these needs. These assets include Social Security benefits and death benefits from employment, such as group life insurance. Other assets may come from personal investments and savings, including proceeds from life insurance policies already owned. Business interests, home equity, and other nonliquid assets are also valuable assets, so long as they can be converted to cash without unreasonable delay.

The need for new life insurance equals the difference between the assets required to complete the life insurance plan and the assets available to meet these needs. Figure 14-1 presents the needs-based equation for life insurance purchases.

We now present a personal life insurance model or plan that shows how to determine the amount of life insurance to purchase in a specific, theoretical case. In developing a plan to deal with premature death, planners must assume that the death is immediate because any other assumption would leave the financial problems of a premature death unsolved for an unspecified time. That is, if the plan assumed that death would not occur for five years, and if a client died during the first five years, then the likelihood of unmet financial needs would arise.

Life Insurance Planning: A Case Study

Louis and Marie Burton are each twenty-six years old. They had their first child, Pete, when they were twenty-four years old. Louis is a teacher, while Marie works in a department store. Their stated goal in the event of Louis's premature death is to have adequate resources to allow Marie to remain at home and raise Pete. Their statement of net worth appears in Table 14-1 and their cash flow statement for 2008 appears in Table 14-2.

Table 14-3 shows the first few years of a life insurance plan for the Burtons. This output reflects estimated results if the current family situation continues until Pete is ten years old.[4] Our example assumes both parents live, continue to work, save, and spend in the same percentages as they did in 2012. If this estimate is accurate, the Burtons will accumulate savings of $62,166.

Table 14-4 is based on the assumption that Louis dies on January 1, 2013. At this time, Marie stops working to stay at home to raise Pete. Both Marie and Pete are eligible for Social Security survivor benefits. Social Security benefits automatically

---

[4] This example is simplified. In practice, most financial planners recommend funding until the child graduates college.

TABLE 14-1 Statement of Net Worth

Assets

Bank account	$ 2,300
House	175,000
2 cars	14,000
400 shares of common stock	24,500
TOTAL	$215,800

Liabilities

Home mortgage	$160,000
Car loan	7,500
Charge card debt	1,750
TOTAL	$169,250
Net Worth	$ 46,550

TABLE 14-2 Cash Flow Statement for 2012

Income

Louis	$40,000
Marie	35,000
Investments	1,200
TOTAL	$76,200

Taxes

Social Security	$ 5,738
Federal income	17,526
State income	3,048
Real estate	1,100
TOTAL	27,412
Disposable Income	$48,789

Expenses

Food	$ 3,903
Shelter	12,197
Autos	4,879
All other	21,955
TOTAL	$42,934
Savings	$ 5,855

increase with inflation.[5] The survivors' benefits are shown as income in Table 14-4. With Louis's death, the family's expenses drop by one-third. Under these assumptions, savings become negative, indicating expenses in excess of income. The present value of the deficit totals $197,056, using a 4 percent assumed discount factor. This amount, $197,056, is the exact amount needed on January 1, 2013, to fund all the deficits projected through 2020, before Pete is eleven. That is, if withdrawals equal the projected deficits between income and expenses each year and if the balance of the fund earns 4 percent interest (after taxes), the final withdrawal will exhaust the fund.

---

[5] See Chapter 20, "Social Security," or the Social Security Web site (*http://www.ssa.gov/*) for a description of this program's benefits.

TABLE 14-3 Burton Life Insurance Plan

| Inflation Rate = 0.04 | | | | | | | | | |
Year	2012	2013	2014	2015	2016	2017	2018	2019	2020
Pete's age	2	3	4	5	6	7	8	9	10
Income (in dollars)									
Louis	40,000	41,600	43,264	44,995	46,794	48,666	50,613	52,637	54,743
Marie	35,000	36,400	37,856	39,370	40,945	42,583	44,286	46,058	47,900
Investments	1,200	1,248	1,298	1,350	1,404	1,460	1,518	1,579	1,642
TOTAL	76,200	79,248	82,418	85,715	89,143	92,709	96,417	100,274	104,285
Taxes (in dollars)									
Social Security	5,738	5,967	6,206	6,454	6,712	6,981	7,260	7,550	7,852
Federal income	17,526	18,227	18,956	19,714	20,503	21,323	22,176	23,063	23,986
State income	3,048	3,170	3,297	3,429	3,566	3,708	3,857	4,011	4,171
Real estate	1,100	1,100	1,100	1,100	1,100	1,100	1,100	1,100	1,100
TOTAL	27,412	28,464	29,559	30,697	31,881	33,112	34,393	35,724	37,109
Disposable income (in dollars)	48,788	50,784	52,859	55,018	57,262	59,597	62,024	64,550	67,176
Expenses (in dollars)									
Food	3,903	4,063	4,229	4,401	4,581	4,768	4,962	5,164	5,374
Shelter	2,197	12,696	13,215	13,754	14,316	14,899	15,506	16,137	16,794
Autos	4,879	5,078	5,286	5,502	5,726	5,960	6,202	6,455	6,718
All other	21,955	22,853	23,787	24,758	25,768	26,819	27,911	29,047	30,229
TOTAL	42,934	44,690	46,517	48,415	50,391	52,446	54,581	56,803	59,115
Savings (in dollars)	5,855	6,094	6,342	6,602	6,871	7,151	7,443	7,747	8,061
Total savings	5,855	11,949	18,291	24,893	31,764	38,915	46,358	54,105	62,166

Using the equation for a needs-based life insurance purchase shown in Figure 14-1, if Louis and Marie currently own no individual life insurance, they should purchase $197,056 to meet the goal of allowing Marie to stay at home and raise Pete until he is ten. Assuming that Louis already owns $100,000 of individual life insurance, then he should purchase $97,056 ($197,056 − $100,000) of new life insurance. Assuming that Louis also qualifies for $25,000 of group life insurance from work and that the Burtons are convinced this insurance will be available during the period of Pete's dependency, $25,000 could be subtracted from $97,056, leaving $72,056 ($97,056 − $25,000) as the amount of new life insurance to be purchased.[6]

This example greatly simplified the planning approach used to calculate the funds needed to support Marie and Pete. In the real world, things rarely follow a plan. Once a spreadsheet is built, however, assumptions can be modified easily. What if the inflation rate changes? What if Marie works after Louis's death? A good financial plan must be flexible, and a professional financial planner must be able to incorporate changes and alternatives into financial plans.

---

[6] The $197,056 is the present value of an "annuity due." That is, the payments are assumed to occur at the *beginning* of the year rather than at the end of the year. The payments from an *ordinary annuity* occur at the end of the year. The reason we assume that the stream is an annuity due is that payments for various items in the Burtons' standard of living will occur during the year. In other words, we conservatively assume all deficits occur at the beginning of the year. The effect of this assumption is to reduce by one year the interest that can be earned on the balance.

TABLE 14-4 The Burton Life Insurance Plan After Louis's Death

Year	2012	2013	2014	2015	2016	2017	2018	2019	2020
Pete's age	**2**	**3**	**4**	**5**	**6**	**7**	**8**	**9**	**10**
Income (in dollars)									
Louis	40,000	0	0	0	0	0	0	0	0
Marie	35,000	0	0	0	0	0	0	0	0
Social Security		7,500	7,800	8,112	8,436	8,774	9,125	9,490	9,869
Investments	1,200	1,248	1,298	1,350	1,404	1,460	1,518	1,579	1,642
TOTAL	76,200	8,748	9,098	9,462	9,840	10,234	10,643	11,069	11,511
Taxes (in dollars)									
Social Security	5,738	0	0	0	0	0	0	0	0
Federal income	17,526	0	0	0	0	0	0	0	0
State income	3,048	0	0	0	0	0	0	0	0
Real estate	1,100	1,144	1,190	1,237	1,287	1,338	1,392	1,448	1,505
TOTAL	27,412	1,144	1,190	1,237	1,287	1,338	1,392	1,448	1,505
Disposable income (in dollars)	48,788	7,604	7,908	8,225	8,553	8,896	9,251	9,621	10,006
Expenses (in dollars)									
Food	3,903	2,576	2,679	2,786	2,898	3,014	3,134	3,260	3,390
Shelter	12,197	12,696	13,215	13,754	14,316	14,899	15,506	16,137	16,794
Autos	4,879	2,439	2,537	2,638	2,744	2,854	2,968	3,087	3,210
All other	21,955	14,490	15,070	15,673	16,299	16,951	17,630	18,335	19,068
TOTAL	42,934	32,201	33,501	34,851	36,257	37,718	39,238	40,819	42,462
Savings (in dollars)	5,854	(24,597)	(25,593)	(26,626)	(27,704)	(28,822)	(29,987)	(31,198)	(32,456)
Present value of the deficit		**197,056**							

Insurance for Spouses and Children

In the Burton case study, Marie's income provides a significant portion of the family's resources. Therefore, the Burtons cannot complete their life insurance plans until they consider the effect of Marie's premature death, in addition to Louis's. Using a spreadsheet similar to the one in Table 14-4 that shows Marie's income and expenses eliminated, the impact of Marie's premature death can be estimated. Thus, in dual-income households, planners should consider the income earned by both wage earners when developing family life insurance plans.

Even if one member of a couple does not work outside the home, he or she still makes a vital contribution to the household that needs to be considered when purchasing life insurance. A homemaker supplies valuable economic services in the work he or she does within the home. If the homemaker dies prematurely, the need for services in the home continues. Someone would have to raise the children and help with the household chores. Insurance proceeds can be used to purchase many of the replacement services, such as day care and housekeeping, that would be needed to keep the family unit operating without a homemaker. The amount of insurance purchased should be related to the financial need created by the absence of the homemaker.

Each family faces different circumstances. In some cases, grandparents or other family members can supply needed services and help. In other cases, there may be no dependent children. Often, if the source of secondary income dies, the primary income continues. Thus, with a needs-based approach, the amount of life insurance appropriate for the secondary wage earner usually is less than the amount required for the primary wage earner. If insurance dollars are limited, they should be spent to insure the family's main source of income, whether provided by the wife or the husband. In many cases, life insurance on a secondary wage earner meets a definite economic need and is a logical purchase.

Because they do not produce current income for the family, there is much less economic reason for insuring children than there is for insuring either husband or wife. The premature death of a child means funeral expenses, but beyond that, only seldom are there unfavorable economic consequences from a child's death. Only after the wage earner and spouse have been insured adequately should life insurance on children be considered. Many financial planners believe that life insurance proceeds should fund economic needs. If such needs are not present, the purchase of life insurance cannot be justified logically.

Financing a College Education

Financing college tuition is one of the three largest financial problems facing many middle-income Americans. The other two are financing a residence and financing retirement. The federal government accords each of these financial problems special tax advantages. Developing a financial plan to finance a college education requires current knowledge of state and federal tax provisions; therefore, people often consult with professional financial planners to develop appropriate funding strategies. College funding plans often require life insurance because it provides certainty that money will be available even if a wage earner dies prematurely.

TAX-ADVANTAGED FUNDING STRATEGIES

Financial planners note that college tuition funding plans that use tax-advantaged strategies are usually are more efficient (produce more funds) than non-tax-advantaged strategies. Most tax-advantaged strategies let investors earn income on funds that they otherwise would use to pay taxes. The earlier a family starts saving for college, the better the results, since tax-advantaged compound interest builds higher values over time.

A **Section 529** plan, also known as a *State Tuition Assistance Plan*, is a state-sponsored education savings program that allows parents, other relatives, and friends to contribute to a child's college education. The 529 plan allows for significantly higher contributions than other tax-advantaged options. In some states, the contribution limit was over $200,000 for each beneficiary in a recent year. Contributions to the 529 plan are not tax-deductible, but investment income may escape both state and federal tax income taxation at withdrawal if used for qualified education expenses.[7] The general features of 529 plans include the following points:

- The contributor owns the account.
- The account owner selects the investment strategy when making the initial contribution. The owner can make changes in the initial investment strategy once a year under current rules. If investments perform poorly, of course, college funding goals may not be achieved, so 529 plan investments must be reviewed regularly for both risk and return results.
- The account owner is entitled to select or change the designated beneficiary (to a member of the student's family) or even take funds back if that beneficiary elects not to attend college or receives a full or partial scholarship.

---

[7] Readers can find much relevant information, including specific details of various state plans, at *http://www.savingforcollege.com/* or at *http://www.sec.gov/investor/pubs/intro529.htm*.

- Withdrawals of earnings for nonqualified educational expenses (such as transportation expenses or room and board fees in excess of plan limits) are taxed as ordinary income and may be subject to a 10 percent penalty.

The following three questions are among the most important ones that parents and planners must consider when analyzing college funding decisions:

1. If the annual cost of college is ($15,000) when the child is age (five), what will be the estimated cost of tuition if costs inflate at an annual rate of (6) percent? The numbers in the parentheses are just examples, but using spreadsheets can provide the needed savings goal if the values in parentheses change over time.

2. If a parent dies prematurely, what amount of death benefits is needed to fund college tuition? While family wage earners generally survive to see their children finish college, sometimes they do not. Every college savings plan thus should include an adequate amount of life insurance to pay for the children's college education in the event of a premature death.

3. What amount of annual savings is needed to fund tuition payments fully if the parent survives? Once the cost of a college education has been estimated, it usually is wise to begin to save to accumulate the needed funds. As noted, federal (and state) governments provide tax-advantaged savings alternatives that produce the best results when savings begin before the student needs the tuition payments.

THE MIDDLE ADULT YEARS: FINANCING RETIREMENT

At some point in the financial life cycle, children become independent, mortgages are repaid, and families accumulate savings. A family's main financial concern shifts from the problems that result from the premature death of the wage earner to financing the retirement years. This change often occurs between ages forty and sixty. We call this period the *middle adult years*. Some aspects of retirement funding occur long before middle age. Participation in Social Security and employer-sponsored pension plans begins in the early stages of employment. However, sometime during middle age, the focus of financial planning changes from the concerns of early adult life to the concerns of middle adult life, with an emphasis on saving for retirement.

The evolution is gradual and arises from a series of modifications to existing financial plans. The availability of savings and the proximity of retirement are key factors. Generally, each person surviving to midlife faces the problem of planning to finance a retirement period. In recent years, this problem has become more severe for many Americans. Many employers have reduced their commitment to funding retirement programs, and Social Security has increased the normal retirement age and lowered benefit targets. Increases in longevity have placed greater burdens on retirement savings, and retirees are responsible for a greater portion of their health care expenses.

Spreadsheets can be used to estimate the need for retirement income in the same way as presented in the Burton case. Some Web sites also have retirement income needs calculators. In any case, the logical solution involves estimating the assets available at retirement, subtracting the cost of living for the longest period of expected life, and funding the difference between available assets and need for income with some form of pre-retirement savings. To complete the solution to the problem, estimates must be made of several variables: inflation rates, investment returns, spending needs in retirement, length of life, and tax rates before and after retirement. If these factors change, a financial plan will need to be reviewed and modified before retirement

TABLE 14-5 Life Expectancy (in Years) at Age 65 (Middle Mortality Assumption)

Year of 65th Birthday	2005	2010	2015	2020	2025	2030	2035	2040	2045	2050
Male	16.4	16.8	17.2	17.6	18.0	18.5	18.9	19.3	19.8	20.3
Female	19.7	20.0	20.3	20.6	20.9	21.2	21.5	21.8	22.1	22.4

Based on U.S. Department of Commerce, Economics, and Statistics Administration; U.S. Bureau of Census: *Current Population Reports: Population Projections of the United States . . . 1995–2050*, p. 1130 (*http://www.census.gov*).

begins. The potential for outliving one's wealth or spending down one's assets too quickly in retirement is a serious issue, with dire consequences if mistakes are made.

Planners follow the same general sequence of steps for the middle years as for the early years. Financial plans requiring early and regular savings will be the most likely to allow people to maintain their standard of living during retirement. Table 14-5 presents some estimates of expected retirement periods by the Bureau of the Census.

Table 14-5 shows that for every year projected, women are expected to outlive men. This statistical fact has serious implications for women's financial plans. Experts have paid special attention to women's financial planning problems, and the Web site of the Women's Institute for a Secure Retirement (*http://www.wiserwomen.org/*) provides access to some of this literature.

In summary, a person planning for retirement must solve the following problems:

- Estimating the length of his or her life and future health status (and that of a spouse, if applicable)
- Forecasting the amount and sources of pre-retirement and postretirement income
- Predicting the amount and type of retirement expenses
- Estimating the age of retirement
- Gauging the impact of inflation on pre-retirement and postretirement finances
- Anticipating the possibility of dependent children, parents, or both.

The Role of Life Insurance and Annuities in the Middle Adult Years

Life insurance products can be used to fund both premature death and retirement financial needs.

PREMATURE DEATH PROTECTION

While planning retirement finances should receive priority attention during middle age, plans for premature death or disability remain important in many cases. Usually, people need a fund to pay the costs of a last illness and all other final expenses. Survivors typically require emergency funds. Sometimes a debt retirement fund may be required to repay outstanding debts. In other cases, the financial future of children, parents, or a spouse with physical or mental problems is a concern. Such needs should be met by a dependent support fund backed by adequate life insurance.

Individual savings are likely to be greater in middle age than during the young adult period. Available savings reduce the need for life insurance. Social Security survivor benefits also meet a portion of the need for postdeath resources.

The most logical way to determine the amount of life or disability insurance needed during middle age is to construct a financial model similar to the models presented in the preceding section of this chapter. As always, immediate death or disability is the basic premise. Spreadsheet models of postdeath financial requirements can accommodate changes in both financial circumstances and inflation estimates.

RETIREMENT FUNDING

The insurance contract designed to provide retirement funds that a person cannot outlive is called an **annuity**. By pooling the mortality exposures of many people, called *annuitants*, insurers are able to guarantee each annuitant a stream of income that will last until death. Annuities also earn investment income that accumulates on a tax-advantaged basis. Chapter 17, "Annuities," provides a complete discussion of annuities. At this point, we note that people have been purchasing larger amounts of annuities in the past two decades.

THE LATER ADULT YEARS: ESTATE PLANNING

At some point, people transfer wealth from one generation to another. The process of planning the transfer of wealth is called **estate planning**. The goal of estate planning is to produce a logical and economic transfer of assets consistent with the owner's desires and lifetime needs.

Wills

Every estate plan requires a will. A **will** is a legal document in which a person directs the disposal of his or her assets at death. **Probate** is the name for the legal (court-supervised) process of transferring property at a person's death. In many states, only an attorney can write wills and provide legal advice on alternative courses of action. Even people with few assets need a will if they want those assets distributed according to their wishes. Families can use their wills to appoint guardians for their children, and a carefully drafted will can minimize probate issues.

The will must be made while the person is competent; that is, "of a sound mind." It must be properly witnessed, and it must be in a form acceptable to the court. Some states accept handwritten wills; others do not. If a person dies without a will, the state determines who receives the decedent's property. A person dying without a will is said to have died **intestate**, and some studies have shown that about 40 percent of all people die without wills. All states have laws prescribing the intestate distribution of property.

Federal Estate Tax

The federal government taxes property transferred at death. This tax is called the **federal estate tax**. The government also taxes lifetime gifts, in part because people often give away assets to reduce their federal estate taxes. This tax is called the **federal gift tax**. Together, both taxes are known as the **uniform transfer tax**. Some states also impose a death tax, while others impose an inheritance tax.[8]

The government calls all the property a person owns at death the **gross estate**. The gross estate includes a person's house and other real property, personal property, trust property, tax-advantaged retirement plans, and the face amount of life insurance policies in which they have an ownership interest. Given the wide scope of the property included in the gross estate, it is common for many upper-middle-income earners to acquire taxable estates. The fair market value of the gross estate at the time of

---

[8] A good description of federal estate taxes can be found at the IRS Web site (*http://www.irs.gov/*). Form 706 and Publication 950 provide a detailed description of this tax.

TABLE 14-6 Federal Unified Transfer (Estate and Gift) Tax Rates for 2011 and 2012

Taxable Estate	*Tentative Tax*
$0 to $10,000	18% of amount
Over $10,000 but not over $20,000	$1,800 + 20% of excess over $10,000
Over $20,000 but not over $40,000	$3,800 + 22% of excess over $20,000
Over $40,000 but not over $60,000	$8,200 + 24% of excess over $40,000
Over $60,000 but not over $80,000	$13,000 + 26% of excess over $60,000
Over $80,000 but not over $100,000	$18,200 + 28% of excess over $80,000
Over $100,000 but not over $150,000	$23,800 + 30% of excess over $100,000
Over $150,000 but not over $250,000	$38,800 + 32% of excess over $150,000
Over $250,000 but not over $500,000	$70,800 + 34% of excess over $250,000
Over $500,000	$155,800 + 35% of excess over $500,000

Based on U.S. Code, Title 26, Subtitle B, Chapter 12, Subchapter A, Section 2502.

death, plus certain gifts made during the decedent's lifetime, is subject to the estate tax. Funeral, administrative, and other expenses, as well as outstanding debts, can be subtracted from the gross estate, yielding a resulting value called the *taxable estate*.

The taxable estate can also be decreased by the value of allowable deductions. An important estate tax deduction is the unlimited **marital deduction**. This deduction allows the first spouse to die to give all his or her property to the surviving spouse without any estate or gift tax liability. The **charitable deduction** similarly subtracts from the taxable estate the value of property that is transferred by a will or other approved arrangements to qualified organizations like charities, universities, or churches.

The Tax Relief, Unemployment Insurance Reauthorization and Job Creation Act of 2010 provides a rate schedule used to calculate federal estate taxes for the 2011 and 2012 tax years, as shown in Table 14-6. The calculation of the estate tax involves two steps. First, an initial value of the estate tax, called the *tentative tax*, is calculated using one of the formulas listed on the right side of Table 14-6. The appropriate formula is selected on the basis of the decedent's taxable estate, as shown in the left column. For example, as shown on the bottom line of the table, if the decedent's taxable estate equals $5.5 million, the tentative tax equals $1,905,800, or $155,800 plus 35 percent of $5 million, the portion of the taxable estate in excess of $500,000.

In the second step, the tentative tax is reduced by the value of an applicable credit amount, also known as the *unified credit*. For 2011 and 2012, the applicable credit amount is set to $1,730,800. The value of this applicable credit is set to eliminate estate taxes for decedents with taxable estates that are less than or equal to $5 million.[9] While the $5 million estate tax exclusion means that most Americans do not have to pay estate taxes, an untimely death to a person with a high taxable estate but limited cash in hand (such as a cash-poor farmer who could sell his farm to a real estate developer for millions of dollars, or a successful small business owner who dies without a buyer for her multimillion dollar enterprise) can be costly. Because large estates often need cash to pay estate taxes, life insurance is purchased to supply the cash needed.

---

[9] To demonstrate using the bottom row of Table 14-6, note that the tentative tax on a taxable estate equal to $5 million is $155,800 plus 35 percent of $4.5 million (the portion of the $5 million taxable estate in excess of $500,000), or $1,730,800.

Life Insurance and Estate Planning

The need to pay the federal estate tax in cash after a person's death, the desire to make cash bequests, and the general need for liquid assets like cash can be met with life insurance. Life insurance supplies cash just when it is needed. Available cash can be important because much of the wealth in large estates will be in land, buildings, antiques, closely held business investments, or other illiquid assets not easily or quickly turned into the cash needed to pay bills.

A common arrangement is for the life insurance proceeds to be paid into a trust for the benefit of the heirs. A **trust** is a legal arrangement allowing a person, called a *trustee*, to manage property for the benefit of another person, called the *beneficiary*. Attorneys call a trust funded with life insurance proceeds a **life insurance trust**. Typically, the cash in a life insurance trust is used to purchase the assets from the estate at set prices. The effect of such an arrangement is to leave the productive assets in the trust and the cash in the estate. The cash in the estate then is available to pay taxes and meet other cash needs. Questions of who is to own the policy and who is to be the beneficiary have significant tax implications.

Another policy type that is especially useful in estate planning is **survivor life insurance**, which is also called *second-to-die* life insurance. These policies insure two lives under one contract. The beneficiary is paid only after the second death. The estate plan involves passing the estate of the first spouse to die to the surviving spouse. The unlimited marital deduction eliminates the federal estate tax on this transfer. At the second death, assuming no remarriage or other significant change in factors, the federal estate tax will apply. At this point, the survivorship life insurance policy matures, producing the cash needed to pay the taxes. After the first death, these policies often have large increases in cash values.

It is important to note that this text has given simplified treatment to a very complex subject. Estate planning is a subject for advanced texts and courses in universities and law schools. Nonetheless, after reading this material, you should understand that life insurance is a useful tool in solving estate planning problems.

LIQUIDATING RETIREMENT SAVINGS

One of the most challenging problems facing professional financial planners is advising clients on how to liquidate the savings that have accumulated for retirement. Where possible, planners recommend using one or more of the following alternatives to save for retirement: qualified pension plans, Individual Retirement Accounts (IRAs), 401(k) plans, or 403(b) plans. These plans are described in Chapter 19, "Employee Benefits." For now, a few financial planning points can be noted. The government encourages people to save for retirement by providing tax incentives that defer taxes, but at some point, presumably in retirement, people must withdraw the funds and pay the taxes.[10] To discourage the pre-retirement withdrawal of tax-advantaged retirement savings, the government applies a 10 percent early withdrawal penalty on most withdrawals made before age 59½. If a participant dies or becomes disabled before this age, the penalty does not apply, but ordinary income taxes may apply. If a participant tries to avoid taxes by keeping funds in a tax-advantaged retirement plan after age 70½, another penalty—50 percent of the required minimum distribution—applies. While a detailed description of the Internal Revenue Code minimum distribution rules is beyond the scope of this text, we note that much financial planning is required between the ages of 59½ and 70½ to allow people to enjoy their retirement savings, achieve their other financial planning goals, and minimize their tax burden.

---

[10] While many retirement programs yield payouts that are subject to taxes, some (e.g., Roth IRAs) do not. Please see Chapter 19 for more details.

BUSINESS USES OF LIFE INSURANCE

Businesses often purchase life insurance for three reasons: to provide benefits for employees, to protect the firm against the financial problems caused by the loss of a key person, and to aid in transferring business ownership.

Life Insurance as an Employee Benefit

Businesses purchase **group life insurance** as an employee benefit. Many employers, including the federal government, provide group life insurance as a benefit. The purpose of this life insurance is to help attract, motivate, and retain employees. We describe employee benefits funded by insurance, including group life insurance, in more detail in Chapter 19.

Protecting the Firm Through the Use of Life Insurance

In Chapter 1, "Introduction to Enterprise Risk Management and Insurance," we noted that if a business were to lose a key person, its earning power could be harmed, perhaps seriously. **Key employee life insurance** can protect firms from financial problems caused by such losses. The first step in the risk management process is to identify the key person. It may be the president, the chief researcher, a top salesperson, or an engineer. The next step is to measure the financial loss that the key person's death would cause. Such a measure will usually involve estimating the cost of replacing the key employee. To measure the loss, firms also need to estimate the effect on profits while a replacement is hired and trained and has achieved the same level of productivity as the original employee. After identifying and measuring the potential loss, the business purchases a life insurance policy on the key employee's life. The business is the *owner* and the *beneficiary* of the policy and the key employee is the *insured*. The business pays the premiums. For this arrangement to work, the key person must be insurable and must give permission for the purchase.

Another business use of life insurance is to provide a means of rewarding and retaining valuable personnel. The **split-dollar life insurance** plan allows firms to achieve this end. With this approach, both employer and employee pay a part of the premium for an insurance policy with a savings feature. The employer's share typically equals the annual increase in savings. As the savings increase each year, so does the employer's premium payment. When the annual increase in savings equals or exceeds the level premium, the employee contributes nothing for the insurance. Employees who terminate employment at this point (several years after the policy had been in force) give up an important fringe benefit.

In a split-dollar plan, the employer receives an amount equal to the savings value at the employee's death. The employee's beneficiary receives an amount equal to the face value minus the savings value. For example, assume that after fifteen years, the split-dollar life insurance policy has a face value of $100,000 and a cash value of $25,000. The total employer-paid premiums over the fifteen years equal $25,000. At the employee's death, the employer receives $25,000 of the death proceeds, and the employee's beneficiary receives $75,000. From the employer's standpoint, the cost of the policy becomes the forgone interest on the premium payments because the absolute amount of premiums is returned at the employee's death.

Funding Business Continuation Agreements with Life Insurance

Partnerships, sole proprietorships, and closely held corporations often need to purchase life insurance to facilitate the transfer of ownership when a proprietor dies. If a proprietorship is sold at a predetermined price at the owner's death, the arrangement relieves the spouse of having to worry about operating the business. Because the buy-out allows the continuation of the business, and because most firms are worth more as going concerns than they would be in liquidation, the heirs benefit from the higher value. Often, the business can be sold to a key employee. In any event, a life insurance policy on the owner provides the cash needed to complete the purchase. The money will be there when it is needed. In general, the person who buys the business will be the beneficiary who also pays the premiums. A legal agreement for the purchase between the buyer and seller, called a **buy-and-sell agreement**, also must be arranged before the plan becomes effective. Thus, people need the services of both an attorney and a life insurance agent to arrange and fund the business continuation plan (a buy-and-sell agreement properly funded by life insurance).

Calculating the appropriate value of the business interest is an important part of the process. The Internal Revenue Service (IRS) requires the value determined in the buy-and-sell agreement to be a fair price because the purchase price ordinarily will be a part of the decedent's estate and subject to the estate tax. This price also sets the buyer's cost basis in the business. As a business grows and prospers, the amount of life insurance needed for purchasing the owner's interest increases. Thus, buy-and-sell life insurance plans should be flexible and be reevaluated regularly.

Partnerships and closely held corporations also present the need for business continuation life insurance. Often the surviving partners or shareholders want to purchase the interest of the member who dies. Life insurance policies can be used to fund the purchase.

The buy-and-sell plans can be arranged in either of two ways. Each partner (shareholder) can purchase life insurance on every other partner (shareholder); this plan is called a **cross-purchase plan**. The partnership (corporation) can purchase the insurance on each partner (shareholder); this plan is called the **entity plan**. The second alternative involves a much smaller number of policies. If there were eight partners involved in a cross-purchase plan, each partner would have to purchase seven policies, and a total of fifty-six policies would be purchased. Under the entity plan, only eight policies would be needed. Tax consequences, however, may favor the cross-purchase arrangement in some cases.

Although this discussion of business life insurance is in terms of dealing with financial problems associated with the death of a business owner, the disability of the owner creates similar challenges, and even more severe difficulties in some cases. Long-term disability income policies, therefore, are a logical part of the risk management approach to solving business continuation problems of closely held businesses.

THE TAXATION OF LIFE INSURANCE

Death Proceeds

Premium payments for individually purchased life insurance are not deductible from a person's federal income tax. On the other hand, when the beneficiary receives the proceeds of a life insurance policy, no federal income tax applies to this amount. If the beneficiary does not take the proceeds as a lump sum of cash (which is one of several *settlement options* described in Chapter 16, "Standard Life Insurance Contract Provisions and Options") and instead takes a series of payments that includes interest earnings, federal income tax is paid on the interest portion. Another exception to the general rule is the **transfer for value rule**. In this case, if a life insurance contract is sold or transferred for value, the difference between the death benefit paid and the purchaser's cost is ordinary taxable income.

If the insured has any legal rights (called *incidents of ownership*) in a life insurance policy, or if the proceeds are payable to the insured's estate, the proceeds of the life insurance policy are included in the gross estate and may be subject to the estate tax. Incidents of ownership include the right to change the beneficiary, the right to take a loan, or the right to any dividends. However, if the gross estate is less than the exempt amount, no federal estate tax will be paid. Thus, for small estates, neither the federal income nor the estate tax applies to life insurance proceeds.

Living Benefits: Dividends, Savings, and Accelerated Death Benefits

The policy owner has three ways to receive cash from a life insurance policy while the insured is living:

1. If the policy is participating, the contract entitles the owner to a share of the profits. Insurers call this share a *dividend*. Dividend options are described in Chapter 16.
2. If a life insurance policy has a savings value, the owner can legally withdraw this value.
3. If the insured is terminally ill, many policies give the owner the right to receive a lump sum settlement based on the policy's death benefit.

Even if the policy owner takes the dividends in cash, which is one of several alternatives that most insurers offer, the dividends received from a participating life insurance policy are not subject to federal income tax because the IRS views these dividends as a return of part of the premium and not as earned income.

Several types of life insurance policies have a savings feature, which Chapter 15, "Life Insurance Policies," describes. The general rule is, if the insured withdraws the savings value and if this value exceeds the insured's adjusted cost basis (premiums paid minus dividends received), the excess is subject to federal income tax in the year of the withdrawal. For example, Bill Shakespeare purchased a whole life insurance policy thirty-five years ago, when he was twenty-five years old. He decides to retire at age sixty, and he withdraws the cash value of his life insurance to buy a recreational motor home. Assume that Bill's total premiums ($50,000) minus dividends he received ($21,000) equal $29,000. If Bill withdraws $35,000 in cash value, $6,000 ($35,000 − $29,000) is subject to tax. For the past thirty-five years, Bill has not had to report the interest income on the savings value of the policy. When he makes the withdrawal, however, the excess of the cash value over his adjusted cost basis is subject to the income tax at ordinary rates.

Summary

Professional financial planning is a five-step process: (1) motivate people, (2) collect data, (3) develop goals, (4) implement goals, and (5) review and update plans. The financial planning process has a different focus throughout the financial life cycle. In the early years, the focus is on premature death. Life insurance also can be used to guarantee funding for college tuition if a parent or parents were to die prematurely. In the middle adult years, life insurance and annuities can be used to provide funds for the retirement period, often on a tax-advantaged basis. In the later adult years, the focus of financial plans is on estate planning, or the efficient passing of property from wealth owners to successors. Life insurance often is used to provide needed cash in estate plans.

People should purchase life insurance to meet specific needs that could not be met by other assets if death were to occur immediately. Needs common to most families include (1) a burial fund, (2) an education fund, (3) an income fund, and (4) a debt-retirement fund.

Spouses working at home provide valuable economic services to the family. Often, it is desirable to purchase life insurance on a homemaker to permit the family to withstand the financial burdens caused by his or her premature death. Much less of a case can be made for insuring the lives of most children. Only after the main wage earner's life has been insured adequately should insurance be considered for other family members.

Three common reasons for businesses to buy life insurance are (1) to provide employee benefits, (2) to indemnify the firm for the financial loss suffered if a key employee dies prematurely (or is disabled), and (3) to finance the transfer of ownership rights from current to future owners.

Generalizations about the taxation of life insurance transactions are not easily made. The chapter described some basic points on taxation of the life insurance transaction.

Review

1. List and explain the different categories of need that life insurance can fill in the event of a premature death. Separate your list into permanent and temporary needs.
2. Other than life insurance, what assets are available to most American families at death?
3. Identify the five steps in the life insurance planning process.
4. What are the advantages of saving for college through a Section 529 plan?
5. What purposes are served when businesses purchase life insurance for their employees?
6. Describe key employee life insurance.
7. What is a buy-and-sell agreement, and what role does life insurance play in such a plan?

8. What is the purpose of a will? What happens if a person dies without a valid will?
9. Define the term *gross estate*, and indicate how it differs from a taxable estate.
10. Describe a second-to-die life insurance policy. What purpose does it serve?
11. Explain the purpose of life insurance in an estate plan.
12. Define the term *split-dollar life insurance*.
13. Explain the difference between the cross-purchase plan and the entity plan.
14. Does the federal income tax apply to life insurance death proceeds? Are there exceptions to the general rule?
15. When does the federal estate tax apply to life insurance proceeds?

Objective Questions

1. The first step in the financial planning process is:
   a. To recommend the right amount of life insurance for a particular client
   b. To recommend the right life insurance policy for a particular client
   c. To motivate and educate clients
   d. To reduce the amount of taxes a client must pay
2. The need for postdeath financial resources includes all the following categories except:
   a. A wealth accumulation fund
   b. An income fund to support dependents
   c. An education fund
   d. A burial fund
3. The text identifies all the following categories of assets as often available to meet postdeath financial needs except:
   a. Social Security benefits
   b. Group life insurance

   c. Tax refunds
   d. Savings accounts and other liquid assets
4. The process of planning the transfer of wealth from one generation to another is called:
   a. Wealth transfer planning
   b. Wealth accumulation planning
   c. Estate planning
   d. Continuation planning
5. The needs-based purchase of life insurance is based on which equation?
   a. Life insurance purchased = financial needs − available assets
   b. Life insurance needs = Social Security benefits − available assets
   c. Financial needs = available assets − life insurance
   d. Life insurance needs = Social Security benefits + burial fund

6. Which of the following would make the best subject for the purchase of life insurance (assuming that none of them currently own it)?
   a. Healthy college senior, no debts, but plans to go to graduate school
   b. Single woman, no debts, good job
   c. Baseball player, large salary, no dependents, no debt
   d. Single mother, two children, good salary, some debts

7. The court-supervised process for transferring property at death is called:
   a. Probate
   b. Estate planning
   c. The will oversight process
   d. Adjunct administration

Discussion Questions

1. Describe how the primary goals of financial planning change from the early, middle, and late years of the planning process.

2. Determine the current state of the unified transfer tax. How has it changed in recent years?

Selected References

G. Victor Hallman and Jerry S. Rosenbloom, 2003 "Personal Financial Planning," 7th ed. (New York: McGraw-Hill).

15

Life Insurance Policies

After studying this chapter, you should be able to

- Identify the markets for group and individual life insurance

- Describe different types of term insurance and explain their uses

- Describe whole life insurance and explain its uses

- Explain how universal life insurance and variable universal life insurance are similar and different from traditional whole life insurance

- Explain the advantages and disadvantages of combining saving with life insurance

One purpose of Chapter 14, "Professional Financial Planning," was to provide a basis for understanding how much life insurance a person or family needs to provide adequate coverage. The purpose of this chapter and the following three chapters is to describe several different types of insurance that people can purchase individually for use in their financial plans. Life insurance policies help to protect against the financial problems associated with premature death. Some life insurance policies also provide a savings fund for retirement or other purposes. Medical expense insurance and disability insurance pay for medical expenses or replace income lost because of disability. Annuities provide a guaranteed income that annuitants cannot outlive.

We begin this chapter by examining two ways that consumers acquire life insurance. Then we describe different types of life insurance, including term, whole, universal, and variable universal life insurance policies. In the final section of this chapter, we examine the advantages and disadvantages of saving with life insurance. As a whole, this chapter thus focuses on identifying the appropriate life insurance policy for the needs and goals of different people.

Throughout this chapter, we will refer to several parties identified in a typical life insurance policy. The **insured** is the person covered for protection under the life insurance policy by the life insurer. Assuming that the death of the insured is covered by the policy, the life insurance company agrees to pay a predetermined amount of money to a **beneficiary**, the person designated in the policy to receive the death proceeds. The amount of death proceeds is sometimes called the **face amount** of coverage, a reference to the practice of listing the amount of death protection on the face page (i.e., the first page) of the policy. The **owner** of the policy is often the insured, such as cases in which a working

TABLE 15-1 Life Insurance Statistics for Selected Years from 1980 to 2009 (in $ Billions)

Value of New Life Insurance Coverage Purchased (by Year) in the United States

Year	1980	1990	2000	2005	2006	2007	2008	2009
Individual	385	1,070	1,594	1,796	1,813	1,891	1,870	1,744
Group	183	459	921	1,040	1,022	1,102	1,073	1,156

Life Insurance Coverage in Force (by Year) in the United States

Year	1980	1990	2000	2005	2006	2007	2008	2009
Individual	1,760	5,391	9,376	9,970	10,057	10,232	10,254	10,324
Group	1,579	3,754	6,376	8,263	8,906	9,158	8,717	7,688

NOTE: Total life insurance in force is measured by the total face amount of potential life insurance claims. Data from the American Council of Life Insurance and the U.S. Census Bureau 2012 Statistical Abstract (http://www.census.gov/compendia/statab/).

spouse buys life insurance to protect his or her spouse and dependent children. In other cases, the owner can buy insurance on the life of another person. For example, two or more partners in a partnership may buy reciprocal insurance on each other to assure that the survivors can pay the deceased partner's family for the deceased's share of the ownership of the firm, thus retaining ownership within the partnership.

TWO WAYS LIFE INSURANCE IS DISTRIBUTED

Insurance companies primarily distribute life insurance in two different ways: as group life insurance or as individual life insurance. Table 15-1 provides a comparison of annual purchases and the amount of life insurance in force for the individual and group insurance categories.

Group Life Insurance

Group life insurance is provided to well-defined groups of people who become members of their groups for purposes other than purchasing life insurance. Common examples of groups that are covered through this type of arrangement include the employees of a local school system or of a large corporate employer. Professional associations, such as the American Medical Association and the American Accounting Association, also can obtain group insurance for their members. We explain group life insurance more completely in Chapter 19, "Employee Benefits."

Credit life insurance is a special type of group life insurance purchased by a lender for its group of debtors. Banks, credit unions, and retail stores that sell merchandise on credit often offer credit life insurance to their customers. If the debtor dies with the loan outstanding, the life insurance proceeds repay the debt.

Financial planners generally do not recommend relying on group life insurance as the exclusive source of post-death funds in a financial plan because it is unlikely to match individual needs and may be unavailable after a job loss. Nonetheless, as shown by the figures in Table 15-1, insurance coverage from group life insurance has grown quickly in recent years.

Individual Life Insurance

In addition to group life insurance, many consumers purchase *individual life insurance*, which also is called **ordinary life insurance**. Unlike group insurance, the purchase of individual life insurance enables consumers to buy insurance that is designed to fit their personal needs for protection. Consumers frequently need much more life insurance protection than is provided under group life policies.

Individual life insurance is sold as several different types of policies. Among the most popular types of individual insurance protection are term life, whole life, universal life, and variable universal life insurance policies. Each is described below.

TERM LIFE INSURANCE

One of the most popular forms of life insurance protection is the term insurance policy. When a life insurer sells a **term life insurance policy**, it promises to pay a specific dollar amount of death protection if the insured dies within a specified term, or period of time. If the insured outlives the period, the insurer makes no payment. Term insurance premium charges are thus based on the insured person's probability of dying during the term of the contract. For adults, this probability of dying increases with age.

Term insurance is often described as providing "pure death protection." Unlike other types of life insurance, the premium charges for term insurance do not include payments into a savings or investment fund. Consumers can thus buy a larger amount of insurance protection when buying term insurance as compared to buying whole life insurance.

Unlike the risk of losing a home or automobile, death is a certainty. The time of death, however, is not. Most term insurance is purchased by people between the ages of 25 and 65. A majority of insureds do not die before age 65, however. Noting that most term policies do not pay any death proceeds, some critics suggest that term life insurance is an ill-advised purchase. This criticism overlooks two important considerations, however. First, a few term life insurance policies pay off on claims that are far larger than the premiums paid, providing valuable life insurance protection to the dependents of the insureds who died during the term of coverage. Second, this criticism ignores the reduction in risk and peace of mind that term life insurance has provided to policyholders and their families, knowing that they have protection if death occurs.

Types of Term Life Insurance

Insurers sell several types of term life insurance policies. Some of these policies are differentiated by the length of the time that the policies provide protection, including the following:

- **Single-year term** policies promise to pay if the insured dies within the one-year policy term. If they have the renewability feature, as described shortly, insurers call these single-year policies **yearly renewable term** or **annually renewable term** policies.
- Multiyear policies, such as **5-year term**, or policies of longer duration, such as **10-, 15-, or 20-year term** policies, pay if the insured dies during the term of the policy.
- Term to a specified age (such as **term to age 65**) policies pay if death occurs before the designated age.

Term insurance policies also can differ on the basis of how the policy specifies the amount of protection. Multiyear term policies may have death benefits that decrease or remain level. A **decreasing term life insurance** policy provides the beneficiary with less protection each year that the policy is in force. If death occurs in the first policy year, the beneficiary receives the face amount, for example, $100,000. If death occurs in a succeeding year, the proceeds will be less. For example, in year 21, the proceeds may equal only $38,100. In a decreasing term policy, the premiums remain the same

TABLE 15-2 Sales Illustration for 20-Year Level Term Insurance Policy

Hypothetical Term Life Insurance
Illustration for Richard L. Heart
(Age 35, Nonsmoking)

Year	Age	Guaranteed Premium	Death Benefit	Nonguaranteed Current Premium	Death Benefit
0	35	$ 450	$250,000	$450	$250,000
5	40	$ 450	$250,000	$450	$250,000
10	45	$ 450	$250,000	$450	$250,000
20	55	$2,700	$250,000	$450	$250,000

each year but purchase less insurance. That is, the death benefit decreases because the chance of death increases with age. Decreasing term insurance is useful, for example, to provide funds to repay a mortgage or provide support for a dependent child until the child reaches age 21. Over time, the funds needed to accomplish each of these goals decreases, and so do the insurance proceeds.

A **level term life insurance** policy pays the same amount of benefits if death occurs at any point while the policy is in force. Table 15-2 presents a sales illustration for a twenty-year level term policy prepared for Richard L. Heart. The insurance company guarantees the premium and death benefit for twenty years. At the end of the twentieth year, Richard may keep the policy, but the premiums may rise steeply to reflect his age at that time. In this scenario, the nonguaranteed premium does not rise in the twentieth year, assuming that the insurer's current experience with mortality and investment results remain favorable. As the column heading indicates, the nonguaranteed premium is subject to change.

Renewable term policies allow the insured to continue the coverage up to a specified age regardless of the status of the insured's health or other relevant factors, including occupation. For example, if a five-year term policy is not renewable, an insurer could cancel the insurance at the end of any five-year period. The insurer could not end coverage if the policy was renewable. Although renewable term policies cost more, the guaranteed renewal feature is worthwhile for many people because it transfers the risk of becoming uninsurable to the insurance company.

Each time a term insurance policy is renewed, the premium increases because the insured is older. Thus, the premiums for yearly renewable term insurance increase each year at renewal. With a five-year term policy, the premiums increase at each fifth anniversary. For example, assume that a 28-year-old insured pays $2 each year for each $1,000 of five-year renewable term insurance. At age 33, on renewal of the policy, his premiums increase to $2.50 a year for the next five years. At age 38, the premiums will increase again to $3.50 per year, and an increase will follow at each renewal until he no longer renews the policy. Many term life insurers do not permit renewability past a certain age, such as age 70 or 80, to minimize their exposure to adverse selection.

Convertible term policies allow the insured the option of converting the policy to a whole life policy. This privilege can be valuable if the term insurance is about to expire and the insured wants to continue the coverage on a permanent basis. When the insured makes the conversion, the premium increases.

Combinations of term insurance features may be purchased. Thus, Thomas Paine may purchase a ten-year, renewable, convertible, level term policy. Such a policy would provide level benefits for ten years, allow him to renew the policy at the end of year 10 (if he was younger than the maximum age for renewability), or allow him to convert to a whole life policy of the same face amount of insurance.

Uses of Term LIfe Insurance

Term life insurance can prove useful in solving many financial problems. It can be used when the need for life insurance is temporary. It is also useful when people need the maximum coverage and have limited financial resources. Because of competition for large policies, the price of term insurance decreased significantly in recent years, when purchased both on the Internet and through the traditional marketing channels using agents and brokers. The price of term insurance is attractive to many people.

In the event of a premature death, the education fund need can be met by a level term policy. Assume that King George has a son, Prince George, and that the son is now 6 years old and shows promise of becoming a scholar. King George thinks that, if he should die prematurely, he would like a fund of $80,000 available for his son's college education. Prince George will enter college in 11 years and remain there for 4 years. Thus, because the need for an education fund exists for only 15 years, it could be met with a 15-year level term policy.

People often use term life insurance to repay debts. The need for life insurance is temporary because most debts are temporary. For example, many home mortgages last from 15 to 30 years. When homeowners use installment payments to retire the mortgage, the amount of debt decreases each year. Thus, a $230,000 mortgage requires only $230,000 of life insurance proceeds before the homeowner makes the first loan repayment. Afterward, less insurance is needed. A decreasing term policy can be coordinated to cover the loan balance outstanding. Many homeowners purchase a decreasing term policy to retire the mortgage if the family wage earner dies. Mortgage balances generally are not payable at the homeowner's death. However, the proceeds of the life insurance can relieve the survivors of having to make monthly mortgage payments.

Term insurance can be used to provide financial support for dependents. The need for funds to support dependent children is temporary. Once the children become financially independent, the need for funds to support them ends. However, if a child, or a spouse, is likely to be a permanent dependent, perhaps because of a permanent disability, then term life insurance is unlikely to be the best choice to fund problems caused by a premature death.

At ages less than 65, term insurance premiums are usually less than whole life insurance premiums. Therefore, term insurance is useful when the need is for maximum life insurance protection—especially if a consumer's life insurance budget is limited. An example of this situation would be a young family with two or more dependent children and limited disposable income.

Term life insurance can be a valuable part of an individual's life insurance plans. Term policies are flexible and initially have lower premiums than other forms of life insurance. Term insurance cannot solve all life insurance problems, however. Generally, it should not be used when the need for life insurance is permanent rather than temporary, as would be the case with a burial fund. Nor can term insurance by itself provide a regular forced savings plan. Insuring permanent needs while accumulating savings requires a whole life plan.

WHOLE LIFE INSURANCE

Whole life insurance policies promise to pay the beneficiary whenever death occurs, and they extend coverage to advanced ages, such as age 100.[1] In addition, the insurer will pay the death proceeds if the insured survives through the end of the coverage period. When life insurers make a claim payment, they say that the policy has *matured*. The insurer thus knows with certainty that it eventually must pay a matured claim on every whole life

---

[1] New whole life insurance policies based on the 2001 Commissioners Standard Ordinary (CSO) Mortality Table mature at age 120. Most policies purchased before 2000 were based on earlier mortality tables, such as the 1980 CSO Mortality Table, and they mature at age 100.

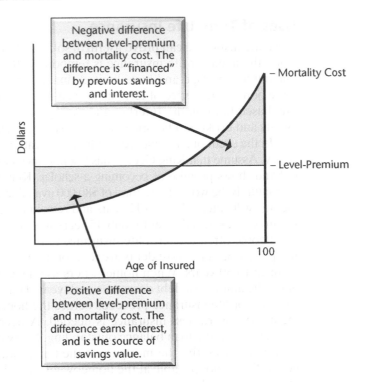

FIGURE 15-1 The Origin of Savings Value in Level-Premium Whole Life Insurance

policy remaining in force. This circumstance is different from both property insurance and term life insurance policies. Because claims are a certainty with whole life policies, the insurer must collect enough premiums to pay them. This fact is one reason that whole life insurance premiums initially are larger than term life insurance premiums.

Cash Values

Because whole life policies provide life insurance protection to older policyholders in their 80s and 90s, a key challenge for insurers is finding a way to pay for the high cost of mortality at such advanced ages. Most whole life insurers finance such costs using the *level premium concept*, a practice in which insurers charge a level premium over the life of the policy that is higher than the cost needed to cover mortality cost at younger ages but is lower than the high cost of mortality at older ages. Figure 15-1 illustrates this concept. Because the insurer initially charges a larger premium than is necessary to pay the early death claims, the level-premium method produces a savings value, called the **cash value** in most whole life insurance policies. With each additional premium payment, the cash value continues to grow during the early years of the policy. Over time, these additional charges and the compound interest earned on them generate a sizable savings value. The increase in cash value is not subject to income taxes in the year that it is earned. The savings accumulated in the cash value are used later in the life of the policy, when the level premium charges are insufficient to cover the high cost of mortality as the insured's age nears 100.

The ability of the level premium concept to finance mortality costs depends heavily on the interest earned by an insurer over the term of the insurance policy. Life insurance policies often cover a policyholder for decades, enabling insurers to earn considerable investment income on the savings accumulated over the life of a whole life policy. Life insurers invest their insureds' cash value in conservative investments such as federal government debt issues or blue-chip corporate bonds. These safe investments allow the insurer to guarantee an increase in cash values, and traditional whole life policies contain a table presenting these guaranteed values.

One purpose for building the savings value is to finance the large premiums needed to keep the policy in force in the years when the probability of death is high. In addition to keeping premiums level, the savings in the whole life policy are the basis of several important contractual rights. Policyowners can withdraw all their cash value at once if they want to end the policy. People can use the cash value to purchase an annuity at older ages when they need retirement income. Some of or all the cash value can be borrowed from the insurer at any time. As these examples suggest, the savings element in a whole life policy enables the policy to serve a variety of flexible roles in many life insurance plans.

Types of Whole Life Policies

Insurers classify whole life insurance policies in the following categories based on the method of premium payment: single premium, continuous premium, and limited payment.

Single-premium whole life insurance policies are those for which, in exchange for one relatively large premium, the insurer promises to pay the claim whenever death occurs. Consumers needing a great deal of life insurance generally cannot use the single-premium method because the size of the single premium becomes unaffordable. For example, if the single premium for every $1,000 of whole life insurance was $350 for a male age 20, then $100,000 of insurance will cost $35,000. In addition to their high cost, Congress classified single-premium policies as **modified endowment contracts (MECs)** in 1988, eliminating the tax advantages that are otherwise available for more traditional forms of cash value insurance.[2]

Continuous-premium whole life insurance policies require insureds to pay the same premium as long as they live or until they reach the specified maturity age. Insurers also call these policies **level-premium whole life insurance** and **straight-premium whole life insurance**. The premiums take into account, mathematically, both compound interest and the probability of the insured's death. An insured's death means that the insurer must pay a claim. It also means that an insured is no longer responsible for making premium payments to the insurer.

The premium schedule of **limited-payment whole life insurance** policies falls somewhere between that of single-premium and continuous-premium policies. In each case, the protection continues until the insured dies. Insureds with limited-payment policies pay premiums for only a limited number of years, after which the policy is "paid up," so it requires no additional premiums. Examples include ten-payment and twenty-payment whole life policies and policies paid up at age 60 or 65. Like most consumer purchases financed over time in a series of payments (such as mortgages or loans), the size of each premium payment is a function of the length of time over which it will be paid. The shorter the payment period, the larger each payment will be. Thus, for a man aged 35, payments for a ten-payment whole life policy will be larger than the payments required for a whole life policy paid up at 65, where thirty annual payments are due. Limited payment policies thus are attractive to people who want long-term death protection but who also wish to finish paying for such protection before their income decreases due to retirement or the scaling back of one's career to part-time employment.

---

[2] As defined by the Internal Revenue Service (IRS), any life insurance policy failing a "seven-pay" test is considered an MEC, thus losing the tax advantage of tax-free policy loans. To avoid being labeled an MEC, premiums cannot be paid more rapidly than necessary to provide the paid-up death benefits that seven level annual payments can purchase. See Chapter 10, "Insurance Regulation," for a discussion of the favorable tax treatment available to whole life policies.

TABLE 15-3 Whole Life Insurance Sales Illustration

Illustration for Vince Vango
Age 35, Nonsmoking
Annual Premium = $3,000
Face Amount = $250,000

Year	Age	Guaranteed Premium	Guaranteed Cash Surrender Value	Death Benefit	Nonguaranteed Cash Surrender Value (current)	Nonguaranteed Death Benefit (current)
0	35	$3,000	$ 0	$250,000	$ 0	$250,000
5	40	$3,000	$ 9,000	$250,000	$ 9,300	$252,000
10	45	$3,000	$27,500	$250,000	$29,000	$254,000
20	55	$3,000	$65,000	$250,000	$86,000	$287,000

A Whole Life Ledger Sheet

Table 15-3 is a summary ledger sheet prepared for Vince Vango. It is for a continuous-premium whole life policy with an excess interest provision. The **excess interest provision** means that the cash values will increase faster than the guaranteed rate if the insurer earns rates of return greater than the guaranteed rate, as it is currently doing. The insurer guarantees the maximum annual premium and a minimum cash surrender value. The nonguaranteed death benefits in this illustration show the effect of nonguaranteed dividends, which are used to purchase paid-up additional death benefits. The company notes that this column is based on its current dividend scale and that actual dividends may be more or less than those illustrated.

The Uses of Whole Life Insurance

Whole life insurance policies meet people's needs for permanent life insurance protection and for savings. Permanent protection needs include a burial fund and an income fund in cases in which a spouse, child, or parent depends permanently on the insured for financial support. The type of life insurance that is used in estate plans and in business continuation arrangements often is cash value insurance. Such permanent needs generally cannot be met by term insurance because term insurance often becomes unavailable or unaffordable after age 65, while these needs frequently continue after that age.

After many years of whole life having wide market appeal, sales of this type of insurance have fallen significantly (as a percentage of all policies sold) in the United States over the past several decades. A portion of this decrease can be traced to the growing popularity of term insurance, especially as increased longevity of adults in the United States has led to intense price competition among term life insurers. Newer types of whole life insurance, such as universal life and variable-universal policies, also have increased in popularity, drawing consumers away from the traditional whole life product. Both of these types are described below.

UNIVERSAL LIFE INSURANCE

Universal life insurance is designed to provide permanent life insurance protection like traditional whole life insurance, but with greater flexibility in paying premiums, accumulating cash value, and modifying death protection. Universal life insurance does not use the level premium concept to finance the high cost of mortality expense at advanced ages; instead, it places the owner in greater control of the cash value account. Premium payments are credited into the cash value, but monthly or quarterly mortality charges and administrative expenses are deducted from the cash value as well. The policyowner thus is not obligated to pay a fixed annual amount every year but assumes responsibility for making certain that the balance of the fund is sufficient to cover both types of expense charges.

As is the case for whole life insurance, universal life insurers invest the premiums paid by customers, using the tax-deferred accumulation of investment income to help pay for part of the cost of mortality expenses. The insurer's investments supporting universal life insurance are typically in short-term (six months or less) federal government debt issues. The underlying investments supporting universal life policies thus are similar to low-risk money market mutual funds.

The policy allows the insured to set both the amount and the frequency of the premium payments within limits. The minimum premium is the amount needed to keep a term insurance policy in force. An IRS formula determines the maximum premium that is eligible for favorable tax treatment (see footnote 2).

Typically, the insurer subtracts a monthly mortality charge and an expense charge from the insured's accumulated premium fund. Neither the mortality charge nor the expense charge is fixed; they may fluctuate based on the insurer's experience. The accumulated premium deposits, minus expense and mortality charges, produce a cash value. This cash value then earns two types of interest. The contract specifies a **guaranteed interest rate**. The guaranteed rate produces a guaranteed minimum cash value. The insurer also credits an **excess interest rate** if certain policy conditions are met. The excess interest rate is determined by a formula or by company declaration. When a formula is used, the formula is usually tied to the interest rate on short-term U.S. Treasury securities. During economic times in which these interest rates are high, insurers often pass along a portion of the higher interest rates to policyowners as excess interest, thus increasing the attractiveness of the universal life insurance product to consumers.

Universal Life Insurance Death Benefits

Universal life insurance death benefits follow one of two patterns, usually identified as Plan A and Plan B. Figure 15-2 shows these plans graphically. Plan A is sometimes called a *level death benefit plan* because the death benefit remains constant over the life of the policy for most insureds. If the insured dies, the insurer pays the face amount of coverage but retains the accumulated cash value from the policy. Because the effective amount of death protection paid out at the time of death equals the face amount minus the cash value, the insurer will bear a decreasing amount of payments as the cash value increases over time. This net payout is often called the insurer's **net amount at risk** because it reflects the actual out-of-pocket payment by the insurer at death after retaining the cash value. Holding cash value and face amounts constant, the policyowner pays a lower monthly mortality charge for Type A plans than for Type B plans because these charges are based on the net amount at risk for Type A plans. Thus, if Al owns a $100,000 Plan A universal life policy with a cash value of $10,000, his monthly mortality charge will be set based on the cost of the net amount at risk of $90,000, not the $100,000 face amount.[3]

---

[3] As noted earlier, the cash value on whole life insurance and universal life insurance grows free of taxes. To prevent investors from depositing excess amounts of premiums in the tax-free account to exploit this tax advantage, the IRS limits the amount of cash value granted this favorable tax treatment in universal life policies, setting the maximum tax-favored cash value below the face amount of coverage on the policy. This tax issue typically arises when the cash value on a policy grows large, such as when the inflows to the policy increase due to accelerated premium payments or favorable investment results. The IRS uses a complex *corridor test* to determine if the cash value of a policy is too large for the amount of death protection. To satisfy this test, insurers often include provisions in Plan A policies that automatically increase the face amount of coverage when the cash value on the policy grows quite large, as shown on the right side of the Plan A illustration found in Figure 15-2.

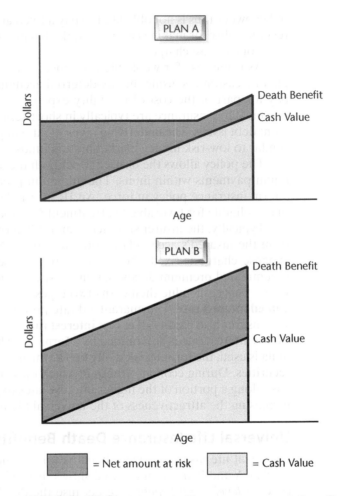

FIGURE 15-2 Universal Life Insurance Death Benefits

Plan B provides a variable death benefit, where the death benefit is equal to the initial face amount of coverage plus any accumulated cash value at the time of the insured's death. Thus, if Sue owns a $100,000 Plan B policy with a cash value of $10,000 at the time of her death, the insurer will pay her beneficiary $110,000. Like Plan A, insurers base the term insurance mortality charge on the **net amount at risk**, but this value is always equal to the face amount of protection for Plan B policies because the insurer pays out the cash value as part of the death benefits. The insurance company guarantees the initial death benefit regardless of operating results.

Uses of Universal Life Insurance

Universal life insurance can be used in place of traditional whole life insurance in most cases. The following features distinguish universal life insurance from traditional whole life policies:

- *Flexibility of premium payments*: Within the minimum and maximum limits, the insured can choose the frequency and amount of premium payments. Most insurers suggest a targeted premium payment to their prospective customers and provide a policy illustration that forecasts the anticipated cash values and death benefits for the policy, assuming that the customer continues to pay the target premium in the future. The insured need not make the suggested payment, and

TABLE 15-4 Universal Life Insurance Sales Illustration

Illustration for W. A. Mozart
Age 35, Nonsmoker
Initial Death Benefit = $250,000
Planned Premium = $2,400
Guaranteed Interest Rate = 4%
Nonguaranteed Current Charges/Current Interest Rate = 5.25%

Age	Year	Premium	Guaranteed Cash Value	Cash Surrender Value	Death Benefit	Nonguaranteed Cash Value	Nonguaranteed Cash Surrender Value	Nonguaranteed Death Benefit
0	35	$2,400	$ 0	$ 0	$250,000	$ 0	$ 0	$250,000
5	40	$2,400	$ 8,800	$ 5,000	$260,000	$ 9,350	$ 5,600	$260,000
10	45	$2,400	$18,000	$17,000	$268,000	$20,000	$18,500	$272,000
20	55	$2,400	$36,000	$36,000	$286,000	$46,000	$46,000	$307,000
30	65	$2,400	$34,000	$34,000	$284,000	$65,000	$65,000	$354,000

a premium is not required so long as the policy has sufficient cash value to cover the mortality and expense charges.

- *Ability to earn a greater return when interest rates rise*: During periods of inflation, short-term interest rates change regularly. In general, short-term interest rates increase when prices rise because the federal government attempts to control inflation using interest rates to restrain the economy. Universal life insurers typically increase the interest income credited to cash values during periods of higher interest rates, passing along a portion of their increased investment income to their customers.

- *Flexibility of death benefits*: By controlling premium payments or switching between Plan A and Plan B, insureds have more control over their insurance death benefit. Insurers may require evidence of insurability from policyowners requesting large increases in coverage.

In terms of legal rights and tax treatment, universal life insurance and whole life insurance policies are similar. Both allow full or partial withdrawals of cash value and both allow the beneficiary to receive the death proceeds free of federal income tax. Many traditional options and riders also are available with the universal life contract. Because it duplicates most of the advantages of traditional whole life contracts and offers the opportunity for greater investment gain and a rising death benefit, universal life insurance is an attractive substitute for the traditional whole life policy, especially during periods of high interest rates.

Ledger Sheet for Universal Life Insurance

W. A. Mozart asked his life insurance agent for an illustration of a universal life insurance policy. The result appears in Table 15-4. This table illustrates a Plan B policy, in which increases in cash values are added to the death benefit. The face amount of insurance equals $250,000. The illustration assumes that Mozart pays an annual premium of $2,400 and that the insurer credits the policy with 4 percent interest. Based on these assumptions, the leftmost six columns of the table project the cash value, surrender value,[4] and death benefits for the policy. In reality, however, these assumptions are unlikely to hold true over the full life of the policy given the changes of our dynamic economy. If the premiums or investment results increase or decrease, the cash values will be different

---

[4] This policy includes a surrender charge, a fee assessed against the policyholder in the event that he or she prematurely terminates the policy. If the owner terminates the policy, this charge is deducted from the cash value, thus explaining the difference between the cash value and the surrender value. The surrender charge disappears after the twentieth year. Chapter 16, "Standard Life Insurance Contract Provisions and Options," more fully discusses the options available to the policyowner if he or she surrenders a whole life policy.

from those illustrated. For example, the figures in the right three columns of the table are calculated under an assumption that the insurer can earn 5.25 percent on these policies, and this nonguaranteed result is illustrated alongside the guaranteed results.

Variable Universal Life Insurance

Variable universal life (VUL) insurance is a cash-value life insurance policy that was designed to provide policyowners more alternatives for investing the cash values in their whole life policies. The design of the VUL policy follows that of a traditional universal life plan. That is, a cash value develops when premiums exceed mortality charges and expenses. When the cash value develops, the insured can choose to invest it in one or more investment funds, called **separate accounts**. The investment alternatives available in the separate accounts typically include money market, common stock, and bond funds. The cash value earns a return (positive or negative) based on the performance of the underlying separate account. Insurers do not guarantee a minimum cash value; however, they do guarantee a minimum death benefit.

VUL insurance can duplicate either universal life insurance or traditional whole life insurance depending on the investment account(s) chosen. For example, it could resemble universal life if the underlying investment is a money market fund. If the underlying investment vehicle is a long-term bond fund, the policy would operate more like traditional whole life insurance. Most insurers selling VUL also provide a variety of investment options involving common stock, similar to the investment options available through a stock mutual fund. These stock funds offer the policyowner the potential to earn higher returns, but with much higher investment risk. Because the VUL policy can be invested in stocks and other securities, insurance agents selling VUL policies must be licensed with the National Association of Securities Dealers (NASD).[5]

REASONS FOR BUYING CASH-VALUE LIFE INSURANCE

Many consumers choose a life policy with a savings value, including whole life, universal, or VUL policies. Buying life insurance with a cash value offers the following advantages:

- Many consumers do not save money unless forced to do so by a regular savings plan, such as the one built into these policies.
- The savings accumulated in these life insurance policies is invested by professional investors, who typically have more training in finance and investments than policyowners.
- People saving with life insurance receive federal income tax advantages. The interest on the savings is tax-deferred. No federal income tax need be paid on the interest earned on the savings element of a life insurance policy unless the policy is surrendered and the owner withdraws the cash value. If the savings are not withdrawn and the policy matures as a death benefit, then no federal income tax applies.
- The savings element of a whole life policy provides some protection from creditors' claims in the event of an insured's bankruptcy. Depending on the beneficiary designation and relevant state and federal bankruptcy laws, the savings in a life insurance policy may not be subject to seizure by creditors of a bankrupt insured. Protection from creditors' claims is a technical and complex issue, so questions on the topic may require guidance from a legal expert.

Some financial planners suggest that buying a whole life policy with a cash value is not the best choice, however, proposing instead that consumers should "buy term

---

[5] Passing the NASD Series 6 examination permits the sale of variable life insurance products and mutual funds. Passing the Series 7 exam allows the sale of listed stocks, bonds, and option contracts.

TABLE 15-5 Representative Annual Life Insurance Premiums for Each $1,000 of Protection

Age	20	25	30	35	40	45
Single-Year Term	$ 2.06	$ 2.16	$ 2.29	$ 2.62	$ 3.56	$ 5.33
Whole Life	$11.34	$12.95	$15.10	$17.51	$20.90	$25.56

NOTE: The term policy is renewable and convertible. Premiums increase each year. The whole life policy pays nonguaranteed dividends that reduce the premium outlay.

insurance and invest the difference" (BTID). The "difference" is the difference in premium between term insurance and some form of permanent insurance.

For example, Table 15-5 shows the difference in cost between the annual premiums for term and whole life insurance for insureds from ages 20 to 45. At every age listed, term insurance requires a smaller premium outlay than whole life insurance. At age 20, the difference is $9.28 ($11.34 – $2.06) for each $1,000 of life insurance. At age 40, the difference is $17.34 ($20.90 – $3.56). Advocates of BTID stress the following points:

- The consumer who buys term and invests the difference not only leaves the insurance death benefits to the beneficiary but also leaves the amount of savings accumulated outside the policy. These savings can reach significant amounts when compound interest is earned. In later years, the outside savings can exceed the original amount of insurance.
- Many needs for life insurance present in the early family years no longer exist at age 65. If a need for life insurance continues, savings will be available to meet it.
- The investment return and accumulated savings outside the life insurance policy each may be significantly greater than returns and accumulations inside the policy.

On the other hand, critics of BTID offer the following counterarguments:

- If consumers invest the difference outside the policy, they forgo the advantages of safety and guaranteed earnings that the insurance provides. In other words, one reason the investment returns and accumulations are greater outside the policy is because there is more risk.
- If the need for life insurance should continue beyond the original plans, the advice could prove costly. If the term policies are not convertible, the advice could produce unmet needs. The savings fund built up outside the policy, however, would prevent a totally unmet need.
- If the savings are outside the policy, insureds may lose the tax advantages and protection from creditors' claims that were described at the beginning of this section.

Summary

People may acquire life insurance in two ways. Some employees are covered by group life insurance, which is a frequent employee benefit provided to workers. In addition, many consumers purchase their life insurance on an individual basis from life insurance agents.

This chapter describes three main types of insurance: term life, whole life, and (variable) universal life. Table 15-6 compares the three policy types. Term insurance, which provides protection for a limited period, involves the lowest premium outlay. Term insurance generally should not be used when the need for protection is permanent or when the insured wants savings benefits. Whole life insurance policies, which have no time limit for the payment of death proceeds, combine a savings element with life insurance protection. Many consumers want to combine these savings features with life insurance protection.

TABLE 15-6 Policy Comparison Chart

	Level Term Life	*Ordinary Whole Life*	*Universal Life and VUL*
Death Benefit	Level	Level	Level or increasing
Cash Value Savings	None	Minimum schedule— guaranteed	Guaranteed, may be supplemented in favorable investment environments
Premiums	Level during term; increases if renewed	Level for lifetime	Flexible premium, within limits
Uses	– Temporary needs – Maximum coverage	– Permanent needs – Combines savings and protection	– Policy can adjust to changing economic conditions – VUL combines insurance and investments
Disadvantages	– No cash value – Premiums can become unaffordable – Uninsurability	– Policy hurt by inflation – High acquisition costs	– VUL policyowner bears risk of declining investment value

Because term insurance premiums are lower than whole life insurance premiums, consumers have been advised to save the difference in premiums outside the insurance policy. Following this advice allows the possibility of leaving more proceeds to survivors. On the other hand, people should be confident of their ability to save regularly, invest wisely, and leave the savings untouched before they consider or follow this advice.

Life insurers sell many policies other than term and whole life insurance. Universal life insurance combines flexibility in premium payments with the opportunity for increased interest earnings. VUL insurance allows the insured an opportunity to invest cash values in one or more separate investment accounts maintained by the insurer.

Review

1. Identify four different types of groups that may purchase group life insurance.
2. Describe the most common type of group that is covered by group life insurance.
3. Describe the conversion privilege found in group life insurance. When is it useful?
4. What is the function of credit life insurance?
5. List some of the differences between group and individual life insurance.
6. Identify the contractual rights that the owner of a life insurance policy may exercise.
7. Describe four different types of term insurance policies based on their potential time span.
8. Why are decreasing term policies used to repay mortgage loans?
9. Explain why the renewability feature makes term insurance more attractive to some buyers.
10. How does convertible term life insurance differ from renewable term life insurance?
11. Develop a set of family circumstances in which term insurance is the most appropriate type of policy to meet the consumer's needs.
12. Develop a set of family circumstances in which traditional cash value, whole life insurance is the most appropriate type of policy to meet the consumer's needs.
13. Why have many consumers found the savings aspect of whole life insurance policies useful?
14. For a healthy man aged 27, rank the following policies in order of their annual premium size, from largest to smallest: continuous-premium whole life, ten-payment whole life, single-premium whole life, and whole life paid up at age 65.
16. Describe some family circumstances in which a consumer logically might choose a universal or variable life insurance policy.
17. Describe the advantages and disadvantages of buying term insurance and investing the difference.

18. Why does a whole life insurance policy require a larger premium than a term insurance policy?
19. What are the main differences between universal life insurance and traditional whole life insurance?
20. Explain the two different types of death benefit plans offered with universal life insurance.
21. How can a variable life insurance policy be operated like a universal or whole life insurance policy?

Objective Questions

1. The simplest form of life insurance is:
   a. Single premium whole life
   b. Term life insurance
   c. Universal life insurance
   d. Variable life insurance
2. Choose the true statement about whole life insurance.
   a. It builds a guaranteed savings (cash) value.
   b. It must be purchased in amounts greater than $100,000.
   c. It is usually the insurance with the lowest premium for a given age.
   d. It provides temporary protection.
3. Each of the following features distinguishes universal life insurance from traditional whole life insurance except what?
   a. Universal life provides higher returns during economic periods of high interest rates.
   b. Universal life allows flexibility of premium payments.
   c. Universal life allows borrowing the face amount after the first five years.
   d. Universal life provides some flexibility in death benefits.
4. Choose the true statement about variable universal life insurance.
   a. Savings values are guaranteed.
   b. The policyowner has flexibility in investment choice.
   c. The investment risk is borne by the insurance company.
   d. None of the above statements is true.
5. The investments supporting the cash values of traditional whole life insurance policies are:
   a. Common stock/equity investments
   b. Short-term government debt issues
   c. Municipal debt
   d. Federal government debt issues and high quality corporate bonds.
6. Choose the true statement about convertible term life insurance.
   a. It is cheaper to convert the older the insured gets.
   b. It allows conversion from individual to group insurance.
   c. It allows the insured to convert to whole life insurance within five years of a spouse's death.
   d. It allows conversion from term to cash value life insurance.
7. Selling which of the following types of life insurance policies requires registering with the NASD?
   a. Variable life insurance
   b. Term life insurance
   c. Whole life insurance
   d. Limited-pay whole life insurance

Discussion Questions

1. Explain how universal life insurance policies are more flexible than traditional whole life policies.
2. What is your position on the BTID argument?

Selected References

Black, Kenneth Jr., and Harold D. Skipper, Jr., 2000, *Life Insurance*, 13th ed. (Upper Saddle River, NJ: Prentice Hall).

Life Insurance Fact Book, published annually (Washington, D.C.: American Council of Life Insurance), *http://www.acli.com*.

Appendix: Simplified Life Insurance Mathematics

Many of my students have indicated that they find basic life insurance calculations interesting. As has been the case several times before in this text, the following material simplifies a complex subject. Readers wanting information that is more detailed should consult a textbook on actuarial mathematics.

We begin this appendix by describing the **mortality table**, the basis of all life insurance premium calculations. Premium calculations for term life insurance and whole life insurance follow. We describe only briefly the calculation of level premiums for term and whole life insurance policies. The concepts are what is important, not the calculations, and certainly not the numbers. We will also limit the numbers to the right of the decimal point to keep the figures simple, recognizing that this may introduce some slight amount of rounding error.

Mortality Tables

Insurers have kept statistics on births and deaths for more than 200 years. Readers interested in recent U.S. birth rates, death rates, and other demographic data can find it at http://www.cdc.gov/nchs/. Actuaries build mortality tables based on observations of the number of deaths in a population. Mortality tables indicate the probability of death in a pool of insured lives.

The **2001 Commissioners Standard Ordinary Mortality Table** is the current mortality table that the various states have adopted for many regulatory purposes, including the minimum valuation standards for life insurance products. Table 15-7 presents a section of the 2001 Commissioners Standard Ordinary Mortality Table. The second and fourth columns are the annual expected number of deaths per 1,000 lives for males and females, respectively. The data show that if a company were to insure 10,000 lives of men age 35, it should expect 1.24 deaths per 1,000 men insured. That means that it should expect 12.4 deaths in a group of 10,000 insureds.

Some Simplifying Assumptions

Before we begin to explore the mathematics of life insurance, we must make some simplifying assumptions:

1. The actual number of deaths will equal the mortality table estimates.

2. There are no transaction costs; the insurer makes only death benefit payments.

3. Insureds pay all premiums on the first day of the year. Insurers pay all death claims on the last day of the year. The effect of this assumption is to allow the insurer to earn a full year's interest on the death claims.

These assumptions are not realistic; actuaries make them to simplify initial premium calculations. In a following stage, the actuaries "load" premiums for transaction costs, unexpected deaths, and lower interest expectations. We call the simplified, unrealistic premiums *net premiums*. They are always less than the actual premiums charged by life insurers, which are called *gross premiums*.

Single-Premium, One-Year Term Insurance

When a consumer purchases a single-premium, one-year term insurance policy, the insurer promises to pay the beneficiary only if the insured dies in the next 365 days. If the insured lives, the insurer makes no payment.

Assume that 10,000 healthy males, aged 35, purchase a $1,000 single-year, term life insurance policy. The mortality table reveals a death rate of 1.24 for each 1,000 lives insured. If 10,000 lives are insured, there thus will be 12.4 (10 × 1.24) death claims. A $1,000 payment is required for each claim. Thus, the insurer pays a total of $12,400 ($1,000 × 12.4 claims). Does the insurer need to collect $12,400 in premiums at the beginning of the year? Not quite. It will earn interest for one year on the money it collects. We assume that interest is earned at a rate of 3 percent.

In our example, the insurer expects to pay benefits of $12,400 at the end of the year. How much money should it have on hand at the beginning of the year to fund the claims? Financiers use present value calculations to answer this question. **Present value calculations** combine interest rates, time periods, and an ending balance of $1 to calculate a beginning amount, the present value of the $1. A present value calculation tells us that if we invest $0.97 at the beginning of the year, we will have $1 at the end of the year, assuming that we earn 3 percent interest.

TABLE 15-7 A Section of Commissioners 2001 Standard Ordinary Mortality Table

Commissioners 2001 Standard Ordinary Mortality Table
Male and Female
Age Last Birthday

Age Last Birthday	Male 1000qx	Male Life Expectation	Female 1000qx	Female Life Expectation
0	0.72	75.67	0.42	79.87
1	0.46	74.73	0.31	78.90
2	0.33	73.76	0.23	77.93
3	0.24	72.79	0.20	76.95
4	0.21	71.81	0.19	75.96
5	0.22	70.82	0.18	74.98
6	0.22	69.84	0.19	73.99
7	0.22	68.85	0.21	73.00
8	0.22	67.87	0.21	72.02
9	0.23	66.88	0.21	71.03
10	0.24	65.90	0.22	70.05
11	0.28	64.91	0.25	69.06
12	0.34	63.93	0.27	68.08
13	0.40	62.95	0.31	67.10
14	0.52	61.98	0.34	66.12
15	0.66	61.01	0.36	65.14
16	0.78	60.05	0.39	64.17
17	0.89	59.10	0.41	63.19
18	0.95	58.15	0.44	62.22
19	0.98	57.21	0.46	61.25
20	1.00	56.26	0.47	60.27
21	1.01	55.32	0.49	59.30
22	1.02	54.37	0.50	58.33
23	1.04	53.43	0.51	57.36
24	1.06	52.48	0.53	56.39
25	1.09	51.54	0.55	55.42
26	1.14	50.60	0.58	54.45
27	1.17	49.65	0.61	53.48
28	1.16	48.71	0.64	52.51
29	1.15	47.77	0.67	51.55
30	1.14	46.82	0.70	50.58
31	1.13	45.88	0.75	49.62
32	1.14	44.93	0.79	48.65
33	1.16	43.98	0.85	47.69
34	1.19	43.03	0.92	46.73
35	1.24	42.08	1.00	45.78
36	1.31	41.14	1.07	44.82
37	1.39	40.19	1.14	43.87
38	1.49	39.25	1.20	42.92
39	1.59	38.30	1.26	41.97

Returning to the $12,400 claims payment, we find the insurer needs about $0.97 for each dollar that it must pay at the end of the year, so the insurer must have $12,028 (0.97 × $12,400) on hand at the beginning of the year to meet its obligations. The insurance pool began with 10,000 premium-paying members. Each member will have to pay $12,028/10,000, or $1.20, as a premium for the one-year term insurance promise of a $1,000 death benefit.

Single-Premium, Five-Year Term Insurance

Assume that a consumer wants to purchase a single-premium, five-year term insurance policy from the insurer. What will the net premium be? The insurer promises to pay a beneficiary $1,000 if death occurs in the five years following the purchase of the policy.

Assume that 10,000 men buy our five-year term insurance policy beginning at age 35. In the first year, 12.4 (10,000 × 1.24) insureds die. The insurance company will need $12,400 at the end of the first year to pay these claims. It needs only $12,028 (0.97 × $12,400) at the beginning of the first year.

In the second year, 13.084 of the original 10,000 insureds die. (This calculation results from the death rate at age 36, multiplied by the 9,988 survivors from the original group of 10,000.) The insurance company needs $13,084 at the end of the second year to pay each $1,000 claim. It needs $12,333 (0.94 × $13,084) on hand at the beginning of the first year to meet these claims. Note that two years of interest is earned on this money, and the present value of $1 for two years at 3 percent interest is $0.94.

In the third year, all the living insureds are age 37, and 13.865 of them die. The insurance company pays $13,865 in benefits at the end of the third year. It needs $12,688 (0.91 × $13,865) at the beginning of the first year to meet these claims.

Following the same mathematical procedure, the company needs $14,841 at the end of the fourth year, or $13,186.37 at the beginning of the first year, to meet fourth-year death claims. The mortality table predicts that 14.841 of the original 10,000 insureds die in the fourth year. The present value table shows that $0.88 is the present value of $1 due in four years. In the fifth year of the insurance, 15.814 insureds die, and the insurer needs $13,641 (0.86 × $15,814) at the beginning of the first year to pay these claims.

Therefore, at the beginning of the first year, the insurer will need to have on hand the present value of all the money that it must pay as death claims. This sum equals $63,876. When the total present value of the claims is divided by the 10,000 people purchasing the insurance, it produces a premium of $6.38. Thus, in exchange for a net single premium of $6.38, a 35-year-old male could purchase a promise from the insurer to pay a beneficiary $1,000 if he should die within the next five years.

As a general formula, the calculation for the premium is as follows:

(Number of deaths in a given year/Number of insureds at the beginning of the plan) × ($1,000 death benefit) × (Present value in a given year, discounted at the specified rate)

Thus, for the first year of the five-year term plan, given a 3 percent interest rate, the formula equals:

$$12.4/10{,}000 \times \$1000 \times 0.97 = \$1.20$$

In the fifth year, the formula calls for the following:

$$15.814/10{,}000 \times \$1000 \times 0.86 = \$1.36$$

The sum of the five annual premiums equals $6.38.

Single-Premium, Whole Life Insurance

Assume that our 35-year-old male consumer wants to purchase a single-premium, whole life insurance policy from the insurer. What is the net single premium? The insurer promises to pay the beneficiary $1,000 whenever death occurs. Furthermore, if the insured is alive at age 120, he collects the policy's maturity value.

To calculate the premium, we must make 85 calculations—one for each year in which the insured may die between the ages 35 and 120. The first five calculations are identical to the ones just completed for the five-year term policy. Another 80 calculations in the same format would follow. Each year the probability of death and the present value amount would change. When we calculate the total amount of premiums for 65 years, it equals $291.

In exchange for $291, the insurer agrees to pay a beneficiary $1,000 whenever death occurs. Once you understand the mathematical concept resulting in the $291 net single premium, we can explore several other interesting concepts.

One conclusion is the high net single premium for whole life insurance keeps this method of payment from being useful to most consumers. If a 35-year-old male consumer needed $500,000 of life insurance, the net single premium would be $145,500.00 (500 × $291). This large outlay is the reason that insurers developed the level-premium method of payment for whole life insurance.

Leveling the Whole Life Premium

Because the single premium required to purchase whole life insurance is impractical for most people to pay, life insurers developed a different system of premium payment: the level-premium (or continuous-premium) plan. The level-premium plan begins with the net single premium. I will abandon mathematical calculations at this point and simply present the concepts. The interested reader should refer to an actuarial textbook.

Two factors are considered when leveling the premium—interest and mortality, which are the same two factors that we used to calculate the net single premium. In arriving at a net single premium of $291 for a 35-year-old man, the insurer assumed that it would have the entire premium on hand at the beginning of the policy period. It assumed that it would earn 3 percent interest on this sum to pay its death claims. If the insured pays level premiums rather than the lump sum of $291, however, not all the interest that would have been earned is available. The missing interest must be included in the level premium.

To be more specific, a man at age 35 could be expected to pay a maximum of 65 continuous premiums. The size of these level premiums cannot be found by dividing $291 by 65, however. A good deal of interest that the insurer would earn on the $291 must be included in the level premiums. A second factor is even more obvious than the missing interest, however. Not all insureds who begin to pay a series of 65 level payments live to complete all the payments. In fact, only a few people live to age 120.

Thus, a charge must be added to the level premiums for those insureds that do not live to age 119 to pay their premiums. These missing premiums, like the missing interest, raise the level premium well beyond the result of $291 divided by 65 ($4.48).

For the purpose of illustration, we assume the annual net level premium for a whole life policy issued to a 35-year-old man is $12.50. That is, the life insurance company is willing to accept from the insured the promise to pay $12.50 so long as he remains alive, in exchange for the promise to pay a beneficiary $1,000 whenever the insured dies.

Some students rather easily understand the actuarial concepts just described. Other students find these ideas challenging. Either way, once readers understand the mathematics of life insurance, it becomes easier to see the differences between the policy types described in this chapter. The main distinction between the various policies centers on whether savings accumulate, and if they do, how insurers invest these savings. The mortality table and compound interest remain the essential building blocks of all the different kinds of life insurance policies.

16

Standard Life Insurance Contract Provisions and Options

After studying this chapter, you should be able to

■ Distinguish between the insured, the owner, and the beneficiary of a life insurance policy

■ Describe some common contractual provisions commonly found in life insurance policies

■ Describe several valuable legal rights held by of the owner of a life insurance policy

■ Describe several options made available to the policyowner, including the dividend options, settlement options, nonforfeiture options, and policy loans

■ Explain why some extra-cost options are more valuable than others

This chapter describes some contractual provisions that are commonly found in many life insurance policies. No standardized life insurance policies exist. However, life insurance policies must include certain contractual provisions that are required by each state's insurance laws, which vary across the country. In comparing state insurance laws, the state of New York is very influential in the regulation of life insurers due to the Appleton Rule (see Chapter 10, "Insurance Regulation"). Thus, New York's insurance regulations apply not only to insurers as they conduct business in that state, but more generally when such insurers are conducting business in other states as well. Portions of this chapter will thus refer to New York's insurance regulation in view of the state's significant role in life insurance regulation.[1]

INSURED, OWNER, AND BENEFICIARY—WHO'S WHO?

A life insurance policy creates three distinct classifications of interest: insured, owner, and beneficiary. The **insured** is the person whose death causes the insurer to pay the claim. The **owner** is the person who may exercise the rights created by the contract.

---

[1] For additional discussion of the extraterritorial regulatory influence of New York, please see Steven W. Pottier and David W. Sommer, "Regulatory Stringency and New York Licensed Life Insurers," *Journal of Risk and Insurance*, 1998, Vol. 65, No. 3, pp. 485–502.

The **beneficiary** is the person receiving the proceeds when the insured dies. A person, a trust, an estate, or a business may be a beneficiary. One person may be both insured and owner, or owner and beneficiary. A person cannot be both insured and beneficiary, however.

The owner of the life insurance policy has the right to name a beneficiary. If the owner retains the right to change beneficiaries after the initial choice, the beneficiary is called a **revocable beneficiary**. The owner cannot change an **irrevocable beneficiary**. Generally, the revocable beneficiary has no rights in the policy while the insured is alive. An irrevocable beneficiary has a vested interest in the death benefit and can prevent the owner from taking any action—such as terminating the policy or borrowing from it—that reduces the beneficiary's interest.

Policyowners should identify the beneficiary clearly. A designation such as "my wife" or "my children" can lead to litigation in cases of multiple marriages, children born of different marriages, or illegitimate children. To prevent confusion, the owner may designate "my wife, Marie Antoinette," or "all the children born of my marriage to Marie Antoinette, share and share alike." Usually, policyowners name *primary* (first) and *contingent* (second, third, etc.) *beneficiaries* to deal with the problems arising if the primary beneficiary predeceases the insured. An example of a successive beneficiary designation is: "Proceeds to my wife (Cathy T. Grate). If my wife predeceases me, then to my children (Tom, Dick, and Harry Grate)—share and share alike. If both my wife and my children predecease me, then to the American Red Cross."

In cases involving frequent beneficiary changes or unclear beneficiary designations, the insurer can transfer the policy proceeds to the court and let the court decide who is rightfully entitled to the money. In other cases of ambiguity, such as the aftermath of catastrophes involving multiple deaths where the order of deaths, or even the fact of death of a missing person, might arise, insurers can use the court system to resolve legal issues. Attorneys call this process **interpleader**. Interpleader relieves the insurer from having to make restitution to an injured party if the "wrong" person is paid the policy benefits.

GENERAL LIFE INSURANCE POLICY PROVISIONS

Most states do not require all life insurance policies to have identical or standard wording. The states instead require that approved policies satisfy at least the minimum provisions of the law. Thus, the wording and the format of life insurance policies sold in a single state by different insurers may differ from one another. Rather than specify exact wording, a state's insurance regulation may simply require that certain legal topics are addressed in the policy but allow the insurer to write its own specific provisions, subject to approval by insurance regulators. For example, life insurance contracts issued in New York are required to include the following provisions: grace period, reinstatement, incontestability clause, entire-contract provision, misstatement of age provision, and a provision requiring the annual apportionment of surplus. In addition to these mandatory provisions, many companies include optional clauses and features.

Grace Period

If the insured neglects to pay a premium when it is due, the policy does not end immediately. Before the due date, the insurer will send the insured a notice of when the premium is due. If the insured forgets to pay the premium or decides to end the contract, the **grace period** provides him or her an amount of time, typically 30 or 31 days, to pay the premium without forfeiting any contractual rights. If the policyholder dies during the grace period, the insurer will pay the proceeds, minus the overdue premium, to the beneficiary. If the policyholder does not pay the premium before the end of the grace period, however, the policy is said to have lapsed.

A **lapsed policy** means that the insured voluntarily has given up the life insurance contract. Letting a life insurance policy lapse usually is expensive to the insured and to the insurer. Because most of the expenses of acquiring the life insurance policy and putting it in force occur in the first year of the policy, these expenses must be recovered in the early years of the contract or the insurer loses money. These acquisition costs include the salesperson's commission, the cost of a medical examination, and administration costs.

When insureds let a policy lapse, it often means they have become displeased with their purchase or cannot afford to pay the premiums. Perhaps the insured purchased the wrong type of policy, found a better offer from another insurer, or no longer needs the insurance. Whatever the reason, a lapsed life insurance policy represents a mistake—often an expensive one.

If an insured allows a policy that has accumulated a cash value to lapse, the policy provides the owner several choices with respect to having the cash value returned. We describe these nonforfeiture options later in this chapter.

The Reinstatement Provision

After a policy lapses, the insured has an opportunity to reinstate (renew) it if specified conditions are met. The opportunity to renew a lapsed policy is called the **reinstatement provision**. For example, New York has a limit of three years from the date of default in which the owner may reinstate the policy. The insured must not have withdrawn the cash surrender value. Other conditions that must be met to reinstate a policy are the following:

- Evidence of insurability, including good health
- Payment of all premiums in default, with interest
- Repayment or reinstatement of any policy loans, with interest

Evidence of insurability means that the insured is in good health and is not engaged in any dangerous occupations or hobbies. Insurers require payment of all defaulted premiums with compound interest. Likewise, the owner must repay any outstanding policy loans with interest.

You may ask why a consumer would want to reinstate a policy rather than purchase a new one because the requirements for reinstatement are the same with respect to insurability. Furthermore, reinstatement usually involves a larger outlay of cash than starting a new policy because all past unpaid premiums must be repaid with interest. The answer is that by reinstating a lapsed policy, the consumer avoids being charged a second time for the large initial expenses of a new policy. Also, after a policy has been reinstated, the cash value is restored immediately. The premium will be lower on the reinstated policy because it was issued at an earlier age. An additional factor may be a change in policy terms from one series of policies to the next, with the original policy having more favorable terms. Two other considerations also may be pertinent. When the policy is reinstated, the suicide clause time period does not restart, and only statements made for the purpose of reinstatement are contestable until a new time period expires. The incontestable clause is discussed just below; the suicide clause (an optional provision) will be discussed shortly.

The Incontestable Clause

Insurance contracts are contracts made in utmost good faith, which means that an applicant may not answer questions untruthfully or conceal information that an honest person would reveal. If an insured (or owner) lies or conceals material facts, the insurer may go to court and contest the policy for the purpose of voiding it. The **incontestable clause** states that if there is a valid contract between the insurer and insured, the insurer may not contest the policy to void it after the policy has been in force for a one-year or two-year period. Thus, a life insurer has only a relatively short period of time in which to discover any fraud. Generally, after the specified time has elapsed, the insurer cannot void the policy even if a notorious fraud is uncovered. This solution balances the right of the insurer to know the truth when entering the contract with the innocent beneficiary's right of recovery.

A life insurance policy may be ended if the premiums are not paid. Also, suspected fraudulent claims for accidental death benefits or disability income benefits can be contested. Likewise, an insurer may go to court and try to establish that a valid contract never existed between the two parties. But in general, the incontestable clause prevents an insurer from avoiding claims payments. It is interesting to note that this clause was included voluntarily in the contracts of some life insurers after 1850. The motive was to establish public confidence. Such a public relations effort was required because a few disreputable life insurers were voiding contracts on the slightest technical grounds.

The Misstatement-of-Age Provision

The incontestable clause prevents an insurer from voiding a policy because of an insured's misrepresentations. Because the applicant's age is a key factor in underwriting and pricing the insurance, a misstatement of age, either intentionally or by mistake, causes pricing errors. The **misstatement-of-age provision** allows the insurer to adjust the face amount of insurance to reflect the insured's true age, rather than allowing the insurer to void a policy if a misstatement is discovered. For example, if the insured, Ann Alitic, reported her age to be three years less than it actually was, the benefits, $100,000, would have to be reduced to $92,000, or whatever amount of insurance the premiums would purchase at the insured's true age.

The Entire-Contract Provision

Most states require that the written policy, including the application for the insurance when attached to the policy, constitute the entire contract between the parties. The **entire-contract provision** serves two purposes. It allows the insured a chance to review the answers as they are recorded in the application, and it prevents the insurer from making any hidden document or undisclosed restrictions a part of the contract. Historically, some companies incorporated their bylaws in their contracts by reference only, thus frustrating beneficiaries seeking death proceeds.

The entire-contract clause explains why the handwritten insurance application is often attached to each contract. Including the application provides a chance for policyowners to verify the statements made in the application, which is now a part of the contract. Only information based upon the attached statements can be contested within the contestable period. An insured should thus review the application carefully, especially to assure that all oral responses were recorded accurately.

Annual Apportionment of Divisible Surplus

Life insurers use two different methods to price their policies. **Participating policies**, typically issued by mutual life insurers, set prices by charging the policyowner a relatively large initial premium, followed at the end of the year by a dividend. The participating premium is relatively large because insurers use conservative estimates of mortality, administrative expenses, and interest earnings to determine the figure. For instance, assumed mortality losses may be 20 percent higher than actuarial estimates. When the bad results do not occur, the excess premium is returned to the policyholder as a dividend. The return of the overcharge is not comparable to the payment of common stock cash dividends, and it is not treated as a dividend for tax purposes.

Nonparticipating (nonpar) policies use more realistic projections of operating results and require a lower initial premium. Nonpar policies do not pay dividends to policyholders at the end of the year, but some modern forms credit excess interest payments if the insurer earns investment returns beyond the guaranteed rate.

Participating dividends or excess interest payments are not guaranteed, a fact that is not well understood by many consumers. For example, many states have adopted insurance regulations that require insurance companies to provide **policy illustrations**, financial projections showing the dividend and cash value accumulations on their life insurance policies based on their current mortality and investment experience, to prospective customers. When presented with computer-generated policy illustrations, many consumers assume that the dividends were guaranteed, rather than nonguaranteed forecasted projections. Thus, if conditions improve, as would be the case if years were added to our life expectancy, dividends would increase. If conditions get worse (say, if life expectancy decreases), dividends would decrease accordingly. Similarly, if investment earnings rise or fall substantially, dividends or excess interest payments are affected.

New York law requires that once a year, the life insurance company issuing a participating policy must determine whether any dividends are payable to its policyholders from the surplus, or earnings, that it generated over the year. If there is a divisible surplus, the insurer must pay dividends. This requirement prevents insurance companies from retaining the dividends and not paying them to policyholders who die or let their policies lapse.[2]

The Suicide Clause and Other Restrictive Clauses

Many state insurance laws allow a life insurer to exclude payment for death by suicide if the suicide occurs within two years from the policy issue date. The purpose of the **suicide clause** is to control the moral hazard. (Many insurance companies have a one-year restriction that is more favorable to the policyholder and is permissible under law.) After the two-year restriction, the company will pay for suicide deaths. One explanation of the two-year restriction is that, after the waiting period, the suicide presumably was not planned by the insured at the time she applied for insurance and therefore, this is not a case of adverse selection.

In addition to the suicide clause, state laws also may allow certain restrictive clauses. Policies including *war restrictions* may exclude death while in the military or

---

[2] Before 1900, many insurers made dividend payments only to the longest-living member of an insurance pool, a plan called the *tontine system*. The tontine led to serious consumer abuses and therefore is forbidden by the divisible surplus requirement. The abuses stemmed from the potentially long time period before the insurer had to pay the accumulated dividends. Under the now-outlawed tontine arrangement, the insurer could control the money and the compound interest thereon for decades, promising to pay (generous) dividends to the small number of survivors.

death caused by military action. A policy with *aviation restrictions* may restrict payments for deaths from accidents involving noncommercial flights. Some policies may include *hazardous occupation restrictions* that reduce or eliminate payment if the insured changes to a more hazardous occupation.

OPTIONS THAT PROVIDE THE POLICYOWNER WITH CHOICES

Life insurers typically provide their policyowners with choices related to several different coverage features, including dividend options, nonforfeiture options, policyholder loans, and settlement options.

Dividend Options

As we noted earlier, participating insurance policies pay dividends to the policyowner. Owners may choose what form the dividends take. The following are four standard dividend options:

- Dividends may be taken in cash.
- Dividends may be used to pay a portion of the next premium.
- Dividends may be left in an account with the insurer to accumulate at interest.
- Dividends may be used to purchase single-premium, paid-up insurance. For example, a $50 dividend may purchase $123 of paid-up whole life insurance at age 40. At the insured's death, the beneficiary receives the sum of the paid-up additions, plus the face amount of the policy. Even if the insured has become uninsurable, the owner still may acquire more life insurance using this dividend option.

Some companies offer other dividend options in addition to these four, including allowing owners to use the dividend to purchase one-year term insurance. This dividend option often limits the additional term insurance the owner can purchase to the amount of the policy's cash value. Some companies allow the purchase of a combination of term and paid-up whole life insurance with dividends. Using dividend options allows insureds to increase coverage without incurring acquisition costs and without having to provide evidence of insurability. Thus, dividend options create flexibility in a consumer's life insurance plan.

Nonforfeiture Options

In general business, if one party fails to complete contractual arrangements as called for, the other party may void the contract and perhaps confiscate property to satisfy a debt. If a life insurance company were allowed to cancel a life insurance policy for nonpayment of premiums, the consumer would be seriously disadvantaged. Insureds in poor health and unable to make payments would be clear losers, as would insureds with large savings accumulated in the life insurance policy. To prevent such injustices, the law provides that life insurance policies that have a savings value are not forfeited if the policies are lapsed. Instead, insurers are required by law to provide to their policyowners **nonforfeiture options**, or options in which the policyowner can use the existing cash value on a terminated or lapsed policy.[3]

---

[3] Elizur Wright, one of the first insurance commissioners of Massachusetts, led the efforts to provide nonforfeiture options to policyowners. Wright was an early champion of the insurance consumer. In addition to the nonforfeiture requirement, he promoted more complete disclosure of financial information on life insurance companies and the legal reserve basis of accounting for the liabilities of life insurance companies.

When an insured stops paying premiums on a continuous-premium whole life policy or other policy that requires more payments, regulations typically require that the insurer must grant the policyowner at least three nonforfeiture options: cash, term insurance, and whole life insurance that is fully paid up, but for an amount less than the original policy.

Assume that 60-year-old Johann S. Bach has a continuous-premium whole life insurance policy on which he has paid premiums for twenty years. The contract requires payments until age 100, but Johann decides to stop making premium payments. The face amount of his insurance is $400,000, and the cash value is $166,800. When he stops making his premium payments, Johann may ask for the $166,800 in a lump sum from the insurer. This situation illustrates the first option, taking the **cash surrender value**. If the cash is withdrawn in this manner, the policy may not be reinstated and ordinary income taxes may be incurred.

As a second option, Johann may choose to convert to a term insurance policy that provides the same face amount as his whole life policy, $400,000. The insurer will determine how long the $400,000 of term insurance will continue if a $166,800 premium were paid. Assume that the answer is 14 years and 4 months. Thus, without paying another premium, Johann could continue with $400,000 of life insurance protection. However, when he reached age 74 and 4 months, the insurance protection and the cash value would be gone, and the term insurance has no cash value. Insurers call this option the **extended-term option**. A policy lapsed under this option may be reinstated under the reinstatement provision.

As a third nonforfeiture option, Johann may choose a reduced amount of paid-up life insurance. That is, he currently has a $400,000 whole life policy with $166,800 cash value. If he stops paying premiums, he may choose a fully paid-up whole life policy with a face amount of $212,500. This option is called the **reduced paid-up insurance option**. A policy lapsed under this option also is subject to the reinstatement provisions.

In our example, Johann S. Bach had a whole life policy; any policy with a cash surrender value would offer a choice of three standard nonforfeiture options. Policies such as ten-pay whole life and life paid up at 65 show cash values after the first few years. All these policies have a nonforfeiture value. If an owner does not choose a nonforfeiture option after lapsing a policy, the insurer automatically chooses one. Frequently, the extended-term option is the automatic choice.

Insurance companies generally allow owners to convert cash-value life insurance to annuities. For example, Hunter Fischer, the famous outdoorsman, buys a $150,000 whole life insurance policy when he is 30 years old. He pays a level premium every year. Assume that Hunter lives to be age 65, he no longer has dependent children, his mortgage is paid, and his need for life insurance no longer exists. He now needs a regular stream of income in retirement. Thus, he converts his life insurance policy to an annuity.

For example, assume that Hunter Fischer's $150,000 whole life policy has a cash value of $130,000 when he reaches age 65, and he uses the cash value to purchase a single-premium immediate pure annuity. The annuity guarantees payment of about $1,000 a month for the rest of his life. It generally is more efficient to convert the cash value contract than to purchase a new annuity contract for the following reasons: (1) no new acquisitions charges and commissions occur, and (2) a cash-value life insurance contract may have more favorable annuity assumptions than a new updated annuity contract, which will predict that people live longer lives.

Policyholder Loans

Life insurance policies with cash surrender values have a **loan provision**. This provision gives the policyowner the right to borrow an amount of money less than or equal to the cash value of the policy. The company generally has the right to delay making the loan for up to six months.

The interest rate charged for the loan is stated in the policy. Unless the policy provides for variable rates, it remains unchanged even though general interest rates fluctuate. While older policies may include interest rates that range from 6 to 8 percent, most new policies use variable rates that change with prevailing market interest rates.

The **policyholder loan** is secured by the cash surrender value of the insurance policy. The insured is not legally required to repay the loan. If the loan is outstanding when the insured dies, the insurer deducts the amount of the loan and accrued interest from the insurance proceeds. If the loan and the accumulated interest exceed the accumulated cash value, then the policy lapses. Taking a loan against a life insurance policy is one alternative to surrendering the policy for its cash value. Taking a loan leaves the policy and some of the life insurance protection in force.

Some insureds may wonder why they must pay interest to the insurer when they are borrowing their own savings. The answer is fairly simple. When the premiums were calculated, the insurance company assumed that it would earn compound interest on the money. If this interest is not earned, the premium calculation becomes inaccurate. Thus, if Johann S. Bach borrows the $166,800 cash value of his policy, interest is charged. Yet he still may not have to pay the interest out of his own pocket. If the policy is a participating policy, the dividends may more than cover the interest charges. However, some insurers calculate differing levels of dividends for borrowed and unborrowed portions of the cash value. That is, if Johann Bach borrows only half of his cash value, he may earn 3 percent interest on the borrowed half and a 6 percent return on the unborrowed half. In either case, the cash value on policies, including those having outstanding loans, continues to increase. However, compound interest on the unpaid loan requires ever-increasing dividends to prevent the policy from lapsing.

The **automatic premium loan (APL)** provision, which typically is found in policies that have a cash surrender value, modifies the policy so that the insurer will advance a policy loan to the insured for the purpose of paying the premium. Thus, if an insured does not pay the premium when due and the grace period expires (and there is sufficient cash value), the insurer makes an automatic loan to the insured to pay the overdue premium. The automatic premium loan thus prevents policies from lapsing due to unpaid premium charges.

Settlement Options

Settlement options specify how the death proceeds are paid to the beneficiary. These options are available in both term and whole life policies and provide considerable payment flexibility to the beneficiary. Five common settlement options are the cash, fixed amount, fixed period, interest, and life income options. Figure 16-1 provides a review of the dividend, nonforfeiture, and settlement options found in life insurance policies.

FIGURE 16-1 Typical Life Insurance Policy Options

DIVIDEND OPTIONS	NONFORFEITURE OPTIONS	SETTLEMENT OPTIONS
• Cash	• Cash	• Cash
• Premium Payments	• Paid-up Whole Life Insurance	• Fixed-amount Payment
• Paid-up Additions	• Extended Term Insurance	• Fixed-period Payment
• Accumulation at Interest		• Interest Only
• Term Insurance		• Life Income

With the **cash option**, the beneficiary simply receives the life insurance proceeds in a single cash payment. Most policies are paid using the cash option. If no other settlement option is chosen, insurers pay the proceeds in cash.

The **fixed-amount option** provides the beneficiary with regular, fixed-income payments. Interest income is earned on balances that remain with the insurer. Federal income tax applies to the interest portion of these payments. The payments continue until the death proceeds and the interest thereon are exhausted. This option is logical when people need income for a limited period, such as while Social Security benefits are unavailable or when they want to create and contribute to an education fund. Using this option, the beneficiary can receive an insurance payment before each tuition bill.

The **fixed-period option** is similar to the fixed-amount option. With the fixed-amount option, the choice of the amount of each payment determines how long the payments will last. With the fixed-period option, the choice of the length of the period determines the size of each payment. This option might be used to fund a college education over a fixed four-year period.

Under the **interest-only option**, the proceeds are left with the insured. The insurer pays the first beneficiary (for example, the widow) regular payments composed entirely of interest earnings. After the first beneficiary's death, the insurer pays the death proceeds to a second beneficiary, such as a child. The interest-only arrangement can be useful, for example, if the first beneficiary has substantial investment, wage, or Social Security income.

The **life-income option** guarantees for a lifetime a series of regular payments to the beneficiary. (This choice is an *annuity* option; the details of annuities are presented in Chapter 17, "Annuities.") In its simplest form, the insurer makes payments under this option only if the beneficiary is alive. Assume that Mrs. Johann S. Bach receives the proceeds of a $400,000 policy under the life-income option, getting $50,000-a-year payments, and that she lives only three years beyond old Johann (after all, they had twenty children, which can take a lot out of a person). So she received only $150,000 of the benefits. The remainder of the money is retained by the insurer, where it is used to pay benefits to other annuitants in the risk pool who live well past their life expectancy.

Despite the potential for "losing" some of the death proceeds, the life-income settlement option can be quite practical. A beneficiary's need for income ends when the beneficiary dies. In some cases, there may be no dependent beneficiaries other than a surviving spouse. The life-income option can provide a sure source of income to the surviving spouse because the payments are guaranteed for life. Because the payments include a portion of principal, they will exceed interest-only payments significantly at later ages. This settlement option makes good sense if the surviving spouse is inexperienced in investing money. It is also useful if the surviving spouse has an unscrupulous relative or friend who may talk the beneficiary out of the money if a large lump sum of cash is paid.

AVAILABLE RIDERS AND OPTIONS

In addition to the more common policy provisions discussed so far in this chapter, life insurance policies also can be purchased with a variety of extra-cost options. Three of the more common options or riders are guaranteed insurability, waiver of premium, and double indemnity.

The Guaranteed-Insurability Option

If insureds purchase the **guaranteed-insurability option**, they obtain the legal right to purchase more insurance at predetermined intervals and at standard rates, regardless

CHAPTER 16   Standard Life Insurance Contract Provisions and Options   **255**

of changes in insurability. For example, this option may provide the right to purchase an additional $20,000 of insurance on every third anniversary of the policy issue date until the insured reaches the age of 38. If the policy was issued at age 20, the insured could purchase an additional $120,000 of life insurance. An option that is not used is forfeited, but any future options remain available. Some companies allow an additional purchase at marriage or at the birth of children.

This option can prove valuable to insureds whose health declines significantly after purchasing the life insurance. The cost of including this option in the policy is relatively modest. With one well-known company, the cost is about $2 for every $1,000 of insurance that can be purchased under the option. This company limits the total amount of insurance available for purchase under the option to twice the face amount of the original policy. With a $50,000 original policy, an additional $100,000 could be purchased, for a maximum total of $150,000 of life insurance. Naturally, each time more insurance is purchased, the premium increases. The increased premium is based on the insured's age at the time he or she exercises the option.

The Waiver-of-Premium Option

The **waiver-of-premium option** provides a valuable right for the insured. If the insured becomes totally disabled, the insurer forgives any premium due during the period of disability, and the life insurance policy remains in force. Usually a six-month waiting period applies to the benefit. Moreover, even though the insured pays no premiums while disabled, participating dividends are paid and cash values continue to increase according to schedule.

The cost for the waiver-of-premium option usually is modest. For a whole life policy on a male aged 25 offered by one well-known company, the cost is about $0.30 a year for each $1,000 of insurance. Some companies include the waiver-of-premium provision as a part of their whole life contracts rather than as an extra-cost option.

The Double-Indemnity Option

The **double-indemnity option** provides that if the insured's death is a result of a specified peril, essentially some form of accident, twice the face value of the policy will be paid. Some companies take this idea one step further and pay higher multiples of the policy face value if death occurs from an accident on a common carrier or in some other specific type of accident or circumstance.

Critics object to this option, claiming it is inconsistent with the needs-based life insurance purchase. If a family needs $260,000 of insurance proceeds if the wage earner dies prematurely, it needs this amount whether the death results from a heart attack or a plane accident.

Other objections to double- or multiple-indemnity provisions include the misdirection of consumer dollars spent for the option. A typical cost is $0.75 a year per $1,000 of insurance. This money may be better spent on increasing the face amount of protection.

In defense of the option, some people believe that it makes the life insurance policy easier to sell to individuals who otherwise would not make the purchase. Also, between the ages of 20 and 40, a higher percentage of deaths are attributable to accidents than to nonaccidental causes. These arguments, however, do not refute the point that informed consumers should not base the amount of life insurance that they purchase on the chance that they will die in an accident.

Summary

Life insurance policies do not have the standardized format, such as those found in homeowners insurance or in personal automobile insurance policies. However, they do have several general provisions required by state law. This chapter has discussed a variety of provisions that are required across a wide number of states, including policy reinstatements and grade periods; incontestability and misstatement of age clauses; entire contract provisions; and the allocation of surplus through dividend payment.

The chapter also describes several of the options that typically are included in many life insurance policies. For example, participating policies provide the policyowner a variety of ways to receive dividend payments: cash, a reduction of the next premium payment, accumulations at interest, the purchase of paid-up whole life insurance, or the purchase of one-year term insurance.

If an insured (owner) allows a policy with cash value to lapse, a nonforfeiture option applies. This option allows the insured three choices: (1) receive the cash surrender value, (2) receive a reduced amount of paid-up whole life insurance, or (3) receive term insurance in an amount equal to the face of the lapsed policy. The length of the term is determined by the cash value of the policy before it was lapsed.

Policyholders have the legal right to borrow their policy's cash value. They are charged interest on such policyholder loans, but the loans (and, in some cases, the interest) need not be repaid in cash. Insurers subtract unpaid loan balances from death proceeds.

After an insured dies, the beneficiary may receive the proceeds in one of five ways. Most beneficiaries take a lump sum of cash. Other choices include regular payments of a fixed amount or regular payments for a limited period of time. Some beneficiaries take just the interest earned on the proceeds and have the principal go to a second beneficiary. The life-income option promises payments as long as the beneficiary lives.

Life insurers sell extra-cost options. The guaranteed-insurability option gives an insured the right to purchase additional amounts of insurance regardless of changes in health. The waiver-of-premium option allows insureds to omit premium payments due while the insured is totally disabled. Even though insureds do not pay premiums, dividends and scheduled increases in cash value continue to be earned. A questionable option is one providing for multiples of the face amount of insurance if an insured dies from accidental causes. Insurers call this option the double-indemnity option.

Review

1. Define the terms *insured*, *owner*, and *beneficiary*.
2. Give the reasons for a life insurance policy containing each of the following provisions:
   a. Grace period
   b. Reinstatement
   c. Incontestable clause
   d. Entire-contract clause
   e. Misstatement-of-age clause
   f. Annual apportionment of divisible surplus
   g. Loan
3. What is a lapsed life insurance policy? What are some possible causes of lapsing? Is a lapsed policy a problem or a benefit to the insured? To the insurer?
4. Give some reasons why an insured might prefer to reinstate an existing policy that has lapsed rather than begin a new one.
5. Does the incontestable clause mean that an insured always "gets away with" fraud against the insurer? Is the purpose of the incontestable clause to protect the insured from fraud? Does the incontestable clause encourage fraud?
6. What will an insurer do if it learns that an applicant misstated his or her age on a life insurance application? Buster Brown knowingly tells the insurer that his age is 28 when he is actually 38. What effect will this lie have on his insurance contract?
7. Describe some of the differences between participating and nonparticipating life insurance. Which plan should a consumer purchase?
8. Are participating dividends guaranteed?
9. Identify four dividend options.
10. Describe the three typical nonforfeiture options. Why do insurers offer nonforfeiture options? Illustrate the three nonforfeiture options in the case of John Brahms, who currently has a policy with $24,000 of cash value. John is 38 years old.
11. Do insureds have a legal right to a loan secured by their cash value? Describe some circumstances when

a policyholder loan provision is an advantage to the insured but a disadvantage to the insurer.
12. What is an automatic premium loan?
13. Explain five different settlement options. Give an example where each alternative might be useful.
14. Describe the benefits provided by the guaranteed-insurability and waiver-of-premium options.
15. What are some objections to the double-indemnity option? What is the justification for this option?

Objective Questions

1. In a life insurance policy, the owner is the party:
   a. Who receives the death benefits
   b. Who can exercise the contractual rights, such as naming the beneficiary
   c. Whose death causes the policy to pay death benefits
   d. None of the above
2. The policy provision that allows premiums to be paid after the due date is called:
   a. The lapse provision
   b. The past-due premium provision
   c. The redemption provision
   d. The grace period provision
3. The effect of the incontestable clause is:
   a. To prevent insurers from contesting policies after a year or two from the policy's beginning
   b. To prevent insureds from suing the life insurer after a year or two from the policy's beginning
   c. To prevent insurers from changing policy provisions after a year or two from the policy's beginning
   d. To allow insurers to change policy provisions after a year or two from the policy's beginning
4. Which of the following alternatives is not a typical dividend option?
   a. A lifetime income annuity
   b. Cash
   c. Accumulation at interest
   d. Reduction of the next premium

5. The settlement option that pays a monthly amount until death is an annuity called:
   a. The fixed-period option
   b. The fixed-amount option
   c. The life-income option
   d. The fixed-death option
6. The person who receives the proceeds of a life insurance policy is called:
   a. The beneficiary
   b. The receiver in due course
   c. The policyowner
   d. The insured
7. If an insured voluntarily gives up the life insurance contract, the policy is:
   a. Reinstated
   b. On extended warranty
   c. Foreclosed
   d. Lapsed
8. If an insured misstates her age, the insurer:
   a. Recalculates the amount of insurance based on the insured's true age
   b. Cancels the policy as soon as the misstatement is discovered
   c. Sues the insured for breach of contract
   d. Withholds payment if the misstatement is discovered after the insured's death, or rescinds the policy if the misstatement is discovered during the insured's lifetime

Discussion Questions

1. Ed Jenner purchased a $400,000 continuous-premium whole life policy fifteen years ago. Today, the policy has a cash value of $230,000. If Ed were to die tomorrow and his beneficiary were to take the policy proceeds as a cash settlement, list several different reasons why the amount of cash could be more or less than $400,000.
2. Do you think that dividends should be paid to policyholders who have borrowed all their cash value? If you believe that dividends should be paid to these borrowers, do you think that the rate on dividends should be the same for nonborrowers if the insurer can earn substantially more income on the money it invests than on the policyholder-loan charge?
3. Can a life insurance company deny a claim on a valid policy if the insured dies?

Selected References

Black, Kenneth Jr., and Harold D. Skipper, Jr., 2000, *Life Insurance*, 13th ed. (Upper Saddle River, NJ: Prentice Hall).

17

Annuities

After studying this chapter, you should be able to

- Explain the purpose of an annuity
- Identify five different ways that annuities can be classified or described
- Explain why some annuities come with guarantees
- Identify the special features of a variable annuity
- Explain the income tax treatment of annuities

An annuity contract makes the accumulation and liquidation of wealth possible. Many people purchase annuities to finance their retirement because insurance companies can guarantee that the annuitant cannot outlive the stream of income. That is, the insurer can guarantee payments to the annuitant until the annuitant dies. The insurer makes this guarantee based on the insurance principles described in Chapter 3, "Risk Assessment and Pooling": the pooling of many similar exposures to loss to increase predictability using the law of large numbers.

Sometimes people mistakenly describe annuities as insurance that provides protection from living a long time. While this description sounds like a loss that many people would like, it is somewhat misleading. Instead, a better description of an annuity is an insurance product that protects the annuitant from outliving her retirement income. Since old age without money can be a calamity, annuities are often an essential component in retirement planning.

Many people acquire annuity protection by participating in a pension plan. When the employer agrees to provide retirement income, the income is an annuity promise to the retiree. Because of tax advantages, the public's awareness of increasing life spans, and the work of professional financial planners and financial services companies, individually purchased annuities have become increasingly popular. This chapter's appendix describes some of the innovations and product developments that are available in the annuity marketplace.

DEFINITIONS

Financiers describe any regular series of periodic payments, such as $1,000 each year for ten years, as an **annuity**.[1] An *annuity insurance policy* (from here on referred to simply as an *annuity*) is a contract in which the insurer promises the insured, called the **annuitant**, a series of periodic payments, often for a lifetime. If, after the death of the annuitant(s), guaranteed payments continue to a second beneficiary, this person is a **successor beneficiary**.

An annuity insurance operation transfers funds from those who die at a relatively early age to those who live to relatively old ages. That is, some annuitants will live to take out much more than they paid in premiums. (Annuity premiums technically are called *considerations*. For simplicity, we will continue to call them *premiums*.) Other annuitants will not live long enough to take out as much as they paid in premiums. An insurance company earns interest on all the money in the pool. Therefore, the annuitant's payments come from three sources: the liquidation of the original premium payment, or *principal;* interest earned on the principal; and funds made available by the relatively early death of other annuitants.

Because the goal of an annuity is to provide a steady stream of payments over many years, annuity purchases often involve significant amounts of premiums, and it is common for the annuitant to pay the insurer a premium that equals hundreds of thousands of dollars. Decisions that involve such a large amount of a consumer's wealth thus require significant financial planning.

It is interesting to note that the mortality table used to predict annuity payments is not the same one used to calculate life insurance. People who purchase annuities generally live longer than people who do not. The explanation of this curious fact is adverse selection.

Adverse selection in life insurance means that those people with a greater-than-average likelihood of premature death try to purchase life insurance at regular rates. Life insurers try to prevent adverse selection by requiring medical examinations and other underwriting precautions. It is more difficult to prevent adverse selection by people purchasing annuities. Theoretically, an insurer could require a medical examination and then reject the super-healthy as poor risks, but many people would probably disapprove of an insurer rejecting healthy people.[2] Instead, insurers recognize that people who purchase annuities are generally in above-average health, which explains why they use a mortality table reflecting better-than-average mortality. Annuity mortality tables thus project longer survivorship than those used in life insurance.

Uses of Annuities and Suitability Issues

Annuity insurers guarantee a steady stream of income that the recipient cannot outlive. This guarantee is particularly valuable to workers nearing the end of their working careers, and most people use annuities to finance their retirement cash flow needs. An annuity can maximize the annual cash flow for people who are willing to liquidate their assets.

Annuities are especially useful to people in good health, as these individuals are especially vulnerable to the financial risks associated with old age. Healthy people have a great need for annuities because they are concerned about their **longevity risk**,

---

[1] The word *annuity* originated from the Latin base *annu*, suggesting a yearly occurrence. The term was first used around 1400 in England to describe a yearly allowance. Most early English municipalities were financed by selling annuities at a profit rather than by collecting taxes.

[2] Theoretically, insurers also could lower payments for people in above-average health or increase payments for people with substandard health—two options that also probably would be rather frowned upon.

the risk that they might run out of money to live on if they live far beyond the normal life expectancy. In this regard, longevity risk relates to the uncertainty about how long a person will live, as a healthy person does not know whether to allocate his or her life savings over a planning horizon of two years or twenty-two years. Annuity insurers can use risk pooling to reduce longevity risk, as it is statistically easier to forecast the mean life expectancy of a large sample of annuitants in an insurance risk pool compared to the life expectancy of a single person.

By contrast, people in poor health or who have limited life expectancies do not buy annuities frequently. In the typical annuity risk pool, the annuitant who dies well before his life expectancy gives up a sizable premium payment, which in turn is used to help pay the annuity payments of annuitants who live well past their life expectancy. People in poor health are generally less interested in buying annuities, fearing that an early death would result in the loss of a significant amount of annuity premiums.

Courts often approve the use of annuities in **structured settlements** in negligence cases. In these instances, instead of the defendant paying a lump sum to a plaintiff, the defendant (using the services of an insurer) promises a series of payments to the injured party. One benefit to the injured party is the professional money management skills that the insurer provides—skills that the injured party may not possess. A second benefit is that, whereas a large lump sum of money could be dissipated by bad decisions, the structured settlement produces guaranteed cash inflow.

CLASSIFICATION OF ANNUITIES

Insurers classify annuities using the following five criteria: the method of premium payment, the time when benefits begin, the guarantees purchased, the number of annuitants covered, and the types of benefits. Thus, a consumer may purchase an annual-premium, cash-refund, fixed-benefit, joint-and-survivor, and deferred-benefit annuity. One purpose of this section is to describe the various types of annuity contracts.

Method of Premium Payment

If an annuity is purchased with a single-premium payment, it is a **single-premium annuity**. An annuity also may be purchased by a series of annual (or more frequent) payments. Insurers call this method of premium payment an **annual-premium annuity**. For example, assume that Charles Lemain, now age 39, wants to purchase an annuity that will pay him $500 a month when he retires in 25 years, at age 65. He has four payment options:

1. One payment of $70,000 on his 65th birthday (described below as a single-premium immediate annuity)
2. A series of 25 payments of $1,600 each, beginning on his 40th birthday (described below as a level-premium deferred annuity)
3. A series of 25 unequal payments, beginning on his 40th birthday (described below as a flexible-premium deferred annuity)
4. One payment of $16,000 on his 40th birthday (described below as a single-premium deferred annuity)

With the second method, 25 payments of $1,600 equal $40,000. Where does the difference between the $70,000 for the single-premium immediate annuity and the total of $40,000 in level premiums come from? It results from the compound interest that the insurer earns on the advance payments. Compound interest also explains the difference between the one-time payment of $16,000 at age 40 and the $70,000 payment required at age 65 to receive $500 a month.

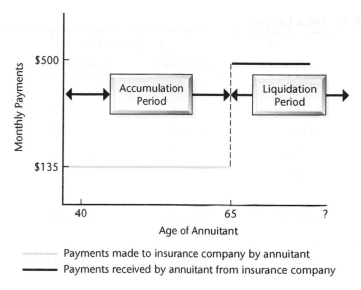

FIGURE 17-1 Annual-Premium Deferred Annuity

Beginning of Benefits

An **immediate annuity** begins to pay benefits as soon as the premiums are paid in full. If a person pays for an annuity and benefits do not begin at once, that is a **deferred annuity**.

Readers might get confused when they consider both the method of premium payment and the time that benefits begin. It is possible to purchase a single-premium *immediate* annuity. For example, Charles Lemain pays $70,000 for benefits of $500 a month beginning immediately, or he may pay a $16,000 premium, wait 25 years, and then collect benefits of $500 a month, illustrating a single-premium deferred annuity. Figure 17-1 illustrates the annual-premium deferred annuity. Insurers call the period during which the annuitant is paying premiums to the insurer the **accumulation period**. Insurers call the period during which the insurer makes payments to the annuitant the **liquidation period**. With most deferred annuities, if an annuitant dies during the accumulation period, a beneficiary is entitled to the return of the premiums, often with interest.

Single-Premium Deferred Annuity If the owner paid a single premium more than one period before the initial receipt of benefits, the contract is called a **single-premium deferred annuity (SPDA)** contract. The deposit earns compound interest at a minimum guaranteed rate, and this interest accrues on a tax-deferred basis until liquidation. In liquidation, only the interest portion of each annuity payment is taxed.

In some cases, if the insurer earns interest on its investment portfolio in excess of the minimum rate guaranteed in the contract, the insurance company credits the **excess interest** (the difference between the actual investment earnings and the minimum guaranteed earnings) to the account. However, even if the insurer's investment earnings decline below the guaranteed amount, the annuitant's earnings credit will not be less than the minimum rate guaranteed.

Typically, insurers guarantee SPDA current interest rates for one year. However, some carriers offer lower current rates but guarantee this rate for up to five years. SPDAs usually are a no-load contract with back-end surrender charges that typically

TABLE 17-1 FPDA Ledger

		8% Current Rate		3.5% Guaranteed Rate	
Year	*Annual Premium*	*Cash Value*	*Surrender Value*	*Cash Value*	*Surrender Value*
1	$1,000	$ 1,083	$ 909	$ 1,035	$ 869
2	$1,000	$ 2,255	$ 1,962	$ 2,106	$ 1,832
3	$1,000	$ 3,523	$ 3,171	$ 3,215	$ 2,893
4	$1,000	$ 4,897	$ 4,554	$ 4,362	$ 4,057
5	$1,000	$ 6,384	$ 6,129	$ 5,550	$ 5,328
...					
10	$1,000	$ 15,878	$ 15,878	$12,142	$12,142
...					
30	$1,000	$128,645	$128,645	$53,429	$53,429

decline and finally disappear over a six- to ten-year period.[3] The surrender charge allows the carrier to recover its acquisition costs if policyholders cancel the contract in its early years.

Flexible-Premium Deferred Annuity People often plan to accumulate the sum needed to purchase an annuity at retirement by purchasing a series of single-premium deferred annuities. Because insurance companies have minimum deposit requirements of about $5,000 for SPDAs, another contract, the **flexible-premium deferred annuity (FPDA)**, must be used for deposits of smaller amounts. The FPDA does not require the annuitant to make an even series of level payments. The annuitant determines the contributions within minimum-amount (typically $25) and maximum-frequency (typically monthly) limits established by the insurer. Because of this flexibility, insurers have higher administrative charges for these contracts than SPDAs. Some FPDA contracts provide for the deduction of an expense charge from each premium payment (a **front-end load**). Other contracts provide for surrender charges (a **back-end load**). And some insurers impose both front-end and back-end loads. Insurers often reduce surrender charges on a straight-line basis over time. For example, a company may assess an 8 percent charge for surrender within the first year and reduce this charge by 1 percent each year until it disappears by the ninth year.

Like the SPDA, FPDA contracts have minimum guaranteed interest rates that are well under current market rates. They also have a provision for crediting excess earnings when available. For example, the guaranteed accumulation rate may be 3.5 percent, but the carrier actually may declare a rate of 5 percent for the first year. On each policy anniversary, the insurer declares an excess interest rate for the upcoming period in keeping with the current investment climate.

Table 17-1 illustrates a ledger for an FPDA contract. In Table 17-1, we assume the annuitant makes annual deposits of $1,000. Level annual deposits are not necessary. In some years, no deposit may be made; in others, a sum much greater than $1,000 may be deposited. The table also shows the difference between the rates the insurer guarantees

---

[3] A no-load contract is one in which no explicit expense charge, known as a "load," is assessed against the first (or only) premium. Such a charge would reduce the net amount that is invested in the annuity. Instead, with a no-load annuity, issuers would recover acquisition expenses over time from the difference between the income that they earn on investments and the rate that they credit on the annuity.

(3.5 percent) and a higher rate (8 percent). This insurer imposes a 16 percent surrender charge on withdrawals during the first year. The insurer then reduces the surrender charge 3 percent each year until no surrender charge remains after the fifth year.

Guarantees Purchased

The basic annuity promise is for the insurer to agree to continue payments only so long as the annuitant is alive. Insurers call this most simple of annuity contracts a **pure annuity** or **straight-life annuity**. There is no guarantee of the total amount of money the annuitant will receive with such a contract.

For example, if Charles Lemain purchases a pure annuity for $70,000 and dies after receiving only one payment of $500, the insurer is not obligated to make any more payments. Even though Charles's estate suffers a large financial loss in our example, there is much logic behind this arrangement.[4] Charles purchased the annuity to provide retirement income, and with the pure annuity, income payments end when the need ends. Moreover, for a given amount of premium dollars, the pure annuity provides the largest monthly payments. Some financial planners suggest that if Charles were concerned about leaving funds for his survivors, he could purchase a life insurance policy in any amount, including the $70,000 amount of the annuity premium. In cases where there were no survivors (or no survivors with financial needs), or if the life insurance premiums were not affordable, then Charles would be unlikely to purchase life insurance to complement the annuity purchase. However, in other cases where survivors' needs for funds were unmet, purchasing life insurance to complement the annuity purchase could be a logical option.

Many people who purchase annuities are not happy with the thought of "losing" most of their premium payment should they die after receiving just a few annuity payments. Therefore, insurance companies allow annuitants to purchase guarantees specifying a maximum amount of dollars going to a successor beneficiary. These guarantees come with an additional price. The larger the value of the money guaranteed to be paid by the insurer, the greater the premium for a given annuity liquidation payment.

If a person wants to specify a minimum total payment to be received from the insurer, two choices are available. The individual may specify a minimum number of years in which the insurer must make a payment or choose either of two refund options.

For example, an annuity, **five-years-certain**, calls for payments for five years or until the annuitant dies, whichever event occurs last. For example, if Charles purchases such a contract and lives only one month after receiving the first payment, a successor beneficiary will receive payments for an additional four years and eleven months. Alternatively, if Charles lives for thirty-two years after the first payment, payments continue for the thirty-two-year period. Insurers call these contracts **period-certain life-income annuities**.

Most companies limit the maximum number of years certain to twenty. The longer the period certain the annuitant chooses, the smaller installment payment each $1,000 of premium will purchase. With one large company, a $1,000 premium for a man aged 65 provides a monthly benefit of $7.03 with a pure annuity. If the ten-years-certain option is purchased, the insurer reduces the monthly benefit to $6.45. If the twenty-years-certain option is purchased, the insurer reduces the monthly benefit to $5.22. Thus, when the annuitant chooses a twenty-year guarantee option at age 65, monthly benefits are about 26 percent less than the benefits provided by a pure annuity.

---

[4] In principle, the $70,000 "loss" suffered by Charles's estate is no different from Charles buying a $70,000 life insurance policy and dying after making only one premium payment, thereby receiving a "windfall gain." In the life insurance case, the life insurance company suffers a large financial "loss." In each case, the transaction is entered knowing that the exchange of dollars will be unequal, but each side receives fair value based on the contingent promises exchanged.

A second method of guaranteeing a minimum return from an annuity is to purchase a refund option. A **cash-refund annuity** specifies that if an annuitant dies before having received a total amount of annuity payments equal to the premium paid, a second beneficiary will receive the difference in cash at the time of the annuitant's death. An **installment-refund annuity** guarantees that if an annuitant dies before having received annuity payments equal to the premium paid, the annuity payments will continue to a successor beneficiary until the insurer pays out a total amount of dollars equal to the premium.

Assume that Charles paid $70,000 for a $500-a-month refund annuity. If he dies after receiving payments for four years, he will have received $24,000 in annuity payments [$500 × 12 months × 4 years]. If he had purchased a cash-refund annuity, a successor beneficiary will receive a $46,000 cash payment ($70,000 − $24,000) at his death. If he had purchased an installment-refund annuity, a successor beneficiary will continue to receive the monthly payments of $500 for seven years and nine months until the sum of both streams of payments equal $70,000. Alternatively, if Charles lives 11.6 years or longer, he will receive at least $70,000 in annuity payments. If he lives beyond this point, he will continue to receive monthly payments, but no refund will be paid at his death.

If you are wondering how an insurer can guarantee to return at least an annuitant's entire premium and also guarantee payments so long as the annuitant is alive, the answer is compound interest. With all annuities for which a minimum return is guaranteed, monthly payments are less than with a pure annuity for each $1,000 of premium paid. The smaller the monthly payment, the greater the interest earned on the remaining principal.

Again, assume that Charles Lemain pays a $70,000 premium for a *pure* annuity. First-year benefits amount to $6,000 [$7.03 × 70 × 12, or (monthly rate per $1,000 × number of $1,000s purchased × 12 months)]. Thus, $64,000 is left to earn interest the second year. If an annuity, *twenty-years-certain*, had been purchased, first-year benefits would have been about $4,400 ($5.22 × 70 × 12). Under this plan, $65,600 would have been left to earn interest the second year. Therefore, the longer the minimum guarantee, the larger part interest earnings play in each annuity payment.

Number of Annuitants

An annuity may be purchased to cover one or more lives. A **single-life annuity** covers one life. A **joint-life annuity** covers two lives. With this contract, payments end at the death of either annuitant. A **joint-and-survivor annuity** provides payment to two annuitants, with the payments continuing so long as either annuitant is alive. If the payments are reduced by one-half (or two-thirds) after the death of one annuitant, the contract is called a **joint-and-one-half-survivor annuity** (or *joint-and-two-thirds-survivor annuity*).

Types of Benefits

An annuity may provide two types of benefits: (1) fixed-dollar benefits or (2) variable-dollar benefits. **Fixed-dollar benefits** mean each regular monthly benefit is the same. Thus, a $500-a-month benefit remains $500 a month for the contract period. In some cases, insurers allow annuitants to participate in excess earnings, which can increase annuity benefits if the insurer earns investment income beyond that guaranteed. In no event do solvent insurers lower annuity benefits.

Insurers call an annuity in which the amounts of regular payments are not fixed a **variable annuity**. The variable annuity is designed to overcome the problems that inflation causes people with fixed-dollar incomes. Consider the problem an annuitant would have with a fixed $250-a-month annuity income that began in 1965. In 1965, the annuity income could probably provide for an adequate standard of living. (Keep in mind that during the mid-1960s, a first-class postage stamp cost 5 cents and gasoline cost 35 cents a gallon). If the annuitant lived to see the next century, his $250-a-month income would not provide for anywhere near the same standard of living. Inflation is a great enemy of fixed-dollar income.

The variable annuity was developed in the 1950s to provide constant purchasing power rather than a constant number of dollars. With one common approach to the liquidation of variable annuities, the dollar amount of the payments may increase or decrease from year to year. Thus, the annuitant may receive $500 a month for the first year and $560 a month for the second year. If prices of consumer goods have risen from the first to the second year, the $60 increase in the annuity payment allows the annuitant to maintain the same standard of living.

A portfolio of common stock is used to provide the varying amount of dollars. In theory, in the long run, the same forces that drive up consumer prices during an inflationary period also drive up the earnings of corporations. The increase in earnings that these companies report theoretically causes their market values to increase. If an insurer were to own a portfolio of many companies with increasing earnings, dividends, and market prices, it thus can pay an increasing number of dollars to its annuitants.

In the nearly 60-year period during which variable annuities have been available, the theory underlying the variable annuity has proved to be mostly correct. In the short run, the theory need not hold true. Thus, in the period from 1973 to 1975, the prices of most consumer goods rose at about a 12 percent rate. The stock market, on the contrary, sustained a severe setback. This result was exactly the opposite of the theory supporting the variable annuity.

The appendix of this chapter describes some of the recent and interesting guarantees that insurers have developed for the variable annuity. The appendix will demonstrate the creative talents of actuaries and financial engineers and will be of interest to readers wanting to know about some current developments in variable annuity design.

Figure 17-2 provides a review of annuity classifications.

FIGURE 17-2 Classification of Annuities

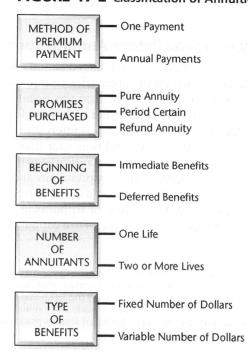

THE EFFECT OF AGE AND GENDER ON ANNUITY BENEFITS

Annuity benefits are determined through the use of a mortality table. The age at which an annuitant begins to receive benefits is an important determinant of the size of each monthly installment. The annuity mortality table shows that men at age 65 are expected to live longer than men at age 70. The longer the life expectancy of an annuitant, the greater the number of benefit payments the insurer likely will have to make. Thus, a man aged 65 receives $7.03 a month in benefits for each $1,000 premium with one large company. A man aged 70 receives $8.45, and a man aged 75 receives $10.41. The older the annuitant is when the annuity begins, the shorter is the average period in which the insurer expects to pay benefits, and thus each benefit payment may be larger.

Women have a longer life expectancy than men. Thus, if a man and a woman of the same age pay a $1,000 premium for an annuity, the male annuitant will receive a greater monthly payment.[5] Because the insurer expects to pay benefits over a shorter period of time to a male annuitant, the size of each payment will be larger. As a practical matter, rather than have separate male and female mortality tables, some insurers treat women the same as men who are four or five years younger. Such treatment reduces their monthly benefits. For example, for a $1,000 premium, one company pays men aged 65 $7.03 of monthly benefits with a pure annuity. A 65-year-old woman will be treated like a 60-year-old man and will receive $5.98 of monthly benefits. The 65-year-old woman, however, is likely to receive her benefits for several more years than the 65-year-old man, so this procedure produces actuarially fair results.

TAXATION OF ANNUITIES

Withdrawals from deferred annuities may be made during the accumulation period or during the liquidation period. The tax consequences of a withdrawal during the *accumulation* period generally are not favorable and may incur a significant tax penalty that we describe shortly. The tax consequences of withdrawal during the *liquidation* period can be favorable because tax deferral continues for the duration of the liquidation.

Withdrawal Before Annuitization

If the annuitant funds a deferred annuity with a series of deposits, there will be a growing accumulation of funds prior to liquidation. No federal income tax is paid on the investment income earned on this accumulation unless funds are withdrawn before age 59½. If an annuity owner withdraws funds during the accumulation period, the first withdrawal is treated as if it is interest income and it is subject to taxation as ordinary income. If the withdrawal is greater than all the investment income earned, however, the difference is treated as a return of principal. For example, assume that Jane Austen deposited $5,000 in annuity premiums and that investment income increased the value of her account by $2,000, so its total current value is $7,000. Now assume that she withdraws $2,500. In the year of withdrawal, she must report $2,000 as ordinary income. The $500 is considered a return of capital. Moreover, a 10 percent penalty tax is applied

---

[5] This statement assumes that the use of gender as a pricing variable has not been prohibited by law. While many employer-sponsored pension plans in the United States traditionally differentiated plan payouts by gender, litigation during the 1970s and 1980s resulted in a ban of this practice. Gender can generally be used in the pricing of individual annuities in the United States, however. In the early part of this century, the use of gender-based annuity pricing was deemed discriminatory in the United Kingdom and European Union.

to the $2,000 taxable withdrawal. Thus, if Jane Austen makes a withdrawal prior to age 59½, she will pay the 10 percent penalty tax ($200) plus any additional ordinary income tax applicable.

Annuity Liquidation Distributions

When the annuitant receives liquidation payments, part of the payment is a return of principal. This part of the return is exempt from federal income tax. The amount of the payment attributed to the return of principal is determined by an exclusion ratio. Most simply, the **exclusion ratio** is the amount paid for an annuity divided by the expected return from the annuity. The mathematics of the exclusion ratio is defined by the Internal Revenue Service (IRS).

As an example of the favorable tax treatment of annuity withdrawals, assume that Jean Valjean paid $70,000 for an annuity. During his expected lifetime, he will receive $100,000 in annuity benefit payments from the insurer, as calculated using IRS annuity tables.[6] In this case, Jean Valjean may exclude 70 percent [70,000 (premium)/100,000 (expected return)] of each payment, paying taxes only on the remaining 30 percent. Thus, if Jean receives $6,000 from his annuity in a given tax year, he reports only (0.3 × $6,000), or $1,800, as taxable income. If he is in the 28 percent marginal rate bracket, he pays only (0.28 × $1,800), or $504, in taxes on $6,000 in cash flow.

Summary

Life annuities provide a steady stream of income that an annuitant cannot outlive. The payment received by each annuitant comes from three sources: (1) liquidation of the principal, (2) interest, and (3) survivorship benefits.

Annuities are used to provide regular income in retirement years. Individually purchased annuities may be used to supplement the income provided by Social Security and company pension plans.

Annuities are categorized by the following five criteria:

1. Method of premium payment—one or more frequent (e.g., annual or monthly) payments
2. Promises purchased—pure, period-certain, or refund annuity
3. Beginning of benefits—immediate or deferred
4. Number of annuitants—one or more lives
5. Type of benefits—fixed or variable

The size of each annuity benefit payment is a function of the premium payment(s), the age and gender of the annuitant, and interest earnings.

Appendix: Recent Developments in Variable Annuity Guarantees

The variable annuity in its accumulation phase is directly comparable to a mutual fund. In both cases, a customer deposits money (mutual fund purchase = annuity premium payment), which results in an accumulation credit (mutual fund shares = annuity accumulation units). The number of shares or accumulation units credited is determined by the value of an underlying portfolio of assets on the day the deposit is made. One significant difference between the mutual fund and the variable annuity,

however, is their tax treatment during the accumulation period. The mutual fund can produce annual taxable income, while taxation of investment gains from the annuity is postponed until the annuitant receives liquidation payments, as we explained in the "Taxation of Annuities" section of this chapter. Offsetting the tax advantages in many cases are the higher expense loadings of annuities compared to mutual funds and the loss of capital gain treatment on distributions.

---

[6] The IRS Web site (*http://www.irs.gov/*) provides detailed information, examples, and worksheets describing annuity taxation.

The variable annuity's tax advantages during the accumulation period, the public's increasing awareness of the problems associated with underfunded retirement periods, and the rising stock market of the late 1990s led to increasingly large amounts of variable annuity sales. The declining stock market results between 2000 and 2003 dampened variable annuity sales and led financial service firms to offer various guarantees designed to increase the contract's appeal.

The following four categories of guarantees are typical of recent developments in the variable annuity market:

- Guaranteed minimum death benefit (GMDB)
- Guaranteed minimum income benefit (GMIB)
- Guaranteed minimum accumulation benefit (GMAB)
- Guaranteed minimum withdrawal benefit (GMWB)

GMDB

Without the GMDB, the policyholder would receive a death benefit equal to the current fund value. If the GMDB were in force, however, the policyholder would be entitled to a refund equal to *at least* the premiums paid, or some other amount determined by a contractual formula. Thus, the GMDB can be seen as a "put option" available if the actual fund value is below the guaranteed amount. One formula used when calculating the GMDB makes the death benefit equal to the premiums paid growing at some rate of interest. Some providers have a formula with a "ratchet" provision. These companies use an initial GMDB equal to the premium paid, but the GMDB is reset on each policy anniversary to the current account value if it is higher than the original GMDB. Some companies have capped their GMDB to some percentage, for example 200 percent, of the premiums paid.

An Example of the GMDB

Hunter Fischer, the outdoorsman, paid a total of $100,000 in annuity premium deposits for a variable annuity between ages 50 and 60, when he died unexpectedly. He had planned to continue making $10,000 annual annuity deposits until he retired at age 65, at which time he would have begun to receive liquidation payments. At the date of his death, the total value in his accumulation account was $75,000. The accumulation

account was affected adversely by a stock market decline the year before Hunter died. The GMDB would add back the $25,000 negative difference between the actual fund value and the sum of Hunter's premiums, providing a $100,000 payment to Hunter's survivors. If the actual fund value in Hunter's account were greater than $100,000 (say, $180,000), then the larger amount would be paid to Hunter's survivors.

If Hunter's GMDB had a more generous formula than just a return of premiums, then Hunter's survivors would be entitled to receive the guaranteed amount at a minimum. For example, assume that the premium deposits growing at some interest rate equaled $118,000 when Hunter died, while the actual accumulation equaled $75,000 on this date. Then the survivors would receive the $118,000.

GMIB

Without a GMIB, the annuitant's liquidation income would be calculated by a simultaneous consideration of the account value when the liquidation begins and the then-current mortality table factors. With the GMIB in effect, interest and mortality table factors can be guaranteed at the date of issue. The GMIB is a put option that can be used if the account value declines or if mortality factors less favorable to the annuitant develop during the accumulation period. Thus, the GMIB can guarantee a minimum amount of income regardless of fortuitous events. Many companies providing this guarantee require a waiting period, often ten years after the GMIB is issued. The waiting period protects the insurer from the adverse selection arising from a precipitous drop in the stock market shortly after the annuity and guarantee is purchased.

An Example of the GMIB

Assume that Hunter Fischer lives to age 65 and has made a total $150,000 in annual variable annuity premium deposits between ages 50 and 65. Hunter retired at age 65 and requested his annuity income payments from the insurer. Unfortunately, the year before he retired, the stock market portfolio in which his accumulations were invested declined significantly, and his actual account value equaled only $75,000. Because he purchased the GMIB, Hunter's insurer made liquidation payments based on the $150,000 total premiums paid, not on the actual account value of $75,000. Of course, if Hunter's accumulation account is worth $200,000 when he reaches age 65, his liquidation payments would be calculated using this larger amount.

GMAB

If policyholders surrender the annuity after some period (e.g., ten years), they are entitled to the then-current value of the contract. If they had purchased the GMAB, however, they would be entitled to a guaranteed minimum value, typically equal to the premiums paid, but some issuers also guarantee a minimum interest rate on the premiums. The GMAB is a put option that can be exercised if the fund value is below the guaranteed value at the option date.

An Example of the GMAB

Assume that Hunter Fischer pays a total of $100,000 in annuity deposits between ages 50 and 60. Originally he planned to continue making premium deposits until age 65, but he changes his mind and decides to end his annuity by withdrawing all his funds at age 60. On the day he terminates his contract, the actual value of his accumulation fund in $80,000. If he had purchased the GMAB, though, the insurer will allow him to withdraw the full $100,000.

Some insurers allow sequential renewals of the guarantee with a "ratchet" provision. That is, if the first option date (e.g., the annuity's tenth anniversary) expires and the GMAB is valuable because the actual account value (e.g., $50,000) is below the guaranteed amount ($100,000), then the GMAB amount remains the same ($100,000) for the next guarantee period. But if the GMAB is not valuable because the actual amount in the account (e.g., $200,000) is more than the guaranteed amount ($100,000), then the GMAB ratchets up to the actual account value on the tenth anniversary date.

GMWB

In a standard variable annuity contract, the policyholder may withdraw some percentage (e.g., 6 percent) of the current account value each year. If the account has had a poor year, the amount available under this formula will decline. The GMWB allows the policyholder to make a minimum withdrawal equal to a percentage of the GMWB balance (which is usually the amount of premiums paid). Of course, if the actual account value is greater than the GMWB balance, the policyholder will withdraw a percentage of the larger amount.

An Example of the GMWB

Assume that Hunter Fischer makes a total of $150,000 in annuity premium deposits between his fiftieth and sixty-fifth birthdays and that Hunter plans to withdraw 6 percent of his account value each year after his sixty-fifth birthday. If the account is worth $150,000 when the withdrawals begin, Hunter receives $9,000 (.06 × $150,000 = $9,000). Assume that in the year of withdrawal, Hunter's actual account value is less than $150,000 (for example, $100,000); in that case, Hunter will receive $9,000 rather than the $6,000 (.06 × $100,000 = $6,000) that he would have received if the guarantee were not purchased.

The Cost of Purchasing the Guarantees

As was the case with the mortality guarantees offered with fixed benefit annuities (recall the cash refund and installment refund guarantees described earlier in this chapter), the guaranteed minimum benefits now being offered with variable annuities have a cost. Issuers have been assessing charges, often calculated as a given number of basis points on the account balance each year, depending on the guarantee chosen. (A "basis point" equals 1/100 of 1 percent.) Whether these charges are fair and adequate is an actuarial issue beyond the scope of this text. To protect themselves against portfolio declines, insurers offering these guarantees have engaged in sophisticated financial hedges that transfer to the capital markets some of the risk of annuitants exercising their options.

Equity-Indexed Annuities

Recent years have seen many new products developed in the annuity market. The equity-indexed annuity (EIA) is one of these developments. Currently there is no standard EIA; each company's contract is likely to have unique features.[7]

---

[7] This brief description is largely drawn from a more detailed description of these products found at the SEC Web site (*http://www.sec.gov/investor/pubs/equityidxannuity.htm/*).

During the accumulation period, EIAs offer policyowners two rates of return: (1) a minimum interest rate (e.g., 3 percent) or (2) a return based on a stock market index such as the Standard and Poors 500 index. The credit for the indexed return usually is limited to some percentage gain in the index, such as 80 percent. This percentage is called the *participation rate*. For example, if the participation rate is 80 percent and the index rises 9 percent, the EIA account would earn only 7.2 percent $(0.80 \times 0.09 = 0.072)$. Product designers have included interest rate caps that limit the amount of interest credited. For example, if there were a 7 percent cap in the previous example, the gain credited would be 7 percent, not the 7.2 percent produced by the formula. Thus, there is a definite upside limit on the amount of gain an EIA purchaser can receive.

Product designers also have been creative in the indexing method contained in these contracts. These methods can be complex and vary across insurers. Consumers without extensive investment experience are advised to research these products carefully or work with qualified professional financial planners. The U.S. Securities and Exchange Commission (SEC) makes two additional points about EIAs: (1) purchasers can lose money with these products if issuers provide for significant surrender charges or if tax penalties apply when contracts are not held to maturity; and (2) most EIAs are not registered with the SEC, unlike variable annuities, which require SEC registration.

Review

1. How do most Americans qualify for annuity payments?
2. Identify the three sources of funds used to pay annuity benefits.
3. Describe adverse selection with respect to an annuity. How is adverse selection related to the fact that the annuity mortality tables show lower mortality at any specified age than do life insurance tables?
4. Define the following terms:
   a. Single-premium immediate annuity
   b. Single-premium deferred annuity
   c. Annual-premium deferred annuity
5. Give some reasons for and against purchasing a refund annuity.
6. How does a cash-refund annuity differ from an installment-refund annuity?
7. Which will provide a larger monthly payment to a male annuitant aged 65: an annuity, five-years-certain, or an installment-refund annuity? Assume that the same amount of money is available for each purchase.
8. Why do some insurers treat female annuitants as if they were male annuitants of a younger age?
9. Describe a structured settlement. What is its purpose?
10. What circumstances favor the purchase of a pure annuity over an annuity twenty-years-certain? What circumstances favor an annuity twenty-years-certain over a pure annuity?
11. Illustrate the difference between a joint-life annuity and a joint-and-survivor annuity.
12. Briefly explain the purpose of a variable annuity and the financial theory that underlies it.
13. Has the theory underlying variable annuities been proved right or wrong during the last several decades?
14. Describe a financial circumstance in which owning a variable annuity would not be a good idea.
15. What are the consequences of Stevie Ray withdrawing all his funds from an annuity as a lump sum of cash before liquidation? Steve is 42 years old.
16. Describe the exclusion ratio and its purpose.

Objective Questions

1. The definition of an annuity insurance policy is:
   a. A promise of a series of payments by insurer to an annuitant, often for a lifetime
   b. A contingent promise to make payments to a beneficiary at the annuitant's death
   c. A series of payments from an insurer used to repay a mortgage loan
   d. A contract made to provide indemnity payments for long-term care
2. An annuitant makes one payment to the insurer fifteen years before he retires. At retirement, the insurer pays the annuitant a lifetime income on a monthly basis. This transaction is an example of a:
   a. Flexible premium annuity
   b. Variable annuity

c. Single-premium deferred annuity
d. Single-premium immediate annuity

3. If an annuitant withdraws funds from an annuity during the early years of the accumulation period and receives less than the contract's prewithdrawal value, this result is likely due to a(n):
   a. Accumulation penalty
   b. Discount on deposit
   c. Surrender charge
   d. Lost interest penalty

4. If an annuity contract contains a promise to continue payments until the second of two deaths, it is called a:
   a. Double indemnity annuity
   b. Joint-and-survivor annuity
   c. Joint death annuity
   d. Double life annuity

5. The period when the insurer makes payments to the annuitant is called:
   a. The retirement period
   b. The deferral period
   c. The accumulation period
   d. The liquidation period

6. Which of the following annuities would pay the highest monthly income for a $1,000 premium, holding all other factors constant?

   a. Straight-life annuity
   b. Annuity five-years-certain
   c. Annuity ten-years-certain
   d. Cash refund annuity

7. An annuity that does not have fixed payments during liquidation is the:
   a. Refund annuity
   b. Variable annuity
   c. Immediate annuity
   d. Vested annuity

8. Choose the true statement.
   a. If funds are withdrawn from an annuity during the accumulation period, no federal income tax is paid.
   b. If funds are withdrawn from an annuity during liquidation, no federal income tax is paid.
   c. If funds are withdrawn from an annuity before age 59½, there is a federal income tax penalty in addition to the ordinary income tax.
   d. If funds are withdrawn from an annuity, and the annuitant is older than age 75, no federal income tax is paid.

Discussion Questions

Harry Ito is about to retire. He plans to sell his business sometime in the next five years and is considering using the $100,000 proceeds from the sale to purchase an annuity.

1. Under what set of circumstances would the annuity be desirable?

2. If an annuity is purchased, what features should it have with respect to guarantees?

3. If Mr. Ito doesn't purchase an annuity, what alternative uses of the $100,000 could provide him with a life income in retirement?

Selected References

Black, Kenneth Jr., and Harold D. Skipper, Jr., 2000, *Life Insurance*, 13th ed. (Upper Saddle River, NJ: Prentice Hall).

18

Health Insurance and Disability Income

After studying this chapter, you should be able to

■ Compare the health care system in the United States to other industrialized countries

■ Explain why health insurance costs have been increasing in the United States

■ Describe why private individual health insurers are vulnerable to adverse selection

■ Describe five different types of individual health insurance policies

■ Identify some common contractual provisions found in individual health insurance policies

■ Describe the differences between traditional fee-for-service health insurers and managed care organizations

This chapter provides an overview of the health insurance system in the United States and describes individually purchased medical expense and disability insurance. Individuals suffering a serious accident or illness often encounter two broad categories of financial losses: a loss of income resulting from their inability to work and the extra costs owed to medical providers, such as hospitals, physicians, and other related costs, after receiving medical treatment. Medical expense insurance, also known more broadly as health insurance, pays for the extra medical expenses. Disability insurance provides partial wage replacement to the insured.

We begin by examining some of the issues affecting the current U.S. health care system. This background is needed to understand individual health insurance coverage, as well as employer-sponsored health care coverage, a topic covered in Chapter 19, "Employee Benefits." The next section of the chapter describes several types of health care coverage, including basic medical, major medical insurance, and health savings accounts. Disability insurance and long-term care insurance are discussed as well. Different types of health insurance organizations are described at the end of the chapter.

HEALTH CARE INSURANCE: AN INTERNATIONAL COMPARISON

Three central concerns that the United States and other countries must confront when providing health care to its citizens are affordability, quality of care, and access to care. In assessing these considerations, it is helpful to compare the performance of the U.S. health care system to those of other industrialized countries.

Health care spending in the United States accounted for 16.4 percent of the country's gross domestic product (GDP) in 2008, or $7,720 per person when measured on a per capita basis. While these figures demonstrate the high cost of health care, it is helpful to compare them to measures of health care costs in other industrialized countries. As shown in Table 18-1, the per capita cost of health care in the United States is more than 50 percent higher than in countries like Canada, France, and Germany, and nearly double the cost of health care in Japan and the United Kingdom. All the countries shown in Table 18-1 except the United States provide medical care to their citizens mostly outside the private market, typically through the use of government-sponsored universal health care programs that are less reliant on the pricing mechanisms found in a free market system.

Despite spending more on health care than other countries, the United States does not rank highly in several key measures of quality of health care. For example, as shown in the third and fourth rows of Table 18-1, an international comparison of statistics related to longevity indicates that Americans have shorter life expectancies. As shown in the fifth row of Table 18-1, birth statistics also indicate that infant mortality is higher in the United States than in other industrialized countries.[1] These results suggest that despite the money spent on health care, the effectiveness of the U.S. health care system often lags behind many other countries.

Access to health care is also an issue in the United States. Approximately one out of every six Americans does not have health insurance. The data in Table 18-2 show the percentage of non-elderly Americans (those not covered by Medicare) without health insurance, as well as the source of health insurance for those with insurance protection. The data show that most Americans receive health insurance as an employee benefit from their employers, as we discuss in Chapter 19. From 2000 to 2009, however, the percentage of non-elderly Americans receiving health insurance from an employment-based health insurance program decreased from 66 percent to 57 percent. Over the

TABLE 18-1 An International Comparison of Health Care Statistics: 2008

2008	Canada	France	Germany	Japan	United Kingdom	United States
Health care spending per capita	$4,024	$3,809	$3,963	$2,878	$3,281	$7,720
Health care spending (as % of GDP)	10.3	11.1	10.7	8.5	8.8	16.4
Life expectance at birth, females	83*	84.3	82.7	86	81.9	80.5**
Life expectance at birth, males	78.3*	77.6	77.6	79.3	77.8	75.5**
Infant mortality / 1000 live births	5.1*	3.8	3.5	2.6	4.7	6.5

Data from Organization for Economic Cooperation and Development (OECD) Health Statistics for 2007 (www.oecd.org/), accessed October 14, 2011.

Note: All data are from 2008 except those denoted by *, which are 2007 data; 2008 data denoted by ** are estimated.

---

[1] Some researchers caution that these measures of health care quality are subject to measurement error, may be related to factors beyond the control of the health care system, and are difficult to compare across countries. For example, see Chapter 1 in Ohsfeldt and Schneider (2006).

TABLE 18-2 Health Insurance Coverage of the Nonelderly Population: 2000 and 2009

Year	Employment-based	Medicaid	Private Non-Group	Uninsured
2000	66%	13%	5%	16%
2009	57%	19%	5%	19%

Data from Kaiser Commission on Medicaid and the Uninsured, "Health Insurance Coverage in America," 2001 and 2010 data updates.

same time period, the percentage of non-elderly Americans insured through Medicaid[2] increased from 13 to 19 percent, and the portion of the non-elderly population without health insurance increased to 19 percent.

INCREASING HEALTH CARE COSTS

A leading cause for the increased number of Americans without health insurance is the rising cost of medical care. Since the 1980s, medical care costs in the United States have risen more rapidly than the general category of expenses measured by the consumer price index (CPI). Figure 18-1 presents data documenting this increase.

Figure 18-1 shows that in several recent years, medical costs, including physicians, medical equipment, nurses, medicine, and buildings, rose at rates more than twice that of the general CPI. The reasons behind the increase include the high cost of improvements in medical technology, an aging population, moral hazard associated with health insurance, and fee-for-service medicine.

FIGURE 18-1 Comparing the U.S. Consumer Price Index to the Inflation Index for Medical Expenses (1983 = 100)

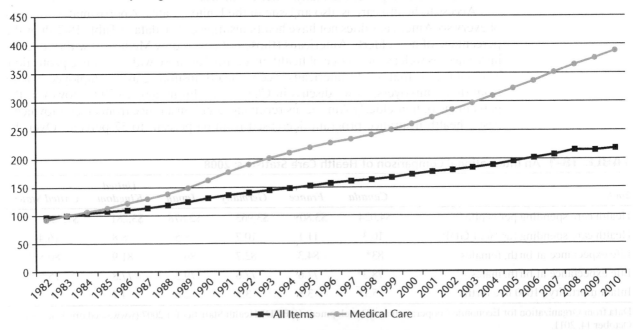

Data from U.S. Department of Labor, Bureau of Labor Statistics (http://bls.gov/data/).

---

[2] Medicaid is a social insurance program that provides health care to the poor. A recipient's eligibility is based on demonstrating financial need. Medicaid is discussed in greater detail at the Official U.S. Government Site for Medicaid, www.medicaid.gov.

Cost of Technology Technological improvements in health care have proved to be expensive. The costs of medical research, development of new equipment and pharmaceuticals, and certifying this technology for government approval costs billions of dollars each year. While it is likely that technological improvements, such as new drugs or new surgical techniques, result in more rapid cures, these costs help to fuel health care inflation.

The Aging of the U.S. Population Many economists expect the demand for health care to increase as the large number of "baby boomers" born in the United States between 1946 and 1964 leave the workforce. The oldest baby boomer turned 65 in 2011, signaling a transition in the U.S. population. As people get older, their medical expenditures generally increase. Thus, if the above trends hold true, an increase in demand for health care as our society ages seems likely.

Moral Hazard The existence of employer-sponsored health insurance also results in greater **moral hazard** by health care consumers. As shown in Table 18-2, most Americans covered by health insurance receive this protection through employer-sponsored plans. Under these arrangements, an employee's health care costs are primarily borne by their employers. Thus, employees have traditionally paid only a portion of the full cost of the medical care that they use, effectively decreasing the employees' out-of-pocket cost for health care to very low prices. Holding other factors constant, consumer demand for a product or service typically increases as the price of that good decreases. Thus, because insured employees pay far less for medical services than they would without health insurance, they tend to use more health care.[3] The additional use of health care that results from this decrease in price is attributable to moral hazard (see Pauly, 1968), as employees with health insurance behave in ways that increase the expected loss borne by their insurers.

In cases where the patient does not pay the bill, or even a portion of the bill, the consumer (patient) will be indifferent about the medical costs involved. This indifference was true for many group health insurance plans until employer-provided group insurance plans began cost-shifting efforts that resulted in placing more of the cost on employees. Employer-to-employee **cost shifting** involves larger deductibles, larger participation percentages, and other changes that increase the price paid by the employee for that good. If employer efforts at cost shifting succeed, patients will respond by reducing their consumption of health care.

Fee-for-Service Health Care In addition to leading to moral hazard, the existence of health insurance can result in an environment in which patients and medical providers have little incentive to improve the cost effectiveness of the delivery of health care. Traditionally, medical services have been financed through a **fee-for-service** health care delivery system, where health care providers like physicians and hospitals are reimbursed by health insurance plans after delivering medical services to the patient. These medical providers greatly influence the demand for health care services, as they are the parties responsible for diagnosing and treating their patients' medical needs. The efforts of medical providers to provide quality medical care routinely involve the use of additional medical services.

The traditional fee-for-service health care system included few incentives for providers to improve the cost effectiveness of alternative medical treatment options. Many health insurers simply reimbursed providers for their services after they treated the patient, and medical providers had little reason to limit the use of expensive services

---

[3] The health economics literature often refers to this problem as the overutilization of health care. In this context, consumers should theoretically use medical services up to the point where the marginal benefit from an additional unit of health care equals its marginal cost. This concept is difficult to implement in real life, however, in part because consumers are not well informed about health care prices or their benefits.

because the cost of the services was primarily borne by the health insurer. Unless they were subject to cost-shifting devices like deductibles, patients also had little incentive to limit their use of health care. In addition, it was common for many patients to select expensive treatment options like hospitalization or specialist care instead of less costly alternatives. As a result, fee-for-service plans were criticized for their failure to control the use of costly medical procedures and for their high utilization of health care services.[4]

In response to the criticisms of fee-for-service health insurance and its failure to control costs, health insurers introduced a variety of managed care organizations (MCOs) during the 1990s, including health maintenance organizations (HMOs) and preferred provider organizations (PPOs; both are described later in this chapter). MCOs attracted a large share of the health insurance market during the 1990s. As a result, the traditional "pre-1990s" fee-for-service health insurance plans described above account for only a small fraction of today's U.S. health insurance market.

ADVERSE SELECTION

Efforts to improve the U.S. health insurance system are complicated by the fact that health care spending is heavily concentrated on a comparatively small number of Americans. The graph in Figure 18-2 shows the cumulative distribution of health care expenditures across all Americans. The graph indicates a majority of Americans require little if any health care. The least costly 70 percent of Americans account for only 10 percent of the country's health care spending, and the health care needs of half of all Americans could be paid for using only 3 percent of the country's current health

FIGURE 18-2 Distribution of Total US Healthcare Costs

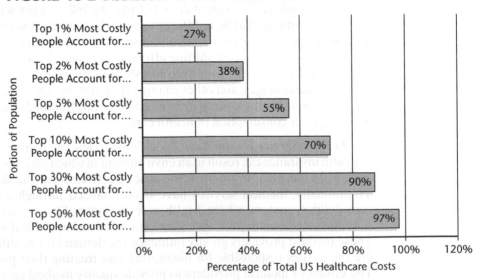

Data from K. Swartz, "Reinsuring Health: Why More Middle-Class People Are Uninsured and What Government Can Do" (New York: Russell Sage Foundation, 2006), pp. 9. 60–65; M. L. Berk and A. C. Monheit, "The Concentration of Health Care Expenditures, Revisited," Health Affairs, (Bethesda, MD: Project HOPE, 2001), 20, No. 2, pp. 9–18; and the 1996 Medical Expenditures Panel Survey (MEPS) (Rockville, Md.: Agency for Health Care Policy and Research, 1997).

---

[4] A related reason that medical providers may encourage the increased use of medical services is to better protect them from medical malpractice lawsuits, which are lawsuits filed against medical providers by their patients. For example, to minimize the chance of injury to the patient, physicians and hospitals may conduct more tests, such as X rays or magnetic resonance imaging (MRI), and keep patients hospitalized longer than they might otherwise, a practice known as *defensive medicine*.

care expenditures. By contrast, 10 percent of Americans consume 70 percent of all health care spending in the United States. Over a quarter of U.S. health care costs are spent on 1 percent of the population.

The dramatic difference in health care consumption between healthy and unhealthy Americans explains why private health insurers often use medical underwriting to screen insurance applicants. Private health insurers are particularly concerned about their vulnerability to **adverse selection,** the tendency for unhealthy individuals to apply for health insurance more frequently than healthy people. Adverse selection is less problematic for workers covered by employer-sponsored group health insurance plans, as these plans typically cover a large group of workers, assuring that the losses of the unfortunate handful of unhealthy workers are spread across a larger group of healthier workers. Employment groups also serve as an effective screening device to reduce the probability of adverse selection, as such plans are typically provided to full-time workers who are healthy enough to hold a full-time job. Without such means to protect them from adverse selection, private health insurers rely heavily on medical screening and underwriting to reduce adverse selection.

How can individuals protect themselves from the high costs that result from a loss of health? In the next section, we describe several types of health insurance protection designed for individuals. In Chapter 19, we discuss employee benefits.

HEALTH INSURANCE COVERAGE FOR INDIVIDUALS

Consumers can buy several different types of individual health insurance policies, including basic medical expense insurance, major medical insurance, health savings accounts, disability income insurance, and long-term care insurance. Figure 18-3 provides an outline of the five types of health insurance policies described in this section.

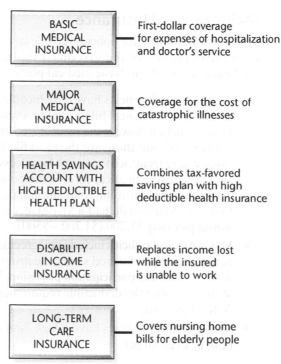

FIGURE 18-3 Five Types of Medical Expense and Disability Insurance Policies

BASIC MEDICAL INSURANCE — First-dollar coverage for expenses of hospitalization and doctor's service

MAJOR MEDICAL INSURANCE — Coverage for the cost of catastrophic illnesses

HEALTH SAVINGS ACCOUNT WITH HIGH DEDUCTIBLE HEALTH PLAN — Combines tax-favored savings plan with high deductible health insurance

DISABILITY INCOME INSURANCE — Replaces income lost while the insured is unable to work

LONG-TERM CARE INSURANCE — Covers nursing home bills for elderly people

Basic Medical Expense Insurance

Basic medical expense insurance includes several types of health insurance policies that provide fairly low limits of coverage with small deductibles. Traditionally, separate policies were sold to cover different types of medical treatments. For example, *hospitalization insurance* typically provides coverage for the cost of a semiprivate hospital room, limiting coverage to a specified period of time, such as 60 or 90 days. Some hospitalization policies pay up to a specific limit of coverage, while others are based on the usual, customary, and reasonable cost of hospitalization. *Surgical expense contracts* provide coverage for the costs of surgical procedures, reimbursing physicians based on the usual, customary, and reasonable cost of the procedure. Newer basic medical expense policies often extend coverage across both types of coverage, as well as for outpatient coverage and certain diagnostic tests.

As noted above, basic medical expense insurance policies often reimburse providers on the basis of the usual, customary, and reasonable, or UCR, fee for services. Under this arrangement, the insurer pays the charges billed by the medical provider up to the UCR charge for the service. Based on statistical surveys of hospital and physician charges, the UCR charge is typically set as the fee corresponding to a specific percentile of the charges by providers, such as 80 percent. Thus, if the charge related to the 80th percentile was $2,000 for a particular medical service, UCR reimbursement would pay a majority of providers in full, up to a $2,000 payment limit. On the other hand, the reimbursement for the 20 percent of providers charging above the 80 percentile would be capped to equal the $2,000 UCR fee. Under both types of policies, the insured may be responsible for the portion of the medical charges not covered by insurance.

Originally designed in the mid-1900s as a fee-for-service insurance arrangement, basic medical expense policies account for a small portion of today's health insurance market. The use of basic medical expense policies plummeted in the 1980s, replaced by major medical insurance.

Major Medical Insurance

Major medical insurance policies provide coverage for potentially large medical expenses rather than paying for the first dollar of loss. Three characteristics distinguish major medical coverage from basic medical plans:

- Major medical policies have a *deductible provision*. They cause insureds to pay an amount of medical bills equal to a specified deductible, such as $500 or $1,000. This deductible lowers the insurer's costs because the first dollars of all losses are not covered, and these are the most likely to be incurred. Second, in marginal cases where treatment may not be necessary, the insured has a strong incentive to avoid overusing medical care. Some policies apply the deductible to each illness or accident but limit the total amount deducted to some annual maximum. If Florence Nightingale had a $1,700 medical bill with a $500 deductible, the insurer would pay only $1,200 ($1,700 – $500).

- Major medical policies include an agreement where the insurer pays only a percentage of the insured's bills; the insured must pay the difference. This sharing of costs is called the **participation provision**. Typically, the insurer pays 75 to 80 percent of the bills after the deductible requirement is met. The insured pays the remaining 20 to 25 percent.

- Major medical policies have a *high limit of liability*, such as $1 million to $5 million, or even larger.

As an example of a major medical plan, assume that Nick Romanoff incurs $28,000 in medical expenses while being treated in a hospital and that he has a $1,000,000 major medical policy with a $500 deductible and an 80 percent participation provision. Under these circumstances, Nick collects $22,000 from his major medical insurance, calculated as follows:

$28,000	Medical expense
(−)$500	Deductible
$27,500	Covered expense
$22,000	Covered expense × covered percentage (80%) equals the **insurance payment** (0.8 × 27,500) = $22,000
$ 5,500	Covered expense × patient's copayment percentage equals the patient's responsibility (0.2 × 27,500) = $5,500

Some major medical plans place a cap on the insured's payments. In the above example, Nick collected $22,000 from the insurer, but he also paid $6,000 ($5,500 in participation payments plus the $500 deductible). If his major medical policy capped the insured's payments at $5,000, for example, his participation payment responsibility would have ended after he paid $4,500 because at this point, the deductible ($500) plus his participation payment equaled the cap ($5,000).

Health Savings Accounts and High Deductible Health Plans

The passage of the Medicare Modernization Act in 2003 created a new form of health insurance, a two-part coverage consisting of a high-deductible health care plan and a health savings account. A **high-deductible health care plan (HDHP)** provides health insurance protection to the insured, incorporating a very high deductible to limit the moral hazard common in traditional health insurance plans. The **health savings account (HSA)** is a tax-favored savings fund designed to pay for the cost of qualified medical expenses borne by the account holder under the deductible provision of the HDHP. HDHPs that satisfy requirements set by the Department of the Treasury are referred to as *qualified* plans. When a qualified HDHP is paired with an HSA, the combination is eligible for favorable tax treatment.

By depositing tax-deductible contributions into an HSA, account holders are provided a tax-favored way to save money for future medical costs. Because account holders are spending their own savings, they have a financial incentive to be prudent consumers, carefully choosing the medical services that they use to treat their health care needs and monitoring the price and quality of such care. By taking an active role in choosing their medical providers, account holders are more likely to demand that medical providers provide quality care at reasonable prices, helping to slow the rate of cost inflation for medical services. Account holders are also less likely to use unnecessary medical services because they personally pay a greater portion of their medical costs. HSAs are thus an example of **consumer-driven health plans**, plans designed to increase the cost-effectiveness of the health care industry by providing financial incentives to patients to become better consumers of health care.

The HDHP portion of coverage is designed to pay for medical expenses after the insured has satisfied the deductible for the plan. HDHP plans typically provide high coverage limits; a recent survey indicated that the average lifetime maximum benefit for its best-selling products for individual consumers was more than $5 million.[5]

---

[5] America's Health Insurance Plans, 2010 AHIP HSA/HDHP Census Report.

The minimum size of the deductible built into the HDHP is set by law. In 2012, the minimum deductible was set at $1,200 for an individual and $2,400 for a family. Like other types of insurance, consumers can decrease the cost of their HDHP premium by agreeing to assume a larger deductible. To limit the amount of money that an insured may have to pay toward their medical expenses, qualified HDHPs also include a maximum limit on out-of-pocket expenses. In 2012, this maximum limit for out-of-pocket expenses was set equal to $6,050 for an individual and $12,100 for a family in 2012.[6] The minimum and maximum deductible limits are provided in the Internal Revenue Code and adjusted as necessary for inflation.

Account holders can reduce their taxable incomes by the amounts that they contribute to their HSAs up to a maximum annual contribution limit. The maximum contribution permitted by law was capped at $3,100 for individual plans and $6,250 for family plans in 2012. Account holders over the age of 55 are also permitted to make an additional "catch-up" contribution above the standard limits to enable them to accumulate additional savings for future medical costs. The maximum tax deductible catch-up contribution was set equal to $1,000 in 2012. The contribution limits are adjusted for inflation. Savings accumulated in an HSA account can be carried over from one year to the next. The account holder can invest the money in her HSA, earning investment income toward the cost of future health care expenditures.

HSA funds can be used to pay for qualified medical expenses, as defined by section 213 of the Internal Revenue Code. Qualified medical expenses include the typical medical expenses covered under traditional health insurance plans, as well as a wider variety of related expenses that can be difficult to cover in a health insurance policy in a cost-effective manner (such as dental care, prescription drugs, chiropractic care, eyeglasses, hearing aids, and psychiatric care). The high deductibles of these plans do not apply to preventive medical services (such as immunizations, weight loss programs, or routine physical exams) to increase the incentives of account holders to use such cost-saving services. People are not eligible for coverage under a HDHP/HSA plan if they are covered by Medicare or any other comprehensive health care plan.

Disability Income Insurance

Disability resulting from illness or accident may be an even greater peril to a family than premature death because disability not only cuts off income but also may create large medical expenses. Moreover, a six-month or longer period of disability is a more likely cause of loss to people in their working years than is premature death. **Disability income insurance** replaces income not earned because of illness or accident. Disability income insurance policies are designated as either short or long term, depending on the period for which coverage is provided. Short-term policies provide a specific number of weeks of coverage (perhaps 30 weeks) after a brief (for example, one-week) elimination period. An **elimination period**, also called a *waiting period*, is a period that must pass before an insured is eligible to receive insurance payments. The purpose of the elimination period is to exclude payments for minor illness. The elimination period is consistent with the purpose of insurance to cover severe losses but not expenses. This provision also helps keep premiums affordable.

Long-term disability income insurance policies provide a number of years of protection after a substantial elimination period (for example, six months of continuous disability) has elapsed. Coverage typically ends at age 65, the age when many people retire.

---

[6] See *http://www.irs.gov/pub/irs-drop/rp-11-32.pdf.*

Disability income insurance is a logical complement to life insurance, although people do not purchase it as often. One explanation for the less frequent individual purchase of disability insurance is that benefits from workers' compensation, Social Security, and successful negligence lawsuits (if a person is disabled by another's negligence) may provide disability income. Nevertheless, individually purchased disability income insurance can be important in cases where other sources of funds are inadequate or unavailable.

DEFINITION OF DISABILITY

The definition of the term *disability* is one of the most important contractual features. Some contracts have an "own profession" clause, while others have an "any profession" clause. Even among these categories, different insurers can have varied contractual language. Consider the following clause defining the term "totally disabled":

> The insured is totally disabled when he is unable to perform the principal duties of his occupation. After the initial period, the insured is totally disabled when he is unable to perform the principal duties of his occupation and is not gainfully employed in any occupation.

The previous definition states that after the initial period defined by the contract, the insured remains disabled if he or she still cannot perform the principal duties of his or her occupation and is not employed. Under this definition, the insured can choose not to work in another occupation. Contrast this definition with "the inability to perform any occupation that the insured is reasonably fitted for by education, training, and experience." Under this definition, if the insured is able to work in *any* reasonable profession, the insurer makes no disability payments. This first definition is rarely used by insurers (and if they do allow it, they charge a lot for the privilege).

Insurers can use a combination of definitions. For example, insurers may define disability as "the inability to engage in (all or principal) duties of one's own occupation," and then after a period of years, redefine disability as "the inability to engage in an occupation that the insured is reasonably fit for by training, education, and experience."

BENEFIT PERIOD AND AMOUNT

Insurers generally state disability benefits as a dollar amount per week or month, for a stated number of weeks, months, or years. Disability contracts also vary according to the length of each benefit period and the amount of each monthly benefit. Benefits can be paid for nearly any length of time, including for life. Insurers often terminate or modify benefits at age 65, however, to integrate with Social Security and private retirement plans. In general, the longer the potential benefits for a covered disability, the more expensive the policy is.

Insurers restrict the amount of the benefit to 60 or 70 percent of the insured's gross wage (earned income) for total disability benefits. The percentage set by underwriters is typically a function of the absolute level of wage income and the taxation of the benefits. The reduced benefit is necessary to encourage rehabilitation and reduce malingering. The wage-replacement percentage typically declines for higher wage earners. For example, a professional earning $300,000 per year may be allowed only a 50 percent replacement rate by the underwriters. The $150,000 (50% × $300,000) earned income replacement is considered sufficient income to cover expenses but also encourages rehabilitation.

Some disability income policies include a definition of **partial disability**. The term **residual disability benefit** is commonly used to describe a partial disability payment. A residual disability benefit allows payments to be made to a person working only part time while recovering from an illness. The insurer uses a formula comparing pre-disability and post-disability income to calculate insurance payments, making up the difference between the two. Insurers call this provision a **rehabilitation benefit**.

In addition to purchasing a separate disability income policy, a second way to acquire disability income protection is in the form of an extra-cost rider attached to a life insurance policy. **Disability income riders** on life insurance policies provide for payments, such as $10 a month for each $1,000 of life insurance, if an insured becomes totally disabled. Insurers may apply an upper limit, such as $500 a month.

Long-Term Care Insurance

Long-term care (LTC) insurance provides coverage for the cost of several types of LTC facilities, such as nursing homes or assisted living facilities. LTC facilities can be expensive. The annual cost of a nursing home approaches $100,000 in many areas of the country. The average length of stay in a nursing home is between 24 to 30 months, and an estimated 10 to 15 percent of nursing home residents live in the facility for more than two years.

While some young people with medical conditions may need LTC coverage, the use of LTC facilities is more common among the elderly. The demand for LTC in the United States is expected to grow over the next twenty years with the aging of the baby boomers. Other factors contribute to the anticipated increase in demand for LTC as well. Many American families have fewer children than previous generations, making care of elderly parents by family members more difficult. The mobility of American families also means that many children do not live close enough to their parents to provide care if it is needed.

LTC INSURANCE COVERAGE CHARACTERISTICS

Most LTC policies reimburse the insured for the cost of care up to a specific daily dollar limit of coverage, such as $100, $200, or more per day. Thus, if the cost per day for coverage in an LTC facility equals $250, a policy with a $200 per day limit would cover all but $50 of the daily cost. Most policies specify a maximum amount of coverage, typically ranging from $100,000 to $1 million. Some policies specify the coverage maximum as a number of years (or months) in a long-term care facility.[7]

LTC policies generally specify an elimination period, a time period that commonly ranges from 0 to 90 days. During this time period, insureds residing in a LTC facility pay their own costs out of pocket. The elimination period thus serves as a deductible against the LTC coverage, controlling moral hazard.

Some older LTC policies require medical certification of need from a physician as the event that triggers the beginning of claims payment by the insurer. More recent policies define the peril insured against as an inability to perform a specified number of **activities of daily living (ADL)**, which include shopping, preparing meals, doing light housework,

---

[7] In addition to nursing home care, a number of different LTC services have become increasingly popular in recent years. **Home health care** refers to skilled nursing care and related medical treatment provided in a patient's home. **Adult day care programs** offer residents personal care and supervision for short durations, such as several hours in a day. **Respite care** provides relief for the primary caregiver of an ill or disabled person. It provides services in either the provider's or the disabled person's home, allowing the primary caregiver to be absent for a time. A **hospice** is a facility caring for the terminally ill. A life expectancy of six months or less certified by a physician is the basic criterion for entry into a hospice. Most hospice facilities have 24-hour staffing by medical and nursing personnel; counseling, including bereavement counseling; and physical therapy facilities. Coverage for these facilities varies across LTC policies. *Facilities coverage* provides protection for LTC institutions like nursing homes, assisted living facilities, and hospices. *Home care coverage* provides coverage for treatment outside of LTC institutions, such as home health care, adult day care, or respite care. Many comprehensive LTC policies offer coverage for both institutional and home health care coverage.

bathing, dressing, getting in and out of bed, and walking outside. Thus, a policy may specify that the insured will be eligible for benefits if she is unable to perform two ADLs. Some policies mention the loss of cognitive capability, thus covering mental impairment.

The general pricing pattern for LTC insurers is to require level premiums payable for life using gender-neutral rates that increase rapidly with age. Premiums also are based on the applicant's health when the policy is purchased, with discounts offered for people in above-average health, and surcharges applied for people in substandard health.[8] Often, discounts are available to married couples when both spouses purchase coverage. Some insurers sell LTC policies that provide insureds protection from inflation, but such coverage is often quite expensive.

Long-term care insurance policies are not standardized. However, the National Association of Insurance Commissioners (NAIC) has developed and regularly modified model legislation that specifies minimum standards and other guidelines for LTC policies. For example, NAIC model regulations provided such consumer protections as requiring insurers to offer inflation protections and preventing insurers from (1) not renewing policies because of age or deteriorating health; or (2) increasing premiums because of a person's age or having filed a claim.

THE FINANCIAL PROBLEM

Private LTC insurance currently finances less than 1 percent of all LTC expenses. By contrast, about one-third of all LTC expenses are financed by families, and about two-thirds are financed by the federal and state governments, primarily as part of the **Medicaid** program. As a needs-based program, Medicaid is designed to insure only economically poor individuals. The program therefore requires many people to exhaust, or "spend down," their financial assets before they are qualified for LTC coverage from Medicaid. The spend-down provision often leaves many Americans with little savings for other losses and expenses and can result in an embarrassing loss of dignity for many LTC residents. It also contributes to the financial problems experienced by both state and federal governments.

Several reasons might explain why LTC insurance has not been widely purchased. Some people do not correctly understand the likelihood or the cost of the peril, while others mistakenly believe their individual health insurance or group health insurance will cover the potential loss. Many people plan to spend down or give away their assets and rely on Medicaid to finance their LTC needs. The government has tightened restrictions on this strategy, but some financial planners still promote this ethically questionable plan. And many people simply believe that currently available LTC insurance policies are too expensive or restrictive in coverage.

COMMON HEALTH INSURANCE CONTRACTUAL PROVISIONS

Unlike property insurance, standard health insurance policies do not exist. Rather, all states have passed, with some variation, model health insurance legislation that specifies both mandatory and optional provisions applying to individual accident and sickness policies. Many of these provisions are comparable to those in life insurance policies, as described in Chapter 16, "Standard Life Insurance Contract Provisions and Options." As a result, this discussion is simplified to avoid repetition.

---

[8] LTC policies also receive favorable tax treatment. Unreimbursed medical expenses are tax deductible when they exceed 7.5 percent of a taxpayer's adjusted gross income. Most LTC insurance premiums are considered tax-deductible medical expenses, and thus can be included as unreimbursed expenses. The Internal Revenue Service (IRS) sets limits on the portion of the LTC premium that can be included as unreimbursed medical expense. The deduction limits increase with age. For example, a person younger than age 40 could deduct up to $340 in premiums in 2011, while a person over 70 could deduct up to $4,240 in that year.

Entire Contract

This provision states that the written policy, its application, and endorsements constitute the entire agreement. No other documents or unattached applications may be incorporated by reference to modify the contract's terms. In addition, if there are any changes, they must be written and are valid only if the company agrees to them. Agents cannot modify the terms of the written contract.

Grace Period and Reinstatement

The grace period allows the policy to remain in force for a short period while the premium is past due, typically 31 days for annual premium policies. If the premium remains unpaid after the grace period expires (and the insurer properly notifies the insured), the policy terminates. The insured may reinstate the lapsed contract under certain conditions. Typically, the insured must submit an application with the past-due premium. The insurer then issues a conditional receipt pending a reinstatement decision by the company's underwriters. Under the uniform provisions, reinstatement is assumed automatically if the insurer fails to respond within 45 days.

Incontestable Clause

Health insurance contracts contain either a time limit on certain defenses or an incontestable clause limiting an insurer's right to contest the claim. A time-limit-on-certain-defenses clause provides a two- or three-year period after the contract starts for the insurance company to contest the contract. After the stipulated period, the contract cannot be contested except for fraudulent misstatements. Insurers must pay even if there were fraudulent misstatements at the time of the application if a policy contains an incontestable clause.

Claims

The insured must file a claim notice and submit a proof of loss within specified time limits. The insurer has specified time limits to pay the claim. The time limits allow insurers a period to investigate and validate the claim. Insurers retain the right to examine an insured as often as necessary to determine claim legitimacy; however, insurers cannot harass the insured by imposing unreasonable requirements. If an insured dies, insurers may require an autopsy to settle cause-of-loss disputes.

Renewability

An important health insurance policy provision relates to renewability. Most states restrict an insurer's rights to cancel health insurance policies. Some contracts, including those identified as **guaranteed renewable**, however, allow the insurer to raise premium charges. Generally, premium increases must affect a whole class of business rather than an individual policy. For greater protection from premium increases, a consumer can purchase a **noncancellable** health insurance policy, one in which the insurer cannot increase the premium during the life of the policy. Not surprisingly, noncancellable policies cost more than guaranteed renewable policies.

Preexisting Conditions

The exclusions in health insurance policies are important, but they are not numerous. A major exclusion pertains to preexisting conditions. To prevent people who are about to enter the hospital from collecting benefits from insurance purchased shortly before hospitalization, most health insurance policies exclude payment for preexisting conditions. The definition of **preexisting conditions** describes an excluded period, typically ranging from six months to two years before the policy was purchased. The insurer then states that no payment will be made for losses arising from health problems the insured was treated for or knew (or had reason to know) about during the excluded period. The longer the specified period, the less desirable the coverage is. Another way of viewing this exclusion is to note that the health insurer intends to cover losses resulting from illness or accident arising after the effective date of the policy.

For example, a person may have recovered fully from the effects of an ear operation occurring six months before the purchase of insurance. If an ear problem again is manifested a week after the policy's effective date and the policy specified a one year preexisting condition exclusion, the cost of treating the illness would not be covered. Thus, it is more desirable to have a relatively short preexisting coverage period so that an illness can be labeled a new problem rather than a preexisting condition.[9]

HEALTH INSURANCE PROVIDERS

A variety of organizations offer health insurance coverage in the United States. These organizations can be classified into two broad categories: traditional health insurers and managed care organizations.

Traditional Health Insurers

Traditionally health insurance has been offered for nearly a century by Blue Cross and Blue Shield organizations and by commercial insurers. Blue Cross began in 1929 when the university hospital at Baylor University began accepting prepaid insurance premiums from local teachers. Under the **Blue Cross** arrangement, the insured subscribers (teachers) were protected by a *service* contract, a contract in which insureds were covered for prepaid hospitalization services administered to them as patients at the hospital. The concept of hospitalization service contracts spread quickly, as the American Hospital Association (AHA) began to offer such prepaid hospitalization plans in other cities under the name of Blue Cross coverage. Under the Blue Cross plans, patients were covered for services received at any participating hospital in their city.

The Blue Cross service contract provided direct payments to health care providers on behalf of their insureds. Typically, Blue Cross policies covered charges for semiprivate rooms, other hospital charges, such as use of the operating room, and charges for some types of outpatient care. Blue Cross plans grew quickly in popularity, controlling nearly the entire hospital insurance market through the 1930s.

To complement Blue Cross hospitalization coverage, **Blue Shield** plans began in the late 1930s, offering service contracts that covered payments for physicians' services. Blue Shield benefits often provide coverage based on UCR charges. Although Blue Cross and Blue Shield began as two separate organizations, they combined operations in the early 1980s, resulting in the creation of today's Blue Cross–Blue Shield (BCBS) organizations.

BCBS organizations were formed as nonprofit organizations, serving the public by increasing the number of Americans with health insurance. As nonprofits, BCBS organizations were exempt from most of the state and federal taxes levied upon

---

[9] The Patient Protection and Affordable Care Act of 2010 (PPACA) includes provisions that prohibit health insurers from excluding preexisting conditions and requires them to provide coverage for children age 19 or under in 2010, and for all individuals older than 21 effective at the beginning of January 2014. Additional discussion of the PPACA can be found in Chapter 19, "Employee Benefits."

for-profit commercial insurers. BCBS determined group health insurance premiums based on **community rating**, a system in which the price of health insurance for each employer in a community is based on the combined risk levels of all employers in that community. BCBS plans grew rapidly during the 1940s, when wage and price controls restricted employers from increasing wages. During that time, nonwage compensation was not restricted, and employers expanded their employee benefit programs to attract workers. BCBS plans were also included in many collective bargaining agreements, as the plans were popular among many labor unions.

Commercial health insurers entered the health insurance markets in the 1940s with **indemnity contracts**, fee-for-service hospitalization and surgical expense contracts that reimbursed patients for their health care expenditures subject to specified coverage limits. These early plans typically included cost-shifting features like deductibles and participation provisions that required the insured to pay for a percentage of their health care costs. Unlike BCBS plans, commercial health insurers did not use community rating to price their group insurance products. Instead, commercial insurers set the prices of their policies based on the unique insurance underwriting characteristics of the specific group of workers employed by an employer, a pricing practice known as **experience rating**.

Although BCBS organizations held nearly complete control of health insurance markets during the 1930s, the commercial insurers slowly increased their market share during the mid-twentieth century. Through the effective use of experience rating and selective underwriting, commercial insurers were able to attract an increasing number of low-risk employers who were paying higher premiums for their employees' health insurance coverage under the community rating system. By the mid 1960s, the market share of commercial insurers was comparable to that of the BCBS organizations in many states.

Managed Care Organizations

The figures shown in Figure 18-2 indicate that medical cost inflation grew quickly from the 1980s to the 2000s. Not unexpectedly, health insurance costs increased as well. Traditional fee-for-service health insurers like BCBS and the commercial health insurers were generally unable to slow the health insurance inflation rate during that time. In response to a dramatic increase in health insurance premiums that occurred during the early 1990s, employers focused increased attention on finding alternative ways to control the cost of health insurance. These efforts culminated in an abrupt transition in the employer sponsored health insurance markets, as many employers switched from traditional fee-for-service health care in favor of health insurance plans administered by managed care organizations (MCOs).

Managed care refers to health insurance plans that actively integrate the financing of health-related services with the delivery of health care. By definition, managed care plans actively influence the doctor-patient relationship, the type of care provided, the amount paid for the care, and where the care is delivered. Typically, managed care plans exhibit one or more of the following characteristics that differentiate them from traditional health insurance plans:

- Managed care plans involve contractual arrangements with selected health care providers, or the hiring of employees to provide a broad range of benefits to the insured members of the plan. By negotiating reduced charges with preferred providers or fixing provider payments for a period of time, health care costs can be controlled more effectively than in traditional fee-for-service plans.
- Managed care plans use financial incentives that encourage insured members to use the health care providers associated with the plan. Members typically pay less

out of pocket if they choose to be treated by managed care providers rather than other providers.

- Managed care plans often have a quality assurance plan to monitor the appropriateness and the effectiveness of health care provided as compared to other alternative methods of treatment, which in turn controls health care provider costs.

The two most common types of managed care plans found in today's health insurance market are health maintenance organizations and preferred provider organizations, as described below.

Health maintenance organizations (HMOs) provide members with broad health care coverage in exchange for a set fee called a **capitation payment**. HMOs cover hospital costs, physicians' charges, emergency care, and other related medical care. Unlike fee-for-service plans, which reimburse medical providers for each treatment that they provide to covered insureds, the capitation payment received by the HMO does not change with usage. Because it receives a set fee, the HMO has a profit incentive to keep members healthy and thus minimize its cost of administering care. As a result, HMOs emphasize preventive care, promoting healthy lifestyles and early detection of health issues before they become larger, more costly medical problems.

HMOs focus considerable attention on delivering quality health care in a cost-effective manner. HMOs do not rely on cost shifting to control moral hazard; instead, they contract with physicians and other medical providers to assemble a *provider network* with contractual incentives to deliver care in a cost-effective manner. For example, many HMOs rely upon *primary care physicians* to orchestrate the care for their patients, determining what care is needed and when the patient requires more costly medical care, such as hospitalization or the use of specialists. Primary care physicians typically provide most of the routine medical care required by patients, while referring the patient to specialists in the HMO provider network if such care is needed. Many HMOs also popularized the use of outpatient surgery instead of more costly hospitalization as a means to improve cost-effectiveness. HMOs also encourage preventive care, such as nutritional counseling and smoking cessation programs, as a way to reduce the frequency of high-cost medical events like heart disease.

A large number of HMOs were formed in the United States between the early 1970s and the 2000s.[10] HMOs have been formed by groups of physicians, hospitals, employers, commercial insurers, and BCBS organizations. HMOs can be organized several different ways. In a *staff model HMO*, the HMO hires physicians and related medical providers as salaried employees. Unlike fee-for-service health care arrangements, these providers do not receive additional compensation for delivering more care, and thus they are more likely to support efforts to minimize the cost of health care delivery. Under a *group practice HMO* model, the HMO contracts with physicians in an established medical practice to treat HMO subscribers on a capitation basis, thus creating a financial incentive for providers to deliver health care in a cost-effective manner. HMOs that contract with more than one group practice on a capitation basis are often called *network model HMOs*. Finally, under an *individual practice association HMO*, the organization contracts with selected physicians and hospitals in its coverage area. These providers may provide service to the public in addition to members of other HMOs. Subscribers in the individual practice association HMOs can choose a physician from among those participating in the plan. The physician then charges the HMO a fee

[10] The Health Maintenance Act of 1973 dramatically increased the use of HMOs. This federal law required certain employers with 25 or more employees to offer an HMO option, if available, in addition to their regular health insurance plan. The federal government also offered financial subsidies in support of HMO development during this time.

for each subscriber seen. Under each of these four models, the HMO often assesses the subscribers a small fee or copayment, such as $15, for each physician visit.

Many employers have found HMOs to be a cost-effective choice in providing health insurance to their employees, especially for younger and less wealthy people who often prefer HMOs because of their emphasis on prevention and limited use of cost-shifting. On the other hand, other employees have objected to HMOs for a variety of reasons. For example, members must choose from a limited number of physicians and hospitals, and some members have experienced long waits for certain types of services. Some members also express concern about early release from care facilities like hospitals because longer stays increase the HMO's costs but do not increase revenue. For the same reason, critics are also concerned that HMOs unfairly deny patients' needs for expensive treatments.

Some doctors express reservations about HMOs as well. The administrative burden of processing referrals and requesting approvals for treatment is costly for physicians, taking away time otherwise spent with patients and increasing the expense of running an office. Many physicians object to HMOs having the power to restrict certain (expensive) care options from their patients. Capitation payments can also limit a provider's compensation.

In summary, while the organizational design of HMOs provides them greater ability to control health care costs, both patients and medical providers have expressed concerns about the implementation of such controls. As concerns about HMOs became more widely known, a second type of managed care organization, the preferred provider organization (PPO), has become the most widely used type of health insurer in the United States.

A **preferred provider organization (PPO)** consists of an association of cooperating physicians and hospitals, commonly known as a *PPO network*, that agrees to provide employers with health care services for their employees at discount prices. In exchange for agreeing to accept lower fees for their services, providers in the PPO network benefit from the increased supply of PPO patients who visit them for treatment. Since 2000, PPOs have enjoyed phenomenal growth; approximately two-thirds of all non-elderly Americans are currently covered by PPOs.

Although both are managed care organizations, PPOs differ from HMOs in several ways. First, the employer's cost with PPOs is determined by use. A fee is charged for each use, but the fee is lower than the provider's usual charge for the service. Second, covered employees do not have to use the personnel or facilities of the PPO. If employees use non-PPO providers, however, they pay higher costs. For example, physicians may agree to charge PPO members less than their customary fee for a particular service. In addition, the employer's health care plan may provide reimbursement for 80 percent of the cost if a PPO provider is used, but only 60 percent if the employee uses a non-PPO physician. Third, PPO patients exercise greater autonomy than HMO subscribers in their use of providers in their insurer's networks. PPO patients do not have to use a primary care physician, nor do they typically need referrals to see a specialist.

Summary

Concerns about the U.S. health care system involve questions of affordability, access to care, and quality of care. Americans spend more on health care, both per capita and as a percent of GDP, than many other major industrial countries, and health care costs have increased much more rapidly than other categories of expenses measured by the CPI. Many reasons explain the increase in health care costs, including the cost of technological improvements, moral hazard, and fee-for-service health insurance. The aging of U.S. society is likely to further increase health care costs.

People purchase health insurance to protect against the potentially high cost of paying for health care services and the potentially large loss of income while they are unable to work. Basic medical expense insurance pays for the first-dollar costs of hospitalization and associated expenses. Major medical insurance pays for the costs of catastrophic illness. These policies have high maximum limits and a deductible provision. Major medical policies also have a participation provision that requires the insured to pay a portion of the covered loss. A newer health insurance alternative, high-deductible health plans combined with HSAs, has recently been introduced in the health insurance market in the hopes of moderating the escalating cost of health insurance.

Disability income insurance is purchased to replace income lost while people are unable to work. Long-term care insurance will be needed by an increasing number of Americans in the next few decades as our society ages. Before more private long-term care insurance is sold, many underwriting and educational problems must be addressed.

Common medical expense insurance policy provisions include a grace period, an entire contract clause, and an incontestable clause. Definitions are an extremely important feature of a health insurance policy. Terms such as *disability*, *renewable*, and *preexisting condition* take on specific meanings that may vary from company to company.

The major providers of health insurance in the United States include Blue Cross–Blue Shield plans, commercial health insurers, HMOs, and PPOs. Most employers provide health insurance coverage to the worker through a managed care organization, such as HMOs and PPOs.

Review

1. Compare the per capita cost spent on health care in the United States to other industrialized countries. Explain the differences across countries.
2. Compare the quality of health care in the United States to that of other countries.
3. Why are more Americans uninsured for health care protection than other countries?
4. Identify four reasons that health care costs have been increasing in the United States.
5. How does the existence of health insurance increase moral hazard in health care?
6. Explain why critics argue that fee-for-service health care leads to the inefficient delivery of health care.
7. Do all Americans use equal amounts of health care? If not, explain how costs are distributed.
8. Permanent disability can be a more expensive peril than death. Explain why this is so.
9. Explain the purpose of long-term care insurance.
10. List five activities of daily living (ADLs) used in LTC insurance.
11. Identify the problems with the current U.S. system for delivering long-term care.
12. Define the terms *custodial care*, *intermediate care*, *hospice*, and *skilled nursing facility*.
13. Illness may cause two different types of monetary loss. What are they?
14. Describe two common definitions of disability used in health insurance.
15. Describe three important contractual provisions often found in health insurance policies.
16. Describe five standard clauses found in health insurance contracts.
17. Describe the differences in renewability provisions of health insurance contracts.
18. Define the term *preexisting conditions*. How does time enter into this definition?
19. Describe the methods used by HMOs to control health care costs.
20. Describe the difference in operations between an HMO and a PPO.

Objective Questions

1. Which of the following is not a major type of individually purchased medical expense or disability income policy?
   a. Major medical insurance
   b. Basic medical insurance
   c. Medicare
   d. LTC insurance
2. All the following are reasons given for increasing medical costs EXCEPT:
   a. The cost of technological improvements
   b. Moral hazard
   c. Defensive medicine
   d. Lower deductibles on health insurance contracts

3. The country that spent the most (per capita) on health care in 2008 was …
   a. Japan
   b. Germany
   c. the United States
   d. the United Kingdom
4. Which of the following are examples of traditional fee-for-service health care insurance?
   a. HMOs
   b. PPOs
   c. BCBS major medical plans
   d. All the above
5. Because health insurance decreases a consumer's out of pocket cost for medical coverage, consumers tend to use more health care, a practice commonly known as _____.
   a. moral hazard
   b. adverse selection
   c. asymmetric information
   d. insurance fraud
6. A fee-for-service health care system is one that:
   a. Pays health care providers only when they provide a service
   b. Pays health care providers a regular monthly salary based on seniority
   c. Pays health care providers a capitation payment
   d. Pays health care providers providing services to HMOs
7. The percent of uninsured Americans in 2008 was about:
   a. 2 percent
   b. 4 percent
   c. 10 percent
   d. 16 percent
8. "A facility caring for the terminally ill" is the definition of a:
   a. nursing home
   b. hospice
   c. respite care center
   d. custodial care facility

Discussion Questions

1. Unlike many other countries, the United States relies on several different health insurance providers to cover different types of people. Why is the U.S. system so complicated? In your answer, describe three separate providers.

2. What do you think should be done for the many Americans not covered by private health insurance?

Selected References

AHIP Center for Policy and Research, *AHIP HSA/ HDHP Census Report*, published annually.

American Academy of Actuaries, October 2007 Issue Brief, *FAQs on HSAs: Frequently Asked Questions on Health Savings Accounts*, retrieved December 16, 2011, from *http://www.actuary.org/*

Employee Benefits Research Institute, "Managing Health Care Costs" (2009), Chapter 29 in *Fundamentals of Employee Benefit Programs*, 6th ed. (Washington, DC: Employee Benefits Research Institute).

Ohsfeldt, R. L., and Schneider, J. E., *The Business of Health: The Role of Competition, Markets, and Regulation.* (Washington, DC: AEI Press), 2006.

Pauly, Mark V., "The Economics of Moral Hazard: Comment," *American Economic Review* (1968), 58, 1, pp. 531–537.

Santerre, Rexford E., and Stephen P. Neun, 2007 *Health Economics: Theories, Insights, and Industry Studies*, 4th ed. (Mason, OH: Thomson South-Western).

Simon, Gary. "Can Long-Term Care Insurance Be Fixed?" *Journal of Health Care Finance* (2010) 37, 1, pp. 51–77.

Swartz, Katherine, 2006, *Reinsuring Health: Why More Middle-Class People Are Uninsured and What the Government Can Do* (New York: Russell Sage Foundation).

19

Employee Benefits

After studying this chapter, you should be able to

- Identify the main nonwage employee benefits offered to workers in the United States

- Describe the roles of the government, employer, and employee in employee benefits

- Describe the coverage features commonly found in group life insurance

- Describe the coverage features commonly found in group disability insurance

- Describe the different approaches used by employers to provide health insurance to their employees

- Describe the two main types of employer-sponsored retirement plans

- Identify several types of tax-favored retirement plans for individuals and small businesses

Employers define **employee benefits** as anything of value received by an employee other than wages. Several common employee benefits provide protection from personal risks. Some of these benefits are mandated by the government, including Social Security, workers' compensation, and unemployment. (We describe these benefits in Chapters 20 and 21.) Other employee benefits are not mandated by law, including group life insurance plans, group disability income insurance plans, group health insurance plans, and pension plans. Employee benefits can also include noninsurance benefits, such as paid vacations, day care, employee discounts, and reimbursement for educational expenses. Because many types of employee benefits involve the application of insurance principles to fund the benefit, we cover this topic in this book. Figure 19-1 presents these benefit categories graphically.

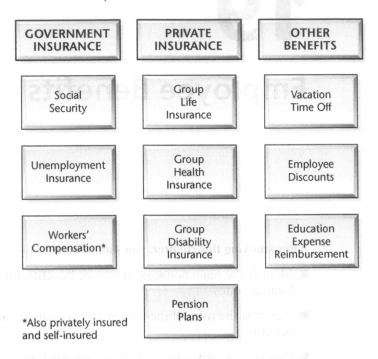

FIGURE 19-1 Categories of Employee Benefits

EMPLOYEE BENEFITS: THE ROLE OF THE GOVERNMENT, EMPLOYERS, AND EMPLOYEES

Understanding employee benefits is becoming increasingly important. Stories about employee benefits appear in the news frequently, and often these stories have had negative implications for employees. For example, as we noted in Chapter 1, many employers have reduced health insurance and pension benefits for their employees in recent years. There also has been much discussion and analysis of the consequences for society of an aging population, global competition, and health care cost increases. Each of these issues has a direct impact on employee benefits.

Traditionally, employee benefits have not been viewed as the sole source of protection from personal risks, but one component in a **tripod of economic security**. This historic tripod anticipated that the employer, the government, and the individual each would provide fairly equal contributions toward the individual's economic security in the United States. Today, however, many people are concerned that the employer-sponsored portion of the tripod may not be sustainable, in part because productivity growth cannot support the rising cost of benefits. Therefore, the material presented in this chapter is especially important because no other major industrialized society relies as much on the private market to deliver the basic framework of economic security to its citizens as the United States.

Table 19-1 presents a clear picture of the increase in benefit costs to employers over a recent twenty-year period. Calculated as the sum of wages and salaries and the total cost of employee benefits, the total cost of employee compensation increased 45 percent from 1991 to 2011. The total cost of employee benefits grew 60 percent over the same time period, a much higher growth rate than wages and salaries. The main driver of this increase has been rising health insurance costs, but the cost of funding retirement income also has contributed to the increase.

TABLE 19-1 Employers' Average Hourly Costs for Employee Total Compensation, Wages, and Total Benefits for All Workers, 1991–2011

	1991	*2011*	*Percentage Increase*
Total compensation	$20.83	$30.11	45
Wages and salaries	$15.07	$20.91	39
Total benefits	$ 5.77	$ 9.21	60

Data from U.S. Government Accountability Office (GAO), "Employer Compensation" (February 2006), GAO-06-285 and Bureau of Labor Statistics (BLS), "Employer Costs of Employee Compensation" (September 2011), USDL-11-1718, and author's calculations.

The Government

Working people in the farming societies that were prevalent in the United States and elsewhere before the twentieth century were assumed to be self-sufficient. If disaster (such as premature death or disability) occurred, the remaining members of the family assumed responsibility. Few people lived long enough to retire from work, and extended families lived close enough to help one another. Industrialization destroyed this agrarian pattern, however. People left the land and lost their self-sufficiency. Society became interdependent and relied on a monetary exchange system for transactions. Families were more likely to be separated geographically. Improved sanitation and health care increased life expectancy. The result was a potentially long retirement period that often involved economic and physical dependency. The use of machinery and fossil fuel shortened workweeks, providing leisure time. Society was revolutionized, and so was the method of providing economic security to its members. The government assumed more responsibility for providing economic security to its citizens. These changes, as well as the change from the view of individual responsibility for one's welfare to collective or social responsibility, did not happen suddenly. Today, however, in all industrialized societies, the government provides some level of economic security for its citizens.

Each society approaches the problem of providing economic security differently. The democratic socialist approach found in Western European countries involves some measure of free enterprise, but with heavy government intervention, regulation, and taxation. These governments also provide economic security directly to their citizens in the form of health care, pensions, disability income payments, and childcare allowances. Because government bureaucrats do not have the competitive incentive to perform, and because the government controls vast amounts of capital to fund benefit plans, the efficiency and quality of this approach are open to question. But one advantage of the democratic socialist approach is universal coverage for all citizens.

The U.S. approach relies on free enterprise, with a foundation of government-provided benefits and extensive regulation, to provide the framework of the national economic security program. This system has many advantages. The competition of free enterprise promotes efficiency. When numerous insurers, hospitals, and health maintenance organizations (HMOs) each can provide coverage and compete for business in terms of price and quality, society benefits from the invisible hand of competition. The large amount of capital required to fund pension plans also remains in private hands, which is consistent with the tenets of the free enterprise system. Taxes are lower than would be the case if government benefits were substituted for benefits coming from the private sector.

The free enterprise system also has several disadvantages. The unemployed, part-time employees, and employees of companies with no (or minimum) benefit programs may be cut off from essential services. Health care access is an especially troublesome social issue. The tax revenues forgone when the government induces employers to provide employee benefits by granting tax breaks also means somebody's taxes must go up if the government is to raise the revenue needed for social programs. Critics maintain that such a tax policy often benefits upper- and middle-income citizens at the expense of lower-income people.

With this background, we can identify three advantages that our government receives from the private employee benefits system besides the economic efficiency associated with free enterprise. First, fewer people depend on the government for support (that is, welfare). Second, the burden on the Social Security program is reduced if people also have private pensions and life insurance. Third, government control of the economy is avoided if the funds that finance the benefits system remain in private hands.

The Employer

If an employer was given the option of paying employees either $14 an hour in wages or $10 an hour in wages and $4 in benefits, why might it choose the second alternative? First, the government provides some tax benefits for the second approach. In both cases, the employer's costs would be deductible from income so long as the compensation were reasonable; therefore, there is no direct tax advantage in the deductibility of expenses. Assume that the employer had a goal of providing a given dollar amount of pension benefit to each employee, such as $500 a month. Then, because there is no tax payable on the investment income during the employee's working years if there is a qualified plan, the employer does not have to put as much into the fund to accumulate the desired amount.

Second, it is argued that employee benefits allow the employer to attract, retain, and motivate employees better than straight wages. In a competitive job market, if one employer's total compensation package is viewed as less desirable than all others, presumably that employer will have difficulty finding and keeping good workers. On the other hand, if one employer has a better compensation program than others, it might be able to hire the best workers. So long as employees view the combination of wages and employee benefits as more desirable than wages alone, competitive employers must provide them to attract the best people.

Third, an efficient pension plan allows employers to facilitate the retirement of older workers, whose salaries might be greater than needed to attract younger workers. Young workers also might have more current job skills, better health, and more enthusiasm for work. Of course, not all young workers have as good job skills, good work habits, or other desirable attributes as older workers. However, many employers believe that orderly retirements allow regular promotions throughout the workforce and can be a useful part of a well-designed human resources program.

The Employee

Like employers, employees also receive favorable tax treatment on the portion of their compensation paid as employee benefits. Some benefits are received tax free, including premiums spent on group disability or health insurance, which often amount to thousands of dollars for workers and their families. Other benefits receive the significant advantage of **tax deferral**. For example, although the employer gets an immediate income tax deduction when contributions are made to a pension plan, the employee does not have to report the income until the pension is received, which may be forty years after the employer's payment is made.

Tax deferral provides several advantages. First, postponing tax payment allows interest to be earned on dollars "owed" to the government. This is the present value advantage of deferring taxes. The employee also may be in a lower tax bracket upon receiving the distribution. Also, deferral allows the compound interest to accumulate on a tax-deferred basis. To understand the importance of these advantages, compare the position of Joe Green, who must pay taxes on his marginal $1,000 of income at a 30 percent rate. He can thus invest $700 after taxes. Each year, he also must pay 30 percent of his investment earnings in taxes. Sue Blue, in contrast, postpones the taxes on the marginal $1,000 that she contributes to her pension plan. The full $1,000 is invested. Furthermore, she also postpones the taxes on all the income the $1,000 produces. In the long run, even though she owes taxes when withdrawals are made, Sue's position will be superior to Joe's. The appendix to this chapter illustrates the advantages of tax deferral in detail.

In addition to favorable tax treatment, employees receive other advantages from employee benefit programs. These include (1) greater incentive to save for retirement; (2) obtaining insurance coverage for a lower cost than if similar coverage were purchased individually; and (3) obtaining insurance coverage when it might be unavailable individually if the worker is uninsurable.

INSURED EMPLOYEE BENEFITS

The government's philosophy is that when it grants tax breaks for employee benefit plans, it also provides regulations to ensure that the employer distributes these benefits fairly to all employees. Put another way, the government does not want to forgo tax revenue to subsidize plans benefiting only upper-income employees. The desire for nondiscriminatory benefits has resulted in complex benefit plan regulations. A significant portion of the federal regulations applying to employee benefits is found in the **Internal Revenue Code (IRC)** and the **Employee Retirement Income Security Act of 1974 (ERISA)**. These laws have two areas of emphasis: qualification rules and nondiscrimination rules. The **qualification rules** are straightforward, detailing what employers must do to receive tax benefits. For example, the rules require that the plan must be in writing and that the plan must create legally enforceable rights for employees. The plan must be for the exclusive benefit of employees, and it must be expected to last indefinitely. By contrast, the **nondiscrimination rules** are not easily summarized. Instead, using guidelines and formulas, the government tries to ensure that employee benefits do not discriminate in favor of the highly compensated group and against lower-paid workers.

General Features

When an insurer provides coverage for many people under one master contract, the result is called **group insurance**. Typical groups covered include the employees of one employer or all the members of a labor union. Group insurance can be written on all the debtors (credit card holders with outstanding balances) of one creditor (a bank or credit union). Group coverage also has been offered to all members of social fraternities, sororities, or the alumni of a particular university. To prevent adverse selection, the most important characteristic of the covered group is that the reason for its existence is something other than the purchase of group insurance.

In employee benefit arrangements, group life, disability, and health insurance require a contract between an employer and an insurer. With an insured plan, each employee receives a **certificate of participation** and an explanation of the benefits provided, but the insured technically is the employer.

Group insurance is lower in cost than comparable individual insurance. Several reasons explain the cost difference. In most group insurance cases, no medical examination is required, though an examination may be required for groups consisting of a small number of members. The insured often provides administrative services, including collecting premiums when employees contribute to the cost. The acquisition cost to the insurer, including the commission paid to the selling agent, is lower than if a comparable amount of individual coverage is sold. For these reasons, the insurer can offer group coverage for a lower price than individual coverage.

Group insurance involves underwriting the group as a whole. Group demographics, size, and stability are key factors in developing a premium. Depending on the type of coverage—life, disability, or health—insurers will adjust the premium if there are large percentages of men or women and old or young people. The insurer also will be interested in the stability of the group. Is there an above-average rate of leaving and joining? Most underwriters also are cautious about cases in which the insured has switched insurers two or more times in the last five years.

If the group is large, the insurer will offer **experience-rated premiums**. In this case, if the employer's data have **credibility** because the group consists of the large number of observations (workers), the insurer has confidence in tailoring the premium to the particular group's outcome. Once a group has credibility, if there are fewer deaths, disabilities, or hospitalizations in a policy year, the group receives lower premiums in future years. An employer with fewer workers may have to wait several years before its data are sufficiently credible for the insurer to experience rate premiums. Before a group achieves statistical credibility, the insurer determines its rates using group averages.

GROUP LIFE INSURANCE

Perhaps the easiest employee benefit to understand is **group term life insurance**. This contract provides a death benefit for a specified period, typically one year. When the term expires, the policy can be renewed. If an employer offers this benefit, when a covered employee dies, a beneficiary receives the death benefit.

The insurer bases the premiums for group term life insurance on the average age of the covered employees. Unlike an individual, a group's average age does not necessarily increase every calendar year. In fact, if several older employees were to retire and were replaced by younger employees, the average age of the group would go down. Thus, the age and number of employees entering and leaving immediately affect the average age of a group. Most employers offering this benefit cover only full-time workers, but some also may offer the coverage to part-time employees. Some employers also offer coverage, often in reduced amounts, to retired employees.

The amount of coverage may be set as a *flat amount*. For example, each beneficiary receives $50,000 if a covered worker dies. Alternatively, the amount of insurance may be based on a *position schedule*. In this case, the benefit may be $50,000 for salaried workers and $25,000 for hourly workers. The amount of insurance also may be a *percentage of earnings*. For example, each employee's benefit equals 100 or 150 percent of one year's salary. Combinations of these approaches are possible. For example, in one company, benefits equal 200 percent of annual salary for senior managers, 150 percent for middle managers, and 100 percent for all other employees.

The employee generally is allowed free choice when designating a beneficiary and may assign contract rights if proper notification is given to the insurer. The employee or beneficiary has several settlement options, comparable with the settlement options available with individual insurance: namely, lump-sum payment, lifetime income, or payments for a limited period.

Most contracts allow for conversion of the group insurance coverage to individual insurance if the employee leaves the group. This right is exercised rarely, except by people otherwise uninsurable. One reason for the relatively small number of conversions is that the conversion may be from the group term policy to a cash-value type of coverage with premiums calculated at the insured's age at the time of conversion. If the employee is older when converting from group term to individual coverage, these premiums tend to be costly. If the employee leaves one employer's group to enter another employer's group, an expensive conversion would be unattractive. If the employee left the group and is unemployed, an expensive conversion may not even be affordable.

The federal income taxation of group term life insurance allows the employer a deduction for premiums paid, so long as an employee's total compensation is reasonable. The employee does not have to report the premium paid as income, so long as the insurance benefit is less than $50,000. If the benefit is greater than $50,000, the premium for the insurance in excess of $50,000 is included in the employee's taxable income.

There are several reasons why people should not rely solely on group term life insurance, or even a combination of group term life insurance and Social Security survivor benefits, for their life insurance program. First, the benefits may be inadequate to meet all financial needs and goals. This outcome is likely because employers set benefit amounts without considering employee needs. Second, the benefits may be unavailable if employment ends or the employer cancels the plan due to bankruptcy, merger, or other reasons. We explained previously why the conversion of group insurance to individual insurance is unlikely. Finally, group term life insurance involves no savings, and this feature of individual cash-value life insurance may be important to some people. Thus, most people recognize employer-provided life insurance as one leg of a tripod, with Social Security and individual life insurance as the other two legs.

GROUP DISABILITY INCOME INSURANCE

If an employee is disabled by a work-related accident or illness, workers' compensation benefits are available to provide indemnity and rehabilitation payments. Workers' compensation benefits, however, generally are inadequate to replace all lost income. Moreover, not all permanent disabilities are work-related. Thus, for work-related or non-work-related disability, many people need disability income insurance to provide economic security. Insurers categorize these programs as short- or long-term programs.

Short-Term Disability

Short-term programs continue the employee's salary for six or fewer months. Employers may call these plans **sick-leave plans**, and often the plans are not insured. Employers that offer this benefit often provide employees with a certain number of sick days for a given period worked. For example, an employee may earn one sick day for each month of employment. If more sick days are taken than are earned, the employee's pay is reduced accordingly. Some employers coordinate a sick-leave plan with an insured short-term disability income plan that provides covered employees with up to six months of coverage.

Long-Term Disability

Long-term disability benefits, when offered by an employer, typically will be insured. Long-term benefits may begin after a waiting period (for example, three or six months) and last for a period of years (for example, five or ten years) or until a specified age, such as age 65, is reached.

Several problems must be solved when offering long-term disability insurance. The plan must define the term **permanent disability**. As we described in Chapter 18, "Health Insurance and Disability Income," the definition may be liberal (unable to perform the tasks of the occupation for which the person is trained) or strict (unable to perform the tasks of any occupation for which the person might be trained in the future). Some policies combine definitions, applying the liberal definition for the first few years of disability and then shifting to the strict definition if the disability persists. Thus, a teacher who suffers a permanent voice loss may meet the liberal definition but may not be able to continue to qualify for disability benefits under the strict definition if the requirements of an administrative position could be met.

The compensation provided must not be so great as to encourage malingering. The usual approach to achieving this goal is to limit the compensation paid to some percentage of the predisability income, such as 66 percent. Generally, the employer considers all sources of disability income, including Social Security, when calculating the amount of disability insurance benefit provided. Plans that consider Social Security benefits when determining disability insurance benefits are called **integrated plans**.

Only a few exclusions are likely to be found in group disability contracts. Typical exclusions are (1) losses arising out of self-inflicted injuries (including suicide attempts), (2) losses arising out of the commission of a felony, and (3) losses arising from war.

The federal taxation of disability income benefits allows the employer to deduct the cost of purchasing the insurance coverage. The employee does not have to report the cost of the employer's contribution as taxable income. If the employee receives payments as a result of disability, however, these payments are included in the employee's taxable income in the year received. There is an exception to this rule. If the employee paid the premium for the disability income protection, then there is no federal income tax on the benefits. If the premiums were paid in part by the employer and in part with employee contributions, then the amount of disability income attributed to the employee's contribution is not subject to income tax. For example, if the employer paid 60 percent of the premium and the employee paid 40 percent, then only 60 percent of the disability income payments the employee receives is included in taxable income.

GROUP HEALTH INSURANCE

As we discussed in Chapter 18, employers are the leading provider of health insurance to a majority of working-age Americans, who receive such coverage as non-wage employee benefits. Employers providing group health insurance typically cover the employee and eligible dependents. Eligible dependents include a married spouse and dependent children under 26 years old.

Many of the recent changes in the health insurance industry have been driven by employers searching for ways to decrease the cost of providing such coverage to their employees. For example, the data shown in Figure 19-2 demonstrate how employers have dramatically shifted from fee-for-service indemnity health insurance coverage to managed care organizations (MCOs) in a relatively short period of time. While a majority of employers used fee-for-service health insurance as recently as the mid-1990s,

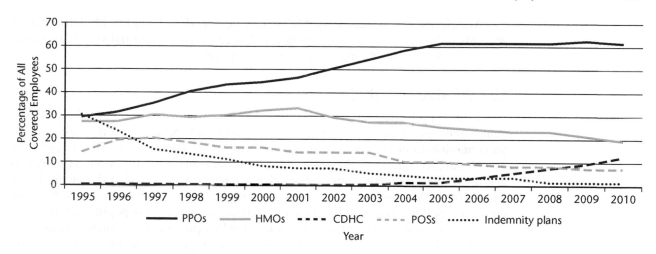

FIGURE 19-2 Distribution of Health Plan Enrollment (as a percentage of all covered employees), by Type of Plan, 1995–2010

Data from Mercer's National Survey of Employer-Sponsored Health Plans (published annually), Kaiser/HRET Survey of Employer-Sponsored Health Benefits (published annually), and author calculations.

such plans currently account for only a small fraction of all employer-sponsored health insurance. Since that time, employers have turned to MCOs, most commonly HMOs and preferred provider organization (PPOs), to control the cost of health insurance.

HMOs provide extensive health care services, including preventive care (such as physical examinations, vaccinations, and wellness programs), in exchange for monthly payments made by the employer called **capitation payments**. Once the HMO sets the capitation payment (set as a specified dollar amount each month for each employee), the amount does not change because of use. The HMO will use this rate for a specified period, such as six months or a year. Employees covered under an employer-sponsored HMO receive treatment from the medical providers who are part of the HMO's provider network. HMOs include financial incentives in their contracts with medical providers to encourage the providers to deliver care in a cost-effective manner. A second type of MCO closely related to HMOs is the **point of service (POS)** plan. POS plans control cost through the use of an HMO-like medical provider network, but they do not restrict coverage to network providers. Covered employees can receive treatment from providers affiliated with the POS network for little or no cost, but they also can be treated by providers outside the network, subject to deductibles and coinsurance provisions. PPOs provide services on a contract basis to employers. They do not provide prepaid benefits like HMOs, but they bill the user (employer) at prearranged discounted prices when service is rendered. Employers use disincentives, such as reduced coverage if employees use a non-PPO provider, to encourage employees to use PPO providers to meet their health care needs.[1]

---

[1] For example, if the employee uses the PPO's hospital and physicians for a medical condition, the bill may be $10,000, and the employee may be reimbursed for 90 percent of this amount ($9,000). If the employee uses non-PPO providers, however, the bill may be 20 percent higher, or $12,000, because PPO medical providers agreed to reduce their fees when joining the PPO. Moreover, the reimbursement for the non-PPO providers may be at a lower level than the PPO provider, say 60 percent rather than 90 percent. A 60 percent level of reimbursement provides payment of $7,200 (0.6 × 12,000), rather than the $9,000 paid when the PPO provider is used. Thus, using the PPO costs the employee $1,000 ($10,000 − $9,000), while using the non-PPO costs $4,800 ($12,000 − $7,200).

Additional details regarding MCOs can be found in Chapter 18. This chapter presents only a brief review of this material because group and individual insurance contracts are comparable in most important respects.

Self-Funded Health Care

Rather than purchase insurance, many employers currently self-fund (self-insure) their health benefits. The employer with a self-funded health benefit typically hires a **third-party administrator (TPA)**, which might be an insurance company or a Blue Cross–Blue Shield plan, to administer the program, carrying out such activities as verifying coverage for claims, calculating appropriate claims payments, and paying the medical provider. The TPA administers the program, but the payments to providers come from the employer. Self-funding health benefits have become increasingly popular for financial and other reasons. In particular, a portion of ERISA preempts self-funded plans operating in multiple states from state regulation, enabling the employers to avoid certain costly regulatory requirements (such as mandated benefits).

Some employers use **stop-loss insurance** arrangements to assure that their self-funded health insurance plans do not produce catastrophic loss results. An employer can buy stop-loss coverage from an insurer on a *per-person* basis, protecting the employer from a catastrophic loss suffered by a single employee. When the medical expenses of that employee exceed the per-person stop-loss limit, the insurer pays all expenses in excess of the limit. Alternatively, an *aggregate* stop-loss insurance arrangement sets a coverage limit based on the total losses of the employer. If the total of all self-insured medical expenses exceed a specified coverage limit, often specified as 125 to 150 percent of the expected losses for the employee group, the insurer pays the claim in excess of the aggregate limit.

Consumer-Driven Health Care

An increasingly popular trend in employer-sponsored health insurance is **consumer-driven health care (CDHC)**, health insurance arrangements that provide employees financial incentives to minimize moral hazard by becoming more actively involved in the decision to consume medical services. As was shown previously in Figure 19-2, CDHC is one of the fastest-growing methods used by employers, particularly employers with large numbers of employees, to control the cost of employer-sponsored health care.

While CDHC plans can be designed in several ways, one of the most common arrangements combines a high-deductible group health insurance policy with a tax-favored savings account that can be used by the employee to pay for medical expenses not covered by the group policy. The group policy typically covers employees as subscribers in a preferred provider organization. The tax-favored savings account is often designed as a health savings account (HSA), as was described in Chapter 18. Employees can make tax-deductible contributions into the HSA, earning tax-free investment income on the account balance. The employee can use the money in his HSA to pay for uninsured medical expenses, expenses that fall below the deductible limit or medical treatments not otherwise insured under the group policy. Unspent balances in the HSA can be accumulated over time for use in future years.[2] To receive tax-favored

---

[2] As an alternative to HSAs, the employer can design CDHC plans using health retirement accounts (HRAs) to pay for uninsured medical expenses. An HRA receives the same favorable tax treatment as an HSA, but it is financed by tax-deductible payments made by the employer, not the employee. The employer can specify the types of medical benefits that can be paid for by the employee through the HRA.

treatment, the minimum and maximum size of the deductible must fall within limits set by the Internal Revenue Service (IRS; see Chapter 18).

Because the employee is spending her own savings from the HSA, she has a financial incentive to be careful about the price and the amount of health care consumed, thus controlling moral hazard. In theory, these incentives should make the market for health care more competitive as employees compare the price and quality of medical care across medical providers. To date, it has been difficult to determine if CDHC is meeting its goals. Although employers can reduce the cost of group health insurance coverage by using very large deductibles, studies offer contradictory conclusions about employee satisfaction with CDHC. Some critics question whether consumers can gather sufficient health care pricing information to make informed decisions. Others caution that low-income employees may forego necessary treatment because they cannot afford to contribute enough money into their HSAs.

General Provisions of Group Health Insurance Contracts

Several exclusions or limitations may apply to group health insurance policies. For example, cosmetic surgeries often are excluded unless they are made necessary by a non-elective medical need (such as to treat an injury from a car accident). There is no coverage for custodial care, such as a nursing home that is not designed to improve the status of a patient's health. Some group health insurance policies may place limits on the amounts that they will pay for substance abuse or mental health services because it is difficult to determine when the insured loss event begins or when the patient has recovered.

Another area of concern in group health insurance policies is **coordination of benefits**. With many families having two working spouses and medical expense coverage provided by personal automobile policies (when hospitalization results from automobile accidents), insurers need to determine which policy pays first (provides primary coverage) and which policy pays second (provides excess coverage). Either the policies themselves or an appropriate state law will determine the issue. The purpose of these rules is to allow the insured to be indemnified but not allow more compensation than the costs incurred.

Cost-containment measures have become increasingly common in recent years. Such measures as wellness programs (including emphasis on physical fitness and elimination of unhealthy habits such as smoking and drinking), precertification before surgery (when a medical technician reviews and approves the anticipated length of stay), second opinions before surgery, and post-claim audits of medical bills all have been used to reduce the rapid rise in employers' health care costs.

Federal Health Insurance Regulations[3]

Group health insurance is heavily regulated on a state and federal level, with much of this regulation affecting the terms of coverage provided to employees. In this section, we examine three specific federal regulations with which employees and risk managers should be familiar.

---

[3] Several federal Web sites offer detailed information about these regulations. For information on COBRA, see *http://www.dol.gov/dol/topic/health-plans/cobra.htm*. For information about the FMLA, see *http://www. dol.gov/whd/regs/compliance/1421.htm*. For information about HIPAA, see *http://www.dol.gov/dol/topic/ health-plans/portability.htm*.

THE CONSOLIDATED OMNIBUS BUDGET RECONCILIATION ACT OF 1985 (COBRA)

COBRA rules require employers to allow workers leaving the group, spouses of deceased employees, children who are no longer dependent, and divorced spouses to continue group health insurance coverage for up to 36 months after a qualifying event, including separation from work, death, or divorce. The person continuing the coverage must pay the group premium to the employer, but this cost typically is less than individually purchased coverage. COBRA benefits may be terminated for a few reasons, including if the employer stops providing health insurance benefits for all its employees, the insured does not pay the required premiums on time, or the beneficiary obtains group health insurance coverage under another plan.

THE FAMILY AND MEDICAL LEAVE ACT OF 1993 (FMLA)

The FMLA assures that employees will be permitted to leave their jobs temporarily to tend to urgent family situations, such as the care of a child, spouse, or parent with a serious health condition, or to care for a personal serious health condition suffered by the employee that prevents him or her from performing job duties. The act also allows employees time off from work to care for newborn or newly adopted children. When family leaves are completed, employers must reinstate employees to their previous or equivalent position with no loss of benefits. The act applies to employers having fifty or more employees. Employers are not required to pay compensation for periods of leave taken under the act.

THE HEALTH INSURANCE PORTABILITY AND ACCOUNTABILITY ACT OF 1996 (HIPAA)

HIPPA prohibits employers from excluding newly hired workers from their health insurance plans due to **preexisting conditions**, recent health issues that could require the new employer to pay for the medical treatment of problems that occurred prior to hiring. Workers with preexisting medical conditions often are reluctant to switch jobs out of fear that the new employer may not cover their medical expenses if the medical problem recurs. Economists believe that labor mobility increases the overall performance of an economy. A primary purpose of HIPAA is to promote labor mobility.

Assume, for example, that Anne Chovie currently is a fishing boat captain but has the skills to qualify as a computer systems administrator. If she could move from her current job to a new job of computer systems administrator, not only could she double her salary, the entire economy benefits from the better use of her skills. However, also assume that Anne has a serious health condition for which she currently is receiving treatment. If her new employer's group health insurance policy excludes coverage for "preexisting conditions," Anne might not be eligible for coverage of this condition under her new employer's group insurance policy, and therefore she might not change jobs.

HIPPA applies to group health plans that cover two or more employees and prohibits employers from excluding an employee or her dependents from coverage for more than twelve months due to medical history—health status, claims experience, medical history, genetic information, or disability—including a medical condition that was treated or diagnosed within the previous six months.

INSIGHT BOX 19-1

The Patient Protection and Affordable Care Act

In March 2010, President Barack Obama signed into law the Patient Protection and Affordable Care Act (PPACA), federal health care legislation that will dramatically change the way that many Americans receive health insurance. The factors leading to this legislation are well documented. The cost of health care has increased steadily over the past two decades (see Figure 18-1), and aging baby boomers are expected to fuel this trend further. Due in part to increased health care costs, 1 in 6 Americans currently do not have health insurance.

Most Americans with health insurance receive it as a tax-favored, employer-sponsored employee benefit. Many Americans without health insurance are not a part of a large employer group, and therefore, they must purchase coverage through the individual health insurance markets. Underwriting in the individual health insurance markets is rigid, as insurers are wary that the individuals most likely to seek insurance also are most likely to have health problems. For insurers, this form of adverse selection can be costly. Over a quarter of all health care expenses incurred by patients in the United States are consumed by only 1 percent of all Americans (see Figure 18-2)—a fact that explains why individual health insurers have used extensive medical underwriting screening to identify high-risk applicants and exclude costly preexisting conditions.

In an effort to address some of these issues, the PPACA makes the following changes to the U.S. health insurance markets:

- Employers with fifty or more employees will be mandated to offer health care protection to their employees or pay a penalty. This so-called "play or pay" provision increases the odds that most Americans receiving health insurance from employers will continue to receive such coverage.

- All Americans are required to have health insurance. If a person is not covered in an employer-sponsored health plan, he or she will have to buy individual coverage or pay a penalty. This "individual mandate" provision is built into the PPACA to assure that the health insurance pool includes a maximum number of Americans, including many uninsured Americans who may not need protection currently, but probably will need it in the future. By expanding the size of the insurance pool, the total cost of health care is spread across the largest number of insureds,

with the intent of lowering the overall cost per insured. These cost reductions, however, may be offset by an increase in moral hazard, as increasing the number of people with health insurance is expected to increase the demand for health care.

- Tax credits will be available to individuals with incomes up to 400 percent of the federal poverty level (up to $43,000 for individuals and $88,000 for a family of four, based on 2010 figures) who are ineligible for affordable health insurance coverage, thus making it easier for them to comply with the individual mandate.

- Eligibility for Medicaid, the welfare program that provides health care to the poor, will be expanded to include a greater percentage of low-income, uninsured Americans. State-administered health insurance exchanges will be established for the individual and small-group markets. Insurers offering products in the exchanges will be restricted in their use of medical underwriting practices. Product design will be limited to a select number of coverage "tiers," or types of health insurance products.

For the health insurance industry, the passage of the PPACA ushered in an era of heightened regulation. Miller (2010, p. 1102) notes that in the political debate leading up to the passage of the PPACA, health insurers were portrayed as "political villains primarily responsible for unaffordable or unavailable private insurance coverage," and the act includes regulation to address these issues. For example, insurers are prohibited under the PPACA from excluding applicants for preexisting conditions or other forms of medical underwriting. To address the affordability issue, the PPACA requires insurers to spend at least 85 percent (for small group coverage) or 80 percent (for individual coverage) of the premium for coverage of medical costs, paying excess premiums back to consumers if necessary to meet the percentage standards.

In 2011 the Supreme Court agreed to hear a constitutional challenge to the PPACA after opponents of the Act won several lower court rulings. The Court upheld the legality of most of the Act in June 2012. In particular, the Court ruled that penalties assessed on people who failed to meet the individual mandate were valid under Congress' authority to tax. The Court ruled against a portion of the Act, however, that penalized states that fail to expand Medicaid eligibility.

The design of the PPACA relied heavily on a wide body of health economics research. Please see Harrington (2010a, 2010b) and Monheit (2010) for useful reviews of these studies and more detailed discussion of the design of the PPACA. See Miller (2010) for an interesting commentary on the political process involved in the passage of the PPACA.

Based on S. E. Harrington, "The Health Insurance Reform Debate," Journal of Risk and Insurance, 2010a, Vol. 77, No. 1, 5–38; S. E. Harrington, "U.S. Health-Care Reform: The Patient Protection and Affordable Care Act," Journal of Risk and Insurance, 2010b, Vol. 77, No. 3, pp. 97–102; T. P. Miller, "Health Reform: Only A Cease-Fire in a Political Hundred Years' War," Health Affairs, 2010, Vol. 29, No. 6, 1101–1105.

INSURED PENSION PLANS

A **pension plan** is an employee benefit that provides workers with retirement income. **Retirement** occurs when an employee permanently ends active employment. The **normal retirement age** is the youngest age when full retirement benefits are available. Some plans allow participants to retire before the normal retirement age, but early retirement reduces the annual pension benefits. The objective of a pension plan is to replace some percentage of the employee's preretirement income. The **replacement ratio** is calculated as retirement income divided by preretirement income. Replacement ratios of less than 100 percent are typical because the retired worker presumably has no work-related expenses, such as commuting expenses, and pays no Social Security tax on pension income. Thus, a replacement ratio of 60 percent might allow retired workers to maintain a standard of living comparable to that which they enjoyed during their working years.

Many retirement plans are **contributory plans** that require the covered employee to make payments toward their own retirement plan. A smaller number of programs are **noncontributory plans**, retirement plans for which the employer assumes full financial responsibility.

A pension plan may be qualified or nonqualified. A **qualified plan** meets the requirements of the relevant sections of the IRC, and the employer and employee each receive substantial tax advantages. If the plan does not qualify, the employee reports income as soon as the employer makes a payment into the plan. **Nonqualified pension plans** can be more flexible than qualified plans. For example, they can discriminate in favor of, or pay larger benefits to, highly compensated employees. Qualified pension plans cannot discriminate unfairly. The tax advantages offered to qualified plans have been sufficient to induce many employers to meet the qualification criteria, which we describe shortly.

Pension plans are either defined-benefit plans or defined-contribution plans. **Defined-benefit plans** calculate pension benefits based on a specific formula, which is often based on the employees' final compensation in the year(s) immediately prior to retirement. For example, a formula may call for 2 percent of the employee's last year of salary for each year of employment. An employee with twenty years of employment would receive 40 percent (2 percent/year × 20 years) of his or her final salary under this formula. In a defined-benefit plan, pension obligations are a legal liability of the employer providing the pension, and the employer must provide adequate funding to finance the promised result.

The **cash balance plan** is a special, or hybrid, type of defined-benefit plan. The inputs are a specified percentage of the employee's annual salary while working, such as 5 percent, plus a guaranteed interest credit on the employee's hypothetical account.

The account is hypothetical because the employer actually pools all employees' accounts. The employer guarantees the interest credit and bears the investment risk if actual earnings are less than the guaranteed percentage. If actual earnings exceed the guaranteed rate, the employer can adjust future deposits.[4]

A **defined-contribution plan** requires the employer to make a specified input payment. Unlike defined-benefit plans (including cash balance plans), defined-contribution plans make no promises regarding output. The simplest type of defined-contribution plan is a **money purchase plan**. A money purchase plan, for example, may call for the employer to deposit 6 percent of the employee's annual salary into the plan. These contributions can be invested in a variety of investments, including stocks, bonds, and securities issued by the government. The investment earnings on a money purchase plan could vary widely over a working career, and the employer guarantees no particular rate of return. At retirement, the employee receives the sum of all the input amounts plus the investment earnings. Each employee has a separate account, and the employee bears the investment risk. That is, the employee suffers the financial losses resulting from poor investment experience in a defined-contribution plan, while the employer bears the investment risk in a defined-benefit plan. A 2011 survey indicated that 28 percent of American civilian workers were participating in defined-benefit plans, while 37 percent were participating in defined-contribution plans.[5]

The Decline of Defined-Benefit Plans

Since the 1980s the popularity of defined-benefit plans has decreased, while the popularity of contribution plans has increased. The number of private-sector defined-benefit plans reached a peak of 112,000 in the mid-1980s. By the late 2000s, that number had shrunk to below 30,000.[6] Employers shifted from defined-benefit plans to defined-contribution plans for several reasons. Defined-contribution plans tend to be simpler and less expensive to administer than defined-benefit plans. For example, actuaries are not needed to determine if the plan is overfunded or underfunded. In addition, once an employer has made its contribution to the defined-contribution plan, it has no further liability. The employer guarantees no future benefit. Defined-contribution plans are also popular among workers who switch jobs frequently because the departing workers can remove their vested defined-contribution assets easily from their former employers.

The switch from a defined-benefit to a defined-contribution plan also results in a significant shifting of risk from employer to employee. The employee assumes the **investment risk** in a defined-contribution plan. Because the employer does not guaranteed a specific pension benefit from a defined-contribution plan, adverse investment experience affects only the worker's individual account. The employee may also bear greater **longevity risk**, because retirees are living longer and thus require more assets to live on. Employers sponsoring defined-benefit plans bear the responsibility of paying pension payments to the retiree for life (an obligation that is often satisfied by the purchase of an annuity on the life of the retiree), but the longevity risk is shifted to the worker in a defined-contribution plan.

---

[4] For more information on this type of plan, see U.S. Government Accountability Office (GAO), "Private Pensions: Information of Cash Balance Pension Plans," November 2005 (GAO-06-42).

[5] Figures published in the March 2011 National Compensation Survey, as reported by the Bureau of Labor Statistics (data collected December 31, 2011, from *http://www.bls.gov/ncs/ebs/benefits/2011/ownership/civilian/table02a.htm*.

[6] Pension Benefit Guarantee Corporation (PBGC), "An Analysis of Frozen Defined Benefit Plans," December 2005, p. 1.

Requirements for Tax-Qualified Plans

The requirements for plans to become "tax qualified" can be understood in terms of two overriding government goals. First, plans should not discriminate in favor of highly compensated employees. This goal is enforced primarily by IRC regulations. IRC regulations also place maximum limits on contributions to pension plans and provide other rules to limit the revenue loss to the government. Second, plans should be operated in a financially sound manner. This goal is achieved primarily by ERISA regulations.

Among the requirements established by the IRC and ERISA are the following:[7]

- *Participation and Eligibility.* Plans should cover all full-time employees over age 21 with one full year of service.
- *Nondiscrimination.* Plans should not provide unfairly large benefits to highly compensated employees. Employer contributions to the plan also must not be unfair. The IRS determines the meaning of "unfair" using formulas and safe harbor provisions.
- *Funding.* Defined-benefit plans must be funded in advance according to the requirements of ERISA. Regular payments must be made to defined-contribution plans. The employer must give up control of any funds used to finance qualified pension plans.
- *Vesting.* Tax-qualified plans must include **vesting** provisions—conditions that grant employees the legal rights to the contributions paid by employers into the workers' accounts. Employees become vested in these contributions based on their years of service, or the number of years that they worked for the employer. A plan sponsor can meet its vesting obligations to its employees by satisfying one of two vested standards. Under the *three-year cliff vesting* standard, the sponsor of a defined-contribution plan must provide 100 percent vesting to an employee who completes three years of service. By contrast, under a *graded vesting* standard for defined-contribution plans, the employer must offer at least 20 percent vesting to a worker after two years of service, with an additional 20 percent vested for each additional year of service.[8] Vested benefits are not generally available at the time the employee becomes vested; they are instead payable to the vested employee when he attains the normal retirement age for the plan. A worker is 100 percent vested in the contributions he or she makes into the pension plan.

Federal Regulation of Pension Plans

Pension plans are subject to considerable federal regulation. Over the years, pension regulations have evolved to maintain consistency with the country's efforts to limit discrimination. For example, an amendment to the **Civil Rights Act of 1964**[9] bans employers from discriminating in pension plan benefits based on gender or race. As a result of U.S. Supreme Court rulings, plans may not collect unequal contributions or pay unequal benefits based on gender. Amendments to the **Age Discrimination in**

---

[7] IRC and ERISA regulations are complex; these four general requirements are summaries of some very detailed requirements. For a more detailed description of these requirements, please see McGill et al. (2010), listed in the references cited at the end of the chapter.

[8] The vesting provisions for defined-benefit plans are slightly different. Cliff vesting can require five years of service, and graded vesting standards allow the plan sponsor to require three years of service (not two years) before granting the employee 20 percent vesting.

[9] For more information, see the Web site *http://www.justice.gov/crt/about/cor/coord/titlevi.php*.

Employment Act of 1967 (ADEA)[10] prohibit discrimination against employees in the protected age group (ages 40 to 70). This act prevents employers from forcing employees to retire before age 70. It also prevents plan provisions, such as those relating to contributions or benefits, from discriminating against individuals in the protected group.

The most far-reaching federal law covering pension plans is ERISA.[11] Its overall purpose is to protect the rights of pension plan participants. To accomplish this goal, it has four core features:

1. Reporting and disclosure requirements—that is, employers are required to provide employees with easily understood plan descriptions and benefit statements.

2. Fiduciary requirements, so that those responsible for holding and investing pension assets must be careful to protect the assets and minimize risk of loss.

3. Minimum plan requirements (the requirements for qualification just discussed previously).

4. Plan termination insurance. This part of ERISA created the **Pension Benefit Guarantee Corporation (PBGC)**. The PBGC is a government agency that collects an insurance premium from all plan sponsors and in return stands ready to assume the liabilities of insolvent plans. Only defined-benefit plans create liabilities of the type that the PBGC assumes.[12]

PROFIT-SHARING, 401(K), 403(B), AND CAFETERIA PLANS

Profit-Sharing Plans

Profit-sharing plans are one type of defined-contribution plan. Unlike money purchase plans, the employer is not committed to a regular annual contribution. Rather, in years when the firm's profits permit, the employer credits each employee with a share of the profit. The payments may be in cash or may be deferred (like pension plans). Deferred profit-sharing plans may be qualified like pension plans. If qualified, they get the same tax-deferral advantages and must meet similar qualification requirements as pension plans. Because profit-sharing plans do not produce predictable benefits on which to base retirement income, they usually supplement other pension plans. The maximum tax-deductible contribution is 25 percent of an eligible employee's compensation, subject to a contribution limit that is indexed annually for inflation.

401(k) Plans

Most employers, including nonprofit organizations (except state and local governments), can establish a 401(k) plan. A 401(k) plan allows an employee a choice between taking income in cash and deferring the income by putting it in a qualified plan. If the employee chooses to put the income in a qualified 401(k) plan, all the advantages of tax deferral are available. That is, the employee can make contributions on a pre-tax basis, which lowers current taxable income, and investment income is earned on a

---

[10] For more information, see the Equal Employment Opportunity Commission Web site (*http://www.eeoc.gov/*).

[11] A Department of Labor Web site (*http://www.dol.gov/dol/topic/health-plans/erisa.htm#doltopics/*) provides more details about ERISA.

[12] The PBGC has endured a long history of financial problems, due in part to the bankruptcies of several large companies sponsoring defined-benefit pension plans and a tradition of charging inadequate premiums to high-risk employers. For a detailed discussion on the financial issues that plagued the PBGC during the 1980s, see Harrington and Niehaus (2004), listed in the references cited at the end of the chapter.

tax-deferred basis. Tax law limits the annual contributions to 401(k) plans to $17,000 in 2012.[13] Once funds are deposited in this arrangement, withdrawals before age 59½ are subject to a 10 percent penalty unless attributed to the employee's death, disability, or hardship. Some employers match all or part of their employees' contributions, presumably as an inducement to increase plan participation. Some plans allow employees to borrow from their 401(k) accounts. Some plans also allow hardship withdrawals for contingencies like emergency medical expenses.

403(b) Plans or Tax-Deferred Annuities (TDAs)

The employees of nonprofit (tax-exempt) organizations such as universities, schools, hospitals, and museums have a special section of the IRC devoted to them. Congress justifies this special tax advantage because nonprofit employers do not have the same tax incentives as tax-paying employers to provide for their employees' welfare.

Originally, the law allowed the employees of the specified nonprofit institutions to reduce their salaries (and their income tax liability) voluntarily to purchase deferred annuities. Subsequently, the law was amended to allow contributions to be made to mutual funds. Money placed into tax-deferred annuities (TDAs) has all the advantages of tax deferral discussed throughout this chapter. There are limits on the total amount an employee can contribute to a 403(b) plan and its related TDA—$17,000 in 2012. Early withdrawal from these plans results in a 10 percent penalty.

Cafeteria Plans

In recent years, some employers have given employees a choice of benefits by giving them an amount of money to spend, with minimum participation required in each alternative. Such choice-oriented plans may allow an employee, for example, to trade eyeglass and vision coverage for increased dependent-care allowance. Each person or family will have a different priority of needs, and it is difficult to design a single employee benefit program that satisfies the wide range of needs of a diverse workforce. Because they can be modified to fit the unique needs of the covered employees, cafeteria plans are also known as *flexible benefit plans*.

One of the most common examples of a cafeteria plan is the **flexible spending account**. Under this arrangement, employees can elect to reduce their pretax compensation voluntarily, diverting the compensation into their personal flexible spending account. In turn, the employee can use this money to pay for medical benefits not covered by group health insurance, such as orthodontia, eyeglasses, or many types of uninsured medical care. Using this approach, services not covered by group plans can be financed on a tax-advantaged basis. It should be noted, however, that the IRC applies a "use it or lose it" rule to money in a flexible spending account. This provision states that any money remaining in an employee's flexible spending account at the end of the plan year is forfeited to the employer.

INDIVIDUAL RETIREMENT ACCOUNTS (IRAS)

The federal government wants to encourage people to save for retirement and has passed several laws to achieve this result. One tax law allows qualified people to make limited tax-deductible contributions to an **Individual Retirement Account (IRA)**. This provision of the tax code allows IRA accounts to earn tax-deferred investment income. Congress passed the original IRA provisions as part of ERISA.

---

[13] These limits are subject to change by Congress. Readers can find current information at the Internal Revenue Service Web site: *http://www.irs.ustreas.gov/*).

Current tax rules distinguish between deductible and nondeductible IRA contributions. Deductible contributions can be made only by people in categories to be described shortly. Other people can make nondeductible contributions. Deductible contributions lower taxable income in the year made. The advantage of making nondeductible contributions lies in the tax deferral that is accorded to the investment income.

The maximum limits on contributions are the same for deductible and nondeductible contributions. The maximum limits, which are subject to change, are set equal to $5,000 ($6,000 if over age 50) in 2012. After 2012, the limit will be indexed to inflation and increase in $500 increments. Money invested in an IRA earns investment income free of taxes until it is withdrawn. The money in an IRA cannot be withdrawn without penalty before age 59½.

Eligibility for Deductible Contributions

Currently, people in the following categories can make deductible IRA contributions:

- Single people not covered by an employer-provided pension.
- Married couples where neither spouse is covered by an employer-provided pension.
- Single people or married couples covered by an employer provided pension but with lower or middle incomes may make deductible IRA contributions determined by a formula tied to their total income.

Investment Alternatives

IRA funds must be held by qualified trustees or by a life insurance company. If a life insurance company holds the funds, the IRA contracts must be in the form of annuities and no death benefit may be provided. Qualified trustees include banks, other savings institutions (including federal credit unions), mutual funds, and stock brokerages that provide self-directed IRA accounts. Most of the investment alternatives provided by these institutions are available for IRA use.

Rollovers

Money may be placed in an IRA by a rollover. A **rollover** occurs when money from an IRA or other retirement plan is placed with a new trustee. For example, a rollover occurs if an investor takes IRA funds from one mutual fund and places them with another fund. Rollovers may occur when an employee switches jobs and takes vested retirement benefits from a pension plan, or when an employer terminates a pension plan and makes payments of vested benefits to individual employees. If the employee takes the vested benefits and places them in an IRA, this transaction is considered a rollover. A rollover also would occur if a person switched from one investment medium to another, such as from a mutual fund to a bank.

Taxation

As described above, traditional IRA withdrawals are taxed as ordinary income in the year received. Any portion of a payment attributed to a nondeductible contribution is not taxed a second time. In other words, only deductible contributions and tax-deferred interest are taxed. In general, age 59½ is the earliest date of withdrawal without penalty. If the owner of an IRA withdraws funds from an IRA prior to age 59½, the owner incurs a 10 percent tax penalty in addition to the ordinary income tax arising when the withdrawal is added to the person's taxable income. Exceptions to the premature withdrawal penalty exist in cases of death or disability before age 59½. Withdrawal of funds must begin by age 70½.

Roth IRA

The preceding material describes what now has come to be known as the "traditional IRA." A more recent version of the IRA is known as the "Roth IRA." Contributions to a Roth IRA are not tax deductible, but the funds in the account are tax free when withdrawn. Under current rules, withdrawals of contributions at any time are not subject to tax, as would be expected because the contributions were made with after-tax dollars. Withdrawals of investment earnings also are tax free if IRC rules are followed. To avoid taxation, withdrawals of investment earnings must occur after the taxpayer is at least age 59½, and the Roth IRA must have existed for at least five years before that. Tax-free withdrawals of investment earnings also are possible if the Roth IRA has existed for at least five years, and the taxpayer becomes disabled, has died, or uses up to $10,000 for qualified first-time home-buyer expenses.

Table 19-2 provides a comparison of the major features of traditional and Roth IRAs.

TABLE 19-2 A Comparison of a Traditional IRA and a Roth IRA

Feature	*Traditional IRA*	*Roth IRA*
Eligibility	Working taxpayers under age 70½ can contribute up to $5,000 ($6,000 if age 50 or older), as of 2012. *Phase-out rules and limits may apply.*	Up to $5,000 ($6,000 if age 50 or older) of earned income may be contributed, as of 2012. *Phase-out rules and limits may apply.*
Tax deductibility of contributions	Yes, subject to income limits and phase-out restrictions	None
Taxation of annual investment earnings	None	None
Maximum age for contributions	70½	None
Mandatory age for withdrawals	April 1 of the year after the year in which the taxpayer reaches 70½	None
Taxation upon distribution	All taxed at ordinary income tax rates	No tax if account is five years old and withdrawn after 59½.
Penalty for early withdrawal	10 percent penalty on amount of earnings distributed before age 59½ (unless exception applies)	Contributions may be removed without tax penalty or tax if account is open for 5 or more years. 10% penalty on amount of earnings distributed before age 59½ (unless exception applies). Income tax also applies to earning withdrawn prematurely.

Summary

Employers define the term *employee benefits* as anything of value received by an employee other than wages. Major employer-provided benefits include group life insurance plans, group disability income insurance plans, group health insurance plans, and pension plans, all of which involve the use of insurance principles.

Proponents argue that employee benefits allow the employer to attract, retain, and motivate the employee better than straight wages. Employees receive many advantages from employee benefit programs, including (1) forced saving for retirement accompanied by professional money management, (2) getting insurance coverage for a lower cost than if purchased individually, and (3) getting insurance coverage when it might be totally unavailable individually.

Employee benefit plans must not discriminate in favor of highly compensated employees. Several federal laws, including ERISA and the IRC, are designed to prevent such discrimination with tax-subsidized dollars.

A pension plan is designed to provide employees with retirement income. A pension plan may be qualified or nonqualified. If it qualifies under relevant sections of the IRC, the employer and employee receive substantial tax advantages centering on tax deferral. If the plan does not qualify, the employee reports income as soon as the employer makes a payment to the pension.

The chapter also described profit-sharing plans, IRAs, and 401(k) plans, among other investment options.

Review

1. Define the term *employee benefits*. Describe some of the benefits included in this category.
2. Why is it important to learn about employee benefits?
3. Describe the concept of the tripod of economic security as it applies to employee benefits.
4. How does the U.S. approach to providing society with economic security differ from other national governments' approaches?
5. Describe the employer's goals in offering employee benefits.
6. Why do employees prefer employee benefits to straight wage income?
7. What are two main objectives of federal employee-benefits legislation? Briefly describe how these purposes are achieved.
8. Describe the four basic requirements for a benefit plan to be qualified for tax benefits.
9. Explain some important characteristics of group insurance.
10. List three different approaches for determining a group life insurance benefit.
11. How is group term life insurance taxed while the insured is alive?
12. Most financial planners do not recommend that employees rely exclusively on group life insurance for family survivor death benefits. Explain their reasons.
13. What is an integrated group disability plan?
14. Give two different definitions of permanent disability.
15. What is the difference between short-term disability and long-term disability?
16. Identify some expenses typically excluded by group health insurance contracts.
17. What is the most common approach used by employers to provide health insurance to their employees?
18. Describe the concept of self-funded health insurance.
19. Describe the main reason for qualifying pension plans from the point of view of the employer.
20. Explain the difference between defined-benefit and defined-contribution pension plans.
21. List four requirements for qualifying a pension plan.
22. Describe three of the federal laws that apply to pension plans.
23. What is the general rule regarding the taxation of pension benefits?
24. Describe two important tax advantages accruing to people making traditional IRA contributions. Why would an employee be willing to make a nondeductible contribution to an IRA?
25. Compare the tax advantages of the Roth IRA to a traditional IRA.
26. What is an IRA rollover?

Objective Questions

1. All the following rules apply to qualifying a benefit plan except:
   a. The employee must receive all the tax benefits.
   b. The plan must be in writing.
   c. The plan must be for the exclusive benefit of employees.
   d. The plan must be expected to last indefinitely.
2. "Credibility" with respect to experience-rated group insurance premiums means:
   a. The employer is well known to the insurer.
   b. The employer losses have been verified by a claims auditor.
   c. The insurer has charged the lowest rates permitted by regulation.
   d. The insurer has observed the employer's loss data for a sufficiently long period to have confidence in the results.
3. All the following exclusions are common in group health insurance plans except:
   a. No coverage of cosmetic surgery

b. No coverage of the expenses of the emergency room
c. No coverage for intentional losses
d. No coverage of custodial care

4. In a defined-benefit plan:
   a. The employee's pension is determined by a formula.
   b. The employer makes a flat amount annual payment for each employee.
   c. The employer receives no immediate tax advantage but gets a deduction after the employee retires.
   d. The employee makes the investment choices and bears the investment risk.

5. One advantage of tax deferral on qualified pension plan contributions is:
   a. The employee never has to pay taxes on the contribution.
   b. Taxes are deferred until withdrawal and investment income can be earned on money that would otherwise have been paid in taxes.
   c. Only the employer can earn tax-free investment income; the employee pays taxes immediately, but at a reduced rate.

d. The employee pays taxes in the year the employer makes contributions, but then taxes on investment earnings are deferred until withdrawn in retirement.

6. HMOs charge employers a monthly fee called:
   a. A coverage fee
   b. The pro rata plan fee
   c. The subrogation payment
   d. The capitation payment

7. In a _____ plan, an insurer provides coverage for many people under one master contract.
   a. Reinsurance
   b. Multiple insurance
   c. Group insurance
   d. Combination

8. Which of the following retirement plans does not allow the covered employee to reduce his taxable income voluntarily by the amount he deposits into his retirement account while earning tax-deferred investment income on the account balance?
   a. Roth IRA
   b. 403(b) plan
   c. 401(k) plan
   d. Traditional IRA

Discussion Questions

1. What are the advantages and disadvantages of using the free enterprise system to provide economic security to society?
2. Would you prefer a 10 percent increase in your before-tax salary or 10 percent of your salary contributed to a qualified pension plan? Explain your choice. (If you are an unemployed student, assume that you earn the average full-time salary in your chosen profession.)

Selected References

Harrington, S. E., and G. R. Niehaus, 2004, *Risk Management and Insurance*, 2nd ed. (New York: McGraw-Hill Higher Education).

McGill, D. M., K.N. Brown, J. J. Haley, S. J. Schieber, and M. J. Warshawsky, 2010, *Fundamentals of Private Pensions*, 9th ed. (New York: Oxford University Press).

Appendix: Tax Deferral

The benefit of tax deferral is critical to the understanding of qualified pension plans. In this appendix, we continue our example of tax deferral from earlier in this chapter, extending the example over a 30-year time frame. Again, assume that Joe Green and Sue Blue each receive $1,000 in marginal income. Joe takes his income in cash. Sue takes hers in a tax-qualified pension plan. Joe and Sue each pay 30 percent in taxes. Each earns 8 percent on investments.

Sue's tax-deferred fund grows at a faster rate than Joe's taxed fund. Due to the 30 percent tax, Joe paid $300 in taxes on his $1,000 in income, and $16.80 in taxes on the $56 dollars of investment income by the end of year 1. He begins year 2 with $739.20. Sue earned $80 in income on the $1,000. She has no tax liability until the money is withdrawn. As a result, Sue's balance at the beginning of year 2 is $1,080, a much larger fund than Joe's.

Once you can explain the difference derived from tax deferral, examine Table 19-3, which compares the growth in Sue and Joe's pension accounts over thirty years. Note that Sue must pay taxes at the 30 percent rate at the end of the period, whereas Joe pays annual taxes. Even after paying taxes, the balance in Sue's account is ***nearly double*** that in Joe's. This is due to the advantage of tax deferral. Sue earned income on dollars that otherwise would have been paid in taxes (the initial $300). She also earned income on the portion of the annual investment returns that otherwise would have been paid in taxes.

TABLE 19-3 The Advantage of Tax Deferral in Retirement Plans

	Joe Green					Sue Blue				
Year	Deposit ($)	Taxes ($)	Interest ($)	Taxes ($)	Fund Balance ($)	Deposit ($)	Interest ($)	Fund Balance ($)	Taxes ($)	Balance After Tax ($)
1	1,000	300	56.00	16.80	739.20	1,000.00	80.00	1,080.00		
2			59.14	17.74	780.60		86.40	1,166.40		
3			62.45	18.73	824.31		93.31	1,259.71		
4			65.94	19.78	870.47		100.78	1,360.49		
5			69.64	20.89	919.22		108.84	1,469.33		
6			73.54	22.06	970.69		117.55	1,586.87		
7			77.66	23.30	1,025.05		126.95	1,713.82		
8			82.00	24.60	1,082.45		137.11	1,850.93		
9			86.60	25.98	1,143.07		148.07	1,999.00		
10			91.45	27.43	1,207.08		159.92	2,158.92		
11			96.57	28.97	1,274.68		172.71	2,331.64		
12			101.97	30.59	1,346.06		186.53	2,518.17		
13			107.68	32.31	1,421.44		201.45	2,719.62		
14			113.72	34.11	1,501.04		217.57	2,937.19		
15			120.08	36.03	1,585.10		234.98	3,172.17		
16			126.81	38.04	1,673.87		253.77	3,425.94		
17			133.91	40.17	1,767.60		274.08	3,700.02		
18			141.41	42.42	1,866.59		296.00	3,996.02		
19			149.33	44.80	1,971.12		319.68	4,315.70		
20			157.69	47.31	2,081.50		345.26	4,660.96		
21			166.52	49.96	2,198.06		372.88	5,033.83		
22			175.85	52.75	2,321.16		402.71	5,436.54		
23			185.69	55.71	2,451.14		434.92	5,871.46		
24			196.09	58.83	2,588.40		469.72	6,341.18		
25			207.07	62.12	2,733.35		507.29	6,848.48		
26			218.67	65.60	2,886.42		547.88	7,396.35		
27			230.91	69.27	3,048.06		591.71	7,988.06		
28			243.84	73.15	3,218.75		639.04	8,627.11		
29			257.50	77.25	3,399.00		690.17	9,317.27		
30			271.92	81.58	3,589.35		745.38	10,062.66	3,018.80	7,043.86

20

Social Security

After studying this chapter, you should be able to

■ Explain why the Social Security system was developed

■ Describe the differences between Social Security, public assistance, and private insurance

■ Describe how Social Security benefits are financed

■ Describe the different categories of benefits that Social Security provides

■ Describe some of the current issues affecting the operations of the Social Security programs

The Social Security program affects virtually all Americans, either as beneficiaries or as covered workers who are currently paying into the system. The designers intended this essential social insurance program to be the floor of protection for the financial security of our society. Thus, questions about its solvency, its efficiency, and its future are of the utmost importance. In recent years, these questions have been at the forefront of public debate. This chapter contains a comprehensive description of the Social Security program and provides the background needed to understand the critical but complex arguments about the future economic security of Americans.[1]

The Social Security program has been operating for more than seventy-five years. Despite its longevity, Social Security is facing an uncertain future, and many critics have serious concerns about the system's stability. Some people believe that it is inadequately financed and, in the long run, will be unable to deliver all the benefits promised unless substantial changes are made soon. Many young workers believe that Social Security will not provide them with benefits. Some critics find the benefits too liberal; others believe the benefits are inadequate. The aim of this chapter is to provide the background to readers so they can understand the issues raised by the system's critics and defenders and form their own opinions about the important issues pertaining to its benefit levels and financing.

---

[1] The Social Security Administration (SSA) Web site (*http://www.ssa.gov/*) provides current data and information on this all-important part of the U.S. social safety net. Readers can find current Medicare information at the Medicare Web site (*http://www.medicare.gov/*).

SOCIAL INSURANCE BACKGROUND

During the Industrial Revolution, the focus of the economy changed from agricultural to industrial. This change occurred first in Europe, in the latter half of the nineteenth century, and later in the United States. There were several distinct factors behind this change, including the appearance of steam-powered machinery, a movement of the population from the country to the city, and a devotion to applied technological research. Among the changes in society caused by this revolution were a separation of people from the land and growing interdependence among people, with far fewer families capable of self-sufficiency. Moreover, laborers living in rapidly growing urban areas often no longer could look to their relatives for financial or other support. Industrial society, therefore, created greater economic insecurity.

To note that the Industrial Revolution caused great suffering as well as great material benefits is to state the obvious. Today's relatively high standard of living, which machinery and scientific advances made possible, follows a period of great economic distress for many workers. Low wages and unsanitary living conditions preceded the greatly increased life span and the amount of leisure time people presently enjoy. In the United States and numerous countries in Europe, the widespread human suffering associated with the Industrial Revolution, combined with the decline of self-sufficiency and the great disparities in wealth between the upper and lower classes, led to the introduction of social insurance programs.[2]

Interestingly, social insurance was developed as a response to socialism rather than being a part of it. The most conspicuous player in the early development and implementation of a social insurance system was Otto von Bismarck, the chancellor of Germany. As chancellor, he saw growing opposition to his party from the socialist movement. The economic misery of the masses of people was what fed the socialist cause in Germany and elsewhere in Europe. Bismarck, viewed by some as the devil and by others as a diplomatic and political genius, was unrelenting in his approach to opponents. After an unsuccessful attempt to destroy the socialist movement by force, he changed tactics and implemented the first Social Security system. The purpose of his scheme was to cut at the taproot of the economic problems that fed his rival political party. Funding his program by taxing current workers, he accomplished his goal of undermining the socialist movement without cost to the wealthy members of society who supported his party.

Bismarck's system became law in stages. Medical insurance was provided in 1883, accident insurance in 1884, and old-age and disability insurance in 1889. Unemployment insurance was not a part of Bismarck's program. The rest of industrialized Europe, which faced the same political and economic problems, soon followed Bismarck's lead. At the beginning of the twentieth century, social insurance programs were the rule in European industrialized countries.

In the United States, we refer to the time of our most serious economic problems as the Great Depression. The stock market crash of 1929 was a dramatic and clearly visible symptom of these problems. From an economic standpoint, however, the greatest number of people felt the worst consequences in the early 1930s. President Franklin D. Roosevelt responded with the New Deal program, part of which included the Social Security Act. More formally, the program was called the Old-Age Benefits Program. Today, it is known as the **Old-Age, Survivors, Disability Insurance (OASDI)** program. Congress passed the Social Security Act in 1935, and the program took effect

---

[2] See Abe Bortz, "Historical Development of the Social Security Act," retrieved on April 12, 2012, at *http://www.socialsecurity.gov/history/bortz.html.*

in 1937. Thus, some forty-five years after the implementation of Bismarck's program, the U.S. government began to apply the principles of insurance to the solution of society's greatest economic problem—the provision of economic security.

The History and Philosophy of the U.S. Social Security System

In the Depression of the 1930s, about 25 percent of all Americans were unemployed. Many banks failed, and people lost not only their current income but past savings as well. No wonder the term *Social Security* was chosen rather than *social insurance*. In those troubled days, people needed the promise and hope of economic security.

The Social Security Act represented a great break with past political philosophy in the United States. The principle of individual responsibility typified the prevailing political philosophy before 1935. Each family was responsible for its own financial security. However, moving from the farm to the city substituted economic interdependency for self-sufficiency. Thus, a vacuum existed in society's economic safety net, and after 1935, the government assumed part of the family's role in providing economic security.

The Social Security Act of 1935 marked the federal government's acceptance of some of the responsibility for the provision of individual economic security. The key word here is *some*. According to the original concept of Social Security, benefits were to be the floor upon which people were to complete the remainder of their economic building. While the *floor-of-protection* concept remains the current philosophy of the program, the appropriate height of the floor is subject to debate. Some people want a relatively high level of benefits; others prefer a more moderate level. Those critics who continue to stress individual responsibility favor a relatively low level of benefits, relying more heavily on private sources of retirement benefits, such as personal savings and employer-sponsored retirement plans. (See Chapter 19, "Employee Benefits," for a more detailed discussion of the latter two programs.)

Since 1935, the expansion of the original program has been continuous. New groups, such as physicians and members of the armed forces, have been added to the program, and new benefits, such as disability coverage and health insurance for the aged, were added. The amount of benefits has increased steadily. Today, almost all Americans either pay Social Security taxes or are eligible to receive benefits.

SOCIAL SECURITY, PRIVATE INSURANCE, AND PUBLIC ASSISTANCE

Both **public assistance programs** and Social Security are solutions to social and economic problems, but public assistance, or welfare, is not social insurance. What these two programs have in common is that they both are government-operated transfer payment systems. The government takes money from all taxpayers to fund welfare payments to people in need, and the government takes money from the currently employed to fund benefits for eligible workers and their dependents. In each case, the government takes money from one group and gives it to another group.

Two characteristics distinguish public assistance from Social Security. First, people who receive Social Security benefits made contributions for their benefits, as is the case with any insurance program. No such payment is expected of welfare recipients. Second, recipients of Social Security do not have to demonstrate financial need to receive benefits. Social Security benefits are a legal right for all eligible people. The wealthiest Americans are entitled to Social Security benefits as soon as their eligibility, which is *not* a function of financial need, is established.

While Social Security and public assistance are different types of programs, they share some common threads. That is, some aspects of the Social Security system spring from the same goals as a welfare program. For example, the total amount of survivor benefits a family receives is determined in part by the number of dependent children. Thus, the greater the need, the greater the benefits paid. Also, the current Social Security benefit structure provides lower-income people more than their actuarially fair share of the benefits. Providing benefits based in part on need reflects the goal of supplying **socially adequate** benefits. Paying benefits based on individual earnings, regardless of need, reflects the goal of providing **individual equity** in benefits.

Two important examples of public assistance in the United States provide health care coverage to the non-elderly poor. **Medicaid** is a public assistance program that provides health insurance to beneficiaries who can demonstrate that their family income levels fall below certain prescribed income (or asset-level) thresholds. Financed jointly on a state and federal level, eligibility varies across the states. **Children's Health Insurance Programs (CHIP)** are Medicaid programs that provides health coverage to children in families that are not eligible for Medicaid but who cannot afford private health insurance coverage.

Social Security and Private Insurance Are Different

Several important distinctions can be made between private insurance and Social Security, including the following:

- Participation in Social Security is compulsory for all eligible workers; private insurance purchases are a matter of free choice.
- Social Security benefits are predetermined by a formula set by law; private insurance benefits are a matter of choice between insurers and policy owners.
- The Social Security system, with the taxing power of the government behind it, can operate on a self-supporting, pay-as-you-go basis. By contrast, regulators demand private insurance companies be fully funded to protect the public against insolvencies. Theoretically, a private life insurance company could be liquidated at any point and all its liabilities could be met. By contrast, the Social Security system never has been fully funded, as we describe more fully in the next section of this chapter.
- Benefits of the Social Security program can be changed (either increased or decreased) by legislation; private, contractual benefits generally are not subject to change.

Social Security Is an Insurance System

Social Security is unique. It is not a public assistance program, and it is different from private insurance. It is a social insurance program operated by the federal government. The major perils covered by the Social Security program are premature death, disability, outliving one's income, and medical expenses of the aged. These are the same perils insured by private life insurance companies. Social Security, as is true of all insurance systems, transfers costs from the few people who experience losses to all the other participants in the system. The system uses the pooling technique of combining loss exposures and then using actuarial statistics to predict losses. If the system predicts losses accurately, it can operate on a financially sound basis even if it is not fully funded.

Because the essential features of an insurance system underlie its operations, insurance experts conclude that the Social Security program is an insurance program, despite having some aspects comparable to public assistance. Because the government operates the Social Security system, and because it is different from private insurance in several important respects, we call Social Security a social insurance program.

TABLE 20-1 Comparison of Social Security, Private Insurance, and Public Assistance

	Social Security	*Private Insurance*	*Public Assistance*
Recipient pays for benefits	Yes	Yes	No
Benefits subject to change	Yes	No	Yes
Compulsory program	Yes	No	No
General tax support	No	No	Yes
Fully funded program	No	Yes	No
Benefits based on need	No	No	Yes

A **social insurance program** is a government-run insurance program that is defined by legislative statute. While it relies on the taxing power of the government to guarantee solvency, it is operated soundly using actuarial techniques, funded primarily by current contributions. Table 20-1 reviews some of these ideas.

HOW SOCIAL SECURITY IS FINANCED

This section describes the benefits available from Social Security and how they are financed. The payments available to Social Security beneficiaries change frequently, and readers are advised to visit the Social Security Web site (*http://www.ssa.gov*) for updated figures. Although the numbers change regularly, the general ideas and rules forming the Social Security program change much less frequently.

The Program Is Compulsory for Almost Every Worker

Since it began in 1935, the Social Security program has considerably expanded the scope of covered employment. Today, almost every wage earner pays the Social Security tax via the **Federal Insurance Contributions Act (FICA)** deduction from paychecks. The program now covers wage earners, self-employed people, members of the U.S. armed forces, farmers, and people whose income comes from tips. It is easier to cite the few groups excluded from the program than to cite the covered groups. Full-time civilian employees of the federal government who were hired before 1984 are not covered. Special provisions of the Social Security law also allow railroad workers, employees of a few state and local governments, specified religious occupations, and children under 18 working for a parent to avoid participation in the program.

A Tax on Wages Is the Main Source of Funds

Where does the government get the money to pay Social Security benefits? Almost all the money comes from a tax on the wages of covered employees. The tax applies only until a covered maximum wage is reached; wages above this level are not taxed. This **maximum taxable earnings** level is subject to change each year to allow for inflation. For example, in 2012, the maximum taxable earnings were $110,100. Both the employer and employee pay the Social Security tax. In a recent year, each party paid 7.65 percent of the covered wage up to the covered maximum. Employees who earn more than the covered maximum pay 1.45 percent of all additional earnings to support the hospital insurance (HI) portion of the Social Security program. The tax on self-employed people is 15.3 (2 × 7.65) percent.

As an example of how the Social Security tax applies to earned income, consider three brothers. The first, Moe Shun, a bus driver, earned $40,000 in 2012 and paid $3,060 (0.0765 × 40,000) in Social Security taxes. The bus company also paid $3,060 in Social Security taxes for its employee. His brother, Dick Shun, a doctor specializing in speech therapy at a hospital, earned $120,100 in 2012, when the maximum covered wage was $110,100. Dick's Social Security tax is calculated as follows:

$$0.0765 \times 110{,}100 = \$8{,}423$$
$$0.0145 \times (120{,}100 - 110{,}100) = \underline{\quad 145\quad}$$
$$\text{Total tax} = \$8{,}568$$

The third Shun brother, Penn, is retired but not receiving Social Security benefits. He received $25,000 in dividend and interest income in 2012 but had no income from employment. Because the Social Security tax applies only to earned income, Penn pays no Social Security tax.

Benefits Are Not Fully Funded

The government operates Social Security on a pay-as-you-go or current-income basis. The taxes collected from currently employed workers and their employers are used to pay benefits to the current recipients.[3] Unlike private life insurance companies, the invested assets of the Social Security system are small relative to the system's liabilities. Therefore, investment earnings play a much smaller role in financing Social Security benefits than they do in financing private life insurance benefits.

Since the late 1980s, the system has accumulated a surplus that will be used to cushion the impact of the retirement of the baby-boom workers who were born after 1946 and will begin to retire around the year 2012. These accumulating funds are invested in government securities as required by law. The securities issued to the Social Security system earn interest based on the prevailing rate that the U.S. government pays to borrow money from other sources.

General tax revenue plays almost no part in funding the system. One exception is the government contribution toward Part B benefits of the Medicare program. Social Security was designed originally, and continues to be operated, as a self-supporting, pay-as-you-go system.

Insured Status and Eligibility for Benefits

To be **eligible** for benefits, a person must be (1) fully insured, (2) currently insured, or (3) disability insured.

People are **fully insured** after they accumulate forty quarters (ten years) of covered employment. Once attained, fully insured status cannot be lost. A person is **currently insured** if six of the thirteen quarters prior to death were in covered employment. Currently insured status makes a worker eligible for survivor benefits but not retirement benefits. To be **disability insured**, the worker must have been in covered employment for twenty of the forty quarters before disability and be fully insured. Special provisions apply to relatively young or old workers.

Quarters of Coverage (QC)

Workers earn one **quarter of coverage (QC)** when their covered earnings exceed a stated minimum. In the year 2012, $1,130 in wage or self-employment income was required for each QC earned. Workers earning $4,520 or more during this year earned

---

[3] This funding arrangement was a good fit for the population demographics of the United States in the 1930s because pay-as-you-go financing dominates pre-funding when the population is growing faster than the economy.

four QCs. No more than four QCs can be earned in one year. Workers do not need to earn covered income in four separate quarters to receive four QCs; some highly paid baseball players could earn four QCs in one inning. The amount required to earn one QC is subject to change annually.

Calculation of Benefits

The amount of Social Security benefits paid to recipients and their families is based on the amount of **covered earnings**—earnings on which Social Security taxes have been paid. Not all earnings are subject to the Social Security tax. Only the earnings up to a stated maximum taxable earnings amount are subject to the tax. The maximum earnings amount has changed in each of the past several years. Earnings in excess of these amounts do not count in the determination of the amount of Social Security benefits a worker receives.

Since 1977, workers' wages have been indexed to allow for the effects of inflation. A shortened and simplified view of how a benefit can be calculated using a five-step process:[4]

- *Step 1.* The number of years after 1950 (or a person's 21st birthday, if later) up to but not including the year of death, disability, or 62nd birthday (whichever comes first) is calculated.
- *Step 2.* Five years are subtracted from the forgoing total, allowing elimination of the five years of lowest earnings.
- *Step 3.* The actual earnings for the remaining years are entered, limited by the maximum amount of covered earnings.
- *Step 4.* The earnings are then indexed—that is, adjusted for inflation—to levels on par with today's compensation rates.
- *Step 5.* The total earnings, after indexation, are divided by the total number of months in the worker's career. For example, assume that in step 4, the worker's total indexed earnings equal $1 million over a thirty-five-year career. Thirty-five years equals 420 months. The formula calls for $1,000,000 / 420, or about $2,381.

That $2,381 outcome is called the worker's **average indexed monthly earnings (AIME)**. The AIME is then used to determine the worker's **primary insurance amount (PIA)**. The transformation from the AIME to the PIA is done by a formula that is updated annually.[5] Retirement, disability, and survivor benefits are expressed as a percentage of the worker's PIA. The PIA also determines the **maximum family benefit**, the greatest amount payable on one Social Security account. Thus, if Johann Bach died leaving twenty dependent children, each child's benefit and the widow's benefit would have to be reduced proportionately so that the maximum family benefit is not exceeded.

---

[4] The SSA Web site (*http://www.ssa.gov/*) includes a calculator that people can use to estimate their benefits.

[5] The 2012 PIA formula is calculated as the sum of three dollar amounts: 90 percent of the portion of the beneficiary's AIME that is less than or equal to $767 (the first PIA "bend point"), plus 32 percent of the portion of the beneficiary's AIME that is greater than $767 but less than $4,624 (the second PIA "bend point"), plus 15 percent of the beneficiary's AIME in excess of $4,624. Thus, a person whose AIME equals $5,624 will have a PIA equal to .9(767) + .32(4,624 − 767) + .15(5,624 − 4,624), or $2,074. The income level corresponding to each bend point (that is, the income level at which the percentages in the formula change, or "bend") are adjusted for inflation over time. The three percentages in the PIA formula do not change, however. By use of this formula, low-wage earners thus receive a higher proportion of their AIME as PIA than high-wage earners.

Since 1975, Social Security benefits have received annual increases called a **cost-of-living adjustment (COLA).** That is, Social Security benefits increase each year by the same percentage as the increase in the **consumer price index (CPI)**. Such annual increases allow Social Security recipients to maintain their purchasing power.

CATEGORIES OF BENEFITS

Social Security benefits fall into four broad categories: retirement benefits, survivor benefits, disability benefits, and medical care benefits for the aged and disabled.

Retirement Benefits

Retirement benefits are available to workers, their spouses, and dependent children.

WORKER

The **retirement benefit** is similar to a pure annuity—that is, Social Security sends out regular monthly checks during the recipient's lifetime. A full retirement benefit is available to *fully insured* workers at the "**normal retirement age.**" An increase in the normal retirement age from 65 to 67 began to be phased in in 2003 (67 is the normal retirement age for people born in 1960 or later). For simplicity's sake, however, we will continue to illustrate examples using age 65 as the normal retirement age. When a worker retires between the ages of 62 and 65, a reduced retirement benefit is available. The reduction is based on actuarial statistics.

SPOUSE

If the retired worker is married, the spouse, if age 65, is entitled to a retirement benefit equal to 50 percent of the worker's benefit. If the spouse is 62 to 64, an actuarially reduced benefit is available. If the spouse also is entitled to a benefit due to his or her own covered employment, he or she may take the larger of the two benefits but not both.

For example, assume both John and Gail Adams are employed and are entitled to Social Security retirement benefits based on their own employment records. If John's monthly benefit is $800 and Gail's is $650, Gail will have the choice of $400 (half of $800) or $650. Clearly, she will choose her own retirement benefit. Had she worked only intermittently and therefore earned a minimum monthly benefit of $350, she still would be able to receive $400, which is one-half of her husband's benefit. If the retired worker has a **dependent child**—one who is younger than 18—the child also is entitled to a monthly benefit equal to 50 percent of the worker's benefit.

BENEFIT EXAMPLE

To illustrate the retirement benefit provisions and calculations, assume that Francis Bacon, a swine breeder, retires in 2012 with a PIA of $1,500. If he is 65 years old, he can receive $1,500 per month as a retirement benefit. His wife, Etta (if she is 65 or older), can receive a monthly benefit of $750 (half of $1,500) based on her husband's earnings and PIA. If Francis is 62, his benefit is reduced to $1,200 (80 percent of $1,500). If Etta is 62, her benefit is reduced to $562.50 (75 percent of $750). For ages between 62 and 65, benefits are reduced by 5/9 of 1 percent for each month that the worker is under age 65. Therefore, retirement 36 months early causes a 20 percent reduction in benefits ($5/9 \times 36 = 20$). A spouse's benefit is reduced by 25/36 of 1 percent for each month the spouse is under 65.

Table 20-2 provides a review of the retirement benefits available from Social Security.

TABLE 20-2 Social Security Retirement Benefits

Worker	
Normal retirement age	100 percent of PIA
Age 62–65	PIA reduced
Spouse	
Normal retirement age	50 percent of worker's PIA
Age 62–65	50 percent of PIA reduced
Eligible child	50 percent each

Survivor Benefits

If fully insured or currently insured workers die, their survivors are entitled to Social Security benefits. These benefits do not take the form of a single cash payment, which is the typical way that life insurance policy death claims are paid. Rather, Social Security survivor benefits involve a regular monthly check paid to the dependent survivors. The only one-time payment that Social Security makes is a $255 lump-sum death benefit, which is one feature of the program that has not changed.

A mother's or father's benefit is payable so long as the parent is caring for a dependent child—defined in this case as someone younger than 16. A dependent child's benefit is payable so long as the child is younger than 18 (unless attending high school and then benefits last until age 19), or over 18 but disabled before age 22. A widow's or widower's benefit is payable at and after age 60. If the deceased worker's parents depended on the worker, they are eligible to receive benefits when they are 62 or older.

BENEFIT EXAMPLE

Returning to our previous example of Francis and Etta Bacon, assume that instead of retiring at age 65, Francis Bacon died prematurely at age 45, with the same PIA of $1,500. In this case, Etta Bacon receives a survivor's widow's benefit of 75 percent of her husband's PIA, or $1,125, so long as she is caring for a child under age 16. Each child also receives a benefit of $1,125 while under age 18. To illustrate just this set of facts, assume that there is a maximum family benefit of $1,875, so if there are two or more children, each beneficiary's benefit will be reduced so as not to exceed the maximum family benefit.

THE BLACKOUT PERIOD

A review of the combination of retirement and survivor benefits reveals a potentially serious gap in the coverage provided by the Social Security program. Retirement benefits are first fully payable at age 65. They are payable at age 62 on a reduced basis. Survivor benefits are payable only so long as the mother or father is caring for a child younger than 16 or disabled before 22. There is a potential time gap between the receipt of these two benefits, as illustrated in the following example.

Assume that Jacob and Rachel are both 25 years old. They have one son, Joseph, who is 2 years old. If Jacob were to die at age 25, Rachel would receive survivor benefits for as long as Joseph was under age 16—that is, 14 years. When Joseph reaches age 16, Rachel would be 39 years old and the survivor benefits would end. At age 60, Rachel would be eligible for a widow's benefit. If she were permanently disabled, she could receive benefits as early as age 50. There would be a period from age 39 until benefits are resumed when Rachel would receive no benefits from the Social Security system. This gap in income, often called the **blackout period**, can be bridged with a private life insurance purchase.

THE EARNINGS TEST

A reduction of survivor benefits occurs when a beneficiary under age 65 (or whatever his or her normal retirement age is, if it is greater than 65) earns more than the permissible limit, which is subject to annual change.[6] Each \$2 of earnings beyond the limit reduces benefits by \$1. If one survivor loses benefits because of earned income, however, it does not affect other survivors. Thus, if Rachel goes to work after Jacob's death, she may lose her survivor benefits, but Joseph would continue to receive his.

The effect of the **earnings test** is to reduce the cost of the Social Security program. The cost is reduced when people who are willing and able to earn substantial wages forgo their Social Security benefits.

Table 20-3 provides a review of Social Security survivor benefits.

Disability Benefits

In 1956, Congress added disability benefits to the old-age and survivor benefits of Social Security. What had been OASI became OASDI. Since 1956, the original disability program has been broadened several times. Currently, if a worker is fully insured and was in covered employment for twenty of the forty quarters preceding total disability, that person is entitled to Social Security disability benefits. Special, more liberal provisions apply to younger workers. In addition to the eligible worker, the spouse and dependent children of a disabled worker also are entitled to benefits (subject to a maximum limit on a family's total benefits).

In an individually purchased disability insurance policy, the definition of the term *disability* is a key feature. The definition of **disability** used in the Social Security program is "the inability to engage in any substantial gainful activity by reason of any medically determinable physical or mental impairment which can be expected to last for a continuous period of not less than twelve months." This definition is not as favorable as a definition such as "unable to engage in one's own occupation." Determinations of disability are made by state agencies, not by the Social Security Administration (SSA); thus, there may not be national uniformity in applying the definition of disability.

If workers are disabled by a work-related accident, they usually will be entitled to workers' compensation benefits. Social Security and workers' compensation benefits are coordinated, which limits the total amount that an injured worker can receive from both systems. Thus, if the total benefit available from both sources exceeds 80 percent of the average earnings before the disability, Social Security benefits are reduced until the 80 percent level is reached.

TABLE 20-3 Social Security Survivor Benefits

Spouse	
Caring for dependent child	75 percent of deceased worker's PIA
Starting at age 65	100 percent of deceased worker's PIA
Age 60–64	Deceased worker's PIA, reduced
Disabled, 50–65	50 percent + deceased worker's PIA
Child	75 percent of deceased worker's PIA
Dependent Parent	
One	82.5 percent of deceased worker's PIA
Two	75 percent of PIA, each

---

[6] A table showing the income thresholds applied toward the earnings test can be found at *http://www.ssa.gov/oact/COLA/rtea.html.*

TABLE 20-4 Social Security Disability Benefits

Disabled worker	100 percent of PIA
Spouse	
Caring for dependent child	75 percent of disabled worker's PIA
Age 65	50 percent of disabled worker's PIA
Age 62–65	50 percent of disabled worker's PIA, reduced
Eligible child	50 percent of disabled worker's PIA

Like retirement and survivor benefits, only limited amounts of earnings are permitted for totally disabled workers, with one very important exception. As an incentive for personal rehabilitation efforts, the program provides a twenty-four-month trial work period.

Social Security pays disability benefits at any age and benefits continue until the worker recovers, dies, or reaches age 65. At age 65, the disabled worker's disability benefits stop and retirement benefits begin. The insured will never know the difference, but the accounting requirements of the Social Security system direct this change. Table 20-4 outlines Social Security disability benefits.

Medicare (Health Insurance for the Aged and Disabled)

In 1965, Congress passed the Medicare program, and OASDI became Old-Age, Survivors, Disability, and Hospital Insurance (OASDI-HI). If one considers the OASDI program to be a jungle of rules, regulations, interpretations, exceptions, and questions, the Medicare program is a jungle within a jungle. This section presents a broad outline of the program. Readers who want detailed information will find many details at *http://ssa.gov/* and *http://www.medicare.gov/*.

The Medicare program has four main parts:

- Part A: basic hospital insurance benefits
- Part B: voluntary supplementary medical benefits
- Part C: Medicare Advantage plans
- Part D: Medicare prescription drug coverage

In general, insureds who are eligible to receive Social Security benefits because they are 65 or older or because they are disabled are eligible to participate in the Medicare program. Special provisions apply to those insureds with chronic kidney disease. Part A is compulsory and requires no premium payment from most insureds, but Parts B and D are voluntary and require premium payments that are subject to annual change. Part C offers a managed care option, such as a preferred provider organization (PPO) or a health maintenance organization (HMO) option, as a substitute for Parts A and B.

PART A—HOSPITAL INSURANCE BENEFITS

This coverage pays for a variety of inpatient hospital service benefits, including room and board in a semiprivate hospital room, nursing services, drugs furnished in the hospital, and operating room costs. In addition to these benefits, the program provides coverage for some outpatient expenses, including the following:

- *Skilled Nursing Care.* A physician must certify that skilled nursing care is needed following a condition that was treated in a hospital. Long-term custodial care is not provided.
- *Home Health Care Benefits.* If a patient can be treated at home instead of a hospital or nursing facility, Part A pays for the cost of visits by an eligible home health agency.
- *Hospice Benefits.* If a person is terminally ill and certified to be within six months of death, Part A will pay for hospice care.

PART B—VOLUNTARY SUPPLEMENTARY MEDICAL INSURANCE BENEFITS

Part B provides benefits for medical expenses not covered by Part A, especially payment for physician's services. Participation in the program is voluntary, and insureds must pay a monthly premium. One interesting aspect of this program is that, while the participant pays a premium, the government uses general tax revenues to subsidize at least half the cost. Thus, this part of the Medicare program is not funded directly by taxes on current workers, but by premiums paid in part by the insureds and in part by the government. Should a person participate and then drop out, strict reinstatement restrictions prevent adverse selection.

The benefits provided by Part B of Medicare include payments for a broad range of medical services, including doctor's bills, hospital diagnostic studies, outpatient care, and home health care. Although Part B covers a broad range of services, several important exclusions apply to this coverage, including dental care, eyeglasses, and hearing aids.

MEDICARE SUPPLEMENTAL INSURANCE POLICIES (MEDIGAP INSURANCE)

Medicare recipients often purchase Medicare supplemental insurance to cover the deductibles, coinsurance requirements, and other provisions of the Medicare program requiring cash outlays by insureds. The deductible and coinsurance requirements are complex and subject to annual change. The deductibles and copayments can involve expenses of hundreds of dollars each day, and many thousands of dollars during one spell of illness, which makes Medicare supplemental insurance an expensive, but often necessary, purchase by Medicare insureds.

PART C—MEDICARE ADVANTAGE PLANS

The Part C Medicare option provides coverage to recipients through a managed care option, such as an HMO or PPO. By accepting coverage through an HMO or PPO as a replacement for traditional benefits, the insured generally can avoid the deductibles and most of the copayment provisions of Medicare. They also are eligible for Medicare Part D prescription drug coverage.

Some Medicare insureds have been reluctant to switch to Part C coverage. Although the number of eligible health care providers is growing, some insureds live in areas with few plan options. Other people have objected to the "long lines" and waiting time at some managed care plans. Some insureds object to having to accept care from only the managed care physicians and other providers because they already have longstanding relationships with health care providers who are not part of these plans. Moreover, many managed care plans have not found the reimbursement schedule provided by Social Security to be adequate or attractive. As a result, a majority of Medicare participants have not chosen these alternatives to the traditional program.

PART D: PRESCRIPTION DRUG COVERAGE

In December 2003, the **Medicare Prescription Drug Improvement and Modernization Act of 2003** became law. This law provides limited coverage of a Medicare beneficiary's prescription drug bills, subject to a deductible amount and a sequence of different copayment percentages. Beneficiaries also must pay a monthly premium for coverage. The basic facts of the program are the following:

- Everyone with Medicare coverage is eligible for it, regardless of income, health status, or current prescription expenses.
- People get coverage by joining a Medicare prescription drug plan or a Medicare health plan that offers drug coverage. Beneficiaries must pay a monthly premium for coverage.

- The plan does not offer full coverage for prescription drugs; instead, it includes a deductible, copayment, and corridor deductible known as the Medicare "donut hole." For example, in 2012, beneficiaries were responsible for paying a $320 deductible, as well as 25 percent as a participating deductible, or copayment, on costs between $320 and $2,930. If costs exceed $2,930, the beneficiary pays 100 percent of the amount in the corridor deductible in excess of $2,930 up to $6,657.50, a deductible charge more commonly known as the donut hole. After the beneficiary has paid the maximum amount required in the donut hole, Medicare pays a catastrophic coverage benefit equal to 95 percent of all costs in excess of $6,657.50.

The maximum out of pocket expense that a Medicare beneficiary will pay if he or she incurs $6,657.50 of medical expenses (the maximum threshold of the donut hole) equals $4,700, as shown below.

TABLE 20-5 Calculating a Beneficiary's Out-of-Pocket Expenses in Medicare

Drug Costs $	Plan Pays	Individual Pays	Out of Pocket $
$320	0 percent	$320.00	$320.00
$321–2,930	75 percent	25 percent	$652.50
$2930–6,657.50	0 percent	100 percent	$3,727.50
		Total of $4,700	$4,700.00

CURRENT ISSUES

In recent years, many Americans have become increasingly concerned about the financial health of the country. To help to balance a growing federal budget deficit, some critics have suggested a reexamination of the role of Social Security in the United States. In 2010, OASDI and Medicare accounted for 20 percent and 13 percent of federal spending, respectively, or one third of the total budget.[7]

A formidable task facing the United States is finding a strategy to control the growth in retirement spending through OASDI. Much of this spending increase is attributable to the aging of America as baby boomers born between 1946 and 1964 transition from the workforce to retirement. The cost of this demographic shift is exacerbated by increased longevity risk, as retirees are living longer than ever. Policymakers are considering a variety of ways to address these costs. Should the normal retirement age be increased? Should Americans have more control over the choice of how their Social Security contributions are invested while they are working? Can American workers afford to quit working when many have inadequate retirement savings?

The financial problems plaguing Medicare are more urgent, as forecasts anticipate that the Medicare Hospital Insurance trust funds will be exhausted in 2024.[8] The cost of Medicare is expected to grow quickly in the near future, as a larger percentage of the American population will consist of retirees, and employers in the United States do not offer retiree health care nearly as often as they did in prior years. Questions abound regarding how to contain the cost of retiree health care. Can the government slow health care inflation by transitioning Medicare away from its fee-for-service roots? Will federal

---

[7] Congressional Budget Office, 2011, *The U. S. Federal Budget: Infographic* retrieved January 20, 2012, from *http://www.cbo.gov/ftpdocs/125xx/doc12577/budgetinfographic.htm.*

[8] Social Security and Medicare Boards of Trustees, *Status of Social Security and Medicare Programs, A Summary of the 2011 Annual Reports*, 2011, retrieved January 20, 2012, from *http://www.ssa.gov/oact/TRSUM/index.html.*

programs encouraging Americans to save for future medical needs (such as health savings accounts) be successful? Will efforts to control health care costs (such as reducing payments to medical providers or setting fee limits on certain medical services) decrease the quality of care? Can increased monitoring effectively detect overcharging and fraud?

Summary

Social insurance first appeared in Germany in the late nineteenth century. In an effort to stop the growth of the Socialist Democratic Party, Chancellor Otto von Bismarck introduced a social insurance plan designed to reduce the economic hardship caused by the Industrial Revolution.

President Franklin D. Roosevelt proposed the Social Security Act of 1935 as a part of the New Deal economic plan designed to cure the economic problems of the United States. The program was designed as a "floor of protection" for U.S. workers. Constant expansion has taken place from the beginning: New groups of workers have been added to the program, new types of benefits have been added, and benefit amounts have been raised regularly.

Social Security is neither a welfare program nor a private insurance system. Unlike welfare, benefits are not based solely on economic need. The more survivors or dependents a worker has, the greater the benefits received (up to the family maximum). Unlike private insurance, benefits are not based on a contract but on a law; neither is the system operated on a fully funded basis.

Social Security provides four categories of benefits for eligible recipients: (1) retirement benefits, (2) survivor benefits, (3) disability benefits, and (4) Medicare benefits. For the first three categories, the benefits a worker receives are determined by the amount of average monthly earnings. The average monthly earnings, in turn, determine the worker's primary insurance amount.

Social Security operates on a self-supporting, current-income basis. The system currently is building up surplus funds to be used when workers born between 1946 and 1964 (the so-called baby boomers) begin to retire.

Certain questions about the Social Security program (including Medicare) continue to receive public attention. How should the system be financed? Will a declining birth rate combined with increased longevity destroy the self-supporting operations of the system? Some experts estimate that the open-ended Medicare promises will cause greater funding problems than the better defined and more controllable portions of Social Security. Debate on these and other issues should focus the public's attention on a very important part of its financial security program.

Review

1. What is the connection between a society that moves from an agricultural to an industrial base and the development of a social insurance system?
2. Who was Otto von Bismarck? What role did he play in the development of social insurance?
3. When was the Social Security Act passed? What was the political philosophy that determined its level of benefits, both initially and currently?
4. What aspects of Social Security are similar to a welfare program? How is Social Security different from public assistance?
5. List four similarities and differences between Social Security and private insurance.
6. What is FICA, and what role does it play in the Social Security program?
7. What is the maximum taxable wage?
8. Using the same factors that applied in the Shun brothers example, calculate the Social Security tax for Larry (earned wages of $60,000), Michael (earned salary of $2 million), and Sam (dividend income of $25 million).
9. Describe two major categories of insured status and their requirements.
10. What role does general tax revenue play in funding Social Security benefits?
11. What does "pay as you go" mean with respect to Social Security retirement benefits?
12. Identify three different categories of insured status for Social Security benefits.
13. What is an AIME? Describe what a PIA is.
14. Who is entitled to retirement benefits under the Social Security system? Who is entitled to survivor benefits? Disability benefits? Medicare benefits?

15. What is meant by the blackout period for Social Security benefits?
16. Identify the different types of benefits provided by the hospital insurance part of Medicare and by the supplementary medical insurance portion of the program. What are the deductible and participation provisions of these programs?
17. What problems will a declining birth rate and increasing longevity cause for the Social Security system?
18. Identify some solutions that have been offered to help maintain the Social Security OASDI system's solvency.

Objective Questions

1. The man whose name is associated with the development of the first social insurance program is:
   a. Philip Morris
   b. Albrecht Dürer
   c. Rolf von Winkle
   d. Otto von Bismarck
2. The main source of funding for the Social Security program is:
   a. The federal income tax
   b. The federal estate and gift tax
   c. A tax on wages
   d. The capital gains tax
3. How many quarters of coverage are required to be fully eligible for Social Security benefits?
   a. 60
   b. 55
   c. 40
   d. 25
4. All the following are main categories of benefits provided by Social Security except what?
   a. Welfare benefits for poor people
   b. Retirement benefits
   c. Survivor benefits
   d. Disability benefits
5. The U.S. Social Security program has been operating for more than _____ years.
   a. 65
   b. 75

c. 85
d. 105

6. Choose the false statement regarding the Social Security program.
   a. Participation in Social Security is compulsory.
   b. Social Security benefits are predetermined by a formula.
   c. Social Security operates mostly on the pay-as-you-go basis.
   d. Social Security benefits cannot be changed by legislation.
7. Candy Kane has worked for 42 years in the business that she founded and owns, Candy's Candies. She has paid into Social Security for her entire working life. When she retires, who will be eligible to receive retirement benefits based on Candy's Social Security contributions?
   a. Sandy Kane, Candy's husband
   b. Mandy Kane, Candy's daughter, who is 14 years old at the time Candy retires
   c. Candy Kane
   d. All the above
8. Which of the following is not a public assistance program?
   a. Children's Health Insurance Programs (CHIP)
   b. Medicare
   c. Medicaid
   d. All the above are public assistance programs.

Discussion Questions

1. Do you think Social Security retirement benefits will be there for you when you retire? Argue both sides of this question.
2. Do you think that Social Security should have a greater welfare component, less welfare, or about the same? Explain your reasons. Cite specific changes that you would like to see made.

Selected References

Myers, R. J., 1975, *Social Security*. Homewood, IL: Published for McCahan Foundation, Bryn Mawr, Pa., by R. D. Irwin.

Social Security Administration, The Official Website of the U.S. Social Security Administration, *http://www.ssa.gov*.

21

Unemployment and Workers' Compensation Insurance

After studying this chapter, you should be able to

- Describe the characteristics of the federal-state unemployment insurance program

- Explain how the unemployment insurance program currently is financed

- Describe the workers' compensation insurance program

- Explain the historical reasons for workers' compensation insurance

- Identify five broad objectives of current workers' compensation laws

- Identify some of the current problems facing the workers' compensation insurance program

Insurance proceeds typically do not compensate for happy events. Stolen cars, burned houses, premature deaths, and prolonged illnesses are some of the tragedies of life. Unemployment has a deserved place on this list of calamities. Like premature death, unemployment cuts off a family's income. Like a prolonged disease, there are daily and hourly reminders of the problem that can be terribly depressing. Unemployment causes frustration, anger, and feelings of helplessness that make its contemplation terrible. No wonder people and governments have tried to manage this risk.

The first part of this chapter describes the federal-state unemployment insurance program. We present the philosophy and purpose of the program, together with its general provisions. Few national economic problems receive more public or political attention than widespread unemployment. Therefore, an understanding of the problem's causes and its solutions is important in most industrialized societies.

The second part of this chapter describes the workers' compensation system for compensating victims of work-related accidents and illnesses. Workers' compensation programs provide injured workers with wage replacement, rehabilitation benefits, and medical benefits. Workers' compensation programs also provide survivor benefits for dependents of workers whose deaths are work-related.

Early in the twentieth century, a change took place that affected the party that bears the financial impact of such losses. No longer do injured workers and their families face a future of either no income or extended litigation. Accident compensation generally comes automatically and quickly. This chapter presents the reasons for this change, along with a description of the workers' compensation system. Like the costs of our health care delivery system, the costs of our workers' compensation system have increased greatly in recent years. The two problems are related because medical expenses make up a large component of workers' compensation insurance claims. Beyond medical inflation, workers' compensation costs also have increased because courts and administrative boards introduced new definitions of compensable injuries and illnesses. While costs have increased, some critics have expressed concern about the adequacy of benefits to replace the wages lost by injured workers. Thus, workers' compensation insurance is not just a subject of historical interest; it remains an important and controversial topic.

UNEMPLOYMENT INSURANCE[1]

Unemployment insurance compensates workers who have lost their jobs and therefore have no source of income. The program was established in 1935 with two primary objectives:

1. To replace temporarily a portion of earnings for workers who become unemployed through no fault of their own
2. To help stabilize the economy during recessions by providing unemployed workers with money to purchase needed goods and services

Unemployment insurance covers almost all workers, except for self-employed workers, who do not participate in the program, and employees who work in a handful of exempt industries (such as domestic or agricultural workers). People lose their jobs for many reasons. The business cycle of economic expansion and contraction causes some workers to be unemployed, often for prolonged periods. Importing manufactured items previously made domestically also causes unemployment. In recent years, some U.S. companies have employed foreign workers to do a variety of relatively high skilled jobs. This "outsourcing" of high-quality jobs is another source of unemployment for U.S. workers and a source of concern for politicians and dislocated workers. Automating manufacturing processes typically involves machines replacing working people. New inventions can cause unemployment in an industry whose products become obsolete. Seasonal workers often are unemployed for some portion of a year. These are examples of causes of unemployment that are mostly beyond individual control.

Some Background Information

A historical perspective adds much understanding to the current program. Many of the same factors that led to the Social Security program also produced our first national unemployment insurance program. Indeed, the unemployment insurance program was a part of the 1935 Social Security Act. But for political and legal reasons, its administration was separated from the Social Security program.

About 25 percent of the work force was unemployed during the early 1930s. The New Deal was developed to counteract the economic effects of the Great Depression. In one sense, the economy was drying up, and the New Deal was supposed to return needed liquidity—money—to the economy. One direct way for the government to

---

[1] The U.S. Department of Labor Web site provides extensive information on the unemployment program (*http://www.dol.gov/dol/topic/unemployment-insurance/*).

put money into the economy and create needed employment is for the government to hire people to build bridges, schools, and other public works projects. The Works Progress Administration of 1935 demonstrated this fiscal policy by adding liquidity to the economy. **Fiscal policy** describes direct government actions of putting money into the economy (spending) or taking it out (taxation).

Another way for the government to add money to the economy is to exercise control over interest rates and bank reserve requirements. If it costs less to borrow money, private businesses will undertake more projects and thus create jobs in the private economy. Economists call using government power over the money supply to stimulate employment **monetary policy**. For many complicated reasons, including the psychological effect of consumer expectations, government actions to "fine tune" the national economy do not always produce the theoretical effects within the expected time frame.

A third way for the government to assist the economy is through **transfer payments**, defined as taking money from one group of citizens and giving it to another group. If the group receiving the money is more likely to spend it than the group from whom the money was taken, demand for consumer goods will increase, resulting in more employment in industries that produce consumer goods.[2] Because Social Security, public assistance, and unemployment insurance all follow this pattern, they result in the stabilization of consumption.

The unemployment insurance program is designed to meet the peril of short-term unemployment caused by the business cycle and other factors over which workers have little control. Because unemployment insurance payments allow unemployed workers to retain some purchasing power, aggregate demand for consumer goods does not take as severe a downward spiral as otherwise would be the case. A severe downward spiral begins with a lack of demand for consumer goods caused by some unemployed people, who in turn are unable to purchase goods, causing additional groups of workers to be laid off, with the process building momentum at each downward turn. The unemployment insurance program automatically acts to counter the effects of a downturn in the economy by softening the effects on consumer demand. Thus, unemployment insurance is known as an **automatic stabilizer**, one requiring no additional government action to be put into effect. During periods of severe unemployment, Congress can extend the short-term (twenty-six-week) benefit period to soften the impact of unemployment on families and the national economy.

The administration of Franklin D. Roosevelt decided that, to avoid a political and legal challenge to the constitutionality of the unemployment insurance program, it should be separate from the rest of the Social Security program. Thus, the federal government now imposes an unemployment tax on employers but allows a credit for up to 90 percent of the federal tax if employers pay a state unemployment tax. In effect, the federal government encourages the states to impose their own unemployment tax. Under this arrangement, the states determine who is eligible for benefits, how long benefits last, and the amount of benefit payments.

Some employers give permanently terminated employees an amount of money beyond their final wages. Such payment, called *severance pay*, allows workers time to find new jobs. It also allows the unemployed to maintain their purchasing power for a limited time. Yet private approaches to the unemployment problem, however helpful

---

[2] This reasoning is based on the assumption that $1 of the transfer payment will stimulate the economy in ways that result in more than $1 of additional production. Many economists disagree with this assumption, suggesting that the additional economic activity produced may be worth less than $1, or that this logic minimizes the negative impact on the parties (such as taxpayers or employers) who are financing the transfer payments.

they are in individual instances, are inadequate to deal with the national problem of unemployment because they lack the government's control over monetary and fiscal policy.

Operations of the Unemployment Insurance Program

Currently, the unemployment insurance program is a joint federal-state program. The U.S. Department of Labor (*http://www.dol.gov/*) administers the federal portion of the program. The Department of Labor is responsible for ensuring that the states operate their unemployment programs efficiently and also provides technical assistance and training to states.

The unemployment insurance program is financed by a 6.0 percent federal tax on covered wages. The federal tax is offset up to 90 percent if an employer must pay a tax to a state unemployment insurance program. The federal covered maximum wage for unemployment insurance taxation is $7,000, which is far less than the Social Security maximum.[3] State unemployment tax collections allow the states to fund their unemployment insurance programs. If a state unemployment insurance fund is inadequate to continue paying benefits, the states then can borrow money from the federal government without paying interest. Some penalties are involved if the loan balance is not reduced, however.

An interesting question arises concerning who ultimately pays the unemployment insurance tax. Economic theory suggests that employees pay for at least some of the cost of mandated benefits through lower wages.[4] In addition, employers may pay through lower profits, and consumers may pay through higher prices. Some combination of the three is the probable answer, but this answer raises difficulties in analyzing the transfer caused by the insurance mechanism. In the operation of insurance risk pools, all exposed to the potential loss (the whole work force) should share the costs of the unfortunate few who experience the loss (the unemployed). Unfortunately, because many—not just a few—people lose their jobs at the same time during severe recessions, this risk pooling outcome cannot be achieved with unemployment insurance, leading to the following question.

Is Unemployment Insurance Really Insurance?

This question has two sides. In Chapter 6, "Fundamentals of Insurance," we identified an insurance system as one that transfers the cost of loss from the few who experience it to the many who are exposed to it. The transfer is made using a contract between the insured and the insurer. Unemployment insurance fails both these tests. There is a legal rather than a contractual right to benefits, and the effects of the transfer are not clear-cut, as we explained. The unemployment insurance operation lacks predictive accuracy and faces the possibility of catastrophic losses. Both private insurance and the Social Security system have predictive accuracy and do not face catastrophic loss potential. Thus, some economists think that the term *unemployment compensation* is more descriptive than *unemployment insurance*.

The unemployment program, however, does have some aspects of an insurance program. Payments for losses are funded in advance, although the program is not funded actuarially because losses cannot be predicted accurately. Generally, the payments

---

[3] Some states have higher tax rates, and some have higher covered-wage bases. Information on the various state programs can be found on the Department of Labor Web site (*http://www.dol.gov/*).

[4] For example, see Lawrence Summers, 1989, "Some Simple Economics of Mandated Benefits," *American Economic Review,* Vol. 79, No. 2, pp. 177–83.

provided do not replace the total amount of wages lost. Like other insurance transfers, the program makes compensation payments only to those workers who suffer losses from a specified peril: short-term unemployment from causes beyond the recipient's control. These payments are a matter of right and are not based on need. The next section of this chapter describes eligibility requirements to participate in the program and disqualification provisions that preclude adverse selection. Both the eligibility requirements and disqualification provisions have counterparts in private group insurance programs.

Perhaps the most interesting resemblance to a private insurance operation is the experience-rating pricing approach found in almost all state plans. **Experience rating** means that the insurer looks backward over time to determine if an insured has paid a fair premium. For example, if an insured's loss experience was favorable, experience rating results in a refund of a portion of the premium. Experience rating is quite common in private group life and health insurance.

Careful analysis of an experience-rating plan reveals an effect that is just the opposite of the insurance transfer. That is, while insurance transfers the cost of losses from the fortunate many to the unfortunate few, experience-rating refunds transfer money to the fortunate employers with good loss records and not to the employers with average or poor loss records.

The justification given for experience rating is that it encourages or promotes a stable work force. An employer is put in the position of having to balance the savings from laying off employees for short periods against the increase in the employer's unemployment insurance costs. While promoting a stable work force is a worthy objective, the effect of experience rating may be just the opposite of what the economy needs. When the economy is going strong, unemployment insurance premiums are reduced because employers have relatively good loss experience. When the economy is weak, unemployment premiums go up because employers have relatively poor loss experience. Thus, with experience rating, the insurance system takes more money out of the economy during downswings in the cycle than during upswings. More logically, the program should take more money out during upswings, when business is good, than during periods when business is relatively poor.

The safest answer that one may give to the question posed at the beginning of this section is that unemployment insurance is a government-operated transfer payment scheme that has some, but not all, elements in common with private group and individual insurance programs.

General Provisions of State Programs

All state unemployment insurance programs have provisions that cover eligibility to participate in the program, actions that disqualify workers from receiving benefits, and provisions for determining the amount of benefits an unemployed worker receives.

States have three general requirements relating to eligibility to receive benefits: (1) a waiting period, (2) an earnings record, and (3) a continuing interest in employment. A one-week waiting period is a typical requirement before unemployment benefits are available. A previous earnings record is stated in terms of some minimum dollar amount, such as earnings of at least $1,000 in the past twelve months. A continuing interest in employment means the worker must be both able and available to work. These three requirements are designed to keep people who have not worked recently (including people who have already received the maximum coverage from their unemployment insurance) or who do not intend to work in the near future from collecting unemployment insurance.

Certain actions may disqualify a worker from receiving benefits even if the three eligibility tests are met. Disqualification for benefits results if a worker (1) has left employment voluntarily, (2) was fired for misconduct, (3) refuses suitable work, (4) is not legally eligible to work, or (5) is unemployed owing to a labor dispute. Several of these points involve questions of fact. Was the employee really fired for misconduct? Was an employee who "voluntarily quit" really forced out? Is the (noncitizen) worker legally eligible to work? States can make exceptions to these general rules on disqualification.

Traditionally, unemployment claims had to be made in person at state employment offices. Some states also allow claim submissions over the telephone or Internet. After the claim is filed, the state sends a form to the unemployed worker's former employer requesting verification of earnings and the reason for their leaving employment. Each state determines the amount of benefits to which an unemployed worker is entitled. Benefits are subject to federal income taxes. States typically use a formula based on previous earnings. Some states grant dependents' allowances as an increase in the weekly benefit. The states also determine the duration of benefits; most states grant twenty-six weeks. This restriction is in keeping with the principle that unemployment insurance should compensate for short-term unemployment. During periods of high unemployment, however, a federal-state program provides for an extension of benefits beyond the maximum set by the states. This program has some automatic provisions that are activated when national unemployment exceeds a stated level.

Summary—Unemployment Insurance

Unemployment is an awful peril to which all workers are exposed. The results of this peril are lost income, frustration, and possible depression. Much unemployment is due to causes beyond the worker's control. The swings of the economic cycle, changes in methods of production, and new inventions all have caused unemployment. Some unemployment is not beyond a worker's control, and unemployment insurance is not designed to compensate workers for such losses.

The current federal-state approach to unemployment insurance appeared as a part of the Social Security Act of 1935. The unemployment insurance provisions of the federal program were separated from the other coverages to avoid a constitutional challenge. Under the current approach, employers can offset up to 90 percent of the federal unemployment tax if they pay a state unemployment tax. This approach allows the various states, rather than the federal government, to determine eligibility requirements and the amount of benefits paid.

Unemployment insurance has some features comparable to private insurance programs and others that are quite different. Unlike private insurance, there is no contract between insured and insurer, nor is the loss necessarily transferred from those who experience it to those who are exposed to it, because both employers and customers may be paying for the loss. Also, unlike a private insurance arrangement, the unemployment insurance program lacks predictive accuracy and may experience catastrophic losses. Funds for making payment for losses, however, are collected in advance, and requirements restrict the program to cover a specified peril: short-term unemployment arising from causes beyond the worker's control. Many states have experience-rating plans, whereby those employers who have a good record receive the benefit of lower insurance premiums. While the experience-rating plan may encourage a stable employment policy, it has economic implications that can be undesirable.

All states have their own eligibility standards for benefits. The states also determine certain conditions and circumstances that would disqualify workers from receiving benefits. The states determine both the amount and the duration of unemployment insurance benefits.

WORKERS' COMPENSATION[5]

Among the problems that arose when the economy changed from an agricultural to an industrial basis were work-related injuries and illnesses. Agriculture historically was, and remains, a relatively dangerous occupation. However, the move from farm to factory exposed many more workers to new and dangerous occupations and unsafe working environments. The problem in the United States probably reached its peak during the period between 1900 and 1910. New members of the labor force, many from agricultural backgrounds, and many women and children were exposed to machinery for the first time. Under such conditions as then prevailed—long hours, long work weeks, and dangerous working conditions—many factories saw relatively high injury rates.

The cry for reform followed public awareness of the problem. One widely read book, Upton Sinclair's *The Jungle* (1906), dealt with industrial accidents in the meatpacking industry. As was the case with several other economic problems related to the Industrial Revolution, Europeans provided Americans with workable solutions. Compensation for industrial accidents was a part of German chancellor Otto von Bismarck's social insurance program, and other European countries subsequently followed the German pattern.

The Problem

Work-related accidents and illnesses are an unfortunate part of the industrial economy. In addition to physical and emotional problems, industrial accidents cause workers two types of economic problems: (1) medical, rehabilitative, or funeral expenses, and (2) lost wages. The important economic and social question presented by these occurrences is "Who shall bear the economic burden of these costs?" Before workers' compensation laws were enacted, the answer was almost always the injured worker and the family. One objective of the new laws was to transfer (a portion of) this cost from the injured worker to other parties. As we have noted several times throughout this textbook, one of the most effective and efficient means of transferring the cost of losses is through the insurance mechanism. Therefore, it should not be surprising that insurance was the device used to achieve this new objective.

Why were injured workers bearing the cost of most industrial accidents? In essence, it was because of the common-law legal doctrine that prevailed in the United States before the enactment of workers' compensation laws. As a rule, whenever a person is injured because of another's negligence, that person can sue the negligent party for the damage sustained. The defendant in such a case has the right to try to establish that its actions were not responsible for the plaintiff's injuries. Before the enactment of workers' compensation laws, the injured worker had a legal right to sue the employer, and the employer had a right to a defense.

Such a legal system, although seeming fair on the surface, really was very lopsided in favor of the employer, thus producing unfair results. In many cases, employees would not or could not sue their employer because they had no money or they feared losing jobs they might never replace. Fellow workers were not eager to testify against their employers for the same reasons. Assuming that one did sue one's employer, the employer had three lines of defense to assert. Establishing any of these defenses would stop an injured worker's recovering from the employer.

The employer could claim **contributory negligence**—that is, the worker's own actions contributed to the injury. The employer might establish that another worker,

---

[5] For the most recent workers' compensation insurance data and information, see the National Council on Compensation Insurance (NCCI) Web site *(http://www.ncci.com/)*.

not the employer, was responsible for the injury—the **fellow servant rule**. The employer also might establish that a reasonable person should have known a line of work such as meatpacking presented some chance of injury. If the worker knew that a job was dangerous before accepting it, the employer could invoke the **assumption-of-risk defense** because the employer compensated the employee for the inherent danger. Thus, the chances of an injured worker collecting damages from an employer under the prevailing legal doctrines at the time varied from slim to none.

The Solution

Faced with public indignation and the European example, many states enacted legislation that changed this situation. The new workers' compensation laws substituted the employer's liability without fault for the prevailing common-law doctrine of negligence. Under the new laws, the employee could not sue the employer to collect for work-related injuries. The workers' compensation claim payment was the **exclusive remedy** available to the injured worker. The employer had to pay the worker for the damages, regardless of fault, but the employer then was protected from employees' civil claims that arose from work-related injuries.

It is unlikely that the employer ultimately bears all the cost of a worker's injuries. More likely, the consumer pays part of the cost through higher prices. (Workers also bear a portion of the cost in the form of lower wages, as already stated.[6]) Because the employer treats workers' compensation insurance premiums as another cost of doing business, these expenses are included in the cost of producing goods and in the price charged for the goods. The result of including claims for workers' injuries in the price of goods is that goods that are relatively dangerous to produce have an additional element of cost that goods that are relatively safe to produce do not have.

Workers' compensation laws established the employer's liability in cases of work-related injury. Employers, exposed to this peril of liability losses, purchase insurance to cover their exposure. Workers' compensation insurance policies promise to pay on behalf of the employer payments for which the employer is legally liable due to injuries to employees during the course of their employment. Premiums for this insurance transfer money to those employers who experience such losses from all the employers exposed to such losses.

As in the case of unemployment insurance, insurance companies use experience rating to adjust an insured's premiums. Thus, employers with good safety records will pay lower insurance rates than employers with poor safety records. Experience rating rewards loss prevention and loss reduction efforts. Generally, only larger employers receive significant benefits from experience-rated premiums; insurers cannot rely on the data from a small employer because its small number of workers does not provide much statistical credibility.

The Purposes of Workers' Compensation Laws

The National Commission on State Workmen's Compensation Laws completed and presented a comprehensive study of existing workers' compensation laws to President Richard Nixon and Congress in 1972.[7] Although it is now more than forty years old, the objectives in the report provide the focus for a modern workers' compensation

---

[6] For example, see P. Fishback and S. Kantor, 1995, "Did Workers Pay for the Passage of Workers' Compensation Laws?" *Quarterly Journal of Economics,* Vol. 110, No. 3, pp. 713–42.

[7] *The Report of the National Commission on State Workmen's Compensation Laws* (Washington, D.C.: U.S. Government Printing Office, 1972).

program. These objectives were expressed as the commission's opinion of what an ideal workers' compensation program should accomplish, as follows:

- Broad coverage of employees and work-related injuries and diseases
- Substantial protection against loss of income
- Sufficient medical care and rehabilitation services
- Encouragement of safety
- An effective delivery system for workers' compensation

BROAD COVERAGE OF EMPLOYEES AND WORK-RELATED INJURIES AND DISEASES

Coverage should be provided for all U.S. workers. Many states have exclusions applying to small businesses, agricultural workers, government workers, household workers, and other groups. Such exclusions are undesirable, in the commission's opinion. Likewise, the commission argued that all occupational diseases should be covered, not just specified illnesses as is the current practice. Such an objective presents problems. How does one determine whether high blood pressure, ulcers, and so forth are work-related illnesses? Presumably, an administrative body would have to judge each case individually, but designing a program to carry out these tasks in an efficient and balanced way requires considerable administrative fine-tuning.

SUBSTANTIAL PROTECTION AGAINST LOSS OF INCOME

Benefits should be equated with the total remuneration of the injured worker. Such things as overtime, employee benefits, and vacation pay should be considered in addition to basic wages and salaries. Minimum and maximum benefit totals should be developed, but the goal should be a close approximation of indemnity. In addition to lost income, indemnity payments would include payment for medical expenses caused by injury or disease. With rapid inflation, benefits should be increased regularly to keep pace with cost-of-living increases.

SUFFICIENT MEDICAL CARE AND REHABILITATION SERVICES

This goal reflects the point that an injured worker is entitled to prompt and continuous medical care, combined with post-accident physical therapy, if necessary, until productive employment can be resumed. The workers' compensation system should provide incentives to restore injured workers to useful lives.

ENCOURAGEMENT OF SAFETY

Employers have great incentive to prevent and reduce workplace injuries because they pay for their employees' workers' compensation benefits regardless of fault. Employers therefore routinely invest in loss control efforts to minimize their workers' compensation costs. Incentives for safety are also built into the workers' compensation insurance pricing system. For example, the use of experience rating rewards employers with low insured losses by reducing their workers' compensation premiums.

AN EFFECTIVE DELIVERY SYSTEM FOR WORKERS' COMPENSATION

This objective reinforces the four goals previously noted. The commission thought that an adequate number of attorneys, physicians, and state administrators was needed to maintain the workers' compensation system's efficiency and effectiveness.

Because there has been an ongoing discussion of the desirability of continuing to provide workers' compensation under more than fifty different administrative jurisdictions, the normative goals set forth by the National Commission serve as a benchmark in evaluating the existing state programs. Many people believe workers' compensation should be administered on a federal basis, arguing that the current system produces inadequate and often unfair results. The commission's report has been a useful source of ideas and information for this debate.

Operations of Workers' Compensation Systems

Including Puerto Rico, Washington, D.C., and other territories under U.S. control, there are more than fifty different jurisdictions that administer workers' compensation laws. We present the general features of these programs in this section. The answers to specific questions about a given state's program should be sought at local administrative offices.

Each state's workers' compensation program has criteria for determining a worker's eligibility to receive benefits. The general test that must be satisfied is that an employee in covered employment (defined by state law) must suffer a work-related injury or illness. The injury must be caused by an accident arising out of employment and in the course of such employment. The "course of employment" rule generally requires that the injury occur on the employer's premises and during working hours. This rule eliminates coverage for employees traveling to and from work. However, employees who are injured when they are off the employer's premises while performing a part of their job, such as delivery drivers, generally receive coverage.

Workers' compensation programs do not cover all types of employment-related injuries and illnesses. Although coverage exclusions vary from state to state, some losses that typically are not covered include (1) injuries that result from intoxication, (2) injuries that are willfully self-inflicted, and (3) injuries that arise from a willful failure to follow safety precautions.

Workers' compensation insurance provides three types of benefits after eligibility has been established:

- Cash payments to replace lost income
- Full payment of medical expenses
- Payment for rehabilitation services

Cash benefits generally begin after injury and a waiting period, typically one week. Cash benefits are determined using three different factors. Some percentage of weekly income, often two-thirds, is paid to injured employees who are unable to work. In addition, there may be a schedule of cash benefits for accidents involving permanent impairment, such as paralysis or loss of a finger or an eye. Third, if a worker is killed because of an accident, dependents of the deceased worker generally are entitled to death benefits. Workers' compensation income benefits are coordinated with Social Security disability benefits, so a total of no more than 80 percent of a worker's average monthly wage is paid from both sources.

The cash benefits available through workers' compensation are frequently classified into several categories of disability. **Permanent partial disability** means that the employee has suffered some permanent injury, such as the loss of an eye or a limb, but still can work. Some "repetitive motion" injuries that affect office workers and other workers who perform the same task throughout the day have been categorized as permanent partial injuries. These painful conditions have been difficult to prevent, and employers have found it expensive to rehabilitate the injured workers. Other loss categories include **temporary partial disability** (the worker will recover and can work part time while disabled), **temporary total disability** (the worker will recover but can do no work until disability ends), and **permanent total disability** (the worker has suffered permanent injury and no longer can work at his or her previous job).

Workers' compensation insurance covers medical expenses for accidents without the worker having to pay for deductible, copayments, or upper limits on coverage. However, medical expenses arising from occupational illness sometimes are not covered completely. This lack of complete medical coverage for occupational illnesses is another complaint about current plans.

Injured workers generally are entitled to rehabilitation after an industrial accident. **Rehabilitation programs** teach workers how to use injured arms and legs or provide training with prosthetic devices. Some of the program's critics think more can and should be done to improve state rehabilitation programs.

The providers of workers' compensation insurance vary from jurisdiction to jurisdiction. Some states require that employers purchase insurance from a state-operated workers' compensation fund. Other states allow competition between private insurers and state-operated funds. Some states have no state-operated funds and private insurers provide all the coverage. Most states allow employers with large work forces and established financial assets to operate self-insurance programs.

In all cases, the insurance premium is based on an employer's payroll. Experience-rating formulas may reduce the premiums. Insurers classify employers by industry, giving recognition to the fact that some industries involve more danger to workers than others. An employer in a relatively dangerous industry would pay a higher rate than an employer in a relatively safe industry. Experience rating provides rewards for employers with good safety records, regardless of an industry's accident record.

If an injured employee thinks an insurer has not handled his or her case fairly, most states provide for settlement of the dispute by a workers' compensation board. Some states have designated a court to oversee the administration of workers' compensation disputes. Workers' compensation boards may judge questions relating to whether an injury was work-related, whether the injured worker was acting within the scope of his or her assignment, or the severity of the injury. One of the original purposes of the workers' compensation laws, however, was to eliminate litigation and provide prompt and fair settlement of claims. Thus, voluminous litigation is to be neither an expected nor a desired part of an effective workers' compensation program.

Some Current Concerns about Workers' Compensation

During the "Great Recession" that began in 2008, total employer spending on workers' compensation declined, reflecting increased job losses and the resulting reduction in employer payrolls. Nationally employer costs for workers' compensation equaled $1.30 per $100 of covered wages, the lowest cost in thirty years.[8] Despite this cost trend, financing the cost of injured workers presents an ongoing problem to many risk managers and insurers. In particular, health care costs have accounted for a growing percentage of all workers' compensation benefits paid nationwide.

Factors causing prices to rise include the following:

- The lack of a requirement for injured or disabled employees in many states to pay a portion of their health care costs because workers' compensation benefits have no deductible or copayment requirements like those found in individual and group health insurance policies. Because employees do not spend any of their own funds, employers and their insurers believe more services are used.

---

[8] National Academy of Social Insurance, "Job Losses Cause Workers' Compensation Coverage and Costs to Fall," August 16, 2011, retrieved February 3, 2012, from *http://www.nasi.org.*

- A large number of fraudulent claims. Attracted by the prospect of receiving "money for nothing," some employees attempt to file bogus workers' compensation claims. For example, they may try to collect workers' compensation benefits for injuries suffered while not working. (A student in one of the author's classes explained that the largest workers' compensation claim filed in his father's construction business was from a worker who claimed that he injured his back while working on a Monday morning, when in fact he was injured in a bar fight two days earlier.) Other common fraudulent claims involve feigning injury or exaggerating the severity of an injury.[9]

- The practice of some health care providers to charge more for services when treating workers' compensation patients than for other patients with the same diagnosis. Such differential charges are especially likely to occur in cases where Medicare pays for service, on the one hand, and workers' compensation insurance, on the other. Some commentators describe this problem as *cost shifting* from the government (Medicare) to private (workers' compensation) insurers.

While employers and their insurers were expressing great concern about the costs of providing workers' compensation coverage, many employees felt their benefits were inadequate. In some states, benefits were significantly less than 80 percent of pre-disability income, a common target replacement ratio. Thus, all concerned parties—employers, insurers, and employees—have expressed dissatisfaction with the workers' compensation system: Employers felt the system was too costly, insurers found the business unprofitable, and many employees felt they were undercompensated for their injuries.

A second issue that affects the provision of workers' compensation insurance is how to compensate victims of cumulative injuries and stress-related claims. **Cumulative injuries** are job-related disabilities that result over many years of employment. Black lung, to cite one example, is a cumulative illness that affects coal miners, and workers' compensation programs compensate injured victims with this disease. Some workers have claimed that their heart attacks or deafness also are job-related cumulative injuries, which raises the issue of how workers' compensation boards should distinguish job-related heart attacks or deafness from non-job-related events. Surely some people would become deaf or have high blood pressure, regardless of their employment.

Summary—Workers' Compensation

Each year, thousands of workers die or are injured permanently, and millions miss one or more days of work because of job-related injuries and diseases. As a result of workers' compensation laws, the economic cost of these injuries no longer falls on the unfortunate worker. Before the Industrial Revolution, the worker and his or her family bore the burden of industrial accidents. Workers had the right to sue employers, and employers had the right to defend themselves against the claim of negligence. Three almost-sure defenses were available to employers: (1) contributory negligence (workers contributed to their own loss), (2) fellow servant rules (the injury was caused by a fellow worker, not the employer), and (3) assumption of the risk (the employee should have known the employment was inherently dangerous when accepting the work). Because of the prevailing legal doctrines, injured workers rarely collected for injuries.

Workers' compensation legislation created liability for employers, regardless of fault. At the same time, it took the right to sue away from the employee. It is often assumed that the transfer of much of the cost of injuries probably went from the worker

---

[9] For descriptions of other real-life workers' compensation fraud cases (as well as other types of insurance fraud), see the list of "real-life_cases" at *http://www.insurancefraud.org.*

to the consumer because the employer passes along all costs, including the costs for workers' compensation insurance, to the consumer.

A national commission outlined the following objectives for a modern compensation program:

- Broad coverage of employees and work-related injuries and diseases
- Substantial protection against loss of income
- Sufficient medical care and rehabilitation services
- Encouragement of safety
- An effective delivery system for workers' compensation

Under current state administration, each workers' compensation program has criteria for determining eligibility and for exclusions from coverage. The types of benefits currently available under workers' compensation programs are (1) cash benefits, (2) medical expenses, and (3) rehabilitation services. State-operated funds or private insurers may provide workers' compensation insurance. In all cases, the premium is based on the amount of payroll and the relative danger to employees in the industry. Experience ratings recognize the safety efforts of particular employers. In the case of a dispute between an injured employee and an insurer, workers' compensation boards are available to settle disputes. Workers' compensation laws were designed to minimize litigation, however, and legal disputes should not be an outcome of these laws.

Current concerns about the workers' compensation program include the rapidly increasing costs of health care; the spreading cost of cumulative injuries; and inadequate rates for insurers.

Review

1. Describe some causes of unemployment. Separate your list into causes that are beyond the worker's control and those that are under the worker's control. Can you identify some gray areas in the categorization of these causes?
2. What alternatives are available to the government for dealing with unemployment?
3. What do Social Security, public assistance, and unemployment insurance have in common?
4. Explain why a downward cycle of unemployment is likely to develop without government action.
5. How does unemployment insurance help to reverse the downward spiral of unemployment? Why is unemployment insurance called an *automatic stabilizer*?
6. What parts do the state and federal governments play in providing the unemployment insurance program?
7. Who do you think ultimately pays the cost of the unemployment insurance program?
8. Why does experience rating reverse the insurance transfer process? What is the explanation for experience rating in unemployment insurance?
9. What are the general provisions of state unemployment insurance programs?

10. Identify four reasons that may disqualify a worker from receiving unemployment benefits.
11. Under current workers' compensation laws in the United States, are employers, employees, or consumers most likely to bear the costs of work-related injuries?
12. What was the fellow servant rule? What role did it play in the development of workers' compensation laws?
13. Why is workers' compensation known as the exclusive remedy available to an injured worker?
14. List the five purposes of workers' compensation laws as outlined by the National Commission on State Workmen's Compensation Laws.
15. Identify three reasons that an injured worker may be excluded from workers' compensation coverage despite being injured while at work.
16. Identify the three general types of workers' compensation benefits.
17. Describe the role that insurance plays in distributing the cost of work-related injuries.
18. If an injured worker thinks that the compensation for the injuries sustained is unfair, what course of action may be pursued to attempt to correct the problem?
19. Give an example of a permanent partial disability.

Objective Questions

1. "Fiscal policy" describes direct government actions to:
   a. Put money into or take money out of the economy
   b. Raise interest rates
   c. Regulate insurance transactions
   d. Increase the supply of money
2. Unemployment insurance is called an *automatic stabilizer* because:
   a. It reduces the tax rates on the unemployed.
   b. It gives purchasing power to people who would not be able to make purchases without these payments.
   c. It transfers money from the upper to the lower income brackets.
   d. It generally reduces the federal deficit in most years.
3. States have three general requirements relating to eligibility for unemployment benefits. These requirements include all the following except:
   a. A waiting period
   b. An earnings record
   c. A continuing interest in employment
   d. Fully insured status for Social Security benefits
4. All the following were legal defenses used by employers before workers' compensation laws existed, allowing employers to avoid making payments to injured workers, except:
   a. The fellow servant rule
   b. Assumption of the risk

   c. Dishonorable discharge of duties
   d. Contributory negligence
5. The workers' compensation claim payment is the _____ available to the injured worker.
   a. Exclusive remedy
   b. Government contribution
   c. Agreed amount
   d. Principal sum
6. _____ is designed to reward loss prevention and loss reduction efforts.
   a. Reduced credibility
   b. Warranty reduction factors
   c. Experience rating
   d. Ex-post factoring
7. Currently, workers' compensation programs are administered by:
   a. The federal government
   b. The state governments
   c. City governments
   d. Labor unions
8. Each of the following is an excluded injury under workers' compensation insurance programs except:
   a. Injuries resulting from intoxication
   b. Injuries that are willfully self-inflicted
   c. Injuries suffered traveling to or from work
   d. Injuries caused by a fellow employee

Discussion Questions

1. Has the cost of workers' compensation increased or decreased in recent years? Explain the factors that have led to this trend. In your answer, describe how the type of workers' compensation benefits paid has changed in recent years.
2. In recent years, states have done a great deal of borrowing from the federal government to finance

unemployment insurance payments. Do you think the political climate has changed sufficiently since 1935 to allow the federal government to take over this program and combine it with Social Security? Do you think such a change would be a good idea or a bad idea?

Selected References

Myers, R. J. (1975). *Social Security*. Homewood, IL: Published for the McCahan Foundation, Bryn Mawr, PA., by R. D. Irwin.

Rejda, G. E. (1976). *Social Insurance and Economic Security*. Englewood Cliffs, NJ: Prentice Hall, Inc.

22

Commercial Property Insurance

After studying this chapter, you should be able to

- Describe the different types of commercial property insurance

- Explain how businesses can use a package insurance policy to protect themselves against direct and indirect losses

- Describe the different types of property coverage available in the Building and Personal Property coverage form

- Identify the need for business income insurance

- Explain how property insurance rates are developed

- Explain how transportation insurance distinguishes between ocean marine insurance and inland marine insurance

- List the major kinds of property insurance needed by owners of cars and planes

In this chapter, we begin a two-part discussion of the loss exposures of commercial businesses and the types of commercial insurance available to cover these needs. This chapter will focus on different types of commercial property loss exposures and the insurance policies designed to insure such risks. Chapter 23, "Commercial Liability Insurance," will focus on commercial liability exposures. Both types of insurance coverage are widely used by risk managers to protect their firms from the adverse financial consequences of accidental property and liability losses.

COMMERCIAL INSURANCE

Commercial and Personal Property Insurance

Both businesses and homeowners need property insurance. When businesses purchase insurance, it is called **commercial insurance**. When individuals purchase insurance, it is called **personal insurance**. Because much of our discussion of personal insurance contracts found in the earlier chapters of this book is applicable to commercial insurance, we need not examine commercial insurance contracts with the same level of detail. Instead, we describe the essential elements of the most useful property and liability insurance policies.

Property and Marine (Transportation) Insurance

For insurance purposes, a broad division is made when describing physical property. Property is either permanently attached to land or it is not. We call property permanently attached to land, such as buildings and fixtures, **real property**. **Personal property**, on the other hand, can be moved. This dichotomy in the nature of property has led to a division in property insurance. Real property historically has been covered by some type of property insurance, such as a fire insurance policy, specifying the location of the covered property. Mobile property, such as property to be exported, is generally covered by **transportation insurance**, historically called **marine insurance**.

Focusing attention on the mobility of property leads to an understanding of how these two basic property coverages have evolved. The perils facing mobile property are broader in scope than the perils facing real property. In addition to perils such as fire, lightning, and windstorm, mobile property may be sunk, confiscated, and hijacked; also, it can be collided with and stolen more easily than property attached to land. The broader scope of the perils, the difference in ability to investigate losses, and the differing potential for salvage operations have resulted in marine insurance practices that are quite distinct from comparable property insurance practices.

We describe both the property and transportation sections of the most frequently used commercial package insurance policy in this chapter. We also cover aviation and automobile property exposures.

COMMERCIAL PACKAGE POLICY

Historically, businesses had to purchase several different insurance policies when weaving together a "complete" insurance program. A small or medium-sized manufacturing or retail firm might have needed several separate policies to achieve its insurance objectives, including property insurance, liability insurance, automobile insurance, and transportation insurance. Specialized companies, such as building contractors, jewelry firms, and firms operating aircraft, needed even more policies. Many commercial insurers issue a **package policy**, a policy in which two or more coverages are combined into one insurance purchase that provides all generally needed coverages. For example, the **Insurance Services Office ISO** designed the **commercial package policy (CPP)** to provide insurance coverage to a broad range of profit and nonprofit organizations, including manufacturing firms, schools, retailers, and apartment building owners. In practice, most property owners except private homeowners can use this policy. Figure 22-1 shows the main insuring components of the CPP. Insureds must purchase at least two of the

FIGURE 22-1 Commercial Package Policy

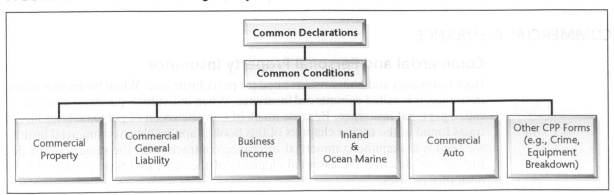

package's components (shown at the bottom of this figure), but they may purchase as many other coverage forms as they need.

The CPP is preceded by declarations and conditions that apply to the entire package. The declarations usually are the first page of most insurance policies. The **declarations** establish the insured's identity and the location of the business. This section also shows the different component coverages purchased and the premium charged. The common **conditions** cover policy cancellation, assignment of the policy, and other legal rights and duties. In addition to the common declarations and conditions, each component part has its own specific declarations page and conditions.

BUILDING AND PERSONAL PROPERTY FORM

Because of its importance, we describe commercial property insurance by focusing on the ISO commercial package policy. The CPP provides property insurance in the **building and personal property coverage form**.

Property Covered

The form for building and personal property coverage identifies the building(s) covered as those listed on the declarations page. Insurers insist on careful identification of the property covered to respect the principle of definite losses. Without such identification, legal disputes would undoubtedly arise between insurers and their policyholders about which buildings are (not) insured.

In addition to covering the building, the CPP covers the insured's **business personal property**, which includes such items as machinery, furniture, and inventory. *Inventory* includes raw material, work in process, and finished goods available for sale. The declarations establish the limit of recovery and the appropriate premium.

The third category of covered property is **personal property** not owned by the business but in its care, custody, or control. This category would be especially important to firms holding or using borrowed property, such as on-site displays or special tools.

Property Excluded from Coverage

The form for building and personal property coverage also specifies property that is not covered. Sometimes property is excluded because providing insurance would violate one of the ideals for coverage. (For example, losses of accounts, currency, and securities are not definite and difficult to verify. Asking a policyholder "How much cash was destroyed in the fire?" could result in an inflated estimate of loss.) Cash and near-cash items can be insured using policies having special conditions and exclusions to deal with the moral hazard. Sometimes property is excluded because the insurer wants to charge an additional premium for insureds having this type of property. (While the basic form excludes personal property while airborne or waterborne, this coverage can be added with an inland marine form for an additional premium.) Other property (vehicles, for example) is excluded because a separate policy is designed for this property.

Earlier in the chapter, we noted the distinction between *real* and *personal property*. The law makes another important distinction between **tangible property** (which includes physical assets such as buildings and machinery) and **intangible property** (nonphysical assets). Intangible property includes intellectual property (for example, chemical formulas and computer software), brand value, and proprietary business methods. In some cases, the value of intangible property can exceed the value of tangible property, making such property a vital (albeit difficult-to-insure) concern to business owners and insurers.

Perils Covered

The property component requires a **causes-of-loss form** to complete the contract. There are three main alternatives: the basic form, the broad form, and the special form. The basic form covers the following perils:

1. Fire
2. Lightning
3. Explosion
4. Windstorm or hail
5. Smoke
6. Aircraft or vehicles (striking the property)
7. Riot or civil commotion
8. Vandalism
9. Sprinkler leakage
10. Sinkhole collapse
11. Volcanic action

The *broad form* extends the coverage by adding more perils, including falling objects and water damage. This form also covers some specific causes of building collapse. The *special form* provides **open-perils coverage**. With this form, the insured is covered unless the peril causing the loss is excluded specifically. With the open-perils form, the legal burden is on the insurer to show that an exclusion applies. With the specified-perils form, the insured has the burden of showing that the proximate cause (as defined in Chapter 6, "Fundamentals of Insurance") of the loss was covered.

Reporting Forms

Many firms have wide swings in their inventory during the course of an operating cycle. For example, many retail stores build inventory before the Christmas season, and food processing companies carry more stock immediately after the harvest. To solve the insurance problems presented by variation in inventory values, insurers use reporting forms. With this coverage, a maximum amount of insurance is purchased and an initial premium set. Subsequently, the insured reports the actual amount of inventory held (on a weekly, monthly, or quarterly basis), and the premium is adjusted based on these reports.

Students frequently ask what happens if the insured underreports the inventory to reduce the premium. Reporting forms require the insured to be scrupulously honest. If the insurer audits the insured's records (most likely after a loss), and if the insured's records do not support the amount of inventory claimed by the most recent report, the insured will collect only the proportion of the claim that the amount of inventory reported bore to the actual amount of inventory on hand. Thus, if only three-quarters of the actual inventory was reported, only three-quarters of the loss will be covered by insurance. This penalty clause presumably reduces the moral hazard.

BUSINESS INCOME COVERAGE

The Business Income (BI) Form of the CPP may be used to cover indirect losses. **Indirect losses** typically occur after insured physical damage and are commonly referred to as *business interruption* losses. Insurers categorize these losses as follows:

1. *Loss of income:* For example, if fire destroys a grocery store, the loss of the building and inventory is a direct loss. The income lost while the building is rebuilt and the business reestablished is an indirect loss.

2. *Continuing expenses:* While a business is being reestablished, fixed expenses such as bond interest payments, property taxes, and salary for indispensable employees continue. Insurance that replaced only lost net income would not cover these expenses. BI, as defined in this policy, includes **continuing expenses**.

3. *Extra expenses:* For some businesses, such as television stations, hospitals, and banks, operations must be uninterrupted. These businesses will not suffer lost income after a direct loss because they will keep operating. They are likely to incur **extra expenses** to stay in operation, and BI insurance can cover these extra costs.

4. *Leasehold interest:* This loss is calculated as the net present value of rent differential between the preloss and postloss rent paid by the insured, and it also would include any unamortized acquisition costs, improvements, or prepaid rent.

The trigger for BI coverage is the necessary suspension of operations caused by insured direct physical loss of or damage to property at the premises described in the declarations. The policy covers the actual loss of BI consisting of net income and continuing normal operating expenses. The insurance usually covers the period beginning 72 hours after the loss and ending when the damaged property could be repaired with reasonable speed and similar quality. Insureds also can purchase an "Extended Period of Indemnity," which can result in an additional period of coverage after the repairs of the insured damage are complete in exchange for an additional premium.

Business Income from Dependent Properties

In some cases, a business suffers no direct physical damage, but its operations still may be halted because other businesses or the transportation system sustain physical loss. Consider the following examples:

- A number of automakers were forced to halt or reduce production in 2011 when an earthquake and tsunami in Japan damaged the production facilities of the companies supplying parts to the automakers.

- The tenants in a shopping mall often experience a significant decline in sales if the lead department store in the mall must close due to a fire, even if the other tenants are undamaged, because they rely on the lead store to attract customer traffic to the mall.

- Assume that the New York Shirt Company buys its entire supply of buttons from the New Jersey Button Company. If a tornado destroys the button company, the shirt company also may shut down until it can find a new supplier of buttons that meet its specifications. Finally, if we reverse the previous example, we can see a situation where a manufacturer depends on one customer to purchase all its output. If the customer were to be destroyed by fire, the manufacturer likely would suffer significant income loss despite remaining physically intact.

The **dependent properties** business income form can cover these contingencies.

PROPERTY INSURANCE RATING

A property insurance **rate** is the cost per hundred dollars of exposed value. Insurers calculate the **premium** by multiplying the rate by the number of hundreds of dollars of value of exposed property. For example, assume that the property insurance rate is $0.80 per each $100 of value. A $16 million factory has 160,000 such units. Therefore, the premium will be 160,000 multiplied by $0.80, or $128,000.

How was this $0.80 property insurance rate developed? Property insurers commonly use two different methods to produce rates: class rating and schedule rating.

Class rating operates by placing comparable units into a group and then charging a class rate reflecting the expected loss experience and expenses of the group. This approach is especially useful with relatively homogeneous property, such as residential homes, small apartment buildings, or churches. For example, several factors influence a class rate for property insurance, particularly the costs related to coverage from fire loss. The first letter of each factor is often remembered using the convenient acronym "COPE":

- *Construction* of the building (e.g., wood or brick frame).
- *Occupancy* (e.g., owner-occupied or not).
- *Protection class,* which refers to a numeric scale used to grade community fire-fighting capability. (Typically, insurers use a 1-to-10 scale to grade a fire protection district. The grade reflects an evaluation of such factors as equipment, personnel training, and water availability.)
- *Exposure* to external sources of loss (e.g., are nearby structures especially flammable and in such proximity that fires will spread quickly to the insured property?).

Figure 22-2 illustrates some possible class rates reflecting these factors. Assume that an owner of an apartment building with a wooden frame structure, in a medium-sized city with an average fire department, whose property was not closely surrounded by homes or businesses, wanted to purchase a property insurance policy. The agent or the insurance underwriter would use the data shown in Figure 22-2 to determine the rate, which is based on insurance industry loss experience and adjusted for differences in risk levels related to factors such as construction, occupancy, and fire protection. Assume that this combination produces a rate of $0.90. If the apartment owner has a $1 million structure and wants to insure its full value against property damage, it will cost $9,000 a year ($1,000,000/100 × $0.90 = $9,000).

FIGURE 22-2 Example of Class Rating

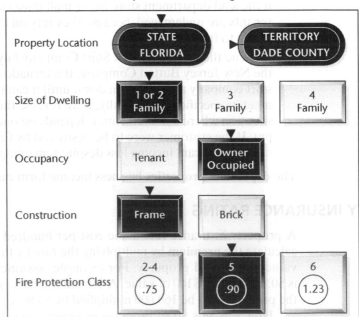

TABLE 22-1 Illustration of Schedule Rating (Based on Universal Mercantile System)

Base rate		$0.60
Charges		
Construction:		
Wooden floors	$0.10	
Deficient floor	$0.20	
Occupancy/Use:		
Mattress factory	$0.20	
Total		$1.10
Credits		
Fire sprinkler (20% credit)		($0.22)
Rate		$0.88

Schedule rating analyzes each property individually and is used primarily in rating commercial buildings. This procedure begins with a rate for a standard building (for example, $0.60 per each $100 of value) in the same city as the building under consideration. Next, charges (for more hazardous conditions) and credits (for less hazardous conditions) are combined, producing a rate for this specific building.

Examples of construction features that would produce schedule rating charges for a building are more flammable floors, walls, or roof than the standard building. Occupancy by a mattress factory, where there is the possibility of combustible dust, is an example of a use that would produce a charge. Credits would be granted for such features as a fire sprinkler system, fire doors, and smoke alarms. By giving careful consideration to the construction, use, and fire prevention devices of a particular building, a unique rate applicable to that building and use is developed. An example of a schedule rate is presented in Table 22-1.

This description of rate making suggests that property insurance rating is scientific and precise. This conclusion is not quite right, however. Judgment still must be used in the schedule-rating approach to produce fair charges and credits. Class rating is fairly mechanical, but constant revision of class rates is called for as new loss patterns develop or as a community's firefighting ability improves. Competitive considerations often enter into the decisions as well. In general, insurance rates are based on shared loss data and estimates. While the mathematical estimating process is refined, insurance rates still involve actuarial and underwriting judgment and estimates.

TRANSPORTATION INSURANCE

Transportation insurance is generally divided into two broad categories: ocean marine insurance and inland marine insurance.

Ocean Marine Insurance

Ocean marine insurance is one of the earliest forms of insurance. Commerce by ship was well established in the Mediterranean Sea before the year 2,000 B.C. The Babylonians, Phoenicians, Greeks, and Romans were great sea traders. Coincident with the development of this trade, insurance transactions emerged as distinct commercial agreements. *Bottomry* was a transaction that protected an owner from financial loss if his ship was destroyed. If the shipowner acquired the ship by means of a loan, an interest rate was paid to a moneylender. The moneylender, for a premium beyond the ordinary interest rate, would agree to forgive the loan if the ship was destroyed.

The bottomry loan was an early forerunner of ocean marine insurance. Recalling the elements of an ideally insurable exposure from Chapter 7, "Insurable Perils and Insuring Organizations," we can see that (1) similar units (ships) were exposed to similar perils; (2) nonaccidental, self-inflicted losses were presumably excluded from coverage; (3) losses were definite and measurable; and (4) catastrophes were not likely. We can see transfer and pooling in the bottomry loan because the moneylender charged each shipowner a premium that presumably was sufficient to pay for the few loans that would have to be forgiven.

Nevertheless, some elements of the modern insurance transaction were missing. Actuarial science was not practiced (even though the Phoenicians were noted mathematicians, they weren't *that* skilled), so premiums were probably not based on mathematical estimates but on intuition and judgment. The early sea traders and moneylenders also lacked a highly developed body of law like the one that provides the environment for the modern insurance transaction.

Respondentia loans were comparable to bottomry loans, but the difference lay in the subject of the loan. In the case of respondentia loans, the ship's cargo, rather than the ship itself, was the subject of the loan. Otherwise, the transaction was comparable. A merchant placing cargo on a ship would take out a loan using the cargo as collateral. The moneylender, for a premium in addition to the regular interest charged, agreed to forgive the loan if the cargo were lost. Again, as shown next, modern ocean marine cargo insurance is very similar to the respondentia loan.

Today, as in historical times, ocean marine insurance is essential to international commerce. The worldwide shipping of petroleum products, manufactured goods, and agricultural products creates a great need for ocean marine insurance. Many people who never think about this insurance actually pay the premiums because they are included in the price of foreign petroleum, imported automobiles, and other imported products.

Ocean Marine Coverages

Four distinct types of loss exposure—**hull, cargo, loss of freight,** and **liability loss**—are insured by ocean marine insurance policies, as follows:

- The *hull* exposure includes the value of the ship and its equipment. This coverage is comparable to the bottomry loan in that the insurer agrees to pay the shipowner if the ship is lost while the policy is in force.
- The *cargo* exposure is the value of the goods being shipped. This coverage is comparable to respondentia loans in that the shipper is compensated for losses suffered while the goods are being shipped.
- The loss of *freight* is the loss of income that the shipowner would have earned if the cargo (or passengers) had been delivered rather than lost. This coverage is comparable to the BI consequential loss coverage of property insurance.
- The *liability* loss exposure is the loss that a shipowner would suffer if the ship were held to be legally responsible for negligently injuring other people or their property.

Much ocean marine insurance terminology is quaint by today's standards, especially those used to describe losses. **Particular average** losses are those borne by the owners of the ship or cargo due to direct damage to their property. **General average** is the loss attributed to the owners of property where there was not necessarily a loss to their property, but other property was thrown overboard to save the ship and the loss was borne proportionately by all who had property exposed to loss during the voyage. For example, if Mr. Washington's $100,000 worth of gears and wheels were thrown overboard to save the ship during a storm, the loss would be shared by all those having an interest in the voyage. The shipowner and the others whose goods were not lost would (or their insurers would on their behalf) have to contribute a proportionate share of the loss. Ocean marine insurance policies may cover either particular or general average losses, as well as freight and liability losses.

The perils covered by an ocean marine insurance policy are broader than the open-perils coverage described earlier in this chapter, and for good reason. If the perils were specific and narrow, it would be very hard to collect insurance coverage for losses because the peril that caused a loss is nearly impossible to establish when the ship is at the bottom of the ocean. While the list of insured perils is comprehensive, today's ocean marine policies do not cover all risks, however. Losses resulting from war or fraud generally are not covered. (War losses can be covered for an extra premium— fraud losses, never.) Nor will the insurance proceeds be paid if the conditions of the policy are breached by the insured.

Ocean Marine Insurance Rating

Unlike property insurance, ocean marine insurance rates often rely heavily on the judgment of the underwriters. An underwriter, such as one operating at Lloyd's of London or a U.S. insurer, will quote an applicant a rate based on a subjective estimate of the risk involved in the particular case, based in part on his experience in pricing similar exposures in the past. The following factors usually are considered:

- The seaworthiness of the ship
- The experience and ability of the captain and crew
- The potential for loss of the cargo—$1 million of glass crystal having more potential for loss than $1 million of sheet steel
- The scheduled route and the season of the year
- The coverage provided by the policy

Competition in the ocean marine insurance marketplace and the potential for war damage (if not excluded by the policy) also would be factors to consider in setting a final premium in ocean marine insurance. Some ocean marine policies are written to cover only one voyage; others cover a specific time period; and some are written on an open-ended basis and are good until canceled.

Inland Marine Insurance[1]

Inland marine insurance is less familiar to most readers than many other property insurance types. This section begins, therefore, with some historical background and a definition of this category of coverage. Inland marine insurance is written as an open-perils contract. This type of coverage provides insurance against "risks of direct physical loss" and then limits the coverage by specific exclusions. Open-perils contracts put a legal burden on the insurer asserting that a claim is not covered by the insurance contract, requiring the insurer to prove that an exclusion applies. War, nuclear hazard, wear and tear, and government action are among several exclusions that apply to inland marine insurance policies. The peril causing the largest amount of inland marine losses is theft.

---

[1]Information about inland marine insurance can be found at the Web site of the Inland Marine Underwriting Association (IMUA; *http://www.imua.org/*).

Inland marine insurance is essentially an American distinction. Other countries have not separated the underwriting powers of insurers to the extent that it is done in the United States. That is, in other countries, if an insurer (underwriter) wants to write property insurance, marine insurance, or perhaps even life insurance, it is a private decision, and the insurer may proceed unconstrained by law. In the United States, however, there was an early tradition of allowing fire insurers to write fire insurance exclusively and marine insurers to write marine coverage exclusively. This separation of underwriting power led to a separation of inland from ocean marine insurance. In the United States, the distinction between the two marine branches remains.

After the Industrial Revolution began in the nineteenth century, commerce moved inland. Trucks, canal barges, and railroads became the vehicles of commerce. The warehouse-to-warehouse approach of the ocean marine policy initially appeared to be adequate to meet the needs of insureds and insurers. Over time, however, the differences in the perils, salvage potential, and loss investigation potential led to the development of inland marine as a separate branch of marine insurance.

The distinction between fire and inland marine insurance is not as clear as that between fire and ocean marine insurance. In the early twentieth century, jurisdictional questions led to considerable controversy between fire and inland marine insurers. The rather mechanical rating approach of the fire insurers was in sharp contrast to the more judgmental rating approach of the inland marine insurers. The latter had much more flexibility in providing coverage and determining premiums. The fire insurers did not like losing business to the inland marine insurers. The inventory of chain stores is an example of the type of property that was subject to jurisdictional dispute.

The 1933 **Nationwide Definition** of marine insurance was developed to settle the dispute between the fire and the inland marine insurers. This definition, in the form of a model law, was adopted by most states. The definition has been modified several times, most recently in 1976, and is currently effective in a majority of states. It provides for six types of property to be the proper subject of inland marine insurance:

- Property designated for export
- Imported property until it reaches its destination
- Domestic property in the process of shipment
- Property used to facilitate (instrumentalities of) transportation, such as bridges, tunnels, pipelines, and electrical transmission towers
- Personal property that is moved easily and is typically of significant value, such as jewelry, furs, and cameras
- Commercial property that is moved easily and is typically of significant value, such as mobile equipment, property of others held by bailees, and electronic data processing equipment

It is very difficult to think of any other type of insurance coverage that is less well known or understood by the general public than inland marine insurance. This lack of recognition cannot be attributed to the subject's lack of importance, however. On the contrary, inland marine insurance is one of our most important types of insurance.

Can you think of any of your property that has not been the subject of inland marine insurance? Consider a pair of blue jeans. Presumably, they are made of blue cotton denim. The cotton bales, frequently transported from location to location, were the subject of inland marine insurance. The processed cotton was probably subject to *cotton buyers' transit insurance*, a special type of inland marine coverage. The finished jeans, when shipped from manufacturer to wholesaler or directly to a chain or department store, most likely were covered by an *annual transit policy*. This very basic and important type of inland marine policy insures incoming or outgoing merchandise against most losses. The *department store transit policy* is used to provide coverage when merchandise is shipped within one company from location to location. As you can see, your blue jeans probably were the subject of not one but several different types of inland marine insurance before you bought them. The same reasoning will reveal that most of the property we own was likewise the subject of inland marine insurance because almost everything we own has been transported on a truck or train several times before its purchase.

In addition to the various types of transportation insurance, inland marine insurance policies include bailees' customers' policies, instrumentalities of transportation policies, and personal and commercial property floaters.

Bailment

In a **bailment**, property belonging to one party (the bailor) is temporarily in the possession of a second party (the bailee), but ultimate possession is to return to the first party. This very common arrangement describes such situations as parking a car in a public garage, leaving clothes at a dry cleaner, shipping goods on a truck, or lending a lawnmower to a neighbor. Although not owning the property in temporary possession, the bailee is legally responsible for its safe return to the bailor. Even if not legally responsible, the bailee may feel morally responsible and not wish to jeopardize public goodwill. Because of these obligations, the bailee often insures the bailed property while it is in its possession. A **bailees' customers' insurance policy** (such as those purchased by dry cleaners or furriers) will pay the bailee if the property is lost, not returned, or damaged. After a loss of customer property, the insurer pays the bailee's (cleaner's) claim, then the bailee will reimburse the bailor (customer) to be relieved of legal liability or moral obligation for the damaged property.

Shipping Cargo on Common Carriers

The **annual transit policy** protects the interest of the shipper (bailor). The **motor truck cargo insurance** (a form of bailee's liability coverage) protects the interest of the trucking company. For example, if a loss occurs while merchandise is being transported by truck, the insured shipper usually will look to its own inland marine insurer for payment. After payment, the shipper's insurer then will seek payment from the motor carrier, which in turn will look to its own inland marine insurer for payment of the loss.

The following example outlines this relationship in sequential order:

1. The Blue Jeans Company places $1 million worth of jeans on a truck.
2. While aboard the truck, the cargo is destroyed because of the trucker's negligence.
3. The Blue Jeans Company looks to its own insurer for payment for the $1 million loss.
4. The insurer pays the Blue Jeans Company under its annual transit inland marine policy.
5. The insurer is subrogated (substituted) to the Blue Jeans Company's right to sue the trucker.
6. The trucker's insurer pays the Blue Jeans Company's insurer on behalf of the trucker because this loss is covered by the trucker's motor cargo insurance policy.

Readers may ask why the shipper needs transit insurance, because payment for losses could presumably be sought from the trucking company that caused the damage. The annual transit policy serves several purposes. Getting payment from the trucking company may be slow and involve legal complications. For example, questions of facts surrounding the loss might have to be litigated. Also, the trucking company might go bankrupt after the loss. Or the loss might have been due to an "act of God" (an unfortunate phrase describing such things as tornadoes, floods, and other natural calamities) for which the trucking company was not legally responsible and hence would not have to pay. For all these reasons, it is simpler for the shipper to purchase an independent policy for the goods, collect payment from the insurer if a loss occurs, and allow the insurer to try to collect from the trucking company through a legal doctrine known as *subrogation*.

Because the shipper's insurer often will succeed in recovering from trucking companies (or their insurers), transit insurance is less costly than otherwise would be the case. The relatively low price is another argument for the shipper to purchase a transit insurance policy.

Property Used in Transportation and Communication

Instrumentalities of transportation may cover a variety of different structures, including bridges, tunnels, piers, pipelines, wharves, dams, and traffic signals. Also covered by inland marine policies, because they are in many respects similar to the foregoing, are television and radio transmission towers and electrical power transmission towers. The inland marine coverage on this property is generally broader (open-perils) than that provided by property insurance.

Personal and Commercial Property Floater Policies

Inland marine insurance **floater policies** cover property that is moved easily and frequently and is generally of high value. The two basic types of floaters are personal and commercial. One type of personal floater, the **personal articles floater**, covers valuable assets such as cameras, jewelry, furs, guns, stamp and coin collections, and silverware. **Blanket floaters** are used when the property as a whole is valuable (e.g., silverware), but no one item is of outstanding value. **Scheduled floaters** can cover items of significant individual value, such as medical equipment, salesperson's samples, livestock, fine art, and other valuable commercial property that may be transported easily.

AVIATION INSURANCE

Aircraft owners and operators, airport operators, and companies that build and supply parts for aircraft (including their navigation equipment) purchase aviation insurance. Not all firms build, own, or operate aircraft, but a significant number of organizations do. The term *aircraft* as used in insurance is quite broad. In addition to airplanes (private and commercial), the term also applies to helicopters, hot air balloons, hang gliders, and space satellites.

Aircraft owners purchase both property insurance to protect against loss caused by physical damage to the plane and liability insurance to protect against lawsuits. Insurers call the airplane itself, including its electronic equipment, a *hull*. An **aircraft hull policy** provides protection, either for damage caused by specified perils or on an open-perils basis. Remember that open-perils coverage does not mean that all losses will be covered. It means that, unless otherwise excluded, all losses will be covered. Typically excluded would be losses due to war or wear and tear. On the other hand, the loss of a plane that simply vanishes (perhaps over the ocean or in Alaska) would be covered by an open-perils policy. The core insurance problem that faces aviation insurers is that the small number of exposure units weakens the application of the law of large numbers, while any single exposure unit is capable of causing a catastrophic loss.

The cost of aircraft insurance is a function of the perils covered. For example, open-perils coverage is more expensive than specified-perils coverage, while ground and flight coverage is more expensive than a not-in-motion policy. The latter coverage would provide property loss damage coverage but not liability coverage. Commercial airlines pay more for liability coverage because their planes generally are in the air more than private planes and represent a much greater exposure to loss because of the number of people onboard a commercial aircraft. On the other hand, light planes are more susceptible to damage or theft while on the ground, which raises the rate for their property coverage. Another important factor that insurers consider when setting rates for a particular exposure is the health, experience, and training of the airplane's pilot(s).

AUTOMOBILE PROPERTY INSURANCE

Figure 22-3 summarizes the types of damage caused by automobile accidents. In this section, we briefly describe the automobile *property* loss exposure. Chapter 23 describes automobile *liability* insurance.

Almost all business organizations own, operate, or authorize the use of vehicles. Thus, every comprehensive risk management plan must consider potential losses caused or sustained by business vehicles. In many cases, large firms will self-insure vehicle property damage. However, they generally insure some of or all the liability exposure associated with vehicles. Businesses wanting to insure their vehicle exposure can add the commercial auto component to their CPP.

The commercial auto component of the CPP provides both liability and property coverage. Special forms are available to firms in the automobile business. Business automobiles are classified in nine different categories, including owned and nonowned vehicles, private passenger cars, and other-than-private passenger autos.

FIGURE 22-3 Damage Caused by Automobile Accidents

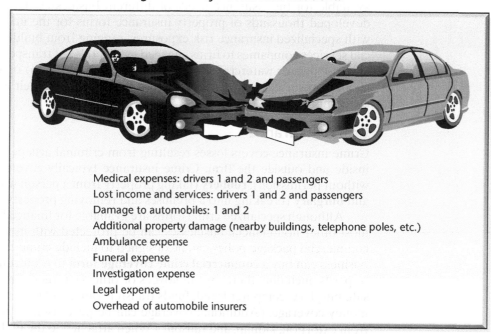

Medical expenses: drivers 1 and 2 and passengers
Lost income and services: drivers 1 and 2 and passengers
Damage to automobiles: 1 and 2
Additional property damage (nearby buildings, telephone poles, etc.)
Ambulance expense
Funeral expense
Investigation expense
Legal expense
Overhead of automobile insurers

When providing physical damage coverage, insurers make an important distinction based on the cause of the loss. A loss either is caused by collision or it is not. Thus, the definition of the term *collision* in automobile insurance takes on great importance.

To get a complete program of automobile property insurance, a business must purchase collision coverage, in which the insurer agrees to pay "for loss caused by collision," and a second part, sometimes referred to as comprehensive coverage, in which the insurer agrees to pay "for loss caused other than by collision." Each of these coverages may be purchased separately (if state law permits), but in so doing, a consumer unknowingly may create a serious gap in automobile property insurance protection.

Collision means the striking of an automobile with another object (a car, a tree, or even standing water), as well as damage resulting from the overturn of the vehicle. The word *object* has a quite broad meaning in this context, and it includes almost anything that can be seen or felt. Losses clearly not caused by collision include theft, vandalism, fire, and windstorm. In some instances, it is difficult to ascertain if a loss was caused by a collision or another peril. If a car is stolen and the thief has a collision, is the loss caused by theft or collision? If a car hits a deer and gets damaged, was the loss due to collision or a loss other than collision? ISO automobile policy forms deal with this issue with the following wording:

> Loss caused by the following is considered other than collision: missile or falling objects; fire; theft or larceny; explosion or earthquake; windstorm; hail, water, or flood; malicious mischief or vandalism; riot or civil commotion; contact with a bird or animal; or breakage of glass.

Thus, if a vehicle is damaged by a cause of loss that is included in this definition of "loss other than collision" (such as theft or collision with an animal), it will not be covered by collision coverage.

OTHER COMMERCIAL PROPERTY INSURANCE

Most people are unaware of the wide variety of property insurance forms that are available for the insurance needs of different businesses. The insurance industry has developed thousands of property insurance forms for the unique needs of industries with specialized insurance risk exposures, ranging from building contractors to financial services companies to firms engaged in all modes of transportation (such as aircraft, automobiles, or watercraft). More generally, however, two other types of specialized property insurance protection warrant discussion due to their wide use by firms *across* different industries.

Crime Insurance

Crime insurance covers losses resulting from criminal acts performed by people both inside and outside the firm. Crime insurance typically covers **theft** (taking property without permission); **robbery** (taking property from a person with a threat of violence); and **burglary** (breaking into a premises and removing property).

Although specialized crime forms are available for financial institutions like banks, most other nonfinancial businesses can be protected with more general policies. The commercial package policy can be designed to include crime coverage. For example, a business can buy a **commercial crime coverage form** to protect itself from a wide range of perils, including theft (by employees or others), forgery or alteration, robbery and safe burglary, computer fraud, funds transfer fraud, and money orders and counterfeit money coverage. (Additional coverage can be purchased to protect from loss arising from extortion, kidnap, and ransom.) When attached to the CPP, the crime forms have their own separate declarations, their own limits of coverage, and their own exclusions. Among the more important exclusions are losses resulting from an insured's dishonesty and indirect losses.

Equipment Breakdown Insurance

Equipment breakdown insurance covers losses resulting from the accidental breakdown of mechanical equipment. Traditionally, this protection was known as boiler and machinery insurance, but the coverage has been expanded over time to include losses to steam boilers and other pressurized equipment; air conditioning and refrigeration equipment; electrical generating and transmitting equipment; engines, pumps, compressors, and turbines; and electrically powered office equipment, such as computer or phone systems. While all these types of equipment can be covered as insured property under the CPP, such coverage is limited to damage caused by a peril listed in the property insurance cause-of-loss form. In addition, the cause-of-loss forms specifically exclude coverage for such events as boiler explosions, mechanical breakdown, or electrical breakdown. Equipment breakdown insurance fills this coverage gap by providing property protection from breakdowns and explosions (both to the specifically insured property and other property damaged by the loss), as well as the resulting business interruption and extra expenses caused by such losses.

Summary

Commercial property insurance is provided as one part of a seven-part commercial property package (CPP). Property coverage falls into three categories: buildings, personal business property, and property of others. Fire and thirteen other perils are specified causes of loss in the basic form. Coverage that is more extensive is available in the broad and special forms.

Indirect loss coverage is available for income lost and extra expenses following a direct loss. Income lost because of direct losses at dependent properties also can be insured. Reporting forms are used in cases of widely varying inventory values.

Property insurance rates usually are determined on a schedule or a class-rating basis. Scheduled rating requires comparing property to a standard exposure and increasing or decreasing the premium for desirable or undesirable features. Class rating involves placing property in a class with similarly situated exposures.

Transportation insurance generally covers mobile property. Ocean marine insurance provides very broad peril coverage if the loss is to the ship (hull), cargo, or freight (the carrier's earnings for transporting cargo), or if it is a liability claim. Inland marine coverage also is used for instrumentalities of transportation and small and expensive personal property, such as furs and jewelry.

Aircraft property insurance protects airplane (and other aircraft) owners from loss of their property (aircraft hull). The coverage may be for all risks (with some perils, such as wear and tear, excluded) or the coverage may protect only if specifically named perils cause the loss.

Automobile property insurance protects car owners against loss to their property. A key consideration in providing this coverage is the definition of *collision* and *losses other than collision*.

Review

1. What is the difference between real and personal property? Why is this difference important in insurance underwriting and pricing (rating)?
2. Briefly explain the format and content of the ISO CPP.
3. Identify several different types of organizations that might purchase a CPP.
4. What role does the ISO play in the commercial property insurance market?

5. Why do insurers insist on exact identification of an insured's covered property?
6. Identify some property that is excluded from coverage under the building and personal property coverage form.
7. What is business personal property?
8. List the fourteen perils covered in the basic causes-of-loss form.
9. Describe the chief difference in coverage between the broad and special policy forms.
10. Explain the difference between extra expenses and continuing expenses in BI coverage.
11. Give some examples of a need for BI coverage from dependent properties.
12. What is a reporting form, and what purpose does it serve?
13. Describe the differences in setting premiums using schedule and class rating systems.
14. Describe the loss exposures insured by hull, cargo, and freight policies in ocean marine insurance.
15. Why is ocean marine coverage so broad in scope? What are the limits on ocean marine coverage with respect to losses not covered?
16. Identify some items in your possession that have been covered by inland marine insurance at some point in time.
17. What factors are considered when insurers develop a rate for an ocean marine exposure?
18. What is the Nationwide Definition of marine insurance?
19. What kinds of property are covered by floater policies?
20. What is a bailment? Describe three bailments in which you have been involved.
21. Describe the difference between the annual transit policy and the motor truck cargo policy.
22. What is the difference between blanket and scheduled floaters?
23. Define the term *collision*.

Objective Questions

1. The basic form of business property coverage provides protection against all the following perils except:
   a. Lightning
   b. Smoke
   c. Theft of currency
   d. Vandalism
2. If a business has large differences in the value of the inventory it has on hand during the year, the cost of its insurance requires the _____ form of insurance policy.
   a. Reporting
   b. Variation
   c. Inventory cycle
   d. Double reduction
3. Choose the true statement.
   a. Ocean marine insurance is a relatively new form of coverage appearing slightly more than 100 years ago.
   b. Ocean and inland marine insurance cover about the same losses and are used for about the same purposes.
   c. Inland marine insurance is found mostly in Europe.
   d. Inland marine insurance is used mostly in the United States.
4. Floater policies:
   a. Cover property usually associated with ships
   b. Cover all property that moves on water
   c. Cover property that is moved easily and frequently
   d. Cover property only when it moves within a warehouse
5. Property that is attached permanently to land, such as buildings, is called:
   a. Real property
   b. Permanent property
   c. Intangible property
   d. Collective property
6. Which of the following is considered when calculating a property insurance rate?
   a. The materials used in the construction of the building
   b. The fire protection available in the community in which the building is located
   c. The proximity of the building to sources of loss from neighboring properties
   d. All of the above are considered.
7. Categories of indirect losses include all the following except:
   a. Loss of income
   b. Advertising
   c. Extra expenses
   d. Continuing expenses
8. A property insurance _____ is the cost per each $100 of exposed value.
   a. Premium
   b. Charge
   c. Fund
   d. Rate

Discussion Questions

1. Why do you think so many expensive fires occur each year in the United States despite technology to prevent or reduce fire loss? Prepare a report on several large fire losses that occurred in the past few years.

2. Do you think most small manufacturers adequately cover losses from dependent properties in their risk management plans? Explain your answer by developing a case study for a hypothetical mail-order clothing company.

Selected References

Rodda, William H. *Marine Insurance: Ocean and Inland,* 3d ed. (Englewood Cliffs, NJ: Prentice-Hall), 1970.

Trupin, J., and A. L. Flitner, *Commercial Property Risk Management and Insurance,* 8th ed. (Malvern, PA:

American Institute for CPCU/ Insurance Institute of America), 2008.

23

Commercial Liability Insurance

After studying this chapter, you should be able to

■ Examine the importance of liability insurance in corporate risk management programs

■ Describe how organizations can insure their general liability exposures with the commercial general liability insurance policy

■ Describe the difference between claims-made and occurrence-based liability insurance policies

■ Explain the function of commercial umbrella liability policies in a risk management program

■ Describe the circumstances in which firms may be held legally responsible for damages caused by faulty products.

■ Identify some of the sources of liability that employers face in their personnel management activities

■ Describe professional liability insurance and identify who needs to purchase it

■ Discuss medical malpractice liability and some solutions to problems caused by the errors of health care practitioners

In Chapter 22, "Commercial Property Insurance," we explained how firms can insure their exposure to property losses. In this chapter, we continue our discussion of commercial insurance by examining how businesses can protect themselves from the damages resulting from lawsuits through the purchase of liability insurance. We begin the chapter by providing some background information about corporate liability exposures. The next section of this chapter focuses on the foundation of most commercial liability insurance programs, the commercial general liability (CGL) policy, and the types of liability claims covered under the CGL. The rest of the chapter examines a variety of more specialized liability exposures.

THE INCREASING COSTS OF CORPORATE LIABILITY RISKS

For businesses both large and small, the financial responsibility associated with corporate liability risks is a large and sometimes catastrophic loss exposure. As we discussed in Chapter 2, "Risk Identification," businesses can be held financially responsible for the injuries and damages that they cause to other parties when they are sued under tort law, a branch of U.S. civil law. Tort law applies to non-contractual legal disputes in which an injured party, called the **plaintiff** or claimant, sues a second party, called the **defendant** or tortfeasor, requesting compensation for his or her damages, typically in the form of a monetary award.

The legal system in the United States plays a key role in determining not only the value of liability awards paid to individual claimants, but, more generally, in motivating firms and individuals to engage in prudent liability risk management. By holding defendants responsible for their actions, the courts create an economic environment that encourages firms and individuals to conduct their daily activities in safe and responsible manner, thus deterring risky behavior. In this regard, the legal system reinforces conduct consistent with sound corporate risk management. By holding defendants financially responsible for their actions, the legal system is also designed to compensate injured parties for their harm.

Over the past several decades, however, the costs resulting from corporate liability risks have increased dramatically. In many corporate boardrooms, executives are concerned that the legal system has failed to maintain an equitable balance between compensating injured parties and assessing too much cost on corporate defendants, who are sometimes viewed as little more than "deep pockets" of money.

Some factors that have led to an increase in corporate liability exposure are discussed next.

Expanding Areas of Liability Exposure

Corporate risk management has historically focused on some traditional areas of corporate liability risk, including the legal duties that the owner of a building or premises owes to its customers or guests, the duty to provide safe products to customers (two types of risk that are covered by a commercial general liability insurance policy, described in the next section of this chapter), and the legal responsibilities of corporate vehicle operators. During the last half of the twentieth century, however, the courts expanded corporate liability standards in other areas of liability. Thus, for example, litigation resulting from the legal duties related to employment liability, professional liability, and directors' and officers' liability has become more common in recent years. In addition, some areas of increased liability exposure have been more heavily concentrated in specific industries, such as lawsuits filed against medical providers like physicians and hospitals, or pollution liability in the chemical, manufacturing, and extraction industries.

Decreased Use of Contributory Negligence

In addition to the expansion of liability risks described previously, other factors have contributed to an increase in the frequency of corporate liability claims. For example, during the late 1900s, most states replaced the contributory negligence standard with a comparative negligence standard. Under the common law defense of **contributory negligence**, a claimant cannot recover an award if he is partly at fault in causing the incident that resulted in his financial harm. By contrast, under the **comparative negligence** standard, the courts determine the percentage of fault that both defendant and claimant bear in causing the incident, awarding the claimant an award that is reduced to reflect his portion of fault. Thus, for common situations in which both defendant *and* claimant are partly at fault in causing the incident that results in the claimant's harm, contributory negligence bars recovery by the claimant while comparative negligence increases the frequency of claims paid by defendants to claimants.

TABLE 23-1 Median and Average Personal Injury Jury Awards (in $1000s)

Type of Liability	2002 Median	2008 Median	2002 Average	2008 Average
Products Liability	$1,548	$2,000	$4,765	$4,885
Medical Malpractice	$ 971	$1,200	$4,379	$3,722
Premises Liability	$ 100	$ 125	$ 559	$ 849
Vehicular Liability	$ 13	$ 20	$ 213	$ 327
All Liability	$ 28	$ 47	$ 800	$1,046

Based on Insurance Information Institute, *The Insurance Fact Book 2011,* 180 (2011); and LRP Publications, *Current Award Trends in Personal Injury* (2010).

High Cost of Corporate Liability Awards

For many organizations, the threat of corporate liability lawsuits represents a potentially catastrophic loss event. As shown in Table 23-1, the average and median jury award for products liability and medical malpractice lawsuits exceeded $1 million in 2008. Lawsuit awards have generally increased across all types of liability from 2002 to 2008.

Class Action Liability Suits

A contributing factor to the growth in corporate liability cost is the increased use of class action lawsuits, suits in which large numbers of plaintiffs band together to jointly file a lawsuit claiming harm against a common plaintiff. Some of the settlement agreements between defendants and class action plaintiffs have been multibillion dollar awards, and the size of these awards has in turn heightened public interest in corporate litigation.[1] Class action lawsuits are especially common in product liability cases, where multiple claimants—sometimes tens of thousands of people—allege harm from a common product defect.

In theory, the economics of class action lawsuits offer potential advantages to all parties involved in such cases. Unlike lawsuits involving single plaintiffs, the thousands of plaintiffs involved in a class action suit can spend far more on evidence to support their case. Rather than attempting to contest multiple individual liability suits over a prolonged period of several years, some defendants may prefer to focus on a single class action lawsuit in the hopes of limiting adverse publicity for their firms. Judges suggest that it is more efficient to hear a single aggregated case instead of tying up courtrooms with a multitude of suits. The large settlements of class action lawsuits and improved odds of winning them are popular among plaintiffs' attorneys.

In practice, the allure of huge liability awards unfortunately has led to abuse of class action lawsuits in the courts, subjecting defendants to increased levels of litigation that overwhelm the theoretical advantages of class action suits. Plaintiffs' attorneys often advertise extensively to increase the number of claimants in class action lawsuits,

---

[1]For example, the drug manufacturer Wyeth agreed to settlements of more than $4.5 billion (and set aside $21 billion in reserves) for claims related to their "Fen-Phen" diet drugs; and a group of defendants, including Dow-Corning, Baxter, 3M, and Bristol-Myer, agreed to a settlement of over $3 billion for claims related to silicone breast implants. Settlements related to asbestos litigation over the past four decades exceed $70 billion. See D. R. Hensler, "Has the Fat Lady Sung? The Future of Mass Toxic Torts," *Review of Litigation,* **26**(4), 883–926.

and then use the large size of the suits as a lever to negotiate large settlements with defendants. In some cases, class action lawsuits have been plagued with questionable evidence and populated by plaintiffs with minimal levels of harm. Although the passage of the Class Action Fairness Act in 2005 addressed some areas of abuse, the specter of huge claims and adverse publicity makes class action lawsuits one of the more troublesome loss exposures facing today's risk managers.

COMMERCIAL GENERAL LIABILITY INSURANCE

Many firms insure their exposure to general liability lawsuits by purchasing a commercial general liability (CGL) insurance policy. The CGL is designed to protect the insured business from non-automobile related bodily injury and property damage liability claims filed against the business by the general public, such as customers or visitors on the insured's property. The CGL can be added as a part of the commercial package policy discussed in Chapter 22, or it can be purchased separately. The policy covers court awards, out-of-court settlements, and related legal defense costs.

Description of Coverage

The types of liability exposures covered under the CGL policy include liability resulting from premises and operations liability, products liability, liability from completed operations, and liability from insured contracts. *Premises and operations liability* refers to lawsuits arising from the ownership, use, and maintenance of business buildings and grounds. For example, assume that an employee neglects to clean an oil spill from a floor, resulting in a patron's slipping and being injured. The patron then sues the firm, alleging the injury resulted from the firm's negligence. Other examples might involve an escalator accident that injures a shopper or an attack on a customer in a poorly lit parking lot.

Products liability refers to lawsuits alleging that a defect in a firm's product caused injuries to the claimant. For example, a drug company can be held legally responsible for customers injured from the harmful side effects of its drugs, as was described in footnote 1. Products liability can result from injuries resulting from product defects, design defects, and failure to instruct consumers on the safe use of the product or to warn them of product hazards.

Many service firms, including contractors, plumbers, and electricians, are sued when plaintiffs claim that their work was improperly done or left undone, resulting in an injury. Because the defect in workmanship is typically discovered after the contractor has completed the job, this type of lawsuit is commonly known as liability from *completed operations*. For example, a heating contractor could be sued if he incorrectly installed a new heating system in a home and the faulty installation resulted in the death of the homeowner due to carbon monoxide poisoning. Note that these losses generally occur away from the firm's premises, so specific coverage is needed for this exposure.

Contractual liability occurs if a firm accepts by contract a liability that it otherwise would not have. Contractual liability is limited to specific types of "insured contracts" that are defined in the CGL, including leases, railroad sidetrack agreements, easements, elevator maintenance agreements, and hold harmless agreements. For example, to get the Rockenroll Railroad to build a track to its warehouse, the Big Tree Lumber Mill agrees to sign a **hold-harmless agreement**. This agreement relieves Rockenroll of liability arising from the use of the tracks on Big Tree's property and places the liability

TABLE 23-2 Exclusions under Section 1, Coverage A: Bodily Injury and Property Damage Liability

a. Expected or intended injury
b. Contractual liability (but not excluding specified "Insured Contracts")
c. Liquor liability
d. Injuries covered by workers compensation
e. Employers' liability (liability for injuries to employees of the insured)
f. Most types of pollution
g. Aircraft, auto, watercraft, and certain types of mobile equipment
h. Mobile equipment
i. War
j. Damage to property owned, rented or in the "care, custody, or control" of the insured
k. Damage to the insured's product
l. Damage to the insured's work
m. Property damage to impaired property
n. Product recall
o. Personal and advertising injury (which is insured in Section 1, Coverage B, of the CGL)
p. Damage to electronic data and damage from the loss of use of such data
q. Liability from distributing material (e.g., spam) in violation of communication laws

for accidents on the tracks with Big Tree. In this example, Big Tree needs liability insurance for the exposure that it assumed from Rockenroll. If a Rockenroll train engineer negligently destroys a truck or injures somebody on Big Tree's property, then the injured party may sue either Big Tree or the Rockenroll railroad, but in either case, Big Tree (or its insurer) will satisfy the legal judgment.

CGL Policy Design

A sample copy of the Insurance Services Office (ISO) 2000 CGL policy is provided in Appendix C. As shown in the appendix, the CGL consists of five sections, as described next. In addition, Section 1 consists of three coverages: Bodily Injury and Property Damage Liability; Personal and Advertising Injury Liability; and Medical Payments.

SECTION 1, COVERAGE A: BODILY INJURY AND PROPERTY DAMAGE LIABILITY.

In this section, an insurer agrees to cover claims for accidental bodily injury or property damage arising from two sources of liability: liability arising from the insured's premises and operations and liability arising from the insured's products and completed operations. The insurer also agrees to provide a legal defense for the insured. The cost of the defense does not reduce the amount available for paying covered losses. If a firm loses a $1 million judgment and defense costs equal $100,000, the insurer pays $1.1 million cost even though the coverage limit of the policy was $1 million.

The CGL does not provide coverage for bodily injury or property damage liability arising from the exclusions listed in Table 23-2.[2] Some of the exclusions shown in Table 23-2, such as war or intentional acts, are not covered because they are uninsurable. Others are excluded from the CGL because they are better covered under other more specialized policies, such as workers' compensation insurance; auto, aircraft, and watercraft policies; property insurance policies; or environmental impairment liability (EIL) policies.[3] Some CGL exclusions, such as liquor liability exclusion, can be modified by endorsement; the insured can obtain coverage for the specific liability

---

[2] Some of the exclusions shown in Table 23-1 are too complex and lengthy to be covered here, so please refer to the exclusions section of Section 1, Part A of the CGL, shown in Appendix C, for a complete description.

exposure and eliminate the exclusion by purchasing the endorsement. The CGL exclusions do not apply to **fire legal liability**—property damage liability that the named insured may owe to the owner of the property in which the insured is doing business.

SECTION 1, COVERAGE B: PERSONAL AND ADVERTISING INJURY LIABILITY

This portion of the CGL covers tort liability arising from false arrest or imprisonment, libel or slander, copyright infringement, and invasion of privacy.

SECTION 1, COVERAGE C: MEDICAL PAYMENTS

This coverage pays for the cost of medical treatment administered to people injured on the insured premises (who are not "insureds" under the policy) or by actions of the insured away from the premises, regardless of the insured's legal liability. This coverage allows the insured business to provide first aid to injured people before questions of fault are litigated. The injury must be the result of an accident, which means the injury was neither expected nor intended by the insured.

SECTION 2

Section 2 of the CGL specifies whom the policy covers. Possibilities include owners of proprietorships, partners, and officers and directors of corporations. The policy also covers employees acting within the scope of their employment.

SECTION 3

Section 3 of the CGL limits the insurer's liability after a loss. The policy has overall (aggregate) limits and sublimits. The general aggregate limit of insurance caps the amount that a policy can pay on behalf of the insured. Each loss payment under Coverage A, B, or C in Section 1 reduces the amount available to pay future claims. For example, assume that an insured has an aggregate limit of $500,000. If three $250,000 losses occur, the insurer will pay for only the first two, for a total of $500,000. After the second $250,000 payment, the aggregate coverage limit is exhausted (explaining why buying a high limit of liability coverage is sound risk management). The coverage limit for fire legal liability is also specified in Section 3. Additionally, a separate aggregate coverage limit is specified in Section 3 toward the cost of product liability.

SECTION 4.

Section 4 of the CGL presents the policy conditions and explains such things as what the insured must do if it is sued, how to file a claim, or how to cancel the policy.

SECTION 5

Section 5 is the policy's glossary. Here, the policy provides definitions of terms that appear throughout the policy.

ISO has developed CGL policies in two formats: an occurrence form and a claims-made form. The occurrence form provides liability protection for events that occur during the time period covered under the policy, recognizing that covered claims may

---

[3]Environmental impairment insurance is a specialty insurance coverage designed to cover the cost of pollution cleanup and remediating hazardous waste sites. During the 1990s, the federal Environmental Protection Agency (EPA) sued many corporations for the cost incurred in remediating numerous hazardous waste sites across the United States. Many of these corporations in turn filed claims with their general liability insurers for these damage awards. The high cost of the pollution liability cleanup prompted CGL insurers to develop a more specific pollution liability exclusion than that found in earlier versions of the CGL. For more detailed discussion of the issues surrounding the pollution liability, see Mark Dorfman, *Introduction to Risk Management and Insurance*, 9th ed. (Upper Saddle River, New Jersey: Pearson Prentice Hall, 2008).

be filed a significant time after the occurrence took place. The claims-made form obligates the insurer to pay only for claims first made against the insured during the policy period and arising from incidents occurring after the retroactive date stated on the policy, as described more fully in the next section.

CLAIMS-MADE AND OCCURRENCE POLICIES

Insurers make an important distinction in liability insurance between policies written on a claims-made or an occurrence basis, as described next.

Claims-Made Policies

Claims-made forms allow the insurer to close the book on the business after the policy period has expired and also relieve the insurer of responsibility for injuries sustained before the retroactive date. If a policy is written on a **claims-made basis**, the insurer will be liable to provide coverage only if the following two conditions are met:

1. The claim arises from a covered event that occurs after the beginning date (or a retroactive date if retroactive coverage is purchased) and before the end of the policy period.
2. The claim is made between the policy's beginning date and its expiration date.

The policy's *beginning date* is the first day that the coverage is in force after the purchase. The policy *coverage period* starts at an earlier time, called the *retroactive date*. The **retroactive date** is a date preceding the beginning date for which coverage is provided for an additional premium. For example, a policy might be purchased with a beginning date of January 1, 2006, while the retroactive date might be January 1, 2002. A two-year policy period would end two years after the beginning date, or December 31, 2008. Therefore, the **policy period** is January 1, 2006 until December 31, 2008. The period in which claims may be reported can be extended by the purchase of tail coverage. The **tail period**, also known as the **extended reporting period**, extends the time during which a claim may be filed for a loss that occurs during the policy period. For example, assume that tail coverage is purchased for three years, making the expiration date of the policy December 31, 2011. The tail coverage will provide insurance for losses occurring after the retroactive date but before December 31, 2008, and reported between December 31, 2006, and December 31, 2011. Both the retroactive date (the earliest date for a covered occurrence) and the tail period (the ending date of the reporting period) are subject to negotiation between the insurer and insured. Figure 23-1 presents this terminology graphically.

FIGURE 23-1 Claims-Made Policy Terminology

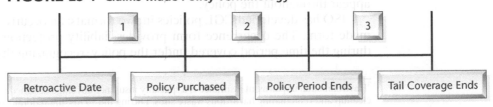

1. If a loss occurs between the retroactive date and the beginning date, **and** is first reported during the policy period, there is coverage.
2. If a loss occurs and is reported during the policy period, there is coverage.
3. If a loss occurs after the retroactive date and before the policy period ends, and is reported during the tail period, there is coverage. There is no coverage for losses occurring during the tail period.

As an example, assume that Leaky Louis, the plumber, installs a gas water heater during September 2005. On January 1, 2006, he purchases a one-year claims-made liability insurance policy with a retroactive date of June 1, 2005. The one-year policy ends on January 1, 2007, and has no tail coverage. On February 1, 2006, the water heater that Louis installed explodes, destroying the house and killing a resident. Leaky Louis is sued after the explosion for $1 million. In August 2008, a jury awards the owner $1 million. Because the occurrence took place after the retroactive date and the claim was filed during the policy coverage period, the insurer must defend the suit and pay the judgment. The award of the judgment after the policy period expired does not affect the insurer's liability in this case.

Occurrence-Based Policies

If a policy is written as an **occurrence-based liability policy**, the insurer is liable to make payment if its policy was in force when the negligence occurred. For example, assume that Dr. Pasteur delivered a baby, Napoleon, in 2004. At the time, he was insured on an occurrence basis by the French Insurance Company (FIC). In 2007, Napoleon's family sues Dr. Pasteur, alleging that negligence during the delivery caused Napoleon to have a pointed head and diminished mental capacities. Assume further that in 2007, Dr. Pasteur no longer is insured by the FIC because he retired. Nevertheless, the FIC must defend the doctor against the claim and pay any adverse judgment because the injury occurred during the period in which the FIC provided coverage. Because it was written on an occurrence basis, the FIC's liability is open-ended. This indefinitely long liability exposure is spoken of as the "long tail of claims."

As a second example, again assume that in 2007, Dr. Pasteur is sued by Napoleon's family for the 2004 injury and that he had not purchased medical malpractice liability insurance before 2004. In 2007, even though he retired, he purchased three years of professional liability tail coverage from the Austrian Insurance Company (AIC) on a *claims-made* basis. The tail coverage ends in 2010. Assume that this policy had a 2005 retroactive date. In this instance, because the alleged injury occurred before the retroactive date, there would be no coverage for the 2004 injury claim. However, if Dr. Pasteur's alleged negligence caused an injury after 2005 that was reported between 2007 and 2010, the tail coverage policy would be available to pay a lawsuit.

Next, assume that the AIC's liability insurance coverage had a retroactive date of January 1, 1999, and a termination date of December 31, 2003. Because it is responsible only for claims made while the policy is in force, the AIC is not responsible for a claim against Dr. Pasteur made in 2004 or later.

BUSINESS LIABILITY UMBRELLA POLICIES

As a risk manager contemplates worst-case loss scenarios, surely the possibility of being sued successfully for an amount in excess of available policy limits must be considered. To deal with this possibility, a commercial **umbrella policy** can be purchased to provide coverage after underlying liability policies have been exhausted. The umbrella policy is often called **excess liability coverage** because the umbrella policy pays only for losses in excess of the underlying limits. For example, assume the Green Bean Factory is held responsible for injuring William M. Rice, a visiting salesperson. The jury returns a $10 million verdict in favor of Mr. Rice. Green Bean's CGL Coverage A limit is $1 million for such bodily injuries. If Green Bean has a $10 million liability umbrella, it would pay $9 million of the award (the excess of the award over the underlying coverage), which, along with the CGL coverage of $1 million, would compensate Mr. Rice fully.

The commercial umbrella policy also may cover some exposures left uncovered by underlying policies. Typically, the insured must pay a prearranged retention limit for cases when the umbrella policy is providing the initial coverage rather than an underlying liability insurance policy. In all other cases, umbrella policies require the insured to maintain certain minimum amounts of underlying liability insurance coverage.

AUTOMOBILE LIABILITY INSURANCE

Americans annually do an alarming amount of economic damage with their automobiles. They injure each other and damage property amounting to billions of dollars each year. Compensation for the damage done to others comes through the tort liability system. Most people rely on a personal automobile insurance policy, which was described in Chapter 12, "The Personal Auto Policy," to protect them against being sued because of an automobile accident.

Commercial Automobile Insurance

Risk managers of most businesses need to consider the liability loss potential presented by the ownership, maintenance, or use of vehicles. As stated in Chapter 22, large firms will often self-insure vehicle property damage (as will many individuals). They almost always will seek to insure some of or all the vehicle liability exposure. Firms wanting to insure their vehicle exposure can add the **business auto coverage form** to their commercial property package.

The business auto coverage form can be used by most firms, except those engaged in the automobile business. This latter group includes garages, repair shops, and car dealerships. These firms must use a special *garage coverage form*. The business auto coverage form provides liability coverage for insureds who face claims from auto accidents. Like the CGL, the insurer agrees to pay to defend the insured and such legal defense costs do not reduce the amounts available to satisfy judgments. Many of this policy's provisions are comparable to those found in Chapter 12.

PRODUCTS LIABILITY INSURANCE[4]

The manufacturer of a product has a legal duty to design and produce a product that will not injure people from normal use. In addition to careful designing and manufacturing, products must be packaged carefully and accompanied by adequate instructions and warnings so consumers may use them properly and avoid injury. If any of these duties are not fulfilled and the result is an injured user, potential for a products liability lawsuit exists. Moreover, not merely the manufacturer or processor may be named defendants in a products liability lawsuit, but the vendor of a product, such as a drugstore or automobile dealer, also may be named.

A key question in products liability cases is whether the plaintiff has the burden of establishing the defendant's negligence (as is usually the case in negligence suits) or

---

[4]For a comprehensive review of this topic, see David W. Lannetti, "Toward a Revised Definition of 'Product' Under the Restatement (Third) of Torts: Products Liability," *Tort and Insurance Law Journal*, Summer 2000 (Vol. 35, p. 4).

whether the defendant has the burden of proving a lack of negligence on its part. If the court applies the doctrine of **res ipsa loquitur** ("the thing speaks for itself"), the burden is on the defendant. If the court adopts the *strict liability* approach, the burden also is on the defendant. Here, however, the producer still can defend itself (for example, by establishing that the injured party modified the product in some irresponsible way or failed to give heed to clearly stated and conspicuous warnings), but in the absence of a valid defense, the producer will be held liable. In several areas of the country, especially in cases involving food and drugs, courts have been moving in the direction of strict liability. Arguments the courts have used that favor imposing strict liability on producers include:

- The party best able to detect and eliminate defects should be responsible for injuries caused by the product.
- The party best able to absorb the costs should be held liable.
- Injured parties often have too difficult a burden proving negligence in product liability cases.

Courts that impose strict liability on producers often support this decision with the rationale that, ultimately, the consumers of a product bear the cost of victims injured by that product. This result occurs if the producers purchase insurance and include the cost in the product price.[5] Injured consumers also bear the cost if no insurance is purchased and the producer is bankrupted by liability claims.

Unfortunately, the costs of product liability awards can sometimes become so large that they cannot be added to the price of the product without making it unaffordable or unavailable. For example, after several American vaccine manufacturers exited the market in response to high liability costs, the National Childhood Vaccine Injury Act was passed by Congress to address vaccine litigation in a no-fault setting.[6] Although these health-related dislocations caused by potential products liability claims indeed are serious, many products manufacturers face comparable problems. Some companies report abandoning research and development of new products. Because many U.S. companies must compete with foreign firms that do not have to build the costs of products liability lawsuits into the price of their products, the U.S. firms may face a competitive disadvantage in the world market.

Products liability insurance protects manufacturers or vendors that have been sued. The insurer agrees to pay the plaintiff on behalf of the insured defendant and to pay the insured defendant's legal defense costs. This coverage is found in Section 1, Coverage A, of the CGL policy. Because the costs of product liability awards are potentially catastrophic, insuring this exposure can be very expensive and complicated. (For example, Insight Box 23-1 describes the complications related to insuring liability from asbestos injuries.) Insurers consider the type of products made and the insured's claims history when pricing this coverage.

---

[5]In his concurring opinion in *Escola v. Coca Cola Bottling Company*, Judge Roger J. Treynor reinforced this concept, recognizing how the liability system can function as an insurance mechanism. "Those who suffer injury from defective products are unprepared to meet its consequences. The cost of an injury and the loss of time or health may be an overwhelming misfortune to the person injured, and a needless one, for the risk of injury can be insured by the manufacturer and distributed among the public as a cost of doing business." The ruling in the case led to greater use of strict liability in products liability cases. See *Escola v. Coca Cola Bottling Co.*, 24 Cal. 2d 453, 150 P.2d 436 (1944).

[6]See B. Kendall, "Vaccine makers shielded from suits," *Wall Street Journal,* February 23, 2011, pp. B.3-B.3; and P. M. Danzon, S. P. Nuno, and S. S. Tejwani, "Vaccine Supply: A Cross-national Perspective," *Health Affairs,* **24**(3), 706–717 (2005).

INSIGHT BOX 23–1

Paying for Asbestos Litigation

The liability arising out of the use of asbestos has a long and complex legal history that has troubled liability insurance companies for decades. Asbestosis and other diseases caused by exposure to hazardous substances are often not recognized until decades after the victim's initial exposure to the substance. For example, a worker may have been exposed to some disease-causing substance from 1960 until 1995, but the first symptoms of disease may not have appeared until several years after 1995. Death may not have occurred until 2005, when the worker was 70 years old. During this period, the employer, its suppliers, and its customers may have had a dozen different insurers that provided products liability insurance. Moreover, the injured employee may have had several different employers during his career and may have smoked two packs of cigarettes a day for many years.

Products liability insurance traditionally has been provided to manufacturers as part of the CGL policy. One problem with this policy is that it does not make clear which insurer is liable for the loss. At least three possibilities exist: (1) the insurer whose policy was in force when the first exposure occurred (the exposure theory); (2) the insurer whose policy was in force when the disease was first recognized (the manifestation theory); and (3) the insurer whose policy was in force when the disease developed (the exposure-in-residence period theory). In one relevant case, *Keene* v. *INA*,[7] the court dealt with the issue of which insurer was responsible for the loss. The court ruled that if several insurance policies were in force when a developing injury is in progress, all the insurers would be responsible for providing coverage. (This decision is called the **triple-trigger theory**. The three triggers are exposure, manifestation, and exposure-in-residence period.) In the Keene case, the court allowed the insurers to determine among themselves how the loss would be shared. It also placed the burden of proof on any insurer that claimed its policy did not apply.

EMPLOYMENT PRACTICES LIABILITY

Another area of corporate liability losses arises when a local or state government or the federal government creates rights for specified classes of citizens and then allows these citizens to sue organizations that abridge these rights. A federal agency, the U.S. Equal Employment Opportunity Commission, enforces laws that make it illegal for employers to discriminate on the basis of such characteristics as race, sex, age, or the disabled.[8] Many federal and state laws also contain whistleblower and anti-retaliation provisions to protect the rights of injured workers and their colleagues further.

Exposure to liability can result from a wide range of employer activities, including hiring, promotion, and discharge from work. In the case of hiring practices, these laws govern an employer's actions between the time a position is created (including rules governing the advertising of the position and the interviewing of job applicants) and the time the position is eliminated. Legal requirements and accompanying litigation also influence promotion policy, pay increases or decreases, and allowing or contributing to an atmosphere where sexual harassment occurs.[9] Some of the reasons that employers have been sued include:

- **Invasion of privacy** (too much pre-employment investigation, causing emotional distress to a job applicant)

---

[7]*Keene Corp. v. Ins. Co. of North America,* 667 F. 2d 1034—Court of Appeals, Dist. of Columbia Circuit 1981.

[8]Refer to the Equal Employment Opportunity Commission Web site (*http://www.eeoc.gov/*) for information about employment and civil rights law as it applies to discrimination on the basis of such characteristics as race, sex, age, and disabilities.

[9]For an instructive discussion on how firms can protect themselves from litigation from sexual harassment, see William J. Warfel and J. Tim Query, "Sex Ed: Insulating Yourself from Sexual Harassment Litigation," *Risk Management Magazine,* February 2005, pp. 14–20.

- **Negligent supervision** (a frequent contention in harassment cases where, even if employers did not know of the offensive activity, juries have held that they should have known about it)
- **Negligent discharge** (claims of age, gender, religious, and sexual orientation discrimination, infliction of emotional distress, and other issues surrounding the discharge of an employee)
- **Wrongful discipline and negligent evaluation, including failure to promote**

As an illustration of the pros and cons of these laws, consider the Americans with Disabilities Act (ADA), a federal law passed in 1990. Before the passage of the (ADA), many capable disabled workers who could contribute positively to society often were denied the opportunity to prove their worth to an employer. Moreover, because they had no opportunity to have a job, they had no access to employee benefits, including health insurance. The ADA addressed these issues, creating an environment in which disabled people gained the valuable legal right to participate in the workforce.

The cost of implementing the ADA has not been trivial, however. Employers bear the cost of providing reasonable accommodations for employees who are disabled (for example, providing wheelchair access to the work site, reconfiguring restrooms to make them accessible to disabled workers, removing physical barriers, and redesigning working areas and equipment). In addition, because these laws have a significant impact on an employer's personnel administration practices, the cost of compliance is quite high. Many employers believe that the rules can lead to fraud and legal "blackmail" in the form of increased threats of litigation. For example, in the first full year of the ADA's enforcement, 25,000 lawsuits were filed. The legal cost to defend an employer charged with a violation of an employee's rights ranges from $20,000 to $200,000, depending on where the legal process stops. Legal defense costs will be incurred in cases where the plaintiff's allegations are true, false, or even frivolous. The costs of this type of litigation also must include the time and stress on the supervisors directly involved in the legal defense. Some of the added costs of complying with these laws are passed on to consumers (in the form of higher prices) or employees (in the form of reduced compensation), and these costs must be compared with the benefits that society receives from the passage of this legislation.

Employers use both insurance and noninsurance techniques to address these risks. **Employment practices liability insurance (EPLI)** is one of the fastest-growing new products offered by property liability insurers. Although EPLI policies are not standardized across insurers, most provide protection for a fairly common set of "wrongful acts." These acts include liability resulting from demotions, failures to promote, and disciplinary actions against employees; wrongful termination or denial of training; negligent hiring and supervision; work-related harassment; work-related libel, slander, invasion of privacy, defamation, or humiliation; and work-related abuse (including verbal, mental, physical, and emotional abuse) from discrimination. EPLI also provides coverage for the cost of defending the insured employer, but unlike many other types of liability insurance coverage, these costs are often subject to a specific coverage limit.

To minimize their exposure to employment-related liability, many employers rely heavily on loss control techniques and a frank self-assessment of their exposure to litigation. Employers can reduce their exposure to loss by developing an understanding of the law, evaluating their compliance with the law, adopting best practices, and taking steps to prevent and reduce losses. A more thorough checklist for compliance is outlined in Figure 23-2.

- *Know the Meaning and Application of the Law*: The risk management and the human resource management departments should maintain current knowledge of how the law is being interpreted and enforced.

- *Self-Evaluation and Adoption of Best Practices*: Organizations should conduct an initial audit to assess their human resource management policies honestly. Thereafter, audits for compliance should be done routinely, with the goal of adopting current standards.

- *Loss Prevention*:
  - Prepare a manual to describe procedures needed for compliance with specific laws. The manual should be available to all affected employees of the organization.
  - Organizations should have a stated policy that they offer equal opportunities for employment and advancement to all qualified individuals regardless of age, gender, race, religion, sexual orientation, or other factors.
  - Work with legal counsel to prepare procedures and written material. Guidelines should be very specific in defining discrimination or harassment, for example. Guidelines should be prepared that outline steps to be followed after a complaint is filed. The rights of the accuser and the accused must be protected.
  - Educate people responsible for compliance, including executive management. Controversial compliance issues may need to be addressed in detail.
  - Identify a contact person should questions arise in specific cases.
  - Develop monitoring programs to ensure that company policy is being followed.

- *Loss Reduction*:
  - Operate on the basis that litigation is inevitable. However, not every incident or complaint must result in litigation.
  - Develop an early warning plan to identify and evaluate potential problems at a stage when remediation is possible.
  - Develop documentation or record-keeping procedures to assist with a legal defense when litigation arises.

- *Insurance*: If considering the purchase of EPLI insurance, gather the policies of the insurers being considered and compare them. Most EPLI policies are not standardized policies, so evaluate their coverage of liability arising from events like unintentional discrimination, wrongful termination, sexual harassment, hiring, promotion and demotion practices, and wrongful discipline. Most of the insurers providing this coverage agree to pay legal judgments and defense costs. Carriers typically exclude coverage for punitive damage awards and acts of malicious intent or willful violations of the law.

FIGURE 23-2 Checklist for Compliance with Nondiscrimination Laws

PROFESSIONAL LIABILITY INSURANCE

The term *professional* refers to a person with special skills, education, or knowledge compensated to provide a service to the public. In many cases, professionals are licensed by the states. Originally the term was restricted to people employed in the areas of theology, law, and medicine, but today the term is applied more widely. Professional liability insurance is a necessary purchase for accountants, actuaries, architects, directors of corporations, pharmacists, hairstylists, insurance agents and brokers, and other professions that require special education or a license.

Sometimes **professional liability insurance** is called **malpractice insurance** or **errors and omissions insurance**. However designated, such insurance typically commits an insurer to pay *all sums that the insured becomes legally obligated to pay as damages* (after any applicable deductibles) resulting from providing or failing to provide professional services.

Claims Settlement

The legal obligation to pay damages implies litigation establishing the professional's negligence. Professional liability policies, unlike personal liability policies, generally do not give the insurer the right to settle suits without the insured's consent. The reason for this "Consent to Settle" clause is that the professional's reputation and future earnings could be affected adversely by settling negligence claims, even though sometimes it might be expedient for the insurer to offer a settlement. The professional would not want an insurer to settle all claims, especially so-called nuisance claims, because too many settlements would imply professional incompetence.

If an insured professional wants to contest a suit that the insurer wants to settle without litigation, some insurance companies insert a contractual agreement that causes their insureds to bear any loss above the amount for which the insurer could settle the claim. This type of clause creates a dilemma for the insured; on the one hand, the insured could allow the insurer to settle nuisance or other claims, thereby risking injury to his or her reputation. On the other hand, the insured could contest such claims and be exposed to the very financial loss for which the insurance was purchased.

Types of Professional Liability Coverage

Among the different professional liability policies available, the more frequently purchased are the following:

- **Physicians', surgeons', and dentists' liability policy.** These policies are often written with coverage limits in excess of several million dollars for the policy period. Policy costs are a function of the city and state of the physician's practice and medical specialty—with surgeons and obstetricians among the most expensive classes. Insurance rates generally are not a function of the practitioner's history, but a poor claims history can lead to nonrenewal or denial of coverage. We address the serious societal issue of medical liability shortly.
- **Hospital liability policy.** This type of policy covers hospitals for tort and vicarious liability arising from the operation of its facilities.
- **Druggists' liability policy.** This type of policy covers a pharmacist for liability arising from the actions as a druggist, such as dispensing the wrong medication or the wrong dose of medication, or improper compounding of drugs and solutions that require manual compounding.
- **Errors and omissions insurance.** Many professions, such as real estate agents, insurance agents, accountants, and architects, need this type of liability protection to cover clients' claims alleging professional negligence.
- **Directors' and officers' liability insurance.** This type of insurance covers directors of corporations and other organizations. It is used to protect directors and officers from liability arising from their mismanagement and failure to carry out their duties with due care. **D&O insurance**, as it is called, is used to attract talented people to serve on boards of directors. This coverage helps board members protect their personal assets which are subject to liability claims. Protection is a necessity. The **Sarbanes-Oxley Act of 2002 (SOX)** added clearly stated responsibilities for directors, auditors, and attorneys of publicly traded companies. The law makes the directors and managers responsible for the effectiveness and efficiency of operations, for the reliability of financial reporting, and for compliance with applicable laws and regulations. Under this law, knowingly certifying a false financial report can lead to large fines and prison.

Medical Liability

One key consideration in the continuing health care debate in the United States has been the effect of lawsuits against medical providers and **medical professional liability**

insurance (MPLI), commonly called *medical malpractice insurance*. Therefore, we will give special attention to this type of professional liability.

In the 1970s, the cost of MPLI, rose rapidly as the number of successful lawsuits against medical practitioners grew both in number and in the size of awards won by successful plaintiffs. MPLI was always expensive, but for some physicians, it was not even available, causing them to risk the possibility of losing their practices after a liability suit. The years following 1970 saw several cycles in the medical liability insurance market. These problems recurred in the 1980s and again in 2000, as some states saw doctors going on strike, emergency rooms of hospitals shutting down, and women having to drive more than fifty miles to be seen by the nearest obstetrician/gynecologist.

The debate about whether the current medical liability system benefits society continues. Proponents of the medical tort laws, especially trial lawyers, argue that the current system discourages poor healthcare practices, compensates victims of medical negligence, and penalizes negligent providers. Opponents claim that the system is very expensive, with the costs being borne by the public. Opponents also cite a reduction in medical services, especially in areas that award large judgments to injured plaintiffs.

The number of liability cases brought in recent years certainly suggests the possibility of a large number of medical mistakes, with claims against physicians including failure to diagnose correctly, failed surgery, and improper treatment.[10] A report by the Institute of Medicine estimated that 1.5 million injuries were caused by medication mistakes each year.[11] However, the Congressional Budget Office (CBO) notes, "Malpractice costs amounted to an estimated $24 billion in 2002, but that figure represents less than 2 percent of overall health care spending."[12]

The costs related to medical liability fall into the following categories:

- *Medical liability insurance*: Commercial insurance premiums, self-insurance contributions, and uninsured losses. The impact of investment earnings on malpractice insurance premiums is significant because an average of almost four years elapses between the time that a lawsuit is filed and when successful claims against a medical provider are settled. This length of time allows good or bad investment earnings to have a noticeable impact on the cost of coverage.

- *Defensive medical costs*: Costs for diagnostic tests and treatments that physicians would not make if there were no threat of lawsuit.

- *Medical device and pharmaceutical liability costs*: Insurance and self-insurance costs of drug firms and manufacturers of medical equipment.

- *Liability-related administrative costs*: Costs incurred to minimize liability exposure including extra record keeping, and time-consuming activities such as participating in the various stages of litigation. Some of these costs can be attributed to weak and sometimes frivolous lawsuits, as evidenced by the fact that well over half of all lawsuits are dismissed by the courts.

---

[10]A CBO study, "Limiting Tort Liability for Medical Malpractice" (January 8, 2004), stated: "Each year, about 15 malpractice claims are filed for every 100 physicians, and about 30 percent of those claims result in an insurance payment." (p. 4). The subject is discussed further in a CBO background paper, "Medical Malpractice Tort Limits and Health Care Spending," April 2006. For additional data on MPLI claims experience and a more general discussion of the financial performance of insurers in the MPLI product line, see R. Hoyt and L. Powell, "Assessing Financial Performance in Medical Professional Liability Insurance," *Journal of Insurance Regulation*, Fall 2006, 25 (1), pp. 3–13.

[11]"Preventing Medication Errors," Institute of Medicine, July 20, 2006, accessed on June 17, 2012 from *http://www.iom.edu*.

[12]CBO study, 2004, p. 6.

Many people and groups have suggested solutions for dealing with the medical tort liability problem, including the following:

- A limitation of the amount of money a jury can award as a judgment. For example, a cap on noneconomic damages, such as jury awards for pain and suffering, mirrors a California law.[13]
- Placing a cap on the size of punitive damage awards in malpractice cases.
- A limitation on contingency fees for the plaintiff's attorney.
- Precertification of lawsuits by an expert panel. This reform requires the plaintiff to submit the claim to a panel of experts (typically doctors, health care administrators, and attorneys) who determine if the claim has merit. The plaintiff may ignore adverse judgments of this panel, but the panel's findings become admissible as evidence if the matter is litigated.
- "Apology" laws. A growing number of states have passed laws that allow medical providers to apologize to patients without having the apology used against them by the plaintiff as evidence in court. The theory behind these laws is that if a doctor shows remorse, many plaintiffs will be less likely to sue or will settle their suits faster and/or more generously.

It is often difficult to determine how effective these proposals are because reform efforts are not consistent across the states. It may also take several years before liability claims reflect the impact of such reforms. Despite these complications, however, recent research suggests that at least some of these efforts may help to control insured medical liability losses.[14]

---

[13]California Civil Code § 3333.2, better known as the Medical Injury Compensation Reform Act.

[14]For example, see P. Born, W. K. Viscusi, and T. Baker (2009), "The Effects of Tort Reform on Medical Malpractice Insurers' Ultimate Losses," *Journal of Risk and Insurance*, 76 (1), pp. 197–219, which suggests that caps on noneconomic and punitive damages are useful in controlling insured medical malpractice losses.

Summary

Firms are exposed to different types of liability lawsuits arising from the following sources: premises and operations liability, products liability, completed operations liability, and contractual liability. The basic business liability insurance policy is the commercial general liability insurance policy (CGL), which can provide coverage against the previously listed categories of liability exposure. The CGL contains many exclusions from coverage, as shown in Table 23-2.

A commercial umbrella policy provides coverage after underlying liability policies have been exhausted. The umbrella policy is called *excess liability insurance* because the umbrella policy pays only for losses in excess of the underlying limits.

Both individual and firms must purchase insurance to protect themselves from liability claims arising from the ownership, maintenance, or use of automobiles. Firms cannot be insured using the Personal Auto Policy (PAP), which was described in Chapter 12, because it is designed for personal vehicle use instead of commercial vehicle use. Instead, firms purchase the business auto coverage form, which provides liability protection needed by commercial vehicle operators.

When people are injured as a result of using a defective product, they are entitled to collect compensation for the damage done. Producers, processors, manufacturers, and vendors can purchase products liability insurance as part of their commercial general liability insurance to pay injured parties on their behalf when a court awards judgments in favor of injured parties.

When physicians, lawyers, accountants, or other professionals injure people through professional negligence, the injured victims often sue to recover damages. The professionals can purchase professional liability insurance to protect themselves against having to pay court-awarded damages because such insurance policies agree to pay such claims on the insured's behalf.

Organizations that hire, supervise, or terminate personnel must do so with caution. Both federal and state governments have created protected classes of citizens whose rights must be protected through laws such as the Americans with Disabilities Act of 1990 (ADA). Should an employer abridge these rights, one result can be expensive litigation and expensive adverse legal judgments.

Review

1. Explain why the replacement of contributory negligence rules with comparative negligence rules leads to an increase in the frequency at which firms are sued.
2. Why are class action lawsuits a particularly challenging risk management exposure?
3. Describe the completed operations risk. In your answer, provide an example of the completed operations risk for an electrician.
4. Explain contractual liability and the nature of a hold-harmless agreement.
5. Does the CGL policy cover the following liability costs for a policyholder: a slip-and-fall jury award for $20,000; a $5,000 out-of-court settlement for a customer badly cut on a shelf; and $3,000 in payment to an attorney representing the named insured in a lawsuit?
6. What is the retroactive date in a claims-made CGL form? Why is the retroactive date important?
7. How can tail coverage help an attorney who has just retired from active practice?
8. What are the requirements for coverage for an incident to be covered under a claims-made liability policy? How do these requirements differ from an occurrence-based policy?
9. How does the retroactive date differ from the tail period in a claims-made liability policy?
10. Explain why claims may still be filed under CGL policies written before 1985.
11. Does an umbrella liability policy require other insurance policies to cover an insured loss first?
12. List several types of organizations that need EIL coverage. Discuss the reason why the insurance industry designed this type of protection.
13. What is products liability insurance designed to do?
14. Describe the insurance companies held liable in the *Keene* case? How did the court reach this decision?
15. Identify some of the major federal laws affecting employment practices.
16. List some of the reasons employers have been sued with respect to the managing of their employees.
17. How do the insurer's interests sometimes conflict with the professional's interest with respect to the opportunity to settle malpractice suits?
18. Give some reasons why each of the following might be sued for professional malpractice: a lawyer, an accountant, an architect, and an insurance agent.
19. What are some of the major costs from health care professionals' errors and omissions?
20. Several suggestions have been made to improve the current tort liability system as it relates to medical malpractice. Explain some of these suggestions.

Objective Questions

1. Dr. Xavier Self, M.D., purchases a one-year, claims-made, professional liability policy on June 1, 2003. It has a retroactive date of June 1, 2000. It also has two years of tail coverage that ends on June 1, 2006. Which of the following incidents would be covered by this policy?
   a. Patient injured December 31, 2003; claim filed July 1, 2005
   b. Patient injured December 31, 1999; claim filed July 1, 2000
   c. Patient injured December 31, 2000; claim filed July 1, 2006
   d. Patient injured December 31, 2003; claim filed July 1, 2006

2. Business CGL policies cover each of the following categories except:
   a. Premises liability
   b. Fire legal liability
   c. Professional liability
   d. Contractual liability
3. An umbrella policy:
   a. Covers wet marine exposures
   b. Covers property exposures
   c. Provides excess liability coverage
   d. Is only available if inland marine insurance has been purchased first

4. Firms engaged in the automobile business must purchase _____ to cover their liability exposure.
   a. Commercial automobile open-perils coverage
   b. Garage coverage form
   c. Retroactive commercial automobile policy
   d. Dealers and Auto Mechanics Specific Coverage Policy (DAMSCP)

5. Professional liability insurance policies would include each of the following except:
   a. Hospital liability policy
   b. Druggists' liability policy
   c. Lumberjack cutoff policy
   d. Errors and omissions insurance

6. A(n) _____ policy requires the insurance company providing the coverage at the time of the negligence to pay the claim.
   a. Occurrence-based liability insurance
   b. Claims-made liability insurance
   c. Sequential claims liability insurance
   d. Double indemnity liability insurance

7. Insurers call claims filed many years after the alleged negligence:
   a. Stale claims
   b. Long-tail claims
   c. Out-of-warranty claims
   d. Extended claims

8. Jan is injured while driving by Dan, who fails to stop at a stop sign. Jan sues Dan for $50,000 in damages. The court finds Dan 90 percent responsible for the accident and Jan 10 percent responsible. Under the doctrine of contributory negligence:
   a. Jan will collect nothing.
   b. Jan will collect $50,000.
   c. Jan will collect $45,000.
   d. Jan will collect nothing and Dan will collect $5,000.

9. Jan is injured while driving by Dan, who fails to stop at a stop sign. Jan sues Dan for $50,000 in damages. The court finds Dan 90 percent responsible for the accident and Jan 10 percent responsible. Under the doctrine of comparative negligence:
   a. Jan will collect nothing.
   b. Jan will collect $50,000.
   c. Jan will collect $45,000.
   d. Jan will collect nothing and Dan will collect $5,000.

Discussion Questions

1. Do you think an injured party should have the burden of proving that a company was guilty of negligence to collect damages? Should the burden be on the company to prove the consumer was negligent for the company to avoid having to pay the victim?

2. Define and describe the different types of liability risks covered under a CGL policy. Give an example of each type of risk.

Selected References

The CPCU Handbook of Insurance Policies, 5th ed., Malvern, PA: American Institute of Chartered Property Casualty Underwriters/Insurance Institute of America, 2003.

The Insurance Fact Book 2011, New York: Insurance Information Institute, 2011.

APPENDIX A

Personal Auto Policy (PP 00 01 01 05)

(Please see Figure 12-2 for PAP Declarations Page)

Reprinted with the permission of Insurance Services Office, Inc.

PERSONAL AUTO POLICY

AGREEMENT

In return for payment of the premium and subject to all the terms of this policy, we agree with you as follows:

DEFINITIONS

A. Throughout this policy, "you" and "your" refer to:
1. The "named insured" shown in the Declarations; and
2. The spouse if a resident of the same household.

If the spouse ceases to be a resident of the same household during the policy period or prior to the inception of this policy, the spouse will be considered "you" and "your" under this policy but only until the earlier of:
1. The end of 90 days following the spouse's change of residency;
2. The effective date of another policy listing the spouse as a named insured; or
3. The end of the policy period.

B. "We", "us" and "our" refer to the Company providing this insurance.

C. For purposes of this policy, a private passenger type auto, pickup or van shall be deemed to be owned by a person if leased:
1. Under a written agreement to that person; and
2. For a continuous period of at least 6 months.

Other words and phrases are defined. They are in quotation marks when used.

D. "Bodily injury" means bodily harm, sickness or disease, including death that results.

E. "Business" includes trade, profession or occupation.

F. "Family member" means a person related to you by blood, marriage or adoption who is a resident of your household. This includes a ward or foster child.

G. "Occupying" means:
1. In;
2. Upon; or
3. Getting in, on, out or off.

H. "Property damage" means physical injury to, destruction of or loss of use of tangible property.

I. "Trailer" means a vehicle designed to be pulled by a:
1. Private passenger auto; or
2. Pickup or van.

It also means a farm wagon or farm implement while towed by a vehicle listed in **1.** or **2.** above.

J. "Your covered auto" means:
1. Any vehicle shown in the Declarations.
2. A "newly acquired auto".
3. Any "trailer" you own.
4. Any auto or "trailer" you do not own while used as a temporary substitute for any other vehicle described in this definition which is out of normal use because of its:
   a. Breakdown;
   b. Repair;
   c. Servicing;
   d. Loss; or
   e. Destruction.

This Provision (**J.4.**) does not apply to Coverage For Damage To Your Auto.

K. "Newly acquired auto":
1. "Newly acquired auto" means any of the following types of vehicles you become the owner of during the policy period:
   a. A private passenger auto; or
   b. A pickup or van, for which no other insurance policy provides coverage, that:
      (1) Has a Gross Vehicle Weight Rating of 10,000 lbs. or less; and
      (2) Is not used for the delivery or transportation of goods and materials unless such use is:
         (a) Incidental to your "business" of installing, maintaining or repairing furnishings or equipment; or
         (b) For farming or ranching.
2. Coverage for a "newly acquired auto" is provided as described below. If you ask us to insure a "newly acquired auto" after a specified time period described below has elapsed, any coverage we provide for a "newly acquired auto" will begin at the time you request the coverage.
   a. For any coverage provided in this policy except Coverage For Damage To Your Auto, a "newly acquired auto" will have the broadest coverage we now provide for any vehicle shown in the Declarations. Coverage begins on the date you become the owner. However, for this coverage to apply to a "newly acquired auto" which is in addition to any vehicle shown in the Declarations, you must ask us to insure it within 14 days after you become the owner.

   If a "newly acquired auto" replaces a vehicle shown in the Declarations, coverage is provided for this vehicle without your having to ask us to insure it.

b. Collision Coverage for a "newly acquired auto" begins on the date you become the owner. However, for this coverage to apply, you must ask us to insure it within:
  (1) 14 days after you become the owner if the Declarations indicate that Collision Coverage applies to at least one auto. In this case, the "newly acquired auto" will have the broadest coverage we now provide for any auto shown in the Declarations.
  (2) Four days after you become the owner if the Declarations do not indicate that Collision Coverage applies to at least one auto. If you comply with the 4 day requirement and a loss occurred before you asked us to insure the "newly acquired auto", a Collision deductible of $500 will apply.
c. Other Than Collision Coverage for a "newly acquired auto" begins on the date you become the owner. However, for this coverage to apply, you must ask us to insure it within:
  (1) 14 days after you become the owner if the Declarations indicate that Other Than Collision Coverage applies to at least one auto. In this case, the "newly acquired auto" will have the broadest coverage we now provide for any auto shown in the Declarations.
  (2) Four days after you become the owner if the Declarations do not indicate that Other Than Collision Coverage applies to at least one auto. If you comply with the 4 day requirement and a loss occurred before you asked us to insure the "newly acquired auto", an Other Than Collision deductible of $500 will apply.

PART A—LIABILITY COVERAGE

INSURING AGREEMENT

A. We will pay damages for "bodily injury" or "property damage" for which any "insured" becomes legally responsible because of an auto accident. Damages include prejudgment interest awarded against the "insured". We will settle or defend, as we consider appropriate, any claim or suit asking for these damages. In addition to our limit of liability, we will pay all defense costs we incur. Our duty to settle or defend ends when our limit of liability for this coverage has been exhausted by payment of judgments or settlements. We have no duty to defend any suit or settle any claim for "bodily injury" or "property damage" not covered under this policy.

B. "Insured" as used in this Part means:
  1. You or any "family member" for the ownership, maintenance or use of any auto or "trailer".
  2. Any person using "your covered auto".
  3. For "your covered auto", any person or organization but only with respect to legal responsibility for acts or omissions of a person for whom coverage is afforded under this Part.
  4. For any auto or "trailer", other than "your covered auto", any other person or organization but only with respect to legal responsibility for acts or omissions of you or any "family member" for whom coverage is afforded under this Part. This Provision **(B.4.)** applies only if the person or organization does not own or hire the auto or "trailer".

SUPPLEMENTARY PAYMENTS

We will pay on behalf of an "insured":
  1. Up to $250 for the cost of bail bonds required because of an accident, including related traffic law violations. The accident must result in "bodily injury" or "property damage" covered under this policy.
  2. Premiums on appeal bonds and bonds to release attachments in any suit we defend.
  3. Interest accruing after a judgment is entered in any suit we defend. Our duty to pay interest ends when we offer to pay that part of the judgment which does not exceed our limit of liability for this coverage.
  4. Up to $200 a day for loss of earnings, but not other income, because of attendance at hearings or trials at our request.
  5. Other reasonable expenses incurred at our request.
These payments will not reduce the limit of liability.

EXCLUSIONS

A. We do not provide Liability Coverage for any "insured":
  1. Who intentionally causes "bodily injury" or "property damage".
  2. For "property damage" to property owned or being transported by that "insured".
  3. For "property damage" to property:
    a. Rented to;
    b. Used by; or

c. In the care of;
that "insured".

This Exclusion **(A.3.)** does not apply to "property damage" to a residence or private garage.

4. For "bodily injury" to an employee of that "insured" during the course of employment. This Exclusion **(A.4.)** does not apply to "bodily injury" to a domestic employee unless workers' compensation benefits are required or available for that domestic employee.

5. For that "insured's" liability arising out of the ownership or operation of a vehicle while it is being used as a public or livery conveyance. This Exclusion **(A.5.)** does not apply to a share-the-expense car pool.

6. While employed or otherwise engaged in the "business" of:
   a. Selling;
   b. Repairing;
   c. Servicing;
   d. Storing; or
   e. Parking;
   vehicles designed for use mainly on public highways. This includes road testing and delivery. This Exclusion **(A.6.)** does not apply to the ownership, maintenance or use of "your covered auto" by:
   a. You;
   b. Any "family member"; or
   c. Any partner, agent or employee of you or any "family member".

7. Maintaining or using any vehicle while that "insured" is employed or otherwise engaged in any "business" (other than farming or ranching) not described in Exclusion **A.6.**

   This Exclusion **(A.7.)** does not apply to the maintenance or use of a:
   a. Private passenger auto;
   b. Pickup or van; or
   c. "Trailer" used with a vehicle described in **a.** or **b.** above.

8. Using a vehicle without a reasonable belief that that "insured" is entitled to do so. This Exclusion **(A.8.)** does not apply to a "family member" using "your covered auto" which is owned by you.

9. For "bodily injury" or "property damage" for which that "insured":
   a. Is an insured under a nuclear energy liability policy; or
   b. Would be an insured under a nuclear energy liability policy but for its termination upon exhaustion of its limit of liability.

   A nuclear energy liability policy is a policy issued by any of the following or their successors:
   a. Nuclear Energy Liability Insurance Association;
   b. Mutual Atomic Energy Liability Underwriters; or
   c. Nuclear Insurance Association of Canada.

B. We do not provide Liability Coverage for the ownership, maintenance or use of:

1. Any vehicle which:
   a. Has fewer than four wheels; or
   b. Is designed mainly for use off public roads.
   This Exclusion **(B.1.)** does not apply:
   a. While such vehicle is being used by an "insured" in a medical emergency;
   b. To any "trailer"; or
   c. To any non-owned golf cart.

2. Any vehicle, other than "your covered auto", which is:
   a. Owned by you; or
   b. Furnished or available for your regular use.

3. Any vehicle, other than "your covered auto", which is:
   a. Owned by any "family member"; or
   b. Furnished or available for the regular use of any "family member".
   However, this Exclusion **(B.3.)** does not apply to you while you are maintaining or "occupying" any vehicle which is:
   a. Owned by a "family member"; or
   b. Furnished or available for the regular use of a "family member".

4. Any vehicle, located inside a facility designed for racing, for the purpose of:
   a. Competing in; or
   b. Practicing or preparing for;
   any prearranged or organized racing or speed contest.

LIMIT OF LIABILITY

A. The limit of liability shown in the Declarations for each person for Bodily Injury Liability is our maximum limit of liability for all damages, including damages for care, loss of services or death, arising out of "bodily injury" sustained by any one person in any one auto accident. Subject to this limit for each person, the limit of liability shown in the Declarations for each accident for Bodily Injury Liability is our maximum limit of liability for all damages for "bodily injury" resulting from any one auto accident.

The limit of liability shown in the Declarations for each accident for Property Damage Liability is our maximum limit of liability for all "property damage" resulting from any one auto accident.

This is the most we will pay regardless of the number of:
1. "Insureds";
2. Claims made;
3. Vehicles or premiums shown in the Declarations; or
4. Vehicles involved in the auto accident.

B. No one will be entitled to receive duplicate payments for the same elements of loss under this coverage and:

1. Part **B** or Part **C** of this policy; or
2. Any Underinsured Motorists Coverage provided by this policy.

OUT OF STATE COVERAGE

If an auto accident to which this policy applies occurs in any state or province other than the one in which "your covered auto" is principally garaged, we will interpret your policy for that accident as follows:

A. If the state or province has:

1. A financial responsibility or similar law specifying limits of liability for "bodily injury" or "property damage" higher than the limit shown in the Declarations, your policy will provide the higher specified limit.
2. A compulsory insurance or similar law requiring a nonresident to maintain insurance whenever the nonresident uses a vehicle in that state or province,

your policy will provide at least the required minimum amounts and types of coverage.

B. No one will be entitled to duplicate payments for the same elements of loss.

FINANCIAL RESPONSIBILITY

When this policy is certified as future proof of financial responsibility, this policy shall comply with the law to the extent required.

OTHER INSURANCE

If there is other applicable liability insurance we will pay only our share of the loss. Our share is the proportion that our limit of liability bears to the total of all applicable limits. However, any insurance we provide for a vehicle you do not own, including any vehicle while used as a temporary substitute for "your covered auto", shall be excess over any other collectible insurance.

PART B—MEDICAL PAYMENTS COVERAGE

INSURING AGREEMENT

A. We will pay reasonable expenses incurred for necessary medical and funeral services because of "bodily injury":

1. Caused by accident; and
2. Sustained by an "insured".

We will pay only those expenses incurred for services rendered within 3 years from the date of the accident.

B. "Insured" as used in this Part means:

1. You or any "family member":
   a. While "occupying"; or
   b. As a pedestrian when struck by;
   a motor vehicle designed for use mainly on public roads or a trailer of any type.
2. Any other person while "occupying" "your covered auto".

EXCLUSIONS

We do not provide Medical Payments Coverage for any "insured" for "bodily injury":

1. Sustained while "occupying" any motorized vehicle having fewer than four wheels.
2. Sustained while "occupying" "your covered auto" when it is being used as a public or livery conveyance. This Exclusion (**2.**) does not apply to a share-the-expense car pool.
3. Sustained while "occupying" any vehicle located for use as a residence or premises.

4. Occurring during the course of employment if workers' compensation benefits are required or available for the "bodily injury".
5. Sustained while "occupying", or when struck by, any vehicle (other than "your covered auto") which is:
   a. Owned by you; or
   b. Furnished or available for your regular use.
6. Sustained while "occupying", or when struck by, any vehicle (other than "your covered auto") which is:
   a. Owned by any "family member"; or
   b. Furnished or available for the regular use of any "family member".
   However, this Exclusion (**6.**) does not apply to you.
7. Sustained while "occupying" a vehicle without a reasonable belief that that "insured" is entitled to do so. This Exclusion (**7.**) does not apply to a "family member" using "your covered auto" which is owned by you.
8. Sustained while "occupying" a vehicle when it is being used in the "business" of an "insured". This Exclusion (**8.**) does not apply to "bodily injury" sustained while "occupying" a:
   a. Private passenger auto;
   b. Pickup or van; or
   c. "Trailer" used with a vehicle described in **a.** or **b.** above.
9. Caused by or as a consequence of:
   a. Discharge of a nuclear weapon (even if accidental);
   b. War (declared or undeclared);

c. Civil war;

d. Insurrection; or

e. Rebellion or revolution.

10. From or as a consequence of the following, whether controlled or uncontrolled or however caused:

a. Nuclear reaction;

b. Radiation; or

c. Radioactive contamination.

11. Sustained while "occupying" any vehicle located inside a facility designed for racing, for the purpose of:

a. Competing in; or

b. Practicing or preparing for;

any prearranged or organized racing or speed contest.

LIMIT OF LIABILITY

A. The limit of liability shown in the Declarations for this coverage is our maximum limit of liability for each person injured in any one accident. This is the most we will pay regardless of the number of:

1. "Insureds";

2. Claims made;

3. Vehicles or premiums shown in the Declarations; or

4. Vehicles involved in the accident.

B. No one will be entitled to receive duplicate payments for the same elements of loss under this coverage and:

1. Part **A** or Part **C** of this policy; or

2. Any Underinsured Motorists Coverage provided by this policy.

OTHER INSURANCE

If there is other applicable auto medical payments insurance we will pay only our share of the loss. Our share is the proportion that our limit of liability bears to the total of all applicable limits. However, any insurance we provide with respect to a vehicle you do not own, including any vehicle while used as a temporary substitute for "your covered auto", shall be excess over any other collectible auto insurance providing payments for medical or funeral expenses.

PART C—UNINSURED MOTORISTS COVERAGE

INSURING AGREEMENT

A. We will pay compensatory damages which an "insured" is legally entitled to recover from the owner or operator of an "uninsured motor vehicle" because of "bodily injury":

1. Sustained by an "insured"; and

2. Caused by an accident.

The owner's or operator's liability for these damages must arise out of the ownership, maintenance or use of the "uninsured motor vehicle".

Any judgment for damages arising out of a suit brought without our written consent is not binding on us.

B. "Insured" as used in this Part means:

1. You or any "family member".

2. Any other person "occupying" "your covered auto".

3. Any person for damages that person is entitled to recover because of "bodily injury" to which this coverage applies sustained by a person described in **1.** or **2.** above.

C. "Uninsured motor vehicle" means a land motor vehicle or trailer of any type:

1. To which no bodily injury liability bond or policy applies at the time of the accident.

2. To which a bodily injury liability bond or policy applies at the time of the accident. In this case its limit for bodily injury liability must be less than the minimum limit for bodily injury liability specified by the financial responsibility law of the state in which "your covered auto" is principally garaged.

3. Which is a hit-and-run vehicle whose operator or owner cannot be identified and which hits:

a. You or any "family member";

b. A vehicle which you or any "family member" are "occupying"; or

c. "Your covered auto".

4. To which a bodily injury liability bond or policy applies at the time of the accident but the bonding or insuring company:

a. Denies coverage; or

b. Is or becomes insolvent.

However, "uninsured motor vehicle" does not include any vehicle or equipment:

1. Owned by or furnished or available for the regular use of you or any "family member".

2. Owned or operated by a self-insurer under any applicable motor vehicle law, except a self-insurer which is or becomes insolvent.

3. Owned by any governmental unit or agency.

4. Operated on rails or crawler treads.

5. Designed mainly for use off public roads while not on public roads.

6. While located for use as a residence or premises.

EXCLUSIONS

A. We do not provide Uninsured Motorists Coverage for "bodily injury" sustained:

1. By an "insured" while "occupying", or when struck by, any motor vehicle owned by that "insured"

which is not insured for this coverage under this policy. This includes a trailer of any type used with that vehicle.

2. By any "family member" while "occupying", or when struck by, any motor vehicle you own which is insured for this coverage on a primary basis under any other policy.

B. We do not provide Uninsured Motorists Coverage for "bodily injury" sustained by any "insured":

1. If that "insured" or the legal representative settles the "bodily injury" claim and such settlement prejudices our right to recover payment.
2. While "occupying" "your covered auto" when it is being used as a public or livery conveyance. This Exclusion (**B.2.**) does not apply to a share-the-expense car pool.
3. Using a vehicle without a reasonable belief that that "insured" is entitled to do so. This Exclusion (**B.3.**) does not apply to a "family member" using "your covered auto" which is owned by you.

C. This coverage shall not apply directly or indirectly to benefit any insurer or self-insurer under any of the following or similar law:

1. Workers' compensation law; or
2. Disability benefits law.

D. We do not provide Uninsured Motorists Coverage for punitive or exemplary damages.

LIMIT OF LIABILITY

A. The limit of liability shown in the Declarations for each person for Uninsured Motorists Coverage is our maximum limit of liability for all damages, including damages for care, loss of services or death, arising out of "bodily injury" sustained by any one person in any one accident. Subject to this limit for each person, the limit of liability shown in the Declarations for each accident for Uninsured Motorists Coverage is our maximum limit of liability for all damages for "bodily injury" resulting from any one accident.

This is the most we will pay regardless of the number of:

1. "Insureds";
2. Claims made;
3. Vehicles or premiums shown in the Declarations; or
4. Vehicles involved in the accident.

B. No one will be entitled to receive duplicate payments for the same elements of loss under this coverage and:

1. Part **A** or Part **B** of this policy; or
2. Any Underinsured Motorists Coverage provided by this policy.

C. We will not make a duplicate payment under this coverage for any element of loss for which payment has been made by or on behalf of persons or organizations who may be legally responsible.

D. We will not pay for any element of loss if a person is entitled to receive payment for the same element of loss under any of the following or similar law:

1. Workers' compensation law; or
2. Disability benefits law.

OTHER INSURANCE

If there is other applicable insurance available under one or more policies or provisions of coverage that is similar to the insurance provided under this Part of the policy:

1. Any recovery for damages under all such policies or provisions of coverage may equal but not exceed the highest applicable limit for any one vehicle under any insurance providing coverage on either a primary or excess basis.
2. Any insurance we provide with respect to a vehicle you do not own, including any vehicle while used as a temporary substitute for "your covered auto", shall be excess over any collectible insurance providing such coverage on a primary basis.
3. If the coverage under this policy is provided:
   a. On a primary basis, we will pay only our share of the loss that must be paid under insurance providing coverage on a primary basis. Our share is the proportion that our limit of liability bears to the total of all applicable limits of liability for coverage provided on a primary basis.
   b. On an excess basis, we will pay only our share of the loss that must be paid under insurance providing coverage on an excess basis. Our share is the proportion that our limit of liability bears to the total of all applicable limits of liability for coverage provided on an excess basis.

ARBITRATION

A. If we and an "insured" do not agree:

1. Whether that "insured" is legally entitled to recover damages; or
2. As to the amount of damages which are recoverable by that "insured";

from the owner or operator of an "uninsured motor vehicle", then the matter may be arbitrated. However, disputes concerning coverage under this Part may not be arbitrated.

Both parties must agree to arbitration. If so agreed, each party will select an arbitrator. The two arbitrators will select a third. If they cannot agree within 30 days, either may request that selection be made by a judge of a court having jurisdiction.

B. Each party will:

1. Pay the expenses it incurs; and
2. Bear the expenses of the third arbitrator equally.

C. Unless both parties agree otherwise, arbitration will take place in the county in which the "insured" lives. Local rules of law as to procedure and evidence will apply. A decision agreed to by at least two of the arbitrators will be binding as to:

1. Whether the "insured" is legally entitled to recover damages; and
2. The amount of damages. This applies only if the amount does not exceed the minimum limit for bodily injury liability specified by the financial responsibility law of the state in which "your covered auto" is principally garaged. If the amount exceeds that limit, either party may demand the right to a trial. This demand must be made within 60 days of the arbitrators' decision. If this demand is not made, the amount of damages agreed to by the arbitrators will be binding.

PART D—COVERAGE FOR DAMAGE TO YOUR AUTO

INSURING AGREEMENT

A. We will pay for direct and accidental loss to "your covered auto" or any "non-owned auto", including their equipment, minus any applicable deductible shown in the Declarations. If loss to more than one "your covered auto" or "non-owned auto" results from the same "collision", only the highest applicable deductible will apply. We will pay for loss to "your covered auto" caused by:

1. Other than "collision" only if the Declarations indicate that Other Than Collision Coverage is provided for that auto.
2. "Collision" only if the Declarations indicate that Collision Coverage is provided for that auto.

If there is a loss to a "non-owned auto", we will provide the broadest coverage applicable to any "your covered auto" shown in the Declarations.

B. "Collision" means the upset of "your covered auto" or a "non-owned auto" or their impact with another vehicle or object.

Loss caused by the following is considered other than "collision":

1. Missiles or falling objects;
2. Fire;
3. Theft or larceny;
4. Explosion or earthquake;
5. Windstorm;
6. Hail, water or flood;
7. Malicious mischief or vandalism;
8. Riot or civil commotion;
9. Contact with bird or animal; or
10. Breakage of glass.

If breakage of glass is caused by a "collision", you may elect to have it considered a loss caused by "collision".

C. "Non-owned auto" means:

1. Any private passenger auto, pickup, van or "trailer" not owned by or furnished or available for the regular use of you or any "family member" while in the custody of or being operated by you or any "family member"; or
2. Any auto or "trailer" you do not own while used as a temporary substitute for "your covered auto" which is out of normal use because of its:
   a. Breakdown;
   b. Repair;
   c. Servicing;
   d. Loss; or
   e. Destruction.

TRANSPORTATION EXPENSES

A. In addition, we will pay, without application of a deductible, up to a maximum of $600 for:

1. Temporary transportation expenses not exceeding $20 per day incurred by you in the event of a loss to "your covered auto". We will pay for such expenses if the loss is caused by:
   a. Other than "collision" only if the Declarations indicate that Other Than Collision Coverage is provided for that auto.
   b. "Collision" only if the Declarations indicate that Collision Coverage is provided for that auto.
2. Expenses for which you become legally responsible in the event of loss to a "non-owned auto". We will pay for such expenses if the loss is caused by:
   a. Other than "collision" only if the Declarations indicate that Other Than Collision Coverage is provided for any "your covered auto".
   b. "Collision" only if the Declarations indicate that Collision Coverage is provided for any "your covered auto".

However, the most we will pay for any expenses for loss of use is $20 per day.

B. Subject to the provisions of Paragraph A., if the loss is caused by:

1. A total theft of "your covered auto" or a "non-owned auto", we will pay only expenses incurred during the period:
   a. Beginning 48 hours after the theft; and
   b. Ending when "your covered auto" or the "non-owned auto" is returned to use or we pay for its loss.

2. Other than theft of a "your covered auto" or a "non-owned auto", we will pay only expenses beginning when the auto is withdrawn from use for more than 24 hours.

Our payment will be limited to that period of time reasonably required to repair or replace the "your covered auto" or the "non-owned auto".

EXCLUSIONS

We will not pay for:

1. Loss to "your covered auto" or any "non-owned auto" which occurs while it is being used as a public or livery conveyance. This Exclusion (1.) does not apply to a share-the-expense car pool.
2. Damage due and confined to:
   a. Wear and tear;
   b. Freezing;
   c. Mechanical or electrical breakdown or failure; or
   d. Road damage to tires.

   This Exclusion (2.) does not apply if the damage results from the total theft of "your covered auto" or any "non-owned auto".
3. Loss due to or as a consequence of:
   a. Radioactive contamination;
   b. Discharge of any nuclear weapon (even if accidental);
   c. War (declared or undeclared);
   d. Civil war;
   e. Insurrection; or
   f. Rebellion or revolution.
4. Loss to any electronic equipment that reproduces, receives or transmits audio, visual or data signals. This includes but is not limited to:
   a. Radios and stereos;
   b. Tape decks;
   c. Compact disk systems;
   d. Navigation systems;
   e. Internet access systems;
   f. Personal computers;
   g. Video entertainment systems;
   h. Telephones;
   i. Televisions;
   j. Two-way mobile radios;
   k. Scanners; or
   l. Citizens band radios.

   This Exclusion (4.) does not apply to electronic equipment that is permanently installed in "your covered auto" or any "non-owned auto".
5. Loss to tapes, records, disks or other media used with equipment described in Exclusion 4.
6. A total loss to "your covered auto" or any "non-owned auto" due to destruction or confiscation by governmental or civil authorities.

This Exclusion (6.) does not apply to the interests of Loss Payees in "your covered auto".

7. Loss to:
   a. A "trailer", camper body, or motor home, which is not shown in the Declarations; or
   b. Facilities or equipment used with such "trailer", camper body or motor home. Facilities or equipment include but are not limited to:
      (1) Cooking, dining, plumbing or refrigeration facilities;
      (2) Awnings or cabanas; or
      (3) Any other facilities or equipment used with a "trailer", camper body, or motor home.

   This Exclusion (7.) does not apply to a:
   a. "Trailer", and its facilities or equipment, which you do not own; or
   b. "Trailer", camper body, or the facilities or equipment in or attached to the "trailer" or camper body, which you:
      (1) Acquire during the policy period; and
      (2) Ask us to insure within 14 days after you become the owner.
8. Loss to any "non-owned auto" when used by you or any "family member" without a reasonable belief that you or that "family member" are entitled to do so.
9. Loss to equipment designed or used for the detection or location of radar or laser.
10. Loss to any custom furnishings or equipment in or upon any pickup or van. Custom furnishings or equipment include but are not limited to:
    a. Special carpeting or insulation;
    b. Furniture or bars;
    c. Height-extending roofs; or
    d. Custom murals, paintings or other decals or graphics.

    This Exclusion (10.) does not apply to a cap, cover or bedliner in or upon any "your covered auto" which is a pickup.
11. Loss to any "non-owned auto" being maintained or used by any person while employed or otherwise engaged in the "business" of:
    a. Selling;
    b. Repairing;
    c. Servicing;
    d. Storing; or
    e. Parking;

    vehicles designed for use on public highways. This includes road testing and delivery.
12. Loss to "your covered auto" or any "non-owned auto", located inside a facility designed for racing, for the purpose of:
    a. Competing in; or
    b. Practicing or preparing for;

    any prearranged or organized racing or speed contest.

13. Loss to, or loss of use of, a "non-owned auto" rented by:
    a. You; or
    b. Any "family member";
    if a rental vehicle company is precluded from recovering such loss or loss of use, from you or that "family member", pursuant to the provisions of any applicable rental agreement or state law.

LIMIT OF LIABILITY

A. Our limit of liability for loss will be the lesser of the:
1. Actual cash value of the stolen or damaged property; or
2. Amount necessary to repair or replace the property with other property of like kind and quality.

However, the most we will pay for loss to:
1. Any "non-owned auto" which is a trailer is $1500.
2. Electronic equipment that reproduces, receives or transmits audio, visual or data signals, which is permanently installed in the auto in locations not used by the auto manufacturer for installation of such equipment, is $1,000.

B. An adjustment for depreciation and physical condition will be made in determining actual cash value in the event of a total loss.

C. If a repair or replacement results in better than like kind or quality, we will not pay for the amount of the betterment.

PAYMENT OF LOSS

We may pay for loss in money or repair or replace the damaged or stolen property. We may, at our expense, return any stolen property to:
1. You; or
2. The address shown in this policy.

If we return stolen property we will pay for any damage resulting from the theft. We may keep all or part of the property at an agreed or appraised value.

If we pay for loss in money, our payment will include the applicable sales tax for the damaged or stolen property.

NO BENEFIT TO BAILEE

This insurance shall not directly or indirectly benefit any carrier or other bailee for hire.

OTHER SOURCES OF RECOVERY

If other sources of recovery also cover the loss, we will pay only our share of the loss. Our share is the proportion that our limit of liability bears to the total of all applicable limits. However, any insurance we provide with respect to a "non-owned auto" shall be excess over any other collectible source of recovery including, but not limited to:
1. Any coverage provided by the owner of the "non-owned auto";
2. Any other applicable physical damage insurance;
3. Any other source of recovery applicable to the loss.

APPRAISAL

A. If we and you do not agree on the amount of loss, either may demand an appraisal of the loss. In this event, each party will select a competent and impartial appraiser. The two appraisers will select an umpire. The appraisers will state separately the actual cash value and the amount of loss. If they fail to agree, they will submit their differences to the umpire. A decision agreed to by any two will be binding. Each party will:
1. Pay its chosen appraiser; and
2. Bear the expenses of the appraisal and umpire equally.

B. We do not waive any of our rights under this policy by agreeing to an appraisal.

PART E—DUTIES AFTER AN ACCIDENT OR LOSS

We have no duty to provide coverage under this policy if the failure to comply with the following duties is prejudicial to us:

A. We must be notified promptly of how, when and where the accident or loss happened. Notice should also include the names and addresses of any injured persons and of any witnesses.

B. A person seeking any coverage must:
1. Cooperate with us in the investigation, settlement or defense of any claim or suit.

2. Promptly send us copies of any notices or legal papers received in connection with the accident or loss.
3. Submit, as often as we reasonably require:
    a. To physical exams by physicians we select. We will pay for these exams.
    b. To examination under oath and subscribe the same.

4. Authorize us to obtain:
   a. Medical reports; and
   b. Other pertinent records.
5. Submit a proof of loss when required by us.
C. A person seeking Uninsured Motorists Coverage must also:
   1. Promptly notify the police if a hit-and-run driver is involved.
   2. Promptly send us copies of the legal papers if a suit is brought.

D. A person seeking Coverage For Damage To Your Auto must also:
   1. Take reasonable steps after loss to protect "your covered auto" or any "non-owned auto" and their equipment from further loss. We will pay reasonable expenses incurred to do this.
   2. Promptly notify the police if "your covered auto" or any "non-owned auto" is stolen.
   3. Permit us to inspect and appraise the damaged property before its repair or disposal.

PART F—GENERAL PROVISIONS

BANKRUPTCY

Bankruptcy or insolvency of the "insured" shall not relieve us of any obligations under this policy.

CHANGES

A. This policy contains all the agreements between you and us. Its terms may not be changed or waived except by endorsement issued by us.
B. If there is a change to the information used to develop the policy premium, we may adjust your premium. Changes during the policy term that may result in a premium increase or decrease include, but are not limited to, changes in:
   1. The number, type or use classification of insured vehicles;
   2. Operators using insured vehicles;
   3. The place of principal garaging of insured vehicles;
   4. Coverage, deductible or limits.
   If a change resulting from **A.** or **B.** requires a premium adjustment, we will make the premium adjustment in accordance with our manual rules.
C. If we make a change which broadens coverage under this edition of your policy without additional premium charge, that change will automatically apply to your policy as of the date we implement the change in your state. This Paragraph (**C.**) does not apply to changes implemented with a general program revision that includes both broadenings and restrictions in coverage, whether that general program revision is implemented through introduction of:
   1. A subsequent edition of your policy; or
   2. An Amendatory Endorsement.

FRAUD

We do not provide coverage for any "insured" who has made fraudulent statements or engaged in fraudulent conduct in connection with any accident or loss for which coverage is sought under this policy.

LEGAL ACTION AGAINST US

A. No legal action may be brought against us until there has been full compliance with all the terms of this policy. In addition, under Part **A**, no legal action may be brought against us until:
   1. We agree in writing that the "insured" has an obligation to pay; or
   2. The amount of that obligation has been finally determined by judgment after trial.
B. No person or organization has any right under this policy to bring us into any action to determine the liability of an "insured".

OUR RIGHT TO RECOVER PAYMENT

A. If we make a payment under this policy and the person to or for whom payment was made has a right to recover damages from another we shall be subrogated to that right. That person shall do:
   1. Whatever is necessary to enable us to exercise our rights; and
   2. Nothing after loss to prejudice them.
   However, our rights in this Paragraph (**A.**) do not apply under Part **D**, against any person using "your covered auto" with a reasonable belief that that person is entitled to do so.
B. If we make a payment under this policy and the person to or for whom payment is made recovers damages from another, that person shall:
   1. Hold in trust for us the proceeds of the recovery; and
   2. Reimburse us to the extent of our payment.

POLICY PERIOD AND TERRITORY

A. This policy applies only to accidents and losses which occur:
   1. During the policy period as shown in the Declarations; and
   2. Within the policy territory.

B. The policy territory is:
1. The United States of America, its territories or possessions;
2. Puerto Rico; or
3. Canada.

This policy also applies to loss to, or accidents involving, "your covered auto" while being transported between their ports.

TERMINATION

A. Cancellation

This policy may be cancelled during the policy period as follows:

1. The named insured shown in the Declarations may cancel by:
   a. Returning this policy to us; or
   b. Giving us advance written notice of the date cancellation is to take effect.
2. We may cancel by mailing to the named insured shown in the Declarations at the address shown in this policy:
   a. At least 10 days notice:
      (1) If cancellation is for nonpayment of premium; or
      (2) If notice is mailed during the first 60 days this policy is in effect and this is not a renewal or continuation policy; or
   b. At least 20 days notice in all other cases.
3. After this policy is in effect for 60 days, or if this is a renewal or continuation policy, we will cancel only:
   a. For nonpayment of premium; or
   b. If your driver's license or that of:
      (1) Any driver who lives with you; or
      (2) Any driver who customarily uses "your covered auto";
      has been suspended or revoked. This must have occurred:
      (1) During the policy period; or
      (2) Since the last anniversary of the original effective date if the policy period is other than 1 year; or
   c. If the policy was obtained through material misrepresentation.

B. Nonrenewal

If we decide not to renew or continue this policy, we will mail notice to the named insured shown in the Declarations at the address shown in this policy. Notice will be mailed at least 20 days before the end of the policy period. Subject to this notice requirement, if the policy period is:

1. Less than 6 months, we will have the right not to renew or continue this policy every 6 months, beginning 6 months after its original effective date.
2. 6 months or longer, but less than one year, we will have the right not to renew or continue this policy at the end of the policy period.
3. 1 year or longer, we will have the right not to renew or continue this policy at each anniversary of its original effective date.

C. Automatic Termination

If we offer to renew or continue and you or your representative do not accept, this policy will automatically terminate at the end of the current policy period. Failure to pay the required renewal or continuation premium when due shall mean that you have not accepted our offer.

If you obtain other insurance on "your covered auto", any similar insurance provided by this policy will terminate as to that auto on the effective date of the other insurance.

D. Other Termination Provisions

1. We may deliver any notice instead of mailing it. Proof of mailing of any notice shall be sufficient proof of notice.
2. If this policy is cancelled, you may be entitled to a premium refund. If so, we will send you the refund. The premium refund, if any, will be computed according to our manuals. However, making or offering to make the refund is not a condition of cancellation.
3. The effective date of cancellation stated in the notice shall become the end of the policy period.

TRANSFER OF YOUR INTEREST IN THIS POLICY

A. Your rights and duties under this policy may not be assigned without our written consent. However, if a named insured shown in the Declarations dies, coverage will be provided for:

1. The surviving spouse if resident in the same household at the time of death. Coverage applies to the spouse as if a named insured shown in the Declarations; and
2. The legal representative of the deceased person as if a named insured shown in the Declarations. This applies only with respect to the representative's legal responsibility to maintain or use "your covered auto".

B. Coverage will only be provided until the end of the policy period.

TWO OR MORE AUTO POLICIES

If this policy and any other auto insurance policy issued to you by us apply to the same accident, the maximum limit of our liability under all the policies shall not exceed the highest applicable limit of liability under any one policy.

APPENDIX B

Homeowners Insurance Policy

This appendix includes…

- Homeowners Policy Declarations Page (HO DS 01 05 11)
- Homeowners 3 – Special Form (HO 00 03 05 11)

Reprinted with the permission of Insurance Services Office, Inc.

POLICY NUMBER: HO 987654321

HOMEOWNERS POLICY DECLARATIONS

Company Name:	Pearson Insurance Company
Producer Name:	Ann Agent
Named Insured:	David Cather
Mailing Address:	22 Main Street, Anytown, USA

The Residence Premises Is Located At The Above Address Unless Otherwise Stated:

Policy Period Year(s)	
Number Of Year(s): one	
From: 1/1/2012	12:01 AM standard time at the residence premises
To: 12/31/2012	12:01 AM standard time at the residence premises

We will provide the insurance described in this policy in return for the premium and compliance with all applicable policy provisions.

Coverage is provided where a premium or limit of liability is shown for the coverage.

Section I – Coverages	Limit Of Liability	
A. Dwelling	$ 200,000	
B. Other Structures	$ 20,000	
C. Personal Property	$ 100,000	
D. Loss Of Use	$ 40,000	
Section II – Coverages		
E. Personal Liability	$ 300,000	Each Occurrence
F. Medical Payments To Others	$ 1,000	Each Person
	Premium	
Basic Policy Premium	$ 800	
Additional Premium Charges Or Credits Related To Other Coverages Or Endorsements: Less: Claims-Free Discount	$ $ −120 $	
Total Premium	$ 680	

Forms And Endorsements Made Part Of This Policy (Number(s) And Edition Date(s))
HO 00 03 05 11

Deductible:	Section I:	$ 1000	Other: $ N/A

Section II – Other Insured Locations (Address): None

Mortgagee(s)/Lienholder(s)		
Name	**Address**	**Loan Number**
1. ZYX Mortgage Co.	222 Corporate Way, Anytown, USA	LN 12345
2.		
3.		

Loss Payee(s) – Personal Property (Name and Address of Loss Payee and Personal Property Involved)		
Name	**Address**	**Personal Property**
1.		
2.		
3.		

Countersignature Of Authorized Representative	
Name:	Ann Agent
Title:	Authorized Representative
Signature:	
Date:	1/1/2012

© Insurance Services Office, Inc., 2010 HO DS 01 05 11

HOMEOWNERS 3 – SPECIAL FORM

AGREEMENT

We will provide the insurance described in this policy in return for the premium and compliance with all applicable provisions of this policy.

DEFINITIONS

A. In this policy, "you" and "your" refer to the "named insured" shown in the Declarations and the spouse if a resident of the same household. "We", "us" and "our" refer to the Company providing this insurance.

B. In addition, certain words and phrases are defined as follows:

1. "Aircraft Liability", "Hovercraft Liability", "Motor Vehicle Liability" and "Watercraft Liability", subject to the provisions in **b.** below, mean the following:

   a. Liability for "bodily injury" or "property damage" arising out of the:

   (1) Ownership of such vehicle or craft by an "insured";

   (2) Maintenance, occupancy, operation, use, loading or unloading of such vehicle or craft by any person;

   (3) Entrustment of such vehicle or craft by an "insured" to any person;

   (4) Failure to supervise or negligent supervision of any person involving such vehicle or craft by an "insured"; or

   (5) Vicarious liability, whether or not imposed by law, for the actions of a child or minor involving such vehicle or craft.

   b. For the purpose of this definition:

   (1) Aircraft means any contrivance used or designed for flight except model or hobby aircraft not used or designed to carry people or cargo;

   (2) Hovercraft means a self-propelled motorized ground effect vehicle and includes, but is not limited to, flarecraft and air cushion vehicles;

   (3) Watercraft means a craft principally designed to be propelled on or in water by wind, engine power or electric motor; and

   (4) Motor vehicle means a "motor vehicle" as defined in **7.** below.

2. "Bodily injury" means bodily harm, sickness or disease, including required care, loss of services and death that results.

3. "Business" means:

   a. A trade, profession or occupation engaged in on a full-time, part-time or occasional basis; or

   b. Any other activity engaged in for money or other compensation, except the following:

   (1) One or more activities, not described in **(2)** through **(4)** below, for which no "insured" receives more than $2,000 in total compensation for the 12 months before the beginning of the policy period;

   (2) Volunteer activities for which no money is received other than payment for expenses incurred to perform the activity;

   (3) Providing home day care services for which no compensation is received, other than the mutual exchange of such services; or

   (4) The rendering of home day care services to a relative of an "insured".

4. "Employee" means an employee of an "insured", or an employee leased to an "insured" by a labor leasing firm under an agreement between an "insured" and the labor leasing firm, whose duties are other than those performed by a "residence employee".

5. "Insured" means:

   a. You and residents of your household who are:

   (1) Your relatives; or

   (2) Other persons under the age of 21 and in your care or the care of a resident of your household who is your relative;

   b. A student enrolled in school full-time, as defined by the school, who was a resident of your household before moving out to attend school, provided the student is under the age of:

   (1) 24 and your relative; or

   (2) 21 and in your care or the care of a resident of your household who is your relative; or

   c. Under Section **II:**

   (1) With respect to animals or watercraft to which this policy applies, any person or organization legally responsible for these animals or watercraft which are owned by you or any person described in **5.a.** or **b.**

© Insurance Services Office, Inc., 2010

"Insured" does not mean a person or organization using or having custody of these animals or watercraft in the course of any "business" or without consent of the owner; or

(2) With respect to a "motor vehicle" to which this policy applies:

(a) Persons while engaged in your employ or that of any person described in **5.a.** or **b.;** or

(b) Other persons using the vehicle on an "insured location" with your consent.

Under both Sections **I** and **II,** when the word an immediately precedes the word "insured", the words an "insured" together mean one or more "insureds".

6. "Insured location" means:

a. The "residence premises";

b. The part of other premises, other structures and grounds used by you as a residence; and

(1) Which is shown in the Declarations; or

(2) Which is acquired by you during the policy period for your use as a residence;

c. Any premises used by you in connection with a premises described in **a.** and **b.** above;

d. Any part of a premises:

(1) Not owned by an "insured"; and

(2) Where an "insured" is temporarily residing;

e. Vacant land, other than farm land, owned by or rented to an "insured";

f. Land owned by or rented to an "insured" on which a one-, two-, three- or four-family dwelling is being built as a residence for an "insured";

g. Individual or family cemetery plots or burial vaults of an "insured"; or

h. Any part of a premises occasionally rented to an "insured" for other than "business" use.

7. "Motor vehicle" means:

a. A self-propelled land or amphibious vehicle; or

b. Any trailer or semitrailer which is being carried on, towed by or hitched for towing by a vehicle described in **a.** above.

8. "Occurrence" means an accident, including continuous or repeated exposure to substantially the same general harmful conditions, which results, during the policy period, in:

a. "Bodily injury"; or

b. "Property damage".

9. "Property damage" means physical injury to, destruction of, or loss of use of tangible property.

10. "Residence employee" means:

a. An employee of an "insured", or an employee leased to an "insured" by a labor leasing firm, under an agreement between an "insured" and the labor leasing firm, whose duties are related to the maintenance or use of the "residence premises", including household or domestic services; or

b. One who performs similar duties elsewhere not related to the "business" of an "insured".

A "residence employee" does not include a temporary employee who is furnished to an "insured" to substitute for a permanent "residence employee" on leave or to meet seasonal or short-term workload conditions.

11. "Residence premises" means:

a. The one-family dwelling where you reside;

b. The two-, three- or four-family dwelling where you reside in at least one of the family units; or

c. That part of any other building where you reside;

and which is shown as the "residence premises" in the Declarations.

"Residence premises" also includes other structures and grounds at that location.

SECTION I – PROPERTY COVERAGES

A. Coverage A – Dwelling

1. We cover:

a. The dwelling on the "residence premises" shown in the Declarations, including structures attached to the dwelling; and

b. Materials and supplies located on or next to the "residence premises" used to construct, alter or repair the dwelling or other structures on the "residence premises".

2. We do not cover land, including land on which the dwelling is located.

B. Coverage B – Other Structures

1. We cover other structures on the "residence premises" set apart from the dwelling by clear space. This includes structures connected to the dwelling by only a fence, utility line, or similar connection.

2. We do not cover:

a. Land, including land on which the other structures are located;

b. Other structures rented or held for rental to any person not a tenant of the dwelling, unless used solely as a private garage;

c. Other structures from which any "business" is conducted; or

d. Other structures used to store "business" property. However, we do cover a structure that contains "business" property solely owned by an "insured" or a tenant of the dwelling, provided that "business" property does not include gaseous or liquid fuel, other than fuel in a permanently installed fuel tank of a vehicle or craft parked or stored in the structure.

3. The limit of liability for this coverage will not be more than 10% of the limit of liability that applies to Coverage **A.** Use of this coverage does not reduce the Coverage **A** limit of liability.

C. Coverage C – Personal Property

1. Covered Property

We cover personal property owned or used by an "insured" while it is anywhere in the world. After a loss and at your request, we will cover personal property owned by:

a. Others while the property is on the part of the "residence premises" occupied by an "insured"; or

b. A guest or a "residence employee", while the property is in any residence occupied by an "insured".

2. Limit For Property At Other Locations

a. Other Residences

Our limit of liability for personal property usually located at an "insured's" residence, other than the "residence premises", is 10% of the limit of liability for Coverage **C,** or $1,000, whichever is greater. However, this limitation does not apply to personal property:

(1) Moved from the "residence premises" because it is:

(a) Being repaired, renovated or rebuilt; and

(b) Not fit to live in or store property in; or

(2) In a newly acquired principal residence for 30 days from the time you begin to move the property there.

b. Self-storage Facilities

Our limit of liability for personal property owned or used by an "insured" and located in a self-storage facility is 10% of the limit of liability for Coverage **C,** or $1,000, whichever is greater. However, this limitation does not apply to personal property:

(1) Moved from the "residence premises" because it is:

(a) Being repaired, renovated or rebuilt; and

(b) Not fit to live in or store property in; or

(2) Usually located in an "insured's" residence, other than the "residence premises".

3. Special Limits Of Liability

The special limit for each category shown below is the total limit for each loss for all property in that category. These special limits do not increase the Coverage **C** limit of liability.

a. $200 on money, bank notes, bullion, gold other than goldware, silver other than silverware, platinum other than platinumware, coins, medals, scrip, stored value cards and smart cards.

b. $1,500 on securities, accounts, deeds, evidences of debt, letters of credit, notes other than bank notes, manuscripts, personal records, passports, tickets and stamps. This dollar limit applies to these categories regardless of the medium (such as paper or computer software) on which the material exists.

This limit includes the cost to research, replace or restore the information from the lost or damaged material.

c. $1,500 on watercraft of all types, including their trailers, furnishings, equipment and outboard engines or motors.

d. $1,500 on trailers or semitrailers not used with watercraft of all types.

e. $1,500 for loss by theft of jewelry, watches, furs, precious and semiprecious stones.

f. $2,500 for loss by theft of firearms and related equipment.

g. $2,500 for loss by theft of silverware, silver-plated ware, goldware, gold-plated ware, platinumware, platinum-plated ware and pewterware. This includes flatware, hollowware, tea sets, trays and trophies made of or including silver, gold or pewter.

h. $2,500 on property, on the "residence premises", used primarily for "business" purposes.

i. $1,500 on property, away from the "residence premises", used primarily for "business" purposes. However, this limit does not apply to antennas, tapes, wires, records, disks or other media that are:

(1) Used with electronic equipment that reproduces, receives or transmits audio, visual or data signals; and

(2) In or upon a "motor vehicle".

j. $1,500 on portable electronic equipment that:

(1) Reproduces, receives or transmits audio, visual or data signals;

(2) Is designed to be operated by more than one power source, one of which is a "motor vehicle's" electrical system; and

(3) Is in or upon a "motor vehicle".

k. $250 for antennas, tapes, wires, records, disks or other media that are:

(1) Used with electronic equipment that reproduces, receives or transmits audio, visual or data signals; and

(2) In or upon a "motor vehicle".

4. Property Not Covered

We do not cover:

a. Articles separately described and specifically insured, regardless of the limit for which they are insured, in this or other insurance;

b. Animals, birds or fish;

c. "Motor vehicles".

This includes a "motor vehicle's" equipment and parts. However, this Paragraph **4.c.** does not apply to:

  (1) Portable electronic equipment that:

    (a) Reproduces, receives or transmits audio, visual or data signals; and

    (b) Is designed so that it may be operated from a power source other than a "motor vehicle's" electrical system.

  (2) "Motor vehicles" not required to be registered for use on public roads or property which are:

    (a) Used solely to service a residence; or

    (b) Designed to assist the handicapped;

d. Aircraft, meaning any contrivance used or designed for flight, including any parts whether or not attached to the aircraft.

We do cover model or hobby aircraft not used or designed to carry people or cargo;

e. Hovercraft and parts. Hovercraft means a self-propelled motorized ground effect vehicle and includes, but is not limited to, flarecraft and air cushion vehicles;

f. Property of roomers, boarders and other tenants, except property of roomers and boarders related to an "insured";

g. Property in an apartment regularly rented or held for rental to others by an "insured", except as provided in **E.10.** Landlord's Furnishings under Section **I** – Property Coverages;

h. Property rented or held for rental to others off the "residence premises";

i. "Business" data, including such data stored in:

  (1) Books of account, drawings or other paper records; or

  (2) Computers and related equipment.

We cover the cost of blank recording or storage media and of prerecorded computer programs available on the retail market;

j. Credit cards, electronic fund transfer cards or access devices used solely for deposit, withdrawal or transfer of funds except as provided in **E.6.** Credit Card, Electronic Fund Transfer Card Or Access Device, Forgery And Counterfeit Money under Section **I** – Property Coverages; or

k. Water or steam.

D. Coverage D – Loss Of Use

The limit of liability for Coverage **D** is the total limit for the coverages in **1.** Additional Living Expense, **2.** Fair Rental Value and **3.** Civil Authority Prohibits Use below.

1. Additional Living Expense

If a loss covered under Section **I** makes that part of the "residence premises" where you reside not fit to live in, we cover any necessary increase in living expenses incurred by you so that your household can maintain its normal standard of living.

Payment will be for the shortest time required to repair or replace the damage or, if you permanently relocate, the shortest time required for your household to settle elsewhere.

2. Fair Rental Value

If a loss covered under Section **I** makes that part of the "residence premises" rented to others or held for rental by you not fit to live in, we cover the fair rental value of such premises less any expenses that do not continue while it is not fit to live in.

Payment will be for the shortest time required to repair or replace such premises.

3. Civil Authority Prohibits Use

If a civil authority prohibits you from use of the "residence premises" as a result of direct damage to neighboring premises by a Peril Insured Against, we cover the loss as provided in **1.** Additional Living Expense and **2.** Fair Rental Value above for no more than two weeks.

4. Loss Or Expense Not Covered

We do not cover loss or expense due to cancellation of a lease or agreement.

The periods of time under **1.** Additional Living Expense, **2.** Fair Rental Value and **3.** Civil Authority Prohibits Use above are not limited by expiration of this policy.

E. Additional Coverages

1. Debris Removal

a. We will pay your reasonable expense for the removal of:

  (1) Debris of covered property if a Peril Insured Against that applies to the damaged property causes the loss; or

  (2) Ash, dust or particles from a volcanic eruption that has caused direct loss to a building or property contained in a building.

This expense is included in the limit of liability that applies to the damaged property. If the amount to be paid for the actual damage to the property plus the debris removal expense is more than the limit of liability for the damaged property, an additional 5% of that limit is available for such expense.

       HO 00 03 05 11

b. We will also pay your reasonable expense, up to $1,000, for the removal from the "residence premises" of:

(1) Your trees felled by the peril of Windstorm or Hail or Weight of Ice, Snow or Sleet; or

(2) A neighbor's trees felled by a Peril Insured Against under Coverage **C;**

provided the trees:

(3) Damage a covered structure; or

(4) Do not damage a covered structure, but:

(a) Block a driveway on the "residence premises" which prevents a "motor vehicle", that is registered for use on public roads or property, from entering or leaving the "residence premises"; or

(b) Block a ramp or other fixture designed to assist a handicapped person to enter or leave the dwelling building.

The $1,000 limit is the most we will pay in any one loss, regardless of the number of fallen trees. No more than $500 of this limit will be paid for the removal of any one tree.

This coverage is additional insurance.

2. Reasonable Repairs

a. We will pay the reasonable cost incurred by you for the necessary measures taken solely to protect covered property that is damaged by a Peril Insured Against from further damage.

b. If the measures taken involve repair to other damaged property, we will only pay if that property is covered under this policy and the damage is caused by a Peril Insured Against. This coverage does not:

(1) Increase the limit of liability that applies to the covered property; or

(2) Relieve you of your duties, in case of a loss to covered property, described in **C.4.** under Section **I** – Conditions.

3. Trees, Shrubs And Other Plants

We cover trees, shrubs, plants or lawns, on the "residence premises", for loss caused by the following Perils Insured Against:

a. Fire or Lightning;

b. Explosion;

c. Riot or Civil Commotion;

d. Aircraft;

e. Vehicles not owned or operated by a resident of the "residence premises";

f. Vandalism or Malicious Mischief; or

g. Theft.

We will pay up to 5% of the limit of liability that applies to the dwelling for all trees, shrubs, plants or lawns. No more than $500 of this limit will be paid for any one tree, shrub or plant. We do not cover property grown for "business" purposes.

This coverage is additional insurance.

4. Fire Department Service Charge

We will pay up to $500 for your liability assumed by contract or agreement for fire department charges incurred when the fire department is called to save or protect covered property from a Peril Insured Against. We do not cover fire department service charges if the property is located within the limits of the city, municipality or protection district furnishing the fire department response.

This coverage is additional insurance. No deductible applies to this coverage.

5. Property Removed

We insure covered property against direct loss from any cause while being removed from a premises endangered by a Peril Insured Against and for no more than 30 days while removed.

This coverage does not change the limit of liability that applies to the property being removed.

6. Credit Card, Electronic Fund Transfer Card Or Access Device, Forgery And Counterfeit Money

a. We will pay up to $500 for:

(1) The legal obligation of an "insured" to pay because of the theft or unauthorized use of credit cards issued to or registered in an "insured's" name;

(2) Loss resulting from theft or unauthorized use of an electronic fund transfer card or access device used for deposit, withdrawal or transfer of funds, issued to or registered in an "insured's" name;

(3) Loss to an "insured" caused by forgery or alteration of any check or negotiable instrument; and

(4) Loss to an "insured" through acceptance in good faith of counterfeit United States or Canadian paper currency.

All loss resulting from a series of acts committed by any one person or in which any one person is concerned or implicated is considered to be one loss.

This coverage is additional insurance. No deductible applies to this coverage.

b. We do not cover:

(1) Use of a credit card, electronic fund transfer card or access device:

(a) By a resident of your household;

(b) By a person who has been entrusted with either type of card or access device; or

(c) If an "insured" has not complied with all terms and conditions under which the cards are issued or the devices accessed; or

(2) Loss arising out of "business" use or dishonesty of an "insured".

c. If the coverage in **a.** above applies, the following defense provisions also apply:

(1) We may investigate and settle any claim or suit that we decide is appropriate. Our duty to defend a claim or suit ends when the amount we pay for the loss equals our limit of liability.

(2) If a suit is brought against an "insured" for liability under **a.(1)** or **(2)** above, we will provide a defense at our expense by counsel of our choice.

(3) We have the option to defend at our expense an "insured" or an "insured's" bank against any suit for the enforcement of payment under **a.(3)** above.

7. Loss Assessment

a. We will pay up to $1,000 for your share of loss assessment charged during the policy period against you, as owner or tenant of the "residence premises", by a corporation or association of property owners. The assessment must be made as a result of direct loss to property, owned by all members collectively, of the type that would be covered by this policy if owned by you, caused by a Peril Insured Against under Coverage **A,** other than:

(1) Earthquake; or

(2) Land shock waves or tremors before, during or after a volcanic eruption.

The limit of $1,000 is the most we will pay with respect to any one loss, regardless of the number of assessments. We will only apply one deductible, per unit, to the total amount of any one loss to the property described above, regardless of the number of assessments.

b. We do not cover assessments charged against you or a corporation or association of property owners by any governmental body.

c. Paragraph **Q.** Policy Period under Section **I** – Conditions does not apply to this coverage.

This coverage is additional insurance.

8. Collapse

a. The coverage provided under this Additional Coverage – Collapse applies only to an abrupt collapse.

b. For the purpose of this Additional Coverage – Collapse, abrupt collapse means an abrupt falling down or caving in of a building or any part of a building with the result that the building or part of the building cannot be occupied for its intended purpose.

c. This Additional Coverage – Collapse does not apply to:

(1) A building or any part of a building that is in danger of falling down or caving in;

(2) A part of a building that is standing, even if it has separated from another part of the building; or

(3) A building or any part of a building that is standing, even if it shows evidence of cracking, bulging, sagging, bending, leaning, settling, shrinkage or expansion.

d. We insure for direct physical loss to covered property involving abrupt collapse of a building or any part of a building if such collapse was caused by one or more of the following:

(1) The Perils Insured Against named under Coverage **C;**

(2) Decay, of a building or any part of a building, that is hidden from view, unless the presence of such decay is known to an "insured" prior to collapse;

(3) Insect or vermin damage, to a building or any part of a building, that is hidden from view, unless the presence of such damage is known to an "insured" prior to collapse;

(4) Weight of contents, equipment, animals or people;

(5) Weight of rain which collects on a roof; or

(6) Use of defective material or methods in construction, remodeling or renovation if the collapse occurs during the course of the construction, remodeling or renovation.

e. Loss to an awning, fence, patio, deck, pavement, swimming pool, underground pipe, flue, drain, cesspool, septic tank, foundation, retaining wall, bulkhead, pier, wharf or dock is not included under **d.(2)** through **(6)** above, unless the loss is a direct result of the collapse of a building or any part of a building.

f. This coverage does not increase the limit of liability that applies to the damaged covered property.

9. Glass Or Safety Glazing Material

a. We cover:

(1) The breakage of glass or safety glazing material which is part of a covered building, storm door or storm window;

(2) The breakage of glass or safety glazing material which is part of a covered building, storm door or storm window when caused directly by earth movement; and

(3) The direct physical loss to covered property caused solely by the pieces, fragments or splinters of broken glass or safety glazing material which is part of a building, storm door or storm window.

b. This coverage does not include loss:

(1) To covered property which results because the glass or safety glazing material has been broken, except as provided in **a.(3)** above; or

(2) On the "residence premises" if the dwelling has been vacant for more than 60 consecutive days immediately before the loss, except when the breakage results directly from earth movement as provided in **a.(2)** above. A dwelling being constructed is not considered vacant.

c. This coverage does not increase the limit of liability that applies to the damaged property.

10. Landlord's Furnishings

We will pay up to $2,500 for your appliances, carpeting and other household furnishings, in each apartment on the "residence premises" regularly rented or held for rental to others by an "insured", for loss caused by a Peril Insured Against in Coverage **C**, other than Theft.

This limit is the most we will pay in any one loss regardless of the number of appliances, carpeting or other household furnishings involved in the loss.

This coverage does not increase the limit of liability applying to the damaged property.

11. Ordinance Or Law

a. You may use up to 10% of the limit of liability that applies to Coverage **A** for the increased costs you incur due to the enforcement of any ordinance or law which requires or regulates:

(1) The construction, demolition, remodeling, renovation or repair of that part of a covered building or other structure damaged by a Peril Insured Against;

(2) The demolition and reconstruction of the undamaged part of a covered building or other structure, when that building or other structure must be totally demolished because of damage by a Peril Insured Against to another part of that covered building or other structure; or

(3) The remodeling, removal or replacement of the portion of the undamaged part of a covered building or other structure necessary to complete the remodeling, repair or replacement of that part of the covered building or other structure damaged by a Peril Insured Against.

b. You may use all or part of this ordinance or law coverage to pay for the increased costs you incur to remove debris resulting from the construction, demolition, remodeling, renovation, repair or replacement of property as stated in **a.** above.

c. We do not cover:

(1) The loss in value to any covered building or other structure due to the requirements of any ordinance or law; or

(2) The costs to comply with any ordinance or law which requires any "insured" or others to test for, monitor, clean up, remove, contain, treat, detoxify or neutralize, or in any way respond to, or assess the effects of, pollutants in or on any covered building or other structure.

Pollutants means any solid, liquid, gaseous or thermal irritant or contaminant, including smoke, vapor, soot, fumes, acids, alkalis, chemicals and waste. Waste includes materials to be recycled, reconditioned or reclaimed.

This coverage is additional insurance.

12. Grave Markers

We will pay up to $5,000 for grave markers, including mausoleums, on or away from the "residence premises" for loss caused by a Peril Insured Against under Coverage **C**.

This coverage does not increase the limits of liability that apply to the damaged covered property.

SECTION I – PERILS INSURED AGAINST

A. Coverage A – Dwelling And Coverage B – Other Structures

1. We insure against direct physical loss to property described in Coverages **A** and **B**.

2. We do not insure, however, for loss:

a. Excluded under Section **I** – Exclusions;

b. Involving collapse, including any of the following conditions of property or any part of the property:

(1) An abrupt falling down or caving in;

(2) Loss of structural integrity, including separation of parts of the property or property in danger of falling down or caving in; or

(3) Any cracking, bulging, sagging, bending, leaning, settling, shrinkage or expansion as such condition relates to **(1)** or **(2)** above;

except as provided in **E.8.** Collapse under Section **I** – Property Coverages; or

c. Caused by:

(1) Freezing of a plumbing, heating, air conditioning or automatic fire protective sprinkler system or of a household appliance, or by discharge, leakage or overflow from within the system or appliance caused by freezing. This provision does not apply if you have used reasonable care to:

(a) Maintain heat in the building; or

(b) Shut off the water supply and drain all systems and appliances of water.

However, if the building is protected by an automatic fire protective sprinkler system, you must use reasonable care to continue the water supply and maintain heat in the building for coverage to apply.

For purposes of this provision, a plumbing system or household appliance does not include a sump, sump pump or related equipment or a roof drain, gutter, downspout or similar fixtures or equipment;

(2) Freezing, thawing, pressure or weight of water or ice, whether driven by wind or not, to a:

(a) Fence, pavement, patio or swimming pool;

(b) Footing, foundation, bulkhead, wall, or any other structure or device that supports all or part of a building, or other structure;

(c) Retaining wall or bulkhead that does not support all or part of a building or other structure; or

(d) Pier, wharf or dock;

(3) Theft in or to a dwelling under construction, or of materials and supplies for use in the construction until the dwelling is finished and occupied;

(4) Vandalism and malicious mischief, and any ensuing loss caused by any intentional and wrongful act committed in the course of the vandalism or malicious mischief, if the dwelling has been vacant for more than 60 consecutive days immediately before the loss. A dwelling being constructed is not considered vacant;

(5) Mold, fungus or wet rot. However, we do insure for loss caused by mold, fungus or wet rot that is hidden within the walls or ceilings or beneath the floors or above the ceilings of a structure if such loss results from the accidental discharge or overflow of water or steam from within:

(a) A plumbing, heating, air conditioning or automatic fire protective sprinkler system, or a household appliance, on the "residence premises"; or

(b) A storm drain, or water, steam or sewer pipes, off the "residence premises".

For purposes of this provision, a plumbing system or household appliance does not include a sump, sump pump or related equipment or a roof drain, gutter, downspout or similar fixtures or equipment; or

(6) Any of the following:

(a) Wear and tear, marring, deterioration;

(b) Mechanical breakdown, latent defect, inherent vice or any quality in property that causes it to damage or destroy itself;

(c) Smog, rust or other corrosion, or dry rot;

(d) Smoke from agricultural smudging or industrial operations;

(e) Discharge, dispersal, seepage, migration, release or escape of pollutants unless the discharge, dispersal, seepage, migration, release or escape is itself caused by a Peril Insured Against named under Coverage **C.**

Pollutants means any solid, liquid, gaseous or thermal irritant or contaminant, including smoke, vapor, soot, fumes, acids, alkalis, chemicals and waste. Waste includes materials to be recycled, reconditioned or reclaimed;

(f) Settling, shrinking, bulging or expansion, including resultant cracking, of bulkheads, pavements, patios, footings, foundations, walls, floors, roofs or ceilings;

(g) Birds, rodents or insects;

(h) Nesting or infestation, or discharge or release of waste products or secretions, by any animals; or

(i) Animals owned or kept by an "insured".

Exception To c.(6)

Unless the loss is otherwise excluded, we cover loss to property covered under Coverage **A** or **B** resulting from an accidental discharge or overflow of water or steam from within a:

(i) Storm drain, or water, steam or sewer pipe, off the "residence premises"; or

(ii) Plumbing, heating, air conditioning or automatic fire protective sprinkler system or household appliance on the "residence premises". This includes the cost to tear out and replace any part of a building, or other structure, on the "residence premises", but only when necessary to repair the system or appliance. However, such tear out and replacement coverage only applies to other structures if the water or steam causes actual damage to a building on the "residence premises".

We do not cover loss to the system or appliance from which this water or steam escaped.

For purposes of this provision, a plumbing system or household appliance does not include a sump, sump pump or related equipment or a roof drain, gutter, downspout or similar fixtures or equipment.

Section I – Exclusion **A.3.** Water, Paragraphs **a.** and **c.** that apply to surface water and water below the surface of the ground do not apply to loss by water covered under **c.(5)** and **(6)** above.

Under **2.b.** and **c.** above, any ensuing loss to property described in Coverages **A** and **B** not precluded by any other provision in this policy is covered.

B. Coverage C – Personal Property

We insure for direct physical loss to the property described in Coverage **C** caused by any of the following perils unless the loss is excluded in Section I – Exclusions.

1. Fire Or Lightning

2. Windstorm Or Hail

This peril includes loss to watercraft of all types and their trailers, furnishings, equipment, and outboard engines or motors, only while inside a fully enclosed building.

This peril does not include loss to the property contained in a building caused by rain, snow, sleet, sand or dust unless the direct force of wind or hail damages the building causing an opening in a roof or wall and the rain, snow, sleet, sand or dust enters through this opening.

3. Explosion

4. Riot Or Civil Commotion

5. Aircraft

This peril includes self-propelled missiles and spacecraft.

6. Vehicles

7. Smoke

This peril means sudden and accidental damage from smoke, including the emission or puffback of smoke, soot, fumes or vapors from a boiler, furnace or related equipment.

This peril does not include loss caused by smoke from agricultural smudging or industrial operations.

8. Vandalism Or Malicious Mischief

9. Theft

   a. This peril includes attempted theft and loss of property from a known place when it is likely that the property has been stolen.

   b. This peril does not include loss caused by theft:

      (1) Committed by an "insured";

      (2) In or to a dwelling under construction, or of materials and supplies for use in the construction until the dwelling is finished and occupied;

      (3) From that part of a "residence premises" rented by an "insured" to someone other than another "insured"; or

      (4) That occurs off the "residence premises" of:

         (a) Trailers, semitrailers and campers;

         (b) Watercraft of all types, and their furnishings, equipment and outboard engines or motors; or

         (c) Property while at any other residence owned by, rented to, or occupied by an "insured", except while an "insured" is temporarily living there. Property of an "insured" who is a student is covered while at the residence the student occupies to attend school as long as the student has been there at any time during the 90 days immediately before the loss.

10. Falling Objects

This peril does not include loss to property contained in a building unless the roof or an outside wall of the building is first damaged by a falling object. Damage to the falling object itself is not included.

11. Weight Of Ice, Snow Or Sleet

This peril means weight of ice, snow or sleet which causes damage to property contained in a building.

12. Accidental Discharge Or Overflow Of Water Or Steam

   a. This peril means accidental discharge or overflow of water or steam from within a plumbing, heating, air conditioning or automatic fire protective sprinkler system or from within a household appliance.

   b. This peril does not include loss:

      (1) To the system or appliance from which the water or steam escaped;

      (2) Caused by or resulting from freezing except as provided in Peril Insured Against **14.** Freezing;

      (3) On the "residence premises" caused by accidental discharge or overflow which occurs off the "residence premises"; or

      (4) Caused by mold, fungus or wet rot unless hidden within the walls or ceilings or beneath the floors or above the ceilings of a structure.

   c. In this peril, a plumbing system or household appliance does not include a sump, sump pump or related equipment or a roof drain, gutter, downspout or similar fixtures or equipment.

   d. Section I – Exclusion **A.3.** Water, Paragraphs **a.** and **c.** that apply to surface water and water below the surface of the ground do not apply to loss by water covered under this peril.

13. Sudden And Accidental Tearing Apart, Cracking, Burning Or Bulging

This peril means sudden and accidental tearing apart, cracking, burning or bulging of a steam or hot water heating system, an air conditioning or automatic fire protective sprinkler system, or an appliance for heating water.

We do not cover loss caused by or resulting from freezing under this peril.

14. Freezing

a. This peril means freezing of a plumbing, heating, air conditioning or automatic fire protective sprinkler system or of a household appliance, but only if you have used reasonable care to:

(1) Maintain heat in the building; or

(2) Shut off the water supply and drain all systems and appliances of water.

However, if the building is protected by an automatic fire protective sprinkler system, you must use reasonable care to continue the water supply and maintain heat in the building for coverage to apply.

b. In this peril, a plumbing system or household appliance does not include a sump, sump pump or related equipment or a roof drain, gutter, downspout or similar fixtures or equipment.

15. Sudden And Accidental Damage From Artificially Generated Electrical Current

This peril does not include loss to tubes, transistors, electronic components or circuitry that is a part of appliances, fixtures, computers, home entertainment units or other types of electronic apparatus.

16. Volcanic Eruption

This peril does not include loss caused by earthquake, land shock waves or tremors.

SECTION I – EXCLUSIONS

A. We do not insure for loss caused directly or indirectly by any of the following. Such loss is excluded regardless of any other cause or event contributing concurrently or in any sequence to the loss. These exclusions apply whether or not the loss event results in widespread damage or affects a substantial area.

1. Ordinance Or Law

Ordinance Or Law means any ordinance or law:

a. Requiring or regulating the construction, demolition, remodeling, renovation or repair of property, including removal of any resulting debris. This Exclusion **A.1.a.** does not apply to the amount of coverage that may be provided for in **E.11.** Ordinance Or Law under Section **I** – Property Coverages;

b. The requirements of which result in a loss in value to property; or

c. Requiring any "insured" or others to test for, monitor, clean up, remove, contain, treat, detoxify or neutralize, or in any way respond to, or assess the effects of, pollutants.

Pollutants means any solid, liquid, gaseous or thermal irritant or contaminant, including smoke, vapor, soot, fumes, acids, alkalis, chemicals and waste. Waste includes materials to be recycled, reconditioned or reclaimed.

This Exclusion **A.1.** applies whether or not the property has been physically damaged.

2. Earth Movement

Earth Movement means:

a. Earthquake, including land shock waves or tremors before, during or after a volcanic eruption;

b. Landslide, mudslide or mudflow;

c. Subsidence or sinkhole; or

d. Any other earth movement including earth sinking, rising or shifting.

This Exclusion **A.2.** applies regardless of whether any of the above, in **A.2.a.** through **A.2.d.**, is caused by an act of nature or is otherwise caused.

However, direct loss by fire, explosion or theft resulting from any of the above, in **A.2.a.** through **A.2.d.**, is covered.

3. Water

This means:

a. Flood, surface water, waves, including tidal wave and tsunami, tides, tidal water, overflow of any body of water, or spray from any of these, all whether or not driven by wind, including storm surge;

b. Water which:

(1) Backs up through sewers or drains; or

(2) Overflows or is otherwise discharged from a sump, sump pump or related equipment;

c. Water below the surface of the ground, including water which exerts pressure on, or seeps, leaks or flows through a building, sidewalk, driveway, patio, foundation, swimming pool or other structure; or

d. Waterborne material carried or otherwise moved by any of the water referred to in **A.3.a.** through **A.3.c.** of this exclusion.

This Exclusion **A.3.** applies regardless of whether any of the above, in **A.3.a.** through **A.3.d.**, is caused by an act of nature or is otherwise caused.

This Exclusion **A.3.** applies to, but is not limited to, escape, overflow or discharge, for any reason, of water or waterborne material from a dam, levee, seawall or any other boundary or containment system.

However, direct loss by fire, explosion or theft resulting from any of the above, in **A.3.a.** through **A.3.d.**, is covered.

4. **Power Failure**

Power Failure means the failure of power or other utility service if the failure takes place off the "residence premises". But if the failure results in a loss, from a Peril Insured Against on the "residence premises", we will pay for the loss caused by that peril.

5. **Neglect**

Neglect means neglect of an "insured" to use all reasonable means to save and preserve property at and after the time of a loss.

6. **War**

War includes the following and any consequence of any of the following:

a. Undeclared war, civil war, insurrection, rebellion or revolution;

b. Warlike act by a military force or military personnel; or

c. Destruction, seizure or use for a military purpose.

Discharge of a nuclear weapon will be deemed a warlike act even if accidental.

7. **Nuclear Hazard**

This Exclusion **A.7.** pertains to Nuclear Hazard to the extent set forth in **N.** Nuclear Hazard Clause under Section **I** – Conditions.

8. **Intentional Loss**

Intentional Loss means any loss arising out of any act an "insured" commits or conspires to commit with the intent to cause a loss.

In the event of such loss, no "insured" is entitled to coverage, even "insureds" who did not commit or conspire to commit the act causing the loss.

9. **Governmental Action**

Governmental Action means the destruction, confiscation or seizure of property described in Coverage **A**, **B** or **C** by order of any governmental or public authority.

This exclusion does not apply to such acts ordered by any governmental or public authority that are taken at the time of a fire to prevent its spread, if the loss caused by fire would be covered under this policy.

B. We do not insure for loss to property described in Coverages **A** and **B** caused by any of the following. However, any ensuing loss to property described in Coverages **A** and **B** not precluded by any other provision in this policy is covered.

1. Weather conditions. However, this exclusion only applies if weather conditions contribute in any way with a cause or event excluded in **A.** above to produce the loss.

2. Acts or decisions, including the failure to act or decide, of any person, group, organization or governmental body.

3. Faulty, inadequate or defective:

a. Planning, zoning, development, surveying, siting;

b. Design, specifications, workmanship, repair, construction, renovation, remodeling, grading, compaction;

c. Materials used in repair, construction, renovation or remodeling; or

d. Maintenance;

of part or all of any property whether on or off the "residence premises".

SECTION I – CONDITIONS

A. Insurable Interest And Limit Of Liability

Even if more than one person has an insurable interest in the property covered, we will not be liable in any one loss:

1. To an "insured" for more than the amount of such "insured's" interest at the time of loss; or

2. For more than the applicable limit of liability.

B. Deductible

Unless otherwise noted in this policy, the following deductible provision applies:

With respect to any one loss:

1. Subject to the applicable limit of liability, we will pay only that part of the total of all loss payable that exceeds the deductible amount shown in the Declarations.

2. If two or more deductibles under this policy apply to the loss, only the highest deductible amount will apply.

C. Duties After Loss

In case of a loss to covered property, we have no duty to provide coverage under this policy if the failure to comply with the following duties is prejudicial to us. These duties must be performed either by you, an "insured" seeking coverage, or a representative of either:

1. Give prompt notice to us or our agent;

2. Notify the police in case of loss by theft;

3. Notify the credit card or electronic fund transfer card or access device company in case of loss as provided for in **E.6.** Credit Card, Electronic Fund Transfer Card Or Access Device, Forgery And Counterfeit Money under Section **I** – Property Coverages;

4. Protect the property from further damage. If repairs to the property are required, you must:

a. Make reasonable and necessary repairs to protect the property; and

b. Keep an accurate record of repair expenses;

5. Cooperate with us in the investigation of a claim;
6. Prepare an inventory of damaged personal property showing the quantity, description, actual cash value and amount of loss. Attach all bills, receipts and related documents that justify the figures in the inventory;
7. As often as we reasonably require:
    a. Show the damaged property;
    b. Provide us with records and documents we request and permit us to make copies; and
    c. Submit to examination under oath, while not in the presence of another "insured", and sign the same;
8. Send to us, within 60 days after our request, your signed, sworn proof of loss which sets forth, to the best of your knowledge and belief:
    a. The time and cause of loss;
    b. The interests of all "insureds" and all others in the property involved and all liens on the property;
    c. Other insurance which may cover the loss;
    d. Changes in title or occupancy of the property during the term of the policy;
    e. Specifications of damaged buildings and detailed repair estimates;
    f. The inventory of damaged personal property described in **6.** above;
    g. Receipts for additional living expenses incurred and records that support the fair rental value loss; and
    h. Evidence or affidavit that supports a claim under **E.6.** Credit Card, Electronic Fund Transfer Card Or Access Device, Forgery And Counterfeit Money under Section **I** – Property Coverages, stating the amount and cause of loss.

D. Loss Settlement

In this Condition **D.,** the terms "cost to repair or replace" and "replacement cost" do not include the increased costs incurred to comply with the enforcement of any ordinance or law, except to the extent that coverage for these increased costs is provided in **E.11.** Ordinance Or Law under Section **I** – Property Coverages. Covered property losses are settled as follows:
1. Property of the following types:
    a. Personal property;
    b. Awnings, carpeting, household appliances, outdoor antennas and outdoor equipment, whether or not attached to buildings;
    c. Structures that are not buildings; and
    d. Grave markers, including mausoleums;
    at actual cash value at the time of loss but not more than the amount required to repair or replace.
2. Buildings covered under Coverage **A** or **B** at replacement cost without deduction for depreciation, subject to the following:

a. If, at the time of loss, the amount of insurance in this policy on the damaged building is 80% or more of the full replacement cost of the building immediately before the loss, we will pay the cost to repair or replace, without deduction for depreciation, but not more than the least of the following amounts:
    (1) The limit of liability under this policy that applies to the building;
    (2) The replacement cost of that part of the building damaged with material of like kind and quality and for like use; or
    (3) The necessary amount actually spent to repair or replace the damaged building.
    If the building is rebuilt at a new premises, the cost described in **(2)** above is limited to the cost which would have been incurred if the building had been built at the original premises.
b. If, at the time of loss, the amount of insurance in this policy on the damaged building is less than 80% of the full replacement cost of the building immediately before the loss, we will pay the greater of the following amounts, but not more than the limit of liability under this policy that applies to the building:
    (1) The actual cash value of that part of the building damaged; or
    (2) That proportion of the cost to repair or replace, without deduction for depreciation, that part of the building damaged, which the total amount of insurance in this policy on the damaged building bears to 80% of the replacement cost of the building.
c. To determine the amount of insurance required to equal 80% of the full replacement cost of the building immediately before the loss, do not include the value of:
    (1) Excavations, footings, foundations, piers, or any other structures or devices that support all or part of the building, which are below the undersurface of the lowest basement floor;
    (2) Those supports described in **(1)** above which are below the surface of the ground inside the foundation walls, if there is no basement; and
    (3) Underground flues, pipes, wiring and drains.
d. We will pay no more than the actual cash value of the damage until actual repair or replacement is complete. Once actual repair or replacement is complete, we will settle the loss as noted in **2.a.** and **b.** above.

However, if the cost to repair or replace the damage is both:

(1) Less than 5% of the amount of insurance in this policy on the building; and

(2) Less than $2,500;

we will settle the loss as noted in **2.a.** and **b.** above whether or not actual repair or replacement is complete.

e. You may disregard the replacement cost loss settlement provisions and make claim under this policy for loss to buildings on an actual cash value basis. You may then make claim for any additional liability according to the provisions of this Condition **D.** Loss Settlement, provided you notify us, within 180 days after the date of loss, of your intent to repair or replace the damaged building.

E. Loss To A Pair Or Set

In case of loss to a pair or set we may elect to:

1. Repair or replace any part to restore the pair or set to its value before the loss; or

2. Pay the difference between actual cash value of the property before and after the loss.

F. Appraisal

If you and we fail to agree on the amount of loss, either may demand an appraisal of the loss. In this event, each party will choose a competent and impartial appraiser within 20 days after receiving a written request from the other. The two appraisers will choose an umpire. If they cannot agree upon an umpire within 15 days, you or we may request that the choice be made by a judge of a court of record in the state where the "residence premises" is located. The appraisers will separately set the amount of loss. If the appraisers submit a written report of an agreement to us, the amount agreed upon will be the amount of loss. If they fail to agree, they will submit their differences to the umpire. A decision agreed to by any two will set the amount of loss.

Each party will:

1. Pay its own appraiser; and

2. Bear the other expenses of the appraisal and umpire equally.

G. Other Insurance And Service Agreement

If a loss covered by this policy is also covered by:

1. Other insurance, we will pay only the proportion of the loss that the limit of liability that applies under this policy bears to the total amount of insurance covering the loss; or

2. A service agreement, this insurance is excess over any amounts payable under any such agreement. Service agreement means a service plan, property restoration plan, home warranty or other similar service warranty agreement, even if it is characterized as insurance.

H. Suit Against Us

No action can be brought against us unless there has been full compliance with all of the terms under Section I of this policy and the action is started within two years after the date of loss.

I. Our Option

If we give you written notice within 30 days after we receive your signed, sworn proof of loss, we may repair or replace any part of the damaged property with material or property of like kind and quality.

J. Loss Payment

We will adjust all losses with you. We will pay you unless some other person is named in the policy or is legally entitled to receive payment. Loss will be payable 60 days after we receive your proof of loss and:

1. Reach an agreement with you;

2. There is an entry of a final judgment; or

3. There is a filing of an appraisal award with us.

K. Abandonment Of Property

We need not accept any property abandoned by an "insured".

L. Mortgage Clause

1. If a mortgagee is named in this policy, any loss payable under Coverage **A** or **B** will be paid to the mortgagee and you, as interests appear. If more than one mortgagee is named, the order of payment will be the same as the order of precedence of the mortgages.

2. If we deny your claim, that denial will not apply to a valid claim of the mortgagee, if the mortgagee:

a. Notifies us of any change in ownership, occupancy or substantial change in risk of which the mortgagee is aware;

b. Pays any premium due under this policy on demand if you have neglected to pay the premium; and

c. Submits a signed, sworn statement of loss within 60 days after receiving notice from us of your failure to do so. Paragraphs **F.** Appraisal, **H.** Suit Against Us and **J.** Loss Payment under Section **I** – Conditions also apply to the mortgagee.

3. If we decide to cancel or not to renew this policy, the mortgagee will be notified at least 10 days before the date cancellation or nonrenewal takes effect.

4. If we pay the mortgagee for any loss and deny payment to you:

a. We are subrogated to all the rights of the mortgagee granted under the mortgage on the property; or

b. At our option, we may pay to the mortgagee the whole principal on the mortgage plus any accrued interest. In this event, we will receive a full assignment and transfer of the mortgage and all securities held as collateral to the mortgage debt.

5. Subrogation will not impair the right of the mortgagee to recover the full amount of the mortgagee's claim.

M. No Benefit To Bailee

We will not recognize any assignment or grant any coverage that benefits a person or organization holding, storing or moving property for a fee regardless of any other provision of this policy.

N. Nuclear Hazard Clause

1. "Nuclear Hazard" means any nuclear reaction, radiation, or radioactive contamination, all whether controlled or uncontrolled or however caused, or any consequence of any of these.

2. Loss caused by the nuclear hazard will not be considered loss caused by fire, explosion, or smoke, whether these perils are specifically named in or otherwise included within the Perils Insured Against.

3. This policy does not apply under Section **I** to loss caused directly or indirectly by nuclear hazard, except that direct loss by fire resulting from the nuclear hazard is covered.

O. Recovered Property

If you or we recover any property for which we have made payment under this policy, you or we will notify the other of the recovery. At your option, the property will be returned to or retained by you or it will become our property. If the recovered property is returned to or retained by you, the loss payment will be adjusted based on the amount you received for the recovered property.

P. Volcanic Eruption Period

One or more volcanic eruptions that occur within a 72-hour period will be considered as one volcanic eruption.

Q. Policy Period

This policy applies only to loss which occurs during the policy period.

R. Concealment Or Fraud

We provide coverage to no "insureds" under this policy if, whether before or after a loss, an "insured" has:

1. Intentionally concealed or misrepresented any material fact or circumstance;
2. Engaged in fraudulent conduct; or
3. Made false statements;

relating to this insurance.

S. Loss Payable Clause

If the Declarations shows a loss payee for certain listed insured personal property, the definition of "insured" is changed to include that loss payee with respect to that property.

If we decide to cancel or not renew this policy, that loss payee will be notified in writing.

SECTION II – LIABILITY COVERAGES

A. Coverage E – Personal Liability

If a claim is made or a suit is brought against an "insured" for damages because of "bodily injury" or "property damage" caused by an "occurrence" to which this coverage applies, we will:

1. Pay up to our limit of liability for the damages for which an "insured" is legally liable. Damages include prejudgment interest awarded against an "insured"; and

2. Provide a defense at our expense by counsel of our choice, even if the suit is groundless, false or fraudulent. We may investigate and settle any claim or suit that we decide is appropriate. Our duty to settle or defend ends when our limit of liability for the "occurrence" has been exhausted by payment of a judgment or settlement.

B. Coverage F – Medical Payments To Others

We will pay the necessary medical expenses that are incurred or medically ascertained within three years from the date of an accident causing "bodily injury". Medical expenses means reasonable charges for medical, surgical, x-ray, dental, ambulance, hospital, professional nursing, prosthetic devices and funeral services. This coverage does not apply to you or regular residents of your household except "residence employees". As to others, this coverage applies only:

1. To a person on the "insured location" with the permission of an "insured"; or

2. To a person off the "insured location", if the "bodily injury":

   a. Arises out of a condition on the "insured location" or the ways immediately adjoining;

   b. Is caused by the activities of an "insured";

   c. Is caused by a "residence employee" in the course of the "residence employee's" employment by an "insured"; or

   d. Is caused by an animal owned by or in the care of an "insured".

SECTION II – EXCLUSIONS

A. "Motor Vehicle Liability"

1. Coverages **E** and **F** do not apply to any "motor vehicle liability" if, at the time and place of an "occurrence", the involved "motor vehicle":

   a. Is registered for use on public roads or property;

   b. Is not registered for use on public roads or property, but such registration is required by a law, or regulation issued by a government agency, for it to be used at the place of the "occurrence"; or

   c. Is being:

(1) Operated in, or practicing for, any prearranged or organized race, speed contest or other competition;

(2) Rented to others;

(3) Used to carry persons or cargo for a charge; or

(4) Used for any "business" purpose except for a motorized golf cart while on a golfing facility.

2. If Exclusion **A.1.** does not apply, there is still no coverage for "motor vehicle liability", unless the "motor vehicle" is:

a. In dead storage on an "insured location";

b. Used solely to service a residence;

c. Designed to assist the handicapped and, at the time of an "occurrence", it is:

(1) Being used to assist a handicapped person; or

(2) Parked on an "insured location";

d. Designed for recreational use off public roads and:

(1) Not owned by an "insured"; or

(2) Owned by an "insured" provided the "occurrence" takes place:

(a) On an "insured location" as defined in Definition **B.6.a., b., d., e.** or **h.**; or

(b) Off an "insured location" and the "motor vehicle" is:

(i) Designed as a toy vehicle for use by children under seven years of age;

(ii) Powered by one or more batteries; and

(iii) Not built or modified after manufacture to exceed a speed of five miles per hour on level ground;

e. A motorized golf cart that is owned by an "insured", designed to carry up to four persons, not built or modified after manufacture to exceed a speed of 25 miles per hour on level ground and, at the time of an "occurrence", is within the legal boundaries of:

(1) A golfing facility and is parked or stored there, or being used by an "insured" to:

(a) Play the game of golf or for other recreational or leisure activity allowed by the facility;

(b) Travel to or from an area where "motor vehicles" or golf carts are parked or stored; or

(c) Cross public roads at designated points to access other parts of the golfing facility; or

(2) A private residential community, including its public roads upon which a motorized golf cart can legally travel, which is subject to the authority of a property owners association and contains an "insured's" residence.

B. "Watercraft Liability"

1. Coverages **E** and **F** do not apply to any "watercraft liability" if, at the time of an "occurrence", the involved watercraft is being:

a. Operated in, or practicing for, any prearranged or organized race, speed contest or other competition. This exclusion does not apply to a sailing vessel or a predicted log cruise;

b. Rented to others;

c. Used to carry persons or cargo for a charge; or

d. Used for any "business" purpose.

2. If Exclusion **B.1.** does not apply, there is still no coverage for "watercraft liability" unless, at the time of the "occurrence", the watercraft:

a. Is stored;

b. Is a sailing vessel, with or without auxiliary power, that is:

(1) Less than 26 feet in overall length, or

(2) 26 feet or more in overall length and not owned by or rented to an "insured"; or

c. Is not a sailing vessel and is powered by:

(1) An inboard or inboard-outdrive engine or motor, including those that power a water jet pump, of:

(a) 50 horsepower or less and not owned by an "insured"; or

(b) More than 50 horsepower and not owned by or rented to an "insured"; or

(2) One or more outboard engines or motors with:

(a) 25 total horsepower or less;

(b) More than 25 horsepower if the outboard engine or motor is not owned by an "insured";

(c) More than 25 horsepower if the outboard engine or motor is owned by an "insured" who acquired it during the policy period; or

(d) More than 25 horsepower if the outboard engine or motor is owned by an "insured" who acquired it before the policy period, but only if:

(i) You declare them at policy inception; or

(ii) Your intent to insure them is reported to us in writing within 45 days after you acquire them.

The coverages in **(c)** and **(d)** above apply for the policy period.

Horsepower means the maximum power rating assigned to the engine or motor by the manufacturer.

C. "Aircraft Liability"
This policy does not cover "aircraft liability".

D. "Hovercraft Liability"
This policy does not cover "hovercraft liability".

E. Coverage E – Personal Liability And Coverage F – Medical Payments To Others
Coverages **E** and **F** do not apply to the following:

1. Expected Or Intended Injury
"Bodily injury" or "property damage" which is expected or intended by an "insured", even if the resulting "bodily injury" or "property damage":

a. Is of a different kind, quality or degree than initially expected or intended; or

b. Is sustained by a different person, entity or property than initially expected or intended.

However, this Exclusion **E.1.** does not apply to "bodily injury" or "property damage" resulting from the use of reasonable force by an "insured" to protect persons or property;

2. "Business"

a. "Bodily injury" or "property damage" arising out of or in connection with a "business" conducted from an "insured location" or engaged in by an "insured", whether or not the "business" is owned or operated by an "insured" or employs an "insured".

This Exclusion **E.2.** applies but is not limited to an act or omission, regardless of its nature or circumstance, involving a service or duty rendered, promised, owed, or implied to be provided because of the nature of the "business".

b. This Exclusion **E.2.** does not apply to:

(1) The rental or holding for rental of an "insured location";

(a) On an occasional basis if used only as a residence;

(b) In part for use only as a residence, unless a single-family unit is intended for use by the occupying family to lodge more than two roomers or boarders; or

(c) In part, as an office, school, studio or private garage; and

(2) An "insured" under the age of 21 years involved in a part-time or occasional, self-employed "business" with no employees;

3. Professional Services
"Bodily injury" or "property damage" arising out of the rendering of or failure to render professional services;

4. "Insured's" Premises Not An "Insured Location"
"Bodily injury" or "property damage" arising out of a premises:

a. Owned by an "insured";

b. Rented to an "insured"; or

c. Rented to others by an "insured";
that is not an "insured location";

5. War
"Bodily injury" or "property damage" caused directly or indirectly by war, including the following and any consequence of any of the following:

a. Undeclared war, civil war, insurrection, rebellion or revolution;

b. Warlike act by a military force or military personnel; or

c. Destruction, seizure or use for a military purpose.

Discharge of a nuclear weapon will be deemed a warlike act even if accidental;

6. Communicable Disease
"Bodily injury" or "property damage" which arises out of the transmission of a communicable disease by an "insured";

7. Sexual Molestation, Corporal Punishment Or Physical Or Mental Abuse
"Bodily injury" or "property damage" arising out of sexual molestation, corporal punishment or physical or mental abuse; or

8. Controlled Substance
"Bodily injury" or "property damage" arising out of the use, sale, manufacture, delivery, transfer or possession by any person of a Controlled Substance as defined by the Federal Food and Drug Law at 21 U.S.C.A. Sections 811 and 812. Controlled Substances include but are not limited to cocaine, LSD, marijuana and all narcotic drugs. However, this exclusion does not apply to the legitimate use of prescription drugs by a person following the lawful orders of a licensed health care professional.

Exclusions **A.** "Motor Vehicle Liability", **B.** "Watercraft Liability", **C.** "Aircraft Liability", **D.** "Hovercraft Liability" and **E.4.** "Insured's" Premises Not An "Insured Location" do not apply to "bodily injury" to a "residence employee" arising out of and in the course of the "residence employee's" employment by an "insured".

F. Coverage E – Personal Liability
Coverage **E** does not apply to:

1. Liability:

a. For any loss assessment charged against you as a member of an association, corporation or community of property owners, except as provided in **D.** Loss Assessment under Section **II** – Additional Coverages;

b. Under any contract or agreement entered into by an "insured". However, this exclusion does not apply to written contracts:

(1) That directly relate to the ownership, maintenance or use of an "insured location"; or

(2) Where the liability of others is assumed by you prior to an "occurrence";

unless excluded in **a.** above or elsewhere in this policy;

2. "Property damage" to property owned by an "insured". This includes costs or expenses incurred by an "insured" or others to repair, replace, enhance, restore or maintain such property to prevent injury to a person or damage to property of others, whether on or away from an "insured location";

3. "Property damage" to property rented to, occupied or used by or in the care of an "insured". This exclusion does not apply to "property damage" caused by fire, smoke or explosion;

4. "Bodily injury" to any person eligible to receive any benefits voluntarily provided or required to be provided by an "insured" under any:
   a. Workers' compensation law;
   b. Non-occupational disability law; or
   c. Occupational disease law;

5. "Bodily injury" or "property damage" for which an "insured" under this policy:
   a. Is also an insured under a nuclear energy liability policy issued by the:
      (1) Nuclear Energy Liability Insurance Association;
      (2) Mutual Atomic Energy Liability Underwriters;
      (3) Nuclear Insurance Association of Canada;
      or any of their successors; or
   b. Would be an insured under such a policy but for the exhaustion of its limit of liability; or

6. "Bodily injury" to you or an "insured" as defined under Definition **5.a.** or **b.**

   This exclusion also applies to any claim made or suit brought against you or an "insured" to:
   a. Repay; or
   b. Share damages with;
   another person who may be obligated to pay damages because of "bodily injury" to an "insured".

G. Coverage F – Medical Payments To Others
Coverage **F** does not apply to "bodily injury":
1. To a "residence employee" if the "bodily injury":
   a. Occurs off the "insured location"; and
   b. Does not arise out of or in the course of the "residence employee's" employment by an "insured";

2. To any person eligible to receive benefits voluntarily provided or required to be provided under any:
   a. Workers' compensation law;
   b. Non-occupational disability law; or
   c. Occupational disease law;

3. From any:
   a. Nuclear reaction;
   b. Nuclear radiation; or

c. Radioactive contamination;
all whether controlled or uncontrolled or however caused; or
   d. Any consequence of any of these; or

4. To any person, other than a "residence employee" of an "insured", regularly residing on any part of the "insured location".

SECTION II – ADDITIONAL COVERAGES

We cover the following in addition to the limits of liability:
A. Claim Expenses
We pay:
1. Expenses we incur and costs taxed against an "insured" in any suit we defend;

2. Premiums on bonds required in a suit we defend, but not for bond amounts more than the Coverage **E** limit of liability. We need not apply for or furnish any bond;

3. Reasonable expenses incurred by an "insured" at our request, including actual loss of earnings (but not loss of other income) up to $250 per day, for assisting us in the investigation or defense of a claim or suit; and

4. Interest on the entire judgment which accrues after entry of the judgment and before we pay or tender, or deposit in court that part of the judgment which does not exceed the limit of liability that applies.

B. First Aid Expenses
We will pay expenses for first aid to others incurred by an "insured" for "bodily injury" covered under this policy. We will not pay for first aid to an "insured".

C. Damage To Property Of Others
1. We will pay, at replacement cost, up to $1,000 per "occurrence" for "property damage" to property of others caused by an "insured".

2. We will not pay for "property damage":
   a. To the extent of any amount recoverable under Section **I**;
   b. Caused intentionally by an "insured" who is 13 years of age or older;
   c. To property owned by an "insured";
   d. To property owned by or rented to a tenant of an "insured" or a resident in your household; or
   e. Arising out of:
      (1) A "business" engaged in by an "insured";
      (2) Any act or omission in connection with a premises owned, rented or controlled by an "insured", other than the "insured location"; or
      (3) The ownership, maintenance, occupancy, operation, use, loading or unloading of aircraft, hovercraft, watercraft or "motor vehicles".

This Exclusion **e.(3)** does not apply to a "motor vehicle" that:

   (a) Is designed for recreational use off public roads;

   (b) Is not owned by an "insured"; and

   (c) At the time of the "occurrence", is not required by law, or regulation issued by a government agency, to have been registered for it to be used on public roads or property.

D. Loss Assessment

  1. We will pay up to $1,000 for your share of loss assessment charged against you, as owner or tenant of the "residence premises", during the policy period by a corporation or association of property owners, when the assessment is made as a result of:

   a. "Bodily injury" or "property damage" not excluded from coverage under Section **II** – Exclusions; or

   b. Liability for an act of a director, officer or trustee in the capacity as a director, officer or trustee, provided such person:

     (1) Is elected by the members of a corporation or association of property owners; and

     (2) Serves without deriving any income from the exercise of duties which are solely on behalf of a corporation or association of property owners.

  2. Paragraph **I.** Policy Period under Section **II** – Conditions does not apply to this Loss Assessment Coverage.

  3. Regardless of the number of assessments, the limit of $1,000 is the most we will pay for loss arising out of:

   a. One accident, including continuous or repeated exposure to substantially the same general harmful condition; or

   b. A covered act of a director, officer or trustee. An act involving more than one director, officer or trustee is considered to be a single act.

  4. We do not cover assessments charged against you or a corporation or association of property owners by any governmental body.

SECTION II – CONDITIONS

A. Limit Of Liability

Our total liability under Coverage **E** for all damages resulting from any one "occurrence" will not be more than the Coverage **E** Limit Of Liability shown in the Declarations. This limit is the same regardless of the number of "insureds", claims made or persons injured. All "bodily injury" and "property damage" resulting from any one accident or from continuous or repeated exposure to substantially the same general harmful conditions shall be considered to be the result of one "occurrence".

Our total liability under Coverage **F** for all medical expense payable for "bodily injury" to one person as the result of one accident will not be more than the Coverage **F** Limit Of Liability shown in the Declarations.

B. Severability Of Insurance

This insurance applies separately to each "insured". This condition will not increase our limit of liability for any one "occurrence".

C. Duties After "Occurrence"

In case of an "occurrence", you or another "insured" will perform the following duties that apply. We have no duty to provide coverage under this policy if your failure to comply with the following duties is prejudicial to us. You will help us by seeing that these duties are performed:

  1. Give written notice to us or our agent as soon as is practical, which sets forth:

   a. The identity of the policy and the "named insured" shown in the Declarations;

   b. Reasonably available information on the time, place and circumstances of the "occurrence"; and

   c. Names and addresses of any claimants and witnesses;

  2. Cooperate with us in the investigation, settlement or defense of any claim or suit;

  3. Promptly forward to us every notice, demand, summons or other process relating to the "occurrence";

  4. At our request, help us:

   a. To make settlement;

   b. To enforce any right of contribution or indemnity against any person or organization who may be liable to an "insured";

   c. With the conduct of suits and attend hearings and trials; and

   d. To secure and give evidence and obtain the attendance of witnesses;

  5. With respect to **C.** Damage To Property Of Others under Section **II** – Additional Coverages, submit to us within 60 days after the loss a sworn statement of loss and show the damaged property, if in an "insured's" control;

  6. No "insured" shall, except at such "insured's" own cost, voluntarily make payment, assume obligation or incur expense other than for first aid to others at the time of the "bodily injury".

D. Duties Of An Injured Person – Coverage F – Medical Payments To Others

  1. The injured person or someone acting for the injured person will:

   a. Give us written proof of claim, under oath if required, as soon as is practical; and

b. Authorize us to obtain copies of medical reports and records.

2. The injured person will submit to a physical exam by a doctor of our choice when and as often as we reasonably require.

E. Payment Of Claim – Coverage F – Medical Payments To Others

Payment under this coverage is not an admission of liability by an "insured" or us.

F. Suit Against Us

1. No action can be brought against us unless there has been full compliance with all of the terms under this Section **II**.

2. No one will have the right to join us as a party to any action against an "insured".

3. Also, no action with respect to Coverage **E** can be brought against us until the obligation of such "insured" has been determined by final judgment or agreement signed by us.

G. Bankruptcy Of An "Insured"

Bankruptcy or insolvency of an "insured" will not relieve us of our obligations under this policy.

H. Other Insurance

This insurance is excess over other valid and collectible insurance except insurance written specifically to cover as excess over the limits of liability that apply in this policy.

I. Policy Period

This policy applies only to "bodily injury" or "property damage" which occurs during the policy period.

J. Concealment Or Fraud

We do not provide coverage to an "insured" who, whether before or after a loss, has:

1. Intentionally concealed or misrepresented any material fact or circumstance;

2. Engaged in fraudulent conduct; or

3. Made false statements;

relating to this insurance.

SECTIONS I AND II – CONDITIONS

A. Liberalization Clause

If we make a change which broadens coverage under this edition of our policy without additional premium charge, that change will automatically apply to your insurance as of the date we implement the change in your state, provided that this implementation date falls within 60 days prior to or during the policy period stated in the Declarations.

This Liberalization Clause does not apply to changes implemented with a general program revision that includes both broadenings and restrictions in coverage, whether that general program revision is implemented through introduction of:

1. A subsequent edition of this policy; or

2. An amendatory endorsement.

B. Waiver Or Change Of Policy Provisions

A waiver or change of a provision of this policy must be in writing by us to be valid. Our request for an appraisal or examination will not waive any of our rights.

C. Cancellation

1. You may cancel this policy at any time by returning it to us or by letting us know in writing of the date cancellation is to take effect.

2. We may cancel this policy only for the reasons stated below by letting you know in writing of the date cancellation takes effect. This cancellation notice may be delivered to you, or mailed to you at your mailing address shown in the Declarations. Proof of mailing will be sufficient proof of notice.

a. When you have not paid the premium, we may cancel at any time by letting you know at least 10 days before the date cancellation takes effect.

b. When this policy has been in effect for less than 60 days and is not a renewal with us, we may cancel for any reason by letting you know at least 10 days before the date cancellation takes effect.

c. When this policy has been in effect for 60 days or more, or at any time if it is a renewal with us, we may cancel:

(1) If there has been a material misrepresentation of fact which if known to us would have caused us not to issue the policy; or

(2) If the risk has changed substantially since the policy was issued.

This can be done by letting you know at least 30 days before the date cancellation takes effect.

d. When this policy is written for a period of more than one year, we may cancel for any reason at anniversary by letting you know at least 30 days before the date cancellation takes effect.

3. When this policy is canceled, the premium for the period from the date of cancellation to the expiration date will be refunded pro rata.

4. If the return premium is not refunded with the notice of cancellation or when this policy is returned to us, we will refund it within a reasonable time after the date cancellation takes effect.

D. Nonrenewal

We may elect not to renew this policy. We may do so by delivering to you, or mailing to you at your mailing address shown in the Declarations, written notice at least 30 days before the expiration date of this policy. Proof of mailing will be sufficient proof of notice.

E. Assignment

Assignment of this policy will not be valid unless we give our written consent.

F. Subrogation

An "insured" may waive in writing before a loss all rights of recovery against any person. If not waived, we may require an assignment of rights of recovery for a loss to the extent that payment is made by us.

If an assignment is sought, an "insured" must sign and deliver all related papers and cooperate with us.

Subrogation does not apply to Coverage **F** or Paragraph **C.** Damage To Property Of Others under Section **II** – Additional Coverages.

G. Death

If any person named in the Declarations or the spouse, if a resident of the same household, dies, the following apply:

1. We insure the legal representative of the deceased but only with respect to the premises and property of the deceased covered under the policy at the time of death; and
2. "Insured" includes:
   a. An "insured" who is a member of your household at the time of your death, but only while a resident of the "residence premises"; and
   b. With respect to your property, the person having proper temporary custody of the property until appointment and qualification of a legal representative.

© Insurance Services Office, Inc., 2010   HO 00 03 05 11

APPENDIX C

Commercial General Liability Policy

This appendix includes...

- Commercial General Liability Declarations Page (CG DS 01 10 01)
- Commercial General Liability Coverage Form (CG 00 01 12 07)

Reprinted with the permission of Insurance Services Office, Inc.

POLICY NUMBER:

COMMERCIAL GENERAL LIABILITY
CG DS 01 10 01

COMMERCIAL GENERAL LIABILITY DECLARATIONS

ABCD INSURANCE COMPANY	**JON'S CAFÉ, INCORPORATED**

NAMED INSURED: __Jon's Café__

MAILING ADDRESS: __22 Restaurant Plaza__

__Anytown, USA__

POLICY PERIOD: FROM __1/2/2012__ TO __1/2/2013__ AT 12:01 A.M. TIME AT YOUR MAILING ADDRESS SHOWN ABOVE

IN RETURN FOR THE PAYMENT OF THE PREMIUM, AND SUBJECT TO ALL THE TERMS OF THIS POLICY, WE AGREE WITH YOU TO PROVIDE THE INSURANCE AS STATED IN THIS POLICY.

LIMITS OF INSURANCE		
EACH OCCURRENCE LIMIT	$ 1,000,000	
DAMAGE TO PREMISES RENTED TO YOU LIMIT	$ 100,000	Any one premises
MEDICAL EXPENSE LIMIT	$ 5,000	Any one person
PERSONAL & ADVERTISING INJURY LIMIT	$ 1,000,000	Any one person or organization
GENERAL AGGREGATE LIMIT		$ 2,000,000
PRODUCTS/COMPLETED OPERATIONS AGGREGATE LIMIT		$ 2,000,000

RETROACTIVE DATE (CG 00 02 ONLY)
THIS INSURANCE DOES NOT APPLY TO "BODILY INJURY", "PROPERTY DAMAGE" OR "PERSONAL AND ADVERTISING INJURY" WHICH OCCURS BEFORE THE RETROACTIVE DATE, IF ANY, SHOWN BELOW. RETROACTIVE DATE: _____ (ENTER DATE OR "NONE" IF NO RETROACTIVE DATE APPLIES)

DESCRIPTION OF BUSINESS
FORM OF BUSINESS:
☐ INDIVIDUAL ☐ PARTNERSHIP ☐ JOINT VENTURE ☐ TRUST
☐ LIMITED LIABILITY COMPANY ☒ ORGANIZATION, INCLUDING A CORPORATION (BUT NOT INCLUDING A PARTNERSHIP, JOINT VENTURE OR LIMITED LIABILITY COMPANY)
BUSINESS DESCRIPTION: __Restaurant, Table service, No Alcohol__

© ISO Properties, Inc., 2000   CG DS 01 10 01

ALL PREMISES YOU OWN, RENT OR OCCUPY	
LOCATION NUMBER	ADDRESS OF ALL PREMISES YOU OWN, RENT OR OCCUPY
1	22 Restaurant Plaza Anytown, USA

CLASSIFICATION AND PREMIUM							
LOCATION NUMBER	CLASSIFICATION	CODE NO.	PREMIUM BASE	RATE		ADVANCE PREMIUM	
				Prem/ Ops	Prod/Comp Ops	Prem/ Ops	Prod/Comp Ops
1	Restaurant	16900	$1,000,000 (gross sales)	$4.100	$0.261	$4100	$261

	STATE TAX OR OTHER (if applicable) $ _____
	TOTAL PREMIUM (SUBJECT TO AUDIT) $ _4361_____
PREMIUM SHOWN IS PAYABLE:	AT INCEPTION $ _xxx_____
	AT EACH ANNIVERSARY $ _____
	(IF POLICY PERIOD IS MORE THAN ONE YEAR AND PREMIUM IS PAID IN ANNUAL INSTALLMENTS)
AUDIT PERIOD (IF APPLICABLE)	☒ ANNUALLY ☐ SEMI-ANNUALLY ☐ QUARTERLY ☐ MONTHLY

ENDORSEMENTS
ENDORSEMENTS ATTACHED TO THIS POLICY:

THESE DECLARATIONS, TOGETHER WITH THE COMMON POLICY CONDITIONS AND COVERAGE FORM(S) AND ANY ENDORSEMENT(S), COMPLETE THE ABOVE NUMBERED POLICY.

Countersigned:	1/2/2012	By:	Ann Agent
	(Date)		(Authorized Representative)

NOTE
OFFICERS' FACSIMILE SIGNATURES MAY BE INSERTED HERE, ON THE POLICY COVER OR ELSEWHERE AT THE COMPANY'S OPTION.

COMMERCIAL GENERAL LIABILITY COVERAGE FORM

Various provisions in this policy restrict coverage. Read the entire policy carefully to determine rights, duties and what is and is not covered.

Throughout this policy the words "you" and "your" refer to the Named Insured shown in the Declarations, and any other person or organization qualifying as a Named Insured under this policy. The words "we", "us" and "our" refer to the company providing this insurance.

The word "insured" means any person or organization qualifying as such under Section **II** – Who Is An Insured. Other words and phrases that appear in quotation marks have special meaning. Refer to Section **V** –Definitions.

SECTION I – COVERAGES

COVERAGE A BODILY INJURY AND PROPERTY DAMAGE LIABILITY

1. **Insuring Agreement**
   a. We will pay those sums that the insured becomes legally obligated to pay as damages because of "bodily injury" or "property damage" to which this insurance applies. We will have the right and duty to defend the insured against any "suit" seeking those damages. However, we will have no duty to defend the insured against any "suit" seeking damages for "bodily injury" or "property damage" to which this insurance does not apply. We may, at our discretion, investigate any "occurrence" and settle any claim or "suit" that may result. But:
      (1) The amount we will pay for damages is limited as described in Section **III** – Limits Of Insurance; and
      (2) Our right and duty to defend ends when we have used up the applicable limit of insurance in the payment of judgments or settlements under Coverages **A** or **B** or medical expenses under Coverage **C.**
      No other obligation or liability to pay sums or perform acts or services is covered unless explicitly provided for under Supplementary Payments – Coverages **A** and **B.**
   b. This insurance applies to "bodily injury" and "property damage" only if:
      (1) The "bodily injury" or "property damage" is caused by an "occurrence" that takes place in the "coverage territory";

(2) The "bodily injury" or "property damage" occurs during the policy period; and
(3) Prior to the policy period, no insured listed under Paragraph **1.** of Section **II** – Who Is An Insured and no "employee" authorized by you to give or receive notice of an "occurrence" or claim, knew that the "bodily injury" or "property damage" had occurred, in whole or in part. If such a listed insured or authorized "employee" knew, prior to the policy period, that the "bodily injury" or "property damage" occurred, then any continuation, change or resumption of such "bodily injury" or "property damage" during or after the policy period will be deemed to have been known prior to the policy period.
c. "Bodily injury" or "property damage" which occurs during the policy period and was not, prior to the policy period, known to have occurred by any insured listed under Paragraph **1.** of Section **II** – Who Is An Insured or any "employee" authorized by you to give or receive notice of an "occurrence" or claim, includes any continuation, change or resumption of that "bodily injury" or "property damage" after the end of the policy period.
d. "Bodily injury" or "property damage" will be deemed to have been known to have occurred at the earliest time when any insured listed under Paragraph **1.** of Section **II** – Who Is An Insured or any "employee" authorized by you to give or receive notice of an "occurrence" or claim:
   (1) Reports all, or any part, of the "bodily injury" or "property damage" to us or any other insurer;
   (2) Receives a written or verbal demand or claim for damages because of the "bodily injury" or "property damage"; or
   (3) Becomes aware by any other means that "bodily injury" or "property damage" has occurred or has begun to occur.
e. Damages because of "bodily injury" include damages claimed by any person or organization for care, loss of services or death resulting at any time from the "bodily injury".

2. **Exclusions**
   This insurance does not apply to:
   a. **Expected Or Intended Injury**
      "Bodily injury" or "property damage" expected or intended from the standpoint of the insured. This

exclusion does not apply to "bodily injury" resulting from the use of reasonable force to protect persons or property.

b. Contractual Liability

"Bodily injury" or "property damage" for which the insured is obligated to pay damages by reason of the assumption of liability in a contract or agreement. This exclusion does not apply to liability for damages:

(1) That the insured would have in the absence of the contract or agreement; or

(2) Assumed in a contract or agreement that is an "insured contract", provided the "bodily injury" or "property damage" occurs subsequent to the execution of the contract or agreement. Solely for the purposes of liability assumed in an "insured contract", reasonable attorney fees and necessary litigation expenses incurred by or for a party other than an insured are deemed to be damages because of "bodily injury" or "property damage", provided:

(a) Liability to such party for, or for the cost of, that party's defense has also been assumed in the same "insured contract"; and

(b) Such attorney fees and litigation expenses are for defense of that party against a civil or alternative dispute resolution proceeding in which damages to which this insurance applies are alleged.

c. Liquor Liability

"Bodily injury" or "property damage" for which any insured may be held liable by reason of:

(1) Causing or contributing to the intoxication of any person;

(2) The furnishing of alcoholic beverages to a person under the legal drinking age or under the influence of alcohol; or

(3) Any statute, ordinance or regulation relating to the sale, gift, distribution or use of alcoholic beverages.

This exclusion applies only if you are in the business of manufacturing, distributing, selling, serving or furnishing alcoholic beverages.

d. Workers' Compensation And Similar Laws

Any obligation of the insured under a workers' compensation, disability benefits or unemployment compensation law or any similar law.

e. Employer's Liability

"Bodily injury" to:

(1) An "employee" of the insured arising out of and in the course of:

(a) Employment by the insured; or

(b) Performing duties related to the conduct of the insured's business; or

(2) The spouse, child, parent, brother or sister of that "employee" as a consequence of Paragraph **(1)** above.

This exclusion applies whether the insured may be liable as an employer or in any other capacity and to any obligation to share damages with or repay someone else who must pay damages because of the injury.

This exclusion does not apply to liability assumed by the insured under an "insured contract".

f. Pollution

(1) "Bodily injury" or "property damage" arising out of the actual, alleged or threatened discharge, dispersal, seepage, migration, release or escape of "pollutants":

(a) At or from any premises, site or location which is or was at any time owned or occupied by, or rented or loaned to, any insured. However, this subparagraph does not apply to:

(i) "Bodily injury" if sustained within a building and caused by smoke, fumes, vapor or soot produced by or originating from equipment that is used to heat, cool or dehumidify the building, or equipment that is used to heat water for personal use, by the building's occupants or their guests;

(ii) "Bodily injury" or "property damage" for which you may be held liable, if you are a contractor and the owner or lessee of such premises, site or location has been added to your policy as an additional insured with respect to your ongoing operations performed for that additional insured at that premises, site or location and such premises, site or location is not and never was owned or occupied by, or rented or loaned to, any insured, other than that additional insured; or

(iii) "Bodily injury" or "property damage" arising out of heat, smoke or fumes from a "hostile fire";

(b) At or from any premises, site or location which is or was at any time used by or for any insured or others for the handling, storage, disposal, processing or treatment of waste;

(c) Which are or were at any time transported, handled, stored, treated, disposed of, or processed as waste by or for:

(i) Any insured; or

(ii) Any person or organization for whom you may be legally responsible; or

(d) At or from any premises, site or location on which any insured or any contractors or subcontractors working directly or indirectly on any insured's behalf are performing operations if the "pollutants" are brought on or to the premises, site or location in connection with such operations by such insured, contractor or subcontractor. However, this subparagraph does not apply to:

(i) "Bodily injury" or "property damage" arising out of the escape of fuels, lubricants or other operating fluids which are needed to perform the normal electrical, hydraulic or mechanical functions necessary for the operation of "mobile equipment" or its parts, if such fuels, lubricants or other operating fluids escape from a vehicle part designed to hold, store or receive them. This exception does not apply if the "bodily injury" or "property damage" arises out of the intentional discharge, dispersal or release of the fuels, lubricants or other operating fluids, or if such fuels, lubricants or other operating fluids are brought on or to the premises, site or location with the intent that they be discharged, dispersed or released as part of the operations being performed by such insured, contractor or subcontractor;

(ii) "Bodily injury" or "property damage" sustained within a building and caused by the release of gases, fumes or vapors from materials brought into that building in connection with operations being performed by you or on your behalf by a contractor or subcontractor; or

(iii) "Bodily injury" or "property damage" arising out of heat, smoke or fumes from a "hostile fire".

(e) At or from any premises, site or location on which any insured or any contractors or subcontractors working directly or indirectly on any insured's behalf are performing operations if the operations are to test for, monitor, clean up, remove, contain, treat, detoxify or neutralize, or in any way respond to, or assess the effects of, "pollutants".

(2) Any loss, cost or expense arising out of any:

(a) Request, demand, order or statutory or regulatory requirement that any insured or others test for, monitor, clean up, remove, contain, treat, detoxify or neutralize, or in any way respond to, or assess the effects of, "pollutants"; or

(b) Claim or "suit" by or on behalf of a governmental authority for damages because of testing for, monitoring, cleaning up, removing, containing, treating, detoxifying or neutralizing, or in any way responding to, or assessing the effects of, "pollutants".

However, this paragraph does not apply to liability for damages because of "property damage" that the insured would have in the absence of such request, demand, order or statutory or regulatory requirement, or such claim or "suit" by or on behalf of a governmental authority.

g. Aircraft, Auto Or Watercraft

"Bodily injury" or "property damage" arising out of the ownership, maintenance, use or entrustment to others of any aircraft, "auto" or watercraft owned or operated by or rented or loaned to any insured. Use includes operation and "loading or unloading".

This exclusion applies even if the claims against any insured allege negligence or other wrongdoing in the supervision, hiring, employment, training or monitoring of others by that insured, if the "occurrence" which caused the "bodily injury" or "property damage" involved the ownership, maintenance, use or entrustment to others of any aircraft, "auto" or watercraft that is owned or operated by or rented or loaned to any insured.

This exclusion does not apply to:

(1) A watercraft while ashore on premises you own or rent;

(2) A watercraft you do not own that is:

(a) Less than 26 feet long; and

(b) Not being used to carry persons or property for a charge;

(3) Parking an "auto" on, or on the ways next to, premises you own or rent, provided the "auto" is not owned by or rented or loaned to you or the insured;

(4) Liability assumed under any "insured contract" for the ownership, maintenance or use of aircraft or watercraft; or

(5) "Bodily injury" or "property damage" arising out of:

(a) The operation of machinery or equipment that is attached to, or part of, a land vehicle that would qualify under the definition of "mobile equipment" if it were not subject to a compulsory or financial responsibility law or other motor vehicle insurance law in the state where it is licensed or principally garaged; or

(b) the operation of any of the machinery or equipment listed in Paragraph **f.(2)** or **f.(3)** of the definition of "mobile equipment".

h. Mobile Equipment

"Bodily injury" or "property damage" arising out of:

(1) The transportation of "mobile equipment" by an "auto" owned or operated by or rented or loaned to any insured; or

(2) The use of "mobile equipment" in, or while in practice for, or while being prepared for, any prearranged racing, speed, demolition, or stunting activity.

i. War

"Bodily injury" or "property damage", however caused, arising, directly or indirectly, out of:

(1) War, including undeclared or civil war;

(2) Warlike action by a military force, including action in hindering or defending against an actual or expected attack, by any government, sovereign or other authority using military personnel or other agents; or

(3) Insurrection, rebellion, revolution, usurped power, or action taken by governmental authority in hindering or defending against any of these.

j. Damage To Property

"Property damage" to:

(1) Property you own, rent, or occupy, including any costs or expenses incurred by you, or any other person, organization or entity, for repair, replacement, enhancement, restoration or maintenance of such property for any reason, including prevention of injury to a person or damage to another's property;

(2) Premises you sell, give away or abandon, if the "property damage" arises out of any part of those premises;

(3) Property loaned to you;

(4) Personal property in the care, custody or control of the insured;

(5) That particular part of real property on which you or any contractors or subcontractors working directly or indirectly on your behalf are performing operations, if the "property damage" arises out of those operations; or

(6) That particular part of any property that must be restored, repaired or replaced because "your work" was incorrectly performed on it.

Paragraphs **(1)**, **(3)** and **(4)** of this exclusion do not apply to "property damage" (other than damage by fire) to premises, including the contents of such premises, rented to you for a period of 7 or fewer consecutive days. A separate limit of insurance applies to Damage To Premises Rented To You as described in Section **III** – Limits Of Insurance.

Paragraph **(2)** of this exclusion does not apply if the premises are "your work" and were never occupied, rented or held for rental by you.

Paragraphs **(3)**, **(4)**, **(5)** and **(6)** of this exclusion do not apply to liability assumed under a sidetrack agreement.

Paragraph **(6)** of this exclusion does not apply to "property damage" included in the "products-completed operations hazard".

k. Damage To Your Product

"Property damage" to "your product" arising out of it or any part of it.

l. Damage To Your Work

"Property damage" to "your work" arising out of it or any part of it and included in the "products-completed operations hazard".

This exclusion does not apply if the damaged work or the work out of which the damage arises was performed on your behalf by a subcontractor.

m. Damage To Impaired Property Or Property Not Physically Injured

"Property damage" to "impaired property" or property that has not been physically injured, arising out of:

(1) A defect, deficiency, inadequacy or dangerous condition in "your product" or "your work"; or

(2) A delay or failure by you or anyone acting on your behalf to perform a contract or agreement in accordance with its terms.

This exclusion does not apply to the loss of use of other property arising out of sudden and accidental physical injury to "your product" or "your work" after it has been put to its intended use.

n. Recall Of Products, Work Or Impaired Property

Damages claimed for any loss, cost or expense incurred by you or others for the loss of use, withdrawal, recall, inspection, repair, replacement, adjustment, removal or disposal of:

(1) "Your product";

(2) "Your work"; or

(3) "Impaired property";

if such product, work, or property is withdrawn or recalled from the market or from use by any person or organization because of a known or suspected defect, deficiency, inadequacy or dangerous condition in it.

o. Personal And Advertising Injury

"Bodily injury" arising out of "personal and advertising injury".

p. Electronic Data

Damages arising out of the loss of, loss of use of, damage to, corruption of, inability to access, or inability to manipulate electronic data.

As used in this exclusion, electronic data means information, facts or programs stored as or on, created or used on, or transmitted to or from computer software, including systems and applications software, hard or floppy disks, CD-ROMS, tapes, drives, cells, data processing devices or any other media which are used with electronically controlled equipment.

q. Distribution Of Material In Violation Of Statutes

"Bodily injury" or "property damage" arising directly or indirectly out of any action or omission that violates or is alleged to violate:

(1) The Telephone Consumer Protection Act (TCPA), including any amendment of or addition to such law; or

(2) The CAN-SPAM Act of 2003, including any amendment of or addition to such law; or

(3) Any statute, ordinance or regulation, other than the TCPA or CAN-SPAM Act of 2003, that prohibits or limits the sending, transmitting, communicating or distribution of material or information.

Exclusions **c.** through **n.** do not apply to damage by fire to premises while rented to you or temporarily occupied by you with permission of the owner. A separate limit of insurance applies to this coverage as described in Section **III** – Limits Of Insurance.

COVERAGE B PERSONAL AND ADVERTISING INJURY LIABILITY

1. Insuring Agreement

a. We will pay those sums that the insured becomes legally obligated to pay as damages because of "personal and advertising injury" to which this insurance applies. We will have the right and duty to defend the insured against any "suit" seeking those damages. However, we will have no duty to defend the insured against any "suit" seeking damages for "personal and advertising injury" to which this insurance does not apply. We may, at our discretion, investigate any offense and settle any claim or "suit" that may result. But:

(1) The amount we will pay for damages is limited as described in Section **III** – Limits Of Insurance; and

(2) Our right and duty to defend end when we have used up the applicable limit of insurance in the payment of judgments or settlements under Coverages **A** or **B** or medical expenses under Coverage **C.**

No other obligation or liability to pay sums or perform acts or services is covered unless explicitly provided for under Supplementary Payments – Coverages **A** and **B.**

b. This insurance applies to "personal and advertising injury" caused by an offense arising out of your business but only if the offense was committed in the "coverage territory" during the policy period.

2. Exclusions

This insurance does not apply to:

a. Knowing Violation Of Rights Of Another

"Personal and advertising injury" caused by or at the direction of the insured with the knowledge that the act would violate the rights of another and would inflict "personal and advertising injury".

b. Material Published With Knowledge Of Falsity

"Personal and advertising injury" arising out of oral or written publication of material, if done by or at the direction of the insured with knowledge of its falsity.

c. Material Published Prior To Policy Period

"Personal and advertising injury" arising out of oral or written publication of material whose first publication took place before the beginning of the policy period.

d. Criminal Acts

"Personal and advertising injury" arising out of a criminal act committed by or at the direction of the insured.

e. Contractual Liability

"Personal and advertising injury" for which the insured has assumed liability in a contract or agreement. This exclusion does not apply to liability for damages that the insured would have in the absence of the contract or agreement.

f. Breach Of Contract

"Personal and advertising injury" arising out of a breach of contract, except an implied contract to use another's advertising idea in your "advertisement".

g. Quality Or Performance Of Goods – Failure To Conform To Statements

"Personal and advertising injury" arising out of the failure of goods, products or services to conform with any statement of quality or performance made in your "advertisement".

h. Wrong Description Of Prices

"Personal and advertising injury" arising out of the wrong description of the price of goods, products or services stated in your "advertisement".

i. Infringement Of Copyright, Patent, Trademark Or Trade Secret

"Personal and advertising injury" arising out of the infringement of copyright, patent, trademark, trade secret or other intellectual property rights. Under this exclusion, such other intellectual property rights do not include the use of another's advertising idea in your "advertisement".

However, this exclusion does not apply to infringement, in your "advertisement", of copyright, trade dress or slogan.

j. Insureds In Media And Internet Type Businesses
"Personal and advertising injury" committed by an insured whose business is:
(1) Advertising, broadcasting, publishing or telecasting;
(2) Designing or determining content of web-sites for others; or
(3) An Internet search, access, content or service provider.

However, this exclusion does not apply to Paragraphs **14.a., b.** and **c.** of "personal and advertising injury" under the Definitions Section.

For the purposes of this exclusion, the placing of frames, borders or links, or advertising, for you or others anywhere on the Internet, is not by itself, considered the business of advertising, broadcasting, publishing or telecasting.

k. Electronic Chatrooms Or Bulletin Boards
"Personal and advertising injury" arising out of an electronic chatroom or bulletin board the insured hosts, owns, or over which the insured exercises control.

l. Unauthorized Use Of Another's Name Or Product
"Personal and advertising injury" arising out of the unauthorized use of another's name or product in your e-mail address, domain name or metatag, or any other similar tactics to mislead another's potential customers.

m. Pollution
"Personal and advertising injury" arising out of the actual, alleged or threatened discharge, dispersal, seepage, migration, release or escape of "pollutants" at any time.

n. Pollution-Related
Any loss, cost or expense arising out of any:
(1) Request, demand, order or statutory or regulatory requirement that any insured or others test for, monitor, clean up, remove, contain, treat, detoxify or neutralize, or in any way respond to, or assess the effects of, "pollutants"; or
(2) Claim or suit by or on behalf of a governmental authority for damages because of testing for, monitoring, cleaning up, removing, containing, treating, detoxifying or neutralizing, or in any way responding to, or assessing the effects of, "pollutants".

o. War
"Personal and advertising injury", however caused, arising, directly or indirectly, out of:
(1) War, including undeclared or civil war;
(2) Warlike action by a military force, including action in hindering or defending against an actual or expected attack, by any government, sovereign or other authority using military personnel or other agents; or

(3) Insurrection, rebellion, revolution, usurped power, or action taken by governmental authority in hindering or defending against any of these.

p. Distribution Of Material In Violation Of Statutes
"Personal and advertising injury" arising directly or indirectly out of any action or omission that violates or is alleged to violate:
(1) The Telephone Consumer Protection Act (TCPA), including any amendment of or addition to such law; or
(2) The CAN-SPAM Act of 2003, including any amendment of or addition to such law; or
(3) Any statute, ordinance or regulation, other than the TCPA or CAN-SPAM Act of 2003, that prohibits or limits the sending, transmitting, communicating or distribution of material or information.

COVERAGE C MEDICAL PAYMENTS

1. Insuring Agreement
a. We will pay medical expenses as described below for "bodily injury" caused by an accident:
(1) On premises you own or rent;
(2) On ways next to premises you own or rent; or
(3) Because of your operations;
provided that:
(a) The accident takes place in the "coverage territory" and during the policy period;
(b) The expenses are incurred and reported to us within one year of the date of the accident; and
(c) The injured person submits to examination, at our expense, by physicians of our choice as often as we reasonably require.
b. We will make these payments regardless of fault. These payments will not exceed the applicable limit of insurance. We will pay reasonable expenses for:
(1) First aid administered at the time of an accident;
(2) Necessary medical, surgical, x-ray and dental services, including prosthetic devices; and
(3) Necessary ambulance, hospital, professional nursing and funeral services.

2. Exclusions
We will not pay expenses for "bodily injury":
a. Any Insured
To any insured, except "volunteer workers".
b. Hired Person
To a person hired to do work for or on behalf of any insured or a tenant of any insured.
c. Injury On Normally Occupied Premises
To a person injured on that part of premises you own or rent that the person normally occupies.

d. **Workers Compensation And Similar Laws**
   To a person, whether or not an "employee" of any insured, if benefits for the "bodily injury" are payable or must be provided under a workers' compensation or disability benefits law or a similar law.

e. **Athletics Activities**
   To a person injured while practicing, instructing or participating in any physical exercises or games, sports, or athletic contests.

f. **Products-Completed Operations Hazard**
   Included within the "products-completed operations hazard".

g. **Coverage A Exclusions**
   Excluded under Coverage **A**.

SUPPLEMENTARY PAYMENTS – COVERAGES A AND B

1. We will pay, with respect to any claim we investigate or settle, or any "suit" against an insured we defend:
   a. All expenses we incur.
   b. Up to $250 for cost of bail bonds required because of accidents or traffic law violations arising out of the use of any vehicle to which the Bodily Injury Liability Coverage applies. We do not have to furnish these bonds.
   c. The cost of bonds to release attachments, but only for bond amounts within the applicable limit of insurance. We do not have to furnish these bonds.
   d. All reasonable expenses incurred by the insured at our request to assist us in the investigation or defense of the claim or "suit", including actual loss of earnings up to $250 a day because of time off from work.
   e. All court costs taxed against the insured in the "suit". However, these payments do not include attorneys' fees or attorneys' expenses taxed against the insured.
   f. Prejudgment interest awarded against the insured on that part of the judgment we pay. If we make an offer to pay the applicable limit of insurance, we will not pay any prejudgment interest based on that period of time after the offer.
   g. All interest on the full amount of any judgment that accrues after entry of the judgment and before we have paid, offered to pay, or deposited in court the part of the judgment that is within the applicable limit of insurance.

   These payments will not reduce the limits of insurance.

2. If we defend an insured against a "suit" and an indemnitee of the insured is also named as a party to the "suit", we will defend that indemnitee if all of the following conditions are met:
   a. The "suit" against the indemnitee seeks damages for which the insured has assumed the liability of the indemnitee in a contract or agreement that is an "insured contract";
   b. This insurance applies to such liability assumed by the insured;
   c. The obligation to defend, or the cost of the defense of, that indemnitee, has also been assumed by the insured in the same "insured contract";
   d. The allegations in the "suit" and the information we know about the "occurrence" are such that no conflict appears to exist between the interests of the insured and the interests of the indemnitee;
   e. The indemnitee and the insured ask us to conduct and control the defense of that indemnitee against such "suit" and agree that we can assign the same counsel to defend the insured and the indemnitee; and
   f. The indemnitee:
      (1) Agrees in writing to:
         (a) Cooperate with us in the investigation, settlement or defense of the "suit";
         (b) Immediately send us copies of any demands, notices, summonses or legal papers received in connection with the "suit";
         (c) Notify any other insurer whose coverage is available to the indemnitee; and
         (d) Cooperate with us with respect to coordinating other applicable insurance available to the indemnitee; and
      (2) Provides us with written authorization to:
         (a) Obtain records and other information related to the "suit"; and
         (b) Conduct and control the defense of the indemnitee in such "suit".

   So long as the above conditions are met, attorneys' fees incurred by us in the defense of that indemnitee, necessary litigation expenses incurred by us and necessary litigation expenses incurred by the indemnitee at our request will be paid as Supplementary Payments. Notwithstanding the provisions of Paragraph **2.b.(2)** of Section **I** – Coverage **A** – Bodily Injury And Property Damage Liability, such payments will not be deemed to be damages for "bodily injury" and "property damage" and will not reduce the limits of insurance.

   Our obligation to defend an insured's indemnitee and to pay for attorneys' fees and necessary litigation expenses as Supplementary Payments ends when we have used up the applicable limit of insurance in the payment of judgments or settlements or the conditions set forth above, or the terms of the agreement described in Paragraph **f.** above, are no longer met.

         CG 00 01 12 07

SECTION II – WHO IS AN INSURED

1. If you are designated in the Declarations as:
   a. An individual, you and your spouse are insureds, but only with respect to the conduct of a business of which you are the sole owner.
   b. A partnership or joint venture, you are an insured. Your members, your partners, and their spouses are also insureds, but only with respect to the conduct of your business.
   c. A limited liability company, you are an insured. Your members are also insureds, but only with respect to the conduct of your business. Your managers are insureds, but only with respect to their duties as your managers.
   d. An organization other than a partnership, joint venture or limited liability company, you are an insured. Your "executive officers" and directors are insureds, but only with respect to their duties as your officers or directors. Your stockholders are also insureds, but only with respect to their liability as stockholders.
   e. A trust, you are an insured. Your trustees are also insureds, but only with respect to their duties as trustees.

2. Each of the following is also an insured:
   a. Your "volunteer workers" only while performing duties related to the conduct of your business, or your "employees", other than either your "executive officers" (if you are an organization other than a partnership, joint venture or limited liability company) or your managers (if you are a limited liability company), but only for acts within the scope of their employment by you or while performing duties related to the conduct of your business. However, none of these "employees" or "volunteer workers" are insureds for:
      (1) "Bodily injury" or "personal and advertising injury":
         (a) To you, to your partners or members (if you are a partnership or joint venture), to your members (if you are a limited liability company), to a co-"employee" while in the course of his or her employment or performing duties related to the conduct of your business, or to your other "volunteer workers" while performing duties related to the conduct of your business;
         (b) To the spouse, child, parent, brother or sister of that co-"employee" or "volunteer worker" as a consequence of Paragraph (1) (a) above;
         (c) For which there is any obligation to share damages with or repay someone else who must pay damages because of the injury described in Paragraphs (1)(a) or (b) above; or

   (d) Arising out of his or her providing or failing to provide professional health care services.
      (2) "Property damage" to property:
         (a) Owned, occupied or used by,
         (b) Rented to, in the care, custody or control of, or over which physical control is being exercised for any purpose by
      you, any of your "employees", "volunteer workers", any partner or member (if you are a partnership or joint venture), or any member (if you are a limited liability company).
   b. Any person (other than your "employee" or "volunteer worker"), or any organization while acting as your real estate manager.
   c. Any person or organization having proper temporary custody of your property if you die, but only:
      (1) With respect to liability arising out of the maintenance or use of that property; and
      (2) Until your legal representative has been appointed.
   d. Your legal representative if you die, but only with respect to duties as such. That representative will have all your rights and duties under this Coverage Part.

3. Any organization you newly acquire or form, other than a partnership, joint venture or limited liability company, and over which you maintain ownership or majority interest, will qualify as a Named Insured if there is no other similar insurance available to that organization. However:
   a. Coverage under this provision is afforded only until the 90th day after you acquire or form the organization or the end of the policy period, whichever is earlier;
   b. Coverage A does not apply to "bodily injury" or "property damage" that occurred before you acquired or formed the organization; and
   c. Coverage B does not apply to "personal and advertising injury" arising out of an offense committed before you acquired or formed the organization.

No person or organization is an insured with respect to the conduct of any current or past partnership, joint venture or limited liability company that is not shown as a Named Insured in the Declarations.

SECTION III – LIMITS OF INSURANCE

1. The Limits of Insurance shown in the Declarations and the rules below fix the most we will pay regardless of the number of:
   a. Insureds;
   b. Claims made or "suits" brought; or
   c. Persons or organizations making claims or bringing "suits".

2. The General Aggregate Limit is the most we will pay for the sum of:

   a. Medical expenses under Coverage **C;**

   b. Damages under Coverage **A,** except damages because of "bodily injury" or "property damage" included in the "products-completed operations hazard"; and

   c. Damages under Coverage **B.**

3. The Products-Completed Operations Aggregate Limit is the most we will pay under Coverage **A** for damages because of "bodily injury" and "property damage" included in the "products-completed operations hazard".

4. Subject to Paragraph **2.** above, the Personal and Advertising Injury Limit is the most we will pay under Coverage **B** for the sum of all damages because of all "personal and advertising injury" sustained by any one person or organization.

5. Subject to Paragraph **2.** or **3.** above, whichever applies, the Each Occurrence Limit is the most we will pay for the sum of:

   a. Damages under Coverage **A;** and

   b. Medical expenses under Coverage **C**

   because of all "bodily injury" and "property damage" arising out of any one "occurrence".

6. Subject to Paragraph **5.** above, the Damage To Premises Rented To You Limit is the most we will pay under Coverage **A** for damages because of "property damage" to any one premises, while rented to you, or in the case of damage by fire, while rented to you or temporarily occupied by you with permission of the owner.

7. Subject to Paragraph **5.** above, the Medical Expense Limit is the most we will pay under Coverage **C** for all medical expenses because of "bodily injury" sustained by any one person.

The Limits of Insurance of this Coverage Part apply separately to each consecutive annual period and to any remaining period of less than 12 months, starting with the beginning of the policy period shown in the Declarations, unless the policy period is extended after issuance for an additional period of less than 12 months. In that case, the additional period will be deemed part of the last preceding period for purposes of determining the Limits of Insurance.

SECTION IV – COMMERCIAL GENERAL LIABILITY CONDITIONS

1. **Bankruptcy**

   Bankruptcy or insolvency of the insured or of the insured's estate will not relieve us of our obligations under this Coverage Part.

2. **Duties In The Event Of Occurrence, Offense, Claim Or Suit**

   a. You must see to it that we are notified as soon as practicable of an "occurrence" or an offense which may result in a claim. To the extent possible, notice should include:

   (1) How, when and where the "occurrence" or offense took place;

   (2) The names and addresses of any injured persons and witnesses; and

   (3) The nature and location of any injury or damage arising out of the "occurrence" or offense.

   b. If a claim is made or "suit" is brought against any insured, you must:

   (1) Immediately record the specifics of the claim or "suit" and the date received; and

   (2) Notify us as soon as practicable.

   You must see to it that we receive written notice of the claim or "suit" as soon as practicable.

   c. You and any other involved insured must:

   (1) Immediately send us copies of any demands, notices, summonses or legal papers received in connection with the claim or "suit";

   (2) Authorize us to obtain records and other information;

   (3) Cooperate with us in the investigation or settlement of the claim or defense against the "suit"; and

   (4) Assist us, upon our request, in the enforcement of any right against any person or organization which may be liable to the insured because of injury or damage to which this insurance may also apply.

   d. No insured will, except at that insured's own cost, voluntarily make a payment, assume any obligation, or incur any expense, other than for first aid, without our consent.

3. **Legal Action Against Us**

   No person or organization has a right under this Coverage Part:

   a. To join us as a party or otherwise bring us into a "suit" asking for damages from an insured; or

   b. To sue us on this Coverage Part unless all of its terms have been fully complied with.

   A person or organization may sue us to recover on an agreed settlement or on a final judgment against an insured; but we will not be liable for damages that are not payable under the terms of this Coverage Part or that are in excess of the applicable limit of insurance. An agreed settlement means a settlement and release of liability signed by us, the insured and the claimant or the claimant's legal representative.

4. **Other Insurance**

   If other valid and collectible insurance is available to the insured for a loss we cover under Coverages **A** or **B** of this Coverage Part, our obligations are limited as follows:

   a. **Primary Insurance**

   This insurance is primary except when Paragraph **b.** below applies. If this insurance is primary, our obligations are not affected unless any of the other insurance is also primary. Then, we will share with all that other insurance by the method described in Paragraph **c.** below.

b. Excess Insurance

  (1) This insurance is excess over:

  (a) Any of the other insurance, whether primary, excess, contingent or on any other basis:

  (i) That is Fire, Extended Coverage, Builder's Risk, Installation Risk or similar coverage for "your work";

  (ii) That is Fire insurance for premises rented to you or temporarily occupied by you with permission of the owner;

  (iii) That is insurance purchased by you to cover your liability as a tenant for "property damage" to premises rented to you or temporarily occupied by you with permission of the owner; or

  (iv) If the loss arises out of the maintenance or use of aircraft, "autos" or watercraft to the extent not subject to Exclusion **g.** of Section **I** – Coverage **A** – Bodily Injury And Property Damage Liability.

  (b) Any other primary insurance available to you covering liability for damages arising out of the premises or operations, or the products and completed operations, for which you have been added as an additional insured by attachment of an endorsement.

  (2) When this insurance is excess, we will have no duty under Coverages **A** or **B** to defend the insured against any "suit" if any other insurer has a duty to defend the insured against that "suit". If no other insurer defends, we will undertake to do so, but we will be entitled to the insured's rights against all those other insurers.

  (3) When this insurance is excess over other insurance, we will pay only our share of the amount of the loss, if any, that exceeds the sum of:

  (a) The total amount that all such other insurance would pay for the loss in the absence of this insurance; and

  (b) The total of all deductible and self-insured amounts under all that other insurance.

  (4) We will share the remaining loss, if any, with any other insurance that is not described in this Excess Insurance provision and was not bought specifically to apply in excess of the Limits of Insurance shown in the Declarations of this Coverage Part.

c. Method Of Sharing

If all of the other insurance permits contribution by equal shares, we will follow this method also.

Under this approach each insurer contributes equal amounts until it has paid its applicable limit of insurance or none of the loss remains, whichever comes first.

If any of the other insurance does not permit contribution by equal shares, we will contribute by limits. Under this method, each insurer's share is based on the ratio of its applicable limit of insurance to the total applicable limits of insurance of all insurers.

5. Premium Audit

  a. We will compute all premiums for this Coverage Part in accordance with our rules and rates.

  b. Premium shown in this Coverage Part as advance premium is a deposit premium only. At the close of each audit period we will compute the earned premium for that period and send notice to the first Named Insured. The due date for audit and retrospective premiums is the date shown as the due date on the bill. If the sum of the advance and audit premiums paid for the policy period is greater than the earned premium, we will return the excess to the first Named Insured.

  c. The first Named Insured must keep records of the information we need for premium computation, and send us copies at such times as we may request.

6. Representations

By accepting this policy, you agree:

  a. The statements in the Declarations are accurate and complete;

  b. Those statements are based upon representations you made to us; and

  c. We have issued this policy in reliance upon your representations.

7. Separation Of Insureds

Except with respect to the Limits of Insurance, and any rights or duties specifically assigned in this Coverage Part to the first Named Insured, this insurance applies:

  a. As if each Named Insured were the only Named Insured; and

  b. Separately to each insured against whom claim is made or "suit" is brought.

8. Transfer Of Rights Of Recovery Against Others To Us

If the insured has rights to recover all or part of any payment we have made under this Coverage Part, those rights are transferred to us. The insured must do nothing after loss to impair them. At our request, the insured will bring "suit" or transfer those rights to us and help us enforce them.

9. When We Do Not Renew

If we decide not to renew this Coverage Part, we will mail or deliver to the first Named Insured shown in the Declarations written notice of the nonrenewal not less than 30 days before the expiration date.

If notice is mailed, proof of mailing will be sufficient proof of notice.

SECTION V – DEFINITIONS

1. "Advertisement" means a notice that is broadcast or published to the general public or specific market segments about your goods, products or services for the purpose of attracting customers or supporters. For the purposes of this definition:
   a. Notices that are published include material placed on the Internet or on similar electronic means of communication; and
   b. Regarding web-sites, only that part of a web-site that is about your goods, products or services for the purposes of attracting customers or supporters is considered an advertisement.
2. "Auto" means:
   a. A land motor vehicle, trailer or semitrailer designed for travel on public roads, including any attached machinery or equipment; or
   b. Any other land vehicle that is subject to a compulsory or financial responsibility law or other motor vehicle insurance law in the state where it is licensed or principally garaged.
   However, "auto" does not include "mobile equipment".
3. "Bodily injury" means bodily injury, sickness or disease sustained by a person, including death resulting from any of these at any time.
4. "Coverage territory" means:
   a. The United States of America (including its territories and possessions), Puerto Rico and Canada;
   b. International waters or airspace, but only if the injury or damage occurs in the course of travel or transportation between any places included in Paragraph **a.** above; or
   c. All other parts of the world if the injury or damage arises out of:
      (1) Goods or products made or sold by you in the territory described in Paragraph **a.** above;
      (2) The activities of a person whose home is in the territory described in Paragraph **a.** above, but is away for a short time on your business; or
      (3) "Personal and advertising injury" offenses that take place through the Internet or similar electronic means of communication
   provided the insured's responsibility to pay damages is determined in a "suit" on the merits, in the territory described in Paragraph a. above or in a settlement we agree to.
5. "Employee" includes a "leased worker". "Employee" does not include a "temporary worker".
6. "Executive officer" means a person holding any of the officer positions created by your charter, constitution, by-laws or any other similar governing document.

7. "Hostile fire" means one which becomes uncontrollable or breaks out from where it was intended to be.
8. "Impaired property" means tangible property, other than "your product" or "your work", that cannot be used or is less useful because:
   a. It incorporates "your product" or "your work" that is known or thought to be defective, deficient, inadequate or dangerous; or
   b. You have failed to fulfill the terms of a contract or agreement;
   if such property can be restored to use by the repair, replacement, adjustment or removal of "your product" or "your work" or your fulfilling the terms of the contract or agreement.
9. "Insured contract" means:
   a. A contract for a lease of premises. However, that portion of the contract for a lease of premises that indemnifies any person or organization for damage by fire to premises while rented to you or temporarily occupied by you with permission of the owner is not an "insured contract";
   b. A sidetrack agreement;
   c. Any easement or license agreement, except in connection with construction or demolition operations on or within 50 feet of a railroad;
   d. An obligation, as required by ordinance, to indemnify a municipality, except in connection with work for a municipality;
   e. An elevator maintenance agreement;
   f. That part of any other contract or agreement pertaining to your business (including an indemnification of a municipality in connection with work performed for a municipality) under which you assume the tort liability of another party to pay for "bodily injury" or "property damage" to a third person or organization. Tort liability means a liability that would be imposed by law in the absence of any contract or agreement.

   Paragraph **f.** does not include that part of any contract or agreement:
      (1) That indemnifies a railroad for "bodily injury" or "property damage" arising out of construction or demolition operations, within 50 feet of any railroad property and affecting any railroad bridge or trestle, tracks, road-beds, tunnel, underpass or crossing;
      (2) That indemnifies an architect, engineer or surveyor for injury or damage arising out of:
         (a) Preparing, approving, or failing to prepare or approve, maps, shop drawings, opinions, reports, surveys, field orders, change orders or drawings and specifications; or
         (b) Giving directions or instructions, or failing to give them, if that is the primary cause of the injury or damage; or

(3) Under which the insured, if an architect, engineer or surveyor, assumes liability for an injury or damage arising out of the insured's rendering or failure to render professional services, including those listed in **(2)** above and supervisory, inspection, architectural or engineering activities.

10. "Leased worker" means a person leased to you by a labor leasing firm under an agreement between you and the labor leasing firm, to perform duties related to the conduct of your business. "Leased worker" does not include a "temporary worker".

11. "Loading or unloading" means the handling of property:
    a. After it is moved from the place where it is accepted for movement into or onto an aircraft, watercraft or "auto";
    b. While it is in or on an aircraft, watercraft or "auto"; or
    c. While it is being moved from an aircraft, watercraft or "auto" to the place where it is finally delivered;

    but "loading or unloading" does not include the movement of property by means of a mechanical device, other than a hand truck, that is not attached to the aircraft, watercraft or "auto".

12. "Mobile equipment" means any of the following types of land vehicles, including any attached machinery or equipment:
    a. Bulldozers, farm machinery, forklifts and other vehicles designed for use principally off public roads;
    b. Vehicles maintained for use solely on or next to premises you own or rent;
    c. Vehicles that travel on crawler treads;
    d. Vehicles, whether self-propelled or not, maintained primarily to provide mobility to permanently mounted:
        (1) Power cranes, shovels, loaders, diggers or drills; or
        (2) Road construction or resurfacing equipment such as graders, scrapers or rollers;
    e. Vehicles not described in Paragraph **a., b., c.** or **d.** above that are not self-propelled and are maintained primarily to provide mobility to permanently attached equipment of the following types:
        (1) Air compressors, pumps and generators, including spraying, welding, building cleaning, geophysical exploration, lighting and well servicing equipment; or
        (2) Cherry pickers and similar devices used to raise or lower workers;
    f. Vehicles not described in Paragraph **a., b., c.** or **d.** above maintained primarily for purposes other than the transportation of persons or cargo.

However, self-propelled vehicles with the following types of permanently attached equipment are not "mobile equipment" but will be considered "autos":
(1) Equipment designed primarily for:
    (a) Snow removal;
    (b) Road maintenance, but not construction or resurfacing; or
    (c) Street cleaning;
(2) Cherry pickers and similar devices mounted on automobile or truck chassis and used to raise or lower workers; and
(3) Air compressors, pumps and generators, including spraying, welding, building cleaning, geophysical exploration, lighting and well servicing equipment.

However, "mobile equipment" does not include any land vehicles that are subject to a compulsory or financial responsibility law or other motor vehicle insurance law in the state where it is licensed or principally garaged. Land vehicles subject to a compulsory or financial responsibility law or other motor vehicle insurance law are considered "autos".

13. "Occurrence" means an accident, including continuous or repeated exposure to substantially the same general harmful conditions.

14. "Personal and advertising injury" means injury, including consequential "bodily injury", arising out of one or more of the following offenses:
    a. False arrest, detention or imprisonment;
    b. Malicious prosecution;
    c. The wrongful eviction from, wrongful entry into, or invasion of the right of private occupancy of a room, dwelling or premises that a person occupies, committed by or on behalf of its owner, landlord or lessor;
    d. Oral or written publication, in any manner, of material that slanders or libels a person or organization or disparages a person's or organization's goods, products or services;
    e. Oral or written publication, in any manner, of material that violates a person's right of privacy;
    f. The use of another's advertising idea in your "advertisement"; or
    g. Infringing upon another's copyright, trade dress or slogan in your "advertisement".

15. "Pollutants" mean any solid, liquid, gaseous or thermal irritant or contaminant, including smoke, vapor, soot, fumes, acids, alkalis, chemicals and waste. Waste includes materials to be recycled, reconditioned or reclaimed.

16. "Products-completed operations hazard":
    a. Includes all "bodily injury" and "property damage" occurring away from premises you own or rent

and arising out of "your product" or "your work" except:

(1) Products that are still in your physical possession; or

(2) Work that has not yet been completed or abandoned. However, "your work" will be deemed completed at the earliest of the following times:

(a) When all of the work called for in your contract has been completed.

(b) When all of the work to be done at the job site has been completed if your contract calls for work at more than one job site.

(c) When that part of the work done at a job site has been put to its intended use by any person or organization other than another contractor or subcontractor working on the same project.

Work that may need service, maintenance, correction, repair or replacement, but which is otherwise complete, will be treated as completed.

b. Does not include "bodily injury" or "property damage" arising out of:

(1) The transportation of property, unless the injury or damage arises out of a condition in or on a vehicle not owned or operated by you, and that condition was created by the "loading or unloading" of that vehicle by any insured;

(2) The existence of tools, uninstalled equipment or abandoned or unused materials; or

(3) Products or operations for which the classification, listed in the Declarations or in a policy schedule, states that products-completed operations are subject to the General Aggregate Limit.

17. "Property damage" means:

a. Physical injury to tangible property, including all resulting loss of use of that property. All such loss of use shall be deemed to occur at the time of the physical injury that caused it; or

b. Loss of use of tangible property that is not physically injured. All such loss of use shall be deemed to occur at the time of the "occurrence" that caused it.

For the purposes of this insurance, electronic data is not tangible property.

As used in this definition, electronic data means information, facts or programs stored as or on, created or used on, or transmitted to or from computer software, including systems and applications software, hard or floppy disks, CD-ROMS, tapes, drives, cells, data processing devices or any other media which are used with electronically controlled equipment.

18. "Suit" means a civil proceeding in which damages because of "bodily injury", "property damage" or "personal and advertising injury" to which this insurance applies are alleged. "Suit" includes:

a. An arbitration proceeding in which such damages are claimed and to which the insured must submit or does submit with our consent; or

b. Any other alternative dispute resolution proceeding in which such damages are claimed and to which the insured submits with our consent.

19. "Temporary worker" means a person who is furnished to you to substitute for a permanent "employee" on leave or to meet seasonal or short-term workload conditions.

20. "Volunteer worker" means a person who is not your "employee", and who donates his or her work and acts at the direction of and within the scope of duties determined by you, and is not paid a fee, salary or other compensation by you or anyone else for their work performed for you.

21. "Your product":

a. Means:

(1) Any goods or products, other than real property, manufactured, sold, handled, distributed or disposed of by:

(a) You;

(b) Others trading under your name; or

(c) A person or organization whose business or assets you have acquired; and

(2) Containers (other than vehicles), materials, parts or equipment furnished in connection with such goods or products.

b. Includes:

(1) Warranties or representations made at any time with respect to the fitness, quality, durability, performance or use of "your product"; and

(2) The providing of or failure to provide warnings or instructions.

c. Does not include vending machines or other property rented to or located for the use of others but not sold.

22. "Your work":

a. Means:

(1) Work or operations performed by you or on your behalf; and

(2) Materials, parts or equipment furnished in connection with such work or operations.

b. Includes:

(1) Warranties or representations made at any time with respect to the fitness, quality, durability, performance or use of "your work", and

(2) The providing of or failure to provide warnings or instructions.

APPENDIX D

Answers to the Objective Questions
(Printed at the End of Each Chapter)

Chapter	Objective Questions (Found at the End of Each Chapter)										
	1	2	3	4	5	6	7	8	9	10	11
1	d	a	d	c	b	a	e	c	c	b	
2	c	c	a	c	d	b	c	b	d	a	
3	d	d	c	c	c	a	a	b	a	d	
4	a	b	c	c	c	c	b	c	c	c	
5	a	a	a	b	d	b	d	a	a	a	
6	c	d	c	c	a	b	d	a	d	e	
7	c	c	d	d	d	c	a	c	d	b	a
8	b	a	b	d	b	d	b	a	c	d	
9	a	b	c	b	d	b	a	c			
10	d	c	c	b	b	d	a	d			
11	c	a	d	a	b	a	c	b	d		
12	answers to the odd questions are shown below										
13	answers to the odd questions are shown below										
14	c	a	c	c	a	d	a				
15	b	a	c	b	d	d	a				
16	b	d	a	a	c	a	d	a			
17	a	c	c	b	d	a	b	c			
18	c	d	c	c	a	a	d	b			
19	a	d	b	a	b	d	c	a			
20	d	c	c	a	b	d	d	b			
21	a	b	d	c	a	c	b	d			
22	c	a	d	c	a	d	b	d			
23	a	c	c	b	c	a	b	a	c		

ANSWERS TO ODD-NUMBERED QUESTIONS IN CHAPTER 12

1. Insurer will pay the limit of Coverage A, which is $100,000 plus $10,000 in legal costs (damage = $101,000, leaving $1,000 uncovered).

3. As a property liability claim, $4,000 damage to the other car is covered; $4,000 damage to Herb's car is covered as a collision claim; $250 deductible applies to the claim for Herb's car. The total paid by the PAP = $4,000 + $3,750.

5. Herb's PAP provides $100,000 coverage for Emmy Lou, who is an insured under Coverage A. When the limit is exhausted, Emmy Lou may look to her own insurer for excess coverage. If the claim is still not satisfied, Emmy Lou's assets (and perhaps Herb's, if it is asserted Herb was negligent in lending the car to a reckless driver) will have to be used to pay the claim. Bankruptcy may follow this chain of events.

7. The deer damage is considered other-than-collision damage and Herb receives the actual cash value, which is $14,500 less the $250 deductible.

ANSWERS TO ODD-NUMBERED QUESTIONS IN CHAPTER 13

The first step I recommend is to check the recovery ratio. Bill is required to have Coverage A equal to or greater than 80 percent of $130,000 ($104,000). Because he has $120,000 in Coverage A, he will collect in full on all losses, up to the face amount of his coverage, $120,000. If he has a total loss, he will pay the difference between the $130,000 in damage and the $120,000 limit of liability.

1. The Coverage A loss is total, so Bill receives the limit of coverage, $120,000, not the replacement cost of the damage, $130,000. The contents, Coverage C, limit is $60,000, so Bill again cannot fully replace the damaged property (of $70,000). Bill can collect the $12,000 in additional living expenses under Coverage D, which has a $24,000 limit. The Section 1 deductible, $250, would come from the $130,000 Coverage A claim (making the claim equal to $129,750). Because the limit of Coverage A is less than the amount claimed, Bill receives $120,000 without reduction for the deductible. Bill's total recovery is $120,000 + $60,000 + $12,000 = $192,000.

3. Tool shed = $7,000 destroyed; equipment = $3,000 also destroyed. Answer: Tool shed is covered under Coverage B. Limit = $12,000; deductible = $250; $7,000 damage − $250 deductible = $6,750 damage. Recovery = $6,750.

   Lawn care equipment is covered under Coverage C, personal property. Recovery = $3,000 (deductible does not apply twice).

5. The fire caused to the neighbor's home will result in a property damage liability claim of $170,000. Coverage E has a $100,000 limit, which is the maximum recovery.

7. Assuming dependency and residency of the daughter, recovery under Coverage C = $1,500 − $250 deductible = $1,250.

9. The business exclusion applies to Bill's accounting activities; thus, there will be no recovery in this instance.

Glossary

This section of the text is neither an exhaustive dictionary of insurance terms nor a complete listing of all the definitions used in this text. Rather, it will help readers who want to look up insurance terms that can be explained by short definitions. Readers can find definitions of other terms requiring longer explanations using the index.

Accumulation period The time period when payments flow from the owner of a deferred annuity to the insurance company and remain on deposit, prior to the liquidation period. See also *Liquidation period*.

Activities of daily living (ADLs) The usual activities of mobile individuals, including bathing, eating, and dressing. The typical insured peril in long-term care insurance is the inability to perform a specified number of ADLs.

Actual cash value (ACV) An amount typically calculated as the replacement cost of property at the time of the loss, minus an allowance for depreciation. Using this definition, property that could be replaced for $100 and that had been used for one-quarter of its expected life would have an ACV of $75 ($100 – $25).

Actuary An insurance company mathematician who compiles statistics of losses, develops insurance rates, calculates dividends, and evaluates the financial standing of an insurance company.

Additional living expenses (loss of use) The extra costs of food and lodging incurred after an insured loss while the homeowner's property is being replaced or repaired.

Adjuster The person whom an insurance company appoints to determine the value of an insured's claim for loss recovery.

Admitted assets Those assets that the state allows an insurer to use in meeting tests of solvency. Typically, these assets can be realized easily as cash and are used to pay claims. *Nonadmitted assets* are things that ordinarily could not be used to satisfy insureds' claims, such as office furniture.

Admitted insurer An insurer licensed to conduct business in a state.

Advance premium mutual In terms of volume of insurance written, the most important kind of mutual insurance company. Under the advance premium system, policyholders pay their premiums when their insurance begins and become eligible for a dividend (and often the subsequent premium is reduced) when the insurance period ends.

Adverse selection Selection against the insurer. The tendency of less desirable exposures to loss, such as people in poor health or people with bad driving records, to try to purchase insurance protection at standard (average) rates. One possible result of asymmetric possession of information.

Agency contract or agency agreement A contract between an agent and an insurer establishing the rights and duties of each party.

Agent A person authorized to act for another person, known as a *principal*. In the typical insurance transaction, the individual dealing with the consumer is an agent acting for the insurer, the principal.

Aleatory contract A contract in which both parties knows from the inception that the monetary value exchanged will not be equal. Insurance is an aleatory contract in which the insured can receive more or less than the premium paid for the coverage.

Alien insurance company An insurer from another country. Contrast this with a *foreign* insurance company, which is one doing business in a state other than the one in which it is incorporated. An Ohio-based insurer doing business in Indiana is a foreign insurer in Indiana, while a Canadian insurer doing business in Indiana is an alien insurer.

Annual transit policy An inland marine policy that covers all shipments made during a specified year.

Annuity A regular series of payments (sometimes called *rent*). If payments are made for a lifetime, the contract is called a *pure annuity* or a *straight life annuity*. If payments are guaranteed for a specified period, regardless of the annuitant's survival or death, the arrangement is called an *annuity certain*. If payments are guaranteed for a lifetime or a certain period, whichever event lasts longer, the arrangement is called a *life annuity, period certain*. Annuities covering two or more lives are called *joint life annuities* if payments end at the first death. If payments end at the second of two deaths, the contract is called a *joint-and-last-survivor annuity*. Contracts that call for a refund when the total amount of rent received by the annuitant (for example, $25,000) is less than the premium paid for the contract (for example, $60,000) are called *refund annuities*. If the refund is made in a lump sum ($35,000 in this example), the contract is called a *cash refund annuity*. If the refund is made by continuing the regular installment payments (for example, $6,000 a year until the $35,000 refund is paid) to contingent beneficiaries, the contract is called an *installment refund annuity*.

Appleton rule   A part of the New York insurance code that says that insurance companies doing any business in the state of New York must be in substantial compliance with all New York's rules in whatever state they do business, not just in New York.

Assessment mutual   An insurer with the legal right to demand additional premium payments from its insureds if insufficient funds are available to meet the insurer's obligations to claimants. These mutuals are sometimes called *farm mutuals*.

Asset allocation plan   In financial planning, a strategy for determining the percentage of a person's assets that will be held in different types of investments.

Assigned risk   An applicant for insurance that could not get coverage in the voluntary market and thus was assigned by state law to an insurer that otherwise would not accept the insured. This arrangement is found predominantly in the high-risk automobile insurance market.

Assignment   The legal transfer of contractual rights and duties from one party to another, which may or may not involve consideration. Assignment of insurance contracts is governed by policy language. Assignment of fire insurance policies is possible only with the consent of the insurer. Assignment of life insurance policies requires only the proper notification of the insurer.

Assumption of risk   A legal defense in negligence litigation. When the plaintiff knew, or should have known, that a course of behavior could lead to his or her own injury, and persisted in such behavior despite this knowledge, the defendant can assert this defense in attempting to avoid compensating the plaintiff for injuries sustained.

Attorney-in-fact   The title of the person who manages an insurance reciprocal exchange

Automatic premium loan (APL)   An optional contractual feature of cash value life insurance policies. The insurer agrees to make a loan equal to any missed premiums to keep a policy in force. The total amount of loans made, plus interest, must be supported by the available cash values of the contract.

Automobile insurance plans   The result of state rules that require insurers to insure some percentage of poor drivers who are unable to buy insurance from other sources. The percentage of bad drivers assigned to an insurer by the automobile insurance plan typically is based on its market share in the personal auto insurance market. Also known as *assigned risk plans*.

Avoidance   A risk-handling technique in which the organization consciously chooses not to engage in a risky activity that could result in financial loss.

Bailment   Possession of property by a party other than the owner, with the intent of the property being returned to the owner. Examples of bailments include property left with dry cleaners, stored in warehouses, or placed on common carriers. The party owning the property is the *bailor*; the party in temporary possession of the property is the *bailee*.

Beneficiary   The person who is designated to receive the proceeds of a life insurance policy. A *revocable (irrevocable)* beneficiary can(not) be changed by the owner of the policy at a later time.

Binder   A temporary insurance contract used to provide property insurance coverage until the actual contract can be issued. See also *Conditional receipt* for a comparable life insurance term.

Breach of contract   A failure, without legal excuse, to fulfill one's contractual duties.

Broker   A legal representative of the applicant for insurance. The broker may be authorized to design coverage and/or shop for insurance coverage.

Building and personal property coverage form   A common type of commercial property insurance policy

Business interruption (or income) insurance   This coverage provides protection from indirect losses, such as lost profits or extra expenses, that arise after a direct loss of property.

Buy-and-sell agreement   An arrangement made to allow the continuation of a partnership or a close corporation after the death of one of the owners. The agreement sets the price at which the sale will be made. It also forces the owners to sell and the buyers to buy the property at this price. Such an agreement is often accompanied by the purchase of life insurance, which provides the funds to complete the transaction.

Call option   An option to buy an underlying asset that can be exercised by the option holder.

Capacity   (1) The legal ability to make a binding contract. (2) The amount of insurance an insurance company can write. (3) The ability of the property-casualty insurance industry to pay claims in the event of a catastrophe.

Captive insurer   An insurance company operated by a non-insurance company or group of companies to insure its own risks. A part of a self-insurance plan.

Cash value   The saving feature associated with permanent life insurance. The result of an initial period when premium payments exceed mortality and other charges.

Cash-refund annuity   See *Annuity*.

Catastrophe   An incident or series of closely related or highly correlated incidents that cause extremely large amounts of property losses. Floods, earthquakes, and volcanoes can produce natural catastrophes, which makes them generally uninsurable by private insurers.

Catastrophe reinsurance An excess-of-loss reinsurance arrangement distinguished by very high retentions by the primary insurer before the reinsurer becomes liable. Catastrophe reinsurance also has very high upper limits on the reinsurance policy, with increments of coverage often being expressed in the millions of dollars.

Cause of loss form A form included in a commercial property insurance policy that specifies the perils covered under the policy.

Ceding company See *Primary insurer*.

Certified Financial Planner (CFP) A professional designation earned by individuals who demonstrate their expertise in financial planning by passing a series of examinations administered by the Certified Financial Planner Board of Standards.

Chartered Financial Consultant (ChFC) A professional designation earned by individuals who demonstrate their expertise in life insurance, health insurance, and financial planning by passing a series of examinations administered by The American College.

Chartered Life Underwriter (CLU) A professional designation earned by individuals who demonstrate their expertise in life and health insurance by passing a series of examinations administered by The American College.

Chartered Property Casualty Underwriter (CPCU) A professional designation earned by individuals who demonstrate their expertise in property and liability insurance by passing a series of examinations administered by the American Institute for Chartered Property Casualty Underwriters.

Chief risk officer (CRO) A common title for the senior executive who is responsible for carrying out the enterprise risk management function in an organization.

Children's Health Insurance Program (CHIP) A public assistance program that provides health coverage to children in families that are not eligible for Medicaid but who cannot afford private health insurance coverage.

Claim A demand for payment made for a covered loss by an insured on an insurer.

Claims-made form A type of liability policy in which the insurer agrees to pay only for claims made during the period covered by the policy. Thus, this format is designed to eliminate coverage for incidents that occur during the policy period but which result in litigation after the policy period expires. This format is the opposite of an *occurrence-basis* liability policy, which pays for losses occurring during the policy period regardless of when the claim is filed.

Class action lawsuit A lawsuit in which a large number of plaintiffs band together to sue a common defendant under a single legal action.

Class rating An insurance pricing technique in which an insurer places comparable units into a group and then charges a class rate that reflects the overall expected loss experience and expenses of the group.

Coinsurance A requirement in an insurance policy that the insured pay a portion of a claim if the insured purchases an inadequate amount of insurance.

Collision In automobile insurance, this term means contact of a vehicle with another object. However, several types of vehicle/object contacts, such as contact with a bird or animal, are deemed not to be collision in the personal auto policy (PAP). These events are covered by the other-than-collision provisions.

Combined ratio The sum of the loss and the expense ratio. It is calculated roughly as the sum of the losses and expenses divided by the premiums for a given period of time.

Commercial general liability (CGL) insurance An Insurance Services Office (ISO) package policy that covers many different liability exposures of small and large businesses.

Commercial lines insurance Insurance for businesses, governmental units, or nonprofit organizations.

Commodity price risk The risk of financial loss resulting from fluctuations in the price of commodity products (such as oil or grain). For example, buyers (sellers) of commodities suffer losses from input (output) price risk when the price of the commodity increases (decreases).

Community rating In health insurance, a system in which the price of health insurance for each employer in a community is based on the combined risk levels of all employers in that community.

Comparative negligence A modification of the contributory negligence doctrine. The comparative negligence doctrine allows the plaintiff some recovery for injuries sustained, despite the fact that the plaintiff contributed to the loss.

Compensatory damages Payments set by the court to restore the victim to the same financial condition after an injury that he or she was in before the injury.

Compulsory insurance laws Statutes that require the purchase of insurance, including such examples as mandated workers' compensation coverage or compulsory auto liability insurance laws.

Concealment Silence when obligated to speak. A duty is imposed on applicants for insurance to reveal all material facts, even if specific information is not requested by the insurer. Neglect of this duty is called *concealment*.

Conditional receipt An arrangement used in life insurance to provide coverage to an applicant before an actual contract can be issued. These agreements typically require the applicant to submit the first premium payment and are conditioned on the insured meeting all the requirements for acceptance by the insurer, including passing a medical examination.

Confidence interval A statistical technique used to set a range between two values (the upper and lower confidence limits) located around the estimate of a random variable such that, with repeated sampling, the actual value of random variable falls within that range a given percentage of the time.

Consolidated Omnibus Budget Reconciliation Act of 1986 (COBRA) A federal law that affects a large number of matters, including rules requiring employers to extend group health insurance coverage to qualified employees for up to thirty-six months after a qualifying event, such as a spouse's death, divorce, or separation from employment.

Consideration The amount of economic value given up in making a valid contract.

Consumer-driven health plans Health insurance plans (such as high-deductible health care plans) designed to increase price competition among medical providers as a means to limit health care cost inflation.

Continuing care retirement community A group-living arrangement for the elderly with independent living units and a nursing facility. Admission usually involves a large front-end fee.

Contract An agreement between two parties. A valid contract is one whose terms a court will enforce. A void contract lacks one or more requirements of a valid contract. A voidable contract is one that has been breached by one of the parties.

Contract of adhesion rule A rule pertaining to insurance law that construes any ambiguities found in an insurance contract against the writer of the contract.

Contractual transfer agreement Contractual arrangements that shift the financial responsibility for losses from one party in the contract to another.

Contributory negligence A legal doctrine applied in negligence litigation that allows the defendant to avoid payment for the plaintiff's injuries once it is established that some action of the plaintiff (however slight) contributed to the loss.

Contributory plan In employee benefits, a plan in which the employee pays a portion of the cost. Plans financed entirely by the employer are called *noncontributory* plans.

Conversion privilege A contractual right of the employee to convert group life insurance into an individual (permanent) policy after terminating employment. This privilege also applies to some group health contracts.

Convertible term life insurance A term insurance policy that allows the insured to convert to a permanent form of insurance without providing evidence of insurability.

Convolution A statistical method used to model an organization's losses by calculating all possible combinations of losses using probability distributions for loss frequency and loss severity.

Coordination of benefits (COB) clause A clause found in health insurance policies that prevents insureds from collecting a full insurance recovery from each of several insurers covering the same loss exposure. The COB clause is designed to limit the total recovery to the amount of damage sustained and determines which insurance contract or contracts pay for the loss.

Corporate risk management The process of protecting the earnings power and the assets of a firm from the financial losses resulting from pure risk events.

Correlation coefficient A measure of how two random variables change relative to each other, equal to the covariance of the two random variables divided by the product of the standard deviations of both variables.

Covariance A measure of how two random variables change relative to each other. See also *correlation coefficient.*

Covered earnings A Social Security term describing the amount of earnings subject to taxation. In recent years, this amount has been indexed for inflation.

Credibility An actuarial concept used in experience-rated group insurance. The more reliable an employer's loss data is, the more its peculiar results are reflected in its premium calculations.

Credit life insurance A type of group life insurance that covers all the debtors of one creditor—a retail store or automobile financing company, for example. The purpose of this coverage is to repay unpaid credit balances if the debtor dies with an outstanding loan balance.

Credit risk Loss potential caused by a borrower defaulting on a loan.

Crime insurance Insurance that provides payments when a crime loss (e.g., theft or burglary) is caused by non-employees. Fidelity bonds cover employee-caused crime losses.

Criminal act An act in violation of penal law. An offense against the state.

Currency risk The risk of loss associated with fluctuations in one currency's value against other currencies. Importers and exporters face this risk.

Currency swap A derivative contract in which two parties lend each other currencies.

Cumulative injury Job-related disabilities and injuries resulting from prolonged exposure to hazardous activities over many years of employment.

Currently insured An insured status category of the Social Security program providing survivor benefits to dependents of workers with covered earnings in six of the thirteen quarters prior to death. See also *Fully insured.*

Custodial care Care for the activities of daily living (bathing, dressing, and toileting, for example). There is no expectation that this care will improve a person's health. It is designed to maintain a person at his or her current level. Providing this care requires no medical training. To be covered by insurance, custodial care requires a doctor's authorization.

Declarations The first part of the insurance policy, in which the property, people, and insurance coverages purchased are set forth.

Decreasing term life insurance A term insurance policy that has a level premium but provides regular reductions in the face amount of coverage. This coverage often is used to repay the decreasing balance on home mortgage loans if the homeowner dies prematurely.

Deductible The first dollars of loss that are deducted by the insurer from the amount that it pays to the insured. For example, if a policy has a $250 deductible and there is a covered loss amounting to $10,000, the insured collects $9,750. Deductibles may be worded in terms of a dollar amount or as a percentage of the loss.

Defendant The party allegedly causing the plaintiff's loss in a lawsuit.

Defensive medicine Medical procedures or tests that would not be carried out in the absence of potential legal liability litigation.

Deferred annuity A contract in which payments to the annuitant begin some time after the premium payments to the insurer have ended. Thus, a person aged 40 who purchases an annuity with payments to begin on his 65th birthday has purchased a deferred annuity.

Defined-benefit plan A pension plan in which the employee's benefit is predetermined by a formula. The defined benefit in turn determines the actuarial contributions required to fund the benefit.

Defined-contribution plan A pension plan in which the employer's contribution is established by a formula but no predetermined benefit amount is guaranteed.

Demutualization The process of converting a mutual insurance company to the stock form of ownership.

Dependent properties A non-owned property whose loss would interrupt or reduce an insured's profitability. For example, the loss at a supplier's (or customer's) premises could interrupt an insured's operations if inputs could not be delivered or output could not be shipped. This exposure can be insured with dependent properties coverage.

Derivative security A financial instrument whose value is based on (derived from) the value of an underlying financial asset or commodity.

Direct loss The physical damage that occurs as a consequence of a covered peril, such as the damage to property caused by a fire. See also *Indirect loss.*

Direct marketing An insurance marketing system based on solicitation of applicants using nonagent marketing techniques, such as mail, telephone, and Internet solicitation.

Direct writer An insurer that markets its products using agents who are employees who generally represent only one insurer.

Disability (total) Although definitions vary, one of the strictest definitions of this term is "the inability to engage in any gainful employment." A more liberal definition would be "the inability to engage in the employment one is trained for."

Disability income rider An extra-cost option that can be added to life insurance policies that provides payment if an insured meets the definition of *disability* found in the contract. For example, a disability income rider may provide $10 per month of income for each $1,000 face amount of life insurance.

Disability insurance This coverage replaces lost income while an insured is unable to work (that is, meeting the definition of disability found in the contract).

Diversifiable risk Financial risks that can be reduced across the members of a risk pool or portfolio.

Diversification A method of handling risk within a group of individuals such that the financial losses of a few group members are shared across all the members of the group.

Dividend An amount paid on participating insurance policies. When dividends are paid to policyholders of mutual insurers, the dividends represent a nontaxable return.

Domestic insurance company A licensed insurer doing business in the state in which it was legally formed. See also *alien insurance company.*

Double indemnity An option on some life insurance contracts that causes the insurer to pay twice the face value of the policy if death is caused by a specified circumstance, such as an accident.

Duplication A process in which an individual or firm reduces its exposure to risk by holding multiple copies of a key resource or asset, also known as *redundancy.*

Earned premium The percentage of an advanced premium belonging to the insurer, based on the passage of time. For example, if the insured pays an annual premium in advance, the insurer earns one-twelfth of the premium each month.

Economic damages A measure used in negligence cases to compensate a plaintiff for monetary costs of an injury. Examples include medical bills and loss of income. *Noneconomic damages,* in contrast, are a measurement used for losses such as pain and suffering, where there have been no out-of-pocket costs. Also see *compensatory damages.*

Elimination period A time specified by disability income insurance policies that must pass before the insured is entitled to benefits.

Employee benefits Any nonwage benefit provided by an employer to employees, including pensions, life, health, and disability insurance.

Employment Retirement Security Act of 1974 (ERISA) Federal legislation designed to guarantee certain aspects of pension plans of private employers.

Endorsement A written modification of an insurance policy that changes the original (often standardized) contract of insurance. Endorsements may either broaden or narrow the original policy language.

Enterprise risk management A senior-level corporate process involving the identification, assessment, and treatment of all sources of risk within a firm or organization.

Entire-contract provision A clause required by state law to appear in life insurance policies, which makes the printed contract and the application attached thereto the entire contract between the parties. The purpose of this provision is to prevent incorporation of other documents (such as a corporate charter) by reference.

Environmental impairment liability (EIL) An insurance coverage that provides protection to manufacturers, transporters, disposal firms, municipalities, or others for legal liability arising from activities resulting in the destruction of the environment.

Experience rating In health insurance, a pricing arrangement in which commercial insurers set the prices of their policies based on the unique insurance underwriting characteristics of the specific group of workers employed by an employer.

Errors and omissions insurance Liability coverage designed to protect professionals, such as accountants or insurance agents, from claims that their professional actions resulted in losses to their clients.

Estate planning The development of a financial plan designed to cover the liquidation and disposal of assets before and at a person's death. Such a plan may involve living considerations (gifts), death considerations (identifying in a will which people will receive property), and tax considerations (including the federal unified transfer tax).

Evidence of insurability In life insurance, whatever evidence an applicant for insurance must provide to induce an insurer to offer a life insurance contract. The term includes, but is not limited to, good health.

Excess coverage In cases in which two or more insurance policies cover a loss, the policy that pays after primary coverage has been exhausted.

Excess of loss reinsurance A contract in which the reinsurer must pay the primary insurer only for the amount of loss in excess of the retention limit of the primary insurer. For example, if the primary insurer retains $40,000 of a $100,000 exposure, ceding the remainder on an excess of loss basis, and if a $60,000 loss occurs, then the reinsurer must pay only $20,000 ($60,000 − $40,000).

Exclusion A clause in an insurance policy in which the insurer specifies losses (circumstances, types of property, ineligible people, etc.) not covered by the policy.

Exclusive remedy A workers' compensation rule making workers' compensation the sole source of funds for injured workers. This rule provides for the absolute liability of employers and eliminates the need (ability) of employees to recover damages by litigation.

Exculpatory clauses Clauses in business contracts in which one party agrees to give up its right to sue another party under specific circumstances.

Expected value A statistical term that refers to the mean or average value of a future unknown random variable, such as the expected loss that a firm's risk manager should anticipate from its exposure to risky activities like worker injuries or auto accidents.

Expense ratio The ratio of all the expenses (such as sales commissions or credit investigations, but not including the costs of covered losses) incurred in writing insurance, divided by the premiums realized from selling the insurance.

Experience rating A plan found in group insurance that gives recognition in premium costs to the specific claims of the particular group being insured.

Exposure unit The person or object exposed to a risk that could result in a financial loss.

Extended-term option A nonforfeiture option found in life insurance policies that provides for the continuation of the face amount of coverage for a period funded by available cash values.

Face amount The amount of life insurance shown on the face page of a life insurance policy to be paid at the insured's death.

Facultative reinsurance A reinsurance arrangement in which the reinsurer has the right to reject submissions of business from the primary insurer.

Fair Access to Insurance Requirements (FAIR) plan A plan adopted in several states that requires insurers to offer insurance if applicants meet specific requirements. Reasons for rejecting business must be stated and are limited by state law.

Family and Medical Leave Act of 1993 (FMLA) This law requires employers with fifty or more employees to offer up to twelve weeks of unpaid leave to eligible employees for the birth or adoption of a child, to care for a sick family member, or for the employee's own illness.

Federal Insurance Contributions Act (FICA) Provides for the familiar Social Security tax deduction on paychecks.

Fee-for-service health care The traditional health insurance reimbursement arrangement where health care providers like physicians and hospitals are reimbursed by health insurance plans after delivering medical services to the patient.

Fellow servant rule A common law defense used by employers prior to the introduction of workers' compensation laws that stated that employers should not be held liable for injuries to their workers if caused by a negligent coworker.

File and use rating A form of insurance rate regulation that allows an insurer to use a new price rate without delay after filing the rate and supporting statistics with the regulator. Also known as *competitive rating*.

Financial responsibility laws State laws that require drivers to show proof that they can satisfy legal judgments arising out of negligence in operating their motor vehicles.

Financial risk management A term used in enterprise risk management that refers to loss exposures associated with fluctuations in financial markets—in particular, losses associated with interest rate changes and currency fluctuations.

Flexible premium deferred annuity An annuity in which accumulations result from a series of payments prior to liquidation. For example, some policies allow owners to make monthly payments (of irregular amounts) for many years prior to liquidation during retirement.

Flexible spending account (FSA) An employee benefit program in which employees can elect to reduce their pretax compensation voluntarily, diverting the compensation into their FSA to pay for medical expenses not covered by their health insurance plans.

Floater A type of inland marine insurance policy that covers mobile property. Floaters may be scheduled (specific property is identified, as by serial number) or nonscheduled (the type of property covered is identified, but individual items are not).

Foreign insurance company An insurer licensed in the state of the policyholder, but whose state of domicile is outside the state of the policyholder.

Forward contracts Contracts similar to futures contracts, but forward contracts are not traded on organized exchanges. See also *Futures contracts*.

Fraud An act, such as lying or other deception, designed to cheat an insurer. Fraud against an insurer generally allows the insurer to void the insurance contract.

Frequency of loss A measure of the number of losses that occur over a given period of time.

Fully insured A category of the Social Security program that provides a broad range of benefits to workers accumulating at least forty quarters of covered earnings. Special rules allow younger workers to attain fully insured status before acquiring forty quarters of coverage. See also *Currently insured*.

Funded risk assumption A risk retention arrangement in which a party exposed to financial loss makes financial arrangements (such as securing a contingent lending agreement from a bank or setting cash aside) to pay for the losses that it assumes.

Futures contracts Contracts for orders to be placed in advance to buy or sell a commodity or financial asset at a specified price.

General damages Compensatory damages awarded to the plaintiff in a lawsuit for hard-to-measure items like pain and suffering or emotional distress.

Grace period A limited period of time, such as thirty days, in which an insured can pay a past-due life insurance premium without having to go through the formalities of reinstating the policy.

Gramm-Leach-Bliley Act of 1999 (GLB) Federal legislation that allows the formation of financial service holding companies with component parts that may include commercial banks, insurance companies, and securities dealers. This act revoked the Glass-Steagall Act, legislation passed in the 1930s that separated commercial banking from other financial services.

Gross estate The property owned by a decedent at death. For federal estate tax purposes, this amount may include some transfers made within three years of death.

Gross negligence Cases in which the defendant in a lawsuit willfully disregards the potential harm inflected upon the defendant by his or her actions, potentially resulting in the courts awarding punitive damages to the plaintiff.

Gross premium A mathematical concept that recognizes all costs of marketing and administering the insurance coverage. See also *Net premium*.

Group insurance plans Insurance contracts designed to protect multiple people as members of a designated group under a single insurance contract.

Guaranteed insurability option A life insurance provision that allows insureds to purchase additional coverage, regardless of their insurability, at specified intervals (e.g., the fifth anniversary of the policy) or at specified events (for example, the birth of a child or a marriage).

Guaranteed renewable A health insurance term that recognizes the insurer's limited rights to cancel in-force contracts. These are renewable at the insured's option to a certain age, but the premium can be changed (for the entire class of insureds) by the insurer.

Guaranty fund A fund created by insurance regulators to pay the unpaid claims of insurance policyholders in the event of an insurance company insolvency.

Hazard A circumstance that increases either the frequency or the severity of losses.

Hazard risk A term used in enterprise risk management that refers to the adverse financial loss exposures associated with pure risks.

Health Insurance Portability and Accountability Act (HIPAA) A federal law, passed in 1996, designed to promote labor mobility. One main feature of the act was to allow workers to change jobs without the preexisting conditions exclusion of group health insurance being applied. See also *Preexisting conditions.*

Health maintenance organization (HMO) A medical organization that typically allows subscribers (usually members of employee groups) to pay one annual fee in exchange for the right to all needed health care services. HMOs stress preventive care (loss prevention).

Hedging Taking two simultaneous and offsetting financial positions so that an increase in one position is matched by a decrease in the other position, typically taken to reduce risk.

High-deductible health care plan A health insurance arrangement that combines a high-deductible insurance policy (to control moral hazard) with a *health savings account* (HSA; a savings account designed to pay for the health care costs not covered by the policy)

High-deductible insurance protection Insurance coverage incorporating an exceptionally large deductible (such as $100,000 to $500,000 per loss), designed for large corporations with considerable financial strength.

Hold-harmless agreement A contract transferring one party's legal liability to another. For example, a railroad may ask a lumberyard to sign a hold-harmless agreement before building a spur on the yard's site. The agreement would transfer the railroad's liability for accidents on the spur to the lumberyard.

Hospice A facility that cares for the terminally ill, usually for only a brief period (such as six months before death).

Hull coverage Marine and aircraft insurance that provides payment for direct losses of the ship or aircraft. Separate coverage is needed for losses of cargo or liability losses.

Human resource risk Source of financial loss to an organization that can result from the death, injury, or discontinuation of employment of key employees.

Immediate annuity A contract in which the first payment begins after only a short delay, such as one payment period.

Impairment A term indicating that an insurer's capital and surplus falls below minimum standards and thus is financially weakened.

Incontestable clause A part of the life insurance contract that prevents the insurer from denying a claim for alleged fraud occurring at the policy's inception. The insurer has a limited period of time to discover any such fraud, after which time there can be no defense for nonpayment by the insurer. This means the insurer must pay even if fraud can be proved after this time has elapsed.

Incurred but not reported (IBNR) reserve A loss reserve that reflects the insurer's estimated obligation for future payments that result from insured loss events that have occurred, but for which no request for payment has been filed or reported.

Indemnity A payment by the insurer to the insured that leaves the insured in the same financial position occupied before the covered loss took place.

Independent adjuster A person who acts as an agent for an insurer but is not an employee of the insurer. Insurers use independent adjusters because it would not be practical or cost-effective to send employees to all loss locations.

Independent agent (independent agency system) An approach to marketing property insurance in which the selling agent is not an employee of an insurer, but instead represents several insurers and owns the rights to renew the policies placed with any one company.

Indirect loss The loss of income following a direct loss. For example, if fire destroys a motel, the structural damage is the direct loss; the lost income, continuing expenses, or extra expenses to keep operating are the indirect losses.

Individual retirement account (IRA) A personal savings account, with favorable federal tax treatment, that individuals can use to finance their investments for retirement.

Inland marine insurance Insurance coverage for exported or imported property; small valuable items (such as furs and jewelry); property transported by planes, trains, or trucks; and tunnels and bridges (instruments of transportation).

Installment refund annuity See *Annuity.*

Insurable interest The ability to demonstrate that the insured event is capable of causing a financial loss to the person owning the insurance. To collect from a property insurance contract, the insurable interest must be demonstrated at the time of the loss. In life insurance, the insurable interest must exist when the policy is begun.

Insurance (1) A contractual relationship between two parties in which one party, the *insurer*, is paid a premium by the other party, the *insured*. In return for the premium, the insurer promises to indemnify the insured in the event of a covered loss. (2) A money transfer scheme in which those exposed to a loss voluntarily put money into a pool from which losses are paid to those pool members that experience loss.

Insurance Services Office (ISO) A national property and liability statistical collection and dissemination organization in the United States and its territories. The ISO creates model policy forms and publishes statistics for its member companies to use in setting prices.

Insured A noun referring to the person or organization whose loss obligates the insurer to pay for the loss claim. Also known as *policyholder* or *policy owner*.

Insuring agreement The part of the insurance contract that describes the insurer's duty to indemnify the insured.

Intangible property The nonphysical assets of value in an organization, such as intellectual property or legal rights.

Interest option A life insurance settlement option that provides payments to the beneficiary derived from the interest earned on the death benefit. Any remaining principal is paid to a second beneficiary at the first beneficiary's death.

Interest rate risk An exposure to losses caused by changes in prevailing interest rates. See also *Financial risk management*.

Interpleader A legal method for an insurer to avoid litigation by remitting insurance proceeds to a court, allowing the court to determine rightful ownership of the proceeds.

Investment income An important source of revenue for insurers that is earned from their investment holdings.

Irrevocable beneficiary A beneficiary in a life insurance policy whose rights cannot be impaired by the policyowner without the beneficiary's permission.

Joint-and-survivor annuity A type of life income annuity that is based on two lives, with payments while both people are alive and ending when the last survivor dies.

Joint-life annuity An annuity in which payments end at the death of the first of two covered lives. See also *Annuity*.

Joint underwriting associations An arrangement designed to provide insurance to high-risk applicants by setting up a pool of insurers (whose profits and losses are often shared by other insurers in the industry) to serve this market.

Judgment The finding of the court in a lawsuit, such as a suit seeking damages due to negligence.

Key employee life insurance Coverage purchased by a business to indemnify it if a key employee dies prematurely.

Lapse The expiration of a life insurance policy because of nonpayment of the premium.

Large-loss principle A principle indicating that the insurance mechanism works best when losses are large and uncertain.

Last clear chance A legal doctrine that creates liability for the party with the "last clear chance" to avoid injuring another. The rule is applied, for example, after a defendant establishes that the plaintiff contributed to a loss. The last clear chance doctrine allows the plaintiff to collect, even if the plaintiff contributed to the loss, if the defendant had the last clear chance to avoid the injury.

Law of large numbers A statistical process used by insurers to diversify risk. When an event based on chance is observed, the larger the number of observations is, the more likely it is that the actual result will coincide with the expected result.

Legal liability A liability recognized and enforced by a court. In insurance, legal liability often results from an insured's (defendant's) negligence that results in a court-awarded judgment for an injured third party (plaintiff). The liability insurer agrees to pay its insured's legal judgment.

Legal reserve The reserve (liability) required by state law to promote the solvency of life insurers. The reserve may be calculated on a prospective or retrospective basis and is a function of the insurer's contractual liabilities under the policies it has written.

Level-premium whole life insurance A form of permanent, cash-value life insurance that requires equal annual (or more frequent) premium payments for the insured's life or until the policy matures—for example, at age 100.

Liability risk The risk that an individual or organization may be held legally and financially responsible for the harm that it caused to another person.

Life income option A life insurance settlement option that provides annuity payments.

Life insurance trust A form of trust often used in estate planning cases to decrease the federal transfer tax liability. The trust is the owner and beneficiary of a life insurance policy.

Limited liability A legal doctrine that prevents creditors or business claimants from attaching to the personal assets of the owner of an incorporated firm, thus limiting the size of the claim to the assets of the firm.

Limited payment whole life insurance A form of permanent, cash-value life insurance in which the number of premium payments is limited to a number of years (for example, ten years) or until a specified age (often age 65) is reached. When the payment period ends, the policy is designated as "paid up."

Liquidation period The period when payments flow from the insurer to the annuitant. See also *Accumulation period*.

Lloyd's of London An association of independent underwriters operating in Great Britain. Lloyd's of London is not an insurer; rather, it is a marketplace for insurance where brokers representing applicants for insurance can contract with underwriters offering insurance.

Loading expense Charges included in an insurance premium that pay for a variety of administrative expenses incurred by insurers in carrying out the insurance function.

Longevity risk The risk associated with the tendency of people to live beyond the normal life expectancy.

Long-term care (LTC) insurance Personal insurance that provides coverage for the cost of several types of LTC facilities, such as nursing homes or assisted-living facilities.

Loss control A risk-handling technique designed to limit financial loss by reducing the frequency of loss, the severity of loss, or both.

Loss financing A risk-handling technique in which the organization makes arrangements to pay for their incurred losses. Examples include buying insurance or designing a self-insurance program.

Loss of use A homeowners insurance provision that provides payment for the additional living expenses that property owners experience after a covered loss. The term *loss of use* is also used to distinguish between direct and indirect losses.

Loss other than collision coverage A coverage in the personal auto policy (PAP) that pays for damage to the covered vehicle caused by a variety of perils (such as fire or theft) other than by collision.

Loss prevention An activity designed to reduce the frequency of loss. Examples of loss prevention include driver training programs, better design of equipment, and better lighting in factories. See also *Loss reduction*.

Loss ratio The total incurred losses experienced by an insurer in a year divided by the premiums earned from writing that insurance during that year.

Loss reduction An activity designed to reduce the severity of losses. Examples of loss reduction include automatic fire sprinklers, directions for first aid found on containers of poisons, and separating a large exposure to loss into smaller units.

Loss reserves Estimates of the claims owed to policyholders, which represent most of an insurer's liabilities.

Major medical health insurance A contract typified by a large upper limit of coverage (such as $50,000), a participation provision (causing the insured to pay some percentage of the claim, such as 20 percent), and a deductible provision (such as $500).

Managed care A term used in health insurance to describe a system of providing health care with an emphasis on cost efficiency. Typical features of a managed care system include preventive examinations and controlled access to medical specialists, often through use of a "gatekeeper."

Marine insurance A type of property insurance covering property while in transit, also known as *transportation insurance*.

Maximum family benefit A Social Security provision that limits the total benefits received by a family unit with several eligible beneficiaries of one wage earner.

McCarran-Ferguson Act A federal law that authorizes the continuation of state regulation of insurance so long as state regulation continues to be in the public interest.

Mean loss distribution A probability distribution showing the possible losses that a member of a risk pool may have to pay to cover its share of the losses covered under the pool.

Medicaid A joint federal/state program providing health care to low-income people.

Medical Information Bureau (MIB) A nonprofit trade association of life insurance companies formed to conduct a confidential interchange of underwriting information. The purpose of the MIB is to prevent fraud.

Medicare A part of the Social Security program that provides health insurance to those receiving retirement benefits.

Medigap insurance Private insurance designed to supplement Medicare by filling in or modifying some of the Medicare limitations and participation features.

Misstatement-of-age-provision A mandatory feature of life insurance contracts that causes insurers to adjust the amount of coverage to the appropriate benefit (given the paid premium) after a misstatement of age is discovered, rather than invalidating the entire contract.

Money purchase plan The most popular type of defined-contribution pension plan. The employer's responsibility ends after it makes the contribution, and no guaranteed benefit is provided.

Moral hazard A behavioral activity that increases the frequency or severity of a loss.

Mortgage clause A homeowners (and other property) insurance provision that covers a lender by creating special rights and duties relative to the mortgaged property. For example, this clause precludes the insured's actions from depriving the lender of coverage; it also commits the lender to paying unpaid premiums if the lender wants to continue coverage.

Mutual insurance company An insurer owned by its policyholders for the purpose of obtaining insurance at affordable premium rates.

Named insured The individual insured whose name appears on the declarations page of an insurance policy.

Needs-based purchase of life insurance An approach to buying life insurance in an amount sufficient to fill the gap between the size of the need and the assets available to fill the need. Needs are classified as *permanent* (needs that exist at all ages) and *temporary* (needs that exist for only a portion of a person's life and will end eventually).

Negligence Doing something that a reasonable person would not do (e.g., speeding in a car) or failing to do something that a reasonable person would do (e.g., failing to remove snow or ice from a sidewalk), such that the act or omission results in injury to another.

Net amount at risk The amount of the insurer's exposure to loss. This amount differs from the face amount of insurance in cash-value life insurance contracts because some of the death benefits received by the beneficiary may be considered to arise from the savings value of the contract. Thus, the amount at risk ($700) is the difference between the face amount of insurance ($1,000) and the cash value ($300).

Net premium A mathematical concept used to illustrate only the loss costs in developing insurance premiums. No overhead or other expenses are included.

No-fault insurance A first-party compensation scheme in which the insurer agrees to compensate its own insured, regardless of whose negligence caused a loss.

Nonadmitted insurance Insurance purchased by a policyholder from an insurer that is not licensed in the insurer's home state.

Noncancellable A health insurance term that recognizes the insurers' limited right to cancel in-force contracts. The contract must be renewed to a specified age at the insured's option, and premiums may not be changed. See also *Guaranteed renewable*.

Non-diversifiable risk Risk that cannot be reduced through the use of risk pooling or other means of risk diversification.

Nonforfeiture value The amount to which the insured is entitled upon surrender of a cash-value life insurance policy. The *nonforfeiture options* include a lump sum of cash, extended term insurance, or a reduced amount of paid-up whole life insurance.

Nonparticipating (nonpar) insurance A for-profit insurance scheme that does not provide for dividend payments to policyholders. Nonpar insurance uses more realistic projections of losses and expenses than participating insurance; thus, initial premiums for nonpar insurance often are lower than participating premiums. See also *Participating insurance*.

Nonqualified pension plan A pension plan that does not meet federal requirements for tax advantages.

Normal distribution A statistical distribution for a random variable that is shaped like a bell and symmetrical around the mean at the midpoint of the distribution. In risk pooling, each pool member's share of the losses owed to the pool is normally distributed.

Ocean marine insurance Insurance covering property transported by ship.

Occurrence-basis form See also *Claims-made form*.

Old-Age, Survivors, Disability Insurance—Hospital Insurance (OASDI-HI) Better known as Social Security, this is a federal insurance program begun in 1935 that provides death, retirement, survivors', disability, and health insurance benefits to qualified recipients.

Open perils contract A term used in newer property insurance contracts to replace the term *all risks*. These policies cover a broad range of perils on a nonspecified basis but contain explicit exclusions restricting coverage for specific reasons.

Operational risk A term in enterprise risk management that refers to financial losses that result from the failure of an organization's systems or processes, technology, or people.

Option The legal right to buy or sell a commodity or a financial asset at a prespecified price for a specific period of time.

Ordinance-or-law exclusion A property insurance provision that excludes coverage for losses to undamaged portions of buildings when total destruction of property is required by law, or if current zoning laws prevent rebuilding.

Ordinary life insurance A term that describes individual life insurance purchases in relatively large amounts paid for with annual (or more frequent) premiums. Ordinary life insurance is distinguished from debit or group life insurance.

Package policy A policy in which two or more coverages are combined into one insurance purchase providing all generally needed coverages.

Paid-up life insurance A whole life policy that has no additional premium payments due.

Participating insurance An insurance scheme that allows the policyholder to share in the favorable or unfavorable operating results of the insurance company. The policyholder/owner is entitled to an annual distribution of dividends based on the company's operating results. Typically, unrealistically high initial estimates of expected losses and expenses are made; when actual results are more favorable than the initial estimates, dividends are paid to the policyholders.

Participation provision A major medical insurance policy clause that causes insureds to pay a portion of each claim. It is sometimes identified as a *coinsurance provision*, but the parallels are not exact because the coinsurance penalty (property insurance) can be avoided, while participation provision (health insurance) payments cannot.

Pension Benefit Guarantee Corporation (PBGC) A federal agency established by the Employee Retirement Income Security Act of 1974 (ERISA), whose purpose is to guarantee that payments are made to retired workers covered by defined-benefit pension plans.

Pension plan   A benefit plan designed primarily to provide retirement income to individuals. These plans commonly are tied to employment and included in an employee's benefit plan. Some pension plans include ancillary benefits, but the main focus of pension plans is providing income to retirees.

Peril   The cause of a loss.

Permanent disability   A term defined in a disability income policy. Some definitions of this term can be relatively liberal (e.g., "unable to engage in one's own profession"), while others can be relatively strict (e.g., "unable to engage in any profession").

Personal injury protection (PIP)   A type of auto insurance coverage that pays for the medical expenses of the named insured, family members, and passengers that is used in states with no-fault auto insurance laws.

Personal property floater   An inland marine coverage that protects the insured for loss of valuable items, such as furs, jewelry, guns, and silverware.

Personal risk exposure   A peril that can cause financial harm to an individual person.

Personal lines insurance   Insurance that is designed to serve the personal risk needs of individuals and families.

Physical hazard   A condition related to the physical environment that increases the frequency or severity of a loss event.

Plaintiff   The individual alleging injury in a negligence lawsuit.

Point of service plan   In health insurance, a managed care arrangement that controls costs through the use of a medical provider network like a health maintenance organization (HMO) but does not restrict coverage to network providers. See also *health maintenance organization (HMO)*.

Policy   The contract between the insurer and insured.

Preexisting conditions   A health insurance policy provision that excludes coverage for health care problems experienced (diagnosed) before the policy became effective.

Preferred provider organization (PPO)   An organization of doctors, hospitals, and other medical providers that are contracted to provide health care for an employer group or insurer at reduced rates. Financial incentives are provided to encourage participants to use services in the network; for example, services provided outside the network cost more than those provided within the network. See also *Managed care organization*.

Premium   The payment made by insureds to insurers for their policies.

Price risk   Losses incurred by an organization that are attributable to changes in the cost of key inputs (such as interest rates or the cost of commodities used in production) or changes in the price at which the organization's output can be sold.

Primary insurance amount (PIA)   A Social Security term that describes the basis of all a worker's benefits based on his or her *average indexed monthly earnings*. That is, benefits are described as a percentage of the worker's PIA. For example, a retirement benefit at age 65 is 100 percent of the worker's PIA.

Primary insurer   The insurer who first markets the insurance to a consumer/insured. The primary insurer, also known as the *ceding company*, in turn purchases insurance in an arrangement known as *reinsurance*.

Prior approval   An approach to state insurance rate regulation that requires insurers to gain approval for proposed rates before implementing them.

Primary coverage   In cases where two or more insurance policies cover a loss, the policy that pays first.

Private insurance   Insurance provided by nongovernmental insuring organizations, such as stock or mutual insurers, with terms of protection defined by terms set in a private contract.

Probability distribution   A statistical term referring to a table or graph that shows all possible outcomes for a random variable, as well as their respective probabilities of occurring.

Probate   The name for the legal (court-supervised) process of transferring property at a person's death.

Products liability   The liability of manufacturers and vendors that arises from products that injure people who use them. Products liability claims arise from claims of negligent design, manufacture, or failure to provide adequate warnings, packaging, or instructions. Sometimes called just *product liability*.

Professional liability   The legal liability of people with special knowledge, training, or a license to practice who injure clients in the course of providing their services. Also called *malpractice insurance* or *errors and omissions insurance*.

Property risk   Losses to a firm that result from the damage of the assets of the firm.

Proximate cause   The first cause in an unbroken chain of events leading to a loss; also, the cause without which the loss would not have occurred.

Public assistance program   A government-sponsored program providing welfare benefits to individuals who can demonstrate financial need.

Public adjuster   An individual who works for an insured after a loss has occurred to arrive at a fair claims settlement.

Punitive damages   Damages awarded by courts in addition to the compensatory damages, for cases in which the defendant's outrageous conduct requires special punishment. The purpose of punitive damages, in part, is to discourage similar future conduct, both by this defendant and by others who might find themselves in a similar situation.

Pure risk A loss exposure in which the only outcome is a loss or no change in condition.

Put option An option to sell an underlying asset that can be exercised by the option holder.

Qualified pension plan A pension plan that meets federal nondiscrimination laws, funding specifications, and other requirements. Qualified pension plans receive valuable tax benefits not available to non-qualified plans, such as allowing the employer to recognize the pension plan payment as an expense in the year made but not requiring the beneficiary to recognize income until the year received.

Random variable A statistical term referring to a variable whose future value is not known with certainty.

Rate The cost per hundred dollars of exposed value, as used in pricing insurance.

Rating bureau An organization that collects and organizes insurance loss data from its member companies and then provides these organized data back to its member companies to facilitate the forecasting of loss costs.

Real property A term that refers to land and anything permanently attached to land.

Reasonable person A legal standard applied in negligence cases that allow the court to evaluate the facts in particular cases.

Reciprocal exchange A type of insurer that is unincorporated and operates on a nonprofit basis. Each insured provides insurance to all other members of the reciprocal exchange.

Reduced paid-up life insurance option A nonforfeiture option (of a permanent life insurance contract having a cash surrender value) that provides the policyowner with a lower face-value amount of life insurance but relieves him or her of the need to pay further premiums.

Reinstatement The right of a life insurance policyholder to return a lapsed contract to its original terms. Reinstatement must occur within the specified time limits provided in the policy. Reinstatement requires evidence of insurability and payment of all policy financial obligations, such as outstanding loan balances and missed premium payments.

Reinsurance The purchase of insurance on some portion of a covered exposure by an insurance company. The company purchasing the insurance is called the *primary insurer* or *ceding company*; the company providing the insurance is called the *reinsurer*. Two typical reinsurance arrangements are *pro rata reinsurance* (where both premiums and losses are shared on a proportional basis) and *excess-of-loss reinsurance* (where the reinsurer pays only when covered losses exceed some predetermined amount and then pays only the excess above this amount).

Renewable term life insurance A policy that the insured can renew without presenting evidence of insurability.

Replacement-cost insurance A property insurance policy in which the insured pays for the replacement cost of the insured property rather than the actual cash value. A typical requirement causes the insured actually to repair or replace the damaged property in order to receive this amount.

Replacement ratio The ratio of retirement to preretirement income.

Representation A statement made by an applicant in an insurance application. The insurer relies on the truth of the applicant's representations in underwriting the policy. A material misrepresentation generally allows the insurer to avoid the contract.

Reservation of rights Notice from the insurer to the insured that the insurer is not certain that coverage exists but plans to proceed with the loss adjustment, and perhaps the legal defense, as if the coverage existed, but that certain events may occur in the future that may cause the insurer to reevaluate its position.

Res ipsa loquitur Literally meaning "the thing speaks for itself," a legal doctrine applied in negligence cases in which the only explanation for the plaintiff's injuries is the defendant's actions. For example, the doctrine is often applied in commercial airplane accidents, in which passengers could not conceivably have contributed to the loss. The application of the doctrine relieves the plaintiff of the duty to establish the defendant's negligence, but it does not preclude the defendant from establishing a defense.

Retention (1) A risk-handling technique in which an organization makes a conscious decision to use internal capital to pay for the losses that it suffers resulting from a risk. (2) The amount of insurance kept by the primary insurer in a reinsurance arrangement. See also *Primary insurer* and *Reinsurance*.

Retroactive date In a claims-made liability policy, the retroactive date determines the first point in time where a covered loss may occur. The retroactive date may be subject to change or negotiation.

Retrocession The purchase of reinsurance by a reinsurer.

Risk assumption or risk retention A loss-financing technique in which the party exposed to the risk of loss pays for its own losses if they occur.

Risk aversion A behavioral tendency exhibited by many individuals faced with risky decisions in which the person prefers the alternative that involves the least risk.

Risk-based capital (RBC) requirement A statutory requirement that calculates an amount of capital, based on the riskiness of the insurer's operations, that must be held by an insurer to maintain its financial strength.

Risk-bearing financial institution A financial institution such as an insurer or mutual fund that assumes (a portion of) its customers' risk exposure, which is typically reduced through diversification.

Risk charge In the calculation of an insurance premium, an amount that is added and subtracted to the estimate of the mean loss in a risk pool to allow a margin for measurement error.

Risk classification system A method commonly used by insurers to achieve larger risk pools by sorting applicants into homogeneous pricing categories based on variables that are related to risk or loss.

Risk management process A systematic approach by which an organization can identify and manage its exposures to risk in ways that best fit its strategic goals.

Risk pooling A process used by insurers involving the diversification of risk across a group or pool of homogeneous firms or individuals.

Risk-return trade-off In financial markets, the tendency for investments offering higher returns to exhibit higher levels of risk.

Schedule rating An approach to property insurance rate making in which the specific characteristics of the covered property are compared to a standard, and then credits or charges are applied for above- or below-standard features when developing a final rate.

Self-insurance A risk-handling technique in which an organization pays for its risk management losses internally through the use of financial risk pooling.

Separation A loss-reduction practice in which a firm designs its operations around multiple locations that are physically far from each other, thus reducing the chance that a single adverse event, like a fire or storm, could disrupt all operations.

Settlement options The different ways that the death proceeds of a life insurance policy can be paid to the beneficiary.

Severity of loss A measure of the size of a financial loss.

Skilled-nursing care Daily nursing and rehabilitative care ordered by a physician. This level of care is performed under the supervision of skilled medical personnel.

Social insurance Insurance protection available to individuals and firms through programs administered and funded by governmental bodies.

Social Security See *Old-Age, Survivors, Disability Insurance—Hospital Insurance (OASDI-HI).*

Solvency The ability of an insurance company to pay all its legal obligations.

Special damages Compensatory damages awarded to the plaintiff in a lawsuit for monetary or economic losses, including such items as medical expenses or lost wages.

Specified perils contract An insurance contract that identifies a list of covered perils. Also known as a *named-perils contract.*

Speculative risk An exposure to loss that could result in a loss, gain, or no change as a result of fortuitous circumstances. For example, investing in common stocks creates a speculative risk.

Split-dollar life insurance A method of paying for permanent life insurance coverage in which two parties (often an employer and employee) each pay a portion of the annual premium, with one party paying an amount equal to the increase in cash value in a given year (the employer) and the other party (the employee) paying the remainder.

Standard deviation A statistical term used to measure the degree to which the outcomes of a random variable may differ from its expected value, calculated as the square root of the variance.

Stare decisis The legal principle of abiding by already-decided cases, which provides continuity to legal decisions. The decision of the court when it first encounters a particular set of circumstances sets a precedent for deciding future cases involving similar circumstances.

State of domicile The state in which an insurer is legally formed.

Stock insurance company An insurer organized as a for-profit venture, with owners who are not necessarily policyholders.

Stop loss insurance An arrangement used by employers to limit the cost of self-insured health plans by transferring the cost of catastrophic losses to an insurer.

Strategic risk A term in enterprise risk management that refers to the risk that an organization cannot successfully compete with its competitors to achieve its goals or mission statement.

Strict liability Liability without fault. This rule of law creates a heavy burden for defendants in liability suits.

Structured settlement In negligence cases, instead of the defendant paying a lump sum to a plaintiff, the defendant (using the services of an insurer) promises a series of annuity payments to the injured party.

Subrogation The substitution of one party (the insurer) for another party (the insured) in that party's rights. The substitution occurs because the first party has made a payment for which another is responsible. In insurance, subrogation occurs when the insurer pays a claim while the insured has a right of action against a third party for causing a loss. After making the claims payment, the insurer is subrogated to the insured's right to sue the third party.

Subsidization A result of insurance operations when one group of insureds pays more than its mathematically fair share of losses, while another group pays less than its mathematically fair share.

Succession planning   A process used to minimize the cost of losing a key employee by making plans to replace the missing executive through the promotion of an internal subordinate.

Suicide clause   A clause that excludes payment for death by suicide if the suicide occurs within a specific time (one or two years typically) from the policy issue date. The insurer pays for suicides that occur after the exclusion period.

Surplus   An insurance accounting term referring to the excess that is available after subtracting an insurer's liabilities from its assets.

Surplus line   Insurance on an exposure for which no coverage is available in the normal market.

Survivor life insurance   A life insurance policy covering two lives that provides a death payment at the second death. (If more than two lives are covered, payment is made at the last person's death.) Survivor life insurance frequently is used in estate planning cases based on plans leaving the entire estate at the first death to the surviving spouse, with life insurance proceeds providing liquidity for estate taxes at the second death. (Also known as *second-to-die life insurance*.)

Swap   A transaction in which two companies lend each other different currencies (a currency swap) or lend at different interest rates, one fixed and one floating (an interest rate swap).

Tangible property   The physical assets of an organization, such as real estate, vehicles, or inventory.

Term life insurance   A policy that promises to pay a specific dollar amount of death protection if the insured dies within a specified term, or period of time.

Third-party administrator   An organization that is hired by an employer to administer a self-insurance plan (like self-insured health insurance or workers' compensation), carrying out such activities as verifying coverage for claims, calculating claims payments, and paying the medical provider.

Tort   A wrongful act, other than a breach of contract, that results in another's injury.

Traded option   The creation of a legal right to buy or sell a commodity or a financial asset at an agreed-upon price for a specific time period.

Transfer   A risk-handling technique in which an organization shifts the financial consequences of a loss onto a third party.

Treaty (or automatic) reinsurance   A type of reinsurance in which a portfolio of the primary insurer's exposures is covered by reinsurance, without specific arrangements for any particular exposure.

Tripod of economic security   An underlying assumption in the design of employee benefits that an individual's economic security in the United States will come from three sources: the employer, the government, and the individual.

Twisting   An illegal replacement of life insurance based on incomplete or deceptive comparisons between existing and proposed policies.

Unearned premium reserve   A liability account on an insurer's balance sheet that reflects the portion of prepaid premiums held by the insurer that cannot yet be considered revenues for the insurer.

Umbrella liability policy   A policy, usually with large limits, that covers losses in excess of the limits provided by underlying liability insurance. For example, a personal umbrella liability insurance policy provides people with excess coverage over the liability coverage provided by their homeowners and automobile insurance policies.

Underinsured motorists' insurance   An automobile insurance policy option that provides payment when the insured is injured by a negligent motorist who has less insurance than the insured, and the insured cannot recover for all damage sustained because of the defendant's inadequate coverage.

Underwriting   The process of selecting and rating applicants for insurance for the purpose of calculating a premium.

Underwriting cycle   A pricing cycle common in the insurance industry, characterized by sudden spikes of high premiums followed by gradual price reductions fueled by price competition until the cycle completes with another wave of price spikes.

Unearned premium   The percentage of an advance premium not yet earned by the insurer by the passage of time. For example, assume that an insured pays a one-year premium for a policy in advance. After the policy has been in force for two months, ten-twelfths of the premium remains unearned.

Uniform transfer tax   The combination of federal gift and estate taxes that are assessed on property transferred at death.

Universal life insurance   A type of permanent life insurance that allows the insured flexibility in choosing premium payments and death benefits during the contract period.

Unsatisfied judgment fund   A state fund designed to make payment to injured victims harmed by uninsured motorists.

Utmost good faith (Uberrima fides)   This term refers to the standard of behavior imposed on the insured by an insurance contract—that is, the requirement that the insured deal with the insurer without making material misrepresentations or concealing material facts.

Valued policy   A type of insurance policy in which the insurer agrees to pay the face amount in the event of a total loss, regardless of the actual damage sustained. Valued insurance policies often are used to insure artwork and similar items because the market value at the time of loss may be difficult to estimate when the insurance policy begins.

Variable annuity An annuity with a flexible liquidation payment determined by the performance of an underlying (common stock) investment portfolio.

Variable universal life insurance A type of cash-value life insurance policy that gives the insured flexibility in choosing the underlying investment for the policy.

Variance A statistical term used to measure the degree to which the outcomes of a random variable may differ from its expected value.

Vested benefit The right of an employee to the employer's contribution to a pension plan. Federal law specifies vesting schedules for qualified pension plans.

Vicarious liability Legal liability that arises out of another's actions. For example, a contractor may have vicarious liability if a subcontractor injures another party.

Waiver-of-premium option An extra-cost life insurance policy provision that provides for the insurer to forgo collecting premiums while the insured is permanently disabled. Despite the forgone premiums, the policy remains in force, with benefits calculated as if premiums had been paid.

Warranty A statement made by an insured that induces the insurer to enter into the insurance contract. The statement must be absolutely true, or else the insurer can avoid its contractual obligations. If the statement covers the future (for example, "There always will be at least two guards on duty"), it is a *promissory warranty*. If the statement represents a current condition (for example, "This ship is seaworthy"), it is an *affirmative warranty*.

Well-diversified portfolio A group consisting of a large number of items (e.g., investments) whose losses exhibits little or no correlation, allowing for the effective reduction of risk.

Whole life insurance A contract that promises payment whenever death occurs, or at a predetermined age specified in the policy, whichever comes first. Ages that are commonly specified in most policies include 100 or 120 years old. Whole life contracts involve savings and often are called *permanent insurance*.

Will A legal document in which a person directs the disposal of his or her assets at death.

Workers' compensation Benefits required by law and provided by employers that pay lost wages and medical expenses to employees injured on the job.

Written premium The total premium collected by an insurer during a specific period, such as a year.

Yearly renewable term insurance A life insurance policy that can be renewed over time and promises to pay if the insured dies within the one-year policy term.

Index

Numbers

A